A CHAUCER GL

A CHAUCER GLOSSARY

COMPILED BY
NORMAN DAVIS, DOUGLAS GRAY
PATRICIA INGHAM, AND
ANNE WALLACE-HADRILL

OXFORD
AT THE CLARENDON PRESS
1979

Oxford University Press, Walton Street, Oxford OX2 6DP

OXFORD LONDON GLASGOW
NEW YORK TORONTO MELBOURNE WELLINGTON
KUALA LUMPUR SINGAPORE JAKARTA HONG KONG TOKYO
DELHI BOMBAY CALCUTTA MADRAS KARACHI
NAIROBI DAR ES SALAAM CAPE TOWN

© *Norman Davis, Douglas Gray, Patricia Ingham*
Anne Wallace-Hadrill, 1979

British Library Cataloguing in Publication Data
A Chaucer glossary
  1. Chaucer, Geoffrey – Language – Glossaries, etc.
  I. Title II. Davis, Norman, b. 1913
  821'.1   PR1941   78–40245
  ISBN 0–19–811168–1
  ISBN 0–19–811171–1

*Printed in Great Britain
at the University Press, Oxford
by Eric Buckley
Printer to the University*

PREFACE

THIS Glossary is designed as a practical aid to the reading of Chaucer, providing fuller references than most editions can find room for but remaining of modest proportions. It necessarily depends heavily on the earlier work of many scholars. We have used the Tatlock–Kennedy *Concordance* as the primary guide to Chaucer's vocabulary, the *Oxford English Dictionary* and the *Middle English Dictionary* edited at Ann Arbor (as far as L) as the essential sources of information about usage and meaning. We have consulted Skeat's glossary constantly and those of other editions frequently; the latest we have been able to use is the 1974 edition of *The Tales of Canterbury* by Robert A. Pratt. We have tried also to take account of the multitude of studies, mostly in scattered articles, of particular words in Chaucer's work. To all our predecessors we are much indebted, but we have endeavoured always to arrive at opinions and definitions of our own.

The initial work of compilation was divided as follows:

Anne Wallace-Hadrill	A–C, GODSIB–RESPORT
Patricia Ingham	D–GOBET, THEE to the end
Douglas Gray	RESTE–THEDOM

The whole was edited by Norman Davis, who also compiled the preliminary notes and the list of names.

Introduction

THE primary aim of this Glossary is to explain the meanings of words and phrases in Chaucer's works which are used in ways unfamiliar in modern English, and to refer them to a number (necessarily limited) of typical instances. It also illustrates Chaucer's use of many expressions not necessarily unfamiliar but characteristic of his language. It is intended to be serviceable with any of the widely read editions. Readers are assumed to have at hand one of the complete texts of Chaucer, so that they can readily refer to passages mentioned. The only quotations given are therefore of brief phrases.

The Glossary does not give a complete account of Chaucer's vocabulary, because that is available in the *Concordance* compiled by J. S. P. Tatlock and A. G. Kennedy (The Carnegie Institute of Washington, 1927, reprinted Gloucester, Mass., Peter Smith, 1963). It covers all the works generally accepted as Chaucer's, and the doubtfully ascribed short poems; it does not treat *The Romaunt of the Rose* beyond Book I, or *The Equatorie of the Planetis*. A considerable number of words are omitted because they are used by Chaucer very much as they are today; yet a great many now familiar do appear, because they had in his use a different range of senses or took part in phrases of special interest. In such cases the current senses are briefly noticed, usually with not more than five references, for the sake of comparison.

Within entries senses are given in approximate order of frequency or importance, so far as these can be judged, not of historical development; and an attempt is made to analyse the longer entries by numbering senses that can be effectively distinguished —there is sometimes doubt about the appropriate classification of individual examples.

Text and arrangement

The spelling of headwords is primarily that of Skeat's six-volume edition (Oxford, 1894, second edition 1900), except that *i* or *I* when used with the value of modern *j* is replaced by *j* or *J*. Different spellings in other editions—especially Robinson's second edition of the *Works* (1957), the *Canterbury Tales* edited by Manly and Rickert (1940), and Root's edition of *Troilus and Criseyde* (1926)—

are also entered if they seem likely to cause a reader difficulty. The letter *y* when it represents a vowel is given the same order as *i*, but when it represents a consonant it has its usual place. Words with initial *k-* which have variants with *c-* are listed under *C*. When a word is spelt in more than one way, whether in different parts of Skeat's edition or in different editions, the principal alternatives are given at the head, separated by /. Minor variants such as *-ance/-aunce*, *-cion/-cioun*, *con-/coun-*, *oght/ought*, *ou/ow* are sometimes ignored, but (except for the last) generally shown by parentheses enclosing the optional letter.

The many words which contain a long vowel, *ā*, *ē*, or *ō*, commonly but not regularly written with a double letter, are printed with the second letter in parentheses and ordered according to the longer spelling; and occasional alternatives of the same kind in consonants are similarly treated. Optional endings *-n* and *-e* (or consonant+*-e*) are marked off by (, and variable prefixes by). Regular inflectional endings are not recorded unless they are the only forms of the word which occur, or are of some special interest; the normal grammatical inflections are shown below, p. xv. Verbs are listed in the infinitive form if it occurs; if it does not, the forms that do appear are given, in order of present and past tenses and of person. Irregular or variant forms are usually collected, to aid identification, at the end of an entry.

The form and the order of references to the texts are based, for convenience of comparison, on those of the *Concordance*. For *The Canterbury Tales* the system of reference to both the group letter and the teller of the tale is followed, but Doc is replaced by Phs. For *Boece* and the *Astrolabe* the numbering is adjusted to the editions used. *The House of Fame* is numbered continuously throughout, not by books. Since references to the *Tales* by group letter and line number, used by Skeat and many other books concerned with Chaucer, are given by Robinson beside his own numbering, they will present no difficulty to readers accustomed to either system. In *Troilus and Criseyde*, however, Root's text of Book III follows an order of its own from line 1324 to line 1414, and here both line-numbers are given, separated by /. The prose texts of the *Tales* offer no problems because they are numbered by sentences, but *Boece* and the *Astrolabe* are troublesome because the editions number only by lines, which differ greatly. For these texts references are given both to Skeat's and to Robinson's edition, separated by /; more than this would have been impracticably cumbrous. When a particular reference is to a word which appears in some but not all of the major editions because of editorial choice of reading, it is marked *var*. Emendations are marked *em*. In passages quoted within entries, ∼ represents the headword. Words found only in Chaucer's works are marked †.

Etymologies

Each etymon is normally given in the form which best accounts for the form in the text, but 'dictionary' forms are sometimes given if the derivation of particular inflections is obvious. If the spelling of an etymon does not differ from that of the word glossed it is not repeated, and only the language abbreviation is given. An asterisk marks a form theoretically reconstructed, not recorded. Long vowels are marked by macrons, except in Old Norse words where the usual acute accent is used. In Old English words the acute marks a vowel originally short but lengthened in Old English. The sign + means that a compound or derivative is first recorded in Middle English. Words in bold type refer to other entries in this Glossary; 'from' is used when the word glossed either has affixes not present in the etymon or is derived by a change of function; 'cf.' indicates uncertain relation; words for which no convincing etymology has yet been put forward are marked [?].

ABBREVIATIONS

absol.	absolute(ly, i.e. without some usual construction	obl.	oblique
acc.	accusative	occas.	occasional(ly
adj.	adjective	OED	*The Oxford English Dictionary*
adv.	adverb(ial		
app.	apparently	opp.	opposed to
art.	article	orig.	originally
attrib.	attributive	pa.	past tense
auxil.	auxiliary	part.	partitive
cf.	compare	pass.	passive
cl.	clause	perh.	perhaps
coll.	collective	pers.	person(al
comp.	comparative	person.	personified
condit.	conditional	phr.	(in) phrase(s
conj.	conjunction	pl.	plural
cons.	consonant	poss.	possessive
constr.	construction	p.p.	past participle
dat.	dative	ppl. adj.	participial adjective
def.	definite	pr.	present tense
demons.	demonstrative	prec.	preceding (word)
deriv.	derivative	predic.	predicative
dial.	dialect(al	pref.	prefix
em.	emendation	prep.	preposition; (applied to noun forms) prepositional (case)
emph.	emphatic		
esp.	especially	prob.	probably
exclam.	exclamation	pron.	pronoun
fem.	feminine	prov.	proverb(ial
fold.	followed	pr. p.	present participle
fig.	figurative(ly	qual.	qualified
fut.	future	refl.	reflexive
gen.	genitive	rel.	relative, related
her.	heraldic	rubr.	rubric
imit.	imitative	s-e.	south-eastern
imper.	imperative	sg.	singular
impers.	impersonal	sim.	similarly
ind., indic.	indicative	spec.	specifically
indef.	indefinite	sthg.	something
infin	infinitive	str.	strong
infl.	influenced	subj.	subjunctive
infl. infin.	inflected infinitive	suff.	suffix
interj.	interjection	sup.	superlative
intr.	intransitive	tr.	transitive
introd.	introducing	transf.	transferred
iron.	ironical	ult.	ultimately
lit.	literally	uninfl.	uninflected
n.	noun	usu.	usually
neg.	negative	v.	verb
nom.	nominative	var.	variant
nth.	northern dialect	vbl. n.	verbal noun
num.	numeral	wk.	weak
obj.	object		

LANGUAGES AND DIALECTS

A	Anglian dialects of Old English	ML	Medieval Latin
		MLG	Middle Low German
AN	Anglo-Norman	Nb	Northumbrian
Arab	Arabic	Norw	Norwegian
CF	Central (Old) French	OA	as A
Dan	Danish	OE	Old English
Du	Dutch	OF	Old French
Fris	Frisian	OI	Old Icelandic
Gmc	Germanic	OIr	Old Irish
Gr	Greek	ON	Old Norse
It	Italian	ONb	Old Northumbrian
L	Latin	ONF	Northern dialects of Old French
LL	Late Latin		
LOE	Late Old English	Scand	Scandinavian
LWS	Late West Saxon	Sw	Swedish
MDu	Middle Dutch	W	Welsh
ME	Middle English	WS	West Saxon

ABBREVIATED TITLES

Canterbury Tales:

A.Prol	The General Prologue	Mars	The Complaint of Mars
A.Kn	The Knight's Tale	CompL	A Complaint to his Lady
A.Mil	The Miller's Tale	Anel	Anelida and Arcite
A.Rv	The Reeve's Tale	PF	The Parlement of Foules
A.Co	The Cook's Tale	Bo	Boece, book shown by simple number, metre and prose by m and p with number and line numbers
B.ML	The Man of Law's Tale		
B.Sh	The Shipman's Tale		
B.Pri.	The Prioress's Tale		
B.Th	The Tale of Sir Thopas	TC	Troilus and Criseyde, numbered by book and line
B.Mel	The Tale of Melibeus		
B.Mk	The Monk's Tale		
B.NP	The Nun's Priest's Tale	Adam	Chaucer's Words unto Adam
C.Phs	The Physician's Tale		
C.Pard	The Pardoner's Tale	HF	The House of Fame, numbered consecutively throughout
D.WB	The Wife of Bath's Tale		
D.Fri	The Friar's Tale		
D.Sum	The Summoner's Tale	LGW	The Legend of Good Women. LGW G. designates the form of the Prologue in Cambridge University Library MS. Gg.4.27.
E.Cl	The Clerk's Tale		
E.Mch	The Merchant's Tale		
F.Sq	The Squire's Tale		
F.Fkl	The Franklin's Tale		
G.SN	The Second Nun's Tale		
G.CY	The Canon's Yeoman's Tale	Rosem	To Rosemounde
		FormA	The Former Age
H.Mcp	The Manciple's Tale	Fort	Fortune
I.Pars	The Parson's Tale	Truth	Truth
		Gent	Gentilesse
		LSt	Lack of Steadfastness
BD	The Book of the Duchess	Scog	Chaucer's Envoy to Scogan
Pity	The Complaint unto Pity		
ABC	Chaucer's ABC	Ven	The Complaint of Venus

Buk	Chaucer's Envoy to Buk-	CompA	Complaint d'Amours
	ton	BalCh	Balade that Chaucer made
Purse	Chaucer's Complaint to		(Womanly Noblesse)
	his Purse	Astr	Treatise on the Astrolabe
MercB	Merciless Beauty	RR	The Romaunt of the Rose,
WUnc	Against Women Uncon-		book I
	stant		

NOTES ON INFLECTIONS

SOME editions, following the practice of some manuscripts, usually represent a long vowel $\bar{e}$ or $\bar{o}$, less often $\bar{a}$, by a double letter in a closed syllable (i.e. before a consonant not followed by a vowel) or at the end of a word, but by a single letter in an open syllable (i.e. before a single consonant and another vowel): *hoot* 'hot', but pl. *hote*. A short vowel before a consonant and another vowel is usually indicated by doubling the consonant letter: *sadde*, pl. of *sad*.

Nouns and adjectives ending in *-f* voice the consonant and spell it *v* before the vowel of an ending: *lyve*, *wyves*, *caytyves* from *lyf*, etc., *leve* from *le(e)f*. Conversely, verbs with stems ending in *-v* may unvoice it to *f* in the imperative where no vowel follows: *le(e)f*, TC 4.896, 5.1518, *yif* A.Kn 2420, C.Phs 238, from *le(e)ve(n, yeve(n* respectively.

NOUNS

Many nouns in Chaucer's English end their basic or common form in a consonant, some in a stressed vowel (native words such as *tre(e, fo(o*, French ones such as *meynee*), many in unstressed *-e* (e.g. *ende, sunne, dette, compaignye*). A few have alternative forms with and without *-e*, such as *blis* (rhyming with *this* A.Kn 1684) or *blisse* (rhyming with infin. *kisse* TC 3.181). The only regular inflections are those of the genitive or possessive singular and of the plural. These are in most nouns the same in both these cases; they differ according to the form and the length of the noun. Monosyllabic nouns ending in a consonant add *-es*, which forms a second syllable; nouns ending in a vowel, and most of those of more than one syllable ending in a consonant (especially those of French origin) add only *-s*: e.g. poss. *lordes, shires, sowes*; pl. *croppes, londes, songes*; but *endes, trees, frankeleyns*, usually *maydens, naciouns, servauntz, significaciouns*. Words of more than one syllable are sometimes written with *-es* in the plural, but metre shows that this was not pronounced as a syllable (*grehoundes* A.Prol 190, *housbondes* 460). Some words have alternative forms (*tavernes* A.Prol 240 and C.Pard 465, *laxatyves* B.NP 4152 and 4344).

A few possessives without ending descend from OE genitives without *-es*: notably the nouns of relation which were unchanged in the genitive in OE: *brother* TC 1.678 *var* (*brotheres* G.SN 296), *fader* (in phrases as at A.Rv 4038, but *fadres* D.WB 301), *suster* LGW 2365 *var*; also *lady* (OE *hlæfdīgan*) A.Prol 88, etc. Of similar origin, though now functioning rather as elements of compounds, are *hevene* in *hevene blisse* TC 3.704, *hevene king* G.SN 542, *herte* in *herte blood* C.Pard 902. Proper names ending in *-s* add no ending in the possessive: *the king Priamus sone* TC 1.2.

A small number of nouns have plural forms in -(*e*)*n* either regularly or occasionally: *brethren* invariably, *doghtren* and *sustren* as alternatives, *e*)*yen* invariably, *asshen, been, foon, hosen, oxen, shoon, toon* more than once, *keen* or *kyn, pesen* once each. *Men, wommen, feet, gees* are as in modern English.

A few nouns have plural forms the same as the singular. These are (a) words unchanged in the pl. in OE: *deer, hors, neet, sheep, swyn,* and sometimes *thing*; (b) terms of measure of time or space constructed with numerals: *foot, myle, pound, night, winter, yeer, sithe, tyme*; (c) words of French origin ending in -*s*: *ca*(*a*)*s, pa*(*a*)*s, vers, harneys*; also *maner* with numerals and in phrases like *alle maner thinges* A.Kn 2181.

In some prepositional phrases certain nouns add the ending -*e* (and double a final consonant of the stem after a short vowel): e.g. *to bedde, to shippe, on fire, on fo*(*o*)*te, of lyve,* and most frequently *on lyve. Lyve* without preposition is also used adverbially in phrases like *al hir lyve* A.Prol 459, *my lyve* 'in my life' TC 2.205.

ADJECTIVES

Some adjectives end in their basic form in -*e*: e.g. *grene, lene, swete,* descended from OE, and a large number of words from French such as *able, povre, possible.* Monosyllabic adjectives ending in a consonant do not usually inflect for case; but they add -*e* in the plural (e.g. *smal* sg. A.Prol 153, 158, *smale* pl. 146), and also in the singular when preceded by a defining word (e.g. *the, this, that,* or a possessive) and in vocative use: *an old man* but *this olde man* C.Pard 713–14, *the grete strengthe, his grete cost* A.Kn 1943, 2090; *O grete god* B.Pri 1797, *leve brother* A.Mil 3151, but not when the adjective follows the noun: *lady bright* TC 3.39. Disyllabic adjectives do not take the ending: *this gentil cok, gentil sire* B.NP 4055, 4474, *O lufsom lady bright* TC 5.465.

In some phrases an adjective takes the ending -*e* without any of the usual conditions: *of olde tyme* B.ML 50, HF 1155, *with harde grace* D.Sum 2228, G.CY 1189, *no more harde grace* TC 1.713. *Alle* appears with singular nouns in *alle trouthe and alle gentillesse* TC 2.160, and with a noun of ambiguous form but a singular verb in *alle thing was wel* TC 3.696.

There are occasional plurals of French adjectives in -*s*: two in verse, *places delitable*s F.Fkl 899, *romances that been royale*s B.Th 2038, and a number in prose such as *weyes espirituel*s I.Pars 79.

An occasional survival is the genitive plural in -*er*: *aller* A.Prol 586, 799, etc., *bother* TC 4.168.

In predicative use the adjective is sometimes but not regularly inflected: *whan that they were seke* A.Prol 18, but *they were as fayn* A.Kn 2707.

Comparison of the simpler adjectives is usually effected by the suffixes -*er* for the comparative and -*est* for the superlative: *frendlier, frendliest*(e. Monosyllables ending in a consonant double it before the comparative ending, and those with a long vowel in the stem syllable often shorten it: *hoot, hotter, greet, gretter*; and the short vowel is extended to the superlative *grettest*. The adjectives *good, yvel, muchel, litel* have irregular comparison as in modern English. *O(o)ld, long*, and *strong* change their vowel to *e*. The superlative, since it commonly occurs after the definite article or another defining word, is often written with the ending *-e*, as *in his beste wyse* F.Fkl 731; but this is not generally pronounced after disyllabic forms: *The gretteste clerkes been noght the wysest men* A.Rv 4054; after trisyllables it is: *the ferfulleste wight* TC 2.450. Comparison may also be expressed by *more* and *most*, not necessarily with the longer adjectives: *more delicat, more pompous, more proud* B.Mk 3661–2, *more sweet* TC 3.1219, *the moste free* F.Fkl 1622, TC 1.1080.

ADVERBS

Adverbs are often derived from adjectives by means of the suffix *-e*, as *brighte, harde, hye*, as well as by *-ly/-liche*.
They may be compared in the same way as adjectives, with suffixes as *the lighter merciable* LGW 410 or with *more/most* as *most felingly* A.Kn 2203. *Murierly* A.Prol 714 *var* is alone in adding the comparative suffix before the adverbial ending.

PRONOUNS

Inflected forms of the personal pronouns are entered separately in the Glossary.
In the first person singular nominative *I* (*y*) immensely predominates, *ich* occasionally surviving with some variation in different manuscripts: it appears within the line in places like *ich have* A.Mil 3277, *ich assente* B.ML 39, and is certified by rhyme in the suffixed form (evidently colloquial or vulgar) *theech* C.Pard 947, G.CY 929. *Ik* occurs only twice, and once suffixed in *theek*, in the speech of the Reeve from Norfolk.

The second person *thow* is often suffixed and assimilated to the ending of a preceding verb, especially with short and familiar verbs such as *artow, shaltow, wiltow*, occasionally other verbs as in *seydestow* G.SN 334, *proferestow* TC 3.1461. The objective *thee* is reduced and treated almost as an enclitic to the verb in *I allow the*, rhyming on *youthe*, F.Sq 676. It is prefixed, with elision of the vowel, in *thalighte* B.Pri 1660, *thexcuse* D.Fri 1611.

When used as possessive adjectives *myn* and *thyn* lose *-n* before consonants other than *h-*: *myn heed* A.Prol 782 but *my bane* A.Kn 1097. As pronouns they retain *-n*: *It is my good as wel as thyn* D.WB 310.

In the third person the masculine *his* is usually treated as a possessive adjective. It functions also as a true genitive, in *his face that was bistad* B.ML 649. The neuter nominative is mostly written *it*, but *hit* also occurs: *hit am I* BD 186. The possessive is *his: ech contree hath his lawes* TC 2.42.

The objective and possessive case forms of the feminine pronoun (*she* in nom.) when within the line are usually written in good manuscripts *hir, hire*. At the line-end they are often written *here*, and rhyme only on words like *bere* A.Kn 1421, *swere* F.Fkl 790.

In the plural, in the second person nominative *ye* and objective *yow/you* are always distinguished. In TC 1.5 *fro ye* 'from you', rhyming with *Troye*, is the only example of the use of a weakened form of *yow* after the stressed preposition. In the third person the nominative is always *they*; in possessive and objective the consensus of good manuscripts regularly shows *here* and *hem* respectively, though scribes occasionally write *th*- forms.

Objective cases of the personal pronouns are used as reflexives, but are sometimes reinforced by forms of *self*—the three forms *self, selve, selven* interchange, *self* in plural as well as singular, as *hanged hemself* D.WB 761.

Demonstrative. That has plural *tho*; *this* has *thise* or *these*, both monosyllabic. Chaucer makes much use of the third demonstrative, *thilke*, which has the same form in sg. and pl.

Relative. Relatives applied to both persons and things are *that, which, which that, the which*; a possessive is sometimes expressed by means of a personal pronoun: *the kinges dere sone . . . which alwey for to do wel is his wone* TC 2.318. *Who*—which is the usual interrogative of persons—does not function as a relative in the nominative, but the other cases *whom* and *whos* often do: *on whom we truste* A.Prol 501, *the gode man whos that the place is* D.Sum 1768.

Of the other pronouns, *everich* appears mainly in partitive phrases such as *as everich of us* A.Kn 1186, but also independently as *everich hath of God a propre yifte* D.WB 103. *Other* has plural *oth(e)re*, as *amonges othere* B.Mk 3344.

VERBS

The infinitive of most verbs ends in *-en* or *-e*, but some monosyllabic verbs contract, as *go(o)(n, sle(e)(n*. Verbal forms ending in *-n* (infin., pr.pl. ind. and subj., pa.pl. ind. and subj., and p.p.) may always have alternative forms without *-n*. A few verbs retain an inflected infin. in special uses: *to do(o)ne* A.Mil 3544, *to se(e)ne* A.Kn 1035.

In the present tense of all regular verbs the personal endings are: 1. *-e*, 2. *-est*, 3. *-eth*, pl. all persons *-e(n*. The ending of the second person singular is exceptionally *-es* in *bringes* HF 1908. The ending of the third singular is *-es* in some passages of the Reeve's Tale as a mark of the students' northern dialect; also exceptionally in three other places, BD 73, 257, HF 426. Words with stems ending in a dental consonant often syncopate and assimilate the ending -eth: rist = riseth, writ = writeth, wryth = wrytheth; forbet = forbedeth, fleet = fleteth; bint = bindeth, fint = findeth, yelt = yeldeth; tret = tredeth, et = eteth, sit = sitteth; stant = stondeth; halt = holdeth; list = listeth, sent = sendeth, tit = tideth, set = setteth, put = putteth. An exceptional contracted form of 2 sg. appears in lixt = liest D.Fri 1618, D.Sum 1761.

The present subjunctive is formed on the stem of the infinitive, with singular ending -e, plural -e(n.

The ending of the present participle, and of the verbal noun, is -ing(e.

In the past tense there is a major difference beween 'strong' and 'weak' verbs. Strong verbs descend from OE types which formed the past tense by change of stem vowel. In the past they have the same form for first and third persons singular, often a different vowel in the plural as well as the ending -e(n, and in the second singular the same vowel as in the plural, with the ending -e. Chaucer's usage shows some variation from the inherited pattern. For instance, the expected forms of the past of bere(n are: 1, 3 sg. bar, 2 sg. bēre, pl. bēre(n. These indeed occur, bar and bēren in rhyme; but baar also occurs in 3 sg., as well as be(e)r B.ML 722, B.NP 4526 (in rhyme), bare in 2 sg. E.Cl 1068, and haren in pl. A.Prol 721. Of speke(n the expected 1, 3 sg. is spak, which duly appears; but in pl. in addition to spēken (not in rhyme) the form spāken appears in rhyme TC 1.565. Many verbs preserve the distinction between singular and plural in stem vowel as well as in ending: e.g. rood sg., riden pl.; gan sg., gonne(n pl.; fo(o)nd sg., founde(n pl. But forms proper to the singular are sometimes applied to the plural: ran B.NP 4571, sat C.Pard 664. The past subjunctive should historically have the stem vowel of the plural, with the endings -e and -e(n in sg. and pl. respectively. It is not frequent. The expected form occurs in bre(e)ke B.NP 4578, but the vowel is altered in yāve TC 2.977. These notes cannot comprehend all variants; individual forms will be found in the Glossary.

The past participle ending of strong verbs alternates freely between -en and -e.

Weak verbs form the past tense by means of the suffix -de or -ed(e according to the stem, and in part to earlier conjugation. After a long syllable -de appears as in herde, seyde, wende 'thought' from wēne(n, but -ed in some verbs as dēmed, eyled, sailed; after a short syllable -ed(e as in loved(e, wered(e, which for the most part are treated metrically as two syllables, occasionally as one. The ending becomes -te after voiceless consonants and in some special cases: kepte, sette, wente 'went' from wende(n. In conjugation 1 and 3 sg. are identical, pl. has -e(n, and 2 sg. is like the present in ending in -est as seydest. The past participle is like the past tense but without -e: seyd, went, engendred. The past subj. has sg. -e, pl. -e(n.

Past participles of both strong and weak verbs may have the prefix i-/y-: ibore, yseyd.

Some weak verbs change their stem forms in the past. Most are like modern English, as *taughte* from *teche(n*, but some differ as *raughte* from *reche(n* A.Prol 136, *straughte* from *strecche(n* A.Kn 2916.

Imperatives of both strong and weak verbs generally have no ending in the singular: *ber, he(e)r, ley, tel*. The plural often ends in *-eth*, but may also have the same form as the singular; *lat* is especially common in phrases like *lat be, lat se*. In weak verbs the imperative is frequently written with *-e*, but this is rarely supported by metre; places requiring it are *knokke* (sg.) A.Mil 3432, *pleye* (pl.) TC 2.1729. A few verbs having a consonant group before the ending take *-e*: *herkne* D.Fri 1551, *folwe* (some MSS.) TC 3.739.

A small group of verbs, mainly functioning as 'modal auxiliaries', is conjugated irregularly. The present tense forms are like those of the past of some strong verbs, except that the second person singular ends in *-st* or *-t*: e.g. 1, 3 sg. *can, may, shal*, 2 sg. *canst, mayst, shalt*, pl. *conne(n, mowe(n, shul(len*. Singular forms are often used in plural function. The past is formed like that of weak verbs: *coude/couthe, mighte, sholde*. The forms of such verbs, and of others showing irregularities of various kinds—*do(o)(n, go(o)(n, wil/wol, wite(n, have(n*—are given in the Glossary; the forms of *be(e)(n* which differ from modern use are listed each in its own place.

A

a *prep.* on A.Mil 3516, B.Sh 1370, LGW 2166; in A.Kn 2934, A.Mil 3134, TC 1.363 *var*; ~ *Goddes half(e* for God's sake D.WB 50, BD 370, ~ *Goddes name* in God's name A.Prol 854, C.Phs 250; with verbal forms in -*ed* C.Pard 406, D.WB 354, F.Fkl 1580. [weakened form of **on**]

a/an *indef. art.* a, an A.Prol 43, B.NP 4280, TC 2.1369; one D.Fri 1396, *(up)on* ~ *day* one day D.Sum 2047, G.CY 1022, TC 4.34, LGW 631, *on* ~ *tyme* LGW 583; at a, in *dere ynogh* ~ *jane* not worth a half-penny E.Cl 999; ~ *certein* (with pl.) a number of B.Mk 3367; (with num.) some C.Pard 771, F.Sq 383; *many* ~ see **many**; *everich* ~ see **everich**. **an** (before vowels and *h*-) A.Prol 447, B.ML 705, D.Sum 1667, TC 5.116. [OE *ān*]

a(a)s *n.* ace B.ML 124 (see **ambes as**), B.Mk 3851. [OF]

abaysschinge *see* **enbasshinge**.

abaissen/abasshe *v.* **1.** *intr.* fear, be dismayed Bo 4. p7. 56/76, RR 1552. **2.** *tr.* **abaysed/abaysshed/abayst** *p.p.* abashed, dismayed B.ML 568, PF 447, TC 3.94; frightened, timid TC 3.1233; amazed Bo 3. m12. 23/32; confused E.Cl 1108. [AN *abaiss-* from stem of OF *e(s)bair*]

abak *adv.* backwards A.Mil 3736, B.Th 2017, LGW 864. [OE *on bæc*]

abakward *adv.* backwards Bo 3. m12. 41/58. [from prec.]

abasshe *see* **abaissen**.

abate *v.* abate, reduce B.Mk 3780, I.Pars 730, *p.p.* Bo 3. p5. 33/46 (L *lapsa*); put down, degrade I.Pars 191; subtract Bo 2. p7. 24/34, Astr 2. 10. 9/12, 25. 16/18. [OF *abatre*]

aba(u)ndoune *v.* devote I.Pars 713, B.Mel 2767; give I.Pars 874. [OF *abandoner*]

abaved *p.p.* made wretched BD 614. [? OF *abaubir* disconcert]

abedde *adv.* in bed B.Sh 1355, 1367, D.WB 407; to bed D.WB 1084, E.Mch 1818. [a prep.+OE *bedd*]

abegge *see* **abye(n**.

a-begged *phr.* a-begging F.Fkl 1580. [from **on**+*beggeth*, vbl. n. from *beg*, prob. OE *bedecian*]

abeye *see* **abye(n**.

abet *n.* incitement TC 2. 357. [OF]

abhominable *adj.* abominable, hateful B.NP 4243, H.Mcp 343, I.Pars 910. [OF]

abhominacioun *n.* disgust D.Sum 2179, I.Pars 687; disgusting vice B.ML 88. [OF]

abyde(n *v.* **1.** stay, remain A.Kn 2554, B.Sh 1350, E.Mch 1616, TC 3.1432, LGW 180; reach a decision, settle E.Mch 1588. **2.** wait A.Mil 3129, D.WB 169, TC 2.1158. **3.** *tr.* await A.Kn 927, E.Cl 757, Bo 4. p6. 256/372, TC 5.1175, HF 1086. **4.** abstain F.Fkl 1522. **abideth**

pr. 3 sg. B.NP 3967; **abit** G.CY 1175, TC 1.1091. **abideth** *imper. pl.* B.Sh 1175. **abo(o)d** *pa. sg.* BD 247, TC 1.127. **abiden** *p.p.* A.Kn 2982, TC 1.474. [OF *abidan*; see **byde**]

abydinge *vbl. n.* expectation Bo 2. p3. 41/59; duration p7. 68/98.

abye(n/abegge/abeye *v.* pay for, suffer for A.Rv 3938, B.Th 2012, D.Sum 2155; *deere* ~ pay dearly for A.Kn 3100, C.Phs 100, G.CY 694. **aboughte** *pa.* A.Kn 2303, TC 5.1756. **abo(u)ght** *p.p.* A.Kn 3100, LGW 1387, Ven 37. [OE *abycgan*; see **bye(n**]

abit *see* **abyde(n, habit**.

a-blakeberyed *phr.* blackberry-picking C.Pard 406. [cf. **a-begged**]

able *adj.* fit, competent (with infin.) A.Prol 167; effective D.Fri 1472; fit (with *to* 'for') BD 779; able (absol.) A.Kn 1241, I.Pars 787; capable A.Prol 584, E.Mch 1912, BD 786; inclined, disposed TC 2.903; deserving (with *to* 'of') ABC 184. [OF]

ablinge *pr.p.* making fit Bo 1. m6 12/18; enabling, raising Bo 3. m9. 24/34 (L *aptans*). [from prec.]

ablucions *n. pl.* washings G.CY 856. [OF]

abo(o)d *n.* waiting A.Kn 965; staying HF 1963; delay TC 3.854. [from OE *bād* and **abyde(n**]

abo(o)d *see* **abyde(n.**

abo(u)ght(e *see* **abye(n.**

abounde, -inge *see* **habounde.**

aboute *adv.* about, around A.Kn 2493, B.Mk 3364, PF 194, TC 5.85; in turn A.Kn 890; *bring* ~ cause TC 4.1275, G.CY 607; *be* ~ *(to)* go about, endeavour A.Kn 1142, be on the point of D.WB 166, busy oneself in I.Pars 643. [OE *abūtan*]

aboute *prep.* round, around A.Prol 158, B.ML 879, PF 80, (following obj.) A.Kn 2952, G.CY 914, TC 2.734 *var*; near, approximately at A.Kn 2189, A.Mil 3645, E.Cl 981; about, on the subject of E.Cl 5; concerned with E.Mch 2019; *ben* ~ been engaged in TC 5.1645. [as prec.]

above(n *adv.* above G.CY 1200, Bo 3. p2. 43/62; in addition F.Fkl 1155. [a prep.+ OE *bufan*]

above(n *prep.* above A.Prol 53, B.Mel 2216, C.Phs 8, D.Sum 1715, TC 1.154; (following obj.) D.WB 1040, F.Fkl 772. [as prec.]

abregge *v.* abridge, shorten A.Kn 2999, E.Mch 1614, TC 3.262, 4.426, 925; (with *of*) reduce I.Pars 243. [OF *abregier*]

abregginge *vbl. n.* reduction Bo 5. p1. 57/83; lessening I.Pars 568.

abreyde *v.* wake, start up A.Rv 4190, BD 192, TC 1.724, HF 110, 559; come to one's senses E.Cl 1061. **abrayd** *pa. sg.* (str.) BD 192, HF 110; **abrayde** (wk.) B.NP 4198, TC 1.724. Cf. **breyde**. [OE *abreġdan*, *abræġd*]

abroche *v.* broach D.WB 177. [OF *abrochier*]

abro(o)d *adv.* wide open F.Sq 441. [a prep.+ **brood**]

absolut *adj.* (only in Bo) complete Bo 3. p10. 20/28, p11. 16/21; free, absolved Bo 5. p4. 74/107, p5. 13/18. [OF]

absolutly *adv.* unconditionally Bo 4. p2. 147/199. [from prec.]

abundaunce *see* **hab-.**

abusioun *n.* perversion of truth, deception B.ML 214; falsehood TC 4.1060; absurdity TC 4.990; disgrace I.Pars 445. [OF]

a-caterwawed *phr.* caterwauling D.WB 354. [?; cf. **a-begged**]

accesse *n.* sudden illness, fever TC 2.1315, 1543, 1578. [OF]

accident *n.* **1.** occurrence TC 3.918; chance happening HF 1976. **2.** attribute (opp. substance) C.Pard 539; something inessential (with pun on sense 1) TC 4.1505; appearance E.Cl 607. [OF]

accidental *adj.* incidental, subsidiary B.Mel 2588. [from prec.]

accidie *n.* sloth I.Pars 388, 677, etc. (only here). [OF]

ac(c)oye *v.* soothe TC 5.782, Bo 2. p3. 45/66. [OF *acoier*]

accomplice/acompliss(h)e(n *v.* accomplish, perform A.Kn 2864, I.Pars 734, Bo 4. p2. 191/263; fulfil Bo 3. p10. 122/164. [OF *acompliss-*, stem of *acomplir*]

accompte *see* **ac(c)ounte.**

ac(c)ord *n.* agreement A.Prol 838, PF 668, LGW 159; *bi oon* ~ unanimously B.Mel 2486; *of his* ~ to an agreement with him F.Fkl 741, *see* **falle(n**; *pl.* HF 695; harmony B.NP 4069, PF 197. [OF]

ac(c)ordable *adj.* harmonious, concordant Bo 2. m8. 1/2, 14/20. [OF]

ac(c)orda(u)nce *n.* concord, agreement Bo 2. m8. 9/13, RR 496. [OF]

ac(c)orda(u)nt *(to) adj.* in keeping (with) A.Prol 37, B.NP 4026; in harmony (with) A.Mil 3363, PF 203; favourable (to) F.Fkl 1290; in agreement Bo 1. p4. 164/229. [OF]

ac(c)orde(n *v.* **1.** agree, consent B.Mel 2137, F.Fkl 798, LGW 3; *refl.* B.Mel 2972, Bo 3. p12. 58/75; correspond A.Prol 830, G.CY 638, *the word moot need* ~ *with the dede* H.Mcp 208; (with *to*) concern TC 3.1409/1395, LGW 955. **2.** *tr.* bring to agreement E.Mch 2130, LGW 1635; reconcile I.Pars 623; arrange, settle TC 4.808, LGW 2027. [OF *acorder*]

ac(c)ording *ppl. adj.* agreeing, suiting B.Pri 1737, D.WB 924, Astr 2.14.5/6. [from prec.]

ac(c)ounte/accompte *v.* **1.** reckon, value B.Mel 2505, BD 1237, ~ *for* reckon as Bo 2. p5. 71/99. **2.** recount B.Mk 3591. [AN *acunter*, OF *aconter*, *ac(c)ompt-*]

accountes *n. pl.* accounts B.Sh 1277; account I.Pars 253, 378. [AN *acunt*]

accuse(n *v.* accuse E.Mch 2270, LGW 350; blame A.Kn 1765, B.Mk 3319, TC 2.1081; reveal RR 1591. [OF *ac(c)user*]

accusement *n.* accusation TC 4.556. [OF]

acha(a)t *n.* buying A.Prol 571, Bo 1. p4. 64/89. [OF]

achatours *n. pl.* buyers A.Prol 568. [OF]

achekked† *p.p.* checked HF 2093. [cf. OF *eschequier*]

acheve *v.* achieve I.Pars 734, TC 2. 1392, succeed in LGW 1614. [OF]

achoken *v.* choke, stifle Bo 2. p5. 57/81, LGW 2008 var. [OE *acēocian*]

acloyeth *pr. 3 sg.* overloads PF 517. [AN *acloyer*]

acorse *see* **acurse.**

acquitaunce *n.* receipt or deed of release A.Mil 3327; discharge A.Co 4411. [OF]

acquite *v.* discharge, release D.Fri 1599; repay, reward TC 2.1200; *refl.* do one's part, behave E.Cl 936; clear oneself I.Pars 179; ~ *of* make good B.ML 37 var. [OF *aquiter*]

act *n.* act E.Mch 1975, action Bo 1. p4. 30/41, *pl.* deeds HF 347; records, histories B.NP 4326. [L *āctus*]

actue(e)l *adj.* practical, in deed I.Pars 357. [OF]

acurse/-corse *v.* curse B.NP 4420, I.Pars 680, TC 3.1072. [*a-* pref.+ OE *cursian*]

acustomaunce *n.* habit HF 28: *hadde of* ~ was accustomed B.Mk 3701. [OF]

aday *adv.* by day, in the daytime TC 1.1075 var, 2.60; see **oft(e.** [a prep.+ **day**]

adamant/atthamaunt *n.* adamant (hard rock) A.Kn 1305, 1990; lodestone PF 148, RR 1182. [OF]

adawe *v.* awake TC 3.1120; arouse E.Mch 2400. [*a-* pref.+ OE *dagian*]

adjeccioun *n.* addition Bo 5. p6. 134/190 [from L *adjectiōn-*]

adjuracioun *n.* charging (spirits in exorcism) I.Pars 603. [OF]

adoun *adv.* down, downwards A.Prol 393, B.Pri 1697, F.Fkl 1402, TC 5.532, LGW 738; down below G.CY 779, H.Mcp 105, HF 889. [OE *of dūne*]

adoured *p.p.* worshipped B.Mk 3753 var. [from OF *adourer*]

adrad/adred *ppl. adj.* afraid A.Prol 605, BD 493, 1190, TC 2.115. [LOE *adrǣd(de*]

adressinge *vbl. n.* directing Bo 5. p4. 63/90. [from OF *adresser*]

adversarie *adj.* opposed, hostile I.Pars 697. [OF]

advertence *n.* attention TC 4.698, 5.1258, HF 709; mind G.SN 467. [OF]

afer *adv.* afar Bo 3. p3. 4/5, TC 1.313, LGW 212; far TC 2.516. [OE *of+feor*]

afere *see* **afir(e.**

afer(e)d *ppl. adj.* afraid, terrified A.Prol 628, B.NP 4109, TC 1.974, (by death) C.Phs 284. [from OE *afǣran*]

affeccioun *n.* affection B.Sh 1526, TC 1.296, Bo 3. m1. 10/14, LGW 44; emotion A.Mil 3611, LGW 1522, B.ML 586; inclination, will B.Mel 2363, I.Pars 293, LGW 793. [OF]

affectes *n.pl.* desires TC 3.1391; (prob. intended also in 3.15, cf. **effect**). [L *affectus*]

afferme(n *v.* affirm Bo 2. p2. 23/32, TC 2.1588; establish A.Kn 2349, LGW 790, confirm B.Mel 2246; assert the value of B.NP 4315. [OF *afermer*]

affiance *n.* trust B.Sh 1330. [OF]

affile *v.* file, polish A.Prol 712, TC 2.1681. [OF]

affinitee *n.* relationship by marriage I.Pars 907; relation Bo 1. p4. 196/275. [OF]

afforced *p.p.* forced I.Pars 974. [from OF *aforcer*]

affray *n.* fright, fear B.ML 1137, Anel 334, HF 553; disturbance D.Sum 2156; attack B.Mk 3273. [AN]

affraye *v.* frighten E. Cl 455, B.ML 563, B.NP 4475; arouse BD 296, RR 91. [AN]

afir(e *adv.* on fire TC 3.856, 5. 1466, LGW 2493; (fig.) inflamed TC 4.509; *sette* ~ set fire to, inflame, arouse D.Sum 1982, TC 3.24; **afere** (s-e.) TC 1.229. [a+**fyr**]

aforyeyn *prep.* opposite TC 2.1188. [OE *on foran*+*gegn*]

afounde *v.* be chilled Rosem 21. [OF *enfondre*]

afright *p.p.* frightened B.NP 4085. [OE *afyrht*]

after *adv.* afterwards, then A.Prol 162, A.Kn 2898, B.ML 603, E.Cl 553, TC 2.1746. [OE *æfter*]

after *prep.* **1.** after (of time) A.Kn 1467, B.ML 1161, TC 2.1185; *at* ~ (point in time) B.Sh 1445, E.Mch 1921, F.Fkl 918; after, following B.NP 4571, PF 400, TC 2.978. **2.** for A. Kn 1266, 2699, Bo 1. m4. 11/15, 2. p5. 124/174, TC 1. 619, 3. 1585, 5. 1133, LGW 1827; *wayte*(*n* ~ look for A.Prol 525, expect B.ML 467. **3.** according to A.Prol 125, A.Kn 2573, F.Sq 205; ~ *oon* alike, equally A.Prol 341, A.Kn 1781; suitably for F.Sq 389. **4.** ~ *that* (*conj.*) after A.Kn 2522, D.Sum 1853, F.Sq 477; as B.Mel 2649, E.Cl 203. [as prec.]

afterward *adv.* afterwards A.Prol 497, C.Pard 884, TC 4.1531. [OE *æfterweard*]

agayn/ageyn/ayein *adv.* **1.** back A.Prol 801, B.ML 23, B.NP 4599, D.WB 718, TC 2.1141, 3.1516; in return A.Kn 1197, A.Rv 4274, in reply A.Kn 1092. **2.** again A.Kn 892, B.Sh 1571, E.Cl 1110, F.Sq 670, TC 2.52. [OE *ongēan* and ON *í gegn*]

agayn/ageyn/ayein *prep.* **1.** against A.Prol 66, B.ML 580, C.Phs 181, E.Mch 1610, TC 1.902. **2.** towards, facing A.Kn 2680, F.Sq 53, LGW 48; to meet D.WB 1000, (following obj.) B.ML 999 *var*; ~ *the sonne* in the sun A.Kn 1509, B.NP 4459, H.Mcp 110, LGW 112. **3.** (of time) towards B.NP 4262, 4268; with a view to F.Sq 142; in anticipation of H.Mcp 301. [as prec.]

again(e)s/ayeyns *prep.* against, contrary to A.Kn 1787, C.Phs 181, BD 16, LGW 330; compared with A.Mil 3155; instead of I.Pars 187; in answer to LGW 344, in return for I.Pars 154; beside, in front of E.Mch 2325, Astr 2.39.27/31; approaching PF 342, LGW 1356; to meet (following obj.) B.ML 999 *var*; in the presence of B.Mk 3702. [from prec.+adv. *-es*]

againward/ayenward *adv.* backward, back again B.ML 441, Bo 4. p5. 23/34, TC 3.750. [cf. OE *ongēanweard*]

agame *adv.* in jest TC 3.636, 650; lightly Mars 277. [a prep.+**game**(n]

agaste *v.* frighten B.NP 4278, TC 2.901, Bo 3. m12. 24/35. *pa.* B.Mk 3395, LGW 1221, *refl.* A.Kn 2424. **agast** *p.p.* and *adj.* afraid A.Kn 2341, B.NP 4111, D.WB 798, TC 1.715, HF 557. [a- pref.+OE *gǣstan*]

age *n.* **1.** age, time of life A.Kn 2592, B.NP 4011, E.Cl 241, E.Mch 1601, TC 5.826; *of* ~ adult B.Mel 2353; (with years specified) A.Prol 82, D.WB 4, E.Mch 1421. **2.** life D.WB 24, E.Cl 627, HF 1986. **3.** old age A.Rv 3867, C.Pard 724, E.Cl 121, E.Mch 1738, TC 2.395; *greet* ~ C.Pard 719, Bo 1. p1.7/10. **4.** era, period of history B.Mk 3177, D.WB 59, TC 2.27. **5.** one of the seven ages of the world Bo 2. m5. 1, FormA 2. **6.** time Bo 3. m9. 3/4. [OF]

ageyn *see* **agayn.**

agilte(n *v.* **1.** *intr.* do wrong I.Pars 150, TC 5.1684, LGW 436. **2.** *tr.* wrong, offend I.Pars 132, ABC 122, TC 3.840. **agilte** *pa.* D.WB 392, I.Pars 946. **agilt** *p.p.* B.Mel 3008, ABC 122. [OE *agyltan*]

ago(n *p.p.* gone E.Mch 2158; gone away, departed A.Kn 2802, B.NP 4396, C.Pard 810, D.Sum 1953, TC 4.1090; gone out A.Kn 2336. *ppl. adj.* (in phrases of time) past B.Pri 1876, C.Pard 436, D.WB 863, TC 2.722. *adv.* ago A.Mil 3537, B.Th 1899, TC 5.317, LGW 443. [OE *āgān*]

agreable *adj.* pleasing, pleasant Bo 3. m2. 19/28, HF 1097; pleasing, suited (*to*) B.ML 767, Ven 68. [OF]

agreablely *adv.* agreeably Bo 2. p4. 92/126, 3. m1. 5/7. [from prec.]

agreabletee *n.* equability Bo 2. p4. 83/115. [OF]

agree(n *v.* **1.** agree PF 409, TC 3. 131. **2.** suit, please TC 1.409. [OF]

agref *see* **agr(i)ef.**

agregge *v.* aggravate, make worse B.Mel 2209, I.Pars 892, 1017. [OF *agreg(i)er*]

agreved *p.p.* distressed, annoyed A.Kn 2057, E.Cl 500, LGW 345; injured A.Rv 4181 *var.* [from OF *agrever*]

agr(i)ef *adv.* in *take* (*it*) ~ take it hard, be upset B.NP 4083, PF 543, TC 3.862, 4.613, (with *of*) D.WB 191. [a *prep.*+ **grief**]

agrise(n *v.* be frightened, shudder Bo 1. p3. 15/20 (L *perhorrescerem*), (with *of*) C.Phs 280, TC 2.1435; *pass.* Bo 3. p1. 12/16; loathe Bo 2. p1. 45/64; tremble D.Fri 1649, Bo 1. m6. 7/10; be deeply moved, melt B.ML 614. **agro(o)s** *pa. sg.* TC 2.930, LGW 830. **agrisen** Bo 3. p1. 12/16. [OE *agrisan, -grās, -grisen*]

agroted *p.p.* surfeited LGW 2454. [?]

agu *n.* ague, acute fever B.NP 4150. [OF]

ay *adv.* always A.Prol 63, B.Mk 3377, TC 1.449; all the time A.Mil 3472, B.Pri 1825, TC 2.643; ~ *whil that* as long as A.Rv 3876; *for* ~ *and o* for ever and ever TC 2.1083. [ON *ei*]

ayel *n.* grandfather A.Kn 2477. [OF *aiuel*]

aylen *see* **eylen.**

air *see* **eir.**

ajourne *v.* summon (a person) on another day ABC 158. [OF *ajourner*]

ajuged *ppl. adj.* in ~ *biforn* prejudged Bo 1. p4. 72/99 (L *praeiudicatae*). [from OF *ajuger*]

ajuste *v.* correct, remedy Bo 2. p3. -/23. [OF *ajuster*]

ake *v.* ache B.Mel 2113, TC 3. 1561, LGW 705. [OE *acan*]

aketoun *n.* tunic B.Th 2050. [OF]

akinge *vbl. n.* aching TC 1.1088.

aknowe *p.p.* conscious: *ben* ~ acknowledge Bo 1. p4. 109/152, 4. p4. 1/2. [OE *oncnāwan*]

al *n.* awl, pricker Truth 11. [OE *æl*]

al *n.* all, everything A.Prol 319, A.Kn 2613, G.CY 1248, HF 272, TC 3.1764; ~ *and som* everything, the whole thing D.WB 91, F.Fkl 1606, PF 650, TC 2.363, LGW 998; *and* ~ and everything else B.Mk 3275, BD 116, TC 5.1319; *at* ~ altogether B.Sh 1360, C.Pard 633, at all D.WB 1078, D.Sum 1763, in every way E.Mch 1222; *in* ~ completely D.WB 46. [OE *eal(l)*, A *al(l)*]

al(le) *adj.* all, the whole of B.ML 907, F.Sq 137, TC 1.100, 2.139; ~ *a* A.Prol 584, G.CY 996. *pl.* A.Prol 26, 53, A.Mil 3636, B.NP 4592, BD 350, Pity 26. ~ *tyme* high time A.Rv 3908. ~ *and some* one and all A.Mil 3136, C.Pard 336, Anel 26, TC 3.607, 5.883. See **aller**. [as prec.]

al *adv.* **1.** entirely, altogether A.Kn 1410, B.Mk 3215, F.Sq 597, G.SN 210, PF 432; ~ *right* exactly TC 1.99; ~ *only* simply B.Mel 2662; Bo 4. p1. 20/27; ~ *so* as Bo 2. p5. 75/106, see **also**; ~ *hayl* A.Rv 4022. **2.** (with subj. and inversion) although A.Prol 734, A.Kn 2999, C.Pard 371, G.CY 861, TC 1.17, 3.87, whether G.CY 839; ~ *be (that)* A.Prol 297, PF 436, ~ *be/were it (so) that* B.Mel 2173, D.WB 1172, I.Pars 382; (with indic. and inversion) D.WB 497. [as prec.]

alayes *n. pl.* alloying, debasing E.Cl. 1167. [AN]

alambyk *n.* alembic TC 4.520*em* (see **lambic**), G.CY 794. [OF]

alaunts *n. pl.* wolfhounds A.Kn 2148. [OF]

albificacioun *n.* turning white G.CY 805. [OF]

alday *adv.* all the time, always A.Kn 1380, A.Rv 3902, TC 2.733, RR 1506; every day, constantly A.Kn 1168, A.Co 4398, TC 4.1563; at any time Mars 237. [**al**+**day**; cf. OF *toz jorz*]

alder *see* **aller**.

alderbest *adv.* best of all A.Prol 710, BD 87, TC 1.1008 [**aller**+**best**].

alderbeste *adj.* best of all BD 1279, TC 3.1597. [**aller**+**beste**]

alderfairest *adj.* fairest of all BD 1050, Bo 3. m9. 8/11, RR 625. [**aller**+**fair**]

alderfirst *adv.* first of all B.Mel 2393, TC 1. 1069, RR 1000; for the first time Bo 1. p3. 17/22. [**aller**+**first**]

alderfirste/alther- *adj.* first of all, very first BD 1173, TC 3.97. [**aller**+**firste**]

alderlast *adv.* last of all RR 449. [**aller**+**last**]

alderlest *adv.* least of all TC 1.604. [**aller**+**le(e)st**]

alderlevest *adj.* very dearest TC 3.239, 5.576. [**aller**+**leef**]

aldermost *adv.* most of all Bo 4. p4. 37/51, TC 1.152, LGW 2117. [**aller**+**mo(o)st**]

aldernext *adv.* nearest of all PF 244. [**aller**+**next(e**]

alderwisest *adj.* wisest of all TC 1.247. [**aller**+**wise**]

alderworst *adj.* worst of all Bo 5. p3. 113/160. [**aller**+OE *wyrresta*]

ale *n.* ale, beer A.Prol 341, B.Th 2062, C.Pard 315, H.Mcp 60; *atte nale* at the alehouse D.Fri 1349. [OE *(e)alu*; *nale* from *at then ale* from OE *æt þæm*]

aley *n.* alley, path B.Pri 1758, E.Mch 2324, TC 2.820. [OF]

aleys *n. pl.* service-berries RR 1377. [OF]

alenge/elenge *adj.* miserable B.Sh 1412, D.WB 1199. [OE *ælenge*]

algate(s *adv.* at any rate C.Pard 292, E.Cl 855, BD 887, TC 5.1071; all the same, nevertheless I.Pars 364, Bo 1. p4. 171/238, 3. p2. 86/124, at all costs HF 943; always, in every case A.Prol 571, B.Mel 2841, D.WB 756. [ON; cf. OI *alla gǫtu*]

aliene *v.* alienate Bo 1. p6. 43/54. [OF *aliener*]

alighte *v.* alight, dismount A.Prol 722, E.Cl 981, TC 5.513; descend E.Cl 909, B.Pri 1660, TC 5.1017. **alighte** *pa.* ABC 161, TC 5.513. **alight** *p.p.* A.Prol 722, A.Kn 2189. **thalighte** (**thee**+*pa.*) B.Pri 1660. [OE *alihtan*]

alkamistre *n.* alchemist G.CY 1204. [from OF *alkemiste*]

Alkaron *n.* Koran B.ML 332. [cf. ML *Alcorānum* from Arab]

allegeaunce *n.* alleviation BalCh 21. [OF]

allegge *v.*[1] allege, adduce A.Kn 3000, E.Mch 1658, TC 3.297. [AN *alegier*]

allegged *v.*[2] *p.p.* lightened Bo 4. p4. 12/17. [OF *aleger*]

aller/alder *adj., n. gen. pl.* of all: *oure* ~ of us all A.Prol 799, ABC 84, LGW 298, *hir* ~ of them all A.Prol 586. See **al**. [OA *alra*]

alleskinnes *quasi-adj.* of every kind, all kinds of HF 1530. [OE *ealles cynnes* gen.; cf. **kin**]

allye *n.* relative, kinsman B.Mk 3593, G.SN 292. [OF *allié*]

allie(n *v.* **1.** *tr.* link, associate C.Pard 613, join TC 1.87; *ben* ~*d* have friends B.Mk 3720; *refl.* C.Pard 618. **2.** *intr.* make an alliance, marry A.Rv 3945, E.Mch 1414. [OF *alliier*]

allon(e/aloon *adj.* alone: *al* ~ A.Kn 1410, E.Mch 1326, TC 2.555; ~ *withouten any compaignye* A.Kn 2779, A.Mil 3204, B.Mel 2750; ~ *as he/she/I was born* A.Kn 1633, D.WB 885, TC 4.298; *her* ~ all by herself LGW 2378; *lat me* ~ leave it to me TC 1.1028, 2.1401, 3.413; all to yourself D.WB 444. [**al** *adv.*+**o(o)n**]

allow *v.* **1.** commend, applaud F.Fkl 676. **2.** admit, accept Bo 5. p3. 20/26. [AN *al(l)ouer*]

almanderes *n. pl.* almond-trees RR 1363. [OF]

almesdede *n.* almsgiving, charity B.ML 1156, I.Pars 386. [next+**dede**]

almesse *n.* alms B.ML 168, I.Pars 377; charity D.Fri 1609; *doon* ~ give alms I.Pars 1035; *eten the* ~ live on the charity B.Mel 2757; *pl.* works of charity I.Pars 1030, 1033. [OE *ælmesse*]

almest *var.* of **almost**, almost B.Th 1948 (rhyming *est*), Bo 4. p2. 103/138 *var.* [OA *al mæst*]

almicanteras *n. pl.* almacanters (circles parallel to the horizon) Astr 1.18.2, 19.3/4, etc. [Arab]

almury *n.* pointer Astr 1.22.4/6, 23.1, etc. [Arab]

alofte *see* **onlofte**.

along *adj.* in ~ on owing to, because of G.CY 922, 930, TC 2.1001, 3.783. [OE *ġelang*]

aloon *see* **allon(e**.

alose *v.* commend TC 4.1473. [OF *aloser*]

aloutrely/-utterly *adv.* (or as two words) entirely, absolutely TC 1.382, HF 296, Bo 3. p12. 82/110. [from **al**+**utterly**]

alpes *n. pl.* bullfinches RR 658. [?]

als *adv.* **1.** also A.Rv 4317, B.NP 3976, F.Fkl 1598, TC 2.726, HF 2071. **2.** as B.Mel 2851. [reduced form of next]

also *adv., conj.* **1.** also A.Prol 64, B.ML 555, TC 4.757; **alswa** (nth.) A.Rv 4085. **2.** as B.Mk 3473, E.Mch 1226, 2109, BD

1064, TC 3.1633, LGW 528; (introd. asseveration) B.Mel 2112, E.Cl 822, BD 683, HF 1067. [OA *al swā*]

altherfirste see **alder-**.

alum *n*. ~ (*de*) *glas* rock alum G.CY 813, HF 1124 *var*. [OF]

alwey *adv*. always A.Prol 185, F.Sq 26, PF 3, TC 1.782; progressively A.Rv 4222. [OA *alne weġ*]

amadrides *n.pl*. hamadryads, wood-nymphs A.Kn 2928. [L *hamādryades*]

amayed *p.p*. amazed TC 1.648, 4.641. [from AN *amaier*]

amalgaming *vbl. n*. making an alloy with mercury G.CY 771. [from OF *amalgamer*]

amased *ppl. adj*. dismayed, daunted G.CY 935. [OE *amāsod*]

ambages *n. pl*. ambiguities TC 5.897. [OF]

ambel *n*. ambling pace B.Th 2075. [OF]

ambes as *n*. double ace (lowest throw at dice) B.ML 124. [OF]

amblere *n*. ambling horse A.Prol 469. [from OF *ambler* v.]

ameled *p.p*. enamelled RR 1080. [from AN *amel*, OF *esma(i)l*]

amende *v*. improve, improve upon A.Kn 2196, A.Mil 3799, B.NP 4048, F.Sq 197, Anel 84; put right D.WB 1106, E.Cl 441, TC 5.692; remedy BD 551, F.Sq 468; mend, make well TC 2.1731, LGW 2418; make amends (for) A.Mil 3799, TC 2.245. [OF]

amendement *n*. amends A.Rv 4185; *don* ~ make amends I.Pars 443; improvement, correction I.Pars 683, 903. [OF]

amender(e *n*. improver D.WB 1197. [from **amende**]

amendes *n. pl*. amends, compensation BD 526, *make* ~ (*of* 'for') TC 2.342, *maken his* ~ make amends to him B.Mel 2936. [OF]

amenuse(n *v*. (only in prose) diminish, reduce I.Pars 360, 1044, Bo 2. p4. 31/41, 3. p10. 19/26, belittle I.Pars 481, 496; *intr*. become less Astr. 1.21.47/65. [AN *amenuser*]

amenusinge *vbl. n*. diminution Bo 2. p5. 19/27, 3. p10. 13/18.

amerciments *n. pl*. fines I.Pars 752. [AN]

amesureth *pr. 3 sg*. measures Bo 2. p1. 62/86 *var*. [OF]

ameve see **am(o)eve**.

amy *n*. friend C.Pard 318. [OF]

amiable *adj*. agreeable, courteous A.Prol 138, kind, comforting B.Mel 2168; pleasant I.Pars 629 (L *placabilis*); favourable Bo 3. p8. 12/18. [OF]

amidde *adv*. in the middle RR 147. [OE *on middan*]

amidde *prep*. in the middle of A.Mil 3810, F.Fkl 1502, TC 1.417. [as prec.]

amiddes *adv*. in the midst PF 277; ~ *of* A.Kn 2009, HF 714, 845. [from **amidde**]

amiddes *prep*. amidst, in the middle of B.Mk 3919, Astr 1.18.4/5, 21.29/39. [as prec.]

amis *adv*. amiss, wrongly A.Mil 3181, TC 3.845, HF 2079; *do* ~ F.Fkl 783, TC 3.1629, HF 269; *fare* ~ fail F.Fkl 1298; *seye* ~ PF 446, TC 2.1048; *take* ~ TC 2, 229. [prob. ON *á mis*]

am(m)onicioun *n*. reminding Bo 1. p4. 7/9. [OF]

am(o)eve *v*. **1**. move (cause emotion in),

provoke I.Pars 670, Bo 1. p1. 33/45. **2**. *intr*. change E.Cl 498. [OF *amo(u)veir*, *-muev-*]

amoneste *v*. admonish I.Pars 583, Bo 5. m5. 14/21; inculcate B.Mel 2484. [OF *amonester*]

amonestinge *vbl. n*. admonition I.Pars 518, Bo 5. p1. 3/4.

among *adv*. mixed in TC 3.1816; in a group BD 298. [OE *on ġemang*]

among *prep*. among, in the middle of A.Kn 2939, TC 3. 860, HF 1687, (following obj.) G.CY 931; between C.Pard 814. [as prec.]

amonges *adv*. together, mingled Bo 2. p1. 77/106 (L *inter se*). [**among**+adv. *-es*]

amonges *prep*. amongst A.Prol 759, B.Mk 3344, TC 1.900. [as prec.]

amorettes *n. pl*. love-knots RR 892. [OF]

amortised *p.p*. deadened I.Pars 247 *var*. [OF]

amorwe *adv*. in the morning E.Mch 1214, BD 1103, TC 2.405, 4.1443; next morning A.Prol 822, A.Kn 1621, D.WB 593, TC 3.552. [a prep.+**morwe**]

amounteth *pr. 3 sg*. amounts to, means A.Kn 2362, B.ML 569, Astr 1.16.4/6. [OF *amo(u)nter*]

amour see **par amour**.

amphibologies *n. pl*. ambiguities TC 4.1406. [OF]

an see **a**, **on**.

ancille *n*. maid ABC 109. [L *ancilla*]

ancre/anker *n*. anchor LGW 2501, Fort 38, Bo 2. p4. 40/54. [OE *ancor*, OF *ancre*]

and *conj*. if B. Mk 3140, E. Mch 2433, G. SN 145, TC 1.125, 2.289, LGW 217; even if F.Fkl 1471. [OE]

anes see **ones**.

angle *n*. angle F.Sq 230; corner HF 1959; (astrol.) 'house' at compass point F.Sq 263, Astr 1.12.5/7. [OF]

angle-hook *n*. fish-hook Mars 238. [prec.+ OE *hōc*]

anguissh/angwyssh *n*. anguish, distress A.Kn 1030, I.Pars 678, TC 4.155; *pl*. worries Bo 3. p9. 84/111. [OF]

anguissheth *pr. 3 sg*. hurts Bo 3. m7. 1. [OF *anguissier*]

anguiss(ch)ous *adj*. sad, anxious I.Pars 304, Bo 3. p3. 18/26; painful, distressing Bo 2. m5. 22/30, TC 3.816. [OF *anguissus*]

anhange *v*. hang B.NP 4252, C.Phs 259, TC 2.1620. [OE *a-hōn* (str.) with altered pref., and *hangian* (wk.)]

any *adj*. a, any at all (often emphatic, esp. in comparisons) A.Prol 198, A.Mil 3246, A.Rv 3926, LGW 745, *withouten ~ lye* for certain A.Kn 3015; *withouten ~ drede* undoubtedly G.CY 1229, TC 3.418; *best of ~ man* better than anyone C.Phs 85, F.Fkl 997; *for ~ man* in spite of anyone C.Phs 129. [OE *æniġ*]

anientissed *p.p*. annihilated B.Mel 2438. [OF *anientiss-*, stem of *anientir*]

anight *adv*. at/by night A.Kn 1042, B.Mk 3758, D.Sum 1827, E.Cl 464, LGW 1414, in the night B.NP 4357. ~**es** A.Mil 3214, RR 18. [a prep. + **night**, and adv. *-es*]

anything *adv*. at all G.CY 1477, TC 1.848. [**any**+**thing**]

anker see **ancre**.

anlas *n*. dagger A.Prol 357. [cf. OF *alenaz*, from Frankish]

annexed *p.p.* attached, linked C.Pard 482, D.WB 1147, Bo 4. p4. 80/111. [from v. from OF *annexer*]

annueleer *n.* chantry priest G.CY 1012. [AN]

annunciat *adj.* foretold B.Mk 3205. [L *annunciātus*]

anoy *n.* **1.** annoyance, displeasure (*of* 'at') I.Pars 678, 680. **2.** trouble, vexation B.Sh 1320, TC 4.845; *do ~* cause trouble B.Mel 2679; torture Bo 3. m12. 25/35. [OF *en(n)ui, an(n)ui*]

anoye(n *v.* annoy, offend B.Mel 2459, D.Sum 1848, I.Pars 1051, displease, weary B.NP 3979, I.Pars 687; disturb B.ML 494, TC 4.1304; harm F.Fkl 875, I.Pars 640; do damage (*to*) B.Mel 2187, F.Fkl 884, I.Pars 557, 847. **anoyeth** *imper. pl.* B.ML 494. [OF *anoier*]

anoyful† *adj.* tiresome B.Mel 2222. [from **anoy**]

anoynte(n *see* **enoynte.**

anoyous *adj.* annoying, distressing B.Mel 2433, I.Pars 365, Bo 2. p5. 60/84, harmful I.Pars 728. [OF *anoious*]

anoyously† *adv.* annoyingly, harmfully Bo 3. p8. 11/15. [from prec.]

ano(o)n *adv.* at once, immediately A.Prol 32, B.NP 4467, TC 2.540; *right ~* C.Pard 826, H.Mcp 84; *~ as* as soon as I.Pars 250, *right ~ as that* F.Sq 615. [OE *on ān*]

anonright *adv.* immediately A.Mil 3847, G.SN 169, LGW 115. [prec.+**right**]

answere *v.* answer, reply A.Rv 3911, F.Sq 436; *~ of* be responsible for LGW 2212; *~ to* B.ML 472, D.WB 1077, E.Mch 2186, TC 4.540. [OE *andswarian*]

antartik *adj.* south Astr 2.25.7/9. [OF]

antiphoner *n.* book of antiphons B.Pri 1709. [OF *antiphon(i)er*]

anvelt *n.* anvil BD 1165. [OE *anfilte*]

aornement *n.* adornment I.Pars 432. [OF]

apay(e)d *ppl. adj.* pleased, satisfied A.Kn 1868, I.Pars 901, TC 5.1249; *yvele ~* B.Sh 1580, G.CY 921, LGW 80; *wel ~* E.Mch 1512, F.Fkl 1548, TC 3.421. [from OF *apaier*]

apaire *see* **apeyre.**

apayse *see* **ape(y)se.**

apassed *p.p.* passed away Bo 2. p5. 22/31. [from OF *apasser*]

ape *n.* ape, monkey A.Rv 3935, TC 2.1042, HF 1806; dupe A.Prol 706, A.Mil 3389, G.CY 1313; *goddes ~* born fool TC 1.913; see **wyn.** [OE *apa*]

apeyre *v. tr.* injure, damage A.Mil 3147, I.Pars 1078, TC 1.38. *intr.* grow worse, decline HF 756; perish TC 2.329. [OF *ampeirier* with altered pref.]

ape(y)se/apayse *v.* appease, assuage B.Mel 2290, TC 3.22, 5.117, *refl.* become calm B.Mel 3051; mitigate, remedy E.Cl 433, H.Mcp 98. [OF *apaisier*]

aperceyve *v.* perceive, realise E.Cl 600, I.Pars 294, TC 4.656. [stem of OF *aperceveir*]

aperceyvinges *vbl. n. pl.* noticing F.Sq 286. [OF]

apert *adj.* open, manifest I.Pars 649. [OF]

apert *adv.* openly: *pryvee and/or ~* in private and/or in public D.WB 1114, F.Sq 531, HF 717. [OF]

apertenant/-tinent *adj.* belonging, suitable B.Mk 3505, E.Cl 1010, Pity 70. [AN and ML]

apertene(n *v.* **1.** appertain, belong G.CY 785, I.Pars 85, 485; be connected with B.Mel 2525; apply, be relevant Bo 3. m12. 43/60. **2.** *impers.* befits, is fitting (to) B.Mel 2171, I.Pars 1069, Bo 1. p4. 125/173; (without expressed subject) B.Mel 2202. [OF *apertenir*]

apertly *adv.* openly Bo 1. p4. 126/175, 3. p.10. 38/53; plainly I.Pars 294. [from **apert**]

apyked *p.p.* trimmed A.Prol 365. [?*a*- pref.+ **pike** v.[1]]

apointe *v.* decide TC 3.454; appoint, assign TC 5.1620; *refl.* fix, settle TC 2.691, E.Mch 1595. [OF *apointier*]

apoplexie *n.* apoplectic stroke B.NP 4031 *var.* [OF]

apot(h)ecarie *n.* druggist A.Prol 425, B.NP 4138; **pothecarie** C.Pard 852. [OF]†

ap(p)alled *p.p.* faded, enfeebled A.Kn 3053, B.Sh 1292; vitiated I.Pars 723; grown pale F.Sq 365.[from OF *apalir*]

ap(p)araille *n.* clothes E.Cl 1208, RR 575; adornments Bo 2. p4. 46/62, attire ABC 153 (F *atour*); dressing-up I.Pars 432. [OF]

ap(p)arailements *n.pl.* ornaments Bo 2. p5. 114/160 (L *ornamentis*). [from next]

ap(p)araille(n *v.* prepare B.Mel 2532, I.Pars 829; adorn I.Pars 462; clothe I.Pars 933, Bo 2. p2. 29/40, p5. 113/166; *refl.* dress D.WB 343. [OF *apareillier*]

apparailling *vbl. n.* preparation A.Kn 2913, I.Pars 833.

apparaunt *adj.* manifest RR 5. [OF]

apparence *n.* appearance, look HF 265, LGW 1372; apparition, illusion F.Sq 218, F.Fkl 1140, 1265. [OF]

appere(n *v.* appear A.Kn 2346, G.SN 200, TC 2.909. [stem of OF *apareir*]

appetyt *n.* desire A.Kn 1670, 1680; appetite E.Mch 1250, H.Mcp 189, I.Pars 818, TC 5.1851. [OF *apetit*]

appetiteth *pr. 3 sg.* seeks after, desires LGW 1582. [from prec.]

applyen *v.* be attached to Bo 5. p4. 9/12. [OF *aplier*]

apposed *pa.* interrogated G.SN 363. *p.p.* objected Bo 1. p5. 34/50 *var.* [from OF *aposer*]

apprentice/-tys *n.* apprentice D.WB 303. *adj.* unskilled RR 687. [OF *aprentis* learner]

appreve *see* **approve.**

approche(n *v. tr.* and *intr.* approach B.Mel 2524, TC 5.1, (with *to*) HF 1115; be concerned F.Sq 556. [OF *aproch(i)er*]

appropred *p.p.* appropriated, reserved Gent 18. [from OF *aproprier*]

approve/appreve *v.* approve E.Mch 1349; approve of Bo 2. p1. 44/61; attest LGW 21, prove, try B.Mel 2353. [OF *aprover*, tonic stem *ap(p)ruev*-]

ap(p)rowours *n. pl.* agents D.Fri 1343. [AN]

aqueyntaunce *n.* acquaintance, familiarity, friendship A.Prol 245, D.Fri 1342, G.CY 988; circle of friends D.Sum 1991 *var*; *pl.* friends D.Sum 1991 *var.* [OF]

aqueynte *v.* become acquainted B.Sh 1219, HF 250, RR 600; *refl.* introduce oneself BD 532. [OF *acointier*]

aqueyntes *n. pl.* friends D.Sum 1991 *var.* [OF *acoint(i)é p.p.*]

arace v. snatch, pull away E.Cl 1103, Bo 1. p3. 30/42; uproot, tear up TC 3 1015, WUnc 18. [AN]

arbitracioun n. discretion, power of decision B.Mel 2943. [OF]

arbitr(i)e n. will, choice Bo 5. p3. 12/16, p.6 141/199. [OF arbitre, L arbitrium]

arch/ark n. arc B.ML 2, E.Mch 1795, Astr 2.7.9/10. [OF]

archewyves† n. pl. arch-wives, women's champions E. Cl 1195. [arch- pref. + wif]

are/arn pr. ind. pl. are A.Rv 4045, E.Cl 342, TC 1.1006, HF 1008. See **be(e)(n**. [ONb aron, OM earun]

arede v. interpret, explain BD 289, TC 2.132; guess TC 2.1112, TC 4.1570. [OE arǣdan]

are(e)ste n. arrest, detention A.Kn 1310, restraint E.Mch 1282; made ~ upon seized B.NP 4090; delay, stopping LGW 806; in ~ into rest, fewtered A.Kn 2602. [OF]

are(e)ste(n v. stop A.Prol 827, B.NP 4210, Bo 1. m7. 8/11; arrest, seize F.Fkl 1370. [OF arester]

areise(n v. **1.** raise Bo 5. m5. 15/22, p6. 217/305, Astr 2.2.5/6; exalt Bo 2. p6. 3/4, LGW 1525; refl. Bo 4. m1. 7/9. **2.** arouse Bo 4. m2. 7/11. **3.** levy I.Pars 567. [a- pref. + reyse(n]

arewe adv. in succession D.WB 1254. [a prep. + rewe]

Argeyes n.pl. Argives, people of Argos TC 5.1501. [L Argēus from Gr]

argoille n. argol (crude tartar) G.CY 813. [AN]

argument n. reasoning A.Rv 4123; argument PF 538; inference Bo 4. p4. 52/71 (L inlatione); discussion A. Co 4329; make ~ reason, dispute B.ML 1040, B.NP 4172, E.Mch 1619. TC 4.477; an angle or arc used to calculate planetary movement F.Fkl 1277. [OF]

argumente(n v. argue B.ML 212; reason (with oneself) TC 1.377. [OF argumenter]

aright adv. right, rightly, properly A.Mil 3115, G.SN 259, HF 50; the right way A.Rv 4254; correctly B.NP 4086, TC 5.364, 1288, HF 79; well A.Mil 3426, TC 1.878, 2.999; just, exactly A.Prol 267, Bo 4. p2. 96/127; indeed A.Prol 189, B.Mk 3135. [a prep. + right]

aryse v. arise, rise A.Prol 249, TC 2.221, HF 209, Astr prol 70/97. **ariseth** pr. 3 sg. B.Sh 1265, etc.; **arist** B.ML 265. **arisen** pa. pl. TC 2. 1598. **arise(n** p.p. A.Kn 1041, TC 2.1462. [OE arīsan; see **rise(n**]

arysing vbl. n. rising, rise F.Fkl 1287, Bo 2. m6. 11/15, Astr prol 71/98; pl. Bo 1. m5. 9/13, 4. m5. 6/8.

arist n. in sonne ~ sunrise Astr 2.12.10/14. [OE ǣrist]

arivaile n. disembarkation HF 451. [OF]

aryvé n. landing A.Prol 60 var. [OF]

ark see **arch**.

arm n. arm (of the body) A.Prol 111, A.Kn 2726; ~ in ~ TC 2.823, 1116; in his ~ in his arms A.Mil 3406, A.Rv 4204. pl. in oaths: Goddes ~ C. Pard 654, 692, D.WB 833, sim. A.Mil 3125. [OE earm]

armee n. military expedition A.Prol 60 var. [OF]

armen v. arm A.Kn 1651, E.Cl 1202, refl.

G.SN 385. **armeth** imper. pl. G.SN 385. [OF armer]

arm-greet adj. as thick as an arm A.Kn 2145. [arm + gre(e)t]

armipotente adj. powerful in arms A.Kn 1982, 2441. [L armipotent-]

armlees adj. without an arm B.Mk 3393. [from arm]

armoniak see **bole, sal**.

armonye n. harmony BD 313, PF 63, TC 5.1812, HF 1396. [OF harmonie]

Armorik adj. Armorican F.Fkl 1061. [L Armoricus]

armure n. armour B.Th 2009, G.SN 385, RR 1271; armaments B.Mel 2523; cote ~ see **cote**; pl. A.Kn 1016, Bo 2. m5. 17/25. [OF]

aroume adv. at large, in an open space HF 540. [a prep. + roum]

arowe adv. in a row, in succession D.WB 1254, HF 1835, LGW 554. [a prep. + rowe]

ar(o)we n. arrow A.Prol 104, TC 2.641, RR 939. [OE arwe]

ar(r)ay n. **1.** (state of) dress, clothing, garb A.Prol 41, B.Sh 1204, E.Cl 1116, G.CY 890, I.Pars 430, HF 228; equipment, gear B.ML 393, TC 2.1264, baggage B.Sh 1244. **2.** display, splendour A.Kn 1932, 2199, D.WB 1075, F.Sq 63, TC 4.1670; of greet ~ B.Mk 3272. **3.** arrangement, preparation A.Mil 3630, TC 3.536. **4.** state, condition A.Kn 934, A.Mil 3447, B.ML 299, 972, D.WB 902; appearance B.ML 775; in ~ in order E.Cl 262; way of behaving D.WB 235, (ill-)treatment E.Cl 670. [OF]

ar(r)aye v. clothe, equip A.Kn 2046, B.Sh 1202, E.Cl 267, LGW 1207; arrange, appoint A.Kn 2867, B.ML 1098, E.Cl 980, F.Fkl 1187. [AN araier]

arrerage n. lateness of payment: bringen in ~ find to be behind with accounts A.Prol 602. [OF arerage]

ar(r)ette v. impute A.Prol 726, A.Kn 2729, I. Pars 1081; lay blame (upon) I.Pars 580; find fault (to 'with') Bo 2. p4. 9/12. [OF aretter]

arrivage n. coming to shore, in took ~ landed HF 223. [OF]

arrive(n v. come to shore, land B.ML 469, TC 1.526, LGW 959; drive ashore Bo 4. m3. 1. [OF ariver]

ars-metrik(e n. arithmetic A.Kn 1898, D.Sum 2222 (? pun on **ers**). [as if from L ars metrica; OF arismetique]

art pr. 2 sg. are (often with suffixed pron. **artow**) A.Kn 1141, E.Cl 310, TC 1.731; **arte** weakened form of artow TC 5.1161. [OE eart]

art n. **1.** 'arts' curriculum in the university A.Mil 3191, (esp. disputation) A.Rv 4122; science F.Fkl 1120, TC 1.659; craft, technique A.Mil 3209, F.Sq 39, G.CY 1424; art (of love) A.Prol 476, D.WB 680, TC 3.1333, RR 40. **2.** art, skill F.Sq 197, TC 2.11, 257, HF 335, LGW 2546; means, way A.Kn 2445, D.Fri 1486. [OF]

artelries n. pl. engines for shooting B.Mel 2523 var. [OF artillerie]

arten v. urge on TC 1.388. [L artāre]

artik adj. arctic; pool ~ North Pole Astr 1.14.6/8, 2.21.3/4, etc. [OF]

arwe see **ar(o)we.**

as *adv., conj.* **1.** in asseverations, as, so A.Rv 4177, D.WB 805, BD 838, TC 3.790. **2.** introd. imper. (no modern equiv.) A.Kn 2302, A.Mil 3777, B.NP 4133, E.Cl 7, TC 5.523. **3.** introd. expressions of time: ~ *now* for the present A.Kn 2264, B.Mel 2667, G.CY 944, TC 3.190, ~ *nowthe* A.Prol 462; ~ *for a certein tyme* B.Mel 2167, ~ *in his tyme* B.Mk 3688; ~ *faste*, ~ *swithe* see these advs. **4.** with preps., mainly of reference: ~ *of*, ~ *to*, ~ *touching* F.Fkl 928, PF 26, TC 3.432, ~ *fro* I.Pars 220. **5.** appended to conjs.: *ther* ~ A.Prol 34, BD 197, TC 2.690, *wher* ~ B.ML 647, D.WB 923. **6.** as if (with subj.) A.Kn 2340, C.Phs 287, H.Mcp 347, TC 3.64, HF 546. **7.** expressing concession: ~ *many a year* ~ *it is passed* .. *sin* many years as it is since, though many years have passed since A.Rv 3889. **8.** in phr. with pron.: ~ *he that* as one who E.Mch 2404. [reduced form of **also**]

ascaunce(s *adv., conj.* as if D.Sum 1745, G.CY 838, LGW 2203; as if to say TC 1.205, 292. [? OF]

ascendent *n.* (astrol.) ascendant A.Prol 417, D.WB 613, Astr 2.3. rubr., 3.40/35, etc. [OF]

ascensioun *n.* rising, ascending degree B.NP 4045, 4146, Astr 2.26.2/3, etc.; distillation G.CY 778. [OF]

ascry *n.* outcry, alarm TC 2.611. [AN; cf. OF *escri*]

aseuraunce see **assurance.**

ashamed *ppl. adj.* ashamed B.Sh 1411, I.Pars 1061, TC 2.1047, *for pure* ~ see **for**; put to shame, disgraced A.Kn 2667. [cf. **shame(n]**

aske(n/axe(n *v.* ask A.Kn 1347, G.SN 426, TC 3.858; ask for, beg B.Mel 2224, 2759; need, require A.Kn 2777, E.Mch 1543, Bo 2. p2. 41/57, TC 2.227. **naxe** = **ne axe** TC 5.594. [OE *āscian, āxian*]

askinge/axinge *vbl. n.* question G.SN 423, BD 33, Buk 3; request, what is asked A.Kn 1826, HF 1541.

aslake *v.* slacken, diminish A.Mil 3553; assuage A.Kn 1760; satiate LGW 2008 var. [OE *aslacian*]

asonder *adv.* asunder, apart A.Prol 491, BD 425, TC 5.983. [OE *on sundran*]

asp *n.* aspen tree A.Kn 2921, PF 180, LGW 2648. [OE *æspe*]

aspect *n.* aspect, disposition (of planets) TC 2.682, Astr 2.4.24/38; (with qualifying adj.) *badde* ~ TC 3.716, LGW 2597, *frendly* ~ Astr 2.4.31/48, *wikke* ~ A.Kn 1087. [AN]

aspen *adj.* of an aspen tree ~ *leef* D.Sum 1667, TC 3.1200. [from **asp.**]

aspre *adj.* bitter, sharp Bo 4. p4. 186/259, p6. 190/274, TC 4.827; harsh, severe Bo 2. p1. 72/99; fierce Anel 23. [OF]

asprenesse *n.* sharpness, bitterness Bo 4. p4. 106/150, p7. 62/86. [from prec.]

assay *n.* **1.** attempt PF 2, *don his* ~ do his best LGW 1594. **2.** trial, test E.Cl 697, BD 552, LGW 9; *make(n* ~ *(of)* D.WB 290, G.CY 1249, 1383; *putte(n in* ~ test E.Cl 1138, TC 4.1508. [OF]

assaye(n *v.* **1.** try, attempt B.Mel 2406, E.Mch 1740, TC 5.784, LGW 477; experience A.Kn 1811. **2.** tempt, test

B.Mel 2637, B.Mk 3149, E.Cl 454, BD 346. **assayeth** *imper. pl.* E.Mch 1740. [AN.; cf. OF *essaier*]

assaille *v.* **1.** attack B.Mk 3953, D.WB 256. **2.** test E.Cl 1180. [OF *assaillier*, sense 2 infl. by prec.]

assaut *n.* assault A.Kn 989, B.Mel 2613, Bo 3. p1. 9/13. [OF]

assege *n.* siege TC 1.464, 2.107, 123 var, 4.62, 5.875. [from next]

assegeden *pa. pl.* besieged TC 1.60. **asseged** *p.p.* A.Kn 881. [OF *asseg(i)er*]

assemblee *n.* assembly, concourse B.ML 403, RR 505; copulation I.Pars 907. [OF]

assemble(n *v.* **1.** *tr.* collect together A.Kn 1286, PF 367; unite D.WB 89; amass Bo 3. p8. 5/7. **2.** *intr.* come together A.Prol 717, TC 2. 1567; have sexual intercourse I.Pars 909, 939. [OF]

assembling *vbl. n.* convening B.Mel 2431; copulation I.Pars 904, 917.

assent *n.* consent B.Mel 2201, B.ML 35, TC 4. 165; opinion A.Kn 3075, E.Mch 1532; *by oon* ~ with one accord, by general agreement A.Prol 777, C.Pard 801, TC 4.346; *of oon* ~ in league D.Fri 1359, *his* ~ those in league with him C.Pard 758. [OF]

assente *v.* **1.** agree, assent A.Kn 3092, B.Mk 3355, PF 526; agree to A.Prol 374, C.Phs 146. **2.** consent B.Mk 3469, LGW 1596; consent to LGW 730. [OF *assenter*]

asshe *n.* ash, cinders A.Kn 1302, C.Phs 209, LGW 2649. **asschen** *of fern* see **fern-asschen. asschen** *pl.* A.Kn 1302, A.Rv 3882, TC 4.119; **assches** G.CY 807. [OE *æsce*]

assyse *n.* assize, sessions A.Prol 314; *grete* ~ Last Judgement ABC 36; position RR 900. [OF]

assoile(n *v.* **1.** absolve C.Pard 387, 913. **2.** release Bo 5. p1. 9/13; loosen Bo 5. p3. 21/29. **3.** solve, resolve E.Mch 1654, Bo 5. p4. 17/25. [AN *assoilier*, OF *assoil-*, stem of *asoldre*]

assoiling, *vbl. n.* absolution A.Prol 661.

assurance *n.* promise, pledge B.ML 341; **aseuraunce** confidence TC 5.1259. [OF *aseurance*]

assure *n.* assurance Anel 331. [from next]

assure *v.* **1.** assure PF 448, TC 3.1395/ 1381, Ven 15; promise, pledge B.Sh 1231, E.Cl 165, LGW 2119. **2.** ensure, make safe Bo 1. p4. 77/106, LGW 1633. **3.** confirm A.Kn 1924, B.Mk 3378. **4.** trust TC 1.680, 5.1624; *refl.* be confident enough LGW 908. **5.** entrust E.Mch 2191. Cf. **ensure(n.** [OF *assurer*]

assured *ppl. adj.* confident Pity 40, TC 1.182, HF 581. [from prec.]

asterte(n *v.* escape A.Kn 1595, F.Fkl 1022, BD 1154, TC 5.1343. **asterted** *pa.* B.ML 437, **asterte** TC 1.1050. **astert** *p.p.* A.Kn 1592. [OE *astyrtan,* cf. **sterte(n]**

astonieth *pr. 3 sg.* stuns, bewilders PF 5, HF 1174. **aston(i)ed** *pa.* E.Cl 316. *p.p. adj.* stunned, stupefied F.Fkl 1339, TC 1.274, 2.427, astonished Bo 4. m5. 23/35, bewildered, baffled, dumbfounded A.Kn 2361, E.Cl 337, PF 142; dazed LGW G.164; deadened I.Pars 233; stupid Bo 4. p3. 82/118. [AN = OF *estoner*]

astonynge *vbl. n.* astonishment Bo 1. p2. 9/13, 4. p5. 21/31.

astored *p.p.* provided A.Prol 609. [AN; cf. OF *estorer*]

astrelabie/astro- *n.* astrolabe A.Mil 3209, Astr *passim*. [OF]

astrologer *n.* astronomer TC 3.1415. [from L *astrologus*]

astrologien *n.* astronomer D.WB 324, Astr prol 53/73, 2.4.2/3. [OF]

aswage(n *v.* **1.** *tr.* soften, moderate B.Mk 3834, RR 1230; soothe, ease Bo 3. m12. 12/16. **2.** *intr.* diminish E.Mch 2082, TC 4.255. [OF *as(s)ouagier*]

asweved *p.p.* dazed HF 549. [OE *aswefed*]

aswown(e *adv.* in a swoon, unconscious A.Mil 3823, C.Phs 245, TC 3.1092; **aswowe** Anel 354. [OE *geswogen*]

at *prep.* **1.** (of place) at A.Prol 20, E.Cl 57; by, beside A.Prol 358, TC 2.1696; at the hands of, by D.Sum 2095, from E.Cl 653, G.SN 542; to E.Mch 1489; ~ *eye* see **eye**. **2.** (of time) at A.Prol 23, A.Mil 3516, B.Sh 1445; see **after**; ~ *erste* see **erst**. **3.** (of price) A.Prol 815, TC 3.1161. **4.** in phrases: ~ *ese* comfortable D.Sum 2101, TC 3.1279; ~ (*one's*) *large* freely A.Kn 1283, HF 745; ~ *on* agreed (cf. **ato(o)n**) A.Rv 4197; ~ *o word* in a word B.ML 428, ~ *shorte wordes* briefly TC 2.956, 4.636, LGW 2462; ~ *his power* to the best of his ability I.Pars 306; ~ *regard of* see **regard**; ~ *the beste* in the best manner A.Prol 749. **atte** = at the: ~ *beste* A.Prol 29, ~ *fulle* completely A.Prol 651, ~ *laste* at last D.WB 799, finally G.SN 360. [OE *æt*]

atake *v.* overtake G.CY 556, 585, Mars 55, LGW 2182 *var.* **atake** *p.p.* D.Fri 1384, Mars 55. [a- pref.+**take**]

atanes *see* **atones**.

ataste *v.* taste Bo 2. p1. 26/36. [OF *ataster*]

atazir *n.* influence (of a planet) B.ML 305. [OF from Arab]

athinken *v.* displease TC 5.878; (impers. with dat.) regret A.Mil 3170 *var*, TC 1.1050. [OE *ofþyncan*]

atyr *n.* attire, dress I.Pars 430, PF 225, TC 1.181. [from OF *atirer*]

atones *adv.* at once, instantly A.Mil 3280, B.ML 670, H.Mcp 10, LGW 102; together, at the same time E.Cl 1178, LGW 1815; **atanes** (nth.) A.Rv 4074. [at+ones]

ato(o)n *adv.* (or as two words) at one, in(to) agreement A.Rv 4197, E.Cl 437. [at+o(o)n]

atrede† *v.* out-counsel, advise better than A.Kn 2449, TC 4.1456. [at+rede(n²)]

atrenne *v.* outrun A.Kn 2449, TC 4.1456. [at+renne(n; cf. OE *ætirnan*]

atte *see* **at**.

at(t)emperaunce *n.* temperament Bo 4. p6. 134/195, *pl.* 136/199; balance, mixture Bo 4. p6. 144/210, m6. 23/34; moderation C.Phs 46, I.Pars 833. [OF]

at(t)empree *adj.* moderate, controlled B.NP 4028, BD 1008; temperate, mild BD 341, PF 204, LGW 1483; modest I.Pars 932. [OF *atempré* p.p.]

at(t)emprely *adv.* temperately, moderately B.Sh 1452, D.Sum 2053, I.Pars 861. [from prec.]

at(t)empreth *pr. 3 sg.* moderates, assuages B.Mel 2704, Bo 1. m2 15/21; controls Bo 4. m1. 20/29, p5. 32/46. [OF *atemprer*]

at(t)empringe *vbl. n.* controlling Bo 5. p4. 62/89.

attendance *n.* service, ministration D.WB 933, Bo 4. p4. 203/284; *pl.* attention TC 1.339. [OF]

atthamaunt *see* **adamant**.

attry *adj.* poisonous I.Pars 583. [OE *ættrig*]

attricioun *n.* regret, imperfect sorrow for sins (short of contrition) TC 1.557. [OF]

atwinne *adv.* apart A.Mil 3589, G.CY 1170, TC 3.1666. [from a- pref+OE *twinn*]

atwixe(n *prep.* between TC 4.821, 5.472, RR 854. [from **bitwixe(n** with altered pref.]

atwo *adv.* in two A.Mil 3569, H.Mcp 263, TC 5.530; open B.ML 600. [OE *on twā*]

auctoritee *n.* **1.** authority, power B.NP 4165, G.SN 471, TC 1.65. **2.** authoritative text B.Mel 2660, D.Fri 1276, D.WB 1208; opinion, judgement B.Mel 2355, E.Mch 1597, F.Sq 482. [OF]

auctour *n.* author, writer B.NP 4174, E.Cl 1141, LGW 88; authority TC 1.394; originator, inventor H.Mcp 359, I.Pars 882, BalCh 27; creator TC 3.1016, 1765. [AN]

audience *n.* hearing E.Cl 329; *have* ~ get a hearing B.Mel 2237, B.NP 3991; *in* ~ in open court D.WB 1032, G.SN 466, *in general* ~ in the hearing of all B.ML 673, in public B.Mel 2239, *in open* ~ E.Cl 790, 1179; *yeven* ~ listen (to) B.Mel 2227, I.Pars 39, PF 308, TC 4.70, 5.235. [OF]

aught/o(u)ght *n.* **1.** anything A.Kn 1571, F.Fkl 1469, TC 5.1737; anything of value G.CY 1333; *as stille as* ~ BD 459; *for* ~ *I can espye* for all I can see Mars 221, TC 3.1135, 4.1469; *for* ~ *that may bitide* whatever may happen TC 3.1736, 5.59; *for* ~ *that may bifalle* A.Kn 1805, LGW 561. **2.** *as adv.* at all, in any way B.ML 1034, B.Pri 1792, TC 1.864, 3.316. [OE *āwiht, ōwiht*]

augrim *n.* arithmetic Astr 1.8.4/6, 9.4; ~ *stones* counters A.Mil 3210; *noumbres of* ~ arabic numerals Astr 1.7.4/6 [OF *augorisme*]

aunce(s)tre *n.* ancestor D.WB 1156, PF 41, LGW 2536. [OF]

auncetrye *n.* ancestry, lineage A.Rv 3982. [OF]

auntre *v.* venture, risk A.Rv 4209, *refl.* 4205. [OF *aventurer*]

auntrous *adj.* adventurous B.Th 2099. [OF *aventureus*]

autentyke *adj.* trustworthy, authoritative B.ML 1086. [OF *authentique*]

auter *n.* altar A.Kn 1905, B.ML 451, TC 5.1466. [OF]

availle(n *v.* **1.** *intr.* avail, be effective A.Kn 2401, B.NP 4336, I.Pars 88, Pity 78, PF 538, have power A.Kn 3040; (with *to*) benefit I.Pars 128; (with infin.) assist towards I.Pars 241; *impers.* B.ML 589, H.Mcp 147, Anel 216. **2.** *tr.* be of use to B.Pri 1765, TC 1.20, 604, help D.Fri 1366, HF 1616; *impers.* (with subject *it*) E.Mch 2107, (without expressed subject) MercB 15, be profitable to D.Fri 1324. [from *vail* v. from stem of OF *valoir*]

avale *v.* pull off A.Mil 3122; sink down Bo 4. m6. 19/22; come down TC 3. 626. [OF *avaler*]

avaunce(n *v.* advance, promote C.Pard 410, TC 1.518, LGW 2022; be profitable A.Prol 246. [OF *avaunc(i)er*]

avaunt *n.* boast TC 1.1050; *make* ~ boast A.Prol 227, E.Mch 1457, F.Fkl 1576, TC 2.727. [from v.]

ava(u)ntage *n.* advantage A.Kn 1293, G.CY 731, I.Pars 609; *at his* ~ well placed F.Fkl 772; profit I.Pars 851; *don his* ~ suit his own interest B.ML 729; (predic.) advantageous B.ML 146. [OF]

ava(u)nte(n *v. refl.* boast B.Mel 2741, D.WB 1014, PF 470, TC 3.318. [OF *avanter*]

avaunting *vbl. n.* boasting A.Rv 3884. I.Pars 391; *refl.* Bo 1. p4. 160/223.

avauntour *n.* boaster B.NP 4107, PF 430, TC 3.314. [from **avaunte(n**]

avenant *adj.* graceful, pleasant RR 1263. [OF]

aventaille *n.* mail neck-guard on helmet E.Cl 1204. [OF]

aventure *n.* **1.** chance A.Kn 1186, Mars 21, TC 4.388; *by* ~ A.Prol 25, B.ML 754; *par* ~ B.Sh 1205; *of* ~ F.Fkl 1501, HF 2090. **2.** fortune, lot B.NP 4189, F.Fkl 940; misfortune, accident A.Kn 2703, B.NP 4376, F.Fkl 1483, TC 1.35; (good) fortune TC 1.368, 2.224, Ven 22; event LGW 1907. **3.** risk, peril E.Mch 1877, Bo 2. m4. 8/12, Mars 60; *in* ~ in doubt I.Pars 1068, TC 1.784. [OF]

aventurous *adj.* subject to chance B.Mel 2857, Bo 1. p6. 68/88; accidental, fortuitous Bo 2. p4. 12/15 (L *fortuitae*). [OF]

avys *n.* advice, opinion A.Kn 1868, I.Pars 54, TC 1.620; consideration A.Prol 786; *took* ~ pondered B.Mel 2916. [OF]

avyse *v.* look at, contemplate TC 1.364, 2.276, 1177, 5.1814, consider Bo 5. p6. 79/111 (L *pensare*); plan I.Pars 448; understand E.Cl 797. *refl.* consider, think carefully, deliberate (on) A.Rv 4188, B.Sh 1426, E.Cl 350, PF 648, TC 2.1124, reflect E.Cl 238. **avyseth** *imper. pl.* A.Mil 3185, E.Mch 1555. [OF *aviser*]

avysed *ppl. adj.* wary, careful A.Mil 3584, C.Pard 690, E.Mch 1528; informed, aware TC 3.328, H.Mcp 286; having considered TC 2.605; determined TC 3.1186; *yvele* ~ ill-considered H.Mcp 335. [from prec.]

avisee *adj.* discreet LGW 1521. [OF]

avysely *adv.* advisedly, cautiously B.Mel 2488; seriously, thoughtfully I.Pars 1024; carefully Astr 2.29.18/25. [from prec.]

avysement *n.* deliberation B.ML 86, E.Mch 1531, TC 2.343; *take* ~ deliberate, consider B.Mel 2941. [OF]

avisioun *n.* vision, dream B.NP 4304, D.Sum 1858, HF 7. [OF]

avout(e)rye *n.* adultery D.Fri 1304, I.Pars 840, PF 361. [OF]

avout(i)er *n.* adulterer D.Fri 1372, I.Pars 841 [OF *avoutre*]

avow *n.* vow A.Kn 2237, C.Pard 695, BD 91. [from next]

avowe *v.* vow, affirm G.CY 642, TC 3.855. [OF *avouer*]

avoy *interj.* come! B.NP 4098. [OF]

await *n.* watchfulness, caution TC 3.457, 580; *have / keep in* ~ keep a watch on B.Mk 3915, H.Mcp 149; ambush Bo 3. p8. 11/15, *in (his)* ~ B.NP 4415, D.Fri 1657. [ONF]

awayte *v.* wait BalCo 7, (with *on* 'for') F.Fkl 1299, ABC 111; ~ *on* watch D.Sum 2052; ~ *after* watch for B.Pri 1776; waylay RR 1611. [ONF *awaitier*]

awaitour *n.* lier in wait Bo 4. p3. 77/110. [from prec.]

awake(n *v.* **1.** *intr.* awake, wake up A.Kn 1474, BD 179, TC 1.729; revive TC 1.564. **2.** *tr.* wake, rouse E.Mch 1957, Bo 3. m11. 24/32. *refl.* BD 1324. **awo(o)k** *pa. sg.* A.Mil 3364, TC 3.751. [*a-* pref.+OE *wacan, wacian,* see **wake(n**]

award *n.* decision I.Pars 483. [AN]

awarde *v.* **1.** determine, decree C.Phs 202. **2.** assign, hand over I.Pars 890. [AN. *awarder*]

awey(e *adv.* away A.Kn 1180, D.Sum 2235, TC 2.542, HF 418; gone A.Rv 4071, F.Fkl 1064, BD 655; astray B.ML 609, Anel 319, TC 4.357; away from home TC 2.1194; out of the way B.ML 593; finished TC 2.123; *exclam.* go away TC 3.1321, 5.1525; *don* ~ abolish Bo 2. p6. 10/17, 3 p3. 66/88; *dryve* ~ occupy (time) C.Pard 628, BD 49; *falle* ~ *fro* leave TC 3.1306. [OE *on weg*]

aweyward *adv.* away, aside H.Mcp 262. [from prec.]

awen *see* **owen.**

awepe *adv.* in *breste* ~ burst out weeping TC 2.408. [a prep.+*wep* n. from **wepe(n**]

awerk(e *adv.* to work A.Co 4337, D.WB 215; see **sette(n.** [a prep.+**werk**]

awhaped *ppl. adj.* amazed, confounded Anel 215, TC 1.316, LGW 132. [? from *w(h)ap* blow]

awreke *v.* avenge D.Sum 2211 var, H.Mcp 298, Pity 11. **awreke** *p.p.* D.Sum 2211, H.Mcp 298; **awroken** A.Mil 3752. [OE *awrecan;* cf. **wreke(n**]

awrie *adv.* on one side RR 291. [*a-* pref.+ **wrie(n**]

axe *see* **aske.**

axinge *see* **askinge.**

aye(i)n *see* **agayn.**

ayenward *see* **againward.**

B

ba *v.* kiss A.Mil 3709 *var,* D.WB 433. [imit.; cf. **pa**]

baar *see* **bere(n.**

babewynnes *n. pl.* baboons, grotesques HF 1189 *em.* [OF]

Babilan *adj.* Babylonian B.ML 63. [modified from L *Babylōnius*]

bacheler *n.* **1.** young man A.Prol 80, H.Mcp 107, RR 918. **2.** unmarried man, bachelor E.Mch 1274, 1278. **3.** knight (of rank below banneret) A.Kn 3085, D.WB 883, F.Sq 24. **4.** holder of a first degree F.Fkl 1126. [OF]

bachelrye *n.* **1.** young men E.Cl 270. **2.** bachelorhood H.Mcp 125. [OF]

bacoun *n.* bacon B.NP 4035; (fig., as of dried meat) D.WB 418. [OF]

bad *see* **bidde.**

badder *adj. comp.* worse F.Sq 224. [ME *badde,* perh. OE *bǣddel*]

baggeth *pr. 3 sg.* ? looks askance BD 623. [?]

baggingly *adv.* leeringly RR 292 (F *en borgnoiant*). [cf. prec.]

baillif *n.* bailiff, steward A.Prol 603, D.Fri 1419, **bailly** D.Fri 1392, 1396. [OF]

baite *v.* **1.** *tr.* bait (hook) Mars 238; torment RR 1612. **2.** *intr.* feed B.ML 466, B.Th 2103, (fig.) TC 1.192. [ON *beita*]

bak *n.* back A.Kn 1050, B.NP 4595, BD 446; ∼ *and side* all over B.Mk 3804, 3934; clothes for the back G.CY 881 *var.* [OE *bæc*]

bake-mete *n.* pie A.Prol 343, I.Pars 445. [from *bake*, p.p. from OE *bacen*,+**mete**]

bakhalf *n.* back Astr 1.4.1, 2.1.6/9. [**bak**+**half**]

balaunce *n.* scales B.Mk 3776; *in* ∼ in suspense, at risk G.CY 611, BD 1021, TC 2.466. [OF]

bale *n.* harm, suffering G.CY 1481, BD 535, TC 4.746; *for bote ne* ∼ for good or ill BD 227. [OE *balu*]

balke *n.* beam A.Rv 3920, A.Mil 3626, LGW 2253. [OE *balca*]

balled *adj.* bald A.Prol 198, A.Kn 2518. [from *ball* n., prob. from OE]

bane *n.* death B.NP 4150, TC 4.774, LGW 2180, 2461; destruction TC 5.602, HF 408; destroyer TC 4.333, LGW 2147. [OE *bana*]

banes *see* **bo(o)n.**

baptyse *v. refl.* receive baptism G.SN 171, 299. [OF *baptiser*]

bar *see* **bere(n.**

barbe *n.* barb (part of woman's headdress) TC 2.110 [OF]

Barbre *adj.* heathen, Saracen B.ML 281. [OF]

bare *adj.* bare, naked F.Fkl 720, TC 2.110, LGW 1859; esp. of knees (when kneeling) B.Pri 1719, E.Mch 1351, F.Fkl 1025, 1545; bareheaded A.Prol 683; uncovered F.Fkl 1580, TC 3.1099; meagre D.Fri 1480; impoverished G.CY 732: deprived TC 4.1168, 5.1547. [OE *bær*]

bareyne *adj.* barren A.Kn 1977, D.WB 372, I.Pars 576; (fig.) destitute A.Kn 1244. [AN *barai(g)ne*]

barge *n.* boat, ship A.Prol 410, A.Mil 3550, LGW 621. [OF]

barm *n.* lap, bosom B.Mk 3256, 3630, E.Cl 551, F.Sq 631. [OE *bearm*]

barm-clo(o)th *n.* apron A.Mil 3236. [prec.+**clo(o)th**]

barre *n.* bar A.Kn 1075. *pl.* I.Pars 433, RR 1103; stripes A.Prol 329. [OF]

barred *adj.* striped A.Mil 3235. [from prec.]

barringe *vbl. n.* striping I.Pars 417.

basilicok *n.* basilisk I.Pars 853. [OF]

hataille *n.* battle A.Kn 879, PF 540, TC 2.630; *mortal* ∼ A.Prol 61, A.Kn 2540. [OF]

batailled *ppl. adj.* battlemented, crenellated B.NP 4050. [OF *bataillier*]

batailen *v.* fight Bo 1. p4. 149/206, 4. p7. 31/43. [OF *batailler*]

bathe *see* **bothe.**

baude *n.* bawd, pimp D.Fri 1354, C.Pard 479, TC 2.353. [? cf. OF *baudetrot*]

baud(e)rie *n.* **1.** (act of) procuring D.Fri 1303, TC 3.397. **2.** gaiety A.Kn 1926. [OF]

baudy *adj.* dirty G.CY 635. [?]

baudrik *n.* baldric, diagonal belt A.Prol 116. [OF *baudrei*, cf. MHG *balderich*]

baume *n.* balm, balsam TC 2.53, HF 1686. [OF *basme*]

baundon *n.* control RR 1163. [OF]

be- *see* **bi-.**

beau sir *n.* (in address) good sir HF 643, RR 800. [OF]

beautee *n.* beauty A.Kn 1114, TC 1.102, MercB 2; (person.) A.Kn 1926, PF 225, TC 2.398; *pl.* I.Pars 858 *var*, Bo 2. p5. 28 *var*/39, LGW 254. [OF]

beblotte *imper.* blot TC 2.1027. [from *blot* n., origin unkn.]

bechen *adj.* of beech wood G.CY 1160, 1196. [OE *bēcen*]

bede *see* **bidde.**

bedes *n. pl.* in *peire of* ∼ rosary A.Prol 159. [OE *bedu* prayers]

bedote *v.* make a fool of LGW 1547. [from **dote(n)**]

bedrede *adj.* bedridden D.Sum 1769, E.Mch 1292. [OE *bedreda*]

bee *n.* bee F.Sq 204, TC 2.193, HF 1522; *bisy* ∼ G.SN 195, E.Mch 2422. **been** *pl.* F.Sq 204, Bo 3. m7. 3, TC 2.193; **bees** B.NP 4582, D.Sum 1693. [OE *bēo*, pl. *bēon*]

be(e)de *v.* offer E.Cl 360, Anel 304, TC 5.185. [OE *bēodan*]

be(e)l amy *n.* good friend C.Pard 318. [OF]

be(e)m *n.* **1.** beam, ray (of light) D.WB 868, BD 337, TC 3. 1. **2.** beam, balk B.NP 4132, 4362; *rode* ∼ Cross D.WB 496. [OE *bēam*]

be(e)(n *v.* be: *lat* ∼ let alone, give up, cease A.Prol 840, D.WB 242, D.Fri 1289, TC 2.1056, 1286; ∼ *as* ∼ *may* however it may be B.Mk 3319, G.CY 935, TC 4.638 *var*, LGW 1145. *auxil.* (with intr. vs.) ∼ *assented* Pity 53, ∼ *kist* B.ML 1074, ∼ *went* E.Mch 1701. **be(e)n** *pr. pl.* A.Kn 887, C.Pard 774, D.Fri 1426, TC 2.235, LGW 782; **be(e** E.Cl 351, BD 674, TC 2.113, 3.1207, LGW 529, Purse 12; **beth** E.Mel 2350 *var*, F.Sq 648 *var*; *see* **are. beth** *imper. pl.* B.Sh 1397, B.Mk 3281, E.Cl 1191, G.CY 937, TC 2.302, 5.145, Purse 14. **be(e)n** *p.p.* A.Kn 929, D.WB 428; **be** E.Mch 1371, LGW 840; **ybe(e)n** B.NP 4487, Bo 5. p6. 63/88; **ybe** E.Mch 2401, LGW 6. [OE *bēon*]

been *see* **bee.**

be(e)r *see* **bere(n.**

be(e)re *n.*[1] bier A.Kn 2871, B.Pri 1815, TC 2.1638. [OA *bēr*]

be(e)st(e *n.* animal A.Kn 1309, B.Mk 3363, E.Mch 1281, PF 196; ∼ *roial* Leo F.Sq 264; beast, brute D.WB 1034, G.SN 288, ABC 45, LGW 1928. [OF]

be(e)te(n *v.*[1] **1.** beat, strike A.Rv 4308, F.WB 511, (the breast) TC 1.932, 3.1416, 4.738; (wings) flap B.NP 4512, F.Fkl 766; beat upon Bo 4. m5. 15/21; assail TC 4.910 *var.* **2.** hammer (esp. gold) A.Kn 979, C.Phs 14, Anel 24; mint LGW 1122. **3.** *intr.* (of heart) beat HF 570, (of spirit in the heart) TC 4.910 *var.* **bet** *pa. sg.* TC 4.738. **beete** *pl.* A.Rv 4308; **bette(n** A.Rv 4316, B.Mel 2694. **bete(n** *p.p.* B.Pri 1732, I.Pars 838, HF 1150; **ybete(n** A.Kn 979, TC 1.741, 2.940, LGW 755; **bet** D.WB 511 *var*; **ybet** D.Fri 1285. [OE *bēatan*, *bēot,-on, ġe)bēaten*]

be(e)te *v.*[2] mend, cure A.Rv 3927, CompL 73, TC 1.665, 4.928; relieve I.Pars 421; kindle A.Kn 2253, 2292. **betten** *pa. pl.* fed (fire) G.SN 518. [OE *bētan*]

beggarly adv. like a beggar RR 223. [from beggar, from begge(n v., prob. OE bedecian]
beggestere n. beggar A.Prol 242. [from begge(n v. (see prec.)+OE fem. suff. -estre]
behewe p.p. carved HF 1306. [OE behēawen]
beye see **bye(n.**
bekke v. nod C.Pard 396, H.Mcp 346, TC 2.1260. [from OA bēcnian]
bele adj. good, beautiful B.Sh 1599, TC 2.288, HF 1796. [OF]
bele chose n. phr. lit. 'beautiful thing': favours D.WB 447, 510. [OF]
bely n. **1.** belly D.Sum 2267; ∼-naked completely naked E.Mch 1326. **2.** bellows I.Pars 351. [OA bel(i)ġ]
belweth pr. 3 sg. bellows HF 1803. [OA *belgan]
beme n. trumpet, bugle B.NP 4588, HF 1240. [OA bēme]
benched p.p. provided with benches TC 2.822, LGW 204; also **ybenched.** [from OE benĉ]
bend n. band RR 1079. [OF bende]
bendinge vbl. n. decorating with bands or stripes I.Pars 417. [from v. from prec.]
bene n. bean; as measure of worthlessness E.Mch 1263, 1854; nat a ∼ A.Mil 3772, B.NP 4004, TC 5.363. [OE bēan]
benedicite/bendiste exclam. bless you! bless us! A.Kn 1785, D.WB 241, TC 1.780. [L]
benestraw n. beanstraw, dried beanstalks E.Mch 1422. [prec.+stree]
benigne adj. kind, gentle, considerate A.Prol 483, B.ML 615, TC 3.26, LGW 243, gracious B.Mel 2933, E.Cl 411, Pity 58, TC 5.1869, well-disposed TC 1.431, 3.1802, favourable F.Sq 52. [OF]
benignely adv. kindly B.Mel 3017, courteously, modestly E.Cl 21, tenderly E.Mch 2093, patiently I.Pars 109. [from prec.]
benignitee n. goodness, graciousness B.ML 446, TC 3.39; your ∼ (as humble address) B.Mel 2428. [OF]
benisoun n. blessing B.Mel 2288, E.Mch 1365. [OF beneiçun]
bent n. grassy slope A.Kn 1981, LGW G. 234. [OE beonet]
berd n. beard A.Prol 270, A.Mil 3742, B.NP 4110; in the ∼ face to face TC 4.41; make (one's) ∼ deceive, hoodwink A.Rv 4096, D.WB 361. [OE beard]
bere n.² cover BD 254. Cf. **pilwe-beer.** [?]
bere n.³ bear A.Kn 1640, B.NP 4125, TC 3.1780, LGW 1214. [OE bera]
bere(n v. **1.** carry A.Kn 1422, B.Mk 3815, D.Fri 1614, HF 662; wear F.Sq 43; (a name, with dat.) attribute to LGW 2135; ∼ the belle come first, lead TC 3.198; ∼ compaignye (with dat.) keep (someone) company I.Pars 967, Bo 3. m12. 33/46, TC 4.1202, LGW 2058; ∼ in minde remember B.ML 1127; ∼ on hond see **hond;** ∼ witnesse F.Fkl 1367, G.CY 1450, I.Pars 931. **2.** refl. behave, conduct oneself A.Kn 1523, D.WB 1108, I.Pars 929, TC 2.401, 1498. **3.** push, thrust: ∼ (a)doun overthrow A.Kn 2644, E.Mch 2270; pierce A.Kn 2256. **4.** give birth to B.ML 722, B.Pri 1652, E.Cl 612, TC 4.763; see **bore(n.** **5.** endure, suffer B.Mel 2654, LGW 2524; sikly ∼ dislike, resent E.Cl 625, ∼ so(o)re E.Cl 85. **berth** pr. 3 sg. B.ML 620.

ba(a)r pa. 1, 3 sg. A.Prol 105, A.Rv 4165, D.WB 224, HF 169; **be(e)r** B.ML 722, LGW 216. **bare** 2 sg. E.Cl 1068, Bo 2. p3./ 67 var; **bere** Bo 2. p3. 46/var, TC 4.763.
baren pl. A.Prol 721; **bere(n** HF 1332, RR 1374. **boren** p.p. D.WB 1153; **y)bore** A.Prol 378, F.Sq 178; **y)born** A.Prol 87, B.ML 995, F.Sq. 340. [OE beran, bær, bæron/bēron, ġe)boren]
beringe vbl. n. behaviour, demeanour B.Th 2022, E.Mch 1604, I.Pars 737, 936.
berkinge vbl. n. barking B.NP 4576. [OE beorcan]
berm n. yeast G.CY 813. [OE beorma]
bern n. barn A.Mil 3258, B.Mk 3759, D.WB 871. [OE bern from bere ern]
besaunt-wight n. weight of a bezant RR 1106. [OF besan from Byzant-ium+wight n.²]
besy, besye see **bisy, bisie.**
besmoked p.p. smoke-blackened Bo 1. p1. 19/27. [OE besmocian]
best adv. sup. best A.Prol 206, E.Mch 1460, TC 1.47; as ∼ I can/coude BD 517, TC 1.459, 2.1673; me was ∼ I should PF 152, yow was ∼ you should TC 4184. [OE betst]
beste adj. sup. best A.Prol 252, D.WB 608, BD 1049; atte/at the ∼ in the best possible way, excellently A.Prol 29, 749, A.Rv 4147; for the ∼ as the best thing to do (often almost a tag) A.Prol 788, A.Kn 1847, B.ML 412, D.WB 427, E.Cl 489, E.Mch 1518, TC 4.808; (as) for (one's) ∼ in one's best interests, to one's advantage B.Sh 1537, B.Mel 2427, D.Sum 1986; thy/your ∼ your best course TC 1.1028, 2.382, 5.392. [OE betsta]
bet adj. comp. better B.ML 311, B.Mel 2566, G.CY 1410, I.Pars 497, TC 1.257. [from next]
bet adv. comp. better A.Prol 242, F.Sq 600, HF 13; the ∼ BD 668, TC 4.1358, never the ∼ D.Sum 1951, BD 671, TC 3.1564; go ∼ go as fast as you can C.Pard 667, BD 136, LGW 1213; ∼ than never is late better late than never G.CY 1410. [OE]
beth see **be(e)(n.**
beting n. beating HF 1034, (pl.) Bo 3. m2. 8/12. [from be(e)te(n]
bettre -er adj. better A.Prol 256, E.Cl 7, LGW 446; ∼ arm right arm TC 2.1650; the smallere the ∼ Astr 2.38.6/9. [OE betera]
bettre adv. better A.Prol 608, B.ML 881, PF 200, TC 2.1531. [from prec.]
bever n. attrib. beaver A.Prol 272. [OE beofor]
bi adv. beside, nearby B.NP 4458, faste ∼ close by A.Kn 1688, B.Mk 3116, (of time) near, at hand A.Kn 1476, TC 4.117, see **faste;** ∼ and ∼ side by side A.Kn 1011, alongside A.Rv 4143, one after another LGW 304. [OE bi]
bi/be prep. **1.** (of place) by, beside A.Rv 4036, F.Sq 643, TC 2.1228, ∼me (stressed, rhyming tyme) TC 2.991; with, see **lye(n;** past BD 388; along LGW 1497; faste ∼ close to A.Prol 719, E.Mch 1928, (following obj.) F.Sq 504, RR 1274 (see **faste**); through, over B.Th 1986, C.Pard 694, TC 5.1144; on A.Prol 467, B.ML 543; (of direction) in A.Prol 388, TC 5.1193. **2.** (of time) at, in, during A.Prol 97, PF 357, TC 1.452,

HF 1951, ~ *the morwe* in the morning
A.Prol 334, B.Mk 3586, TC 2.961, ~ *this*
by this time TC 3.793, ~ *tyme*(*s* see **tyme**.
3. (of cause) by, through A.Prol 25, A.Kn
2488, E.Mch 1967, F.Sq 406; ~ *force of*
necessity A.Kn 2554. **4.** (of means) A.Mil
3625, C.Pard 387, BD 1271; *as* ~ to judge
by E.Cl 924; *live* ~ live on A.Prol 581; *~oon*
accord/*assent* in full agreement B.Mel 2486,
C.Pard 801; ~ *me* by my example G.CY
737. **5.** (of agent) D.WB 1262, F.Sq 666,
I.Pars 322. **6.** (in oaths) A.Prol 120, BD 6,
TC 3.589. **7.** (of succession) *yeer* ~ *yeer*,
etc. A.Kn 1033, B.Mk 3249, F.Fkl 993, ~
rewe in turn G.SN 92, (with num.) in
groups of F.Sq 354. **8.** (of reference) of,
about D.WB 229, D.Sum 1922, PF 4,
according to B.Sh 1396, B.Pri 1824,
C.Pard 601, D.WB 622, by advice of B.Mel
2395, with respect to A.Kn 2021, Mars
263, TC 1.225, in view of A.Prol 244; ~ . .
selve(*n* by (one's) self A.Rv 4142, D.WB
812, BD 419, LGW 1759. **9.** ~ *that* as
conj. by the time that G.CY 971, I.Pars 1,
LGW 2359. [OE]
bibbed *p.p.* drunk A.Rv 4162. [? L *bibere*,
or imit.]
bible *n.* Bible A.Prol 438, D.WB 650; book
G.CY 857, HF 1334. [OF]
bibled *ppl. adj.* covered with blood A.Kn
2002, Bo 3. m2. 9/13. [from **blede**]
bycause (mss. and editions vary in treating
as one word or two: cf. **cause**) **1.** *adv.*:
with *of* forming *prep.* because of B.Sh 1597,
TC 4.688; with infin., in order to Bo 4.
p7. 7/11; with *that* forming *conj.* because
Bo 1. p4. 197/276, TC 4. 717. **2.** *conj.*
because TC 3.991, 5.1215. [**bi** + **cause**]
bicched *adj.* cursed, in ~ *bones* = dice
C.Pard 656. [from OE *bicce* bitch]
biclappe *v.* grab hold of G.SN 9. [from OE
clappian]
bicome(*n* *v.* **1.** become C.Pard 698, D.Fri
1644, E.Mch 2098, LGW 1238. **2.** go,
depart, change state: *wher* ~*th it* what
happens to it TC 2.795, *wher he* ~ what may
become of him TC 2.1151, sim. LGW
2214; *wher is* ~ what has become of Anel
247. **3.** suit D.WB 603. [OE *becuman*, see
come(*n*]
bidaffed *ppl. adj.* made a fool of E.Cl 1191.
[from **daf**]
bidde *v.* **1.** command, tell E.Mch 1387,
F.Sq 321, BD 141, TC 1.357, 2.1554. **2.**
ask, beg TC 1.112, 1027; pray G.SN 140,
TC 2.118, 3. 342, 875, say (prayer) A.Mil
3641. **3.** wish, desire TC 3.1249, (with
infin.) TC 2.406. **biddeth** *pr. 3 sg.* LGW
647; **bit** A.Prol 187, F.Sq 291. **biddeth**
imper. pl. TC 1.36. **bad** *pa. sg.* A.Prol 787,
TC 1.112. **bede**(*n* *pl.* B.Mel 2233, I.Pars
65. **bede** *p.p.* BD 194; **bode**(*n* D.WB
1030, LGW 366. [OE *biddan, bæd, bædon,
beden* and *bēodan, bēad, budon, boden*]
byde *v. intr.* wait B.NP 4275, TC 3.740;
stay A.Kn 1576, E.Mch 1888, TC 4.162.
tr. await TC 2.1519. **bood** *pa. sg.* A.Co
4399, TC 5.29. **biden** *p.p.* E.Mch 1888.
[OE *bīdan, bād, biden*]
bideweth *pr. 3 sg.* bedews Bo 4. m6. 23/33.
[from OE *dēaw*]
bidolven *p.p.* buried Bo 5. p1. 51/73. [OE
bedolfen, see **delve**(*n*]

bye(*n*/**beye** *v.* **1.** buy B.Sh 1246, C.Pard
845, RR 237. **2.** pay for (esp. ~ *dere*)
D.WB 167, Anel 255, TC 5.1801; redeem
TC 5.1843, I.Pars 132; ~ *again* C.Pard
501. **bo**(*u*)**ghte** *pa. sg.* C.Pard 293, E.Cl
1153. **bo**(*u*)**ghten** *pl.* TC 5.1801, LGW
258. **y**)**boght** *p.p.* B.Sh 1534, E.Mch 1648.
[OE *bycgan*, pr. 3 sg. *bygþ; bohte, ģe)boht*]
bifalle(*n* *v.* happen, come about A.Prol 795,
A.Kn 1805, E.Cl 84, E.Mch 1232, PF 664,
(with *of* 'because of') I.Pars 587; (often
impers. fold. by *that*-cl., without expressed subject) A.Prol 19, B.Mk 3613,
TC 1.271, (*and*) *so bifel* B.ML 150, D.WB
543, F.Sq 42, TC 5.1234, (with subject *it*)
A.Mil 3399, B.Mel 2676, D.WB 882, TC
3.511; happen to (with dat.) Bo 3. p4.
17/24, Adam 1, HF 101, LGW 2535;
fayre yow ~ good luck to you I.Pars 68.
bifel *pa.* A.Prol 19, B.NP 4072, D.WB 543;
bifil B.Mk 3613, E.Mch 2133, RR 1455.
bifille *subj.* Bo 1. p4. 22/30. **bifalle**(*n* *p.p.*
A.Prol 795, Bo 1. p3. 15/21, TC 4.1069.
[OA *befallan*, see **falle**(*n*]
biforn/**bifore** *adv.* in front A.Prol 377, 590,
A.Kn 1376; in a favourable position A.Prol
572; before, previously A.Mil 3535, B.Mel
2146, D.Sum 1759, TC 2.966, beforehand
A.Kn 1665, B.Sh 1184. [OE *beforan*]
biforn/**bifore** *prep.* before, in front of
A.Prol 100, A.Rv 3952, D.Sum 2022, TC
1.110; (of time) earlier than BD 198, Astr
2.3. 15/21; in preference to I.Pars 751,
above B.Mel 2490; (following obj.) A.Kn
1634, B.Mk 3526, D.WB 886, E.Cl 65,
G.CY 680. [as prec.]
bigamye *n.* marrying twice D.WB 33, 96. [OF]
bigan see **biginne**.
bigat *pa.* begot, fathered B.Mel 2157, LGW
1562. **bigete**(*n* *p.p.* B.Mk 3138, TC 1.977.
[OA *beġæt, -ġeten* and **gete**(*n*]
bigyle(*n* *v.* deceive, trick A.Mil 3300, G.CY
985, TC 4.3, LGW 2545, RR 1055, trap
B.ML 582; wile away (time) TC 5.404; destroy C.Phs 274; deprive deceitfully (*of*)
TC 1.716. **bigylestow** *pr. 2 sg.* (with suffixed pron.) I.Pars 1022. [from **gyle**]
bigyleres *n. pl.* deceivers I.Pars 299. [from
prec.]
biginne *v.* **1.** begin *tr.* (with obj.) A.Prol
853, B.Mk 3926, *nas nat newe to* ~ did not
need to be initiated, i.e. was long established
A.Prol 428, *was ay span-newe to* ~ had to
be started over and over again TC 3.1665;
~ *the bord* see **bord**; (with (*for*) to and
infin.) TC 2.874, 5.247. *intr.* A.Prol 836,
A.Kn 892, TC 1.868, ~ *at* A.Prol 42, ~
(*up*)*on* I.Pars 53, TC 1.389. **2.** as quasi-
auxil. (cf. **ginne**): *pr. 3 sg.* does B.Mk
3872, TC 4.239 *var, 2 sg.* dost ? LGW
G.261. **bigan** *pa. 1, 3 sg.* A.Prol 44, A.Kn
1354. **bigonne**/**-gunne** *2 sg.* G.SN 442,
Bo 2. p3. 23/32; **bigan** LGW 2230.
bigonne *pl.* D.Fri 1560, TC 4.257.
bigonne(*n* *p.p.* A.Prol 52, B.Mel 2872.
[OF *beginnan, -gann, -gunnon, -gunnen*]
bigon *p.p.* beset, surrounded RR 943; (with
dat.) *him is wo* ~ sorrow has assailed him,
he is sad A.Mil 3372, F.Fkl 1316; sim. B.ML
918; (hence with neom., as if adj.) *wo* ~ *ben
hertes trewe* TC 3.117; sim. *sorwfully* ~
TC 1.114; *wel* ~ happy D.WB 606, TC
2.597, RR 580. [OE *begān*]

bihalve *n.* (only in *on* (*one's*) ~) behalf B.Mel 2987, TC 2.1458, LGW 497. [blend of phr. *bi halve* and *on* . . *halve*, see **half**]

bihated *p.p.* hated Bo 3. m4. 4/5. [from *hate* v., OE *hatian*]

bihe(e)ste *n.* **1.** promise B.ML 37, F.Fkl 698, D.WB 1059; ~ *is dette* a promise is binding B.ML 41. **2.** command TC 2.359, B.Mel 2419. [OE *behǣs*]

bihete(n/bihote *v.* promise A.Kn 1854, I.Pars 290, TC 3.319; *I yow* ~ I assure you G.CY 707. **bihight** *pa. sg.* F.Fkl 788, TC 3.319; **bihette** PF 436. **bihighten** *pl.* F.Fkl 1327, TC 5.496. **bihight** *p.p.* B.Mel 2256, TC 4.445. [OE *behātan*, see **hote(n**]

bihinde *adv.* at the back A.Mil 3239; afterwards B.ML 427; to come G.CY 1291; left out of account, neglected I.Pars 1010. [OE *behindan*]

biholde(n *v.* **1.** see, look at A.Kn 1301, E.Cl 60, TC 1.177, RR 143; gaze, look (with prep.) C.Phs 191, F.Fkl 863, PF 18, LGW G.92. **2.** notice, observe TC 5.533, HF 539, Bo 4. p6. 211/305; consider TC 5.1748, Bo 3. p1. 35/47. **biheld** *pa. sg.* H.Mcp 241, TC 5.730. **bihelden** *pl.* TC 1.177. **bihelde** *subj.* TC 2.378. **biholde(n** *p.p.* G.SN 179, Bo 4. p6. 149/217, TC 5.1252. [OA *behāldan*, see **holde(n**]

biholder *n.* observer Bo 5. p6. 121/171, 209/295. [from prec.]

bihote *see* **bihete(n.**

bihove *n.* profit RR 1092. [OE *behōf*]

bihove *v.* **1.** belong, be necessary I.Pars 83, F.Sq. 602. **2.** *impers.* (with dat.) be proper, right, necessary: (subject not expressed) F.Fkl 1359, I.Pars 634, TC 1.858, Truth 5, RR 1479, (subject *it*) B.Mel 2360, Bo 5. p3. 56/77, p6. 127/180, TC 4.1004, **boes** *pr. 3 sg.* (nth.) A.Rv 4027. [OE *behōfian*]

bihovely *adj.* useful, needful I.Pars 107, 387, TC 2.261. [OE *behōflič*]

bijaped *p.p.* tricked, fooled A.Kn 1585, H.Mcp 145; mocked TC 1.531. [from **jape(n**]

bikenne *v.* commit C.Pard 292 *var.* [from **kenne**]

biknowe(n *v.* acknowledge, confess A.Kn 1556, B.ML 886, (sins) I.Pars 170, 586. **biknew** *pa. sg.* LGW 1058. **biknewe** *pl.* B.NP 4251. **biknowen** *p.p.* in *am* ~ acknowledge Bo 3. p10. 58/80. [OE be- pref. + **knowe(n**]

bile(e)ve *n.* belief, faith F.Fkl 1133, G.SN 427, TC 5.593. [OE *ǧelēafa*, with altered pref.]

bile(e)ve(n *v.*[1] believe: *tr.* A.Mil 3162, TC 2.1502, HF 990; with *on*, *in* B.ML 574, D.WB 1178, I.Pars 605. **bileveth** *imper. pl.* B.Mel 2701. [LOE *belēfan*]

bileve/bleve(n *v.*[2] remain, stay F.Sq 583, TC 4.539, 5.1180. [OE *belǣfan*]

bille *n.* **1.** petition, complaint C.Phs 166, Pity 44, *putte a* ~ submit a petition E.Mch 1971; writ D.Fri 1586; deed ABC 59. **2.** letter E.Mch 1937, TC 2.1130.[AN]

bilongeth *pr. 3 sg.* is proper, appropriate (*to*) B.Mk 3820, E.Mch 1459. **bilongen** *pl.* pertain I.Pars 319. [from **longe(n**[2]]

binde *v.* **1.** bind, fasten B.Pri 1810, TC 5.812, A.Rv 3953; bind (as a book) D.WB 681. **2.** keep fast, hold A.Kn 2414, F.Sq 620, TC 2.359; oblige A.Kn 1149. **bindeth**

pr. 3 sg. Bo 2. p8. 14/20; **bynt** Mars 47, 48. **bo(o)nd** *pa. sg.* A.Kn 2991, E.Mch 1262. **bounde** *pl.* B.Mk 3260. **bounde(n** *p.p.* TC 1.859, LGW 600; **ybounde(n** A.Kn 1149, 2151. [OE *bindan*, *bánd*, *búndon*, *ge*)*búnden*]

bynethe(n **1.** *adv.* beneath, below A.Rv 4041, B.NP 4143, Astr 1.18.7/10. **2.** *prep.* under, below D.Sum 2142, Mars 219, Bo 2. p5. 109/153. [OE *beneoþan*]

binime(n *v.* take away I.Pars 566, Bo 2. p4. 101/138, 4. p3. 18/32. **benomen** *p.p.* Bo 3. p3. 50/65. [OE *beniman*, see **nam**[2]]

bint *see* **binde.**

biquethe *v.* bequeath A.Kn 2768, TC 4. 786. *p.p.* D.WB 1164. [OE *becweþan*, p.p. -*cweden*]

biraft(e, bireft(e *see* **bireve(n.**

byrde *n.* lady RR 1014. [OE **byrde*, deriv. of -*byrdan* embroider, cf. *byrdestre* embroideress]

bireyned *pa.* showered TC 4.1172. [from *reyne.*]

bireve(n *v.* remove, seize, from (with dat. of person and direct obj.), so deprive (person) of D.WB 461, 475, D.Sum 2071, I.Pars 796, PF 87, TC 2.1722; deprive, rob (with direct obj. of person and *of*) B.ML 83, B.Mk 3359, I.Pars 867, TC 4.228, *me wo* ~ relieve my misery CompL 12; prevent (with obj. and infin.) TC 1.685; take away D. Sum 2111, I.Pars 369, TC 3.1340. **birafte** *pa.* B.ML 83, B.Mk 3404; **birefte** Bo 3. p2. 57/81. **biraft** *p.p.* A.Kn 1361, TC 4.225; **bireft** Bo 2. p2. 5/6; **bireved** D.Sum 2071. [OE *berēafian*; cf. **reve(n**]

biscorned *p.p.* mocked I.Pars 278. [from **scorne(n**]

biseche/biseke *v.* beseech, ask, beg (*of* 'for') A.Kn 918, B.Sh 1431, G.SN 55, TC 4.1632; make supplication (*to*) B.Mel 2306. **biso(u)ght(e** *pa. sg.* A.Rv. 4118, B.ML 993, TC 1.769; **biso(u)ghten** *pl.* HF 1706. [EME from **seke(n**]

biseye/-seyn *p.p.* beseen, -looking (with adv.): *wel* ~ BD 829, RR 821; *yvel* ~ E.Cl 965; *richely* ~ E.Cl 984. [OE *besēne* from *besēon*]

bisemare *n.* scorn, mockery A.Rv 3965. [OE *bismer*.]

bisette *v.* employ, apply A.Prol 279, TC 3.471, LGW 1069; bestow A.Mil 3715, BD 772, TC 1.521, dispose of D.Sum 1952. **bisette** *pa.* B.Sh 1565. **biset** *p.p.* A.Mil 3299, I.Pars 279. [OE *besettan*]

bishende *v.* ruin LGW 2696. [from **shende**]

bishet *p.p.* shut up TC 3.602. [from **shet-te(n**]

bishrewe *v.* curse D.WB 844, 845. [from **shrewe**]

bisy/besy *adj.* **1.** busy, industrious A.Prol 321, E.Cl 1029, ~*bee* G.SN 195, cf. E.Mch 2422; occupied TC 5.989; active, restless LGW 103; ~ *ynogh* fully occupied, hard put to it E.Mch 1560. **bisier** *comp.* A.Prol 322. **2.** attentive, careful A.Kn 2442, B.Pri 1779, BD 1265; anxious E.Cl 134, Pity 2, Bo 2. p5. 126/178 (L *sollicitus*), ~ *cure* anxious care A.Kn 2853, B.ML 188, PF 369, TC 3.1042. [OE *bisiǧ*]

biside(s *adv.* **1.** near, in the neighbourhood, often quasi-*prep.* in *ther* ~ near that place

A.Kn 1478, B.ML 398, F.Fkl 902, BD 1316, TC 2.76, see **ther**; sim. *wher* . . ∼ near which B.Pri 1796; with him F.Fkl 1241. **2.** in addition A.Kn 967, E.Cl 416. **3.** by, past TC 3.1781; aside, off the road G.CY 1416. [OE *be sīdan*]

biside(s *prep.* **1.** near A.Prol 402, 445; beside, next to (following obj.) A.Kn 874, B.Mk 3937, B.NP 4293, E.Cl 777, BD 208, PF 241. **2.** against, contrary to TC 2.734, 3.622, HF 2105. [from prec.]

bisie/besye *v. refl.* busy oneself, endeavour, B.Mel 2677, G.CY 1146, 1258, PF 192. [OE *bisġian*]

bisily *adv.* diligently, zealously A.Prol 301, A.Mil 3763, PF 74, TC 4.486, earnestly A.Rv 4006, TC 1.771, 3.1153; eagerly F.Sq 88, F.Fkl 1051; attentively RR 143, intently B.ML 1095. [from adj.]

bisinesse/besi- *n.* **1.** being busy, activity A.Mil 3643, E.Cl 1008, C.Pard 399, I.Pars 684, Truth 10, occupation A.Mil 3654, TC 2.1174 *var.* **2.** employment, occupation B.Mel 2781, PF 86, business B.Sh 1415, *in his* ∼ occupied G.CY 1270. *pl.* employments TC 2.1174 *var.* **3.** what is to be done, duties, part E.Mch 1904, TC 2.1316, task TC 1.1042. **4.** endeavour A.Prol 520, *do (one's)* ∼ strive, make an effort, endeavour B.Mel 2822, E.Cl 592, G.SN 24, F.Sq. 642, TC 4.1488, devote attention, apply oneself A.Kn 1007, B.Mel 2205, take care TC 1. 795; diligence TC 3. 165, *in* ∼ diligent C.Phs 56. **5.** attention Anel 250, TC 3.1413; concern E.Mch 1577, anxiety D.WB 1196, Bo 1. m2. 3/4 (L *cura*), 3. p5. 21/29 (L *sollicitudinum*); difficulty, trouble Anel 99. [from **bisy**]

bismotered *p.p.* bespattered A.Prol 76. [? cf. **smoterliche**]

biso(u)ght *see* **biseche**.

bispet *p.p.* spat upon, spattered I.Pars 276, 279. [from **spete**]

bispotten *pr. pl.* stain Bo 3. p4. 38/55. [from **spot**]

bistad *p.p.* hard pressed, endangered B.ML 649, RR 1227. [from ON *staddr*, p.p. of *steðja* place]

bistrood *pa.* bestrode B.Th 2093. [OE *bestrād* from *-strīdan*]

bit *see* **bidde**.

bitake *v.* commit, entrust A.Mil 3750, E.Cl 559, Bo 2. p 1. 74/102 (L *committeres*), LGW 2297; *refl.* Bo 2. p1. 78/108 (L *te dedisti*). **bitook** *pa.* G.SN 541. **bitaken** Bo 2. p1. 78/108. [ME re-formation of next after **take(n**]

biteche *v.* commit B.Mel 2114. [OE *betǣċan*]

byte(n *v.* bite B.NP 4121, TC 3. 737; (fig.) cut F.Sq 158, burn A.Prol 631, consume Anel 12, spur TC 3.1651. **boot** *pa. sg.* B.Mk 3791, Bo 2. p6. 40/57. **biten** *p.p.* B.Mel 2733, LGW 2318. [OE *bītan, bāt, biten*]

bithenke(n/-thinke(n *v.* **1.** think, imagine D.WB 772, H.Mcp 166, Pity 107, LGW 1439; remember BD 1304; think of, consider TC 1.982. **2.** *refl.* consider B.Mel 2635, RR 521, (with *on*) I.Pars 700; (with *of*) call to mind, remember A.Co 4403. **3.** put in mind: *I am bithoght of* I have

thought of A.Prol 767. **bitho(u)ghte** *pa.* TC 1.545. **bitho(u)ght** *p.p.* TC 2.225. [OE *beþenċan*, see **thenke(n**]

bitide(n *v.* happen, come about A.Mil 3450, D.Fri 1523, TC 2. 623; ∼ *of* become of B.Mel 2592; ∼ *what* ∼ come what may B.Th 2064, TC 5.750; *for aught that may* ∼ E.Cl 595, E.Mch 2330, TC 3.1736. **bitydeth** *pr. 3 sg.* B.Mel 2414 (and always in prose); **bitit** TC 2.48, 5.345. **bitidde** *pa. sg.* B.Th 1949, TC 2.55, RR 1548. **bitid(d)en** *pl.* Bo 5. p3. 64/89. **bitid** *p.p.* D.Sum 2191, TC 3.288. [from **tyde(n**]

bitidinge *vbl. n.* (only in Bo 5) occurrence, event Bo 5. p1. 23/33, p3. 35/49, p5. 72/105, etc.

bitymes *adv.* in good time, soon G.CY 1008; see **tyme**.

bitit *see* **bitide(n**.

bitokeneth *pr. 3 sg.* means, symbolizes B.Mk 3942, D.WB 581, I.Pars 843, TC 5.1513. [OE **betācnian*, cf. **tokneth**]

bitore *n.* bittern D.WB 972. [OF *butor*]

bitraye *v.* betray, deceive G.CY 897, TC 5. 1247, HF 294. [from OF *traïr*]

bitrayse *v.* betray B.Mk 3570, BD 1120, LGW 266. **bitra(i)sshed** *p.p.* RR 1520, 1648. [form of prec., from lengthened stem of *traïr*]

bitrent *pr. 3 sg.* entwines, encircles TC 3.1231, 4.870. [from OE *tréndan* turn]

bitwixe(n *prep.* between A.Prol 277, C.Pard 494, PF 40, TC 1.135. [OE *betwēox(n*]

biwail(l)e(n *v. tr.* bewail, lament B.Mk 3181, B.NP 3975, I.Pars 1090, TC 1.755 *var*; lament the loss of B.ML 26, TC 4.272. *intr.* lament B.Mk 3952, I.Pars 176. [from **waille(n**]

biwared *p.p.* expended, laid out TC 1.636. [from ON *verja*]

biwepe *v.* lament I.Pars 178, TC 1.762. **biwepte** *pa. sg.* Bo 4. m7. 13/18. **biwopen** *p.p.* in tears TC 4.916. [OE *bewēpan*]

byword *n.* proverb TC 4.769. [re-formed from OE *bīwyrde* after **word**]

biwreye(n *v.* divulge, reveal A.Kn 2229, B.Sh 1328, B.Mk 3219, B.NP 4241, E.Mch 1873, TC 3.377; *refl.* reveal one's thoughts TC 2.537 *var*; betray B.Sh 1323, C.Pard 823, D.WB 974, G.SN 150; **biwryen** PF 348, TC 2.537 *var.* [from **wreye**]

biwreyinge *vbl. n.* revealing B.Mel 2338, I.Pars 645.

biwryen *see* **biwreye(n**.

blabbe *n.* tell-tale TC 3.300 *var.* [? imit.]

blaked *p.p.* blackened D.Mk 3321. [from *v.* from OE *blæc* adj.]

blame *n.* **1.** reproach, censure G.SN 455, TC 2.15; blame I.Pars 494, *have* ∼ be blamed G.CY 1004, TC 4.551, *putte me out of* ∼ don't blame me A.Mil 3185; disgrace, scandal Anel 275, TC 3.265, slander RR 979, *false* ∼ B.ML 640, 827; charge, accusation Bo 1. p4. 106/148 (L *crimen*). **2.** fault, guilt TC 5.1068, LGW 1844; *in* ∼ at fault TC 4.594, ∼ *have I* I am at fault TC 2.210, *renneth in a* ∼ makes a mistake G.CY 905, *out of* ∼ guiltless C.Pard 385. [OF *bla(s)me*]

blameful *n.* critical, carping B.Mel 2317 *var.* [from prec.]

blame(n *v.* reproach, censure, find fault

with A.Rv 3863, B.ML 372, B.NP 4451, TC 4.527, Ven 7, *ben to* ~ be at fault, guilty A.Prol 375, A.Mil 3710, B.Mel 2452, D.WB 450, TC 2.287; impute Bo 2. p4. 9/12 (L *imputare*). **blameth** *imper. pl.* A. Mil 3181. [OF *bla(s)mer*]
blancmanger *n.* mousse (chopped chicken or fish with rice, etc.) A.Prol 387. [OF]
blandishe/blandise *v.* flatter, fawn I.Pars 376. [OF *blandiss-*, stem of *blandir*]
blanket *n.* undyed woollen cloth D.Sum 1751. [OF *blancquet*]
blase *n.* fire TC 4. 184. [OE]
blasen *v.* blow HF 1802. [prob. ON *blása*]
blaspheme *n.* blasphemy, blaspheming C.Pard 593, Scog 15. [OF]
blast *n.* gust of wind, Bo 2. m2. 4/5, TC 2.1387. [OE *blǽst*]
blaunche *adj.* white, in ~ *fevere* 'white fever', i.e. love-sickness TC 1.916. [OF]
blaundiss(c)hinge *ppl. adj.* flattering, favourable Bo 2. p1. 20/28 (L *blandientem*); pleasant, sweet Bo 3. m.12. 14/20 (L *blanda*), gentle 2. p2. 32/44. [from **blandishe**]
blede *v.* bleed A.Kn 1801, TC 1.502. **bledde** *pa.* A.Prol 145, TC 2.950. [OE *blēdan*]
bleynte *pa.* blenched, started A.Kn 1078, turned TC 3.1346/1332. **ybleynt** *p.p.* turned away, ducked A.Mil 3753. [OE *blencan, blenc̣te*]
blende *v.* blind A.Mil 3808, PF 600, Truth 4; (fig.) lead astray G.CY 1077; deceive, delude Bo 1. m7. 14/19, TC 2.1496, 4.5, 5.526. **blendith** *pr. 3 sg.* Bo 4. p4./187 *var*; **blent** G.CY 1391, PF 600. **blente** *pa. sg.* TC 5.1195. **y)blent** *p.p.* A.Mil 3808, TC 2.1743. [OE *blēndan*]
blere *v.* make dim: ~ *(one's) eye* deceive A.Rv 4049, H.Mcp 252; ~*d is myn eye* my eyes are bleary (with play on above) G.CY 730. **bleryng** *vbl. n.* A.Rv 3865. [?]
blesse(n *v.* bless B.Mel 2112, D.WB 525, E.Mch 1916, HF 629; protect A.Mil 3484, H.Mcp 321, TC 1.436; (*refl.*) cross oneself A.Mil 3448, B.ML 449, 868 *var*. **blisse** B.ML 868 *var*, E.Cl 552. **blessed** *ppl. adj.* B.ML 950, C.Pard 709; **blissed** C.Phs 248 *var*, C.Pard 474. [OE *blētsian*, infl. by **blis(se)**]
bleve(n *see* **bileve** *v.*²
blew *adj.* blue A.Prol 564, BD 340, TC 3.885. [OF *bleu*]
blinne *v.* cease, leave off G.CY 1171, (with *of*) TC 3. 1365. [OE *blinnan*]
blis(se *n.* joy, happiness A.Kn 1449, B.NP 4390, F.Fkl 1552, TC 2.849; *joye and/or* ~ A.Kn 1684, B.ML 409, B.NP 4256, D.WB 830, E.Mch 1712, Mars 74; ~ *of hevene* C.Pard 912, I.Pars 792, *hevene* ~ PF 72, TC 3.704,1322, cf. B.NP 4636, HF 492, LGW 516; *born to* ~ carried to heaven D.Sum 1857; (in asseverations) *as/so have I* ~ B.Sh 1541, D.WB 830, LGW 505. [OE *bliss*]
blisse(d *see* **blesse(n.**
blis(s)ful *adj.* blissful, happy B.ML 726, B.NP 4391, TC 3.230; blessed A.Prol 17, B.ML 920, E.Mch 1347, TC 3.705 *var*; fortunate Bo 2. p3. 51/74 (L *felicem*); beneficent TC 2.680; splendid B.ML 403. [from prec.]
blis(s)fulness *n.* happiness (only in Bo) Bo 2. p4. 75/103, 3. p1. 37/50, 4. p1. 43/60

(all L *beatitudinis*), 3. p10. 4/5 (L *felicitatis*), etc. [from prec.]
blythe *adj.* happy, pleased A.Prol 846, PF 504, LGW 647; joyous TC 3.1318. [OE *blīþe*]
blythely *adv.* gladly BD 749, 755. [from prec.]
blytheness *n.* happiness Bo 2. p3. 37/53. (L *alacritate*). [from **blythe**]
blyve *adv.* quickly, hastily A.Kn 2697, BD 152, TC 2.1605, HF 1521; *as/also* ~ as soon as possible TC 2.1513, HF 1106, at once TC 1.965, 2.137, 208. [**bi** prep.+*lyf*]
blo *adj.* blue (of smoke) HF 1647. [ON *blár*]
blondreth *pr. 3 sg.* blunders G.CY 1414; **blondren** *pl.* confuse (ourselves) G.CY 670. [prob. Scand.; cf. ON *blunda* shut the eyes]
blood *n.* **1.** blood A.Prol 635, A.Co 4346, BD 490; (the humour) F.Sq 352. **2.** lineage, family, race A.Rv 3945, TC 5.600, ~ *roial* A.Kn 1018, 1546, B.Mk 3341, Anel 65, TC 1.435; kin, relative A.Kn 1583, TC 2.594. [OE *blōd*]
blood-shedinge *vbl. n.* bloodshed HF 1241.
blosme *n.* blossom A.Mil 3324, LGW 143, 157. [OE *blōstm*]
blosmed *adj.* flowery PF 183 *var*, RR 108. [from prec.]
blosmeth *pr. 3 sg.* blooms E.Mch 1462. [OE *blōstmian*]
blosmy *adj.* flowery E.Mch 1463, PF 183 *var*, TC 2.821. [from **blosme**]
blowe(n *v.* **1.** *intr.* blow F.Fkl 888. **2.** *tr.* blow, play A.Prol 565; blow up G.SN 440; make known TC 1.384, 530, 4.167, spread abroad A.Kn 2241, HF 1139. **blew** *pa.sg.* B.NP 4263, G.CY 1260. **blewe** *pl.* B.NP 4589. **blowe(n** *p.p.* G.SN 440, HF 774; **yblowe** TC 4.167, LGW 1475. [OE *blāwan, blēow, blēowon, ġe)blāwen*]
bobance *n.* pride, presumption D.WB 569, boast ABC 84. [OF]
boce *see* **bos.**
boch *n.* ulcer Bo 3. p4. 9/12. [ONF]
bocher *n.* butcher A.Kn 2025. [AN]
bode *n.*¹ delay, hesitation. [OE *bād*; cf. **abo(o)d**]
bode *n.*² presage, foreboding, PF 343. [OE *ġe)bod*]
bode(n *see* **bidde.**
bodeth *pr. 3 sg.* forebodes B.Th 2072, Bo 4. m6. 11/16. [OE *bodian*]
body *n.* **1.** (human) body A.Kn 2283, I.Pars 146, Bo 4. p4. 103/144; *dede* ~ corpse A.Kn 942, 1005, D.Fri 1508, I.Pars 1031; *dette of hir* ~ marital relations I.Pars 941. **2.** person: *every* ~ B.ML 672; *lyves* ~ creature HF 1063; one's person G.CY 1289, *my* ~ I, me B.Sh 1185, 1613, B.NP 4087, D.WB 1061, myself C.Pard 338, *thy* ~, *your* ~ you B.Mel 2216, TC 1.122; *pl.* people B.Mk 3278, F.Fkl 877. **3.** main part E.Cl 42. **4.** substance, element G.CY 820, 825; *celestial* ~ planet Astr prol 64/89. [OE *bodiġ*]
bodily *adj.* of the body, corporal I.Pars 1038, Bo 3. p7. 11/16; material, physical I.Pars 564, 777, 962; carnal E.Mch 1249, I.Pars 886. [from prec.]
boes *see* **bihove.**
boght(e *see* **bye(n.**
boy *n.* servant C.Pard 670; villain, knave

D.Fri 1322; urchin, brat B.Pri 1752; (in address to a horse) lad D.Fri 1563. [? AN *embuié*]
boydekin *n.* dagger A.Rv 3960, B.Mk 3892. [? Celt.]
boiste *n.* box C.Pard 307, I.Pars 947, HF 2129 *var.* [OF]
boistous *adj.* rough, plain H.Mcp 211. [OF]
boistously *adv.* roughly, rudely E.Cl 791. [from prec.]
bokele *n.* buckle RR 1086. [OF *boucle*]
bokeler *n.* buckler, small shield A.Prol 112, A.Mil 3266, A.Rv 4019. [OF *boucler*]
boket *n.* bucket A.Kn 1533. [AN *buket*, perh. from OE *būc* belly]
bolas *n. pl.* bullaces, plums RR 1377. [OF *buloce*]
bolde *v.* grow bold PF 144. [OA *báldian*]
boldely *adv.* confidently B.Sh 1591, B.Pri 1736, G.SN 319; with assurance F.Sq 581, certainly HF 581; brazenly, insolently D.WB 227, LGW 316; strongly D.Fri 1301; immediately A.Mil 3433, B.NP 4210. [OA *báldlíče*]
boldnesse *n.* confidence, courage BD 617; self-assurance C.Phs 71; insolence G.SN 487. [OA *báldnesse*]
bole *n.* bull A.Kn 2139, B.Mel 2515, I.Pars 898; the zodiacal sign Taurus TC 2.55.
boles *gen.* G.CY 797. [ON]
bole armoniak *n. phr.* Armenian clay G.CY 790. [L *bōlus armeniacus*]
bolle *n.* bowl G.CY 1210. [OE *bolla*]
bolt *n.* crossbow-bolt, quarrel A.Mil 3264; as *adv.* in ~ *upright* flat A.Rv 4266, B.Sh 1506. [OE]
bombleth *pr. 3 sg.* booms D.WB 972. [imit.]
bon *adj.* good HF 1022, Truth rubr. [OF]
bond *n.* band, chain, fetter TC 3.1766; formal pledge, covenant, obligation A.Kn 1604; (fig.) binding force TC 3.1261; controlling force (in magic) F.Sq 131. [ON *band*]
bonde *adj.* unfree, in slavery B.Mk 3460, D.WB 378, I.Pars 149, TC 1.255. [OE *bónda* assoc. with ON *band*]
bondemen *n. pl.* serfs I.Pars 752. [from prec.]
bood *see* **byde**.
bo(o)ld *adj.* bold, brave TC 4.33; *made hir* ~ encouraged her B.ML 566; *be so* ~ (with infin.) venture, dare A.Rv 4271, C.Pard 339, Mars 35, LGW 879, *make (oneself)* ~ Astr 2.3.44/64; confident, assured A.Prol 755, B.Sh 1215; rash, forward TC 3.88; aggressive B.NP 3998. [OA *báld*]
bo(o)n *n.* bone A.Kn 1177, C.Pard 350, TC 1.805; *pl.* (in phrases expressing completeness) *blood and* ~ B.NP 4617, *body and* ~ D.Fri 1544, *fel and* ~ TC 1.91, 3.591; (in swearing) *Goddes* ~ B.Sh 1166, B.Mk 3087; *corpus* ~ (nonsensical) B.Mk 3096, C.Pard 314; *cokkes* ~ (= *Goddes*) H.Mcp 9; I.Pars 29; *bicched* ~ dice C.Pard 656; **banes** (nth.) A.Rv 4073. [OE *bān*]
bo(o)nd *see* **binde**.
bo(o)ne *n.* wish, prayer A.Kn 2269, BD 129, LGW 2340, *bad a* ~ made a request E.Mch 1618. [ON *bón*]
bo(o)st *n.* noise LGW 887; clamour, parade B.ML 401; loud talk, bluster A.Rv 4001, C.Pard 764; boasting Mars 37, TC 3.248, 298, LGW 267; pride, arrogance B.Mk 3799, G.SN 441. [AN *bost*]

boot *n.* boat E.Mch 1424, TC 1.416, LGW 2215. [OE *bāt*]
boot *see* **byte(n**.
bo(o)t(e *n.* remedy, benefit A.Prol 424, G.CY 1481, BD 38; salvation B.Pri 1656; *do* ~ benefit, heal D.WB 472, F.Sq 154, TC 2.345, PF 276; *for* ~ *ne bale* see **bale**. [OE *bōt*]
bo(o)teles *adj.* without remedy TC 1.782. [from prec.]
boras *n.* borax A.Prol 630, G.CY 790. [OF]
bord *n.* **1.** table B.NP 4033, E.Cl 3, F.Sq 85, *the* ~ *bigonne* sat in the place of honour A.Prol 52; food G.CY 1017; *to* ~ boarding A.Mil 3188, D.WB 528. **2.** (ship) board A.Mil 3585, *over* ~ overboard B.ML 922, HF 438, LGW 644. **3.** board, plank A.Mil 3440, BD 74. [OE]
bordel *n.* brothel I.Pars 885, 976. [OF]
bordure *n.* border Bo 1. p1. 20/28, 22/31; rim Astr 1.4.5/7, 1.5.3/4, etc. [OF]
borel *see* **burel**.
bore(n/born, ybore(n/-born *p.p.* born A.Kn 1542, D.WB 1153, A.Kn 1073, E.Cl 484, 626, A.Kn 1019. *adj.* by birth C.Pard 704, E.Cl 72, E.Mch 1790, G.SN 425, TC 4.332, LGW 2090; living TC 2.298, 5.155. [OE *ǥe)boren*, see **bere(n**]
borneth *pr. 3 sg.* polishes TC 1.327. [from OF *burnir*, cf. **burned**]
borwe *n.* surety B.Mel 2997, TC 1.1038, 2.134; *to* ~ as a pledge A.Kn 1622, F.Sq 596, F.Fkl 1234, Mars 9, TC 2.1524. [OE *borg*]
borwe *v.* borrow B.ML 105, G.CY 735, TC 1.488. [OE *borgian*]
bos/boce *n.* boss, protuberance A.Mil 3266, I.Pars 423. [OF]
bosteth *pr. 3 sg.* boasts D.Sum 1672, I.Pars 393. [AN]
botel *n.*[1] bottle C.Pard 886, D.Sum 1931. [OF]
botel *n.*[2] ~ *hey* bundle of hay H.Mcp 14. [OF]
boteler *n.* butler B.NP 4324, HF 592. [AN *buteler*]
bothe *adj.* both A.Kn 1631, C.Pard 523, TC 5.1134; ~ *two* B.NP 4616, D.WB 1062, D.Fri 1361, G.CY 851, TC 2.487; (of more than two things) D.Fri 1547, D.Sum 2035, H.Mcp 268, HF 1229, D.WB 1131. as *gen.*, with pron.: *hir* ~ of them both B.ML 221, sim. D.WB 121, TC 1.972. **bothes** *gen.* ABC 83; **bother** TC 4.168. **bathe** (nth.) A.Rv 4087, 4191. [ON *bádir* and perh. OE *ba pa*]
bothe *adv., conj.* both A.Prol 540, D.WB 119, E.Mch 1725, TC 1.984, 2.633. [as prec.]
botme *n.* bottom B.NP 4291, G.CY 1321, TC 1.297. [OE *botm*]
bot(o)melees *adj.* bottomless LGW 1584; (fig.) without foundation, insubstantial TC 5.1431. [from prec.]
bough *n.* bough, branch A.Kn 1980, BD 423. **bowes** *pl.* A.Kn 1642, PF 183, RR 108. [OE *bōg*]
boughte(n *see* **bye(n**.
bouk *n.* body, trunk A.Kn 2746. [OE *būc*]
boun/bown *adj.* ready, about (with infin.) F.Fkl 1503. [ON *búinn*]
bounde(n *see* **binde**.

boundes *n. pl.* boundaries, limits A.Kn 2993, F.Sq 571, LGW 546; boundary marks B.Mk 3308. [AN]
bountee *n.* **1.** goodness, kindness B.Pri 1656, C.Phs 112, ABC 9; good deed I.Pars 393, TC 3.882 *var; pl.* good qualities I.Pars 396, Bo 2. p4. 27/36. **2.** praise, honour B.Pri 1647, E.Cl 415. [OF *bonté*]
bountevous *adj.* bounteous, lavish C.Phs 110, TC 1.883. [from OF *bontif*]
bour *n.* bedroom B.NP 4022, D.WB 300, PF 304, bower (in set phr.) *bright in* ~ B.Th 1932. **boures** *gen.* A.Mil 3367, 3677. [OE *būr*]
bourde *n.* joke H.Mcp 81. [OF]
bourde *v.* joke, jest C.Pard 778, PF 589. [OF *bourder*]
bowes *see* **bough.**
bowges *n. pl.* wallets HF 2129 *var.* [OF]
bragot *n.* drink made of ale and honey A.Mil 3261. [W]
brak *see* **breke(n.**
brake *n.* shoal LGW 1471 *var.* [from **breke(n]**
brasile *n.* brazil wood (red dye) B.NP 4649. [ML *brasilium*]
brast(e *see* **breste.**
brat *n.* cloak G.CY 881 *var.* [OE *bratt*]
brawn *n.* muscle A.Prol 546, B.Mk 3131, LGW 1071; boar meat D.Sum 1750, F.Fkl 1254. [AN *braun*]
brede *n.*¹ roast meat HF 1222. [OE *brǣd(e*]
brede *n.*² breadth A.Kn 1970, B.Mk 3350, BD 956, HF 1494; space TC 1.179; *on* ~ abroad TC 1.530. [OE *brǣdu*]
brede *v.* **1.** *intr.* breed, arise, grow E.Mch 1783, TC 3.1546, LGW 1156. **2.** *tr.* breed B.ML 364. **bredde** *pa.* TC 1.465. [OE *brēdan*]
breech *n.* pair of drawers, pants B.Th 2049, C.Pard 948; buttocks, arse B.NP 4638. *pl.* I.Pars 330. [OE *brēċ*]
breed *n.* bread A.Prol 147, B.NP 4034, TC 2.444. [OE *brēad*]
breyde *v.* **1.** *intr.* start, wake A.Rv 4285, F.Sq 477, TC 5.1243; ~ *out of (one's) wit* go mad Anel 124, TC 4.230, 5.1262. **2.** *tr.* snatch B.ML 837, take up HF 1678. **breyde** *pa.* B.ML 837. **brayd** *p.p.* Anel 124. Cf. **abreyde.** [OE *breġdan, brǣġd*]
breke(n *v.* **1.** *tr.* break A.Prol 551, B.Mk 3090, C.Pard 936; break into I.Pars 879; break out of A.Kn 1468; break (continuity of), check B.Mk 3117, I.Pars 254, break off TC 2.1600, interrupt B.Mel 2233, TC 5.1032; (fig., of agreement, command, promise) break B.ML 40, F.Fkl 698, 1320, TC 1.89, 3.315, 5.355; ~ *(one's) herte* TC 3.908; ~ *(one's) day* fail to meet a date for payment G.CY 1040, BD 730; *p.p.* shipwrecked LGW 1487. **2.** *intr.* break A.Rv 3918, B.NP 4578; break away B.NP 4606; (fig.) Mars 233, *(herte)* A.Kn 954, B.NP 4578, E. Mch 2306; be interrupted TC 3.1403/1389. **brak** *pa. sg.* A.Kn 1468, B.NP 4606, TC 2.1600. **breke** *subj.* B.NP 4578. **broke(n** *p.p.* A.Mil 3571 *var,* BD 730, A.Kn 1168; **ybroke(n** PF 282, HF 765. [OE *brecan, brǣc, ġe)brocen*]
brekke *n.* fault BD 940. [rel. to prec.; cf. MDu *gebrec*]
bremble-/brembul *n.* bramble B.Th 1936. [OE *brembel*]

breme *adv.* fiercely A.Kn 1699, TC 4. 184. [OE]
bren *n.* bran A.Rv 4053, D.WB 478; *bulte it to the* ~ sift it thoroughly B.NP 4430. [OF]
brenne(n/brinne *v.* **1.** *tr.* burn A.Mil 3812, G.SN 313, TC 1.91; (fig.) inflame TC 3.1539. *p.p.* (of gold) refined A.Kn 2162, 2896 (cf. burned). **2.** *intr.* burn A.Kn 2331, B.ML 289, D.WB 52, PF 249; (fig.) glow Rosem 22, be inflamed E.Mch 2075, I.Pars 383, TC 4.704. **brende** *pa. sg.* B.ML 289; **brente** A.Kn 2946. *pl.* **brende(n** B.Mk 3225, A.Kn 2425; **brente** LGW 731. **y)brend** *p.p.* B.NP 4555, TC 5.309; **y)brent** A.Kn 946, 2017. [ON *brenna*, OE *birnan*]
brenning(e *vbl. n.* burning A.Kn 996, I.Pars 221, 445, RR 188.
brenningly *adv.* fervently A.Kn 1564, TC 1.607. [from **brenne(n**]
brere *v.* brier A.Kn 1532, E.Mch 1825, RR 858. [OA *brēr*]
breste(n *v.* **1.** *tr.* break A.Kn 1980, A.Mil 3829, TC 3.1434, LGW 1300, 2416. **2.** *intr.* break E.Cl 1169, TC 3.1637, (of heart) E.Mch 2096, F.Fkl 759, H.Mcp 263, BD 1193, TC 1.599; burst B.ML 671, 697, C.Phs 234, burst out F.Fkl 1480, TC 2.408, 4.373, 5.1078, ~ *out* LGW 1033. **brest** *pr. 3 sg.* A.Kn 2610, TC 1.258, 3.1637. **brast** *pa. sg.* I.Pars 269, TC 5.180; **brest** TC 2.1108 *var.* **broste/bruste** *pl.* B.ML 671, C.Phs 234, TC 2.326 *var;* **braste** TC 2.326 *var.* **brosten** *p.p.* A.Mil 3829, TC 2.976. [OE *berstan, bærst, burston, borsten*]
Bret *n.* Welshman HF 1208. [OE]
bretful *adj.* brimful A.Prol 687, A.Kn 2164, HF 2123. [from ON **bredd*, = OE *brerd/brim*]
breth(e)ren *see* **brother.**
bretherhed *n.* **1.** brotherhood, brotherly relations B.Sh 1232, D.Fri 1399 *var* **brotherhed.** **2.** fraternal society, guild A.Prol 511. [from **brother**+OE suff. -**hǣdu*]
brew *pa. sg.* brewed, contrived B.Mk 3575. [OE *brēaw* from *brēowan*]
brybe *v.* purloin, steal A.Co 4417; extract money D.Fri 1378. [OF *briber* beg]
bryberyes *n. pl.* extortions, ways of robbing D.Fri 1367. [OF]
brid *n.* bird E.Mch 1865, H.Mcp 163, PF 190; young bird PF 192; (as endearment) A.Mil 3699. [OE]
bridale *n.* wedding party A.Co 4375. [OE *brȳd-ealu*]
brige *n.* strife B.Mel 2872. [OF *brigue*]
bright *adj.* bright, shining A.Kn 1700, BD 340; (as conventional epithet for a lady) radiant, beautiful, fair A.Kn 1427, B.ML 841, F.Sq 137, Mars 136, TC 1.166, 3.39. [OA *berht*]
brike *n.* plight B.Mk 3580. [ONF *bricque*]
brimme *n.* (*prep.*) edge, bank LGW 2451. [? ML/Du *brem*]
brymstoon *n.* brimstone, sulphur A.Prol 629, G.CY 824, I.Pars 548. [LOE *brynstān,* rel. to **brenne(n**]
bringe(n *v.* bring, take; conduct A.Prol 566; bring in, introduce Bo 2. m8. 6/8 (L *duxerit*); refer Bo 3. p10. 124/166 (L *referantur*); put E.Cl 915; ~ *aboute* carry

out C.Pard 821, G.CY 803, ~ *it aboute* succeed E.Mch 1560, contrive D.WB 426, TC 4.1275; ~ *adoun* refute PF 537; ~ *forth* produce Bo 3. p12, 30/40 (L *ordo . . procederet*); ~ *in arrerage* see **arrerage**; ~ *of lyve* kill TC 2.1608, 5.1561; ~ *to meschance, meschief* destroy, ruin B.ML 964, B.Mk 3252, G.CY 1072, H.Mcp 233, TC 4.203, LGW 1655. **bringes** *pr. 3 sg.* (nth.) A.Rv 4130, HF 1908. **bringeth** *imper. pl.* B.Mk 3384, TC 2.1750. **bro(u)ghte(n** *pa.* B.NP 4447, 4588. **y)bro(u)ght** *p.p.* A.Kn 1111, 2191. [OE *bringan, brōhte*]

bringere out *n.* remover D.WB 1196. [from prec.]

brink *n.* brink, edge E.Mch 1401, HF 803; seashore F.Fkl 858, 1160. [ON, cf. OI *brekka*]

brinne see **brenne(n.**

bristilede *adj.* bristly Bo 4. m7. 39/55. [from OE *brystel, cf. **brustles**]

Briton *adj.* **1.** British, Welsh B.ML 666. **2.** Breton F.Fkl 711, 1179. [as next]

Britoun *n.* **1.** Briton B.ML 561. **Britons** *pl.* B.ML 545, D.WB 858. **2.** Bretons F.Fkl 709. [L *Britōnes*, OF *Breton*]

brocage *n.* mediation, agents A.Mil 3375. [AN]

brodder see **brood.**

brode *adv.* widely HF 1683; wide-eyed G.CY 1420; plainly A.Prol 739. [OE *brāde*; cf. **brood**]

broghte(n see **bringe(n.**

broided *ppl. adj.* braided A.Kn 1049. [from OE *brogden*, p.p. of *bregdan*; cf. **breyde**]

broiden *ppl. adj.* embroidered A.Mil 3238 *var.* [as prec., blended with OF *brouder*; cf. **brouded**]

broille *v.* grill A.Prol 383 *var.* [OF *bru(s)ler*]

broke(n see **breke(n, brouke.**

brokking *pr.p.* ?warbling, using vibrato A.Mil 3377. [?]

brome *n.* broom HF 1226, RR 902. [OE *brōm*]

brond *n.* brand, torch A.Kn 2338, B.Th 2095, E.Mch 1777. [OE *brānd*]

brood *adj.* broad, wide A.Prol 155, F.Sq 82; large, enlarged F.Sq 394, TC 5. 1017, LGW 829. **brodder/brodere** *comp.* D.Sum 1688, Astr 2.38.1/2. [OE *brād*]

broste(n see **breste.**

brotel/brutel *adj.* brittle, uncertain B.Mel 2640, insecure E.Mch 1279, Bo 2. p5. 4/5 (L *caduca*), TC 3.820. [from stem of OE *brēotan* shatter, p.p. *broten*]

brotelnes *n.* frailty, fickleness E.Mch 2241, Fort 63, TC 5.1832; insecurity E.Mch 1279. [from prec.]

brother *n.* brother A.Prol 529; (sworn) brother A.Kn 1147, C.Pard 808, HF 2101; (fig.) G.CY 1432; (in familiar address) A.Mil 3129, D.Fri 1395, TC 3.330, 5.414. **brother** *gen. sg.* A.Kn 3084, B.Mk 3593, TC 1.678; **brotheres** F.Fkl 1166, G.SN 296. **breth(e)ren** *pl.* C.Pard 416, E.Mch 1475, TC 1.471. [OE *brōþor*, gen. unchanged; pl. unchanged, *brōþru*, and (rare) *broeþre*]

brotherhed see **bretherhed.**

brouded *ppl. adj.* embroidered A.Mil 3238 *var*, B.Mk 3659, LGW G. 159. [OF *brouder*]

broughte(n see **bringe(n.**

brouke *v.* **1.** enjoy, have the use of B.NP 4490, E.Mch 2308, HF 273. **2.** perform, practise: ~ *broken harm* do mischief E.Mch 1425. [OE *brūcan*]

browding *n.* embroidery A.Kn 2498. [as **brouded**]

bruste see **breste(n.**

brustles *n. pl.* bristles A.Prol 556, E.Mch 1824. [OE *byrstel]

brutel see **brotel.**

buf *interj.* (sound of belch) D.Sum 1934. [imit.]

bukke *n.* buck, male (fallow) deer B.Th 1946, PF 195; *blow the ~s horn* go whistle A.Mil 3387. [OE *bucca*]

bulle *n.* bull, papal edict C.Pard 342, 388, E.Cl 748. [L *bulla*]

bulte *v.* sift B.NP 4430. [OF *bulter*]

burdoun *n.* accompaniment, ground-bass A.Prol 673 (perh. indecent pun on homonym from *bourdon* 'pilgrim's staff') A.Rv 4165. [OF]

burel/borel *n.* coarse cloth D.WB 356; as *adj.* rough D.Sum 1872, F.Fkl 716; lay B.Mk 3145. [OF]

burgeys *n.* burgess, citizen A.Prol 369, 754, TC 4.345. [OF]

burghes *n. pl.* boroughs D.WB 870. [OE *burg*]

burned *ppl. adj.* burnished A.Kn 1983, B.NP 4054, HF 1387; shining, radiant C.Phs 38. [from v. from OF *burnir*; cf. **borneth**]

bussh/busk *n.* bush A.Kn 1517, D.WB 879, I.Pars 858 *em*, RR 102. [OE *bysc and ON *buskr*]

but *conj.* except B.NP 4473, F.Sq 638, TC 1.1038; unless B.Sh 1383, E.Cl 938, F.Fkl 803; but that, that . . not (after expressions of impossibility, prohibition, etc.) I.Pars 339, LGW 10; ~ *if* unless A.Prol 656, B.ML 636, ABC 55, TC 4.221, LGW 609; ~ *if ye sholde* than that you should not F.Fkl 1478. *quasi-prep.* (with neg.) only A.Kn 2847, A.Rv 4047, *nat* ~ B.Mk 3476, D.Sum 1728, quite G.CY 601; *I nam* ~ I am as good as A.Rv 4289, D.WB 1006, Pity 21, TC 5.1246. *adv.* only A.Prol 120, BD 39, TC 1.223, simply B.Mk 3105, F.Fkl 1037. [OE *būtan*]

buxom *adj.* yielding, obedient, submissive B.Sh 1367, E.Mch 1287, CompL 120. [from stem of OE *būgan* bend]

buxomly *adv.* obediently E.Cl 186. [from prec.]

buxumnesse *n.* submission Truth 15. [from **buxom**]

C

ca(a)s *n.* **1.** case, circumstance(s), event A.Prol 585, B. Mel 2192, 2452 (*pl.* unchanged), C.Phs 229, TC 2.458, LGW 583; (*as*) *in this* ~ on this matter D.WB 165, here, now (often an almost empty tag) A.Prol 797, A.Kn 2357, A.Mil 3385, B.ML 983, TC 3.283; *in no maner* ~, *for no* ~ in no circumstances D.Sum 1831, TC 4.635, *for swich maner* ~ for such a reason F.Fkl 1430; *in* ~ (*that*) in the event that, if TC 2.758, 4.1509, Astr. 2.3.2/3; (*I*) *sette* ~ suppose B.Mel 3041, TC 2.729; *to dyen in*

the ~ even if I were to die for it E.Cl 859.
2. chance, accident A.Prol 844, A.Kn 1074,
A.Mil 3661, E.Cl 316, TC 4.388; misfortune LGW 1083; *par* ~ by chance
C.Pard 885, *upon* ~ TC 1.271, 4.649. **3.**
case (in law, *pl.* unchanged) A.Prol 323,
C.Phs 163. [OF]
cacche(n *v.* **1.** catch A.Prol 145, G.SN 11,
TC 1.214; win D.WB 76; seize, take hold
of A.Kn 1399, A.Mil 3276, A.Rv 4273,
TC 2.448; overcome I.Pars 823. **2.** take,
come by A.Prol 498, C.Pard 313, I.Pars
689, **kecche** TC 3.1375/1361 *var*, receive
BD 781; perceive Astr 2.17.8/11; meet, in
~ *his deeth* HF 404, *lives ende* TC 5.1554;
~ *a sleep* go to sleep A.Rv 4227. **3.** conceive, feel: ~ *desire* LGW 1750, ~ *lest*
E.Cl 619, ~ *an ire* become angry D.Sum
2003, ~ *a motyf* see **motyf**; ~ *plesance*
take pleasure B.ML 186, E.Cl 993, ~
a pitee/routhe feel pity F.Fkl 740, 1520.
caughte/kaughte *pa.* A.Prol 498, BD 681.
caught *p.p.* A.Kn 1214, C.Pard 313;
ycaught TC 2.583. [ONF *cachier*; pa.
follows *laughte* from *lacchen*, OE *lǣċċan*,
lǣhte seize]
cadence *n.* rhythm HF 623. [OF]
caitif *n.* (*pl.* **caitifs** and **caityves**) captive,
prisoner A.Kn 924, Bo 1. p4. 216/301;
wretch C.Pard 728, I.Pars 214, RR 340.
[ONF]
caitif *adj.* captive A.Kn 1946, I.Pars 344;
wretched I.Pars 271, RR 211. [ONF]
cake *n.* round flat loaf of bread A.Prol 668,
A.Rv 4094, C.Pard 322. [Prob. ON *kaka*]
calcening *vbl. n.* calcining, burning to ash
G.CY 771. [from ML *calcināre*]
calcinacioun *n.* calcining G.CY 804. [OF
from ML]
calcule *v.* calculate F.Fkl 1284, Astr prol
55/76. [OF *calculer*]
calculinge *vbl. n.* calculation TC 1.71,
4.1398.
calle *n.* hairnet D.WB 1018, Astr 1.19.3/4;
maken him an howve above a ~ deceive him
TC 3.775. [? OF]
camaille *n.* camel E.Cl 1196. [AN *cameil*, L
camēlus]
camuse *adj.* snub (of nose) A.Rv 3934 *var*,
3974 *var*. [OF *camus*]
camused *adj.* snub (of nose) A.Rv 3934 *var*,
3974 *var*. [from prec.]
can, canst *see* **conne.**
Cananee *adj.* Canaanite G.SN 59. [OF from
L *Chananaeus*]
canel-boon *n.* neck-bone BD 943. [ONF
canel channel + **bo(o)n**]
canel(le *n.* cinnamon RR 1370. [OF]
canevas *n.* canvas G.CY 939. [ONF]
cankedort *n.* predicament TC 2.1752. [?]
cano(u)n *n.* rule Astr prol 66/94, table
2.32.3/4; (as a book title) C.Pard 890.
[ONF]
cape *v.* gape A.Mil 3444, 3473, 3841, TC
3.558, 5.1133, all *var*. [form of **gape(n**; cf.
LG *kapen*]
caples *see* **capul.**
cappe *n.* cap A.Prol 683, E.Mch 1853; *set
(one's)* ~ deceive, make a fool of A.Prol
586, A.Mil 3143. [OE *cæppe*]
capul *n.* horse A.Rv 4088, D.Sum 2150,
H.Mcp 64. **caples** *pl.* D.Fri 1554. [ON
kapall from L *caballus*]

cardiacle/cardynacle *n.* heart attack, palpitation C.Pard 313. [OF *cardiaque*]
care *n.* **1.** grief, sorrow, (mental) pain
A.Co 4335, E.Mch 1213, F.Fkl 837, TC
3.1565, 4.229; ~ *and wo* A.Kn 1321, 2072,
D.WB 811, G.CY 769, H.Mcp 54; *maken*
~ grieve, lament TC 5.336; ill omen PF
363. **2.** anxiety, concern B.Sh 1313, TC
5.54; *have a* ~ take care LGW 1858; *have
no* ~ don't worry, never fear TC 3.1066.
pl. anxieties, miseries: see **cold.** **3.** trouble
A.Kn 1489, A.Mil 3232, D.WB 990, E.Mch
1547; misfortune B.Th 1949, TC 2.107;
don ~ injure, harm TC 5.958. [OA *caru*]
care *v.* **1.** sorrow, be grieved E.Cl 1212.
2. be anxious, worry D.WB 329, TC 3.670,
1645, 4.462 (*pr. subj.*); *refl.* A.Mil 3298.
[OE *carian*]
careyne *n.* corpse A.Kn 2013, PF 177; carrion I.Pars 214; carcase B.Mk 3814. [AN]
carf *see* **kerve(n.**
cariage *n.* **1.** (means of) transport, vehicles
D.Fri 1570. **2.** *pl.* feudal charges for transport I.Pars 752; taxes Bo 1. p4. 52/72
(L *uectigalibus*). [AN]
carie(n *v.* carry A.Prol 130, C.Pard 665, HF
545. **ycaried** *p.p.* B.Mk 3240. [ONF *carier*]
carl *n.* fellow, chap A.Prol 545, A.Mil 3469,
C.Pard 717, D.Fri 1568. [ON]
carole *n.* round dance with singing A.Kn
1931, LGW 687, RR 744, 759. [OF]
carole *v.* dance and sing (in a round dance)
BD 849, RR 745, 810. [OF *caroler*]
carole-wyse *n.* the manner of a *carole*
LGW G. 201. [prec. + **wyse**]
carolinge *vbl. n.* performing a *carole* G.CY
1345, RR 754.
carpe *v.* talk A.Prol 474. [ON *karpa*]
carrik *n.* carrack, large ship D.Sum 1688.
[OF *caraque*]
cas *n.*[2] case, quiver A.Kn 2080, 2896, LGW
982. [OF *casse*]
cast *n.* contrivance, plot A.Kn 2468, A.Mil
3605; occasion B.Mk 3477; throwing
TC 2.868. [from v.]
castelled *adj.* castellated I.Pars 445. [from
AN *casteler*]
caste(n *v.* **1.** throw A.Kn 2429, B.Pri 1761,
D.WB 782, H.Mcp 48, TC 2.615; ~ *with*
HF 1048, fling A.Mil 3330; cast (lots)
LGW 1933; scatter E.Mch 1770; give off
G.SN 244; *forth* ~ throw out, utter TC
2.1167; turn, direct TC 5.927, 1825, ~
(one's) eye(n look A.Kn 896, B.Mk 3392,
C.Phs 123, E.Mch 2360, F.Fkl 1036; ~ *up*
open BD 185, 212; ~ *out* prevent Bo 1.
p4. 42/58 (L *deieci*); lay down Bo 5. p1. 34/
48; fell TC 2.1389; *refl.* apply oneself
B.Mel 2781, 3048, G.CY 738. **2.** calculate B.Sh 1406, reckon, estimate A.Kn
2172; (absol.) deliberate B.ML 212; consider TC 1.749, 2.659, 1485, 4.161; have
regard to G.CY 1414; plan TC 1.1071;
plot B.ML 406, C.Pard 880, Pity 26,
propose LGW 2605; decide TC 1.75,
4.34, *refl.* B.NP 4265, Anel 208; decide on
B.Mk 3891; contrive HF 1170; ~ *biforn*
premeditate I.Pars 543; attempt Bo 1. p4.
155/215 (L *moliretur*). **casteth** *pr. 3 sg.*
B.Mk 3904; **cast** D.WB 782. **caste** *pa.*
A.Kn 896, 2854. **cast** *p.p.* TC 2.1389;
casten B.Pri 1796. [ON *kasta*]
casuel *adj.* chance TC 4.419. [OF]

casuelly adv. by chance B.NP 4291, HF 679. [from prec.]

catapuce n. caper-spurge B.NP 4155. [OF]

catel n. property, goods A.Prol 373, C.Pard 594, E.Mch 1525, I.Pars 503. [ONF]

caught(e see **cacche(n.**

cause n. 1. cause, reason A.Prol 419, B.Pri 1837, F.Sq 260, G.SN 23, TC 2.727, occasion B.Sh 1342; ~ why the reason (was) A.Rv 4144, E.Mch 2435, F.Sq 185, TC 3.795; by ~ (that) because A.Prol 174, B.ML 220, C.Pard 446, TC 2.1633, cf. **bycause**; by the ~ A.Kn 2488, TC 5.1342, by that ~ F.Sq 4.99; by thise ~s for these reasons B.Mel 2224; (philos.) A.Kn 2987, B.Mel 2585, TC 4.1017, first ~ C.Pard 499, ~ causinge TC 4.829. 2. purpose, interest B.ML 252, E.Cl 387, TC 1.20, 5.1230; sake Bo 3. p1. 32/44. [OF]

causele(e)s adv. without cause, reason B.Mel 3000, PF 590, TC 4.1533. [from prec.]

cause(n v. cause F.Sq 452, TC 4.1448; move, impel I.Pars 460. [OF causer]

causinge ppl. adj. original, primary, in cause ~ TC 4.829 (= L causa causans). [from prec.]

cavillacioun n. quibbling D.Sum 2136. [OF]

ceint n. belt A.Prol 329, A.Mil 3235. [OF]

celebrable adj. worthy of honour Bo 3. p9. 48/64; famous Bo 4. m7. 20/28. [OF]

celebritee n. fame Bo 3. p9. 38/49. [OF]

celerer n. cellar-keeper B.Mk 3126. [AN]

celle n.[1] 1. subordinate monastic house A.Prol 172. 2. a compartment of the brain embodying a particular 'faculty' A.Kn 1376. [OF]

celle n.[2] (= **selle**) flooring A.Mil 3822. [OE syll(e (s-e. form)]

centaure n. centaury B.NP 4153. [ML centaurea]

centres n. pl. table of distances between certain points of an equatorium of the planets F.Fkl 1277. [OF]

cercle n. circle HF 791, Astr. 1.9.1, (fig.) Bo 3. p12. 121/161 (L orbem); sphere Scog 9; orbit Bo 4. m6. 5/7 (L axem). [OF]

cercle(n v. encircle, encompass TC 3.1767, RR 1619; p.p. extended in a circle Rosem 2. [from prec.]

cered ppl. adj. waxed G.CY 808. [from OF cirer, cf. L cēra]

cerial adj. ook ~ evergreen oak A.Kn 2290. [from L (quercus) cerris]

ceriously adv. in due order, in detail B.ML 185. [L seriōsē]

certein adj. 1. fixed, settled A.Prol 815, A.Kn 2993, E.Cl 179, TC 3.539; (a) ~ a certain (definite but unspecified) A.Mil 3494, B.Mk 3364. as n., a ~ a certain number (of) A.Mil 3193, B.Sh 1524, B.Mk 3367, G.CY 776, TC 3.596; a certain amount of B.ML 242, B.Sh 1594. 2. sure, firm B.Mel 2857. Bo 2. m3. 17/21, TC 3. 1030, 4.989 var; unerring F.Fkl 866, Bo 4. m7. 24/33; unfailing Bo 5. p3. 100/142. as n., certainty: in ~ certain Bo 2. p6. 59/83; certainly E.Cl 1182, I.Pars 372, ABC 66, TC 4.908, HF 426, in good ~ B.Th 1918; in no ~ without certainty/no ~ there is no certainty I.Pars 1000 var. [OF]

certein adv. certainly, indeed A.Kn 1139, B.Pri 1853, B.NP 4507, F.Fkl 719, TC 2.724. [from prec.]

certes adv. certainly, to be sure A.Kn 875, G.CY 594, BD 84, TC 5.408. [OF]

ceruse n. white lead A.Prol 630. [OF]

ces(s)e(n v. 1. intr. cease B.ML 1066, F.Sq 257, Mars 11, TC 2.483; ~ of E.Cl 154, G.SN 124, TC 4.1619. 2. tr. stop, put an end to TC 1.445; (with infin.) I.Pars 601, G.SN 538. [OF cesser]

cetewale n. setwall, zedoary (a spice resembling ginger) A.Mil 3207, B.Th 1951, **setewale** RR 1370. [AN zedewale]

cha(a)r n. chariot A.Kn 2138, B.Mk 3550, F.Sq 671, TC 3.1704. [OF]

cha(a)st adj. chaste A.Kn 2051, B.Th 1935, D.Sum 1917. [OF chaste]

chace(n see **chase(n.**

chaffare n. business, trade, A.Co 4389, G.CY 1421; merchandise B.ML 138, B.Sh 1475, D.WB 521. [OE *cēapfaru]

chaffare v. trade B.ML 139. [from prec.]

chayer n. chair B.Mk 3803, (professorial) chair D.Fri 1518; throne Bo 1. m5. 2/3, 4. m2. 3. [OF]

chalange v. claim D.WB 1200, F.Fkl 1324, Bo 2. p6. 23/32. [OF chalanger]

chalanging vbl. n. (false) claim C.Phs 264. [OF]

chalaundre n. lark (Alauda calandra) RR 81, 663, 914. [OF]

chalons n.pl. bedcovers A.Rv 4140 [OF Chalons-(sur-Marne)]

chamberere n. lady's maid D.WB 300, E.Cl 819, 977. [OF]

chamberleyn n. household attendant of a person of rank A.Kn 1418. [OF]

chambre n. room, bedroom A.Kn 1065, C.Pard 735, E.Cl 263, TC 1.358; bridal chamber G.SN 276; ~ of Venus genitals D.WB 618. [OF]

champartie n. shared power A.Kn 1949. [AN, OF champart]

chanoun n. canon (cleric in minor orders) G.CY 573, 992, 1020, etc. [OF]

chaped adj. mounted A.Prol 366. [from OF chape n.]

chapeleyne n. nun serving as assistant to a prioress A.Prol 164. [OF chapelaine]

chapelet n. garland, coronal A.Kn 1054 var, RR 563, 908. [OF]

chapitre n. chapter B.NP 4255, D.Sum 1945, PF 32; subject I.Pars 238; ecclesiastical court D.Fri 1361. [OF]

chapman n. merchant, dealer A.Prol 397, B.ML 135, B.Sh 1444. [OE cēapmann]

chapmanhode/-hede n. bargaining, trade B.ML 143, B.Sh 1428. [prec.+OE suff. -hād, -*hǣdu]

charbocle/c(h)arbuncle n. carbuncle, ruby HF 1363, RR 1120; a heraldic charge (circle with eight rays) representing this B.Th 2061. [OF]

charge n. load Anel 32, RR 1352; heavy weight HF 746; (fig.) burden E.Cl 163, Bo 1. p3. 11/15 (L sarcinam), TC 1.651; weight, importance A.Kn 1284, F.Sq 359, no ~ no matter A.Kn 2287, G.CY 749, LGW 2383; responsibility B.Sh 1622, B.Mel 2404, PF 545; care A.Prol 733, D.WB 321; duty, task E.Cl 193, TC 2.994. [OF]

charge v. 1. load B.Mk 3556, E.Mch 2211, Bo 3. m3. 3/4; (fig.) burden I.Pars 92. 2. order B.ML 802, G.SN 287, TC 2.1437. [OF charger]

chargea(u)nt *adj.* burdensome B.Mel 2433, I.Pars 692. [OF]

charitee *n.* **1.** state of Christian love, good will A.Prol 532, E.Cl 221, G.SN 118; *in ~* I.Pars 235, TC 1.49; *out of ~* A.Prol 452, I.Pars 1043; *for seinte ~* for holy charity A.Kn 1721, B.NP 4510, D.Sum 2119. **2.** kindness A.Kn 1433, PF 508. [OF]

charmeresses *n. pl.* fortune-tellers HF 1261. [OF]

chartre *n.* charter, agreement, deed A.Mil 3327, E.Mch 2173, TC 3.340. [OF]

chase(n/chace(n *v.* drive, expel B.Pri 1756, B.ML 366, D.Sum 1916 (with play on **cha(a)st**, MercB 14, Bo 1. p4. 92/127 (L *pellerentur*); pursue F.Sq 457, I.Pars 355, continue E.Cl 341, 393; harass I.Pars 526; *~ at* harass, attack TC 1.908, 3.1801. [OF *chacier*]

chasted *p.p.* disciplined, reproved F.Sq 491. [from OF *chastier*]

chasteyn *n.* chestnut A.Kn 2922, RR 1375. [OF]

chastise *v.* correct I.Pars 628; admonish TC 3.329; restrain B.Mk 3695. [? new formation from OF *chastier*]

chaunce *n.* **1.** event, occurrence A.Kn 1752, B.ML 1045, TC 5.1668; *for no maner ~* by no means G.SN 527. **2.** fortune, luck A.CY 593, Anel 348, TC 2.464; (in gaming) B.ML 125, C.Pard 653; *par ~* by luck C.Pard 606. [OF]

chaunge *n.* **1.** change, alteration TC 2.22. **2.** exchange F.Sq 535, TC 4.59 var, 665. [AN]

chaunge(n *v.* **1.** (*tr.* and *intr.*) change A.Kn 1400, 1637. **2.** exchange C.Pard 724, TC 4.59 var, 553. [AN *chaunger*]

chaunterie *n.* chantry (endowment for a priest to pray for soul(s)) A.Prol 510. [OF]

che(e)p *n.* ample supply, cheapness HF 1974; *good ~* profitably TC 3.641; *to greet ~* too cheap D.WB 523. [OE *cēap* market, bargain]

che(e)re *n.* **1.** face E.Cl 238, Bo 1. p1. 60/84, LGW 64, RR 813; cheek Bo 2. m3. 3/4; expression, look A.Kn 913, B.Th 1901, D.Sum 2158, TC 1.14, 280; *a ~ make* assume an expression E.Cl 535. **2.** manners, behaviour A.Prol 139, E.Cl 298, F.Sq 103, I.Pars 27, TC 1.181; spirits, humour: *be of good ~* be glad TC 1.879, be confident TC 3.332. *make* (with specifying adj.) *~* behave (in this or that way): *good ~* be cheerful TC 5.913, *mery ~* enjoy oneself B.Sh 1532, *sory, sorwful ~* lament D.WB 588, TC 5.416, *wantoun ~* behave amorously E.Mch 1846, *hevy ~* see **hevy;** delight A.Kn 2683. **3.** hospitality, friendliness, attention: *make (someone) ~* treat in a friendly way A.Prol 747, A.Rv 4132, B.ML 180, TC 2.360, *doon ~* B.ML 1002, B.Sh 1196, TC 2.578. [OF]

che(e)se(n *v.* **1.** *tr.* choose A.Kn 1595, B.ML 227, B.Mel 2745, PF 370, TC 4.189; *for to ~* to be chosen TC 2.470. **2.** *intr.* make a choice, decide A.Mil 3181, D.WB 1237, D.Sum 1748, PF 399. **cheseth** *pr. 3 sg.* I.Pars 276, PF 623 *var;* **cheest** PF 623 *var.* **chese** *subj. sg.* A.Mil 3177. **chees** *imper. sg.* A.Kn 1595, G.SN 458, LGW 1449. **cheseth** *pl.* D.WB 1232, Mars 17; **chese** D.WB 1219. **chees** *pa. sg.*

B.Mk 3706, TC 5.1532, LGW 146. **chose(n** *pl.* LGW G. 290. **chose(n** *p.p.* A.Kn 2109, BD 1004, PF 528. [OE *cēosan, cēas, curon, coren*]

cheeste *n.* wrangling I.Pars 556. [OE *cēast*]

che(e)ve *v.* fare, in *yvele mot he ~* bad luck to him G.CY 1225. [OF *ch(i)ever*]

cheke *n.* cheek D.WB 433; *pl.* A.Prol 633; jawbone B.Mk 3228. [OE *cēoce/cēace*]

chekkere *n.* chess-board BD 660. [AN *escheker*]

chepe *v.* bargain for D.WB 268. [OE *cēapian,* cf. **che(e)p**]

cherice/-ishe *v.* cherish TC 3.175; favour, indulge B.Mk 3710; look after, care for F.Fkl 1554. [OF *cheriss-,* stem of *cherir*]

cherisshinge *vbl. n.* love TC 4.1534.

cherl *n.* common man A. 2459, I.Pars 761, bondman (fig.) I.Pars 463, 763; fellow C.Pard 289, TC 1.1024; churl, boor A.Mil 3169, 3182, A.Rv 3917, B.NP 4599, D.Sum 2206, PF 596. [OE *ceorl*]

cherldom *n.* slavery I.Pars 766 var. [from prec.]

cherlish *adj.* churlish, mean, villainous F.Fkl 1523, RR 177. [from **cherl**]

cheste/chiste *n.* chest, coffer C.Pard 734, D.WB 44b, 317, D.Fri 1400, LGW 510, (fig.) receptacle, holder TC 5.1368; coffin D.WB 502, E.Cl 29. [OE *cest, cist*]

chevauché *see* **chivachee.**

chevesaile *n.* ornamental collar RR 1082. [OF]

chevisance *n.* dealing, lending money A.Prol 282; borrowing B.Sh 1581; *make(n a ~* raise money B.Sh 1519, 1537, LGW 2434. [OF]

chevise *v. refl.* sustain oneself Mars 289. [OF]

chide(n *v.* **1.** *tr.* chide, reproach B.NP 4541, F.Fkl 776, TC 3.1433, 5.1093; scold, nag D.WB 419, I.Pars 632. **2.** *intr.* complain A.Rv 3999, B.Sh 1618, E.Mch 2274, F.Sq 650. **chideth** *pr.3 sg.* B.Mel2898; **chit** G.CY 921. **chideth** *imper. pl.* D.Sum 1824. **chidde** *pa. sg.* A.Rv 3999, D.WB 223. [OE *cīdan, cīdde*]

chideress *n.* scold RR 150. [from prec.]

chidestere *n.* scold E.Mch 1535. [from **chide(n** + OE fem. suff. *-estre*]

chidyng *vbl. n.* rebuke, scolding I.Pars 525, 631. *pl.* I.Pars 206, HF 1028, quarrels I.Pars 793.

chiertee *n.* fondness B.Sh 1526, D.WB 396, F.Fkl 881. [OF]

chiknes *n. pl.* chickens A.Prol 380. [OE *cīcen*]

child *n.* child, baby A.Kn 2019, B.Pri 1706, E.Cl 502, BD 727; unborn baby I.Pars 576; *knave ~* boy B.ML 715, E.Cl 447; *mayde ~* girl B.Sh 1285, E.Cl 446; *(gone) with ~* pregnant A.Kn 2310, B.ML 720, B.Mk 3474; noble youth, knight B.Th 2000, 2007, 2020 var. **childes** *gen. sg.* in *~ pley* child's play E.Mch 1530. **children** *pl.* A.Prol 628, E.Cl 1093, TC 1.132. [OE *cild,* pl. *cildru*]

childhede *n.* childhood B.Pri 1691, B.Mel 2635. [OE *cildhād* with altered suff. *-*hǣdu]

childly *adj.* childlike BD 1095. [OE *cildlīc*]

chilyndre *n.* cylinder, portable sundial B.Sh 1396. [OF from L *cylindrus*]

chimbe *n.* rim (of a cask) A.Rv 3895. [cf. OE *ćimbing* joint]
chimbe *v.* sound, toll A.Rv 3896. [from OF *chimbe* cymbal]
chimenee *n.* fireplace A.Mil 3776, TC 3.1141; chimney Bo 1. m4. 7/10. [OF *cheminee*]
chinche *adj.* as *n.* miser B.Mel 2793, 2809. [OF]
chincherye *n.* meanness B.Mel 2790. [from prec.]
chyning *ppl. adj.* gaping, open Bo 1. p6. 28/36 (L *hiante*). [from OE *ćinan*]
chirche *n.* church A.Prol 708, B.ML 1123, C.Pard 329, D.Sum 1714; *hooly* ∼ A.Rv 3986, D.Sum 2193, I.Pars 93, 94, etc.;∼ *dore* A.Prol 460, D.WB 6; ∼ *hawe*, ∼ *reves* see hawe¹, reve. [OE *ćiriće*]
chirketh *pr. 3 sg.* chirrups D.Sum 1804.
chirkinge *pr. p.* groaning Bo 1. m6. 7/10 (L *stridens*). [cf. OE *ćearćian*]
chirking *vbl. n.* creaking, groaning A.Kn 2004, I.Pars 605, HF 1943.
chisels *n. pl.* cutting blades I.Pars 418. [ONF]
chiteren *v.* twitter A.Mil 3258; chatter G.CY 1397. [imit.]
chivachee/chivachie *n.* cavalry expedition A.Prol 85; feat of horsemanship H.Mcp 50; **chevauché** ride Mars 144. [OF]
chivalrye *n.* **1.** knighthood, chivalry A.Kn 982, F.Fkl 1088, LGW 1822. **2.** knightly pursuits, deeds A.Prol 45, B.Mk 3585, RR 1207. [OF *chevalerie*]
chose *see* bele chose.
chose(n *see* che(e)se(n.
chough/cow *n.* chough, jackdaw D.WB 232, PF 345. [?; orig. imit.]
chuk *n.* 'cluck' B.NP 4364. [imit.]
chukketh *pr. 3 sg.* clucks B.NP 4372. [imit.]
ciclatoun/syklatoun *n.* an expensive thin cloth B.Th 1924. [OF from Arab]
Cimerie *n. pl.* Cimmerians HF 73. [L *Cimmerii*]
cinamome *n.* cinnamon (as endearment) A.Mil 3699. [OF]
cink *n.* five (on dice) B.ML 125, C.Pard 653. [OF]
circuit *n.* circumference A.Kn 1887. [OF]
circumscrive *v.* bound, encompass TC 5.1865. [L *circumscribere* and OF *-scriv-*]
circumsta(u)nce *n.* feature, detail, particular A.Kn 1932, C.Pard 419; *with alle/every* ∼ (*s* in full detail I.Pars 610, 976, with extreme care A.Kn 2263, E.Cl 584; with all ceremony B.ML 317. [OF]
cinor n. strong drink B.Mk 1243, [LL *sicera*]
citole *n.* cithara, stringed instrument A.Kn 1959. [OF]
citryn *adj.* lemon-yellow A.Kn 2167. [OF]
citrinacioun *n.* turning yellow G.CY 816. [OF from ML]
clad *see* clothe(n.
clamb(en *see* climbe(n.
clappe *n.* chatter A.Mil 3144; stroke, clap HF 1040, I.Pars 174. [imit.]
clappe(n *v.* chatter B.NP 3971, G.CY 965, HF 1824*var*; clatter I.Pars 406; clap (hands) F.Fkl 1203; knock D.Fri 1581, 1584; bang A.Mil 3740, E.Mch 2159. **clappeth** *imper. pl.* E.Cl 1200. **clapte** *pa.* E.Mch 2159. [imit.]
clarioning *vbl. n.* playing clarions HF 1242. [from next]

clarioun *n.* clarion, bugle A.Kn 2600, HF 1240, 1247. [OF *clairon*]
clarree *n.* clary, wine sweetened and spiced A.Kn 1471, E.Mch 1807, FormA 16. [OF]
clause *n.* stipulation, condition TC 2.728; particular TC 5.1301; sentence: *in a* ∼ briefly A.Prol 715, E.Mch 1431. [OF]
clawe(n *v.* tear D.Sum 1731; scratch, rub A.Co 4326, D.WB 940, TC 4.728. **clew** *pa.* HF 1702 (or ? an otherwise unrecorded vb. = 'turned'). [OE *clawan, -ian,* ? *clāwan*]
clawes *n. pl.* claws B.Mk 3366; **clowes** HF 1785. [OE *clawu*]
cled(de *see* clothe(n.
cle(e)r *adj.* **1.** bright, shining B.ML 451, B.Pri 1871, I.Pars 1078, TC 4.1548; brilliant (of light) A.Kn 1062, F.Sq 48, TC 3.1, (fig.) gay TC 4.1435; limpid, pure I.Pars 816, HF 522; pure (fig.) G.SN 101, PF 77, innocent C.Pard 914; beautiful, fine B.Th 2048, TC 5.220, LGW 249, 1829; famous Bo 2. m7. 9/13 (L *claris*). **2.** true, resonant (of sound) H.Mcp 115, BD 347. **3.** apparent, plain Bo 4. p2. 25/34 (L *perspicuum*); free, unencumbered TC 3.526, 982. [OF]
cle(e)re *adv.* brightly A.Kn 2331, G.SN 254, TC 4.1575; clearly, loud A.Prol 170, TC 5.578, HF 1722, *loude and* ∼ B.Pri 1845, B.Th 1961, E.Mch 1845. [from prec.]
cle(e)rly *adv.* plainly Bo 2. p5. 70/98, sharply 3. p9. 2/3; entirely B.Sh 1265. [from cle(e)r]
cle(e)rnesse *n.* brightness, radiance G.SN 111, 403, Bo 2. m3. 1/2, LGW 84. [from cle(e)r]
clene *adj.* clean A.Prol 504, C.Pard 873; pure E. Mch 1264, I.Pars 947; free from sin D.Sum 1879; chaste E.Cl 836, G.SN 225, LGW G. 282; neat D.WB 598; free D.WB 944, TC 3.257. [OE *clǣne*]
clene *adv.* completely, clean B.ML 1106, F.Sq 626, G.CY 1425, TC 5.1054. [OE *clǣne*]
clennesse *n.* purity, chastity A.Prol 506, G.SN 160, LGW 1860. [from clene]
clepe(n *v.* call, name A.Prol 620, B.Mk 3169, E.Cl 115, F.Sq 12, TC 1.66; call out A.Mil 3577, TC 1.8, 4.1157; summon D.WB 147, invite I.Pars 444; ∼ *agayn/ayein* recall H.Mcp 354 TC 2.521. **cleped** *pa.* A.Mil 3761, F.Fkl 1487; **clepte** RR 1331. **y)cleped** *p.p.* A.Prol 121, B.NP 4060, A.Mil 3313, TC 1.654; **y)clept** G.CY 863, 772. [OE *clipian, cleopian*]
clere *v.* become clear TC 2.2, 906; grow light TC 5.519; shine brightly LGW 773. [from cle(e)r adj.]
clergeon *n.* schoolboy B.Pri 1693. [OF *clerjon*]
clergial *adj.* learned G.CY 752. [from next]
clergye *n.* learning D.Fri 1277. [OF]
clerk *n.* scholar, writer A.Prol 480, B.Mel 2297, D.WB 706, TC 1.961; student A.Prol 285, A.Mil 3143, A.Rv 4018; priest, church official C.Pard 391, TC 3.41; *parish* ∼ A.Mil 3348. [OE *cler(i)c,* OF *clerc*]
clernesse *n.* brightness, radiance G.SN 111, Bo 2. p5. 29/41, LGW 84. [from cle(e)r]
cleve *v.*¹ split A.Kn 2934, TC 3.375, LGW 758. **clefte** *pa.* BD 72. **clove(n** *p.p.* A.Kn 2934, RR 550. [OE *clēofan, clēaf, clofen*]

cleven/clyven v.² cleave, adhere Bo 2. p6. 62/87, 3. p11. 76/104, 104/143, 5. p4. 105/150. [OE *clifian, cleofian*]

clew n. ball of thread LGW 2016, 2140. [OE *cliwen*]

clew see **clawe(n.**

clifte n. cleft, chink Bo 3. p9. 10/13, LGW 740; cleft of the buttocks D.Sum 2145. [OE *clyft*]

cliket n. latch-key E.Mch 2046, 2117. [OF]

clymat n. zone of the earth between lines of latitude Astr 2.39. 18/25. pl. in *tables of the* ~*s* sets of almacantars calculated for a particular latitude Astr 1.14.2/3. [OF]

climbe(n v. climb A.Mil 3625, F.Sq 106, HF 1119. **clamb** pa. sg. B.Th 1987; **clomb** Mars 271, HF 1118. **clamben** pl. HF 2151; **clomben** A.Mil 3636; **cloumben** B.Mel 2590 var. **clombe(n** p.p. B.ML 12, B.NP 4388, TC 1.215; **cloumbe** B.Mk 3592 var. [OE *climban, clámb, clúmbon, clúmben*]

clinke(n v. tinkle B.Sh 1186, C.Pard 664. [prob. MDu *klinken*]

clippe v.¹ embrace E.Mch 2413, TC 3.1344. [OE *clyppan*]

clippe v.² clip, cut A.Mil 3326, B.Mk 3257, 3261. [ON *klippa*]

clyven see **cleven.**

clobbed adj. club-shaped, knobbed B.Mk 3088. [from *clubbe* n., ON *klubba*]

cloisterer n. monk, enclosed person A.Prol 259, A.Mil 3661, B.Mk 3129. [from **cloistre**]

cloisterlees adj. outside the cloister A.Prol 179 var. [from next]

cloistre n. monastery A.Prol 181, D.Sum 2099; enclosure G.SN 43. [OF]

clom interj. mum! A.Mil 3638, 3639. [imit.]

clomb(en see **climbe(n.**

clo(o)s adj. closed B.NP 4522, H.Mcp 37, RR 1675; shut up B.Mel 2811; secret B.Mel 2336, G.CY 1369; concealed TC 2.1534. [OF]

clo(o)th n. cloth A.Mil 3748; ~ *of gold* A.Kn 2158, 2568, E.Cl 1117; ~ *of Reynes* linen from Rennes BD 255, ~ *of Tars* silk from Tarsia (in Turkestan) A.Kn 2160; garment B.Mk 3663, D.Fri. 1633; clothing D.WB 238, D.Sum 1881. pl. clothes A.Kn 899, cloths (of gold) B.ML 137; draperies, hangings A.Kn 2277, 2281. [OE *cláþ*]

clos n. enclosure Bo 1. p5. 22/32, 2. p7. 36/51; yard B.NP 4550. [OF]

closure n. fence I.Pars 870. [OF]

clote-leef n. burdock leaf G.CY 577. [OE *cláte*+**leef**]

clothe(n v. clothe, dress B.Sh 1202, TC 5.1418, RR 95; deck B.Mk 3495. **clad(de** pa. A.Kn 2873, Anel 145; **cledde** TC 3.1521; **clothede** LGW. G. 117. **clad** p.p. A.Prol 103, PF 173; **yclad** G.SN 133; **cled** BD 252; **clothed** A.Prol 363, TC 1.156. [OE *cláþian* and *clǽþan, ge)cláded*; also ON *klǽþa, klǽdda*]

clothered adj. clotted A.Kn 2745. [cf. OE *clot*]

clothing vbl. n. clothing, clothes B.Mk 3494, E.Cl 256; cloth I.Pars 433.

clothlees adj. without clothing I.Pars 343. [from **clo(o)th**]

clout n. rag, patch C.Pard 348, RR 458; cloth C.Pard 736. [OE *clút*]

clouted adj. dressed in rags RR 223. [from prec.]

clove(n see **cleve.**

clowe-gilofre n. clove B.Th 1952, RR 1368. [OF *clou de girofle*]

clowes see **clawes.**

coagulat ppl. adj. solidified G.CY 811. [L *cóagulátus*]

cod n. bag C.Pard 534. [OE]

coempcioun n. monopoly, cornering Bo 1. p4. 59/82. [OF]

coeterne adj. co-eternal Bo 5. p6. 39/56. [ML *coeternus*]

coffre n. coffer, chest A.Prol 298, F.Fkl 1571, LGW 380; coffin PF 177. [OF]

cogge n. cock-boat, dinghy LGW 1481. [AN]

coy adj. quiet, shy A.Prol 119, E.Cl 2, LGW 1548. [OF]

coye v. cajole TC 2.801. [OF *acoier*]

coillons n. pl. testicles C.Pard 952. [OF]

coynes n. pl. quinces RR 1374. [OF *coin*]

cokenay n. milksop A.Rv 4208. [*coken* prob. adj. from OE *cocc* cock+**ey**]

cokewold n. cuckold, deceived husband A.Mil 3152, D.WB 1214, E.Mch 1306. [AN *cucuald* = OF *cucuault* from *cucu* cuckoo]

cokkel n. corn-cockle B.Sh 1183. [OE *coccel*]

col n. coal A.Kn 2692, TC 2.1332; (piece of) charcoal G.CY 809, 1160. **coles** pl. B.Mk 3323, G.CY 1114. [OE]

cold adj. cold (as one of the characteristic qualities of matter) A.Prol 420, PF 380; (fig.) baleful, hostile A.Kn 2443; disastrous, fatal A.Kn 2467, B.NP 4446; chilling, painful, in *cares* ~*e* F.Fkl 1305, G.SN 347, TC 1.264, 3.1202, 5.1747, LGW 762, *sikes* ~*e* A.Kn 1920, D.WB 602. [OA *cáld*]

colde(n v. grow cold B.ML 579, PF 145, TC 3.800, 4.418, LGW 240. [OA *cáldian*]

cole adj. cool, dull LGW G. 258. [OE *cól*]

colera/-e n. choler, bile B.NP 4118, 4136. [OF]

colerik adj. of a temperament characterized by the 'humour' choler B.NP 4145; favouring such a temperament F.Sq 51; choleric, irascible A.Prol 587. [OF]

colfox n. black fox B.NP 4405. [from **col**]

collacioun n. comparison Bo 4. p4. 49/67; consultation E.Cl 325, Bo 5. p4. 134/193. [OF]

collect adj. collected in groups (of years numbering over 20: see Astr 2.44) F.Fkl 1275. [L *collect-*, p.p.]

colour n. 1. colour A.Kn 1038, C.Phs 28, RR 213; complexion A.Kn 2168, G.CY 727, RR 355. 2. pretence, excuse D.WB 399, F.Sq 511 (with pun on 1), Pity 66. 3. rhetorical ornament E.Cl 16, F.Sq 39, F.Fkl 723. [OF]

colpons n. pl. wisps A.Prol 679; faggots A.Kn 2867. [OF]

colt n. colt A.Mil 3263; ~*es tooth* youthful appetites A.Rv 3888, D.WB 602. [OE]

coltissh adj. eager as a colt E.Mch 1847. [from prec.]

columbyn adj. dovelike E.Mch 2141. [OF from L *columba* dove]

colver n. dove LGW 2319. [OE *culfre*]

comaundement n. order, command A.Kn 2869, HF 2021; commandment I.Pars 887. [OF]

combred *p.p.* encumbered Bo 3. m10. 6/8; impeded TC 3.717 *var*. [OF *(en)combrer*]
combre-world *n*. burden to the world TC 4.279. [cf. prec.]
combust *adj*. burnt G.CY 811; (astrol.) TC 3.717, Astr 2.4.33/51. [L *combust-* p.p.]
come *n*. coming, Advent G.SN 343. [? ON *kváma* replacing OE *cyme*]
come(n *v*. come A.Prol 672; descend A.Rv 3942, B.Pri 1687, B.Mk 3146, D.WB 1101, G.SN 121; ~ *by* attain, discover D.WB 984, F.Fkl 1115, G.CY 1395; ~ *of* come on, hurry up A.Mil 3728, D.Fri 1602, PF 494, TC 2.310, 1738; *to* ~ future, destined I.Pars 224, BD 708, Bo 2. p1. 60/83. 5. p3. 10/12 (L *futurum esse*), TC 1. 784, 4.997. **comth** *pr. 3 sg*. A.Mil 3818, TC 1.402; **cometh** A.Mil 3725. **cometh** *imper. pl.* A.Prol 839, I.Pars 161. **cam** *pa. sg*. A.Kn 983, F.Sq 81; **com** BD 134, TC 2.32. **cam** *pl*. B.ML 178, C.Pard 671; **co(o)me(n** Anel 30, B.Pri 1805, TC 3.205. **come(n** *p.p.* A.Prol 23, 671; **ycome(n** A.Prol 77, E.Mch 1700. [OE *cuman*, *cōm*, *cōmon*, *ȝe)cumen*]
comyn *n*. cummin B.Th 2045. [OF *cumin*]
committe *v*. commit, entrust B.Mel 2495, TC 5.4, 1542. [L *committere*]
commoeve/-meve *v*. move, influence Bo 4. p4. 184/256, TC 3.17, 5.1386; move to pity Bo 3. m.12. 19/27. [OF; cf. **moeve**]
commune *n. pl*. commons, common people E.Cl 70. **communes** common soldiers A.Kn 2509. [from next]
com(m)une *adj*. common, public, shared B.ML 155, C.Pard 601, I.Pars 885, TC 3.1415; widely known B.Mk 3821; common, ordinary B.Mel 2220, Bo 2. p3. 29/42, Astr prol 39/54; ~ *profit* public good E.Cl 431, I.Pars 773, PF 47, Bo 1. p4. 62/86. as *n*., right to use common land E.Mch 1313; commonwealth Bo 2. p7. 7/9, 42/60; *in* ~ generally A.Kn 2681, B.NP 4190, HF 1548. [OF]
com(m)une *v*. converse F.Fkl 693, G.CY 982. [OF *comuner*]
com(m)unly *adv*. in company, together I.Pars 105 *var*; generally B.Mk 3168, D.Sum 2257. [from adj.]
compaignable *adj*. sociable B.Sh 1194, B.NP 4062. [OF]
company/compaignye *n*. company, group A.Prol 24, TC 1.450; companionship, association A.Prol 461, B.Mel 2520; followers B.Pri 1682; *bere (one)* ~ G.SN 315, I.Pars 967, Bo 3. m12. 33/46, TC 4.1202; *holde* ~ keep company D.Fri 1521, F.Fkl 763, I.Pars 584; *departen* ~ part company B.NP 4183; ~ *of man* sexual intercourse A.Kn 2311. [OF]
comparisoned *p.p.* compared Bo 2. p7. 72/104. [from *comparison* n., from OF]
compas *n*. 1. craft, contriving HF 462; plan HF 1170; device, figure HF 1302. 2. circle, ring A.Kn 1889; circuit, circumference Mars 137, Bo 2. m11. 4/5, HF 798; *bi* ~ round about RR 900; *in* ~ in a circle LGW G. 199; *tryne* ~ threefold world (earth, sea, and heaven) G.SN 45. 3. compasses (instrument) Astr 2.5.7/10, 40.17/25. [OF]
compasse *v*. 1. contrive, plot B.ML 591, LGW 1414. 2. enclose MercB 21, Bo 4. p6. 85/121; draw round Astr 1.18.1. [OF]

compassement *n*. plotting LGW 1416. [OF]
compassing *vbl. n*. plotting A.Kn 1996; contrivance HF 1188; measurement, dimension RR 1350.
compeer *n*. comrade A.Prol 670, A.Co 4419. [OF]
compilatour *n*. compiler Astr prol 43/61. [OF]
compiled *p.p.* composed I.Pars 1093. [from v. from OF *compiler*]
compleyne *v*. 1. lament, mourn A.Kn 908, B.Mk 3567, Mars 93, TC 4.23; utter mournfully LGW 1748. 2. complain Pity 5, Bo 4. p1. 23/33. **compleyneth** *imper. pl*. Mars 290, 293. [OF]
compleyning *vbl. n*. lamentation B.ML 929, F.Fkl 945, TC 2.560.
compleynt *n*. lamentation F.Fkl 920, TC 1.541, LGW 2379; complaint, grievance Bo 1. p5. 3/4, LGW 363; song, poem of complaint or grief E.Mch 1881, F.Fkl 1354, Pity 43. [OF]
complexioun/-pleccioun *n*. temperament (determined by 'humours') A.Prol 333, A.Kn 2475, F.Fkl 782, I.Pars 585, HF 21; humour, characteristic B.NP 4114, TC 5.369. [OF]
compline *n*. evening service A.Rv 4171, I.Pars 386. [OF *complie* altered prob. after *matins*]
comporte *v*. endure TC 5.1397. [OF *comporter*]
composicioun *n*. agreement A.Prol 848, A.Kn 2651; combination F.Sq 229. [OF]
compotent *adj*. in possession of itself Bo 5. p6. 33/47 (L *sui compos*). [L *compos+potent-*]
compoune *v*. compound, mix HF 1029, 2108; construct Bo 3. m9. 6/8; compose Bo 3. p10. 144/197; temper LGW 2585; design Astr prol 7/9, mark 1.18.8/11. [OF *compoun-*, stem of *compondre*]
comprehende(n/comprende *v*. 1. understand F.Sq 223, BD 762, Bo 5. p4. 111/159, TC 4.891. 2. include, contain I.Pars 521, Bo 5. p2. 22/31, TC 3.1687. [L *compre(he)ndere* and OF *comprendre*]
comunalitee *n*. community, commonwealth Bo 1. p4. 20/28, 2. p7. 4/6, 4. p6. 250/364. [cf. OF *comunalté*]
conceite *n*. conception, notion G.CY 1078, Bo 3. p10. 28/40, TC 1.692; thought LGW 1764; fancy TC 3.804. [from next, after *deceit(e]*
conceive *v*. 1. conceive B.Mk 3675, I.Pars 576, Bo 2. m6. 6/8. 2. understand F.Sq 336, TC 5.1398, Astr prol 18/24; perceive, observe LGW 1746. [OF *conceiv-*, stem of *concevoir*]
conclude(n *v*. 1. draw a conclusion, infer A.Kn 3067, B.ML 14, Bo 3. p10. 72/98; reach a conclusion E.Mch 1607. 2. sum up A.Kn 1358, 3067, F.Fkl 1152; include G.SN 429. [L *concludere*]
conclusioun *n*. 1. end, ending A.Kn 1869, G.SN 394, HF 103; (*as*) *in* ~ finally, in sum B.ML 215, C.Pard 454, TC 4.452, 5.1003. 2. result, success G.CY 672. 3. conclusion, inference B.NP 4247, F.Fkl 889, PF 620, Bo 4. p2. 159/216. 4. decision, judgement A.Mil 3402, PF 526, TC 5.1310; *for plat* ~ as a firm decision A.Kn 1845. 5. purpose D.WB 115, TC 1.480. 6.

(mathematical) proposition A.Mil 3193, Astr prol 9/12, etc. [OF]

concordinge *ppl. adj.* agreeing TC 3.1752. [from vb. from OF *concorder*]

condescende *v.* come down F.Sq 407, ~ *in especial*, descend, proceed, to the particular B.Mel 2424 (cf. **descende(n)**; agree, settle B.Mel 2447, E.Mch 1605, consent Astr prol 5/7. [OF *condescendre*]

condicioun *n.* **1.** circumstances (of a person), position in life A.Prol 38, B.ML 313, HF 1904; situation B.Mel 2330, 2566; state B.ML 99, I.Pars 755, TC 3.817, Astr 2.35.12/17; form of existence, nature Bo 4. p3. 69/100. **2.** circumstances (of conduct) I.Pars 319. **3.** character, nature A.Kn 1431, B.ML 271, E.Cl 701, G.CY 1039; quality C.Phs 41, TC 5.831. *pl.* Bo 2. p5. 66/92 (L *moribus*), TC 2. 166. **4.** condition, stipulation D.Sum 2132, F.Sq 529, BD 750, *in this* ~ on this condition PF 407. [OF]

conduit *n.* conduit, pipe LGW 852, **condys** *pl.* RR 1414; *saf* ~ safe conduct TC 4. 139 *var*. [OF]

confedred *ppl. adj.* joined Pity 42, 52. [from OF *confederer*]

conferme(n *v.* **1.** strengthen Bo 4. p6. 185/269; confirm, ratify A.Kn 2350, TC 2.1526, 1589. **2.** support HF 761; promote, prosecute B.Mel 2412. **3.** *p.p.* established C.Phs 136. **4.** *refl.* resolve B.Mel 2967. [At Bo 4. p4. 137/194 and p7. 61/85 *conferme* renders L *conform-*.] [OF *confermer*]

confiture *n.* compound, medicine C.Pard 862. [OF]

confounde(n *v.* destroy B.ML 362, TC 4.245; overcome Rosem 10; subdue Bo 2. p6. 36/52; distress B.ML 100, I.Pars 740; condemn G.SN 137. [AN *confundre*]

confus *adj.* confused A.Kn 2230, TC 4.356; perplexed, baffled G.SN 463; obscure Bo 4. m5. 10/13, HF 1517. [OF]

confusioun *n.* **1.** destruction, ruin A.Kn 1545, B.Mel 2296, C.Pard 499, H.Mcp 272, TC 4.186; disgrace I.Pars 187, 820; damnation B.Mk 3133. **2.** mixture, chaos F.Fkl 869, Bo 5. p3. 120/170. [OF]

congeyen *n.* send away, dismiss TC 5.479. [OF *congeër*]

congregacioun *n.* assembly, crowd B.Mel 2194, B.NP 4178; collecting together Bo 3. p2. 13/18. [OF]

conies *n. pl.* rabbits PF 193, RR 1404. [OF *conil*]

conjecte(n *v.* suppose, speculate Bo 1. p6. 20/25, 4. p2. 71/94, TC 4.1026. [from L *coniectāre*]

conjectinge *vbl. n.* conjecture B.Mel 2592, 2598.

conjoignen/-joynen *v.* join, unite: *intr.* Bo 3. p10. 120/161; *tr.* I.Pars 924, Bo 3. p11. 43/57; compose Bo 3. p10. 149/203. **conjoigned** *p.p.* Bo 3. p4. 27/40; **conjoynt** I.Pars 924. [OF *conjoign-*, stem of *conjoindre*]

conjoininge *vbl. n.* composition G.SN 95.

conjuracioun *n.* conspiracy Bo 1. p4. 133/185, 2. p6. 38/55; summoning spirits I.Pars 603. [OF]

conjure *v.* call upon B.Pri 1834; TC 2.1733, LGW 1312. [OF *conjurer*]

conne/cunne/k- (c-/k- vary throughout) *v.* **1.** (with n. or pron. obj.) know, understand A.Prol 110, 210, A.Mil 3193, B.Pri 1735, C.Pard 332, F.Sq 39, G.CY 846, TC 1.647, 3.83, HF 335; learn B.Pri 1730, I.Pars 1041; (absol.) D.WB 56; ~ *craft* be cunning E.Mch 1424; ~ *good* know what is good, have good sense B.Sh 1169, BD 800, 998, TC 2.1178, 3.638; ~ *(one's) good* see one's advantage D.WB 231, TC 5.106, LGW 1182; ~ *reed* know a course of action, see what to do B.Mk 3739, BD 105; ~ *of* know about, be skilled in A.Mil 3200, ~ *on* B.ML 47, F.Fkl 786; experience, feel, in ~ *thank* be grateful, owe thanks (to) A.Kn 1808, 3064, TC 2.1466, Astr prol 39/55. **2.** *auxil.* (with infin.) (I, etc.) can, know how to A.Prol 95, A.Co 4396, B.Mel 2901, D.WB 950, TC 3.377, LGW 2351; be able to A.Rv 3875, C.Phs 13, D.Fri 1518, E.Cl 1042, TC 5.1404; (absol.) A.Prol 588, can do TC 1.776, 2.175, 1078, 1673; *I ~ no more* PF 14 *var*, TC 3.390, 1193, 5.1368; ~ *and/or may* B.Sh 1544, B.Pri 1650, B.Mk 3679, F. Sq 112, *may and* ~ A.Kn 2312, *may ne* ~ E.Cl 304. **can/kan** *pr. 1, 3 sg.* A.Kn 1935, TC 1.11, A.Prol 371, TC 1.147. **canst** *2 sg.* B.Mel 2123, **canstow** (with suffixed pron.) C.Pard 521, TC 4.460. **can** *pl.* A.Kn 1353, A.Rv 3875, E.Cl 937, TC 2.895; **conne(n** B.ML 483, D.WB 950, E.Mch 2438, F.Sq 3. **conne** *subj. sg.* A.Co 4396, G.CY 846, TC 2.1497. *pl.* A.Mil 3118. **con(ne** *imper.* Astr prol 39/55. **coude** *pa.* A. Prol 94, TC 1.193, LGW 2449; **couthe** A.Prol 390, TC 1.984. **coude** *subj.* D.WB 1008, TC 2.59. **coud** *p.p.* BD 787 *var*, 998, I.Pars 1041; **couth** known E.Cl 942, I.Pars 766, TC 4.61; as *adj.*, well-known, celebrated A.Prol 14. [OE *cunnan; cann, cunnon; cūþe*]

conning *n.* skill, understanding B.ML 1099, PF 167, TC 1.83, 662. [from OE *cunnan*, see prec.]

conning *adj.* clever, knowing B.Mk 3690, TC 1.302; ~ *for to pleyne* skilled in composing appeals Pity 97. **conningest** *sup.* TC 1.331. [from **conne**]

conningly *adv.* skilfully E.Cl 1017. [from prec.]

conscience *n.* **1.** conscience B.Mel 2825, C.Phs 280, E.Mch 1635, Bo 1. p4. 181/253, TC 1.554; *good* ~ B.Mel 2822, 2831. **2.** sensibility A.Prol 142, 150, LGW 1255; *spyced* ~ see **spyced, swete** *adv.*; scrupulousness A.Prol 398, D.Fri 1438. [OF]

consecrat *p.p.* dedicated B.Mk 3207. [L *consecrātus*]

conseillour *n.* adviser B.Mel 2305, E.Mch 1501, LGW 1550. [OF]

consentant *adj.* acquiescent (*of* 'in') C.Phs 276. [OF]

consente(n *v.* **1.** *intr.* (with *to*) agree (with) B.Mel 2551; accord, be consistent (with) B.Mel 2572; assent I.Pars 902; give in (to), allow I.Pars 542; acquiesce (in) B.Mel 2552. **2.** *tr.* comply with, submit to E.Cl 537, agree to E.Cl 803. **3.** *refl.* submit TC 1.936. [OF *consentir*]

consentement *n.* agreement I.Pars 967. [OF]

consentinge *vbl. n.* agreement, accord B.Mel 2550; acquiescence I.Pars 293, 296; *pl.* 293, consenting, yielding (to sin) 354, 355.

consequent *n.* result B.Mel 2577, Bo 3. p9. 53/69 *var.* [OF]

conservatif *ppl. adj.* (with obj.) tending to preserve HF 847.

conserve *v.* preserve, keep A.Kn 2329, B.Mel 2185, G.SN 387, TC 4.1664, HF 1160. [OF *conserver*]

considered *p.p.* as *prep.* considering, taking into account B.Mel 3039, TC 2.1290, 4.1271, 5.1348, LGW 225. **considering** *pr. p.* as *prep.* F.Fkl 675. [from *v.* from OF *considerer*]

consistorie *n.* court of justice C.Phs 162; council TC 4.65. [OF]

constable *n.* governor B.ML 512, 521. [OF]

constablesse *n.* governor's wife B.ML 539. [OF]

constance *n.* constancy, faithfulness E.Cl 668, 1000, E.Mch 2283. [OF]

constellacioun *n.* relative position of a planet or planets A.Kn 1088, E.Mch 1969, F.Sq 129; horoscope, state of planets at one's birth D.WB 616, F.Fkl 781, TC 4.752. [OF]

constreine *v.* restrain Bo 4. p6. 113/163 (L *coerceat*); compel, force D.WB 1071, E.Cl 527, TC 2.476, 1232, impel B.Mel 3070; dominate, rule F.Fkl 769; bring together Bo 4. p6. 154/225 (L *perstringam*). [OF *constreign-*, stem of *constreindre*]

constreynt(e *n.* distress TC 2.776, 4.741. [OF *constreinte*]

construe *v.* translate, interpret B.Pri 1718, LGW 152; explain, understand TC 3.33. **construeth** *imper. pl.* LGW 152. [L *construere*]

contek *n.* strife, contention A.Kn 2003, B.NP 4122. [AN]

contemplaunce† *n.* contemplation D.Sum 1893. [from OF *contempler*]

contene *v.* contain, enclose Bo 2. p7. 26/36, TC 3.502, Astr 2.39. 11/16; include, consist of Bo 3. p10. 118/168, 4. p2. 139/189. [OF *contenir*]

continuance *n.* perseverance F.Fkl 680. [OF]

contract *ppl.* contracted, incurred I.Pars 334. [L *contractum*]

contraire *adj.* contrary, opposite BD 1290, TC 1.212, LGW 1360 *var.* [OF]

contrarie *n.* contrary, opposite A.Kn 3057, TC 1.637; hostile act B.Mel 2470, I.Pars 720; opponent A.Kn 1859, B.NP 4470. [OF]

contrarien *v.* oppose, contradict D.WB 1044, E.Mch 1497, 2319, F.Fkl 705. [OF *contrarier*]

contrarious *adj.* adverse, hostile B.Mel 2245, Bo 1. p4. 215/299; mutually opposed D.WB 698, Bo 2. p6. 57/80. [OF]

contrariousnesse *n.* contrary state I.Pars 1077. [OF]

contree *n.* country A.Kn 869, B.Mk 3847, HF 241; homeland A.Kn 1383, C.Pard 610, LGW 2216; countryside, district A.Prol 340, B.ML 434, D.Sum 1710. [OF]

contubernial *adj.* familiar, at home I.Pars 760. [from L *contubernium*]

conveyen *v.* introduce E.Cl 55; conduct, accompany A.Kn 2737, E.Cl 391, LGW 2305. [AN *conveier*]

convenient *adj.* suitable, fitting I.Pars 421, Bo 1. p4. 187/263; appropriate F.Fkl 1278. [L *convenient-*]

convers *n.* in *in* ~ ? on the reverse side TC 5.1810 (but this is unique in Chaucer and does not correspond to Boccaccio *i conuessi*: see *O.E.D.* under *convers*). [L *convers-* p.p.]

conversacioun *n.* manner of life B.Mel 2501. [OF]

converte *v.* **1.** *tr.* convert B.ML 686, G.SN 404; change TC 1.308; reform TC 1.999. **2.** *intr.* turn aside C.Phs 212; change one's mind TC 2.903, 4.1412. [OF *convertir*]

convertible *adj.* equivalent A.Co 4395. [OF]

convict *p.p.* overcome ABC 86; convicted Bo 1. p4. 172/240. [L *convict-* from *convincere*]

co(o)st *n.* coast B.Pri 1626, F.Fkl 995; region D.WB 922; part of the sky Astr 1.19.6/8. [OF *coste*]

cop *n.* tip A.Prol 554; top Bo 2. m4. 4/6, HF 1166. [OE]

cope *n.* cope A.Prol 260; cape, cloak TC 3.724; canopy LGW 1527. [ML *cāpa*]

coppe/coupe/cuppe *n.* cup A.Prol 134, A.Rv 3928, F.Sq 616, LGW 1122; *withouten* ~ abundantly F.Fkl 942. [OE *cuppe* and *copp*, OF *co(u)pe*]

corage *n.* heart, spirit, disposition A.Prol 22, E.Cl 220, F.Sq 22, Bo 1. p4. 2, TC 5.825; nature A.Prol 11; soul Bo 4. p4. 31/42 (L *animus*); courage, fighting spirit B.Mk 3836, Bo 4. p3. 80/115, TC 1.564, *an heigh* ~ a high-spirited thing E.Mch 1513; desire B.Mel 2713, E.Cl 907, E.Mch 1254, 1808; inclination, intention B.Mel 2257, attention H.Mcp 164. [OF]

corageous *adj.* courageous B.Mk 3527, TC 5.800; ardent, passionate I.Pars 585. [AN]

corbets *n. pl.* corbels HF 1304. [OF]

corde *n.* rope, cord A.Mil 3569, LGW 2485; (fig.) cord of a net or snare G.SN 8; string (of a musical instrument) TC 5.443, HF 696. [OF]

cordeth *pr. 3 sg.* agrees TC 2.1043. [from *ac(c)orde*]

cordewane *n.* spanish leather B.Th 1922. [from *Cordoba*]

cordial *n.* heart stimulant A.Prol 443. [OF]

corn *n.* grain of corn B.NP 4365, C.Pard 863; corn, grain A.Prol 562, A.Rv 3939; (fig.) B.ML 702, B.Sh 1183, LGW 74, G. 312. *pl.* crops of grain B.Mk 3225. [OE]

cornemuse *n.* bagpipe HF 1218. [OF]

corny *adj.* malty C.Pard 315, 456. [from *corn*]

corniculer *n.* adjutant G.SN 369. [L *corniculārius*]

corosif *adj.* corrosive: *watres* ~ acids G.CY 853. [OF]

coro(u)ne/croun *n.* crown, garland A.Kn 2290, E.Cl 1118, LGW 220; prize Bo 4. p3. 7/11; (fig.) chief ornament Pity 58, TC 5.547; crown of head B.Sh 1499. [AN]

corporel *adj.* material I.Pars 798. [OF]

corps *see* **cors.**

corpus *n.* body (used in oaths, in error or jest) A.Mil 3743, B.Pri 1625, B.Mk 3082, 3096, C.Pard 314. [L]

correccioun *n.* correction I.Pars 60; punishment C.Pard 404, fine D.Fri 1617; *do* ~ inflict punishment A.Kn 2461, D.Fri 1320; *out of his* ~ out of his jurisdiction to punish D.Fri 1329. [OF]

correcten v. correct G.CY 999; discipline, reprove B.Mel 2663, D.WB 661, G.SN 162, I.Pars 673. [from L *correct-* from *corrigere*]
corrige v. correct Bo 4. p4. 61/84, p7. 26/38. [OF *corriger*]
corrumpable adj. corruptible A.Kn 3010. [OF]
corrumpen v. **1.** tr. corrupt, destroy I.Pars 819, Bo 3. p11. 103/142. **2.** intr. become corrupt LGW 2237, decay, putrefy A.Kn 2746 var, Bo 3. p11. 40/54. [OF *corrumpre*]
corrumpynge vbl. n. disintegration Bo 3. p.12. 57/75.
corrupt p.p. corrupted B.Mk 3579, C.Pard 504, I.Pars 167; as adj. corrupt B.ML 519; infectious E.Mch 2252. [L *corruptus*]
cors n. body H.Mcp 67; (with possessive forming quasi-pron., cf. **body**) *his* ~ him B.Th 2098, *thi* .. ~ C.Pard 304; corpse A.Mil 3429, C.Pard 665, TC 5. 742, LGW 676, **corps** A.Kn 2819, D.WB 768. [OF]
corse see **curse(n.**
corseynt n. saint's shrine HF 117. [OF *cors seint* holy body]
corve(n see **kerve(n.**
cosin n. cousin B.Mel 2562, ~s *germayns* first cousins B.Mel 2558; relative, kinsman or -woman (often as address) A.Kn 1081, B.Sh 1259, 1333; (fig.) akin (to) A.Prol 742, H.Mcp 210. [OF]
cosinage n. kinship B.Sh 1226, 1329, 1599; (? play on sense 'fraud', in F from 15th c.). [OF]
cost n. expense A.Prol 192, 213; expenditure, spending B.Sh 1470; *the* ~ *make* meet the cost LGW 1448; *winne thy* ~ cover your expenses D.Fri 1580. [AN]
costage n. cost, expense D.WB 249, E.Cl. 1126; *doqn* ~ spend money B.Sh 1235. [OF]
costeying pr. p. coasting, moving along, RR 134. [from AN *costeier*]
costlewe adj. costly, sumptuous I.Pars 415, 418. [**cost**+OE suff. *-lǣwe*]
costrel n. flask LGW 2666. [OF]
cote n.[1] hut, cell A.Kn 2454, B.NP 4026, E.Cl 398. [OE]
cote n.[2] tunic (for a man) A.Kn 103, 328; gown (for a woman) RR 459, 573. [OF]
cote-armure n. coat-of-arms (garment embroidered with heraldic device) A.Kn 1016, B.Th 2056, TC 5.1651. [OF]
couche(n v. **1.** intr. lie Astr 2.29.14/20, crouch E.Cl 1206. **2.** tr. place, set A.Mil 3211, PF 216 var; lay (a fire) A.Kn 2933, G.CY 1157. **3.** ornament, embroider A.Kn 2161. [OF *couchier*]
coude see **conne(n.**
co(u)nseil n. **1.** advice, counsel B.Mel 2194, B.NP 4447, C.Phs 285, PF 631, TC 4.1114; *bi* ~ with deliberation A.Mil 3530, E.Mch 1485; decision A.Prol 784; purpose Bo 4. p4. 108/153; pl. plans, intentions B.Mel 2308; *take(n* ~ deliberate B.Mel 2310; concurrence B.Mel 2979. **2.** council, (body of) advisers A.Kn 3096, B.ML 326, B.Mel 2240, confidant A.Kn 1147, *privé* ~ B.ML 204. **3.** secret G.SN 145; secrets A.Prol 665, B.Sh 1323, B.Mk 3282, D.WB 980, PF 348; *kepe* ~ B.Mel 2334, C.Pard 561, (with obj. *it*) TC 1.992; *in* ~ confidentially E.Mch 2431; *of my* ~ in my confidence A.Kn 1141. [OF]

counte pr. 1 sg. account, value (at) (with dir. obj. and n. expressing value) A.Rv 4192, TC 5.363, MercB 29; care (for) (with obj. expressing value and *of*) A.Rv 4056, E.Mch 1568. **counted** pa. BD 718. [OF *counter*]
co(u)ntena(u)nce n. **1.** bearing, behaviour, manner B.Sh 1582, E.Cl 924, F.Sq 94, I.Pars 614, LGW 1738, good manners BD 613, custom, habit E.Mch 2205; appearance A.Kn 1916, F.Fkl 1485, LGW 2076; look, expression F.Sq 284, BD 1022, TC 3.1542; face A.Kn 2010, B.Th 1893, B.Mel 2899, E.Cl 293; gesture B.Sh 1198, B.Mel 2226; self-possession, composure E.Cl 1110; *fond his* ~ assumed an attitude, pretended TC 3.979; *make a* ~ pretend I.Pars 858, assume an appearance TC 2.552, sign, gesture B.Mel 2228; *make good* ~ appear unmoved B.ML 320; *make thi* ~ *upon* give your attention to TC 2.1017. **2.** show, pretence A.Co 4421, G.CY 1264, Fort 34, *feyned* ~ B.Mel 2378. [OF]
countour n.[1] accountant A.Prol 359, arithmetician BD 435. [OF]
countour n.[2] counting-house, office B.Sh 1275, 1403, BD 436 (? or counting-board). [AN *counteour*]
countour-hous n. counting-house, office B.Sh 1267. [prec.]
countrefete v. imitate, counterfeit A.Prol 139, F.Sq 554, TC 2.1532; **countrefeted** ppl. adj. false, affected C.Phs 51. [AN *countrefeter*]
countrepe(i)se v. set against TC 3.1407/ 1393; balance HF 1750. [OF]
countrepleted p.p. argued against LGW 476. [AN *countrepleter*]
countretaille n. counter-tally: *at the* ~ in reply, correspondingly E.Cl 1190. [OF]
co(u)ntrewaite v. watch over I.Pars 1005; watch out for B.Mel 2509. [ONF]
coupable adj. culpable, to blame B.Mel 2731, I.Pars 414. [OF]
coupled p.p. joined E.Mch 1836; **ycoupled** E.Mch 1219. [from OF *co(u)pler*]
cours n. course, path A.Prol 8, orbit A.Kn 2454; course of life G.SN 387; run A.Kn 1694. [OF]
court n. **1.** household of a king or nobleman A.Kn 1181, B.Mel 2996. **2.** court of law: of Rome A.Prol 671, E.Cl 737; of a manor D.Sum 2162. **3.** courtyard F.Sq 171. [OF]
courtepy n. jacket A.Prol 290, D.Fri 1382, RR 220. [MDu *korte pie*]
couthe adv. familiarly HF 757 [OE *cūþe*; cf. **conne**]
coveite(n v. desire, long for D.WB 266, Mars 269, Bo 2. m7. 6/8; intr. lust (L *concupiscit*) I.Pars 336. [OF *coveit(i)er*]
cove(i)tise n. greed, covetousness, avarice A.Rv 3884, B.Mel 2320, C.Pard 424, TC 3.261; excessive desire, craving I.Pars 818, lust 336, *to* ~ *of* in the desire of 845. [OF]
covenable adj. suitable, fitting I.Pars 80, Bo 4. p4. 188/262, TC 2.1137. [OF]
covenably adv. suitably B.Mel 2423, Bo 4. p6. 234/339. [from prec.]
covena(u)nt n. covenant, agreement A.Prol 600, F.Fkl 1587, LGW 688; *in* ~ to mark the contract E.Mch 2176. [OF]

covent n. convent, (members of a) religious house B.Pri 1827, D.Sum 1863, G.CY 1007. [AN]

coverchief n. headscarf A.Prol 453, B.ML 837 var, D.WB 590; see **kerchief**. [OF couvrechief]

covercle n. pot-lid HF 792. [OF]

covere v.¹ cover, veil B.Mk 3956, I.Pars 422. **kevered** p.p. PF 271, HF 275, 352. [OF covrir, pr. stem cuevr-]

covere v.² recover, be cured LGW 762; **kevere** TC 1.917. [OE ācofrian and OF covrer win, reco(u)vrer, stem recuevr-]

coverture n. coverlet, covering I.Pars 198, Bo 4. m2. 1; disguise Bo 5. m3. 15/22, RR 1588. [OF]

covetour n. man who covets Mars 262. [OF]

covyne n. deceit, treachery A.Prol 604, Bo 1.p4. 220/306. [OF]

cow see **chough**.

coward adj. cowardly B.Mel 2517, PF 349, TC 1.792. [OF couarde]

cowardye n. cowardice A.Kn 2730. [OF]

cowardly adv. timidly TC 4.1196. [from adj.]

crabbed adj. bitter, shrewish E.Cl 1203. [from OE crabba crab]

cracchinge vbl. n. scratching A.Kn 2834. [cf. MDu kratsen and **crecche**]

craft n. **1.** skill, artifice A.Prol 401, D.Fri 1468, F.Fkl 909, Bo 1. p1. 14/21; guile, cunning I.Pars 512, LGW 2528; trick, cunning device B.Mk 3258; cf. **conne**. **2.** trade, art A.Mil 3189, C.Phs 84, G.CY 785, PF 1. [OE cræft]

crafty adj. skilled, clever A.Kn 1897, G.CY 1290, BD 319; cunning G.CY 655, subtle G.CY 1253. **craftier** BD 662. [OE cræftiȝ]

craftily adv. skilfully, artfully B.ML 48, TC 2.1026, HF 1203. [from prec.]

craketh pr. 3 sg. cries harshly E.Mch 1850; utters loudly A.Rv 4001 var **craked** pa. [OE cracian]

crakkinge vbl. n. cracking, creaking I.Pars 605.

crampissheth pr. 3 sg. stiffens, contracts Anel 171. [from OF crampiss-, stem of crampir]

crased ppl. adj. cracked, broken G.CY 934, y- BD 324. [from OF acraser]

creat p.p. created B.Mel 2293, I.Pars 218. [L creātus from creāre]

crea(u)nce n. belief, creed B.ML 340, 915, ABC 61. [OF]

crea(u)nce v. borrow on credit B.Sh 1479, 1493, 1556. [OF creancer]

creaunt (interj.) I surrender! I.Pars 698, [shortened from **recreaunt**]

crecche v. scrape together TC 3. 1375/1361 var. [? MDu kratsen, kretsen]

crekes see **crike**.

crepe(n v. creep, move slowly A.Mil 3441, F.Fkl 1614, G.CY 870, BD 391, TC 3.1505. **creep** pa. sg. A.Rv 4226, 4260; **crepte** A.Rv 4193, B.Mk 3806. **cropen** p.p. A.Rv 4259, TC 3.1011. [OE crēopan, crēap, cropen]

crepil n. cripple TC 4.1458. [OE crypel]

crepuscule n. twilight Astr 2.9.1. [OF]

crevace n. crevice, crack I.Pars 363, HF 2086. [OF]

crew see **crowe**.

cry n. shout A.Kn 1080, E.Mch 2364, TC 2.196; calling A.Mil 3417; lament, wailing A.Kn 900, B.NP 4545; crying F.Sq 413. [OF cri]

crie(n v. **1.** intr. shout, scream A.Prol 636, TC 1.753; lament, wail A.Kn 908, B.NP 4566, complain B.NP 4233, F.Fkl 1496; appeal, pray B.ML 850, TC 2.436. **2.** tr. shout, cry out A.Prol 646, A.Rv 4072; proclaim A.Kn 2731, F.Sq 46, HF 1322; beg for A.Mil 3288, B.ML 1111, TC 2.1076; summon loudly HF 2107. **cryde(n** pa. A.Kn 949, TC 1.729. **cryd/cryed** p.p. E.Cl 563 var. [OF crier]

crike n. creek A.Prol 409, Bo 3. m8, 8/10; (fig.) **crekes** pl. devices, wiles A.Rv 4051 var. [ON kriki corner, bend]

crinkled p.p. full of twists and turns LGW 2012 var. [cf. OE crincan yield]

crisp/crips adj. curly A.Kn 2165, D.WB 304, HF 1386. [OE]

cristen adj. Christian A.Prol 55, B.Pri 1679, D.Sum 1820; as n., see **evene-cristen**. [OE]

cristenly adv. in a Christian way B.ML 1122. [from prec.]

cristianitee n. Christian community B.ML 544. [L Christianitas and OF crestienté]

cristned pa. baptized G.SN 217. p.p. B.ML 226, **ycristned** 240. [OE cristnian]

croce n. staff D.WB 484. [OF]

croys n. cross B.ML 451, C.Pard 532, E.Cl 556 (all these in rhyme with voys), A.Prol 699, A.Rv 4286, I.Pars 258, Astr 1.5.3/4 var. Cf. **cros**. [OF]

crokes n. pl crooks, hooks LGW 640. [ON krókr]

crokke n. crock, jar Truth 12. [OE crocca]

cronique/cronycle n. chronicle B.NP 4398 var. [OF]

crop n. top, growing tip, shoot A.Prol 7, A.Kn 1532, Bo 3. m2. 23/33, TC 5.25; ~ and rote everything, whole TC 2.348, 5.1245. [OE]

cropen see **crepe(n**.

croper/croupere n. crupper I.Pars 433; ? hind quarters (of horse) G.CY 566. [OF]

cros n. cross ABC 82, TC 5.1843, Astr 1.5.3/4 var. Cf **croys**. [LOE from OIr]

cros(se)let n. crucible G.CY 793, 1117, 1147, etc. [from AN crosel = OF croisuel]

crouche v. cross, make sign of cross over A.Mil 3479, E.Mch 1707. [from OE crūc]

croude v. push HF 2095, drive B.ML 296, 801. [OE crūdan]

crouding vbl. n. jostling HF 1359, thrust B.ML 299.

oroun see **coro(u)ne**.

crouperes see **croper**.

crowe v. crow A.Mil 3357, B.NP 4048, 4466, C.Pard 362. **crew** pa. B.NP 4048, 4387. **y)crowe** p.p. A.Mil 3357, 3687. [OE crāwan, crēow, crāwen]

crowke n. jug A.Rv 4158. [OE crūce]

crowned ppl. adj. surmounted by a crown A.Prol 161; (fig.) supreme F.Sq 526. [from **coro(u)ne**]

cruel adj. stern, harsh B.Mel 2837; savage E.Cl 1095; fierce, merciless TC 5.1751. [OF]

crul adj. curly A.Prol 81, A.Mil 3314. [? MDu]

curcurbites n. pl. gourd-shaped vessels for distillation G.CY 794. [OF]

culpe *n.* blame, guilt I.Pars 335. [OF]
culter *n.* coulter (for plough) A.Mil 3763, 3776. [OF *coultre*]
cunne *see* **conne.**
cuppe *see* **coppe.**
curacioun *n.* cure B.Mel 2463, TC 1.791. [OF]
curat *n.* parish priest, vicar A.Prol 219, D.Sum 2095, I.Pars 791. [ML *cūrātus*]
cure *n.* **1.** treatment, cure, remedy F.Fkl 1114, PF 128, TC 1.707, 5.49; preserver G.SN 37, Mars 131. **2.** care, attention Bo 2. p3. 21/29, HF 464, 1298; *bisy* ~ see **bisy;** *honest* ~ care for honourable things C.Pard 557; supervision, control D.Fri 1333; concern, pursuit E.Cl 82, endeavour Bo 3. p2. 3/4; *do (one's)* ~ apply oneself, do one's best A.Kn 1007, PF 369, TC 1.369; *do/make no* ~ have no care, care nothing D.WB 1074, LGW 152, 1145; *in (one's)* ~ in one's power B.ML 230, C.Phs 22, TC 2.741, LGW 1176; *take* ~ of pay attention to, take heed of A.Prol 303, D.WB 138, Pity 82, Mars 171, TC 2. 283. [OF]
cure *v.* cure, heal B.Mel 2207, Bo 1. p1. 50/70, TC 1.758, 5.350. [OF *curer*]
curiositee *n.* intricacy, fine workmanship HF 1178, Ven 81; elaboration I.Pars 446, delicacy, epicureanism I.Pars 829: precision Astr 2.14 rubr. [OF]
curious *adj.* **1.** (of persons) skilful, ingenious A.Prol 577; eager, intent E.Mch 1577, HF 29, RR 1052; careful B.Sh 1433. **2.** (of objects) finely wrought A.Prol 196, I.Pars 433, HF 125; elaborate B.ML 402, D.WB 497; intricate, subtle B.Sh 1415; abstruse, occult F.Fkl 1120; eager E.Mch 1577. [OF]
curiously *adv.* skilfully, finely F.Fkl 909. [from prec.]
currours *n.pl.* couriers HF 2128. [OF]
curs *n.* curse, excommunication A.Prol 655, 661; *Cristes* ~ A. Co 4349, C.Pard 946, D.Fri 1347. [OE]
cursed *ppl. adj.* accursed A.Kn 933, D.Fri 1652; ill-omened TC 4.745, 5.1699; abominable, detestable D.WB 789, H.Mcp 39, PF 495; wicked B.ML 80, 958, B.Pri 1760, C.Pard 470, G.CY 830. [from **curse(n)**]
cursedly *adv.* wickedly, sinfully B.Mel 3016, B.Mk 3419, I.Pars 604. [from prec.]
cursedness *n.* sin, wickedness B.Pri 1821, C.Pard 400, F.Fkl 1272, G.CY 1101, TC 4.994; shrewishness, malice E.Mch 1239. [from **cursed**]
curse(n *v.* curse E.Cl 898, **corse** E.Mch 1308; excommunicate A.Prol 486. [OE *cursian*]
cursing *vbl. n.* excommunication D.Fri 1587.
curteis *adj.* courteous, polite A.Prol 99, B.NP 4061, TC 1.81; chivalrous B.Mel 2950, TC 3.26; gracious I.Pars 246. [OF]
curteisye *n.* courtly conduct, courtliness, chivalry A.Prol 46, B.Mk 3686, E.Cl 74, F.Sq 95, (person.) Pity 68, PF 219; good manners, civility C.Pard 739, graciousness B.ML 166, kindness B.ML 179, TC 2.1486; *for/of your* ~ kindly, if you please A.Prol 725, A.Mil 3287, D.Sum 1669, LGW 342. [OF]

curteisly *adv.* courteously, gently, A.Rv 3997, D.Sum 1771, RR 799; correctly B.Sh 1281. [from **curteis**]
custumes *n.pl.* imposts, duties I.Pars 567, 752. [AN]
cut *n.* lot A.Prol 845, C.Pard 794; *draw* ~ draw lots A.Prol 838, C.Pard 793. [?]
cutte(n *v.* cut C.Pard 954, Bo 4. m7. 10/14. **kitte** *pa. sg.* B.ML 600, B.Pri 1761, D.WB 722. **cut** *p.p.* LGW G. 292, **cutted** LGW 973, short-cut I.Pars 422. [OE *cyttan*]

D

daf *n.* fool A.Rv 4208. [cf. OE *dæfte* adj.]
dagged *ppl. adj.* ornamented by incisions I.Pars 421. [from v. based on n.; cf. OF *dague* dagger]
dagginge *vbl. n.* ornamenting (garments) with points I.Pars 418. [cf. prec.]
dagon *n.* scrap (of cloth) D.Sum 1751. [see **dagged**]
day *n.* day **1.** from midnight to midnight Astr 2.1.1/2, 4/7, TC 2.56; ~ *naturel* F.Sq 116, Astr 2.7.13/18; *cercle of* ~ circle on astrolabe listing days of the months 2.1. 7/10. **2.** period of daylight Astr 2.3.1, 3/4; *the arch of the* ~, *the* ~ *artificial* sunrise to sunset 2.7; ~ *vulgare* sunrise to sunset plus morning and evening twilights 2.9; dawn A.Kn 1476, A.Rv 4237, B.Mk 3098, TC 3.1450; *at* ~ at dawn B.Sh 1429, *agayn the* ~ just before dawn B.NP 4268, *a quarter before* ~ three hours before dawn BD 198; *by* ~ in daylight F.Sq 297; ~ *sterre* morning star Bo 2. m3. 4/6; *myn hertes* ~ sun of my life TC 5.1405. **3.** astrological day belonging to a planet A.Kn 1537; *(his) happy* ~ astrologically fortunate day TC 2.621. **4.** appointed day or time B.ML 260, D.WB 1024, E.Cl 183, E.Mch 1998, G.CY 1027, TC 5.84, ~ *set* the appointed day E.Cl 774, TC 4.1441; *pl.* postponed days for settlement of debt F.Fkl 1575, *at certeyn* ~*s* at fixed times 1568; *myn ending* ~ D.WB 507, *thy laste* ~ Fort 71 the day of my/thy death; ~ *of dome* Judgement Day I.Pars 118. **5.** life, time B.Mk 3374, E.Cl 1136, *lyves* ~ lifetime LGW 1624; *tarien forth the* ~ waste time A.Kn 3230, *dryve(n the* ~ *awey* spend the time C.Pard 628; *pl.* F.Fkl 709, *in tholde* ~ of long ago in the time of D.WB 857; *the lyf of this* ~ this present life Bo 5. p6. 18/25 (L *hodierna vita*). **6.** phrases: *al* ~ see **alday**; *fro* ~ *to* ~ A.Mil 3371, B.ML 154, E.Cl 784, TC 1.482; *(up)on a* ~ once, at one time A.Prol 19, A.Kn 1189, 1414; *a* ~ for a whole day B.ML 1135 *var*, and see **aday**; *bi* ~ *or night* A.Kn 1212; *fro* ~ *to night* all day long B.Mel 2205, B.Mk 3098, F.Sq 641, TC 5.1436; ~ *and/ne night* C.Pard 467, E.Mch 1256, F.Fkl 746, *night and/ne* ~ A.Kn 1823, D.WB 669, F.Fkl 824, TC 5.793; *this* ~ today B.ML 90, *this other* ~ a short time ago BD 148; *in o̅ur* ~*es* nowadays F.Fkl 1132; *the longe* ~ all day long A.Prol 354, LGW 650; *gon sithen many a* ~ long ago F.Sq 536; *this* ~ *fifty wykes* a year hence A.Kn 1850; *have good* ~ goodbye A.Kn 2740, B.Sh 1510, B.NP 4287; *yeve*

yow good ~ grant you good fortune TC 5.1074; *allas the/that* ~ how sad that day was F.Sq 621, BD 1244, LGW 658. **dawes** *pl.* in *in olde* ~ F.Fkl 1180. [OE *dæg*, pl. *dagas*]

dayerye *n.* dairy herd A.Prol 597; dairy D.WB 871. [AN from **deye**]

dalf *see* **delve(n.**

daliaunce **1.** small talk, sociableness A.Prol 211, gossip G.CY 592, *have(n* ~ gossip LGW G. 332; company LGW 356, friendly intimacy D.Fri 1406; *do(n* ~ be friendly B.Th 1894, Rosem 8, 16, 24. **2.** flirtation or sexual intercourse C.Phs 66, D.WB 260. [from *dalien* v., OF *dalier*]

damage **1.** (physical) harm, destruction I.Pars 419. *pl.* B.Mel 2213, Bo 2. p6. 5/6. **2.** detriment, injury (to reputation, morals, etc.) I.Pars 520, 609, 645. **3.** disadvantage I.Pars 457; loss LGW 598. [OF]

damageous *adj.* injurious I.Pars 438. [OF *damageus*]

dame *n.* **1.** as title of a woman of rank B.ML 151, B.NP 4312, PF 242; as term of address A.Rv 3956, D.WB 296, D.Sum 1805. **2.** dam A.Mil 3260; mother C.Pard 684, D.WB 576, H.Mcp 317; *our* ~ mistress of this household B.Sh 1546, 1553, D.Sum 1797, 2128. [OF]

dampnable *adj.* worthy of damnation B.Mk 3795, C.Pard 472, I.Pars 679, 695. [OF]

dampnably *adv.* in a manner deserving condemnation B.Mel 3016; in a manner deserving damnation I.Pars 604. [from prec.]

dampne(n *v.* **1.** condemn to eternal damnation C.Phs 88, I.Pars 191, 218, 686; condemn to death A.Kn 1745, D.Sum 2037, LGW 401, 1953. **2.** sentence A.Kn 1175, 1342, D.WB 891, I.Pars 571, Bo 1. p4. 174/243. **3.** make an adverse judgement on D.WB 70, Fort 49. [OF *dam(p)ner*]

dan/daun *n.* (used as title) lord, master (of nobles) A.Kn 1379; (of clerics) B.Sh 1233, 1248; (of ancients) H.Mcp 314, TC. 4.189, HF 434, (of classical gods) HF 199, RR 1616. [OF]

dar *see* **durre.**

dare *v.* lie dozing B.Sh 1293. [OE *darian*]

darreyne(n *v.* **1.** vindicate claim to (something) by fighting A.Kn 1609, 1853. **2.** ~ *the bataille* undertake the combat A.Kn 1631, 2097. [OF *derai(s)nier*]

darst(ou *see* **durre.**

dart(e *n.* **1.** spear, javelin Bo 4. m4. 10/15, TC 4.771; Cupid's weapon A.Kn 1564, (fig.) TC 4.472. **2.** *the* ~ *is set up for the prize is promised for* D.WB 75. [OF]

daswe(n *pr. pl. intr.* grow dim H.Mcp 31, *tr. p.p.* dazzled HF 658. [cf. ME *dasen*, ON *dasa-sk*]

date *n.* in *of latter* ~ lately D.WB 765; *to long a* ~ too long a time G.CY 1411. [OF]

daun *see* **dan.**

daunce *n.* dance: (fig.) *the olde* ~ (of love) all the tricks A.Prol 476, C.Phs 79, TC 3.695 (OF *la vielle dance*); *the newe* ~ 2.553, *the amorouse* ~ 4.1431 love-making. [OF]

daunger *n.* **1.** disdain, reserve (of lady to lover) Anel 186, 195, TC 2.384, 3.1321; (person.) PF 136, TC 2.399, 1376, *of* ~ for (his) disdain RR 1524; *the forme of* ~ public appearance of reserve TC 2.1243. **2.** resistance: *with* ~ with reserve D.WB 521,

withouten ~ without difficulty, freely A.Kn 1849, RR 1147. **3.** power, dominion: *in* ~ in (one's) power A.Prol 663, RR 1049, 1470. **4.** peril *pl.* A.Prol 402. [AN]

daungerous *adj.* **1.** haughty, aloof A.Prol 517, A.Mil 3338; disdainful RR 591, 1492; hard to please B.Mel 2129, D.WB 1090. **2.** niggardly, stingy D.WB 151, 514, D.Fri 1427; unwilling RR 490. [AN]

daunte(n *v.* tame, subdue B.Mk 3799, I.Pars 270, PF 114, TC 2.399; conquer Bo 4. m7. 20/29; frighten (from) D.WB 463. [AN]

dawe *v.* dawn (subject *day*) A.Kn 1676, B.Mk 3872, E.Mch 1842, 2195; (subject *it*) A.Rv 4249. [OE *dagian*]

dawenynge *n.* dawn A.Rv 4234, BD 292. [? cf. Sw *dagning*]

dawes *see* **day.**

deba(a)t *n.* **1.** strife, war B.ML 130, B.Mel 2867, 2872, G.CY 1389; battle A.Kn 1754. **2.** quarrel, dispute D.WB 822, D.Fri 1288, E.Mch 1496, TC 2. 753; *at* ~ at odds, A.Mil 3230. **3.** dilemma BD 1192. [OF]

debate(n *v.* **1.** contest TC 4.166 *var.* **2.** contend, dispute C.Pard 412, FormA 51, Bo 1. p3. 28/38. **3.** engage in combat B.Th 2058. [OF *debatre*]

debonair(e *adj.* submissive A.Kn 2282, H.Mcp 192, meek I.Pars 430, 658, TC 1.214, RR 797; gracious B.NP 4061, kind, gentle BD 860, Bo 1. m5. 15/22; benign Bo 2. p8. 9/12, 3. p12. 99/135; as *n.* courteous one BD 624; benign person ABC 6. [OF]

debonair(e)ly *adv.* meekly B.Mel 2254, I.Pars 660, Anel 127, HF 2013, tamely Bo 4. m3. 11/15; kindly, graciously I.Pars 315, BD 1284, favourably TC 2.1259; modestly 3.156. [from prec.]

debonairete *n.* kindness B.Mel 2811, 3010, I.Pars 467; meekness B.Mel 2129, patience I.Pars 540, 654, BD 986. [OF]

deceit(e *n.* trickery D.WB 401, deceptiveness Fort 21, *pl.* illusions Bo 2. p1. 11/15; *by* ~ Bo 3. p9. 136/184. [AN]

deceivable *adj.* deceptive E.Mch 2058, misleading, false Bo 3. p6. 1, m10. 2/3, 5. p3. 73/102; unreliable Ven 43; treacherous Bo 1. m1. 19/27, 2. m1. 6/8, p8. 3/4. [AN]

deceyvaunce *see* **desceivaunce.**

declamed *pa. pl.* discussed TC 2.1247. [L *dēclāmāre*]

declaracioun *n.* revelation, manifestation I.Pars 595; explanation, elucidation, Astr 2.2.9/12, 4 rubr., 10.11/*var*, 11.14/19; *pl.* corollary Bo 3. p10. 100/135. [OF]

declare(n *v.* **1.** tell B.Pri 1679, G.CY 719, TC 3.575, explain B.Pri 1718, Astr 1.21. 20/28; declare A.Kn 2766; distinguish I.Pars 391; *our wittes to* ~ explain our minds D.Fri 1499; ~ *his confessioun* confess himself I.Pars 1018; ~ *of* expound E.Mch 1687, tell about 2437. **2.** prove Astr 2.11.12/16, 23.6/8. **3.** signify (nonverbally) A.Kn 2356, G.SN 331, Astr 2.6.13/19. [OF *declarer*]

declaring *vbl. n.* explanation B.Mk 3172; *pl.* corollary Bo 3. p10. 114/153.

declinacioun *n.* angular distance north or south of the equator E.Mch 2223, F.Fkl 1033, Astr 1.17.4/6, 37/49; *hote* ~ = summer solstice F.Fkl 1246. [OF]

declyne(n v. **1.** diverge Astr 1.21.57/81, move away 2.17.29/43, 19.8/11. **2.** ~ *fro* deteriorate from Bo 4. p6. 122/176, forsake Bo 4. p7. 32/45. [OF *decliner*]

decoped *p.p.* cut in openwork panels RR 843. [from OF *decopé*]

decre(e n. **1.** ecclesiastical law A.Prol 640, A.Kn 1167, I.Pars 931; *Book of* ~*s* Decretum Gratiani B.Mel 2594. **2.** ruling, judgement I.Pars 17; *in his* ~ by his edict B.Mk 3667. [OF]

decrets n. pl. secular laws Bo 1. p4. 114/157. [OF]

dede v. intr. die HF 552. [OE *dēadian*]

dedica(a)t *p.p.* dedicated I.Pars 964. [L *dēdicātus*]

deduyt n. delight A.Kn 2177. [OF]

de(e)d n. **1.** action B.ML 433, F.Sq 456; act of chivalry, military action B.Th 1999, pl. TC 5.803; battle A.Kn 2636; *in* ~ in practice A.Mil 3591; *in* ~ *of* in the act of I.Pars 356; *lo, which a* ~ what a dreadful act TC 4.1231; *in word and* ~ A.Kn 1775; *in thoght and* ~ G.CY 1275; *do your* ~ act B.Mel 2728; *was parfourned/doon/fulfilled in* ~ was performed, carried out B.Sh 1507, B.Mel 2990, G.SN 516, CY 1140; *putte(n our* ~ *in your wil* submit our future conduct to you B.Mel 2931, *wordes mote be cousin to the* ~ words and actions must match A.Prol 742. **2.** performance I.Pars 297, 846; *with the* ~ at that moment, out of hand G.SN 157, TC 3.1301, by doing so D.WB 70. **3.** effect, result B.Mel 2858. **4.** *in* ~ in truth, in fact A.Prol 659, BD 132, PF 8. [OE *dǣd*, A *dēd*]

de(e)d adj. **1.** dead, lifeless A.Prol 145, E.Mch 1463, H.Mcp 276, *be(n* ~ die A.Kn 1343, E.Cl 364; *wolde han had me* ~ wished to kill me B.NP 4091; *as* ~ like one dead G.SN 204; pale, dead looking TC 4.379, 5.559, *falle(n for* ~ fall swooning 4.733, *wex so* ~ fell into such a deep swoon LGW 1816. **2.** grievous BD 1211. **3.** forgotten, buried in oblivion TC 1. 1083, HF 1701. [OE *dēad*]

de(e)dly/-lich adj. **1.** fatal (to life), mortal B.Mk 3903, I.Pars 998, PF 128, (fig.) RR 1340; subject to mortality Bo 5. p6. 128/181. **2.** destructive, hostile (to soul) I.Pars 200, 206, Bo 2. m7. 7/9; ~ *sinne(s* mortal sin(s B.Mel 2614, I.Pars 99, 234 etc. **3.** deathly A.Kn 913, 1082, LGW 869, 885, languishing F.Fkl 1040, agonizing, grievous Anel 258, TC 4.871. **4.** dull, lifeless (sound) BD 162. [OE *dēadlic*]

de(e)dly adv. bitterly G.SN 476. [OE *dēadlīce*]

deef adj. deaf A.Prol 446, TC 1.753. **deve** pl. G.SN 286. [OE *dēaf*]

de(e)l n. **1.** share, part BD 1001; *every* ~ (sometimes as one word) completely, entirely, all of it A.Kn 1825, 2091, BD 698, TC 2. 590; *eche a* ~ in its entirety TC 3. 694; *al or any* ~ entirely or in part TC 2.1214; *never a* ~ not at all, not a bit, nothing A.Kn 3064, B.NP 4024, BD 937, *bi an hondred thousand* ~ a hundred thousandth part H. Mcp 137, *by a thousand* ~ a thousandth part as RR 1074; cf. **somdel.** **2.** (number) *a gret* ~ many BD 1159, *a ful gret* ~ very many RR 1356. [OE *dǣl*]

de(e)me(n v. **1.** tr. think, suppose F.Fkl 1486, TC 3.763; (with cl.) Bo 1. p6. 58/75, 3. p2. 20/29, TC 1.601; (obj. (to be) sthg.) G.CY 573, TC 2.371, 3.448. **2.** intr. think, conclude E.Cl 133, F.Sq 44, G.CY 595, RR 1012. **3.** tr. judge Bo 5. p6. 221/312; (with cl.) decide, conclude A.Mil 3194, B.ML 1038, B.Pri 1639, D.Sum 2236, PF 166; (with obj.+infin.) give judgement, award C.Phs 199; judge (to be) A.Kn 1881, Bo 3. p4. 21/30, 4. p2. 34/45. **4.** sentence C.Phs 271, Bo 1. p4. 85/117, ~ *to the deeth* D.Sum 2024. **5.** perceive F.Sq 563, distinguish, discern Bo 4. m6. 1 (L *cernere*), interpret Bo 5. p2. 9/12. **6.** intr. make a decision, judgement B.Mel 2220, 2325, F.Fkl 1498, give opinions F.Sq 202, 261; ~ *of* E.Mch 1976, TC 2.461, HF 1746. **deme** pr. subj. E.Mch 1976. **demeth** imper. pl. A.Kn 1353, A.Mil 3172, F.Fkl 1498. [OE *dēman*]

de(e)p adj. **1.** deep A.Kn 3031, F.Sq 155; muddy D.Fri 1541. **2.** heartfelt TC 1.298, 5.675, 1259, CompA 26. **depper** comp. Bo 2. p3. 9/12. **3.** profound, difficult TC 2.151, abstruse, inscrutable B.Mel 2596. [OE *dēop*, *deop(p)ra*]

deepliche adv. (?) seriously Bo 5. m3. 36/52. (erron. for L *alte* on high). [OE *dēopliče*]

de(e)pnesse n. intellectual depths Bo 3. m11. 31/42, mystery Bo 4. p6. 156/227, ? deep sorrow Bo 1. m2. 2. [OE *dēopnes(se)*]

deer n. deer A.Kn 2150, F.Fkl 1190; *wilde* ~ wild animals B.Th 1926. [OE *dēor*, sg. and pl.]

de(e)reling n. darling A.Kn 3793. [OE *dēorling*]

dees/deys n.¹ dais A.Prol 370. [OF *deis*]

dees n.² pl. dice B.Sh 1494, C.Pard 467, F.Fkl 690, TC 2.1347; **dys** A.Kn 1238, A.Co 4384. [from OF *dé*]

de(e)th n. death A.Kn 964, 2829, (person.) A.Rv 3892, C.Pard 675, TC 4.250, *the* ~ A.Kn 1716, B.Mel 3003, LGW 2430; *as the* ~ like the plague A.Prol 605, TC 1.483, fatally I.Pars 997; *from the* ~ ? through death TC 1.469, *almost at the* ~ dying LGW 2436; *ayeins his* ~ near its death LGW 1356, *a maner* ~ a kind of death PF 54; *forfered of his* ~ afraid that he might die F.Sq 527; *a* ~ *was for to see* was grievous to see TC 4.856; *han/cacche his* ~ die B.ML 193, HF 404. [OE *dēaþ*]

deface(n v. **1.** disfigure TC 5.915, 1335; mar (in the telling) TC 4.804. **2.** obliterate E.Cl 510, TC 4.1682, wipe out HF 1164. [OF *de(s)facier*]

defame n. reputation E.Cl 540, bad reputation, dishonour C.Pard 612, E.Cl 730, *for his* ~ to cause him disgrace B.Mk 3738. [OF *dif(f)ame*]

defame(n/diffame(n v. slander A.Mil 3147, D.Sum 2212, TC 2.860; dishonour I.Pars 645, disgrace TC 4.565. [OF *defamer/diff-*]

defaut(e n. **1.** lack I.Pars 186, want 214; lack, absence (*of*) 182, 184, BD 5, 25, Bo 3. p3. 14/20; deficiency E.Cl 1018, TC 5.1796; need I.Pars 99; fault (hunting term) in *on a* ~ *yfalle* checked by loss of scent BD 384. **2.** blemish CompA 56; defect, failing B.Mel 2684, D.Sum 1810. **3.** offence C.Pard 370, I.Pars 165; wickedness B.Mk 3718, sinfulness I.Pars 1030. **4.** *for* ~ *of* through the fault of Bo 2. p7. 38/54, *arette it to the ~ of* blame it on I.Pars 1082. [OF]

defence/diffense 1. act of defending B.Mel 2722, 2727, *in ~ of* LGW 606; *drawen to the ~* urge in support Bo 1. p3. 26/36; *stondeth at ~* protect yourselves E.Cl 1195. **2.** resistance D.WB 467; hindrance RR 1142. **3.** means of defence Bo 1. p4. 226/315; *there helpeth no ~* there is nothing to afford protection TC 4.287, LGW 1931; *no thikker cloth of no ~* no less transparent cloth PF 273; *withouten ~* without a legal hearing Bo 1. p4. 173/243. **4.** *breke(n ~* disobey prohibition TC 3.138, 1299. [OF *defens(e]*

defendaunt *n.* *in his ~* in self-defence I.Pars 572. [OF]

defende(n *v.* **1.** fight in defence of B.Mel 2631, I.Pars 758, 767, Bo 1. p4. 149/207; *refl.* LGW 1996; defend verbally I.Pars 401, 584; *~ thy compleint* support your accusation Bo 2. p3. 3/5. **2.** protect B.Mel 2217, ABC 95, Bo 1. p4. 45/62, 3. p11. 64/87; *refl.* B.ML 933, B.Mel 2724, Bo 3. p11. 105/144; preserve 75/101. **3.** forbid B.Mel 2178, C.Pard 590, D.WB 60, D.Sum 1834, I.Pars 606; (with *that*-cl.) B.Mel 2774, 2947, (someone to do sthg.) 2411, Bo 2. p2. 25/36, p.7. 103/147; *fruyt ~d* forbidden fruit C.Pard 510, I.Pars 332; *God ~* God forbid (*pr. subj.*) TC 4.1647; *(I)... heighly yow ~* (I) strongly urge you against TC 2.1733. **4.** restrain G.CY 1470. **5.** ward off B.Mel 2722. [OF *defendre]*

defet *adj.* altered for the worse TC 5.618, disfigured 1219; **defeted** withered away Bo. 2. p1. 7/10. [OF *desfait/deffet]*

deffyne(n *see* **diffyne(n.**

defye(n/diffye(n *v.* **1.** renounce A.Kn 1604, give up E.Mch 1310. **2.** denounce A.Mil 3758; scorn, repudiate B.Sh 1592, B.NP 4346, D.Sum 1928. **3.** deny the power of B.NP 4361, LGW 138, Fort 8, 16. [OF *desfier]*

defoule(n *v.* **1.** pollute (physically) Bo 4. p1. 33/45; pollute by sexual intercourse F.Fkl 1396, 1418; disfigure Bo 4. m7. 30/43 (L *turpatus*). **2.** pollute (morally or spiritually), violate (conscience, etc.) Bo 1. p4. 181/253, 4. p6. 211/306, I.Pars 882, 911. **3.** afflict, damage Bo 4. p3. 47/67, 48/68; bruise I.Pars 281; dishonour I.Pars 273. **4.** trample on I.Pars 191, Bo 3. m2. 20/28. [**foul** *adj.* and OF *defolor]*

degyse *adj.* elaborate, ostentatious I.Pars 417. [OF *desguisé]*

degysinesse *n.* elaborateness, newfangledness I.Pars 414. [from prec.]

degysinge *vbl. n.* elaborate, newfangled clothing I.Pars 425 *var.* [from v. from OF *desguiser]*

degre(e *n.* **1.** rank, social position A.Prol 40, A.Kn 1434, B.Mk 3166, D.WB 626, LGW 1506, dignity 399; *after/at his/hire ~, in his ~* according to his/her rank A.Kn 2192, 2573, B.Sh 1237; *of smal ~* of lowly rank E.Mch 1625, *in the leste ~* in the lowest position LGW 1313; *as in a low ~* at a low social level A.Co 4397. **2.** condition, reputation, standing E.Mch 1494, LGW 2070, *for shame of his ~* for fear of

harming his reputation F.Fkl 752; *putte(n in this ~* bind by these rules A.Kn 1841; *in swich ~* in such a position H.Mcp 146. **3.** tier, rung, step A.Kn 1890, Bo 1. p1. 24/33, RR 485, *in ~s* in tiers A.Kn 2579; footstep Bo 4. m1. 27/38 (L *gradum*); *upward in ~* higher in its development TC 5. 1360; *lord at al ~s* master of every stage of love A.Mil 3724. **4.** way, extent (in phrases): *in ech ~* in every way D.WB 404, in all ranks of society A.Kn 1168, *in som ~* to some extent A.Kn 2844, *in my ~* in whatever way I can E.Cl 969, *in swich ~* to such an extent LGW 1031, *in no ~* not at all B.Sh 1361, F.Sq 198. **5.** (astron. and math.) $\frac{1}{360}$ of a circle or the angle subtended by that arc Astr 1.21.31/43, 2.4.8/14, etc.; one of a number of equal segments into which a line is divided 1.9.2. [OF]

deye *n.* dairy-woman B.NP 4036. [OE *dǣge]*

deye(n/dye(n *v.* die A.Kn 3034, B.ML 644, TC 1.306; *(for) to ~ in the peyne* on pain of death by torture A.Kn 1133, TC 1.674, 3.1502; *to ~ in the cas* though I were to die for it E.Cl 859. **deyth** *pr. 3 sg.* D.Sum 2039; **dyeth** TC 4.319. **deyde** *pa.* TC 1.56; **dyde** HF 106; **deyed/dyed** A.Kn 2843. **deyed** *p.p.* RR 456; **deyd/dyed** LGW 1677. [prob. ON *deyja]*

deyne(n *v.* **1.** condescend, grant TC 1.435, 3.1281, 1435, 1811. **2.** *impers.* (with dat.) seem proper, fit: *hym/hire ~d* he/she deigned B.Mk 3324, 3460, B.NP 4371, Mars 39, Anel 181, LGW 395. [OF *deignier]*

deynous *adj.* scornful A.Rv 3941, haughty TC 1.290. [OF *disdeignos]*

deyntee *n.* **1.** fine food or drink B.ML 419, F.Sq 301, H.Mcp 179, TC 3. 609; *of (alle) ~s* (the utmost) abundance A.Prol 346, H.Mcp 166, LGW 1100. **2.** pleasure, delight: *for ~ of* because of delight in LGW 206, *have(n ~* be pleased B.ML 139, E.Mch 2043, F.Fkl 681; *take(n ~* take pleasure Anel 143. **3.** value, regard: *holde(n ~ of himself* value himself I.Pars 477, *holde(n it ~* think it honourable TC 2.164; *tolde no ~ of* did not value D.WB 208. [ON *deinté]*

deyntee *adj.* **1.** fine A.Prol 168. **2.** choice, delicious B.NP 4025, C.Pard 520, F.Sq 70, TC 5.438. **3.** pleasing B.Th 1901, E.Cl 1112, LGW 920. [from prec.]

deyntevous *adj.* delicious, choice E.Cl 265, E.Mch 1714. [from **deintee** n.]

deys *see* **dees.**

deitee *n.* God B.Pri 1659, god TC 4.1543; rule F.Fkl 1047, godhead LGW 346; *to his/thy ~* to his/thy godship G.CY 1469, H.Mcp 101, TC 3.1017. [OF]

dekne *n.* deacon I.Pars 891, *pl.* G.SN 547. [OE *diacon]*

dele(n *v.* **1.** *tr.* divide, share out D.Sum 2249. **2.** *~ with* have to do with, have dealings with A.Prol 247, G.CY 1074, TC 2.706, have intimate/close dealings with TC 3.322, 5.1595; have sexual intercourse with I.Pars 907, LGW 1158; *with hem ~ ever lenger the more* become more and more intimate with LGW 1517. **delte** *pa. sg.* G.CY 1074. **deled** *p.p.* D.Sum 2249, I.Pars 907. [OE *dǣlan]*

deliberacioun *n.* deliberation, consideration

B.Mel 2443, TC 3.519; *have* ~ deliberate B.Mel 2219, 2223; *by* ~ carefully,
after due thought I.Pars 355. [OF]
delibere(n *v.* meditate B.Mel 2916; decide
TC 4.169, 211 *var.* [OF *deliberer*]
delicacye *n.* gratification B.Mk 3669;
wantonness PF 359, FormA 58/57. [ML
dēlicācia]
delicat *adj.* **1.** beautiful (limbs) E.Cl 682,
choice, epicurean (food) I.Pars 828,
splendid (horses) 432; luxurious (life)
E.Mch 1646. **2.** fond of luxury B.Mk
3661, E.Cl 927, I.Pars 835. **3.** fastidious
Bo 2. p4. 71/97, sensitive I.Pars 688;
feeble, easily hurt Bo 4. m7. 46/66. [L
dēlicātus]
delices *n. pl.* **1.** delights B.Mel 2601, Bo
4. p7. 66/91; favourite Bo 2. p3. 46/67 (L
delicias). **2.** fleshly pleasures G.SN 3,
I.Pars 186, etc., Bo 3. p2. 81/117, p7. 1,
etc., p8. 14/19, p9. 7/9, 4. p3. 86/123.
(L *voluptates*). **3.** delicacies to eat C.Pard
547, I.Pars 633. [OF]
delicious *adj.* delightful (of music) Bo 2. p3.
8/11, TC 5.443. [OF]
deliciously *adv.* luxuriously I.Pars 377; delightfully (of music) F.Sq 79; *ful* ~ with
every pleasure E.Mch 2025. [from prec.]
delyé *adj.* fine (thread) Bo 1. p1. 14/20 (L
tenuissimis filis). [OF *deliié*]
delyt *n.* **1.** pleasure, joy Bo 3. p1. 7/9, p10.
158/215 (L *iucunditas*), TC 5.138; satisfaction D.WB 945. **2.** sensuous pleasure
A.Prol 337, B.Mk 3590, D.WB 418, E.Mch
2022, Bo 3. p2. 30/43, m7. 1 (L *voluptas*);
(theol.) pleasure of indulging desire for sin
I.Pars 140, 292. **3.** sexual pleasure B.NP
4535, C.Phs 159, LGW 1380; *fulfille hir*
. . . ~ F.Fkl 1372, *parfourne hir* ~ H.Mcp
190, *doon his* ~ LGW 1587 have sexual
intercourse. **4.** delightfulness: *liven in* ~
live a life of pleasure A.Prol 335, B.ML
1135; *holden for* ~ regard as delightful
I.Pars 432; *by* ~ delightfully C.Pard 545;
with ~ beautifully LGW 1199. [OF]
delitable *adj.* pleasing, delightful E.Cl 62,
Bo 1. m1. 2/3, *pl.* F.Fkl 899. [OF]
delite(n *v.* **1.** delight, please PF 27, TC
4.1435, (with (*un*)*to*) Bo 2. p4. 92/127,
p5. 39/55. **2.** take pleasure LGW G. 403;
refl. (with *in*, (*for*) *to*) I.Pars 293, 601, 805,
PF 66, Bo 3. p12. 88/119, 4. m4. 1, LGW
30. [OF *delitier*]
delitous *adj.* delightful RR 90, 489. [OF]
deliver *adj.* active, agile A.Prol 84, RR 831.
[OF *delivre*]
deliveraunce *n.* release TC 4.202. [OF]
deliver(en *v.* **1.** release (someone) TC
4.100, 196, (from parliamentary session)
PF 491; *from*/*out of*/*of* from something:
(concrete) A.Kn 1769, B.Mel 2289, Bo 3.
m1. 1/2; (fig.) B.ML 518, 941, E.Cl 134,
Bo 4. p4. 93/130; ~ *out* rescue D.Sum
1729. **2.** decree TC 4.211 *var.* **3.** *was* ~*ed*
of gave birth to B.ML 750. **delivereth**
imper. pl. D.Sum 1729, TC 5.1400. [OF
delivrer]
deliverly/**-liche** *adv.* quickly, nimbly B.NP
4606, TC 2.1088.[from adj.]
delivernesse *n.* agility, quickness B.Mel
2355, I.Pars 452. [from adj.]
delte *see* **dele(n.**
delve(n *v.* **1.** *tr.* dig (earth) Bo 5. p1. 50/71,

dig up F.Sq 638; *intr.* ~ *in* Bo 5. p1. 55/79.
2. ~ *up* (an object) dig up Bo 2. m5. 24/33,
26/36. **3.** *p.p.* **dolven** *and* **ded** dead and
buried BD 222. **dalf** *pa. sg.* Bo 2. m5. 24/33.
dolve *subj.* Bo 5. p1. 55/79. [OE *delfan,*
dealf, dulf-, dolfen]
delver(e *n.* cultivator Bo 5. p1. 61/87. [OE
delfere]
dema(u)nde *n.* **1.** question B.ML 472,
E.Mch 1870, Bo 1. p6. 25/32, *that is no* ~
TC 4.1295, *this holde I no* ~ 1694 there is
no question about it. **2.** request E.Cl 348,
G.CY 1451, TC 5.859. [AN]
demeyne *n.:* *in his* ~ under his rule B.Mk
3855. [OF *demaine*]
demeine *v.* control HF 959. [OF *demener*]
deminge *vbl. n.* judging, knowing Bo 5. p4.
146/210.
demoniak *n.* madman (possessed by a
demon) D.Sum 2240, 2292. [OF *de-*
moniaque]
demonstratif *adj.* based on logic D.Sum
2272. [OF]
depardieux *interj.* by God, indeed B.ML 39,
TC 2.1058. [OF]
departe(n *v.* **1.** *intr.* go away, depart A.Kn
3060, A.Co 4359, TC 2.990, ~ *away* TC
2.531. **2.** *tr.* separate, part (people)
A.Kn 1134, B.ML 1158, B.Mel 2805,
I.Pars 356, LGW 897, ~ *atwinne* TC
3.1666, ~ *compaignye* B.NP 4183 separate
from each other; (things) Bo 3. p12. 27/36,
5. m1. 5/7, ~ *lif* . . *out of* send life away
from TC 4.470; break F.Fkl 1532; *intr.*
separate, part company D.Fri 1415,
I.Pars 836. **3.** *tr.* divide into parts, share
C.Pard 812, D.Sum 2133, Bo 3. p9.
14/19, 67/88, Astr 2.4.39/61; ~ *shrift* share
confession among different confessors
I.Pars 972; ~ *in othere colours* colour
diversely 426. **4.** differentiate Bo 2. p8.
25/37; ~ *it so* differentiate the matter thus
TC 3.404. [OF *departir*]
departing(e *vbl. n.* **1.** departure B.ML
260, 293, Mars 25, 132. **2.** separation
Bo 2. m7. 22/30, ~ *of our companye* our
separation A.Kn 2774. **3.** division: *in* ~
~ *in whyt and reed* by the division into
white and red I.Pars 425.
depe *n.* sea B.ML 455; depths Bo 3. m11. 27
var/37. [OE *dēop*]
depe *adv.* **1.** deep, deeply A.Prol 129, A.Kn
2640, **depper** *comp.* B.ML 630, G.SN 250;
far (in) A.Mil 3442, TC 1.272; (fig.) B.Mk
3684, ~ *in greyn* intensely (of colour) F.Sq
511; strongly A.Mil 3613. **2.** fervently,
devoutly (sworn) A.Kn 1132, TC 2.570,
LGW 1285; passionately E.Mch 1940, RR
319. **3.** profoundly B.ML 4, Bo 2. p3.
17/24, TC 4.589. **4.** ~ *yholde* seriously
indebted LGW 1954.[OE *dēope*]
depeynt(ed *ppl. adj.* **1.** stained, coloured
C.Pard 950, TC 5.1599. **2.** decorated BD
322, ~ *with* decorated with pictures of
Mars 86. **3.** depicted A.Kn 2027, 2031,
LGW 1025; (fig.) shown, prefigured (in the
stars) A.Kn 2037. [from *v.* from OF *depeint,*
p.p. of *depeindre*]
depper *see* **deep, depe.**
depraven *pr. pl.* calumniate Mars 207. [OF
depraver or L *dēprāvāre*]
depressioun *n.* angular distance below the
horizon Astr 2.25. 6/9. [OF]

depryve(n v. deprive (of) Pity 69, (fro 'of') TC 4.269, ABC 146 var. [OF depriver]
dere(n v. **1.** tr. injure, harm A.Kn 1822, B.Mk 3191, afflict TC 1.651. **2.** intr. do an injury F.Sq 240. [OE derian]
der(e)worth adj. precious Bo 2. p1. 55/75, p4. 37/50, valuable Bo 2. p6. 19/28. [OE dēorwȳrþe]
derk adj. **1.** black, dusky A.Kn 2082, A.Mil 3731, I.Pars 185; dim I.Pars 183; sallow RR 1009. **2.** gloomy, sad F.Fkl 844, TC 2.1307, HF 1512. **3.** obscure, difficult to grasp B.ML 481, Bo 1. m7. 14/19, 5. m4. 3/4; obliterating, obscuring Bo 2. p7. 62/89. **4.** secret and malicious A.Kn 1995, 2468; sinful, vile, ignoble Bo 3. p9. 74/98, m10. 17/25, 5. p2. 26/37. [OE deorc]
derke(n v. **1.** tr. make black or dirty Bo 1. p1. 18/26, m3. 6/8. **2.** obscure (sight) Bo 1. p1. 55/76, p2. 18/26; (understanding, memory) Bo 3. p2. 60/85, 5. m3. 10/14; intr. grow obscure Bo 5. p2. 26/37. **3.** degrade Bo 1. p4. 179/250; lessen Bo 4. p3. 36/52. **4.** ? cower in the dark LGW 816. [OE deorcian]
derkly adv. obscurely HF 51. [OE deorclīce]
derknesse n. **1.** absence of light, gloom A.Kn 1451. **2.** sinfulness, evil G.SN 384, I.Pars 896, Bo 4. m1. 28/40. **3.** obscurity (of mind) Bo 1. p6. 75/96, (of concept) Bo 4. p6. 3/4, ignorance, error Bo 1. m2. 3/4, 3. m11. 18/24. **4.** despair TC 4.300. [OE deorcnes(se]
derne adj. secret (esp. of illicit love) A.Mil 3200, 3278, discreet 3297. [OA dérne]
derre adj. comp. dearer A.Kn 1448. [OE dēorra]
derre adv. comp. with greater loss TC 1.136, as worth more 174. [from prec.]
derth n. costliness I.Pars 414; high cost, dearth HF 1974. [from OE dēore dear]
de(s)ceivaunce n. false impression Bo 3. p8. 34/48. [cf. OF decevance]
descende(n v. **1.** come, go down E.Cl 392, F.Sq 321, RR 1575, or ? condescend B.Mel 2264; ~ down climb down E.Mch 1830; dismount, stop F.Fkl 1242. **2.** ~ of/ fro(m be descended from TC 5. 1480 (cf. 1514); (fig.) derive from Bo 4. p2. 152/207, 5. p1. 67/96; is ~d springs from it A.Rv 3984. **3.** pass, proceed (from general to specific) ~ to B.Mel 2545, ~ doun to TC 5.859, 1511; ~ into the pass to your case Bo 2. p5. 1/2. **4.** decline, deteriorate into Bo 2. p4. 126/175, 3. p10. 21/28. [OF descendre]
descensioun n. decline Astr 2.4.34/53, 35/54. [OF]
descensories n. pl. retorts for distillation G.CY 792. [ML dēscensōrium]
descharge v. unburden, relieve I.Pars 360, 362. [OF descharger]
desclaundred see **disclaundre.**
descryve(n v. **1.** describe B.Mk 3336, TC 2.889, HF 1105, ~ of tell about E.Mch 1737, RR 865. **2.** inscribe, mark Astr 1.17.1. [OF descrivre]
desert n. **1.** what is deserved (with poss.) his ~, pl. in oure ~ what he/we has/have deserved F.Sq 532, TC 3.1267; (with of) the ~ of thinges what things are morally worth Bo 1. p4. 203/285; withouten hir ~ without their having deserved thus B.Mel

2695; bi the ~ of because merited by I.Pars 757; to the ~ of according to what is deserved by Bo 1. p5. 44/64. **2.** meritoriousness, merit, virtue Bo 3. p6. 30/40, through his ~ because of his merit LGW 608, in regard of hise ~ in respect of his merit I.Pars 477. **3.** reward Bo 4. p4. 91/125. **4.** ? services Bo 1. p5. 31/46 (L meritis); good deeds Bo 2. p7. 14/19 (L meritorum). [OF]
desert(e p.p. forsaken, deserted HF 417; ~ of lacking in Bo 4. p2. 8/9. [OF]
deserve v. deserve A.Kn 1726, B.Pri 1822; ~ it unto yow repay you for it G.CY 1352; **disserv-** I.Pars 756; B.Mel 2626, D.Sum 2280, Bo 5. p3./194 all var. [OF deservir]
desespeir/dis- n. despair TC 1.605, 2.6. [OF]
desesperaunce/dis- n. despair TC 2.530, 1307. [AN]
desherited/dis- p.p. dispossessed B.Mel 2941; ~ of deprived of A.Kn 2926, B.Mel 3025; ~ in swich degree so destitute LGW 1065. [from OF des(h)eriter]
desiring n. longing A.Kn 1922, Bo 1. p6. 78/101, craving Bo 3. p7. 2. [from desiren v., OF desirer]
desiring ppl. adj.: to ~ to gete too desirous of acquiring B.Mel 2767. [as prec.]
desirous adj. eager A.Kn 1674; ~ of filled with desire for B.Mel 2951, Bo 3. p1. 2/3, 12/17; ~ to eager to Bo 3. p1. 22/30, TC 1.1058; ~ in armes bold in arms F.Sq 23. [AN]
deslavee adj. unbridled I.Pars 629 (Vulg. Prov. xv. 4 immoderata), 834. [OF]
desola)t adj. **1.** disconsolate, wretched Mars 286; deprived, powerless D.WB 703. **2.** solitary E.Mch 1321. **3.** unpeopled, deserted Anel 62, TC 5.540. **4.** base, vile C.Pard 598. **5.** ~ of lacking B.ML 131, 936. [L dēsōlātus]
desorde(y)nee/dis- adj. inordinate I.Pars 818, 915, Bo 2. m2. 13/18. [OF]
desordinat adj. excessive, improper I.Pars 415, 422. [ML disordinātus]
despeir see **dispeyre.**
despense see **dispence.**
desperacion n. despair I.Pars 1057, ABC 21. [OF]
despised ppl. adj. neglected Bo 1. p1. 18/26. [from next]
despise(n v. **1.** regard with contempt B.ML 115, Bo 4. p7. 71/99, disdain TC 2.720, disparage B.Mel 2209. **2.** speak ill of B.Mk 3859, TC 4. 1478, LGW 135; renounce (deity) G.SN 298; rebuke, find fault with I.Pars 201, revile 663, 3, disregard, neglect Bo 3. p11. 62/85, m12. 28/40. [OF despis-, stem of despire]
despit n. **1.** spite, malice A.Kn 941, D.Sum 2154; in ~ of out of hostility towards TC 3.1705, 4.124; defiance I.Pars 392, 507, PF 281. **2.** scorn, contempt: in your/his ~ in scorn of you/him B.Pri 1753, LGW 134; been in ~ be scorned I.Pars 189; have/take (in) ~ scorn, despise B.Mel 2608, D. Sum 1876, F.Fkl 1395, TC 4.1675, 5.135; halt of it ~ scorns it TC 3.1374/1360; disdain I.Pars 391. **3.** humiliation, insult A.Mil 3752, B.ML 699, B.Mk 3738, D.Sum 2176, in/for ~ as an insult F.Fkl 1371, TC 5.1693; don ~ to violated LGW 1822. **4.** resentment, injured feeling TC 2.1246; for ~

though resentment B.ML 591, TC 1.207, 2.1049; *have in* ~ bear a grudge against TC 2.711. [OF]

despitous *adj.* **1.** scornful, disdainful A.Prol 516, I.Pars 395. **2.** angry A.Kn 1596; cruel BD 624, TC 2.435, 3.1458, RR 156. **3.** (?) sad or fierce D.WB 761, TC 5.199. [OF]

despitously *adv.* angrily A.Kn 1124, B.Mk 3785; cruelly B.ML 605, E.Cl 535, TC 5.1806 *var*, HF 161; violently A.Rv 4274 [from prec.]

desponeth *see* **dispone.**

desport/dis- *n.* **1.** entertainment, recreation A.Rv 4043, A.Co 4420; *make(n/don* ~ provide entertainment A.Prol 775, A.Co 4382, E.Mch 1924; *in* ~ amusing herself PF 260, *for* ~ as recreation B.ML 143. **2.** enjoyment, delight D.WB 839, TC 4.309; *take(n your/oure* ~ enjoy yourself/ourselves D.WB 319, E.Mch 2147; *for* ~ for pleasure D.WB 670. **3.** comfort, solace E.Mch 1332. **4.** deportment: *of greet* ~ dignified in manner A.Prol 137. [OF]

desporte(n *v.* **1.** *refl.* amuse, entertain oneself A.Mil 3660, E.Mch 2040, F.Fkl 849. **2.** *tr.* comfort, cheer TC 2.1673, 3.1133, 4.724. **3.** *intr.* cheer up, take comfort TC 5.1398. [AN *desporter*]

desray *n.* confusion, disorder I.Pars 927. [AN *de(s)rei*]

destinable† *adj.* subject to Destiny (God's instrument) Bo 4. p6. 251/337. Cf. next. [OF]

destinal *adj.* determined by Destiny (God's instrument) Bo 4. p6. 56/81, 70/100, 80/114, 5. p2. 4/6. [ML or from n.]

destinee *n.* Fate, Destiny: **1.** inexorable force controlling men's lives A.Kn 1465, B.NP 4528. **2.** this force as God's instrument A.Kn 1663, Bo 4. p6. 18/27, 39/56, 44/64, etc. (L *fatum*), TC 5.1. **3.** that which happens to someone by virtue of this force (with poss.) A.Kn 1108, 1842, TC 3.734, HF 188. **4.** the Fates LGW 2580. [OF]

desto(u)rbe(n *v.* **1.** distract (from) C.Pard 340. **2.** prevent, impede I.Pars 575, Bo 3. p11. 124/170, 5. p4. 21/30, TC 4.563, 1103, 1403; (with infin.) B.Mel 2167, Bo 1. p4, 104/144. [OF *destourber*]

destourbing *vbl. n.* trouble, distress Ven 44.

destrat/distract *p.p.* troubled, distracted Bo 3. p8. 12/17. [OF *de(s)trait*, L *distractus*]

destroye(n *v.* **1.** devastate, ruin (country, city) A.Kn 2016, TC 1.68, (crops) F.Fkl 1251. **2.** kill (person) LGW 1318, Bo 1. p4. 148/205, 3. p12. 100/136, *refl.* B.Mel 2173; deprive of life I.Pars 544, 731. **3.** damage, injure, impair C.Pard 858, D.Sum 1847, 2080, Bo 3. p11. 50/59, 5. p3. 58/81, bring to distress B.Mel 2941, Bo 3. m12. 27/38. [OF *destruire*]

destroubled *p.p.* disturbed BD 524. [from OF *destroubler*]

destruccioun *n.* **1.** ruin, devastation (physical) F.Sq 210, BD 1247, HF 151; *pl.* Bo 2. p6. 5/7, m6. 1/2; source of damage Bo 2. p5. 66/93. **2.** death A.Kn 2538, LGW 626, Bo 1. p4. 151/210, 3. p11. 65/89. **3.** ruin (mental, moral, spiritual) D.Sum 2007, G.CY 1387, I.Pars 866, Mars 212, Bo 4. p6. 218/313. [OF *destruction*]

determinat *adj.* fixed, definite D.Fri 1459, fixed permanently (of fixed stars) Astr 1.21. 5/6, 2.18. rubr. [L *dēterminātus*]

determyne(n *v.* **1.** end, conclude (doubt, question) Bo 4. p6. 11/17, 5. p4. 6/8. **2.** *intr.* decide HF 343. **3.** ~ *of* discuss Bo 4. p4. 108/153, p6. 136/197. **4.** die TC 3.379. [OF *determiner*]

dette *n.* **1.** indebtedness, (moral) obligation B.ML 41, I.Pars 252, Bo 5. p1. 10/13, *in hire* ~ obliged to her LGW 541; *yelde(n/ paye(n* ~ (to wife or husband) fulfil conjugal duties, i.e. have sexual intercourse (with) D.WB 130, 153, E.Mch 1452, 2048, I.Pars 375, 940. **2.** debt F.Fkl 1578, *in* ~ owing money A.Prol 280, *for* ~ in payment D.Fri 1615, *out of* ~ not owing money B.Sh 1566. [OF]

dettelees *adj.* not owing money A.Prol 582. [from prec.]

dettour *n.* debtor: in money B.Sh 1587, 1603; in duty I.Pars 370; in gratitude D.WB 155. [AF]

deve *see* **deef.**

devyn/dyvyn *n.* **1.** theologian A.Kn 1323, I.Pars 957. **2.** soothsayer, prophet TC 1.66. [OF]

devyne(n *v.* **1.** practise divination PF 182. **2.** *intr.* be suspicious TC 2.1745, 3.765, ~ *upon* suspect 2.1741, ~ *of/on* 3.458. **3.** *tr.* conjecture, suppose B.Sh 1414, B.NP 4456, TC 5.270, 288, anticipate 4.389. **4.** *intr.* speculate, ponder A.Kn 2515, D.WB 26, TC 4.589. **5.** **devyne** *pr. subj. sg.* let him describe HF 14. [OF *deviner*]

devyneresse *n.* prophetess TC 5.1522. [OF]

devys *n.* **1.** scheme LGW 1102, contrivance RR 1413; *pl.* heraldic devices LGW 1272. **2.** phrases: *at his* ~ according to his pleasure A.Prol 816, in his power RR 1326; *at point* ~ perfectly A.Mil 3689, F.Sq 560, RR 830, 1215, clearly HF 917. [OF]

devyse(n *v.* **1.** *tr.* describe A.Kn 1914, TC 4.259, relate B.Mk 3842, talk about, explain C.Pard 423, G.SN 266, TC 1.277; discuss TC 4.1423; *intr.* describe B.NP 4228, G.SN 391, relate B.ML 154, 613, TC 2.31; ~ *of* talk about B.Mk 3693, TC 2.1599, 3.1796; interpret F.Sq 261. **2.** *tr.* imagine A.Kn 1254; D.WB 999, TC 3.41; *intr.* TC 3.56, 5.1363, ~ *of* reflect on, think about E.Mch 1586. **3.** suggest TC 2. 388, 3.160; order A.Kn 1416, LGW 2641. **4.** arrange, contrive A.Kn 1901, 2377, E.Cl 698, 959, TC 3.612; compose E.Cl 739, TC 2.1063. [OF *deviser*]

devocioun *n.* **1.** religious fervour A.Kn 2371, B.ML 257, C.Pard 923, I.Pars 1024, piety HF 33, 494, RR 430; dedication (to religion or other ideal) D.WB 106, (with *of* 'to') G.SN 283, feeling of reverence LGW 109, moral earnestness E.Mch 1447. **2.** prayer, religious observance A.Mil 3640, LGW 1017. **3.** desire, strong inclination LGW 325/G 251, TC 1.187. [OF]

devoir *n.* duty; *do(n) (one's)* ~ perform one's duty, due service A.Kn 2598, B.ML 38, I.Pars 764, do the best one can E.Cl 966; *for my* ~ for my sake TC 3.1045. [OF]

devoure(n *v.* eat, swallow greedily (lit.) LGW 1937, 1947; (fig.) A.Rv 3986, G.SN 21, TC 2.395, Bo 1. p4. 70/96; obliterate

Anel 14; squander D.Sum 1720. [OF *devour-* from *devorer*]
devout *adj.* pious A.Prol 22, deserving of reverence, sacred ABC 145. [OF *devot*]
dewe *see* due.
dewely *adv.* in justice Bo 1. m5. 25/36. [from adj.]
deweté *see* duetee.
dextrer *n.* steed, courser B.Th 2103. [OF *destr(i)er*]
diapred *p.p.* adorned with repeated pattern A.Kn 2158, RR 934. [from OF *diaprer*]
diched *adj.* surrounded by a ditch A.Kn 1888. [from *dich* n., OE *dīc*]
dye(n *see* deye(n.
diete *n.* food A.Prol 435, B.NP 4026, C.Pard 516. [OF]
diffamacioun *n.* disgrace, dishonour D.Fri 1304/1306. [OF]
diffame(n *see* defame(n.
diffense *see* defence.
diffye(n *see* defye(n.
diffyne(n *v.* **1.** *tr.* state PF 529, Bo 3. p2. 49/70; describe the nature of TC 5.271; state in conclusion TC 3.834. **2.** *intr.* turn out finally, behave in the end HF 344. [OF *definer*, ML *diffinire*]
diffinicioun *n.* limitation D.WB 25. [OF]
diffinisshe(n† *v.* define Bo 3. p10. 6/8, 4.p2. 162/220, 5. p1. 22/31 (L *defini-*). [OF *definiss-* from *definir*]
diffusioun *n.* diffuseness, loquaciousness TC 3.296. [OF]
dighte(n *v.* **1.** *tr.* prepare, arrange (dwelling) A. Mil 3205, E.Cl 974, (ships) LGW 1288, 2480; (sacrifices) LGW 2611, (arrows) RR 941; dress, clothe A.Kn 1041, TC 3.1773. **2.** *refl.* go B.Mk 3104, 3719, TC 2.948, LGW 1000, 1712, 2155. **3.** direct, appoint TC 4.1188. **4.** have sexual intercourse with D.WB 398, 767, H.Mcp 312. [OE *dihtan*]
digne *adj.* **1.** worthy of honour, honourable (people) A.Kn 2216, I.Pars 789, Bo 2. p6. 76/108, (things) noble B.Sh 1175, C.Pard 695, TC 3.23. **2.** fitting, suitable E.Cl 818, Bo5. p6. 93/132; ~ *to* LGW 1738, Bo 3. m8. 18/25, ~ *unto* B.ML 778, TC 1.429; ~ *of* appropriate to I.Pars 115, worthy of A.Prol 141, E.Cl 411, I.Pars 493; ~ *to* worthy of TC 5.1868. **3.** haughty A.Prol 517, A.Rv 3964 (or ? honourable, used ironically). [OF]
dignely/-liche, *adv.* **1.** fittingly Bo 2. p6. 63/89, 3. p10. 59/81. **2.** haughtily TC 2.1024. [from prec.]
dignitee *n.* **1.** nobleness, spiritual worth I.Pars 1040; *bi goddes* ~ for God's sake A.Rv 4270, B.Sh 1169, B.Mel 2109. **2.** rank B.Mk 3360, E.Cl 470, I.Pars 190, 895; honour, respect Bo 2. p6. 23/31, Gent 5; *pl.* titles and marks of rank Bo 1. p4. 218/304, 2. p2. 7/9, p3. 30/43. **3.** reputation, esteem Bo 3. p4. 26/38. **4.** gravity Bo 4. p1. 2/3 (L *dignitas, -tates* in all senses). **5.** (astrol.) the situation of a planet in which its influence is heightened Astr 2.4.31/47. [OF *digneté*]
dyke(n *v. intr.* dig ditches, work hard: ~ *and delve* A.Prol 536. [from n., ON *dik*]
dilatacioun *n.* diffuseness, expansion B.ML 232. [OF]
diligence *n.* **1.** persistent effort D.Sum 1818, TC 3.135, 1297, industry B.Mel

2532; *don al/mi/gret*, etc. ~ make every/my utmost/great effort A.Kn 2470, B.Pri 1729, B.Mel 2216, 2460, E.Mch 1298. **2.** eagerness B.Sh 1234. [OF]
diluge *n.* flood Scog 14; the Flood I.Pars 839 *var.* [OF *deluge*]
diluve *n.* Flood I.Pars 839 *var.* [OF, L *dīluvium*]
dyne *v. intr.* dine B.ML 1083, TC 2.1163; *tr.* eat for dinner D.Sum 1837. [OF *diner*]
dint *n.* ~ *of thonder* clap of thunder HF 534. [OE *dynt*]
direct *n.* *in* ~ *of* in a straight line with Astr 2.44. 10/14. [as next]
direct *adj.* (astrol.) proceeding in the same direction as the sun in its ecliptic, i.e. from west to east Astr 2.35 rubr., 11/16, 16/22. [L *directus*]
direct *p.p.* **1.** addressed B.ML 748. **2.** dedicated Ven 75. [L *directus*]
direct *adv.* exactly, directly Astr 2.39.22/30. [from adj.]
dys *see* dees.[2]
disavaunce *v.* repulse, check the advance of TC 2.511. [OF *desavanci(e)r*]
disaventure *n.* misfortune TC 2.415, 4.297, 5.1448. [OF *desaventure*]
disblameth *imper. pl.* exonerate, free from blame TC 2.17. [OF *desblasmer*]
dischevele(e/dis(s)hevelé *adj.* bareheaded, with hair hanging loose A.Prol 683, PF 235, LGW 1720; with hair in disorder LGW 1315, 1829. [OF *deschevelé*]
disciple *n.* pupil G.CY 1448, I.Pars 670; disciple I.Pars 269. [OF]
disclaundre *n.* slander I.Pars 623 *var*; reproach TC 4.564. [from OF *esclandre*]
disclaundre/des- *v.* slander, traduce B.ML 674, D.Sum 2212 *var*, I.Pars 623 *var*, LGW 1031. [from OF *esclandrer* or prec.]
disconfite *v.* **1.** rout, defeat I.Pars 530, 661. **2.** dismay, discourage, discomfited/discoun- *p.p.* Bo 2. m1. 7/10. [OF *desconfit*, p.p. of *desconfire*]
disconfitinge *vbl. n.* *holden no* ~ reckoned no defeat A.Kn 2719.
disconfiture *n.* **1.** defeat A.Kn 1008, dishonour 2721. **2.** thwarting of plans RR 254, dejection Anel 326. [OF *desconfiture*]
disconfort *n.* dismay, distress A.Kn 2010, TC 4.311; grief: *take* ~ grieve, mourn B.Mel 2174; displeasure F.Fkl 896. [OF *desconfort*]
disconforten *v.* dismay A.Kn 2704. [OF *desconforter*]
disconsolat *adj.* cheerless, depressing (of place) TC 5.542. [ML *disconsolatus*]
discord *n.* disagreement B.Mel 2479; enmity I.Pars 642. *pl.* HF 685, Bo 1. p4. 36/50. [OF *descorde*]
discordable *adj.* discordant Bo 4. m6. 14/20, jarring Bo 5. m3. 1, inharmonious TC 3.1753. [OF]
discordances *n. pl.* disagreements, conflicts I.Pars 275 *var.* [OF]
discordaunt *adj.* conflicting, dissonant Bo 2. p7. 50/73, 4. m4. 8/12, TC 2.1037. [OF]
discorde(n *v.* **1.** *intr.* disagree (of judgements) Bo 4. p6. 130/189 (L *depugnant*), (of persons) 3. p10. 178/244 (L *dissentire*). *pr. p.* Bo 3. p2. 86/123 (L *dissidentes*). **2.** *intr.* differ in kind Bo 3. p12. 27/35, 5. m5. 10/14 (L *discrepare*). [OF *descorder*]

discounfited see **disconfite.**

discovere(n v. **1.** reveal B.Mel 2331, 2903, G.CY 696, Bo 2. p8. 4/6; (with dat.) Bo 4. p6. 2/3, **discure** BD 549. **2.** betray, give away E.Mch 1942, TC 1.675. [OF *descov(e)r-, -cuevr-*, from *descovrir*]

discovert n. only in phr. *at* ~ in an exposed condition I.Pars 714. [OF *descovert*]

discrecioun n. **1.** moral discernment B.Mel 3063, *bi* ~ C.Phs 42, I.Pars 733. **2.** judgement, discrimination A.Kn 1779, 2537, C.Pard 559, H.Mcp 182, TC. 3.1334; decision, solution (to a question) Bo 3. p10. 141/191 (L *discretionem*); *bi* ~ in moderation D.WB 622, I.Pars 861. **3.** rational understanding, good sense B.Mk 3822, B.NP 4508, TC 3.894, LGW 1631. [OF]

discreet adj. **1.** judicious A.Prol 312, Astr prol 30/41; circumspect, prudent B.Mel 2986, E.Mch 1909, TC 3.477, 943. **2.** wise (morally) B.Mel 2287, C.Phs 48. **3.** courteous, civil, kind A.Prol 518, B.NP 4061. [OF *discret*]

discreetly adv. **1.** judiciously, prudently B.Mel 2461, B.Mk 3696, I.Pars 1045. **2.** courteously PF 241, pleasantly B.Mel 2303. [from prec.]

discresith see **disencreseth.**

discryving vbl. n. account, description I.Pars 535. [see **descryve(n**]

discure see **discovere(n.**

discussed p.p. **1.** decided PF 624. **2.** dispelled Bo 1. m3. 1 (L *discussa . . nocte*). [ML *discussus*, p.p. of *discutere*]

disdeigne(n v. **1.** disdain E.Cl 98. **2.** be troubled Bo 4. p7. 56/77 (L *indignari*). [OF *desdeignier*]

disdeyn n. **1.** scorn (person.) PF 136, TC 2.1217; *have* ~ *of* hold beneath (one's) dignity G.SN 41, despise, detest I.Pars 142, 149; *have* ~ *to/that* scorn to I.Pars 150, 152. **2.** anger, indignation TC 4. 1191, RR 296; *take/have in* ~ be indignant at A.Prol 789, F.Fkl 700; *have* ~ *that* be angry because Bo 3. p4. 7/9 (L *indignemur*). [OF *desdeigne*]

disencreseth pr. *3* sg. decreases Bo 5. p6. 53/*discresith* 74 (L *decrescit*). [from **encrese(n**]

disese n. **1.** distress (mental), pain, annoyance B.NP 3961, F.Fkl 1314, TC 2.1360, 3.1043, 5.109; *do yow* ~ annoy you TC 2.147. **2.** suffering (physical) B.ML 616, G.CY 747, I.Pars 609, TC 2.987, HF 89. [OF *desaise/dis-*]

disese(n v. **1.** distress TC 1.573, 3.443, 1468, 4.1304. **2.** make uncomfortable TC 2.1650. [OF *desaisier*]

disesperat adj. ~ *of* despairing of HF 2015. [L *dēspērātus* and OF *desesperé*]

disfigurat adj. deformed PF 222 var. [L *disfigūrātus*]

disfigure n. deformity D.WB 960. [from next]

disfigure v. **1.** disguise LGW 2046. **2.** mar, alter for the worse A.Kn 1403, C.Pard 551; *refl.* TC 2.223. [OF *desfigurer*]

disgisynge vbl. n. elaborate clothing I.Pars 425 var. [cf. **degysinge**]

disherited see **desherited.**

dishonest adj. **1.** unjust B.Mel 2418, 2419; dishonourable, shameful I.Pars 777. **2.** immodest E.Cl 876, unchaste H.Mcp 214. [OF *des(h)oneste*]

dishonestee n. dishonour, disgrace I.Pars 833. [OF *des(h)onesté*]

dishonour n. disgrace, shame C.Pard 580, F.Fkl 1358, TC 2.731; *do(n (a)* (with dat.) bring dishonour to TC 5.1066, violate the honour of D.WB 881; subject to indignity C.Pard 691. [OF *des(h)onor*]

disjoynt n. difficulty, straits A.Kn 2962; *stonde(n in* ~ be in a difficulty or dilemma B.Sh 1601, TC 3.496, LGW 1631. [OF]

dismal n. *in the* ~ at an unlucky time BD 1206. [OF = unlucky days]

disobeisaunt adj. disobedient I.Pars 338, PF 429. [OF *desobeïssant*, p.p. of *desobeïr*]

disorde(y)né, disordinat see **desordeynee, desordinat.**

disordenaunce n. disorder I.Pars 267, HF 27, Bo 5. p1. 29/40; immorality I.Pars 275, 277. [OF *desordenance*]

disparage n. dishonour E.Cl 908. [OF *desparage*]

disparage v. dishonour A.Rv 4271; *p.p.* misallied D.WB 1069. [OE *desparagier*]

dispeyre/des- v. **1.** *refl.* despair, lose hope E.Mch 1669, TC 5.1569, (theol.) I.Pars 698. **2.** **dispeyred** *p.p.* in despair B.Mk 3645, F.Fkl 1084. **3.** *be(n* ~*d* F.Fkl 943, TC 1.36, (theol.) I.Pars 705, ~ *of* 1015; ~ *out of* TC 1.42, ~ *from* CompL 7 lack, be deprived of. [OF *despeir-* from *desperer*]

dispence/-se n. **1.** expenditure, spending of money A.Kn 1928, D.WB 1263, RR 1144, *pl.* B.Mel 2842; wasteful expenditure D.Sum 1874; *free of* ~ generous in spending A.Co 4388, B.Sh 1233, E.Cl 1209, *make(n gret* ~ spend freely RR 1141, *leyde on him al the* ~ spent as freely on him HF 260; *esi of* ~ parsimonious A.Prol 441. **2.** costs, expenses A.Kn 1882, B.Sh 1195, 1206, E.Mch 1297. **3.** means of subsistence B.ML 105, D.Fri 1432. [OF *despens(e)*]

dispende(n v. **1.** spend (goods) A.Rv 3983, B.Sh 1270, I.Pars 253, 812, TC 4.921; ~ *in diverse parties* distribute B.Mel 2560; use, consume E.Mch 1403. **2.** squander (goods) B.Mel 2796, I.Pars 849. **3.** spend, pass (time) B.Mk 3500, E.Cl 1123. **4.** waste (time) B.Mel 2121. [OF *despendre*]

dispendours n.pl. stewards, treasurers B.Mel 2843. [cf. OF *despendeor*]

displesance n. displeasure, trouble TC 3.480, 1295; *taketh of my wordes no* ~ do not be offended by what I say C.Phs 74; *do(n us* ~ offend, injure us C. Pard 420. [OF *desplaisance*]

displesant adj. displeasing I.Pars 544, 697. [OF *desplaisant*]

dispoylinge vbl. n. booty, spoil Bo 4. m7. 21/30.

dispoil(l)e(n v. **1.** strip (someone) of clothes E.Cl 374. **2.** ~ *of* rob I.Pars 665, deprive Bo 1. p4. 218/303, 226/315, 4. p4. 27/36. [OF *despoillier*]

dispone/des- v. **1.** order, regulate Bo 3. p12. 33/43, 4. p6. 38/55, TC 4.964. **2.** dispose (of) TC 5.300. [L *dispōnere*]

disport see **desport.**

dispose(n 1. resolve E.Cl 244. **2.** *p.p.* inclined TC 4.230; *ben* ~ be willing E.Cl 639, 707, 755; *am* ~ *bet to* am rather inclined to TC 5.984; *wel* ~ favourable (of a planet) 2.682; *not wel* ~ in ill health H.Mcp

33. **3.** deal with Bo 3. p12. 99 *var*/135 (L *disposuit*); *p.p.* controlled I.Pars 336, arranged Astr 1.21.42/58. **disposeth** *imper. pl.* arrange, set D.Fri 1659. [OF *disposer*]
disposicioun *n.* **1.** arrangement Bo 4. p5. 31/44, p6. 44/64. **2.** frame of mind A.Kn 1378, Bo 5. p6. 184/259, *in lyke* ~ B.Mel 2326. **3.** influence, attitude A.Kn 1087, *for hir diverse* ~ because of their conflicting inclinations, influences D.WB 701; *after hir* ~ according to their nature HF 2113. **4.** *in/at your/thy* ~ at your disposal B.Mel 2915, TC 2.526. [OF]
dispreise(n *v.* disparage B.Mel 2261, 2741, RR 1053. [OF *de(s)preiser*]
dispreisinge *vbl. n.* blame, contempt B.Mel 2876, I.Pars 497.
dispute(n *v.* **1.** *intr.* engage in formal debate Bo 5. m4. 2/3, debate 1. p4. 11/16; argue, reason TC 3.858, 4.1084. **2.** *tr.* discuss (with cl.) BD 505; defend (a proposition) Bo 5. p6. 86/122. [OF *desputer*]
disputisoun *n.* debate B.NP 4428, F.Fkl 890; discussion E.Mch 1474; reasoning Bo 5. p1. 19/27. [OF *desputeisun*]
disserve *see* **deserve.**
disseveraunce *n.* separation Bo 3. p11. 44/59; *make* ~ *of* separate TC 3.1424. [OF *des(s)evrance*]
dissevere(n *v.* **1.** *tr.* separate B.Mel 2805, Bo 4. p3. 12/17; segregate (men) B.Mel 2621; disunite (parts) Bo 3. p11. 49/66, undo, disrupt Mars 49. **2.** *intr.* be divided (from), part (with) G.CY 875, Buk 15. [OF *des(s)evrer*]
dis(s)hevelé *see* **dischevele(e**
dis(s)h-metes *n.pl.* food cooked in dishes I.Pars 445. [OE *disc*+*mete*]
dissimilour/dissymulour *n.* deceiver B.NP 4418, Fort 23. [from next]
dissimule(n *v.* **1.** *intr.* assume a false appearance, pretend G.SN 466, Bo 5. p6. 219/309, TC 3.434; ~ *as* act as if H.Mcp 347. **2.** *tr.* conceal TC 1.322. [OF *dissimuler*]
dissimulinge *vbl. n.* dissimulation, pretences TC 5.1613; *pl.* F.Sq 285; dishonest behaviour G.CY 1073.
dissolveth *pr. 3 sg.* puts an end to Bo 2. p3. 57/83. [L *dissolvere*]
distaf *n.* distaff, in prov. *hadde more tow on his* ~ had more in hand A.Mil 3774. [OE *distæf*]
disteyne *v.* **1.** (fig.) deprive of brightness LGW 255/209, 262/216. **2.** sully TC 2.840 *var.* [OF *desteign*- from *desteindre*]
distemperaunce *n.* **1.** intemperance, lack of moderation Bo 4. p2. 131/178. **2.** bad weather, inclemency I.Pars 421, Bo 3. p11. 88/120. [OF *destemprance*]
distempré *adj.* angry Bo 4. p3. 79/113. [OF *destempré*]
distempre *v.* **1.** upset balance (of humours) I.Pars 826. **2.** *refl.* upset or anger oneself D.Sum 2195; ~ *your herte* B.Mel 2426. [OF *destemprer*]
distille *v.* flow in drops: ~ *in teres* weep profusely TC 4.519. [OF *distiller*]
distinct *p.p.* distinguished, subdivided I.Pars 828. [L *distinctus*]
distingwed *p.p.* made illustrious Bo 2. p5. 47/66. [from v. from OF *distinguer*]
distract *see* **destrat,**

distreyne *v.* **1.** retain B.Mel 2405, hold fast PF 337; arrest I.Pars 269; bind Bo 2. p6. 74/105, overcome TC 2.840 *var.* **2.** constrain, compel I.Pars 104, 109, TC 5.596. **3.** distress, torment A.Kn 1455, 1816, F.Fkl 820; oppress I.Pars 752, TC 1.355, 3.1528. [OF *destreign*- from *destreindre*]
distresse *n.* **1.** distress, suffering A.Kn 919, F.Fkl 737, TC 1.550. **2.** confinement HF 1587; compulsion BalCh 9. [OF *destre(s)ce*]
disturne *v.* avert TC 3.718. [OF *destorner*]
ditee *n.* literary composition, poem or song Bo 1. m1. 2/3, 2. p2. 51/71, 3. p1. 2, HF 622; melody Bo 4. p6. 25/36. [OF]
diurne *adj.* daily E.Mch 1795. [L *diurnus*]
divers *adj.* **1.** various, sundry A.Rv 3857, E.Mch 1469, F.Sq 202, F.Fkl 710, Bo 1. m2. 19/27; *in* ~ *maneres* I.Pars 387, *in* ~ *wyse* of different kinds 564, in different ways TC 1.61, *bi* ~ *weyes* by different routes Bo 3. p2. 5/6, *with colour ful* ~ mottled, livid Pity 17. **2.** different, separate I.Pars 489, Astr 2.14.8/10; aside Bo 5. p1. 13/18. **3.** contrary (of planets) D.WB 701. **4.** unfavourable, cruel TC 4.1195. [OF]
diversely *adv.* **1.** with various opinions A.Rv 3857, E.Mch 1469, RR 1629. **2.** in different ways D.Sum 1877; for different reasons HF 1900. [from prec.]
diverseth *pr. 3 sg.* varies, changes TC 3.1752. [OF *diverser*]
divynailes *n. pl.* arts of foretelling the future I.Pars 605. [OF *devinaille/div*-]
divyn- *see* **devyn-.**
divynis *see* **devyn.**
divinistre *n.* theologian A.Kn 2811. [cf. *devyn*, *devyne(n*]
divinitee *n.* **1.** divine nature G.SN 340, Bo 1. p4. 12/17 (L *diuinarum rerum*), 3. p10. 104/140 (L *diuinitas*). **2.** divine being, God G.SN 316. **3.** study of divinity, theology D.Fri 1512, 1638. [OF]
divynour *n.* foreteller of the future Bo 5. p3. 95/133. [cf. OF *devineor*]
divisioun *n.* **1.** distinction A.Kn 1780, B.Mel 2445, Fort 33. **2.** part, division Astr 1.8.5/7, 12.3/5, 21.33/45; dividing up Astr 2.31.9/13; splitting I.Pars 1009, Bo 3. p9. 13/18, p11. 111/152. **3.** class (of persons) A.Kn 2024. **4.** enmity A.Kn 2476. [OF]
doctour *n.* **1.** authority in theology, Church father B.NP 4431, D.Fri 1648, I.Pars 85, 295. **2.** holder of the highest academic degree A.Prol 411. **3.** scholar, teacher Astr prol 74/102. [OF]
doctrine *n.* **1.** instruction, precepts B.Mel 2422, I.Pars 676, 957, LGW 19; ~ *of* the teachings of B.Mel 2391, Bo 3. m11. 32/44. **2.** learning, knowledge B.Mel 2702, education B.Pri 1689, edification B.NP 4632, Astr prol 45/63. [OF]
doghter *see* **do(u)ghter.**
doing *vbl. n.* **1.** event G.SN 421, Bo 1. m6. 15/22, 3. p12. 31/41; affair, business PF 515. **2.** action Bo 2. p7. 34/48, 4. p2. 155/211, 5. p4. 150/216; behaviour, conduct BD 995, TC 2.34, 40, LGW 1267; *pl.* deeds LGW 1681, ~ *to and fro* machinations 2471.
doke *n.* duck A.Mil 3576, B.NP 4580, PF 498. [OE *duce*]

dolve(n see **delve(n.**

domesman n. judge, magistrate I.Pars 594; assessor, authority B.Mk 3680, Bo 2. m6. 8/12. [from **do(o)m**]

dominacioun n. control, power A.Kn 2758; dominion B.Mk 3409, C.Pard 560; in his ~ dominant F.Sq 352. [OF]

don imper. put on TC 2.954, 3.738. [from phr. do on, see **do(o)(n**]

dongeoun n. tower, keep A.Kn 1057, LGW 937. [OF donjon]

donne adj. dun, grey-brown PF 334; dark TC 2.908. [OE dunn]

do(o)m n. **1.** judgement, opinion E.Cl 1000, Bo 4. p6. 130/188, 5. p3. 99/139; to my ~ TC 4.402, RR 901, as to my ~ in my opinion B.Mk 3127, F.Fkl 677, PF 480, TC 1.100, 4.387. **2.** discrimination Bo 5. p2. 8/12. **3.** judicial decision A.Prol 323, C.Phs 163, PF 308, TC 4.1188, RR 199; in ~ as judicial arbiter C.Phs 257, C.Pard 637, I.Pars 592, 594. **4.** Last Judgement: day of ~ I.Pars 118, 158; **domesday** HF 1284. **5.** destiny, lot LGW 2630. [OE dōm]

do(o)(n v. **1.** used as substitute for a verb or verb phr. A.Prol 812, A.Kn 2795, E.Cl 68, TC 2.1284. **2.** intr. act A.Rv 3881, B.ML 382, B.Mk 3370, D.WB 707, E.Cl 105, F.Sq 600, G.CY 903, TC 2.318. **3.** tr. perform, carry out A.Prol 78, A.Kn 993, B.ML 1087, D.WB 1170, E.Cl 522, G.SN 386, TC 2.75; ~ that I yow praye do what I ask B.Sh 1379, ~ your wil do what you want B.Mel 2908, ~ mi reed do what I advise TC 4.1413; ~ his fantasye carry out his inclination B.Mk 3475, ~ bisinesse B.Mel 2822, ~ forth . . bisinesse make an effort E.Cl 1015; ~ his delyt fulfil his desire LGW 1587, ~ diligence A.Kn 2470, B.Pri 1729, ~ labour make an effort B.Pri 1653; ~ hir nedes carried on their business B.ML 174. **4.** commit, perpetrate B.ML 931, B.Mel 2715, E.Mch 1839, F.Fkl 1366, TC 2.1510. **5.** cause, make (someone (to) do sthg.) A.Kn 2621, B.Mk 3507, C.Phs 59, E.Cl 353, G.SN 32, TC 2.327, 3.1182, ~ come summon B.Th 2035, ~ yow wite let you know TC 2. 1635; make (sthg. act) C.Pard 312, LGW 240, RR 1414; cause (sthg. to be done) LGW 2715, RR 413; (fold. by infin. without expressed subject giving passive sense) B.ML 662, B.Mk 3107, D.Fri 1364, PF 458, TC 1.833, dide ~ D.Sum 2042, leet/lat ~ B.Mk 3342, C.Phs 173, as leet ~ cryen the feste had the feast proclaimed F.Sq 46; (perf., fold. by p.p.) hath ~ wrought caused to be built A.Kn 1913, sim. B.ML 171, E.Cl 1098. **6.** give (pleasure, comfort, respect, etc. to someone) A.Prol 766, A.Kn 2194, B.ML 1001, B.Mel 2539, C.Pard 737; ~ me right give me justice D.WB 1049; ~ no fors (of) pay no heed (to) B.NP 4131, D.WB 1234, D.Fri 1512, I.Pars 721, BD 542, Bo 2. p4. 120/165; ~ no cure take no trouble D.WB 1074, do not care LGW 152; ~ companye accompany LGW 1601; ~ fruit give, bring forth fruit I.Pars 115. **7.** inflict (on) (with dat. of pers.) A.Kn 942, 1555, B.Mel 2470, TC 2.763, 5.1066, ~ on hem correccioun punish them D.Fri 1320; bestow (on) G.SN 346. **8.** advance, improve B.Sh

1598, B.Mel 2782. **9.** put B.Th 2047, TC 4.1643; ~ on G.CY 899; ~ of take off A.Kn 2676, BD 516; ~ awey remove Bo 3. p4. 4/5, TC 5.1068; ~ up open A.Mil 3801; ~ wey put away TC 2.110, take away A.Mil 3287, stop, cease G.SN 487, no more of this! TC 2.893. **10.** p.p. finished A.Kn 2964, D.Sum 2294, E.Mch 2440, G.CY 739, BD 40; have ~ stop PF 492; harm ydoon is ~ past injury cannot be changed TC 2.789. **11.** intr. fare, get on G.CY 654. **12.** auxil. forming periphrastic tense with infin. A.Mil 3410, B.Mk 3622, 3624, CompL 14, TC 2.54, 4.880, 5.350, HF 1036. **13.** imper. (emphatic) with infin. BD 754; (absol.) come! D.WB 853. **14.** han to ~ of occupy oneself with B.NP 4441; have to doone with have something to do with A.Mil 3777, TC 2.213; be(n to ~ be necessary to be done I.Pars 62, Bo 4. p6. 62/89, TC 5.70; na more to ~ nothing else to be done B.ML 770. (for) to **do(o)ne** infl. infin. B.Mel 2191, I.Pars 62, TC 1.1026. **dostow** pr. 2 sg. (with suffixed pron.) D.WB 239. **do(o)th** imper. pl. B.Mel 2785, C.Phs 250, D.WB 1042, E.Cl 568, B.Mch 1517, TC 3.975. **dide** pa. 1, 3 sg. A.Prol 451, B.NP 4613; **dede** TC 1.369 var; **didest/ dedest** 2 sg. TC 3. 363. **dide(n** pl. A.Kn 1007, 1177; **deden** TC 1.82 var. **y)do** p.p. A.Mil 3739, G.CY 899; **y)doon** BD 40, TC 2.789. [OE dōn, dyde, ge)dōn]

dorma(u)nt adj. (table) ~ permanently in place A.Prol 353. [OF]

dortour n. dormitory (of a monastery) D.Sum 1855. [OF]

dossers n. pl. baskets HF 1940. [OF dossier]

dotage n. senility A.Rv 3898, D.WB 709, E.Mch 1253; folly Buk 8. [from **dote(n**]

dotard adj. foolish, senile D.WB 291, **dotardes** pl. I.Pars 857; as n. fool D.WB 331. [from dote n. (from next)]

dote(n v. be feeble-minded, senile E.Mch 1441, LGW G. 261; behave foolishly G.CY 983; p.p. as adj. feeble-minded RR 407, irrational Buk 13. [? OE]

doublenesse n. duplicity G.CY 1300, deceit F.Sq 543, treachery 556, FormA 63/62; faithlessness Anel 159. [from double adj., from OF]

doucet n. a wind instrument HF 1221. [OF]

do(u)ghter n. daughter A.Kn 2222, A.Rv 3969, TC 4.1538; as address to a (related) young woman A.Kn 2453, 2668. **doghter** gen. sg. E.Cl 608. **do(u)ghtren** B.NP 4019, F.Fkl 1429, TC 4.22; **do(u)ghtres** B.NP 4565, C.Pard 486, HF 1007. [OE dohtor, gen. unchanged, pl. dohtru]

doun n. hill: by dale and eek by ~e high and low B.Th 1986. [OE dūn]

doun adv. **1.** yonder ~ down below HF 912; bere(n ~ overcome E.Mch 2270, descende(n ~ to asken proceed to the point of asking TC 5. 859, gon ~ fall A.Kn 2613, A.Rv 4307; doune comp. lower Astr 2. 12. 14/19. **2.** up and ~ everywhere A.Kn 2054, 2513, D.Fri 1283, here and there A.Kn 977, 2241, Mars 210; casten up and ~ consider alternatives B.ML 212; glosen up and ~ interpret in diverse ways D.WB 26; rolle(n up and ~ D.Sum 2217, winde up and ~ TC 2.601 ponder; chaungen up and ~

change from good to bad and bad to good A.Kn 2840. [OE *dūne*]
dounright *adv.* out of hand H. Mcp 228. [prec.+**right**]
doutance *n.* uncertainty TC 1.200; *out of* ~ without a doubt, certainly TC 4.963, 1044. [OF]
doute *n.* **1.** uncertainty: *withoute*(*n* ~ A.Kn 1322, B.ML 734, Bo 2. p5. 53/74, TC 2.735 *var*, *out*(*e of* ~ certainly, surely A.Prol 487, C.Phs 157, TC 1.152, HF 812; *be*(*n in* ~ be uncertain B.Mel 2407, TC 4.1277, *thereof is no* ~ there is no uncertainty about it I.Pars 296, *it nis no* ~ it is certain that Bo 3. p9. 29/39, *putte the out of* ~ dispel your uncertainty HF 598. **2.** difficulty, doubtful point Bo 4. p6. 11/17, 5. p3. 1/2; *pl.* differing interpretations F.Sq 220; ~ *of reson* difficulty based on reason TC 2.366. **3.** peril, danger E.Mch 1721, LGW 1613, fear TC 5.1453, awe I.Pars 1023. [OF]
doute(**n** *v.* **1.** *tr.* hesitate to believe Bo 3. p12. 20/25, 107/144, 4. p2. 78/104; (with *that*-cl.) Bo 2. p4. 36/49, 125/173; ~ *nat but that* . . 114/157. **2.** *intr.* ~ *of* be uncertain about Bo 4. p3. 39/56, ~ *herof* be in doubt about this/that Bo 3. p11. 23/32. **3.** *tr.* fear I.Pars 648, 735, (with infin.) I.Pars 696, 953; *intr.* be afraid B.Mel 2517, *refl.* Bo 1. p6. 69/89, ~ *of* fear on account of I.Pars 880, RR 1089; *be*(*n to* ~ be to be feared Bo 3. p12. 21/27, 5. p1. 14/19. **douteth** *imper. pl.* TC 1.683. [OF *douter*]
doutous *adj.* uncertain, to be doubted Bo 3. p10. 151/205; ambiguous Bo 2. p1. 41/57; unreliable, untrustworthy Bo 2. p8. 26/38, TC 4.992; *of a* ~ *jugement* difficult to judge Bo 1. p1. 9/13. [OF]
doutremer(**e** *adj.* foreign BD 253. [OF phrase]
dowaire/dower *n.* dowry E.Cl 807, 848. [OF *douaire*]
dowe *v.* dedicate, give TC 5.230. [OF *douer*]
dowves *gen.* dove's TC 3.1496 *var.* [ON *dúfe*]
drad, dradde *see* **drede**(**n**.
draf *n.* husks, worthless part I.Pars 35, LGW G. 312. [OE **dræf*]
draf-sek/sak *n.* sack of bran A.Rv 4206. [prec.+**sak**, also ON *sekkr*]
drasty *adj.* foul, crude B.Mel 2113, 2120. [OE *dræstig*]
drat *see* **drede**(**n**.
draught *n.* **1.** drink A.Prol 135, C.Pard 360, ?. move (in chess) BD 653; trick of fate BD 685, *drawe the same* ~ undergone the same fate 682. [from next]
drawe(**n** *v.* **1.** *intr.* go, move A.Mil 3633, A.Rv 4304, B.Th 2017, D.WB 993, PF 490; *refl.* go F.Sq 355, G.CY 685, TC 2.1186, withdraw 3.978; turn TC 3.177, come C.Pard 966; ~ *unto that purpos* decide E.Cl 314. **2.** *tr.* draw, pull E.Mch 1817, TC 3.674, unsheathe (sword) A.Kn 2547, I.Pars 355; drag F.Sq 326, Bo 1. m4. 16/22, 4. m7. 26/36; drag to pieces B.Pri 1823; ~ *to peces* TC 1.833; ~ *cut* draw lots A.Prol 835; ~ *togidere* gather Bo 1. p3. 52/73; ~ *along* protract Bo 1. m1. 20/28; ~ *forth* pull along TC 3.1704; ~ *in*(*to memorie* call to mind A.Kn 2074, A.Mil

3112, I.Pars 239, LGW 1685. **3.** *intr.* pull (cart) D.Fri 1560, TC 1.224; draw water A.Kn 1416. **4.** *tr.* draw out, extract: (of arguments) cite Bo 5. p4. 22/31; ~ *out* pull out B.Mk 3292, (fig.) draw out Bo 4. p6. 234/325 (L *elicit*), 2. p1. 21/30 (L *prolatis*); ~ *with hir* bring about Bo 5. p6. 132/187; ~ *to record* call to witness Scog 22; ~ *on lengthe* extend TC 2. 262. **5.** take in (breath) Bo 3. p11. 115/157, TC 3.1119, (drink) Bo 4. m3. 17/22. **6.** attract A.Prol 519, Bo 2. p5. 27/37, p7. 11/13, 3. p12. 136/183; tempt Bo 1. p4. 49/67, 2. p8. 20/29. **7.** mark out Bo 5. m5. 3; ~ *of* design according to Bo 3. m9. 10/14. **8.** ~ *the same draughte* see **draught**; ~ *the tappe* turn on the tap A.Rv 3892. **draweth** *imper. pl.* A.Prol 835, B.Pri 1632, TC 3.177. **drow** *pa. sg.* A.Mil 3633, **dro**(**u**)**gh** A.Rv 3892. **y**)**drawe** *p.p.* A.Prol 396, B.ML 339. [OE *dragan, drōg/drōh, drōgon, dragen*]
drecche(**n** *v.* **1.** afflict, trouble B.NP 4077, vex TC 2.1471. **2.** delay TC 2.1264, 4.1446. [OE *dreċċan*]
drecchinge *vbl. n.* **1.** prolonging I.Pars 1000. **2.** delaying TC 3.853.
drede *n.* **1.** fear, terror A.Kn 1396, B.Mel 2559, B.NP 4544; *for* ~ *of* for fear of Bo 1. p4. 223/311; *ben in* ~ (*of*) fear F.Fkl 1386, TC 4.1113. **2.** anxiety, concern B.Sh 1313, E.Cl 134, F.Sq 212, *for* ~ *of* through concern about F.Sq 286. **3.** doubt: *withouten* (*any*) ~ F.Fkl 1544, G.SN 329, HF 292; *out of* ~ doubtless B.ML 893, B.Mk 3476, E.Cl 634, TC 5.1751, unquestionable 1.775; *it is no* ~ there is no doubt B.ML 869, C.Pard 507, D.WB 63. **4.** danger B.ML 657, B.Mel 2517. **5.** awe E.Cl 358; *have in* ~ venerate B.Mk 3352. **6.** ? sorrow BD 490, Mars 28, TC 1.529. [from next]
drede(**n** *v.* **1.** *tr.* fear TC 3.328; (with infin.) 322; (with cl.) E.Cl 181, *to* ~ to be feared B.NP 4253, G.SN 437, Bo 2. p1. 65/90, TC 1.84. **2.** hold in awe G.SN 125, Bo 2. m1. 6/8; admire greatly F.Fkl 1312. **3.** abhor B.Mel 2366, 2367. **4.** *intr.* be afraid A.Rv 3874, I.Pars 1005, (with *of*) B.NP 4119; *refl.* D.WB 1214, PF 157, (with *of*) A.Prol 660, B.Mk 3918, HF 1043. **5.** ~ *noght that outher* do not doubt that either A.Kn 1593. **dredeth** *pr. 3 sg.* B.Mel 2381; **drat** TC 3.328. **dredeth** *imper. pl.* B.NP 4159, TC 4.1520. **dredde** *pa. sg.* TC 3, 3.1647, LGW 199; **dradde** B.Mk 3402, E.Cl 523, Anel 185. **dredde**(**n** *pl.* 1.483, 4.56, LGW 1813; **dradden** G.SN 15. **y**)**drad** *p.p.* E.Cl 69, Bo 2. m1. 6/8, TC 3.1775; **dred** Bo 4. p3. 81/117. [LOE *drǣdan*]
dredeles *adj.* fearless Bo 3. m12. 7/9. [from n.]
dred(**e**)**les** *adv.* without doubt, indeed, assuredly E.Mch 1316, BD 764, TC 5.1755. [from n.]
dredful *adj.* **1.** frightened, timorous A.Kn 1479, F.Fkl 1309, PF 195, Bo 2. m2. 16/22, 4. p3. 80/115, LGW 811; reverent TC 2.1045, 5.1331, LGW 109. **2.** anxious, apprehensive PF 3, TC 2.776. **3.** frightening, terrible B.ML 937, B.Mk 3558; **dredfulleste** *sup.* TC 5.248. [from n.]

dredfully adv. timidly TC 2.1138, LGW 2680. [from prec.]

dre(e)m n. dream, vision, B.ML 804, B.NP 4077, PF 31, TC 5.378, HF 35. Cf. **sweven.** [form as OE drēam joy, jubilation; sense as ON draumr and Gmc cognates]

dreye adj. dry A.Kn 3024, B.Mk 3233. [OE drȳġe]

dreye(n/drye v. **1.** suffer Mars 251, PF 251, TC 1.303. **2.** endure, tolerate TC 4.154; ~ forth TC 1.1092 var, 5.1540 var. **3.** experience, feel Anel 333, HF 1879. [OE drēogan]

dreyeth see **dryeth.**

dreynt(e see **drenchen.**

dremed v. impers. pa.; me ~ I dreamt B.Th 1977, RR 51. [OA drēman]

dreminges vbl. n. pl. dreams B.NP 4280.

drenche(n v. **1.** tr. drown A.Mil 3520, 3617, B.NP 4272, LGW G. 293, inundate, submerge I.Pars 839; refl. F.Fkl 1378; (fig.) overcome Bo 1. m1. 18/26, 4. m6. 25/39, Scog 12. **2.** intr. be drowned A.Mil 3521, 3523; ~ in teres be overwhelmed by tears TC 1.543, 4.510, 930, LGW 1919. **3.** sink (ship) I.Pars 363, HF 233. **dreynte** pa. sg. B.ML 923, I.Pars 839, BD 72, Bo 4. m7. 31/44, pl. F.Fkl 1378. **dreynt** p.p. A.Mil 3520, B.ML 69, Mars 89, TC 5.1503, Bo 1. m2. 1. [OE drenčan, drenčte]

drenching(e vbl. n. drowning A.Kn 2456, I.Pars 364.

drery adj. sad E.Cl 514, TC 1.13, HF 179, frightened LGW 810. [OE drēoriġ]

drerinesse n. sadness, grief Bo 1. p6. 31/41, TC 1.701, dejection 971. [OE drēoriġnes(se]

dresse(n v. **1.** prepare A.Prol 106, A.Mil 3635, LGW 1190; arrange E.Cl 381, TC 4. 1182, PF 665; treat, deal with E.Mch 2361; refl. prepare, get ready (to go) B.ML 263, 265, PF 88, TC 2.71, 5.279; clothe oneself TC 2.635; ~ on hors mount TC 5.37; ~d him up took up a position A.Mil 3358, ~d him upward raised himself up TC 3.71, ~ hir adoun sit down LGW 804. **2.** turn, apply (mind) Gent 3, dispose (heart) E.Cl 1049; refl. turn one's attention (to) A.Mil 3468, E.Cl 1007, G.SN 77. **3.** go F.Sq 290; refl. B.ML 416, 1100, E.Mch 1820, G.CY 1271, ~ forthward advance B.ML 263. **4.** guide: ~ thy weyes B.Mel 2308; ~inge hem to goode directing them to a good end Bo 4. p6. 117/169 (L dirigens). [OF drecier]

dryeth pr. 3 sg. dries up A.Kn 1495, Bo 4. m6. 21/31, **dreyeth** I.Pars 848. [OE drȳġan]

drinke(n v. drink. **drank** pa. sg. B.ML 789, NP 4032, **dronk** TC 5.1216 var. **dronken** pl. A.Prol 820, A.Kn 2714. **dronke(n** p.p. A.Prol 135, TC 3.674; **ydronke** B.Mel 2601. [OE drincan, dranc/dronc, druncen]

dryve(n v. **1.** (lit.) drive A.Kn 1859, D.Fri 1540, TC 2.1535, 5.665; shoot RR 950; (fig.) compel, force I.Pars 527, TC 2.576, 5.1332; ~ awey banish F.Fkl 844, Bo 2. p5. 82/115; (with fro, from, out fro, out(e of) banish, expel B.Mel 2311, E.Mch 1980, Bo 1. m7. 12/16, 3. m5. 7/9, TC 4.427, 5.913; persecute, oppress LGW 1924. **2.** force in (nails) A.Kn 2007, D.WB 769. **3.** go TC 3.227, RR 1338, dash D.Sum

1694; ~ forth advance, sail B.ML 505, 969, pursue (way) B.ML 875; ~ aboute circle, go round on Fort 46. **4.** pass (time) LGW 2620; ~ forth TC 5.389, 405, 628; ~ awey C.Pard 628, BD 49, TC 2.983. **5.** pursue, endure ~ forth the world endure life B.Sh 1421, ~ forth as well as he hath might endure as best he can TC 5.1101, ~forth his aventure endure his fate TC 1.1092 var, 5.1540 var. **6.** conclude: ful drive firmly concluded F.Fkl 1230. **dryveth** pr. 3 sg. B.ML 505; **dryfth** TC 5.1332. **dryve** subj. sg. LGW 2177. **dryf** imper. sg. Bo 1. m7. 12/16, TC 4.1615, 5.359, 913. **dro(o)f** pa. sg. D.Fri 1540, Anel 190. **drive(n** p.p. F.Fkl 1230, TC 2.983; **ydriven** A.Kn 2007. [OE drifan, dräf, drifen]

dronkelewe adj. habitually drunk, sottish C.Pard 495, D.Sum 2043. [OE druncen+ suff. -læwe]

dronkenesse n. drunkenness B.ML 771, TC 2.716. [OE drunce(n)nes(se]

dro(o)f see **drive(n.**

droppe(n v. **1.** intr. fall in drops A.Rv 3895; drip G.CY 580. **2.** tr. let fall Bo 1. p4. 185/259. **3.** bespatter A.Kn 2884. [OE droppian]

dropping vbl. n. leaking water I.Pars 632; dripping B.Mel 2276.

dropping(e ppl. adj. leaking D.WB 278, I.Pars 631, 632.

dronk, dronke(n see **drinke(n.**

dro(u)gh see **drawe(n.**

drovy adj. dirty I.Pars 816. [OE drōfiġ]

drow see **drawe(n.**

druerye n. in by ~ from affection RR 844. [OF]

drugge v. labour, do menial work A.Kn 1416. [?]

Duche adj. German HF 1234. [MDu Duutsch]

due/dewe adj. rightful, just I.Pars 561, Bo 1. m5. 23/33; obligatory LGW 603; inevitable A.Kn 3044, ~d deu]

duetee/deweté n. **1.** legal obligation I.Pars 752, of verray ~ as an obligation LGW G. 360; money owing, right D.Fri 1352, 1391. **2.** what is fitting: in the wyse of ~ for fitting courtesy TC 3.970; with ~ and honour with due honour A.Kn 3060; agayns his ~ beyond what he is entitled to I.Pars 408. [AN]

duk n. duke D.WB 1157, prince, leader A.Kn 860, 873, HF 388. [OF]

dul adj. stupid B.ML 202, heavy TC 5.1118. [MDu]

dulcarno(u)n n. dilemma, puzzle TC 3.933, at ~ at wit's end 931. [ML from Arab]

dulle(n v. **1.** tr. weaken Bo 1. p4. 136/188, p6. 32/41, dim m2. 2, diminish Ven 76; nullify I.Pars 233. **2.** bore, satiate G.CY 1093, 1172; intr. be satiated, become bored TC 2.1035, (with of) 4.1489. [from adj.]

durable adj. permanent, eternal I.Pars 1039. [OF]

durabletee n. continuance Bo 3. p11. 127/174. [OF]

duracioun n. fixed period of time A.Kn 2996, HF 2114. [OF]

dure(n v. **1.** last, persist A.Kn 1360, B.ML 189; continue F.Fkl 836; subj. sg. Mars 233. **duryng** pr. p. enduring Mars 228, lasting TC 3.1754. **2.** live A.Kn 1236, TC 4.765. [OF durer]

duresse *n.* suffering, distress TC 5.399. [OF *durece*]

duringe *vbl. n.* duration: *be(n of longer* ~ have a longer life Bo 4. p4. 117/166.

durre *v.* dare: *to* ~ *don that him leste* in daring to perform what he wished TC 5.840. **dar** *pr. 1 sg.* A.Kn 1151, TC 1.16. *3 sg.* B.Mk 3754, C.Pard 380. **darst** *2 sg.* A.Kn 1140, B.ML 860, Bo 2. p5. 46/64, TC 1.768, (with suffixed pron.) **darstou/darstow** B.Mel 2337, LGW 1450. **dar** *pl.* I.Pars 507, TC 2.1747. **dorste** *pa.* A.Rv 3937, 4009; **durst(e** RR 1221. **dorstestow** *2 sg.* TC 1.767. [OF *durran, dearr, dorste*]

durring *vbl. n.* daring: *in* ~ *don that longeth to a knight* in daring to perform knightly deeds TC 5.837. [from prec.]

durst *see* **thar.**

dusked *pa. pl.* grew dim A.Kn 2806. *p.p.* made dark Bo 1. p1. 18/26. [cf. OE *doxian*]

duweliche *see* **dewely.**

dwale *n.* sleeping potion A.Rv 4161. [OE *dwala*]

dwelle(n *v.* **1.** live A.Prol 702, HF 1902. **2.** remain (in a place) A.Kn 2462, D.WB 372, TC 3.651, 4.1449. **3.** remain (in a condition) A.Kn 1661, F.Fkl 1099, Bo 2. p1. 83/114, TC 2.314, 5.615; ~ *(un)to* remain for Bo 2. m7. 21/29, 5. p1. 28/40. **4.** persist, survive B.Mel 2375, 2563, Bo 2. p7. 28/40, 3. p3. 70/93; last Bo 5. p6. 65/90; *ne* ~ *but* only exist as Bo 5. p1. 26/36; ~ *graunted* remain taken as proved Bo 3. p11. 10/13, ~ . . *in hir first grauntynge* remain accepted on their first proof 8–9/11–12. **5.** delay B.NP 4340, TC 2.1595, 1614, 5.1394, HF 1300; wait TC 3.201. **dwelte** *pa. sg.* A.Prol 512, B.ML 134; **dwelled** A.Kn 2804, TC 1.121. **dweltest** *2 sg.* G.SN 48. **dwelten** *pl.* A.Rv 4003. **dwelt** *p.p.* G.CY 720, TC 5.711; **dwelled** Bo 2. p4. 36/48. [OE *dwellan, dwēalde,* and *dwelede, dwēald*]

dwyned *ppl. adj.* withered RR 360. [from OE *dwinan*]

E

Ebraik *adj.* Hebrew B.ML 489, HF 1433, **Hebraik** B.Pri 1750. [LL *Hebraicus*]

ecclesiaste *n.* divine, minister A.Prol 708. [ML *ecclēsiastēs*]

ech 1. *adj.* every A.Prol 660, A.Kn 1168, TC 2.42; ~ *a* D.WB 256, ~ *a del* every detail of TC 3.694. **2.** *pron. each (one)* A.Kn 899, D.WB 702; ~ *other* each . . the other A.Kn 2625; (with *of*) A.Prol 39, PF 662, Bo 3. p11. 14/19 *var* **ich.** [OE *ǣlċ/ylċ*]

eche(n *v. tr.* increase Bo 3. p6. 10/14, TC 1.705, 3.1509, 5.110; *intr.* ~ *in* add TC 3.1329/1406. [OA *ēċan*]

echines/echynnys *n. pl.* sea urchins Bo 3. m8. 14/18. [L *echīnus*]

echo(o)n *pron.* each one, everyone A.Prol 820, A.Kn 2655, TC 4.218; every one (of inanimates) BD 335, HF 1953. [OE *ǣlċ ān*]

ecliptik *n.* apparent path of the sun Astr 2.4. 41/64, 40.1/2; ~ *line* prol 4. 71/99, etc. [L *eclipticus*]

edifice *n.* building B.Mel 2523; structure Bo 3. p11. 93/127, p12. 56/74 (L *machina*). [OF]

edified *p.p.* built up Bo 4. p6. 177/257. [from *v.* from OF *edifier*]

eek *adv.* also, moreover A.Prol 217, A.Kn 1967, B.Mel 2286, BD 339, HF 445. [OE *ē(a)c*]

eem *n.* uncle TC 1.1022, 2.162, etc. (only in TC, but so equally is *uncle*). [OE *ēam*]

eet *see* **ete(n.**

effect *n.* **1.** performance, execution Bo 4. p2. 17/23, p6. 58/84; operation F.Sq 322, Bo 5. p4. 68/97; attainment Bo 3. p10. 170/233, 4. p2. 115/156 (L *obtinere non possunt*), p6. 235/325; fulfilment G.CY 1261, Bo 5. p6. 215/303; *in* ~ in fact, effectively A.Prol 319, E.Cl 856, G.SN 511, PF 619, TC 3.1149, 4.1294, 5.178; actually TC 1.748, 5.1009, in substance 1423, essentially 1621, 1784; to bring about E.Cl 721; *as in* ~ indeed, in fact G.CY 634, 847, I.Pars 419; *what in* ~ of what use TC 2.1379; *of* ~ real Fort 34. **2.** consequence A.Kn 2989, B.ML 893, I.Pars 920, TC 1.212, 3.1815, 5.377, LGW 1924; result, sequel B.NP 4325, HF 5; outcome, end H.Mcp 266, TC 4.144; *take* ~ be concluded Bo 1. p4. 63/88; *taken any* ~ have any result I.Pars 607, *take noon* ~ is not fulfilled 782; *pl.* A.Kn 2228, TC 3.15 (prob. for **affectes**). **3.** purpose: *to this* ~ with this object B.Mel 3073; *to th'* ~ *that* in order that B.Mel 3058; *pl.* Mars 165. **4.** substance, essence A.Kn 1487, 2207, 2259, 2366, D.Fri 1451, E.Mch 1398, TC 3.346, LGW 620, purport Pity 56, TC 2.1220, 4.890; meaning B.Mel 2148; essential matter, point TC 2.1566, 3.1580, LGW 622, matter TC 5.1629; *pl.* LGW 929; *to this* ~ in this sense A.Kn 2851; *to th'* ~ to the conclusion A.Kn 1189, grete ~ conclusion A.Kn 2482, TC 3.505. **5.** quality, attribute Bo 2. p6. 80/114 (L *effectu*), 3. p11. 34/46. **effects** *pl.* Bo 2. p6. 70 *var*/99 *sg.* (L *effectibus*). [L *effectus*, OF *effe(c)t*]

efficient *adj.* effective Bo 5. m4. 29/42. [L and OF]

eft *adv.* **1.** again A.Kn 1669, A.Mil 3271, Anel 331, TC 2.301; another time TC 1.137, 3.1712, 5.265, a second time Buk 13, 24. **2.** afterwards F.Fkl 1553, BD 41, HF 1297; later Bo 1. m5. 9/13. **3.** likewise A.Mil 3647, TC 1.360, HF 401. [OE]

eftso(o)ne(s *adv.* (sometimes as two words) **1.** immediately A.Mil 3489, Bo 3. p12. 39/52, TC 2.1468. **2.** again B.ML 909, D.Sum 1992, HF 359, LGW 2322, another time B.Mk 3476, D.WB 808, G.CY 933, Astr 2.23.11/16. **3.** back Bo 3. m2. 26/38, 4. m6. 39/49. **4.** in return Bo 4. m7. 43/61, in reply TC 4.181. [prec., **so(o)ne**+adv. *-es*]

egal *adj.* equal Bo 2. m7. 12/16, TC 3.137. (cf. **equal**). [OF]

egaly *adv.* equably Bo 2. p4. 92/126; impartially, neutrally Bo 5. p3. 90/127. [from prec.]

egalitee *n.* equanimity Bo 2. p4. 83/115; *in* ~ *as* on a par with I.Pars 949. [OF]

eggement *n.* temptation B.ML 842. [from *v.* next]

eggeth *pr. 3 sg. tr.* entices RR 182. **eggen** *pl. intr.* incite I.Pars 968. [OI *eggja*]

egging *vbl. n.* incitement E.Mch 2135.

egre *adj.* **1.** fierce E.Cl 1199, angry Bo 2. m5. 17/24, 4. p7. 67/93. **2.** bitter, sharp (to taste) I.Pars 117, Bo 1. p5. 53/78, RR 217; painful, biting (words) B.Mel 2367. [OF]

egremoyne *n.* agrimony G.CY 800. [OF *aigremoine*]

ey *n.* egg B.NP 4035, G.CY 806. [OE *æg*]

ei *interj.* ah A.Mil 3768, C.Pard 782, D.Sum 2232, TC 2.87, 3.120 *var*, 4.1087 *var*; I TC 3.120 *var*, 4.1087 *var*. [cf. OF *ahi*]

eye/ye *n.* eye A.Prol 10, A.Mil 3852, **eighe** F.Fkl 1036 *var*; *at* ~ plainly A.Kn 3016, with one's own eyes G.CY 1059, to the eye, to look at E.Cl 1168, G.CY 964; *with* ~ A.Mil 3415, B.ML 280, F.Fkl 1192, TC 2.301. **eyen/yen** *pl.* A.Prol 152, TC 3.1453. [OE *ē(a)ge*, pl. *ē(a)gan*]

eyed/yed *adj.* endowed with eyes TC 4.1459. [from prec.]

eight(h)e *adj.* eighth TC 5.1809 *var*. [OE *e(a)htopa*]

eylen/aylen *v.* ail, afflict, be wrong with (orig. with dat. of pers.) A.Mil 3424, B.NP 4290, F.Sq 501; esp. in *what ~th . .?* A.Kn 1081, A.Mil 3769, E.Mch 2368, with explanatory infin. B.Sh 1171, B.NP 4080, TC 2.211, *~th at me* has against me B.Th 1975. [OE *egl(i)an*]

eir *n.* air A.Kn 1246, LGW 1482: also **air** D.Sum 2254, PF 204, etc. [OF *air*]

eyre *see* **heir(e**.

eyrish *adj.* aerial HF 932, 965. [from **eir**]

eisel *n.* vinegar RR 217. [OF]

eyther **1.** *adj.* each, either A.Kn 2553, B.Pri 1684, Bo 1. m4. 3/4, TC 4.130. **2.** *pron.* TC 4.1033, 5.1764. **3.** *conj.* (usu. correl. with **or**) D.WB 259, Bo 2. p4. 57/77, TC 2.755. Cf. **outher**. [OE *ǣgþer*]

elaat *adj.* arrogant B.Mk 3357. [L *ēlātus*]

elacio(u)n *n.* arrogance I.Pars 391, 400. [OF]

e(e)ld(e *n.* **1.** old age A.Kn 2447, A.Mil 3230, D.WB 1207, Bo 1. m1. 9/13, TC 4.1369, RR 349. **2.** age reached: *twenty yeer of* ~ Anel 78. **3.** passing of time, advancing years TC 2.393, Bo 1. p1. 18/26, 2. p7. 62/89, Anel 12. [OA *ēldo*]

elde(n *v.* **1.** *tr.* make old or feeble RR 391, 396. **2.** *intr.* grow old Bo 2. p7. 5/7. [from prec.]

eldefader/elder- *n.* grandfather Bo 2. p4. 33/45. [OE *ealdfæder*, assoc. with **elder** from **o(o)ld**]

elder, eldest *see* **o(o)ld**.

eldres *n. pl.* ancestors, predecessors B.Mk 3388, D.WB 1118, E.Cl 65, Bo 2. p6. 9/13, 11/16. [OE *eldra*; see **o(o)ld**]

eleccioun *n.* **1.** choice, what is chosen PF 409, power of choice 621; *pleyn* ~ free choice 528, *free* ~ Purse 23. **2.** choice of astrologically appropriate time B.ML 312, Astr 2.4.2 (*pl.*), 44/68. [AN]

element *n.* **1.** one of four primary substances (earth, water, air, fire) G.CY 1460, BD 694, Bo 4. m6. 16/23, TC 3.1753, ? HF 975. **2.** simpler part of complex substance D.Fri 1506. [OF]

elenge *see* **alenge**.

elevacioun *n.* altitude (of north pole above horizon) Astr 2.23.16/23, 24. 5/6. [OF]

elevat *adj.* high above the horizon Astr 2.23. 18/26. [L *ēlevātus*]

elf *n.* (**elves** *pl.*) goblin, evil spirit A.Mil 3479, B.ML 754; incubus D.WB 864, 873; ~ -*queen* queen of supernatural beings D.WB 860, creature of magical beauty B.Th 1978, 1989. [OF *ælf*]

elixir *n.* (alchem.) agent which transmutes to silver and gold G.CY 863. [OF from Arab]

ellebor *n.* hellebore, a medicinal plant B.NP 4154. [L *elleborus*]

elles **1.** *adv.* otherwise, else A.Prol 375, A.Mil 3710, B.ML 1064, D.WB 1223, G.SN 269, (often following *or*) alternatively, at any rate A.Kn 1151, B.Pri 1833, C.Pard 376, TC 1.688, perhaps because E.Cl 88, 90; ~ *God forbede* God forbid it should be otherwise G.CY 1046, 1064, TC 2.1690. **2.** *adj.* other, else, in *nothing* ~ D.Sum 1866, BD 74, *noght* ~ B.Mel 2121, E.Cl 865, *oght* ~ D.Sum 2203, F.Fkl 1469, *no man* ~ HF 60, LGW 2044. [OE]

elleswhere *adv.* elsewhere, somewhere else A.Kn 2113, G.CY 1130, TC 4.698, 5.1044. [OE *elles hwǣr*]

elongacioun *n.* angular distance Astr 2.25.41/58. [L *ēlongātiōn-*]

eloquence *n.* **1.** literary art F.Fkl 678, Bo 2. p3. 40/57. **2.** manner of speech E.Cl 410, 1203, BD 925. [OF]

elvish *adj.* otherworldly, inhuman B.Th 1893, ? mysterious G.CY 751, 842. [from **elf**]

embassadrye *n.* negotiation B.ML 233. [OF *ambassaderie*]

embaume/en- *v.* embalm (corpse) LGW 676; (fig.) impregnate with scent RR 1663. [OF *embaumer*]

embelif (only in Astr) *adj.* oblique, slanting Astr 1.20.2, 2.19.11/15, etc. *adv.* obliquely 2.26.7/9, 28.20/28. [OF *en belif*]

embosed *p.p.* taken refuge in a wood BD 353. [from OF *bos, bois* woods, chase]

embrace/en- *v.* embrace B.Th 1891, TC 5.224; encompass Bo 5. p6. 202/284, TC 5.1816; bring it about, contrive H.Mcp 160. [OF *embracer*]

embroudinge *vbl. n.* embroidering I.Pars 417. [see **enbroude(n**]

embusshements *n. pl.* ambushes B.Mel 2509. [OF]

emeraude *n.* emerald B.Pri 1799. [OF *e(s)meraude*]

emforth *prep.* according to, to the extent of A.Kn 2235, TC 2.243, LGW 2132. [OE *emn = efen* + **forth**]

empeire(n *v.* impair, harm Bo 4. p3. 35/51, p6. 170/247; make worse B.Mel 2209; tarnish E.Mch 2198. [OF *empeirier*]

emplastre *pr.* apply medicinal plaster to, (fig.) gloss over E.Mch 2297. [OF *emplastrer*]

emplyeth *see* **implyeth**.

empoisone *v.* poison B.Mel 2519, I.Pars 514. [OF *empoisoner*]

empoysoner *n.* poisoner C.Pard 894. [from prec.]

empoysoning *vbl. n.* poisoning A.Kn 2460, C.Pard 891.

emprenting *vbl. n.* imprinting, efficacy F.Fkl 834.

emprinteth/-prenteth *imper. pl.* fix E.Cl 1193. **emprented** *p.p.* imprinted E.Mch

2117, F.Fkl 831, Bo 5. m4. 12/14; (fig.) impressed E.Mch 2178, Bo 5. p5. 10/15. [OF *empreinter*]

empryse *n.* **1.** undertaking, enterprise B.ML 348, B.Mel 2412, 2443; task 2258, I.Pars 403, 691, TC 2.73. **2.** chivalric exploit A.Kn 2540, F.Fkl 732; adventure LGW 1452. **3.** aim TC 4.601. **4.** courage B.Mk 3857. [OF]

empte(n *v.* **1.** empty, remove contents of G.CY 741, 1404. **2.** *p.p.* drained, exhausted Bo 1. p1. 6/9, deprived m2. 20/28; emaciated m1. 12/17. [OE *æm(e)tian*]

enb- *see also* **emb-.**

enbasshinge/abaysschinge *vbl. n.* ~ *withouten ende* eternal amazement Bo 4. p1. 28/38. [cf. **abaissen**]

enbatailled *adj.* battlemented RR 139. [from OF *batailles* battlements]

enbibing *vbl. n.* absorption G.CY 814. [from *v.* from L *imbibere* with OF *em-*]

enbossed *p.p.* embossed LGW 1200 *var.* [OF **embocer*]

enbroude *vbl. n.* embroider HF 1327, LGW 2351; *p.p.* decorated LGW 119. [OE *brogden* p.p.+OF *embrodé*]

encens *n.* incense A.Kn 2277, TC 5.1466. [OF]

encense(n *v.* **1.** burn incense G.SN 395. **2.** burn incense to/over, cense G.SN 413, I.Pars 407. [OF *encenser*]

encharged *p.p.* imposed on Bo 5. p6. 219/308. [from OF *enchargier*]

enchesoun *n.* cause, reason B.Mel 2783, F.Sq 456, I.Pars 374, TC 1.348. [OF *enchaison*]

enclyne(n/in- *v.* **1.** *tr.* incline B.Mel 2447, turn Bo 4. p4. 140/197; ~ .. *eres* listen B.Mel 2370. *refl.* inclyneth *nat yow* (*imper.*) do not be disposed B.Mel 2784. *be(n* ~*d* be disposed, inclined B.Mel 2440, I.Pars 361, 691. *intr.* incline, be disposed TC 2.674; condescend B.ML 1082. **2.** *tr.* bend PF 414, Bo 1. m2. 21/30, 5. m5. 10/15; *p.p.* curved Bo 4. m6. 33/50 (L *flexos*), changed Bo 5. p3. 132/188. *intr.* bow B.Mk 3092. **3.** consent B.Mel 2683; submit B.Mel 2342, Bo 3. p12. 72/95. **4.** guide Bo 3. m2. 2/3, 4. m6. 29/43. [OF *encliner*]

enclyning *vbl. n.* inclination, tendency HF 734.

enclyninge *ppl. adj.* sloping Bo 5 m1. 11/16 *var.* [from v.]

enclos *p.p.* surrounded RR 1652. [OF]

enclose(n *v.* **1.** shut up B.Pri 1872, Bo 3. m2. 16/23; contain I.Pars 914. **2.** fence B.NP 4037, E.Mch 2143, enclose Do 1. m6. 1/6 (L *clausit*). **3.** set round RR 607. **4.** include I.Pars 1039. [from prec.]

encomberous *adj.* troublesome HF 862, vexatious Ven 42. [from *encombros*]

encombraunce *n.* hindrance: *dide* ~ (with dat). impeded E.Mch 1960. [OF]

encombre *v.* **1.** trouble A.Kn 1718, I.Pars 687. **2.** bewilder RR 889, 1389. **3.** stick A.Prol 508; choke, clog LGW 2006. [OF *encombrer*]

encorporing *vbl. n.* compounding G.CY 815. [from OF *encorporer*]

encrees *n.* increase, augmenting A.Prol 275, A.Kn 2184, TC 3.1776; spreading Bo 2. m7. 4/6, 4. p7. 60/83, addition HF 2074; result G.SN 18; assistance LGW 1087. [from next]

encre(e)s(s)e(n *v.* **1.** *tr.* increase A.Kn 1338, increase the numbers of B.Mel 2930, enhance Bo 3. p6. 14/18, 15/21; enrich B.Sh 1271; exacerbate B.ML 1068, Bo 5. p2. 29/40; develop, promote B.Mel 2466 *var.* **2.** *intr.* increase, be increased, grow A.Kn 2744, C.Phs 59, E.Cl 50, I.Pars 350, 498; (with dat. pron.) Pity 29; grow worse TC 5.1436. [AN *encres(s)-*, stem of *encreistre*]

endamage(n *v.* injure materially Bo 1. p4. 60/84; ~ *ententes* hinder purposes p1. 46/64. [OF *endomagier*]

ende *n.* **1.** limit (physical) B.Pri 1684, D.Fri 1285, 1537, D.Sum 2263, TC 3.205, (of a zodiacal sign) Astr 2.17.18/25, 27.4/5; extremity of a line Astr 1.6.6/9, 7.1; tip A.Prol 197, G.CY 1266, Anel 184; *every shires* ~ from the region of every county A.Prol 15; *at my wittes* ~ at a loss TC 3.931; *at either* ~ at top and bottom C.Pard 536. **2.** termination, conclusion A.Kn 1392, B.ML 423, Bo 4. p4. 33/45, TC 2.260, Fort 71; (of time) TC 5.499; death CompA 80; *lyves* ~ death B.Sh 1624, D.WB 1257, E.Cl 308, E.Mch 1354, TC 5.1554; *withouten* ~ eternally G.SN 69, I.Pars 214, PF 49, limitless Bo 4. p1. 28/39; *atte* (*laste*) ~ finally D.WB 404, I.Pars 494; *word and* ~ see **word**; *han* (*an*) ~ cease B.Mel 3078, F.Sq 295, be finite Bo 2. p7. 73/106, 75/108; *make(n an* ~ *of* finish, stop A.Kn 2966, B.ML 952, 1116, F.Sq 408, (with of *myself*) commit suicide B.Sh 1312; *dryven to an* ~ spend, pass (time) TC 5.475, LGW 2620; *broght to an* ~ concluded PF 666. **3.** outcome, issue B.ML 925, 928, B.Mel 2230, I.Pars 695, Bo 1. m6. 16/23, TC 2.1235; fate A.Kn 1844, 1869; *this is the* ~ this is the final outcome B.ML 145, 255; *maken of (it) a good* ~ bring about a good result B.Mel 2402, TC 1.973; *han an* ~ *of* achieve E.Cl 188. **4.** aim, purpose A.Kn 2259, B.ML 481, B.Mel 2321, 3073, I.Pars 736, 920, *camen to* ~ achieve objective Bo 3. p2. 6/8; *for this* ~ for this purpose LGW 2397, goal (of creation) Bo 1. p6. 29/38, 39/48, 3. p11. 166/225. **5.** *pl.* conclusions of an argument Bo 3. p12. 89/120. [OE]

endelong *prep.* alongside, along the coast of F.Fkl 992, along LGW 1498, across, over A.Kn 2678, LGW G. 144, down the length of F.Sq 416. *adv.* lengthwise A.Kn 1991, HF 1458; longitudinally Astr 2.40.24/33, 47/66. [OE *andlang* with substit. of *ende-*]

endentinge *vbl n* zigzag border, scalloping I.Pars 417. [from v. from OF *endenter*]

endetted *ppl. adj.* indebted G.CY 734. [OF *endeté*]

ending *n.* conclusion Bo 3. m2. 30/43; outcome A.Rv 4174; death C.Pard 892, ~ *day* day of death D.WB 507, Ven 55. [OE *endung*]

endirken *v.* darken, spoil Bo 4. p3. 36/52 *var.* [*en-*+OA **dircan* from *deorc* adj.]

enditement *n.* indictment, accusation I.Pars 800. [AN]

endyte(n *v.* **1.** *tr.* compose, write A.Prol 95, G.SN 80, TC 2.13, 3.504, LGW 1678; describe, relate G.SN 32, HF 381; ~ .. *a thing* draft a legal document A.Prol 325, draw up Bo 2. m8. 16/24, TC 3.1748. **2.**

intr. compose B.NP 4397, HF 520; tell TC 5.1334; ~ *of* tell of, describe, relate A.Kn 1380, F.Fkl 1550, TC 5. 1767, HF 634. **3.** dictate TC 2.1162, inspire (*to* 'in') Bo 1. m1. 3/4, p1. 32/44. **4.** accuse B.ML 781, B.Mk 3858. [AN *enditer*]

endyting *vbl. n.* composition Ven 77; style Astr prol 31/43, 32/45. *pl.* compositions I.Pars 1085.

endouted *p.p.* feared. *refl.* RR 1664. [from **doute(n]**

endure *v.* **1.** *tr.* suffer, put up with A.Kn 1923, A.Mil 3232, TC 1.34; (with infin.) bear TC 2.864. **2.** *intr.* continue, last B.ML 811, F.Fkl 1062, PF 130, TC 3.14, 4.326; remain, stay A.Kn 1185, B.ML 753, E.Mch 1317; hold out, bear up TC 1.224, 5.239, *up* ~ bear to stay up TC 2.1518. [OF *endurer*]

enduringe *vbl. n.* continued existence Bo 3. p11. 98/134.

enemy *n.*: *be(n* ~ *to* be hostile to I.Pars 681, 866. [OF]

enfamyned *p.p.* starved LGW 2429. [from OF *enfaminer*]

enfecteth *see* **infecte.**

enforce(n *v.* **1.** *refl.* strive, try, labour B.Mel 2365, Bo 3. p1. 33/45, Bo 4. p2. 47/63, 5. p3. 35/48; insist D.WB 340, TC 4.1016. **2.** *tr.* compel, force Bo 3. p12. 77/103, 79/106; bring about Bo 4. p7. 63/87. **3.** strengthen, support (argument, etc.) B.Mel 2148, 2233, Bo 4. p4. 179/248; (soul) I.Pars 730. **4.** *intr.* grow stronger B.Mel 2355. [OF *enforcier* and *enforcir*]

enforme *v.* **1.** inform, instruct B.Mel 2305, F.Sq 335, Bo 3. p1. 34/45. **2.** imbue Bo 1. p3. 43/60, p4. 198/277; inspire I.Pars 658. [OF *enformer*]

enfortuned *pa. sg.* endowed with the power to influence fortune Mars 259. [OF *enfortuner*]

engendre(n *v.* **1.** beget E.Cl 158, E.Mch 1272, I.Pars 333, 909; *intr.* procreate B.Mk 3148; *p.p.* produced A.Prol 4, B.Mel 2399, Bo 4. p6. 98/142 (L *gignitur*), caused A.Prol 421 *var*, A.Kn 1375. **2.** bring about, provoke B.Mel 2581, 2876, D.WB 465, D.Sum 2009, PF 248. **3.** *intr.* originate, arise A.Prol 421 *var*, B.NP 4113. [OF *engendrer*]

engendring(e *vbl. n.* **1.** creation Bo 4. p6. 29/42, ? condition LGW G. 414. **2.** ? cause B.Mel 2580. **3.** ? development HF 968.

engendrure *n.* **1.** (act of) procreation B.Mk 3137, D.WB 128, I.Pars 375. **2.** children, offspring I.Pars 621, 924. **3.** *pl.* results I.Pars 562. [OF *engen(d)reure*]

engyn *n.* **1.** intelligence G.SN 339, I.Pars 453, TC 2.565, ingenuity 3.274. **2.** contrivance F.Sq 184, machine HF 1934. [OF]

engyned *p.p.* tortured, racked B.NP 4250. [OF *enginier*]

engreggen *pr. pl.* burden I.Pars 979. [OF *engregier*]

enhabite(n *v.* **1.** dwell Bo 1. p5. 24/35, 2. p7. 45/65, (fig.) 3. p10. 28/39, m10. 3. **2.** *hen* ~d are settled Bo 2. p7. 36/51. **3.** *p.p.* **enhabit** *is* is devoted TC 4.443. [OF *enhabiter*]

enhaunce(n *v.* **1.** raise, elevate ((in) rank, status, power) A.Kn 1434, B.Mel 2291,

E.Mch 1374, Bo 3. m9. 23/32; strengthen I.Pars 730; ~ *up* support, comfort Bo 2. m1. 6/9 (L *subleuat*). **2.** puff up B.Mk 3773, I.Pars 614. **3.** (astrol.) raise: **enhaused** *p.p.* Astr 2.26.23 *var*/34. [AN *anhauncer*, OF *enhaucier*]

enhaunsing/-hausing *vbl. n.* elevation Astr 2.39.17 *var*/23.

enhorte *v.* encourage, urge A.Kn 2851, LGW 1440. [OF *enorter*, L *inhortāri*]

enjoyne *v.* impose (something on someone, with dat. of pers.) B.Mel 2939, 3041, I.Pars 105, 997. [OF *enjoi(g)n-*, stem of *enjoindre*]

enlaceth *pr. 3 sg. refl.* binds himself Bo 1. m4. 15/21. **enlaced** *p.p.* involved, beset Bo 3. p8. 4/5, 5. p1. 5/6. [OF *enlacier*]

enlumine *v.* **1.** illuminate, embellish ABC 73; (fig.) make illustrious E.Cl 33, TC 5.548. **2.** enlighten I.Pars 244. **3.** *p.p.* coloured RR 1695. [OF *enluminer*]

enluting *vbl. n.* sealing (a vessel) with clay G.CY 766. [from v. from L *lutāre* daub, plaster]

enmitee *n.* **1.** hostility B.Mel 2374, Mars 236. **2.** unfavourable, baleful influence Astr 2.4.24/38. [OF *enemitié*]

enoynte/a- *v.* anoint RR 1057. **enoynte** *pa.* I.Pars 502 *var.* **enoynt** *p.p.* A.Prol 199, A.Kn 2961. [OF *enoint*, p.p. of *enoindre*]

enp- *see* **emp-.**

enpresse *see* **impresse.**

enquere(n *v.* **1.** *intr.* inquire, ask A.Mil 3166, E.Cl 769, TC 5.1538; investigate B.ML 629, D.WB 316. **2.** *tr.* seek, find out E.Mch 1543, Bo 5. p3. 31/43, TC 1.123. [OF *enquerer*]

enqueryng *vbl. n.* investigation B.ML 888.

ensample *n.* **1.** illustrative story, *exemplum* B.Mk 3188, B.NP 4296, B.ML 78, C.Pard 435, E.Mch 1470, H.Mcp 309, TC 1.760, LGW 1258; illustration A.Kn 1953, 2039, 2842; parallel, analogy D.WB 90, I.Pars 363; *by* ~ by analogy Bo 1. m3. 3/4, RR 1181; *for* ~ by way of illustrating Astr 2.25.18/26; ~ *whi* here is a parallel case TC 1.1002. **2.** model, exemplar, pattern G.SN 93, I.Pars 520, TC 5.1590; typical instance LGW 2560; ? symbol G.SN 105; *yive(n* ~ set an example A.Prol 496, 505, B.Mel 2692; *take(n* ~ *of* copy A.Prol 568, D.Fri 1580, learn TC 1.232, *syn yow make this* ~ *of me* if you take me as an argument TC 3.872, *cheef* ~ perfection BD 911, *by* ~ by acting as a model B.Mel 2223. **3.** example, in ~ *as thus* Astr 2.45.6/8. [AN]

ensaumpler *n.* in *of thy* ~ according to your archetype Bo 3. m9. 11/15 (L *exemplo*). [OF *essamplaire*]

enseigne *n.* flag, standard RR 1200. [OF]

enseled *p.p.* ratified TC 4.559; sealed up, kept unopened 5.151. [from OF *enseeler*]

enspire/in- *v.* inspire, enlighten G.CY 1470, TC 3.712; breathe forth, quicken A.Prol 6; move TC 4.187. [OF *enspirer*]

ensure(n *v.* (with pron. obj.) assure, promise HF 2098, Ven 15 *var*; *intr.* give assurance C.Phs 143. Cf. **assure.** [AN *enseurer*]

entaile *n.* ornamentation RR 1081; shape, fashion 162. [OF]

entaile *v.* carve RR 140, 609. [OF *entaillier*]

entalenten *pr. pl.* stimulate, affect Bo 5. p5. 4/5. [OF *entalenter*]

entame v. open (wound) ABC 79. [OF *entamer*]

enteccheth v. afflicts Bo 4. p3. 53/75. **entecched** p.p. infected Bo 4. p3. 47/67, 48/68; endowed, gifted TC 5.832. [OF *entechier*]

entencioun 1. intention, aim, purpose C.Pard 408, E.Cl 703, Bo 3. p11. 62/85, 5. p1. 60/86, TC 1.683, *in hir* ~ as far as their aim is concerned TC 2.258; design TC 1.211; *good* ~ I.Pars 644, TC 1.52, 2.295; *yvel* ~ C.Pard 408. 2. desire, inclination, bent Bo 3. p7. 11/15, p12. 69/90, 4. p2. 103/137, 104/138, 5. m4. 25/37. 3. opinion B.Mel 2982, G.CY 1443, interpretation HF 93. 4. ? operation Bo 3. p11. 113/155. 5. ? attention TC 1.52. [OF]

entendement n. intellect TC 4.1696; comprehension, grasp HF 983. [OF]

entende(n v. 1. intend E.Mch 1791, Bo 4. p1. 5/6, TC 5.469, 478. 2. give heed, apply onself B.Mk 3498, D.Fri 1478, F.Fkl 1097; strive D.WB 1114; ~ (*to*) attend (to), be occupied (with) D.WB 275, TC 3.424, LGW 1155; incline TC 2.853, RR 82; *after a wight* ~*th* according to how a man inclines TC 3.27. 3. perceive, expect TC 4.1649. 4. ~ *to* attend to, notice Bo 1. p2. 2/3, listen to TC 4.893. 5. attend, act as servant E.Mch 1900. [OF *entendre*]

entent(e n. 1. intention, aim A.Kn 1000, B.ML 40, 147, B.Mel 2339, TC 1.738; state of mind G.SN 363; *in (ful/so) good* ~ with good will, kindly A.Kn 958, B.Th 1902, TC 3.1188, LGW 1149, with good intentions B.NP 4176, faithfully TC 4.853, willingly B.ML 824, TC 1.935; *with humble* ~ humbly E.Cl 186, *in hool* ~ completely 861; *in* ~ *to* with the purpose of I.Pars 1006; *to swich* ~ to the end (that) B.Mel 2307; *yvel/wikke(d* ~ A.Mil 3173, B.NP 4613, I.Pars 422. 2. plan, design E.Cl 517, 762, Bo 4. p6. 245/336, TC 5. 1305; *served his* ~ carried out his plan F.Sq 521. 3. desire E.Cl 189, I.Pars 408; ambition B.Mk 3835; attention I.Pars 829; *pl.* endeavours Bo 1. p1. 46/64. *do(o)n (al) (one's)* ~ do one's utmost G.SN 6, H.Mcp 164, BD 752, Anel 28, HF 2132; *sette(n (one's)* ~ (*to*) concern oneself with D.Fri 1374, D.Sum 1822, I.Pars 314, 932, fix one's heart (*on*) B.Pri 1740. 4. mind F.Fkl 1178, ? TC 2.524; spirit B.Mel 3061; *seye(n* . . ~ speak (one's) mind D.Sum 1733, TC 4.173; reason B.ML 942; opinion TC 2.1446. 5. meaning B.Mel 2268, TC 5.150; *so good* ~ such virtuous meaning TC 2.878; *as to commune* ~ in plain language F.Sq 107. 6. occupation Bo 4. p4. 193/268. [OF]

ententif adj. 1. eager E.Mch 1288, I.Pars 781, Bo 2. p2. 13/18, HF 1120. 2. attentive (person) Bo 3. p1. 15/20; ~ *to* (something) RR 339, 436, ~ *about* concerned, occupied with Bo 1. p3. 53/74; ~ *to* (do something) diligent (in doing) Bo 2. p1. 4/6, TC 2.838, RR 685, 1156. 3. diligent (action) B.Mel 2205, 2463. [OF]

ententifly adv. diligently TC 1.332, HF 616; attentively Bo 3. p12. 62/81. [from prec.]

entysinge vbl. n. enticement, allurement I.Pars 353, 520. [from v. from OF *enticier*]

entraille n. bowels B.Pri 1763, inside E.Cl 1188; *pl.* entrails Bo 3. p8. 31/44, inner parts Bo 5. m2. 4/5. [OF]

entrechaunge v. 1. transpose Bo 3. p2. 30/45, 5. p6. 186/262, TC 4.1043. 2. exchange TC 3.1368/1354. [OF *entrecha(u)ng(i)er*]

entrechaungeable adj. mutual, reciprocal Bo 4. p6. 103/149, m6. 13/19. [from prec.]

entrechaunged ppl. adj. confused Bo 5. m4. 24/35. [from v.]

entrechaungynge vbl. n. 1. transposition, reversal Bo 1. m5. 24/35. 2. exchange Bo 4. m4. 10/14.

entrechaungynge ppl. adj. mingling Bo 5. m1. 8/11. [from v.]

entrecomune(n v. ~ *yfere* have dealings with one another TC 4.1354. [AN *entrecomuner*]

entrecomuning(e n. ~ *of marchaundise* commerce Bo 2. p7. 38/55. [from prec.]

entredited p.p. prohibited from use I.Pars 965. [from OF *entredit*, p.p. of *entredire*]

entre(e n. 1. entrance A.Kn 1983, A.Rv 4243, HF 1945; (fig.) open way B.Mel 2229 var; beginning, access Bo 1. p6. 55/70 (L *aditus*). 2. threshold or ? cellar Bo 2. p2. 54/74 (L *limine*). 3. ? record *myn* ~ *that is* . . *myn informacioun* Bo 2. p1. 22/30 [L has *aditus*, usu. said to be confused with *adytum* 'sanctuary', ? secret knowledge']. [OF]

entrelaced ppl. adj. entangled Bo 3. p12. 118/157. [from OF *entrelacier*]

entremedled p.p. mixed, interspersed Bo 2. p6. 70/99, HF 2124, RR 906. [AN *entremedler*]

entremes n. interval PF 665. [OF]

entremette(n v. 1. *refl.* meddle D.WB 834, B.Mel 2731, ~ *of* meddle with B.Mel 2732, Bo 3. p12. 95/130. 2. **entremete** (*of*) imper. sg. concern yourself (with) TC 1.1026. [OF *entremetre*]

entreparten v. share TC 1.592. [OF *entrepartir*]

entreteden pa. pl. treated of, discussed B.Mel 2466 var. [OF *entraiter*]

entryke(n v. entangle, ensnare PF 403, RR 1642. [OF *entrigué*, L *intricāre*]

entring(e vbl. n. act of entering Bo 2. p6. 28/40; place of entrance Astr 1.6.8/11; entrance B.Mel 2229 var.

entune(n v. sing A.Prol 123, TC 4.4. [cf. OF *entoner*, and *tune*, var. of *tone* arising in 14th cent.]

entunes/-tewnes n. pl. melodies BD 309. [from prec.]

envenyme v. impregnate with poison B.Mk 3314, RR 979; spoil D.WB 474. [OF *envenimer*]

enveniminge vbl. n. poisoning E.Mch 2060, I.Pars 854.

envye n. 1. envy, resentment B.ML 1138, Bo 1. p3. 12/16 (L *inuidia*), LGW 358, Astr prol 46/64; envy as one of the 'deadly sins' I.Pars 484, etc., TC 3.1805, FormA 53; *have* ~ (*of*) envy, resent A.Kn 907, D.WB 95, G.CY 1372, TC 5.756, LGW 1409. 2. enmity, hostility, malice A.Kn 2732, TC 5.1479, HF 1476. 3. desire RR 1653. [OF]

envie v.[1] feel ill-will towards, resent D.WB 142, TC 5.1789. [OF *envier* from ML *invidiāre*]

envie(n v.² strive, contend BD 173, 406, HF 1231. [OF *envier* from L *invitāre*]

envyned p.p. provided with wine A.Prol 342. [OF *enviner*]

environ adv. in *acompas* ~ all around LGW 300. [OF]

environe(n v. **1.** encircle Bo 2. p7. 29/42, 3. p5. 26/36, RR 526. **2.** encompass Bo 3. m9. 21/30, comprehend 29/40, 5. p4. 145/208. **3.** endow Bo 2. p2. 15/21. [OF *environner*]

enviro(u)ning(e vbl. n. circle, circumference Bo 2. p7. 17/24, 3. p12. 121/162; roundness 5. p4. 106/152, encircling form 115/165. [from prec.]

envoluped p.p. involved, enwrapped C.Pard 942. [OF *envoluper*]

episicle n. small circle, the centre of which moves along the circumference of a larger one Astr. 2.35.18/25. [OF]

equacio(u)n n. making into equal parts Astr. 1.23/21.3/94; ~ *of houses* (astrol.) partition of the sphere into 'houses' Astr 2.36, 37 rubr., etc., sim. F.Fkl 1279 (or ? allowances for minor motions). [OF]

equal adj. identical in amount or extent I.Pars 9; *houres* ~s Astr 1.16.10/13–14 etc. (In non-technical use the word is **egal.**) [L *aequalis*]

equinoxial n. celestial equator B.NP 4046, Astr 1.16.6/8, 17.12/30, etc. [OF]

equinoxies n. pl. equinoxes Astr 1.17.19/25. [OF]

equitee n. **1.** justice, law C.Phs 181, Bo 4. p6. 158/230; *don* ~ administer justice Bo 4. m6. 28/42. **2.** E.Cl 439, impartiality LGW 398. [OF]

er adv. before, previously A.Mil 3789, G.CY 1273, 1328, TC 3.763, 5.992 var. [OE *ǣr*]

er conj. before A.Prol 255, A.Kn 1040, B.Sh 1251, C.Phs 35, F.Sq 494, lest B.ML 119; ~ *that* A.Prol 36, A.Kn 2688, B.Mk 3748, G.CY 899 var, ABC 16; ~ *than* G.CY 899 var; rather than C.Phs 249, F.Fkl 1322. [OE *ǣr þǣm* (*þe*)]

er prep. before B.Mk 3206, C.Pard 892, RR 120, ~ *this* B.NP 3987, E.Cl 624, ~ *now* A.Rv 4170, D.Fri 1619, ~ *tho* before then LGW 1062, ~ *nightes ten* before the passing of ten nights TC 4.1685 var, ~ *that half a furlong-wey of space* before you could walk 100 yards, i.e. about two and a half minutes had passed D.Sum 1692, ~ *that half an hour/After his deeth* less than half an hour after his death 1856–7. [from adv.]

erand(e n. message BD 134, mission TC 2.72 (with **do(o)(n).** [OE *ǣrende*]

erbe see **herbe.**

erchedeken n. archdeacon A.Prol 655, D.Fri 1300. [OE *erċediacon*]

ere n.¹ ear D.WB 636, PF 519, TC 1.725, *at* ~ in her ear 106. **eres** pl. A.Prol 556, A.Kn 1522, TC 2.1022. [OE *ēare*]

ere n.² ear of corn Bo 3. m1. 3/4, LGW 76. [OE *ēar*]

ere(n v. plough A.Kn 886, Bo 3. m3. 4/6, HF 485. [OE *erian*]

erl n. earl, count A.Kn 2182, B.Mk 3597. [OE *eorl*, sense infl. by ON *jarl*]

erly adv. early A.Prol 33, B.NP 4206; soon A.Prol 809; ~ *and late* continuously A.Co 4401, C.Pard 730. [OE *ǣrlīċe*]

erme v. grieve C.Pard 312, BD 80*em*. [OA *erman*]

Ermyn n. Armenian B.Mk 3528. [from L *Armēnius*]

ernest n. **1.** seriousness A.Mil 3390; *in* ~ seriously B.ML 185, genuinely D.Fri 1627, TC 2.1529; *in* ~ *greet* very seriously TC 2.1703, *for* ~ *or/ne for game* in any event TC 4.1465, LGW 2703, in any circumstances E.Cl 609, whatever the . reason E.Cl 733; *bitwixe(n* ~ *and game/game and* ~ half in jest E.Mch 1594, TC 3.254, *in* ~ *or in pley* seriously or in jest A.Kn 1125. **2.** strong feeling, passion TC 2.452, LGW 1287. **3.** serious matter G.CY 710. [OE *eornust*]

ernestful adj. serious E.Cl 1175, TC 2.1727. [from prec.]

erratik adj. ~ *sterres* wandering stars, planets TC 5.1812. [OF *erratique*]

erraunt adj. in *poune* ~ pawn in chess that mates the king BD 661; *theef* ~ outlaw H.Mcp 224. [OF]

erre(n v. **1.** make a mistake, go wrong B.Mel 2215, 2430 etc., Bo 3. p2. 62/89; ~ *ayeins a law* contravene a law TC 1.1003; *but if that bokes* ~ unless books are misleading TC 3.1774. **2.** wander TC 4.302; ~ *fro* deviate from Astr 2.3.49/72. [OF *errer*]

errour n.¹ **1.** mistaken belief, misunderstanding Bo 1. p3. 35/48, 50/70, p4. 165/231; heresy TC 1.1008, mistake 4.993; mistake of fact Astr. 2.5.8/11; ? ignorance TC 4.200. **2.** sin ABC 157, *falleth in* ~ falls into sin 67, *confounded in* ~ overwhelmed by sin 5. **3.** fickleness, instability Fort 4. [OF]

errour n.² perplexity, confusion PF 146, 156, ? Scog 7. [OF *ir(r)our* confused with prec.]

ers n. arse, behind A.Mil 3734, 3755, D.Sum 1690, 1694. [OE *ærs*]

erst adj. sup. first: *thanne/now at* ~ then/now for the first time, only then/now B.Th 1884, E.Cl 985, G.SN 151, 264, TC 1.842, LGW 2108. [OE *æt ǣrestan*]

erst adv., sup. in sense of comp. before, earlier A.Prol 776, I.Pars 334, ABC 87, TC 3.1683, *never* ~ B.NP 4471, D.Sum 2220, E.Cl 144, 336, F.Fkl 981, I.Pars 766. conj. in ~ *than* A.Kn 1566, ~ *er* C.Pard 662. [OE *ǣrest*]

erthe n. **1.** earth as one of the four elements A.Kn 1246, C.Pard 519, pl. Bo 4. m1. 3/4. **2.** land (opp. sea) I.Pars 174, ABC 50, Bo 2. m8. 9/13, TC 3.8, pl. Bo 2. m8. 8/12. **3.** ground I.Pars 219, 345, Bo 1. p1. 53/73, LGW 125, RR 59, pl. Bo 5. m5. 13/18; *the fruit of the* ~ I.Pars 220; soil, clay, E.Cl 681, G.CY 791, LGW 286, *under* ~ below ground D.WB 1065. **4.** world A.Kn 1896, TC 4.1049, pl. Bo 3. p6. 19/26; (opp. universe) Bo 2. m7. 4/5, Astr 1.18.7/10, 2.7.12/17. **5.** this life (opp. heaven and hell) E.Mch 1639, 1647, PF 33, Bo 2. p7. 107/154, HF 918. [OE *eorþe*]

erthely adj. worldly, fleshly G.SN 74, Bo 3. m1. 10/14, Bo 4. m7. 49/71; worldly, secular (opp. heavenly) I.Pars 598, Bo 2. p7. 108/155, LGW 985; *Paradys* ~ heaven on earth RR 648. [OE *eorþlīċ*]

escape(n v. escape: **1.** gain liberty; *from* A.Kn 1270, *out of* H.Mcp 173, Ven 50, *forth out of* LGW 2320; issue inadvertently (tears) Scog 10; (fig., of time) slip away TC 3.1412/1398, *nis . . ~d* is not lacking Bo 5. p6. 30/43. **2.** get off safely (from death, danger, etc.) B.Mk 3922, I.Pars 168, 227, HF 413, LGW 815, MercB 27; (fig.) ~ *him* avoid his invitation TC 3.557. **3.** recover B.Mel 2172; ? survive Bo 1. p2. 5/6 (L *euaseras*). [ONF *escaper*]

eschaufe(n *v.* **1.** grow hot Bo 1. m6. 1/2, 3. p4. 47/69. **2.** make hot I.Pars 546, Bo 1. m5. 20/28. **3.** become excited Bo 5. m3. 12/18, become angry I.Pars 657; ? rail angrily Bo 1. p5. 43/62. [OF *eschaufer*]

eschaufing(e *vbl. n.* heating I.Pars 537; passionate excitement 916.

eschaunge *n.* exchange TC 4. 146, 158, *in ~* in money changing A.Prol 278. [AN]

eschew/eschu *adj.* averse E.Mch 1812, I.Pars 971. [OF *eschieu*]

eschewe(n/eschue(n *v.* **1.** avoid, shun, keep clear of (things) B.Mel 2362, G.SN 4, I.Pars 632; (person) TC 2.1255; try to avoid B.Mel 2511, Bo 3. p11. 64/88; (with infin.) TC 2.1018. **2.** escape A.Kn 3043, B.NP 4528, Bo 3. p5. 21/29, 46/64, TC 4.1078. **3.** abstain from E.Mch 1451, I.Pars 382, Bo 5. p6. 216/304, TC 2.696. **4.** ? prevent Bo 3. m10. 17/25. [OF *eschiver*]

eschewinge *vbl. n.* avoidance I.Pars 464, PF 140.

ese *n.* **1.** comfort, prosperity B.NP 3962, TC 2.1659, 5.1376, success TC 3.19; *at ~* comfortable, content B.NP 4449, D.Sum 2101, TC 2.750, 3.611, 1279, happy 1406/1392, successful TC 1.43; *lyth in your ~ is convenient* for you B.Sh 1481. **2.** pleasure B.NP 4487, D.WB 127, I.Pars 835, joy G.CY 746, TC 3.1304; *don ~* (with dat.) gratify TC 3.633, 5.116, entertain A.Prol 768. **3.** benefit, advantage I.Pars 609, PF 384, TC 4.86; *an ~* the best course E. Mch 2115. **4.** relief TC 4.726; *don ~* bring relief E.Cl 664, E.Mch 1981, H.Mcp 25, TC 3.109; *for hertes ~ of you* to comfort you TC 5.1740. **5.** rest A.Rv 4119, *take (one's) ~* A.Kn 969, LGW 1112; peace E.Cl 434, *at ~ of herte* with peace of mind TC 4. 1351; leisure E.Cl 217. I.Pars 951. **6.** ease, in *with to greet an ~* too easily TC 1.28. [AN *ese*, OF *eise*, *aise*]

esement *n.* redress A.Rv 4179, 4186. [OF *aisement*]

ese(n *v.* **1.** entertain A.Prol 29, A.Kn 2194, please PF 480, help, benefit TC 2.1400, 3.486. **2.** relieve (someone) TC 3.1790; ease (suffering) TC 3.950, ~ (one's) herte soothe feelings BD 556, I.+W 1704; *hen ~d* be relieved from suffering A.Kn 2670, TC 1.447, 943, be made happy 1.249, comforted 3.445 *var.* **eseth** *imper. pl.* 3. 197. [OF *aaisier*]

esy *adj.* easy, not difficult I.Pars 1042; enjoyable E.Mch 1264, TC 3.1363/1349; gentle PF 382, peaceable BD 1008, tractable A.Prol 223, B.Mel 3046, tractable Bo 1. p5. 52/76, TC 1.1090; suitable LGW 1116; moderate A.Prol 441, G.CY 768; *an ~ pas* at a slow pace TC 2.620, LGW 284, in graceful steps LGW G. 200. **esier** *comp.* more tolerable B.Mel 2690. [OF *aaisié*, *aisé*]

esily *adv.* without difficulty F.Sq 115, I.Pars 1041; comfortably A.Prol 469, E.Cl 423; slowly TC 1.317, 2.988, HF 1675; gently A.Mil 3764, kindly TC 3.156; ~ *a pas* at a slow pace F.Sq 388. [from prec.]

espace *n.* space of time B.Mel 2219; see **space.** [OF]

especes *n. pl.* kinds I.Pars 448. Cf. **spece.** [OF]

especial *adj.* **1.** intimate, esteemed B.Mel 2356; distinctive I.Pars 893. **2.** *in ~* chiefly, above all Truth 25; to detail B.Mel 2424. [OF]

espiaille *n.* spying B.Mel 2509; spies D.Fri 1323. [OF]

espye *n.* spy B.Mel 2216, C.Pard 755, TC 2.1112. [OF]

espye(n/a- v. **1.** *tr.* descry A.Rv 4302, E.Cl 235, TC 1.193, 2.649, (with cl.) HF 1689, Anel 64; notice B.NP 4472, RR 795; *intr.* A.Rv 4195. **2.** discover B.Sh 1374, B.Mk 3258, E.Mch 1413, TC 3.573; (with cl.) B.Pri 1781, TC 2.1507, HF 944; ~ *me* discover my identity LGW 2044; detect B.NP 4513, (fraud) Anel 159; reveal Mars 6; ~ *him a lover* discover him to be a lover LGW 1537. **3.** seek to discover B.Th 1989, E.Mch 1257; *tyme aright/wel ~* find the right time TC 5.556, LGW 1349. **4.** spy on B.NP 4478, D.WB 398, G.CY 1138, attack from ambush (fig.) BD 836; survey (country) LGW 966. [AN *espier*]

espying *vbl. n.* spying Ven 34.

espiritue(e)l/spiritue(e)l *adj.* spiritual I.Pars 455, 516, 547, RR 650, 672; in the Church I.Pars 784. **espirituels** *pl.* (after n.) I.Pars 79, 312, sacred 784. [OF *(e)spirituel*]

essoyne *n.* excuse I.Pars 164. [OF]

esta(a)t *n.* state, condition A.Prol 716, E.Cl 610, I.Pars 325, Bo 1. m5. 21/30 (L *stationis*), TC 2.465, LGW 125, normal state D.Fri 1460, **sta(a)t** A.Prol 572; (astrol.) position E.Mch 1969; rank, social position A.Prol 522, A.Kn 956, A.Mil 3229, B.Mk 3359, TC 2.881; due precedence E.Cl 958; division of society E.Mch 1322; class E.Cl 123, G.CY 1388, H.Mcp 217, TC 5.1749; rank, dignity Pity 41, TC 1.287; display, pomp LGW 1036; office D.Sum 2018. [OF *estat*]

establisse(n v. **1.** ordain, settle by enactment or agreement I.Pars 229, 921, Bo 1. p5. 19/27, 2. m3. 17/21, 5. m3. 3/4; ~ *upon the poeple* imposed upon the people Bo 1. p4. 65/90. **2.** prove Bo 3. p2. 55/79, p10. 42/59. **3.** fix permanently Bo 4. p6. 43/61. [OF *establiss-* from *establir*]

estatlich/-ly *adj.* stately, dignified A.Prol 140, 281, TC 5.823, **statly** LGW 1371; befitting one's rank B.Mk 3902. [from *esta(a)t*]

estimacioun *n.* assessment Bo 2. p5. 105/147, 3. p4. 68/98; understanding, judgement Bo 4. p4. 46/62. [OF]

estorial *see* **historial.**

estraunge *adj.* distant TC 1.1084. Cf. **straunge.** [OF]

Estre *n.* Easter I.Pars 552. [OE *ēastre*]

estres *n. pl.* interior A.Kn 1971, apartment A.Rv 4295, LGW 1715; recesses RR 1448*em.* [OF *estre* to be, confused with *estras* n.]

ete(n *v.* eat A.Kn 947, ~ *of* A.Kn 2048, C.Pard 322, I.Pars 326. **eet** *pa. sg.* A.Kn 2048, B.NP 4023, TC 5.1216. **ete(n** *pl.* BD

432, TC 2.1184, FormA 7. **ete(n** *p.p.*
A.Co 4351, C.Pard 355. [OE *etan, æt,
æton, eten*]
eterne *adj.* **1.** everlasting, perpetual A.Kn
1109, 1304, F.Fkl 865, ABC 56. **2.** *fro(m*
~ from eternity Bo 5. p2. 32/46, TC 4.978.
3. ~ *on lyve* everlastingly living, immortal
D.WB 5, E.Mch 1652, TC 5.1863. [OF]
ethe *adj.* easy TC 5.850. [OE *ēaþe*]
Ethiopen *n.* Ethiopian I.Pars 345. [OF]
evangyle *n.* gospel B.Mel 2269, RR 445,
pl. B.ML 666. [L *ēvangelium*]
evel/yvel *n.* (moral) evil B.Mel 2753, 2767,
Bo 3. p12. 112/149, 114/151, etc.; punishment B.Pri 1822; *mene non* ~ intend no
hurt TC 2.581, 3.1164; *take for/on* ~ take
amiss TC 4.606, 5.1625. [OE *yfel*]
evel/yvel *adj.* bad, wicked A.Mil 3173,
I.Pars 92; dishonourable LGW 2135,
faulty D.WB 247; ~ *thedom* B.Sh 1595, ~
thrift HF 1786 ill success; *with ful* ~ *wil*
reluctantly TC 5.1637; ~ *fare* misfortune
TC 2.1001. [OE *yfel*]
evel(e/yvel(e *adv.* badly G.CY 1225, BD
1204, basely Bo 5. m5. 14/20 (L *male*);
wickedly B.Mel 2718, *me list ..* ~ I am
ill-disposed (to) A.Kn 1127, BD 239; ~
apayd ill-pleased D.Fri 1282, dissatisfied
G.CY 1049, angry E.Mch 1565, 2392, Anel
123; *fare(n* ~ endure suffering BD 501, TC
5.238, get on badly 1.626; *sit* ~ is not
fitting E.Cl 460; ~ *biset* wretchedly cir-
cumstanced A.Mil 3715; ~ *biseye* ill-
looking E.Cl 965; ~ *avysed* ill-considered
H.Mcp 335. [OE *yfele*]
eve(n *n.* evening, twilight D.WB 332, 750,
TC 5.1137, HF 4; *bothe* ~ *and morwe* all
day long, constantly A.Kn 2821, D.WB
152, TC 5.725, *on* ~ *and (a)morwe* E.Mch
1214, TC 1.487; *er that it were* ~ within
a day B.ML 573, G.SN 375; *now sone at* ~
? this very evening LGW 1321. [OE
æfen/ēfen]
even *adj.* **1.** equal B.Mel 2672, BD 1289,
PF 149, Bo 2. m7. 12/17, Astr 1.21.57/80,
2.37.8/11; equally matched A.Kn 2588;
matching PF 381; impartial A.Kn 1864. **2.**
straight A.Mil 3316, Astr 2.38.4/5; level
3/4. **3.** calm E.Cl 811, Bo 2. p1. 67/92, p4.
119/164. **4.** average A.Prol 83. [OE *efen*]
even(e *adv.* **1.** exactly (of time) BD 198,
275; (of position) BD 451, HF 714, Astr
2.17. 17/24, 23. 6/9; (of number) BD 441;
~ *atte fulle* exactly full F.Fkl 1069; ~
joynant to immediately adjoining A.Kn
1060. **2.** evenly, calmly A.Kn 1523. **3.**
equally D.Sum 2249, Astr 1.17.32/43.
4. straight Astr 2.29.15/21. **5.** (emph.)
indeed, right, just BD 120, 458, ? B.ML
1143. [OE *efne/efen*]
evene-cristen *n.* fellow-Christian, neighbour I.Pars 395, 608, 805. [**even**+**cristen**]
even(e)liche *adv.* equally Bo 1. p5. 44/64,
4. p2. 87/116, [OE *efenlīċe*]
even(e)lyk(e *adj.* the same, identical Bo 3.
m9. 23/32; equal 5. p2. 15/22, p6. 50/71.
[OE *efenlīċ*]
evensong *n.* evening service, vespers
E.Mch 1966; (transf.) evening words A.Prol
830. [OF *æfensáng*]
eventyde *n.* (or as two words) evening LGW
770 *var*; *agayn the* ~ towards evening
B.NP 4262; cf. **tyd**. [OE *æfentīd*]

ever *adv.* **1.** always, continually A.Prol 622,
B.ML 866, TC 5. 1861; ~ *in oon* continually A.Kn 1771, E.Cl 677, Pity 9, TC
5.451, throughout Astr 2.2.8/11. ~ *in oon
ylike* constantly, consistently E.Cl 602.
2. always, (for)ever B.Mel 3025, TC 5.756,
Astr 2.3.40/59, 43/64; ~ *in oon* A.Rv 3880.
3. at any time A.Kn 1212, C.Phs 227,
D.WB 614, E.Cl 627. **4.** (intensifying) ~
sith(e continually since A.Rv 3893, TC
3.244, ~ *the hyer .. the more* in proportion
the higher the more C.Pard 597, ~ *the
gretter merit* particularly great merit I.Pars
916; *wepen* ~ *lenger the more* to weep progressively more bitterly B.Mel 2165, sim.
F.Sq 404, F.Fkl 1462, *the wers* A.Rv 3872,
~ *the lenger loved .. tenderly* loved progressively more tenderly Anel 129; *as fast/
soon/wel as* ~ .. as fast (etc.) as .. possibly
A.Kn 1475, B.Sh 1607, A.Co 4342; (in
oaths) *as* ~ *mo(o)t(e I* as I hope to A.Prol
832, A.Rv 4177, E.Cl 172, TC 2.125 (cf.
120). **5.** (giving indef. sense) *wher that* ~
wherever G.CY 733, *whan that* ~ whenever D.WB 45; (added to indef. prons. and
advs.) *who so* ~ Bo 3. p7. 7/10, *what so* ~
Bo 1. m5. 36/50, *wher so* ~ Bo 2. p5. 124/
175, *whoso that* ~ Bo 4. p2. 62/81. [OE *æfre*]
everich *pron.* **1.** each one A.Kn 2096,
B.ML 626, PF 401, RR 1106; (often with
of) A.Kn 1848, I.Pars 261, ~ *of hem* each
one of them B.ML 1004, I.Pars 957, LGW
2381, Astr 1.8.7/10. **2.** every one C.Pard
931, Bo 5. p2. 33/46, ~ *of hem* all of them
Bo 4. m4. 7/11, TC 5.170, FormA 48. [OE
æfre ælċ/*ylċ]
everich/every *adj.* every, each A.Prol 241,
Bo 1. p1. 27/38, TC 4.1518, LGW 1608; ~
maner wight all (kinds of) men A.Kn 1875,
TC 1.844, HF 509, *in* ~ (*maner*) *wyse* in all
respects B.Sh 1435, E.Cl 695; ~ *other day*
each alternate day TC 2.1166, ~ *thridde
yeer* one year in three LGW 1932; ~ *a word*
every word A.Prol 733, *quyten* ~ *grot* pay
back completely D.Fri 1292. [as prec.]
evericho(o)n *pron.* everyone, each A.Prol
31, B.ML 330, D.Sum 1758, TC 1.154,
RR 944. [**everich**+**o(o)n**]
everydeel *see* **deel**.
evermo *adv.* **1.** continually D.WB 834,
E.Mch 2359, TC 4.1110. **2.** perpetually,
always A.Kn 1229, 3072, A.Rv 3961,
eternally B.ML 1076, HF 1403. **3.** *for* ~
constantly E.Cl 754, for ever C.Phs 81,
TC 3.1426. [OE *æfre mā*]
evermo(o)re *adv.* **1.** continually A.Prol 67,
B.Sh 1427, B.Mel 2509, F.Sq 429, ~ *in
oon* E.Mch 2086; ~ *yliche* constantly the
same F.Sq 20. **2.** always A.Kn 1406,
for ~ A.Kn 1032, B.Mel 2308, BD 687;
constantly Astr 2.26.12/16, 28.14/21, on
every occasion 39.8/11 (all *var*). [**ever**+
mo(o)re]
eve-sterre *n.* the evening star Bo 1. m5. 8/11,
2. m8. 5/8. [OE *æfen-steorra*]
evidences *n. pl.* indications Astr prol2. [OF]
evidently *adv.* obviously Bo 3. m11. 18/25,
plainly 4. p2. 156/213, unmistakably Astr
2.23 rubr. [from adj., OF *évident*]
exaltacioun *n.* position of planet in the
zodiac where it was thought to exert its
greatest influence D.WB 702, E.Mch 2224,
F.Sq 49, I.Pars 10. [OF]

exaltat adj. (astrol.) in position of greatest influence D.WB 704. [L exaltātum]

exametron n. hexameter B.Mk 3169. [Gr hexametron (adj. neut.)]

examine v. consider critically B.Mel 2310, 2341, Bo 3. m11. 12/16. **examineth** imper. pl. B.Mel 2456. [OF examiner]

examininge vbl. n. scrutiny, appraisal B.Mel 2392.

excellence n. 1. superiority, surpassing qualities B.Mel 3011, E.Cl 408, G.SN 112, perfection TC 3.1274, ful riche of ~ nobly endowed A.Prol 311, in his ~ at his peak A.Kn 3048; in so greet ~ ? in such beauty C.Phs 10. 2. kindness, doon .. this ~ do this kindness LGW 2049. 3. high position or reputation Bo 1. p4. 189/265. 4. (address) your .. ~ your honour Pity 59. [OF]

excepcioun n. exception LGW 2653; without ~ of bigamye without reservation on grounds of bigamy D.WB 86. [OF]

exces n. 1. intemperance, sin B.Mel 2715, 2717; overindulgence, gluttony C.Pard 514. 2. excessive provision I.Pars 445. 3. excess of feeling, despair TC 1.626. [OF]

excite(n 1. stir up G.CY 744, Bo 5. m4. 33/48; exhort D.Sum 1716; arouse Bo 3. m11. 24/33. 2. incite Bo 1. p4. 225/313. [OF exciter]

excitinge vbl. n. incitement I.Pars 973.

excusacioun n. excuse, plea I.Pars 164, LGW G. 362; false excuse I.Pars 680. [OF]

excuse(n v. 1. make excuses for E.Mch 1903, I.Pars 584, 796, E.Mch 2269; exonerate B.Mk 3317, TC 3.1025, 5.1097, HF 427, refl. B.Mel 2783, TC 3.810, LGW 403. 2. pardon A.Prol 651, D.Fri 1611, TC 3.1036; refl. beg pardon TC 2.12, Scog 36, beg to be excused (from doing something) TC 3. 561; thee ~ of let you off from H.Mcp 29; have ~d pardon B.Mk 3180, F.Sq 7, F.Fkl 718, TC 2.1079, have for ~ pardon Astr prol 30–1/42–3. [OF escuser]

execucioun n. performance Fort 65; putten in to ~ perform, carry out B.Mel 3043, TC 3.521, putten forth in ~ perform Bo 1. p4. 29–30/40–1; doon ~ perform TC 5.4, carry out the law D.Fri 1301, E.Cl 522, inflict punishment H.Mcp 287. [OF]

executeth pr. 3 sg. carries out (what is destined) A.Kn 1664. **execut** p.p. TC 3.622. [OF executer]

executour n. carrier out, agent D.Sum 2010. [AN]

executrice n. (female) administrator, administering goddess TC 3.617. [AN]

exempt p.p. freed Bo 2. p7. 109/156. [OF]

exercen v. ~ any right exercise jurisdiction Bo 2. p6. 30/43. [OF exercer]

exercyse n. 1. physical activity B.NP 4029. 2. training, ?chastising E.Cl 1156. [OF exercice]

exercyse v. 1. put into practice A.Kn 1436, G.CY 750, carry out Bo 4. p6. 65/93. 2. train, chastise Bo 4. p4. 107/152, p7. 26/37. 3. exert I.Pars 689, Bo 4. p3. 75/108. [from prec.]

exercysinge vbl. n. training, ? chastising Bo 4. p6. 220/314, p7. 7/10.

exercitacioun n. practice Bo 4. p6. 186/270. [OF]

exil n. 1. banishment Bo 1. p4. 85/118,

putte(n in ~ send into banishment B.Me 3025, Bo 1. p5. 16/23. 2. place of banishment Bo 1. p5. 5/7, 2. p4. 78/108. [OF]

exyle v. banish A.Kn 1244, C.Phs 273; ~ fro(m A.Kn 1272, Bo 4. m1. 30/43; ~ upon his heed banish on pain of death A.Kn 1344; ~ of deprive of (by banishment) Bo 1. p6. 57/73; p.p. as adj. LSt 17. [OF exilier]

existence n.: in ~ in reality, in fact HF 266. [OF]

exorsisaciouns n. pl. calling up of spirits by magic HF 1263. [cf. ML exorcizāre]

expans adj. individual or in small numbers (of years numbering under 20: see Astr 2.44) F. Fkl 1275. [L expans-, p.p.]

experience n. 1. observing or undergoing A.Kn 3001, B.NP 4168, by ~ D.WB 468, HF 788, 878; old ~ what had been observed or undergone A.Kn 2445, be of old ~ B.Mel 2359. 2. knowledge gained by observing or undergoing something Bo 4. p6. 189/273, TC 3. 1283; to han ~ to have practical proof E.Cl 788. 3. observation, ocular proof Astr 2.1. 17/25, 3.25/35, by ~ by observation 51/75. [OF]

expert adj. 1. experienced: ~ in B.Mel 2353, ~ of D.WB 174, G.CY 1251. 2. learned, skilled (in): ~ of A.Prol 577, B.ML 4 va., ~ in TC 1.67, 2.1367. [OF]

exposicioun n. expounding, interpretation I.Pars 1043. [OF]

expounde(n/expoune v. interpret (dream, vision) B.Mk 3346, 3940, B.NP 4305, TC 5.1278, 1456; paraphrase B.Pri 1716, explain 1725, B.Mk 3398; give the meaning of G.SN 86. [OF espundre]

expres adj. explicit HF 2021; by ~ word specifically D.WB 61. [OF]

expres(se adv. 1. plainly, explicitly D.WB 719, 1169; ~ agayn directly opposed to C.Phs 182, I.Pars 587, 795, 798. 2. woot ~ know clearly D.WB 27. [L]

expresse v. 1. relate, tell, describe B.Pri 1666, C.Phs 105, G.CY 1286, 1305, Buk 5. 2. set forth in writing B.Mel 2975, C.Phs 170, TC 5.790. 3. ~ any word speak, articulate B.Pri 1675. [OF expresser]

expulsif adj. expellent A.Kn 2749. [OF]

extree n. axle Astr 1.14.1/2, 6/7. [OE eax + tre(e]

F

fable n. 1. story HD 52, Bo 3. p12. 97/133, m12. 43/60; fictional story I.Pars 31, 34. 2. falsehood, fiction C.Phs 155, D.Sum 1760, LGW 702, RR 2; withoute(n ~ truly F.Sq 180, RR 705; held it but ~ regarded it merely as fiction HF 1480; holde you in ~ detain you with idle talk RR 1439. [OF]

face n. 1. face, countenance A.Prol 199; (of sun, moon) TC 2.765, LGW 2504, surface Bo 2. p5. 42/60 (L facie); rampeth in my ~ rages with hostility against me B.Mk 3094; I (be)shrewe thy/his ~ I curse you/him D.WB 844, D.Sum 2227. 2. appearance Bo 1. p4. 9/13, p5. 25/37; at pryme ~ at first sight TC 3.919. 3. (astrol.) one of three parts of a zodiacal sign F.Sq 50, Astr 2.4.40/63, 43/66. [OF]

facound *adj.* eloquent PF 521, harmonious BD 926. [OF]

facound(e *n.* eloquence, fluency PF 558; way of speaking C.Phs 50. [OF]

fader *n.* **1.** father A.Rv 3943, B.ML 274; ancestor B.Mel 2293, C.Pard 505, I.Pars 516; source A.Kn 2469; **fadres** *pl.* originators B.ML 129, ~ *olde* men of old E.Cl 61. **2.** God the Father G.SN 208, I.Pars 1037; Christ E.Cl 557, *that* ~*s sone* Christ G.SN 326. **3.** *pl.* senators Bo 1. p4. 150/208. **fader** *gen.* A.Prol 781, A.Rv 4038, B.Mk 3121, 3374, TC 5.665; **fadres** B.ML 861, D.WB 301, G.SN 326, as *adj.* fatherly C.Phs 211. [OE *fæder*, gen. unchanged]

fadme *n. pl.* (with numerals) fathoms A.Kn 2916, BD 422; **fadome** RR 1393.· [OE *fæþm*]

fayerye *n.* **1.** magic, enchantment E.Mch 1743; piece of magic F.Sq 201. **2.** otherworld (of magic) B.Th 1992, 2004, E.Mch 2227, 2316, F.Sq 96. **3.** magic creatures D.WB 859, E.Mch 2039, *pl.* D.WB 872. [OF *faerie*]

failing(e *vbl. n.* diminution I.Pars 214; *for* ~ to prevent lack of success TC 1.928; *han* ~ end Bo 5. p6. 38/54 (L *defectum*).

fail(l)e *n.* in *withouten (any)* ~ for certain A.Kn 1644, G.CY 1163, TC 2.629, Pity 48, TC 4.1596, LGW 1092; *sauns* ~ B.ML 501, HF 188, 429. [OF]

fail(l)e(n *v.* **1.** *tr.* lack, do without A.Rv 3887, B.Mk 3652; (with infin.) TC 4.1313 *var.* **2.** *intr.* be lacking Bo 1. p6. 26/34, 4. p2. 18/25, 21/28, TC 1.764, HF 1098; (with dat. of indirect obj.) Bo 5. p4. 87/125, TC 3.523, (with *to*) I.Pars 80; ~ *of* be deficient, lacking in B.Sh 1438, Bo 4. p2. 113/153, p3. 24/35, 38/55. **3.** lose strength, become exhausted A.Kn 2798, A.Rv 3887, I.Pars 182, cease I.Pars 215, Bo 2. p4. 42/57, TC 4.273, wane PF 85, Bo 5. p6. 52/73; fade, prove ineffective G.SN 388, Fort 56; be unsuccessful HF 1615, ~ *of* fall away from Bo 5. p3. 148/212. **4.** disappoint B.Sh 1378, ABC 112, cheat B.Mel 2642. **5.** fail, fall short in performance: (with cl.) A.Kn 1610, (with infin.) E.Mch 1632, LGW 1646, (absol.) B.Sh 1605, *it wol nat* ~ it will certainly B.Pri 1766. **6.** miss (appointed time) TC 5.642; ~ *of* miss (time) B.Sh 1465, lose (way) Bo 1. p5. 7/10. [OF *faillir*]

fayn *adj.* glad, pleased B.Sh 1241, LGW 1137, eager E.Mch 2017; ~ *of* A.Kn 2437, B.ML 787, TC 5.425; **fawe** D.WB 220 (in rhyme). [OE *fægen, fagen*]

fayn *adv.* gladly, willingly B.ML 173; *wolde* ~ A.Prol 766, B.ML 222, E.Cl 873, TC 1.691. **fawe** anxiously TC 4.887. **fayner** *comp.* more gladly, eagerly CompL 83/77. [from prec.]

fair *adj.* **1.** fine, beautiful, good A.Prol 204, *comp.* 754, *sup.* B.Mk 3341; Bo 2. p5. 74/104; handsome B.Sh 1215, 1218, (separated from n.) A.Prol 165, (following n.) A.Kn 1941, B.NP 4409; shining A.Rv 3976, Astr 2.3.29/43; *foul or* ~ good or bad HF 767, LGW 1818. **2.** favourable A.Kn 1861, 1874, TC 1.907, 2.224; courteous B.Th 1905, 2022, D.WB 1137,

RR 669, 713; flattering LGW 2526. **3.** fine, clement D.Sum 2253, Bo 1. m7. 5/7, LGW 1483; *thurgh foul or* ~ in all weathers, or in all circumstances F.Sq 121. **4.** powerful, convincing B.Mel 2901, Astr 2.23.26/38. **5.** peaceable, ordered A.Kn 2988, 2991, Bo 2. m8. 14/21 (L *pulchris*), 3. m2. 6/9 (L *pulchra*). **6.** desirable, gratifying A.Prol 376, A.Kn 1523, D.WB 439. **7.** *as n.* beauty F.Sq 518; *were a* ~ ? would be a fine thing TC 3.850 (cf. *MED* fair(e). [OE *fæger*]

faire *adv.* **1.** well A.Prol 94, D.WB 1142, D.Sum 2286, I.Pars 68, TC 2.328 (ironic); neatly A.Mil 3210; *endyte* ~ compose skilfully B.NP 4397. **2.** beautifully, elegantly A.Prol 273, G.SN 132, RR 108, 565, 779, pleasingly A.Mil 3322, luxuriously F.Sq 613. **3.** justly A.Kn 2659, duly A.Mil 3568, HF 1050, ~ *and wel* A.Rv 4069, 4226, G.CY 1113, *wel and* ~ PF 594, fittingly HF 1539; ~ *and swythe* ? briefly PF 503; *ful* ~ *and wel* completely A.Prol 539, safely, ~ secretly A.Rv 4062. **4.** courteously A.Mil 3289, B.ML 731, D.WB 803, LGW 1502, RR 592; seemlily B.NP 4062; kindly D.WB 222, flatteringly I.Pars 644. **5.** softly, gently A.Kn 2697, G.SN 536, *take it* ~ take it quietly TC 5.347. **6.** successfully A.Mil 3743, luckily B.Th 2020; ~ *falle yow* see **falle(n.** [OE *fægre*]

faire *n.* market B.Sh 1515, D.WB 221; *nis but a* ~ is only a passing show TC 5.1840. [OF *feire*]

falding *n.* coarse woollen cloth, A.Prol 391, A.Mil 3212. [cf. ON *feldr* cloak]

falle(n *v.* **1.** fall A.Mil 3460, B.Mk 3166, H.Mcp 10, TC 2.105; fall down A.Kn 2662, 2930, B.NP 4591, descend D.WB 702, 705; die B.Mel 2861; drop A.Prol 128, B.Mel 2182, TC 3.1052; come to shore LGW 2423; ~ *on knees/knowe* kneel A.Kn 1758, E.Cl 292, F.Sq 544, TC 2.1202 *var*, HF 1534; ~ *aswowne* faint C.Phs 253, BD 123, TC 3.1092; ~*ing strook* stroke to make (a tree) fall 2.1382. **2.** fall (fig., into a condition or state, often unpleasant) A.Kn 2825, B.ML 616, G.CY 1378, TC 1.813, 3.794; ~ *into a studie* A.Kn 1530, ~ *in love longinge* B.Th 1962, ~ *in prosperitee* LGW 590; ~ *aslepe* A.Rv 4283, BD 275, ~ *on slepe* HF 114; (into captivity) TC 5.252; decline B.Mel 2497, Bo 5. p6. 52/73; come to be placed Astr 2.5.6/8; enter B.Mk 3617; (with infin.) begin A.Mil 3273; ~ *acorded/at oon* agreed D.WB 812, TC 3.565, ~ *of his accord* consented F.Fkl 741; ~ *awey fro* turn from TC 3.1306; ~ *doun* decrease B.Mel 2867; ~ *in* attain, win TC 1.370, come to (agreement) F.Fkl 1219; ~ *in felaweshipe* chance to fall in company A.Prol 25, C.Pard 938; ~ *in office* take service A.Kn 1418; ~ *(forth) in speche* begin to speak F.Sq 238, TC 2.1191, 5.107, sim. 2.498; ~ *in suspecioun* become suspicious B.NP 4222; ~ *upon* seize, afflict A.Rv 4172, B.NP 4600. **3.** decrease TC 1.563, 4.430, 469; fade, diminish BD 564, Bo 4. p3. 17/24; lose influence D. WB 702, 705; be ruined Bo 3. p5. 42/58. **4.** commit sin I.Pars 1025, 1073; ~ *in* (sin, rage, error, etc.) yield to C.Phs 78,

C.Pard 367, ABC 67. **5.** befall, happen A.Prol 324, A.Kn 1669, B.NP 4185, C.Pard 496, TC 1.212; ~ *of* happen because of B.Mel 2618; (of a lot, etc.) ~ *to/on* light on A.Prol 845, C.Pard 803, PF 406; *ne* ~*th nat to purpos* is no part of my intention TC 1.142; be appropriate E.Cl 259, *as fil to hire honour* in keeping with her rank LGW 2474; *as fil to hir plesance* as it pleased them B.ML 149; *as fer as reson fil* as far as was reasonable F.Sq 570; ~ *it foule or faire* whether it turns out badly or well TC 4. 1022. *impers.* (with dat. of pers.): *hem fil* they happened TC 3.1401; *faire/foule* ~ may good, bad luck come to B.NP 4650, LGW 277, RR 798; H.Mcp 40, TC 4.462; *pers.* in *faire(mot)she* ~ LGW 186, G.180; see **faire, foule. falles** *pr. 3 sg.* A. Rv 4042, BD 257 (only). **falle** *subj. sg.* A.Kn 2555, A.Rv 4172, B.NP 4600. **fil** *pa. sg.* A.Prol 845, TC 1.110, **fel** A.Kn 1462, G.CY 1282. **fille(n** *pl.* A.Kn 949, B.Mk 3183, D.WB 812, F.Fkl 1219; **felle(n** TC 1.3, 145. **fille** *subj. sg.* A.Prol 131, TC 1.320. **falle(n** *p.p.* A.Prol 324, A.Kn 2936 (= felled), A.Mil 3231, TC 1.555, LGW 590; **yfalle(n** A.Prol 25, B.Mk 3166, TC 3.859. [OA *fallan, feoll, -on, ġe)fallen]*

falling *vbl. n.* **1.** collapse (physical) A.Kn 2464, B.Mk 3279; (of person) LGW 1858; overthrow A.Kn 2722; ~ *down* ruin, adversity B.Mel 2755. **2.** befalling, occurrence TC 4.1021, 1061.

fals *n.* deceit, treachery TC 3.298. [OF]
fals *adj.* **1.** untrue C.Pard 394, D.WB 382, TC 1.593; erroneous Bo 1. p6. 74/95; wrongful B.ML 827, I.Pars 884, Bo 1. p3. 8/12; spurious (gods, happiness, etc.) B.Mk 3419, E.Mch 2295, TC 3.814, LGW 165, Bo 2. p1. 40/56, p8. 14/20, ? proved wrong TC 5.1526. **2.** disloyal, treacherous A.Kn 1145, B.ML 619, TC 1.93, LGW 486; unfaithful Anel 11, PF 456, TC 4.616, 1537, LGW G. 293, *comp.* LGW 2399. **3.** untrustworthy, deceitful B.Sh 1592, D.Sum 1670, BD 643, TC 5.1832, deceptive G.CY 989, BD 626, LGW 1301, Bo 1. m5. 31/45; cheating A.Rv 4318, G.CY 1028, 1131, 1159. **4.** infamous, evil A.Rv 4268, B.Mk 3095, D.Sum 2213; ~ *livinge* evil liver I.Pars 640. [OF]
fals *adv.* untruthfully B.Mel 2394, D.WB 1057. [from prec.]
fals(e)ly *adv.* **1.** dishonestly A.Kn 1586, C.Phs 228, LGW 666, Bo 2. p7. 89/126. **2.** deceitfully LGW 2427, Bo 1. p4. 124/171, 2. p8. 10/14, 3. p9. 136/183. **3.** unjustly C.Pard 415, TC 1.38, LGW 350; wrongfully Bo 3. p6. 8/11. **4.** treacherously A.Kn 1142, TC 1.89, HF 389, LGW 593, 1658. [from adj.]
false(n *v.* **1.** be unfaithful to (person) BD 1234, Anel 147, TC 3.784, 5.1845, LGW 1377; (pledge) F.Sq 627. **2.** misrepresent A.Mil 3175. [OF *falser*]
fals(e)nes(se *n.* **1.** dishonesty C.Pard 657, G.CY 976, 1086. **2.** treachery F.Sq 506, TC 1.107; faithlessness Anel 160, LGW 473, 1671. **3.** untruthfulness Bo 1. p5. 33/49, 5. p3. 77/107, 105/148. [from adj.]
falshede *n.* cheating G.CY 979, 1051. [**fals** +OE suff. -*hǣdu]*

faltren *pr. pl.* are unsteady B.ML 772. [? rel. to **folde(n]**
falwe *adj.* pale A.Kn 1364, brownish yellow HF 1936. [OE *f(e)alu, f(e)alw-]*
falwes *n. pl.* idle arable land D.WB 656. [OE *fealh,* pl. *fealga]*
fame *n.* **1.** repute, reputation (good or bad) A.Kn 3055, HF 1545, 1560, 1815; (person.) I.Pars 1086, HF 663, 703, 852, etc. LGW 417. **2.** renown, celebrity C.Phs 111, E.Cl 418, Bo 2. p7. 40/57, 48/70, HF 1412, 1436, 1473, 1485, etc. **3.** news B.ML 995, E.Cl 940, public knowledge I.Pars 104. **4.** ill-repute A.Mil 3148. [OF]
familier/famulere *n.* close associate Bo 1. p3. 34/47, 3. p5. 20/27, 34/47; member of household 29/41, 32/44. [from next]
familier/famulere *adj.* **1.** intimate A.Prol 215, B.Sh 1221; belonging to household E.Mch 1784. **2.** courteous LGW 1606. [OF]
familiaritee *n.* friendliness Bo 2. p1. 12/16; *pl.* friendship Bo 3. p5. 1 (L *familiaritas).* [OF]
fan see **vane.**
fantasye *n.* **1.** imaginings F.Fkl 844, TC 3.1032, 5.261, 358, 623, HF 992, *pl.* mental images BD 28; imagination TC 2.482, 5.1523; *heigh* ~ strong fancy E.Mch 1577. **2.** delusion A.Mil 3835, TC 3.1504, 4.1470, 1615, 5.329, HF 593. **3.** desire A.Mil 3191, TC 3.275, inclination FormA 51; *doon his* ~ fulfil his desire B.Mk 3475; *after* . . ~ according to (one's) inclination F.Sq 205, D.WB 190. **4.** caprice B.Mk 3465, D.WB 516, TC 5.461. [OF *fantasie]*
fantastyk *adj.* belonging to fancy or imagination A.Kn 1376. [OF *fantastique]*
fantome *n.* delusion BML 1037; delusory dream HF 11, 493. [OF *fantosme]*
fare *n.* **1.** behaviour, conduct TC 1.1025, 4.1567, 5.53; *nice* ~ foolishness TC 2.1144, 4.532 *var; strange* ~ reserve B.Sh 1453. **2.** condition TC 5.1366, plight Pity 62, Anel 63; well-being HF 682; *yvel* ~ misfortune TC 2.1001. **3.** business, ado, disturbance B.ML 569, TC 1.551, 3.860, 1106, 4.920, 5.335; clamour Bo 2. p5. 82/114; *made* ~ complained loudly A.Rv 3999. [OE *faru]*
fare-carte *n.* cart for sending outside a manor TC 5.1162. [next+ OE *cræt,* ON *kartr]*
fare(n *v.* **1.** go, depart A.Kn 1395, B.ML 512, B.Sh 1245, B.NP 4069, G.CY 733, TC 3.1529; walk LGW 2209; ~ *to mischaunce* go to ruin TC 5.450. **2.** behave D.WB 852, D.Fri 1454, G.CY 662, TC 1.739, 4.1087; behave, seem (with comparison) A.Kn 1372, D.WB 1095, E.Cl 1060, I.Pars 250, 855, BD 967, be B.Pri 1676; ~ *bi/with* treat, act towards D.WB 1088, F.Sq 461, I.Pars 899, TC 4.463, react to PF 599. **3.** get on, fare, do A.Rv 3871, D.WB 330, E.Mch 1461, PF 152, TC 1.666; ~ *wel* prosper, be successful A.Kn 2435, TC 2.163, 3.248, RR 271, (as leavetaking formula) goodbye A.Kn 2740, BD 657, TC 1.1040, 5.1176; ~ *amis* fail F.Fkl 1298, ~ *ful yvele* fail badly TC 1.626, ~ *aright* do well! TC 2.999. **4.** feel (in phrases): ~ *wel* feel happy TC 4.798, RR 249, *ferde so mery* felt so happy RR 499, ~

amis felt ill TC 1.491, suffered 2.1007, ~ *evel* suffered BD 501; *ferd ful wel at ese* felt quite happy TC 4.1094. **5.** *it ~th* turns out, happens, befalls (often with *bi/of/ with* of thing concerned) A.Co 4408, B.Mel 2876, E.Mch 1217, G.CY 966, I.Pars 365, TC 1.963. **fareth** *imper. pl.* B.ML 1159, E.Mch 1688, TC 5.1412. **ferde** *pa. sg.* A.Kn 1372. **ferden** *pl.* A.Kn 1647. **fare(n** *p.p.* B.ML 512, B.NP 4069, **yfare** TC 3.577, LGW 2271, ferd TC 5.1358. [OE *faran*; ON *fara*, p.p. *faren*; OE *fēran*, *fērde*; ON *fara með*]
fasoun *n.* **1.** appearance RR 708, 1001, shape 1028; *of his* ~ as to his appearance 885, *of good* ~ well shaped 551, 932. **2.** established order Bo 2. m8. 13/19 (L *machinam*). [OF *faceon*]
fast *n.* abstinence from food TC 5.370. [OE *fæsten*, ON *fasta*]
fast *adj.* **1.** firm Anel 313, *comp.* more certain Bo 1. p6. 71/92; married D.WB 283. **2.** dense TC 5.1235. **3.** *comp.* swifter F.Fkl 1066, 1068. [OE *fæst*]
faste *adv.* **1.** firmly B.Sh 1275, B.Mel 2159, TC 1.534, RR 1533; *stond* ~ TC 1.969. **2.** swiftly, quickly A.Rv 4090, BD 152, TC 2.906, RR 375, *as* ~ as quickly as possible TC 2.657, very soon 898, *(as)* ~ *as* A.Kn 1469, 1475. **3.** (intensive with various vs.) eagerly A.Kn 1266, zealously HF 1728, LGW 2487, copiously E.Mch 1769, TC 4.130, loudly A.Kn 2359, hard 2558, closely C.Phs 124, TC 2.276, soundly A.Rv 4194, PF 94, RR 25. **4.** ~ *by* close to A.Prol 719, F.Fkl 847, TC 2.1275; close at hand A.Kn 1476, 1688, B.Mk 3116, C.Pard 566, D.WB 970, D.Fri 1389, BD 369, TC 4.117, RR 1206. [OE *fæste*]
faste(n *v.* abstain from food B.Sh 1405, C.Pard 508, D.Sum 1879, F.Fkl 819, I.Pars 257, 1051, TC 2.1166, LGW 1271. **fasted** *pa. sg.* C.Pard 508; **faste** G.SN 139. [OE *fæstan*]
fastne/festne *v.* **1.** tie A.Prol 195, Bo 1. m5. 2. **2.** direct (the eyes) Bo 1. p3. 3/5, 3. p2. 1. **3.** make firm Bo 1. m5. 40/56; place permanently Bo 4. m1. 26/38. **fastnede** *pa. sg.* Bo 1. p3. 3/5, 3. p2.1. **yfastned/festnyd** *p.p.* Bo 1. m5. 2. [OE *ģe)fæstnian*]
fat *adj.* plump, well nourished A.Prol 200, TC 1.222; fine FormA 38; healthy, unscathed MercB 27. [OE *fæt(t)*]
fatal *adj.* predestined, fated B.ML 261, Bo 4. m4. 2/3, TC 5.1; ~ *sustren* the Fates TC 3.733, LGW 2630. [OF, or L *fātālis*]
fate *n.* destiny TC 5.1550 *(the ~)*, 1552; individual lot, destiny 209. [OF]
fatte *v.* nourish D.Sum 1880. [OE *ģefættian*]
fattish *adj.* rounded BD 954. [from **fat**]
faucon *n.* falcon F.Sq 411, PF 337, TC 3.1784. [OF]
fauconers *n. pl.* hunters with hawks F.Fkl 1196. [OF *fauconnier*]
Faunes/fawnes *n. pl.* Fauns, rural gods A.Kn 2928. [OF *faune*, L *Faunus*]
Fauny *n. pl.* fauns TC 4.1544. [L *Fauni*]
fawe see **fayn.**
feblesse/fieblesse *n.* weakness I.Pars 823, 913, TC 2.863. [OF]
fecche(n *v.* **1.** bring A.Mil 3492, B.ML 662, E.Cl 276, G.SN 411, 422; *leet* ~ had

brought D.Sum 2064, ~ *fyr* bring a brand LGW 1347, (fig.) get a light, stay only briefly TC 5.485; *to fer to* ~ impossible to find Anel 338. **2.** come and get B.Pri 1857; take away *(subj. sg.)* B.ML 1064, D.Fri 1544, 1610, 1628, TC 5.322; procure D.Fri 1360. Cf. **fette(n.** [OE *fecċan*]
fecches *n. pl.* vetch-seeds (as type of something valueless), beans TC 3.936. [ONF *veche*]
fecching *vbl. n.* seizing, capture TC 5.890.
fee *n.* **1.** payment for service A.Prol 317, A.Kn 1803, Anel 193; offering BD 266. **2.** tenure D.WB 630; ~ *simple* unentailed tenure, unlimited possession A.Prol 319. [AN *fee* infl. by OE *feoh*]
fe(e)de(n *v.* nourish, feed A.Prol 146, TC 2.1570; *refl.* eat I.Pars 327; (fig.) TC 4.339; bring up E.Cl 397. **fedeth** *imper. pl.* I.Pars 569. **fedde** *pa. sg.* A.Prol 146. **feden** *pl.* I.Pars 901. **fed/yfed** *p.p.* E.Cl 397, RR 471. [OE *fēdan*]
fe(e)ding *vbl. n.* eating: *to* ~ to eat I.Pars 329.
fe(e)ld *n.* **1.** flat country, piece of land A.Kn 1522, E.Cl 223; ~ *of pitee* Elysian Fields TC 4.789; *pl.* open country A.Kn 1503. **2.** (cultivated) field Bo 5. p1. 50/72, *pl.* PF 22. **3.** battlefield TC 1.1074, 2.195, 4.42. **4.** (her.) the surface of a coat of arms B.Mk 3573. [OE *féld*]
fe(e)le(n *v.* **1.** experience, sense D.Sum 1948, TC 1.400, 4.706; *p.p.* in *to ben ~d* sentient Bo 5. p5. 1 (L *sentiendis*). *pr. p.* suffering TC 4.840, sensitive Bo 3. p11. 68/92. **2.** comprehend F.Fkl 727, TC 2.1283, 3.960, LGW 520/508; perceive B.NP 4325, G.SN 155, G.CY 711. **3.** find out TC 2.387. **feled(e** *pa. sg.* BD 492, Bo 3. p1. 14/19; **felte** A.Kn 1575, D.WB 410. **felte(n** *pl.* B.NP 4325, TC 3.1222. **feled** *p.p.* Bo 5. p5. 1; **felt** F.Sq 586, TC 1.25. [OE *fēlan*, *fēlde*]
fe(e)linge *vbl. n.* **1.** feeling TC 3.1090; sensation D.WB 610, Ven 32; passion (of love) BD 1172. **2.** senses PF 4, HF 552; touch I.Pars 959; sensibility Bo 2. p4. 71/97, ? BD 11. **3.** knowledge, understanding TC 1.1333; expressiveness B.NP 4483.
feend *n.* devil, demon D.Fri 1475, *pl.* TC 2.896; monster, enemy ? TC 4.437, LGW 1996. [OE *fēond*, sg. and pl.]
feendly/-lych *adj.* devilish B.ML 783, G.CY 1071, 1158, 1303; monstrous B.ML 751; inhuman BD 594. [OE *fēondlīc*]
feere see **fere.**
fe(e)stlich *adj.* convivial F.Sq 281. [from **feste** n.]
feet *n.* performance, art E.Cl 429. [OF *fet*]
feffe *v.* enfeoff, put in possession (*in* 'of') E.Mch 1698; (fig.) endow, present (*with*) Bo 2. p3. 44/64, TC 3.901, 5.1689. [AN *feoffer*]
fey *n.* faith, fidelity LGW 1365, 2519, credibility Bo 4. p2. 13/17; (in oaths) *by my* ~ on my honour, word A.Mil 3284, D.WB 1002, (as expletive) A.Co 4356, D.WB 215, E.Mch 1505, F.Fkl 1474; *by youre* ~ I.Pars 23, TC 2.1103, *upon hir* ~ LGW 1847; *in good* ~ to tell the truth E.Cl 1032; *in hir* ~ faithfully, with conviction LGW 778. Cf. **feith, par fay.** [OF]

feyne(n/feigne v. 1. dissemble, feign F.Sq
510, TC 2.1558, 4.1463; lie Pity 4, HF
1478; **feyned** ppl. adj. false, insincere
B.ML 362, B.Mel 2208. 2. tr. counterfeit A.Prol 736, B.Mel 2501, D.Fri 1378,
Mars 173, LGW 932; p.p. forged D.Fri
1360. 3. (refl.) pretend to be C.Phs 62,
TC 2.1528, LGW 1266; pretend (with cl.)
E.Mch 1950, TC 1.494, (with infin.) B.ML
351, TC 5.846, LGW 2375. 4. evade ?
E.Cl 529; hesitate, hold back TC 2.997,
3.167. 5. devise, explain Bo 3. p10.
62/86 (L fingat qui potest). [OF feign-,
stem of feindre]
feyning(e vbl. n. dissembling, pretence BD
1100, LGW 1556; ? cajolery F.Sq 556.
feynte v. 1. grow feeble G.CY 753, BD
488, languish TC 1.410. 2. tr. weaken
B.ML 926. [OF feintir]
feynting vbl. n. failing, flagging E.Cl 970.
feith n. 1. belief, trust LGW 31; faith (the
virtue) G.SN 110, I.Pars 734; the ~ religious belief I.Pars 604, Christianity G.SN
538, I.Pars 772, our ~ Christianity A.Prol
62, the ~ of Crist Christian doctrine G.SN
122; taken of the ~ believe you Bo 1. p4.
195/274 (L de te (tanti criminis) fidem
capiunt). 2. faithfulness, loyalty E.Cl 866,
I.Pars 929, TC 2.410, 3.791, 1649. 3.
credibility Bo 3. p12. 136/184, 5. p1. 20/28
(or ? conviction (L fide)); confidence Bo 2.
p3. 59/86 (L fides). 4. ? trust, confidence
Bo 2. m8. 1, 4. m6. 18/26, TC 3.1751
(based on Bo 2. m8). 5. word, pledge
A.Kn 1622, D.Sum 2139, F.Fkl 1234; by
my/thy ~ A.Rv 4209, B.NP 4101, D.Fri
1551; in (good) ~ B.NP 4604, D.WB 360,
PF 24, y ~ A.Rv 4022, upon my ~ indeed,
truly B.Mk 3125; make ~ stand surety
B.Mel 2997. Cf. **fey**. [AN feid]
feythed see **strengest-feythed**.
feithful adj. 1. devout B.Mk 3081. 2.
loyal B.Mel 2345, E.Cl 310, 343. 3. re-
liable D.Fri 1425, Bo 2. p1. 56/76, con-
scientious G.SN 24. [from **feith**]
feithfully adv. 1. truthfully TC 4.114,
MercB 8; truly, indeed D.Fri 1420, 1433,
1504, D.Sum 2203, E.Cl 1066. 2. con-
vincingly TC 2.263, 3.101 var, 5.1076; dutifully
E.Cl 1111; devotedly B.ML 461. [from
prec.]
felawe n. 1. comrade, companion A.Rv
4203, C.Pard 672, D.Sum 1740, G.CY
747; good ~ amiable chap A.Prol 395, 650,
D.Fri 1185; be ~ be a companion I.Pars
928, his ~ his fellow evangelist B.Mel
2135; 'opposite number', opponent A.Kn
2548; see **parting**. 2. friend A.Kn 1031,
1200, Bo 2. p8. 28/39, TC 4.524, 5.1488;
good ~ intimate friend D.WB 618. 3.
equal A.Kn 1624, I.Pars 400; pl. fellows of
a college A.Rv 4112. 4. som old ~ some
man or other F.Fkl 1153; (address) my
good man BD 366. 5. pl. accompaniments
I.Pars 833. [OE fēolaga from ON félagi]
felaweshipe n. 1. band of associates LGW
947, 965; yfalle in ~ having come together
by chance A.Prol 26, sim. C.Pard 938, was
of hir ~ joined their company A.Prol 32;
have no ~ have no companions or equals
A.Kn 1626; household A.Mil 3539. 2.
friendliness I.Pars 967, friendship B.Mel

2379, camaraderie 2749; amity, love TC
2.206, 3.403. [from prec.]
felaweshipe v. join (a journey) accompany
Bo 4. m1. 8/12, (a person) p3. 55/78, refl.
p6. 88/125; ben y~d togidre be joined together Bo 2. p6. 58/81. [from prec.]
feldefare n. thrush; farewel ~ all is over
TC 3.861. [OE feldeware infl. by **fare(n]**
fele adj. many E.Cl 917, PF 329, TC 4.512,
HF 1137, RR 663. [OE fela]
felicitee n. happiness A.Prol 338, B.Mk 3467,
Bo 1. p3. 23/31 (~ that I clepe welefulnesse, no L); favourable aspect (of a planet)
Astr 2.4. 26/40. [OF]
felingly adv. understandingly, sym-
pathetically A.Kn 2203, F.Fkl 676. [from
pr. p. of **fe(e)le(n)**]
fel(l adj. fierce A.Kn 1559, 2630, B.Mk
3290, RR 151; terrible B.Th 2019, TC
1.470, 4.44; violent 5.50. [OF fel]
felle(n v. cut down A.Kn 1702. **felden** pa.
pl. caused to fall RR 911. **feld** p.p. A.Kn
2924. [OA fellan]
felliche adv. bitterly Bo 2. m3. 9/12. [from
fell]
felnesse n. fierceness Bo 1. m6. 7/10. [from
fell]
felon adj. ? angry, sullen TC 5.199. Cf.
feloun. [OF]
felonye n. 1. crime A.Kn 1996, B.ML 643,
Bo 1. p5. 35/52. 2. vice, wickedness Bo 4.
p1. 19/26, p4. 23/33, p5. 15/22; malice,
evil intent I.Pars 543. 3. wrong Bo 4. p6.
174/252, sacrilege 5. p3. 18/24. [OF]
felonous adj. wicked Bo 1. p4. 27/37, 142/197,
5. p3. 122/174; criminal Bo 4. p5. 12/17;
cruel I.Pars 438, Bo 1. m4. 10/14, angry
4. p3. 75/107. [OF feloneus]
feloun n. criminal, evil-doer Bo 1. m5. 30/37,
4. p1. 22/31. [from adj., var. of **felon**]
feminyne adj. female HF 1365. [OF]
femininitee n. female form B.ML 360.
[from prec.]
fen n. chapter (of Avicenna's Canon) C.Pard
890. [ML from Arab fann]
fenix n. phoenix BD 982. [OE from L]
fer adj. distant B.Th 1908, LGW 1418; remote B.Mel 2565, ultimate 2585, 2586; sup.
as n. **ferreste** most distant A.Prol 494.
[OE feorr]
fer adv. far (away), at a distance A.Prol 491,
Anel 17, TC 1.18, ~ or ner TC 1.451; in as
~ as to the extent that BD 960, so/as ~
forth to such an extent ABC 170, as far HF
328 (and as one word); ~ ther see off (in
time) TC 4.1246. comp. in ~ ne ner no
later or sooner A.Kn 1850; **ferre** further
A.Prol 48, A.Kn 2060. [OE feorr, comp.
fyrr]
ferd, ferde(n see **fare(n**.
ferd(e n. fear, only in for/of ~ BD 1214,
TC 1.557, 4.607 var, 1411 var, HF 950.
[prob. from for fered, see **fered**]
fer(e n.[1] 1. fright, fear B.NP 4581, TC
2.770; for the ~ F.Fkl 893, for verray ~
1347, for pure ~ BD 1209; have ~ be
afraid B.ML 803, D.WB 1022, TC 3.753,
HF 607; it was no ~ there was nothing to
fear TC 3.583. 2. danger TC 3.1144.
[OE fǣr]
fere n.[2] companion TC 1.224, LGW 969,
mate PF 410, TC 3.1496, wife 4.791. [OE
ġefēra]

fere *n.*³ company, in *in* ~ together TC 2.1266 *var*, HF 250 *var.* [OE *ġefēre*]
fered *ppl. adj.* afraid: *for* ~ through being afraid, for fear (see **for** *prep.*) F.Sq 527, TC 4.607 *var.*, 1411 *var.* (cf. **ferd(e)**; *of* ~ for fear TC 4.607 *var.* [from **fere(n)**]
fereful *adj.* frightened, cowardly G.CY 660; *sup.* most timid TC 2.450. [from **fer(e)**]
fere(n *v.* frighten, make afraid TC 4.1483. **fered** *p.p.* B.NP 4576, G.CY 924, TC 2.124. [OE *fǣran*]
forforth *adv.* far, in *so* ~ to such an extent, so much (that) B.ML 572, G.SN 40, Anel 290, PF 377, TC 4.1298; *as* ~ *as* as far as, as well as B.ML 19, D.WB 56, G.CY 1087, TC 5.866, LGW 690, as much as if TC 1.121; *as* ~ *as in hem is* as far as in them lies I.Pars 621. [see **fer** adv.]
forforthly *adv. so* ~ to such an extent A.Kn 960, LGW 682; *as* ~ *as* as completely, thoroughly as D.Fri 1545, as far as TC 3. 101 *var.* [from prec.]
ferly *adj.* amazing A.Rv 4173. [app. OE *ᵃfeorlīc* strange]
fermacies *n. pl.* remedies A.Kn 2713. [OF]
ferme *n.* fixed payment, rent A.Prol 252a. [OF]
ferme *adj.* stable, enduring Bo 3. p6. 23/31, p11. 135/185; certain, assured Bo 3. p10. 96/129, p11. 2, 4. p2. 14/18. [OF]
ferme *adv.* firmly: *holde(n* ~ keep resolutely TC 2.1525, *holde(n* ~ *and stable* obey unswervingly E.Cl 663, E.Mch 1499, perform faithfully RR 1500. [from prec.]
ferme *imper. sg.* make firm Bo 1. m5. 40/56. [OF *fermer*]
fermerer *n.* keeper of infirmary D.Sum 1859. [OF *enfermerer*]
fern *adv.* long ago F.Sq 256. [OE *ġe)fyrn*]
fern-asshen *n.* ash produced by burning fern F.Sq 254. [OE *fearn+æsce*, pl. *ascan*]
ferne *adj.* far, distant, remote A.Prol 14, Bo 2. m7. 8/11. [OE *feorran* ᵃadv.]
ferne yere *n.* yesteryear TC 5.1176. [OE *fyrn* adj., and in compds. as *fyrnġēar*; cf. **fern**]
ferre *see* **fer.**
fers *n.* queen in chess BD 654, 681; *pl.* ? pieces 723. [OF *fierce* from Arab]
fers / fiers *adj.* bold, brave A.Kn 1598, 2676, TC 1.225; ferocious A.Kn 2369, G.SN 198, Anel 1; violent A.Kn 2012; dangerous B.ML 300. [OF]
fersly *adv.* violently TC 3.1760. [from prec.]
ferthe *adj.* fourth B.ML 823, D.WB 364. [OE *fēorþa*]
ferther *adj.* far, further B.Pri 1686, E.Mch 2226. [OE *furþra* infl. by **fer**]
ferther *adv. comp.* further A.Prol 36, F.Fkl 1177, TC 3.281, 949; **ferthest** *sup.* Bo 4. p6. 86/123 *var.* **further.** [OE *furþor* and **fer**]
fertherover *adv.* moreover Astr 2.26.8/11. Cf. **fortherover.** [prec.+**over**]
ferthest *see* **ferther.**
ferthing *n.* farthing (small coin worth a quarter of a penny) A.Prol 255, D.Sum 1967 (?pun on *farting*); small round spot A.Prol 134. [OE *fēorþing*]
fervent *adj.* hot I.Pars 536. [OF]
fesaunt *n.* pheasant PF 357. [AN]
fest *n.* fist A.Rv 4275, hand I.Pars 35. **festes/ fistes** *pl.* TC 4.243. [OE *fȳst*]

feste *n.* **1.** entertainment with feasting BD 974, TC 3.1159; banquet D.Sum 1914, I.Pars 444, Bo 3. m8. 6/7; ceremony TC 5.304. *make(n a* ~ hold a feast B.Mk 3270, D.WB 297. **2.** religious festival Mars 22, TC 1.161, 168, 3.150. **3.** (fig.) banquet for the mind or senses I.Pars 47, TC 3.1312; rejoicing, pleasure D.WB 1078, TC 2.421, 3.344, 5.524; *make(n* ~ rejoice, make merry B.Sh 1517; *make(n* (someone) ~(*s* entertain D.Fri 1349, LGW 2302, *joye and* ~ pay joyful attention to E.Cl 1109; *made swiche* ~*s* paid such compliments TC 5.1429. [OF]
festeyinge *n.* feast, festivity TC 5.455, *maketh* ~*s* provides entertainments 3.1718. [from next]
feste(n *v.* **1.** feast, enjoy a banquet LGW 2157. **2.** entertain to a banquet A.Kn 2193. [OF *fester*]
festivaly *adv.* wittily Bo 2. p7. 85/122 (L *festiue*). [from OF *festival* adj.]
festne *see* **fastne.**
fethered *adj.* covered with feathers TC 2.926; provided with feathers RR 942, 951. [from *fether* n., OE *feþer*]
fethered *pa. sg.* covered (with wings), copulated with B.NP 4367. [from *fether* n., OE *feþer*; cf. OE *ge-fiþerian* furnish with feathers]
fetis *adj.* **1.** (of people) well made, graceful C.Pard 478, pretty RR 776, 1017, handsome 821, 829. **2.** (of things) well made RR 532; elegant A.Prol 157, RR 1133. [AN *fetiz*]
fetisly *adv.* skilfully A.Prol 124, D.Sum 1742, RR 1235, handsomely A.Prol 273, A.Mil 3319, elegantly RR 577. [from prec.]
fette(n *v.* fetch, bring A.Prol 819, D.Sum 2159, ~ *forth* TC 5.852; *for to* ~ lacking TC 3.609. **fette** *pa.* B.Sh 1483, B.Th 2041. *2 sg.* TC 3.723. **fet** *p.p.* A.Prol 819, B.ML 667; **yfet** F.Sq 174, G.CY 1116. Cf. **fecche(n.** [OE *fetian*]
fetures *n. pl.* physical qualities H.Mcp 121. [OF]
fewe **1.** *adj.* few B.Mel 2259, B.Mk 3874, *in (a) wordes* ~ briefly C.Pard 820, G.CY 618, TC 4.1280; a few D.Sum 1949, TC 2.1647. **2.** *pron.* few people G.CY 1123; *a* ~ *of* TC 5.1459; *nat .. but a* ~ to only a few people D.Sum 1850; *seid* ~ said little Bo 1. p5. 33/49. [OE *fēawe*]
ficche(n *v.* (only in Bo, nearly all rendering L *figere* or compounds) **1.** fix firmly Bo 4. p1. 47/66, 5. m4. 11/16; (in mind, etc.) 3. p11. 161/218, 4. p2. 46/60. **2.** found, erect Bo 2. m4. 9/13. **3.** fix (eyes etc.) Bo 3. m9. 30/42, m12. 46/65. [OF *fich(i)er*]
fieblesse *see* **feblesse.**
fiers *see* **fers.**
fighte(n *v.* fight, contend A.Kn 984, TC 4.34. **fighteth** *pr. 3 sg.* I.Pars 733; **fight** PF 103. **fighteth** *imper. pl.* A.Kn 2559. **faught** *pa. sg.* A.Prol 399, B.Mk 3519. **foghte(n** *pl.* A.Kn 1660, 2655, **foughten** 1699. **foughten** *p.p.* A.Prol 62. [OE *feohtan, feaht, fuhton, fohten*]
figure *n.* **1.** shape, appearance B.ML 187, B.Mk 3412, D.Fri 1459; form, impression Bo 5. p4. 112/160, 144/207, m4. 9/13, 31/45 (L *notas*); *of our* ~ of our kind Scog 27; *in be divers(e* ~*s* under different appearances D.Fri 1486, Bo 5. m5. 1/2; *hir*

~ her person TC 1.366, HF 132. **2.** comparison A.Prol 499, Bo 5. m5. 14/20; *in* ~ as a prefiguring ABC 94, TC 5.1449, *by* ~*s* by prefiguring HF 48. **3.** picture A.Kn 1916, F.Fkl 831, HF 126; ? representation A.Kn 2043; drawing, diagram Astr 2.26. 25/36,? writing Bo 5. m4.13/19, Buk 25; numbers BD 437, 438. **4.** *pl.* rhetorical figures or ornaments E.Cl 16, HF 858. [OF]

figured *p.p.* set up as a symbol, ? regarded symbolically I.Pars 922; marked Astr 1.9.1/2. [OF *figurer*]

figuringe *vbl. n. in* ~ symbolically G.SN 96; *berth . . . in* ~ symbolizes LGW 298. [from v. as prec.]

fille *n.* enough to satisfy appetite LGW 817; (fig.) as much as one desires A.Kn 1528, A.Mil 3722, D.Sum 1700. [OE *fyllu*]

filth *n.* foulness, infamy Bo 1. p4. 100/139; *pl.* foul things I.Pars 196. [OE *fylþ*]

fin *n.* **1.** end, conclusion B.ML 424, TC 5.1828, 1829, etc., *for* ~ finally 4.477; *this is the* ~ to sum it up, in the end RR 1558. **2.** purpose, aim E.Mch 2106, Mars 218, Bo 3. p3. 4/5, TC 2.757, 3.125. **3.** result B.Mk 3348. [OF]

fyn *adj.* choice, excellent (of food, clothes, etc.) E.Mch 1843, G.CY 1241; ~ *lovinge* true, perfect love LGW 544; *of* ~ *force* by sheer necessity TC 5.421. sup. A.Prol 194. [OF]

final *adj.* ultimate F.Fkl 987, ~ *ende* ultimate conclusion LGW 2101, *for* ~ in conclusion TC 4.145; *cause* ~ ultimate purpose B.Mel 2591, I.Pars 939, ultimate cause TC 1.682. [OF]

fynally *adv.* **1.** eventually, at last F.Sq 576, I.Pars 276, 280, TC 2.1324, 5.1635, 1644. **2.** ? firmly, conclusively Fort 8, 16, 24. **3.** for good TC 3.1006. [from prec.]

finde(n *v.* **1.** discover A.Kn 1627, TC 2.641, LGW 1573; seek out B.Th 1886, D.WB 1212, H.Mcp 184; reveal TC 3.1002; calculate F.Fkl 1270, 1285. **2.** encounter A.Prol 648, A.Mil 3821 (see **selle(n)**, TC 2.838; experience, perceive B.Mel 2152, G.SN 251, PF 318. **3.** devise A.Kn 2244, TC 3.518, ~ *out* BD 319; invent A.Prol 736; create TC 4.1408; compose TC 3.979 (*see* **countenance**). **4.** read, find in writing D.Sum 1920, PF 678, TC 1.399, 5.834, 1758, LGW G. 271; ~ *writen* read G.SN 94, 124, TC 4.1415; read about LGW 917. **5.** provide A.Kn 2413, B.ML 243; provide for B.NP 4019, C.Pard 537, *p.p.* equipped A.Kn 1612. **fyndeth** *pr. 3 sg.* B.ML 1150; **fynt** A.Rv 4071, G.SN 181; **fyndes** A.Rv 4130. **found** *pa. 1, 3 sg.* Anel 154; **fo(o)nd** A.Mil 3821, PF. 374. **founde** *2 sg.* TC 3.362. **founde(n** *pl.* A.Kn 1009, TC 1. 137, **fo(o)nd(e** B.Mk 3259, HF 1810, Astr 2.1.6/9. **founde(n** *p.p.* B.ML 612, 1022; **yfounde** A.Mil 3514, TC 4.594 *var.* [OE *findan, fánd, fúndon, fúnden*]

finder *n.* originator BD 1168, TC 2.844. [from prec.]

finding *vbl. n. in after . . ~* according to the provision, support A.Mil 3220.

fyn(e *adv.* thoroughly TC 1.661, LGW 1715. [from **fyn** adj.]

fyne(n *v.* **1.** end, finish TC 4.26. **2.** desist, stop trying D.WB 788, 1136, TC 2.1460, 5.776. [OF *finer*]

fyr *n.* **1.** fire, flames B.Mk 3920, **fe(e)re** TC 3.978; passion TC 3.484, LGW 106, *pl.* A.Kn 2862; *wild*(*e* ~ blazing fire D.WB 373, I.Pars 445, erysipelas A.Rv 4172. **2.** (one of the four elements) A.Kn 1246. Cf. **afir(e.** [OE *fýr*]

firmament *n.* **1.** sky, heavens E.Mch 2219, I.Pars 421, Astr 2.23.1. **2.** one of the celestial spheres B.ML 295, BD 693, Bo 4. m1. 6/8, 18/26, m5. 3/4. [OF]

first *adj.* **1.** first (in a series) A.Prol 831, A.Mil 3687, B.Pri 1634; ~ *fruit* D.Sum 2277, ~ *matere* opening subject BD 43, ~ *finger* thumb I.Pars 853, ~ *somer* spring Bo 1. m2. 15/22 (L *veris*), 2. m3. 7/9; *the* ~ C.Pard 824; *with the* ~ soon TC 4.63. **2.** original B.Pri 1748, E.Cl 49, F.Fkl 711, BD 1168, Gent 1; ultimate A.Kn 2987, C.Pard 499, Bo 4. p6. 91/131, Astr 1.17. 27/36. **3.** chief BD 218, pre-eminent TC 1.172; *the* ~ the most distinguished TC 3.1773, 5.839. [OE *fyrst*]

first *adv.* in the first place A.Prol 42, BD 789, TC 1.360; for the first time A.Prol 44, TC 2.675; rather TC 3.1495 *var;* ~ *and forward* first of all E.Mch 2187. [OE *fyrst*]

fissh *n.* fish E.Mch 1865, *pl.* PF 188; *the* ~ sign of Pisces F.Sq 273. [OE *fisc,* pl. *fiscas, fixas*]

fisshe(n *v.* fish A.Rv 3927; (fig.) trap TC 5.777, try to catch, hunt D.Sum 1820, seek for TC 3.1162; ~*d faire* (iron.) done a good day's work TC 2.328. [OE *fiscian*]

fit *n.* **1.** bout, episode A.Rv 4184, 4230, D.WB 42. **2.** portion of a song or poem B.Th 2078. [OE *fitt* with sense 2]

fithele *n.* fiddle A.Prol 296. [OE *fiþele*]

fix *p.p.* placed firmly ABC 9; **fixed** Astr 1.21.10/14, 16/22, 42/58. [L *fixus*]

fix(e *adj.* **1.** unvarying (in position) F.Fkl 1282; in a fixed position Astr 1.21.49/69, 23.2/92, 2.38/4/5; fixed: *sterres* ~ Astr prol 57/79, **fixes** *pl.* 1.21.4/5. **2.** unchangeable G.CY 779, TC 1.298. [OF, or L *fixus*]

fix(e *adv.* **1.** in a fixed position Astr 2.40. 20/28, 44/62. **2.** unchangeably G.CY 779. [as prec.]

flayn *p.p.* stripped of skin I.Pars 425. [OE *flǽgen* from *fléan*]

flat *adj.* level, smooth BD 942; as *n.* flat (of a sword) *rather . . ~ than egge* ? rather healing than hurt TC 4.927; cf. **plat** F.Sq 162. [ON *flatr*]

flatere(n *v.* **1.** praise insincerely D.WB 930, D.Sum 1970, B.Mel 2367; cajole I.Pars 376, coax 618, Bo 2. p1. 12/16. **2.** make false promises Mars 188, deceive D.Fri 1294, E.Mch 2059, Bo 2. p1. 39/55. [OF *flater,* and next]

flaterer(e *n.* flatterer, deceiver B.Mel 2197, 2208, I.Pars 613, 615. Cf. **flatour.** [from v.]

flaterye *n.* insincere praise A.Kn 1927, B.Mel 2365, B.NP 4514; deceit A.Prol 705, Anel 125, LGW 2540. [OF]

flateringe *vbl. n.* insincere friendliness B.ML 405, BD 639, Bo 2. p1. 65/90, p8. 20/28; insincere praise I.Pars 612.

flatour *n.* one who curries favour, deceiver B.NP 4515. Cf. **flaterer.** [OF]

fla(u)mbe/flaume, *n.* flame ABC 89, TC 4.118; (fig.) sensation I.Pars 353. [OF]

flaundrish *adj.* Flemish A.Prol 272. [from AN **Flaundres**]

flee(n v.[1] **1.** intr. flee, run away, retreat B.Mk 3507, D.WB 279, TC 2.194, LGW 654; ~inge bataile retreating troops Bo 5. m1. 3. **2.** escape A.Kn 2993; ~ fro I.Pars 211, 216. **3.** avoid tr. B.Mel 2674, 2778, C.Phs 63, G.CY 1408, Bo 3. p9. 72/96; ~ fro B.Mel 2367, Bo 4. p4. 64/88, TC 5.1217. **4.** go away TC 4.868; pass away E.Cl 119, TC 3.828; drain away BD 490, (fig.)~from TC 1.463, ~ oute of 5.1198. **fleeth** imper. pl. fledde pa. sg. B.ML 544, TC 5.1198, **fleigh** B.Mk 3879. **fledden** pl. A.Kn 2930. **y)fled(de** p.p. B.ML 541, TC 1.463, 4.661. [OE flēon, flēah]

flee(n v.[2] **1.** fly B.NP 4132, TC 2.931, HF 921; move through the air RR 951. **2.** move hurriedly BD 178, TC 4.303, leet ~ let loose A.Mil 3806. **fleeth** pr. 3 sg. F.Sq 149. **flying/fleynge** pr. p. BD 178, HF 543. **fley** pa. 3 sg. B.NP 4362; **fleigh** B.NP 4529, HF 2087. **flough/flaugh** 2 sg. B.NP 4421. **flowen** pl. 4581. **flowen** p.p. HF 905. [OE flēogan, flēag, flugon, flogen]

fleen n. pl. fleas H.Mcp 17. [OE flēa, pl. flēan]

fleet see **flete(n.**

flekked adj. spotted E.Mch 1848, G.CY 565. [cf. ON flekkr spot]

fleme(n v. **1.** banish TC 2.852, p.p. G.SN 58. **2.** put to flight H.Mcp 182. [OA flēman]

flemer n. driver-out B.ML 460. [from prec.]

fles(s)h n. **1.** (human) flesh A.Kn 2640, B.Mk 3640, RR 541; ~ and boon B.Mk 3294. **2.** meat A.Prol 147, 344, I.Pars 222. **3.** body D.WB 157, 167, E.Mch 1335, 1386; fleshly desire I.Pars 336, 353; (person. as enemy of man) B.Mel 2611. **4.** ? mind as opposed to soul HF 49. [OE flǣsc]

fles(s)hhook n. meat-hook D.Sum 1730. [from prec. + OE hōc]

flesshy adj. plump, rounded BD 954. [from **fles(s)h**]

fles(s)hly adj. **1.** bodily, human I.Pars 204, 784, 785. **2.** carnal I.Pars 276, 786, 904, 915. **3.** rounded, plump TC 3. 1248. [OE flǣsclić]

fles(s)hly adv. **1.** physically I.Pars 333; in this life 202. **2.** carnally B.Pri 1775; I.Pars 939. [OE flǣsclīce]

flete(n v. **1.** float, drift B.ML 463, 901; pr. p. flowing Bo 1. m7. 7/9, moving Bo 3. p11. 107/147, ? pouring Bo 4. m6. 22/33 (L defluus); (fig.) TC 3.1221, 1671; swim (contrasting with sink) A.Kn 2397, Pity 110, Anel 182, PF 7. **2.** drift Bo 5. m1. 7/10, ~ diversely split Bo 4. p6. 90/129, ~ folyly drift aimlessly 114/165; vacillate Bo 1. p6. 62/79; pr. p. aimless Bo 1. p3. 50/70. **3.** ~ in/with/of abound with Bo 1. m2. 17/25 (L influat), 2. m2. 14/19 (L fluens), 4. p7. 65/91 (L diffluere), 5. m1. 13/19; pr.p. ful of .. is ~ is suffused with TC 2.53. **fleteth** pr. 3 sg. B.ML 901, Bo 1. m2. 17/25; **fleet** B.ML 463. [OE flēotan]

flye n. fly D.WB 835, LGW 392, (as type of something worthless) A.Rv 4192, B.Sh 1361, F.Fkl 1132, G.CY 1150, PF 501; flying insect (bee) I.Pars 467, Bo 3. m7. 2/3. [OE flȳġe]

flikeringe pr. p. fluttering A.Kn 1962. **flikered** pa. sg. fluttered TC 4.1221. [OE flicerian]

flitte v. **1.** move Bo 3. p9. 105/140, TC 5. 1544; **yflit** p.p. having traversed, journeyed Bo 1. m2. 9/13 (L flexa). **2.** vary I.Pars 368, pr. p. changing, variable BD 801, Bo 2. p1. 59/81, 3. p6. 25/34; transitory Bo 2. m3. 16/20, 3. p8. 27/38. **3.** ? govern Bo 3. m2. 2/3 (L flectat). [ON flytja]

flo n. arrow H.Mcp 264. [OE flā]

floytinge pr. p. ? playing the flute, whistling A.Prol 91. [from n., cf. **floute** and MHG floite]

flok n. group, band A.Prol 824, RR 661. [OE flocc]

flokmele adv. in crowds E.Cl 86. [OE floccmǣlum]

flood n. **1.** flood, deluge A.Mil 3518, 3578; on a ~ flooded TC 3.640. **2.** pl. waters Bo 1. m5. 40/56, 2. m3. 11/14, TC 3.1760; flowing, surging B.Mk 3777; (fig.) emotional tumult Bo 4. m2. 8/11. **3.** flood tide F.Sq 259, F.Fkl 1059. **4.** river Bo 4. m7. 30/43, 5. m1. 8/11, HF 72; water Bo 3. m12. 28/40 (L flumina). [OE flōd]

floor n. floor G.CY 936, in the ~ on the floor A.Kn 2205, A.Rv 4277, D.WB 768; inwith the ~ within the domain Bo 2. p1. 67/93 (L aream). [OE flōr]

florissheth pr. 3 sg. grows abundantly I.Pars 636; pr. p. ? happy and healthy B.Mel 2185, abounding in virtue I.Pars 288, eager Bo 1. m1. 2. [OF floriss-, stem of florir]

florisshinges vbl. n. pl. florid ornaments HF 1301.

florouns† n. pl. ? petals or ? small flowers LGW 217, 220, 529. [OF]

floteren pr. pl. waver, vacillate Bo 3. p11. 156/210; pr. p. unstable m9. 6/8. [OE flotorian]

flour n. **1.** flower A. Prol 90, A.Kn 2937, B.Th 2097, LGW 524; ~ of ~s most perfect flower ABC 4; the ~ (cult of) perishable beauty LGW 189, etc.; ornament in form of flower B.Mk 3563. **2.** model, paragon A.Kn 3059, E.Cl 919, F.Fkl 1088, G.SN 29; ~ of most excellent of LGW 1009, most excellent in 2248. **3.** prime peak D.WB 113; in his ~ at his peak A.Kn 3048, hir ~ her perfection (iron.) BD 630; ~ of il endyng the ultimate in bad results A.Rv 4174; prize, in bereth the ~ excels B.Th 2091. **4.** flour, meal A.Rv 4053, 4093. [AN flur/flour]

floure(n v. **1.** flourish E.Cl 120, TC 4.1577, ~ ful of abound in Bo 4. p1. 19/27. **2.** promise flowers Anel 306. [OF florir/flurir]

flourettes n. pl. buds or small flowers RR 891. [OF florete]

floury adj. flowery BD 398, LGW 174, flower-bringing Bo 4. m6. 20/29 (L florifer). [from **flour**]

floute n. flute HF 1223. [OF flaüte]

floutours n. pl. flute players RR 763. [OF flaüteur]

flowe(n v. **1.** run, flow (of water) Bo 2. m8. 6/9, 5. m1. 12/17, TC 3. 1758; (of tide) ebbe and ~ Fort 61, Bo 2. m1. 4/5; ~ togidre joining Bo 5. p1. 59/85. **2.** pr. p. seeping Bo 1. p5. 52/75. **3.** pr. p. wavering Bo 2. p8. 17/24. [OE flōwan]

fneseth *pr. 3 sg.* wheezes H.Mcp 62. [OE *fnēosan*]

fnorteth *pr. 3 sg.* snores A.Rv 4163 *var* **snorteth,** B.ML 790 *var* **snoreth.** [cf. OE *fnora* sneezing]

foyne *v.* thrust A.Kn 1654, 2615, *pr. subj. sg.* 2550. [from OF *foine* n.]

foison *n.* abundance A.Mil 3165, B.ML 504, RR 1359. [OF]

folde *n.*[1] sheepfold A.Prol 512, A.Kn 1308. [OA *fáld*]

folde *n.*[2] fold in cloth, pleat TC 2.697. [from next]

folde *v.* 1. bend (paper) TC 2.1085; **folden** *p.p.* (arms) 4.359. 2. ~ *in armes* embrace TC 3.1201, 4.1230, 1247. 3. join Bo 3. p12. 120/160 (L *complicas*). [OA *fáldan*]

foled *p.p.* born D.Fri 1545. [from OE *fola* n.]

foly *adv.* foolishly BD 874. [from **fool** adj.]

folye *n.* 1. foolishness, stupidity B.Mel 2255, BD 610, TC 4.1504; foolish act A.Kn 1798, BD 737, TC 2.774, 3.762, 986; *don* ~ behave foolishly A.Kn 3045, B.Mel 2894, TC 2.1510; ? buffoonery 1168; foolish trifle B.NP 4628. 2. sin C.Pard 464, I.Pars 315, 404; baseness TC 3.394; *pl.* bad ways I.Pars 972; slander I.Pars 378 (or ? frivolousness). 3. lasciviousness, wantonness A.Kn 1942, A.Rv 3880, B.ML 163, C.Phs 64, E.Cl 236, E.Mch 1655, *don* ~ fornicate LGW 723, ? PF 221. 4. madness TC 3.838, 1382/1368. 5. injury A.Mil 3146. 6. ? confusion Bo 1. p6. 68/87, 4. p6. 240/348, 5. p1. 29/40 (all L *temeritati*); ? nonsense F.Fkl 1131. [OF]

folyen/foleyen *pr. pl.* believe mistakenly Bo 3. p2. 62/89, 66/95. [OF *foleier*]

folily *adv.* foolishly B.Mel. 2639, 2796; wantonly E.Mch 1403; aimlessly Bo 4. p6.114/165. [from **folye**]

folk *n.* 1. persons, people A.Prol 12, C.Pard 420, PF 9; *religious* ~ clergy B.Mk 3150, *cristene* ~ Christians B.Pri 1804, (qual. by *moche(l)* B.Mel 2844, Bo 2. p5. 20/28, 3. p5. 11/15; *pl.* people D.WB 330, PF 278, TC 3.1137, 5.1835. 2. human beings D.WB 1148, HF 1968. 3. company A.Mil 3840, Pity 48, TC 2. 1567, RR 704; congregation B.Mel 2944; (with sg. v.) B.ML 328, TC 2.1743, HF 2055. 4. household, family A.Kn 1286, D.WB 301, F.Sq 379, TC 1.354, 2.1194; followers A.Kn 1537, Bo 1. p3. 41/57, TC 1.319, HF 237. 5. nation, citizens B.Mk 3850, E.Cl 894, F.Fkl 1411, Anel 23, TC 4.55, 112, HF 73; *countrée* ~ fellow countrymen LGW 2161. [OE *folc*]

folwe(n *v.* 1. go/come after E.Cl 897, TC 3.1062, 4.1187; succeed LGW 2549. 2. accompany A.Mil 3260, TC 4.307. 3. obey A.Prol 528, B.Mel 2390, D.WB 583, F.Fkl 749; imitate D.WB 1124, E.Cl 1143, Ven 81; submit to E.Cl 873. 4. pursue BD 585; seek I.Pars 216, 441, Bo 5. m3. 23/34; pursue, practise Bo 4. p2. 126/171, 129/176. 5. result B.Mel 2579, Bo 5. p3. 109/153; result from I.Pars 853; follow as a logical consequence Bo 3. p6. 14/19, p9. 45/60. 6. use as an authority or source Anel 21, Bo 5. p6. 69/97, TC 2. 49, LGW 1002. [OE *folgian*]

fonde(n *v.* try B.ML 347, E.Mch 1410, BD 1020, TC 2.273, 3.1155. [OE *fándian*]

fonge *v.* receive B.ML 377. [OE *fōn,* p.p. *fángen*]

fonne *n.* fool A.Rv 4089. [?]

fontful *n.* (baptismal) fontful B.ML 357. [OE *font*+**full**]

fontstoon *n.* font B.ML 723. [OE *font*+**sto(o)n**]

foo *n.* enemy BD 583; *Cristes* ~ (as oath) the devil! A. Mil 3782. **foos** *pl.* B.Mel 2160, **foon** B.Mk 3896, TC 5.1866. [OE *ge)fā,* pl. *-fān*]

fool *n.* 1. fool, stupid ignorant person A.Kn 1812, E.Cl 1001, RR 1320, TC 1.507; *whiche a* ~ how stupid BD 734, *verrey ~es* truly stupid people TC 1.202; ~ *of fantasye* foolishly imaginative person TC 5.1523, ~ *of alle . . ~es* perfection of stupidity Bo 2. p1. 82/113–14; *holde me . . a* ~ think me an idiot B.Mel 2245; *singe a* ~ *a masse* ?speak too freely, flatter deceptively TC 3.88. 2. jester B.Mk 3271, TC 2.400. 3. ~ *of kinde* natural halfwit TC 2.370. 4. evildoer E.Mch 2278; ? deceiver TC 3.298; lecher E.Mch 1251; ~ *of hire body* whore I.Pars 156. [OF *fol*]

fool *adj.* 1. stupid G.CY 968 (or ? *n.*); senseless Bo 1. m2. 22/32. 2. lascivious I.Pars 853, 885, RR 1253. [as prec.]

fo(o)ld *quasi-n.* times, in adv. phrases: *an hundred* ~ G.CY 1091, *a thousand* ~ B.ML 1120, C.Phs 40, PF 208, TC 1.546, *by twenty thousand* ~ H.Mcp 169. [extracted from OE adj. compds. in *-fáld,* cf. **manyfold**]

fool-large *adj.* improvident, prodigal B.Mel 2789, 2810, I.Pars 814, Bo 2. m2. 8/11. [OF *fol-large*]

fool-largesse *n.* foolish liberality I.Pars 813. [OF]

fo(o)men *n. pl.* enemies B.ML 718, B.Mk 3255. [OE *fāh-mann*]

fo(o)re *n.* path: *folwe(n his* ~ follow in his footsteps D.WB 110, D.Sum 1935. [OE *fōr*]

foot *n.* foot A.Kn 2726; *on fote* A.Kn 2509, F.Sq 390, I.Pars 419; *under* ~ Bo 1. m4. 2; *with dredeful* ~ A.Kn 1479, LGW 811; *at your* ~ at your feet F.Fkl 1315, *him to* ~ at his feet LGW 1314; (of measure) F.Fkl 1103, RR 350, *pl.* unchanged A.Kn 2607, A.Rv 4124. **feet** *pl.* in *beddes* ~ the foot of a bed A.Rv 4156, 4213, TC 1.359, BD 199 *var* **fete;** *him to* **fe(e)te** at his feet B.ML 1104; *under* **fete** BD 400; claws HF 568, 606. [OE *fēt,* pl. *fēt,* dat. pl. *fōtum*]

foot-brede *n.* foot-breadth HF 2042. [prec. + **brede**]

foot-hot *adv.* instantly B.ML 438, BD 375. [**foot**+**hoot**]

foot-mantel *n.* protective garment reaching to the feet A.Prol 472. [**foot**+OF *mantel*]

for *conj.* 1. because A.Prol 102, 427, A.Kn 2681, 3089, A.Rv 4225; ~ *that* B.Sh 1581, TC 3.1667. 2. since A.Mil 3667, TC 3.934, Bo 1. m1. 19/26, ~ *that* D.WB 513, TC 4.1031, 5.1768; ~ *as muche as that* in as much as B.Mel 2457. 3. so that A.Kn 2879, B.Mel 2912, B.NP 4137, D.WB 753, ~ *that* B.Mk 3552, E.Cl 372. 4. if B.NP 4489. [OE *for þon þe,* etc.]

for *prep.* 1. because of A.Prol 264, 492,

B.ML 683, Bo 1. m2. 21/31; ~ *which* on account of which B.Sh 1240; *what* ~ because of B.Mk 3304, *see* **what**; (with adj. or p.p., equiv. to prep.+noun) ~ *blak* because of blackness A.Kn 2144, ~ *drye* because of being dry, withered F.Sq 409, ~ *dronken* because of being drunk A.Mil 3120, A.Rv 4150 (cf. **fordronke**), ~ *old* because of being old, with age A.Kn 2142, ~ *syk* because of illness D.WB 394, ~ *wery* because of weariness PF 93, ~ *wod* to distraction HF 1747, ~ *pure ashamed* out of very shame TC 2.656 *var*, ~ *pure wood* RR 276. **2.** on behalf of A.Prol 62, 301, to benefit 510, LGW 513. **3.** in place of, as A.Prol 667, LGW 2646; *word* ~ *word* literally, word for word LGW 1002, tit for tat D.WB 422; in return for A.Kn 1803, A.Mil 3381, C.Pard 724; *point* ~ *point* point by point E.Cl 577. **4.** in order to procure A.Kn 1177, D.Fri 1455, 1654, LGW 626, *sende(n* ~ A.Kn 2980, E.Mch 2008; ~ *the beste* in order to get the best result A.Prol 788, ~ *his best* in order to serve his interests B.Sh 1537, ~ *noght* to no purpose, in vain A.Kn 2648, D.WB 659. **5.** for the purpose of D.Fri 1369, LGW 2692. **6.** as regards, with respect to A.Prol 387, B.Sh 1292, E.Cl 474; ~ *me* for my part A.Kn 1233, PF 229, HF 2136, TC 2.134 *var*; *as* ~ A.Kn 1619, E.Cl 460, PF 631; ~ *the moore part* as regards most of them A.Rv 3858; ~ *that tyme* as regards that occasion BD 1313; ~ *al the world* in all respects A.Kn 1372, exactly G.CY 886; ~ *erneste or* ~ *game* in any event LGW 2703; ~ *the nones* see **nones. 7.** as, to serve as E.Mch 2148, TC 1.987, 5.315, LGW 1238; *have* .. ~ *excused* regard as excused Astr prol 30/42; *know* .. ~ know to be D.WB 320; *as* ~ *his wyf* as suited his wife LGW 1577. **8.** despite, notwithstanding C.Phs 129, E.Mch 2330; esp. ~ *al* A.Kn 2020, B.ML 982, B.Mk 3760, ~ *al that* .. *he coude poure or pryen* in spite of all the peering and prying he could do E.Mch 2112; ~ *any thing* at all costs A.Prol 276; ~ *my deth* though I were to die for it Mars 186. **9.** against, to prevent B.Th 2052, I.Pars 607, TC 1.928; to avoid PF 468, HF 1359; for fear of B.Mk 3750. **10.** (with *to*+infin.) in order to A.Prol 17, B.Mk 3305, PF 391; ~ *to dyen* though we were to die A.Kn 1133, TC 1.674, sim. B.Sh 1327, E.Cl 364; adding nothing to sense A.Mil 3667, B.ML 1067, etc. **11.** (in oaths and assertions) for the sake of, on the witness of A.Mil 3526, B.NP 4158, 4510, E.Cl 977, TC 4.1286; ~ *sothe* see **so(o)th.** [OE]

forage *n.* animal's food B.Th 1973; rough food, winter feed A.Rv 3868, E.Mch 1422. [OF *fourrage*]

forasmuche(1) as *conj.* (or as four words) seeing that, because I.Pars 179, 191, 270, Bo 3. p1. 27/36, ~ **mechel** Astr prol 4 *var*. [phr.]

forbede(n *v.* **1.** forbid (with direct obj.) A.Mil 3508, C.Pard 633, Scog 17; (with cl.) A.Co 4339, G.CY 996, ~ .. *but* forbid that .. not E.Mch 1665, LGW 910; (with pron. obj. and infin.) I.Pars 327; (without expressed obj.) (*as) God* ~ B.Sh 1398,

E.Cl 1076, TC 2.113. **forbedeth** *pr. 3 sg.* B.Mel 2774; **forbet** TC 2.717. **forbede** *subj. sg.* TC 2.716, 1690. **forbad** *pa. sg.* C.Pard 633, E.Cl 570. **forbode(n** *p.p.* E.Mch 2296. I.Pars 846. [OE *forbēodan*, *-boden*, and *bæd* from *biddan*; cf. **bidde**]

forbere(n *v.* refrain from A.Kn 885, A.Mil 3168, leave alone D.WB 665; (with infin.) B.Mel 3052, I.Pars 1035, TC 3.173; bear, endure E.Mch 2182. **forbar** *pa. sg.* TC 1.437, 3.365. [OE *forberan, -bær*]

forberinge *vbl. n.* (with *of*) abstinence (from) I.Pars 1049.

forby *adv.* by, past B.Pri 1759, TC 2.658. [OE *foran* adv.+**bi**]

forbyse *v.* to instruct by examples TC 2.1390. [from OE *forebysen* n. example]

forblak *see* **for** *prep.*

forbode *n.* prohibition: *Godes* ~ God forbid B.Mel 2248 *var*, LGW G. 10. [OE *forbod*]

forbrak *pa. sg.* interrupted Bo 4. p1. 5/6. [OE *forbræc* from *-brecan*]

forbrused *p.p.* badly bruised B.Mk 3804. [OE *for*+*brȳsan* and OF *bruser*]

force *see* **fors.**

forcracchen† *v.* scratch excessively RR 323. [OE *for-*, and cf. **cracchinge**]

forcutteth *pr. 3 sg.* cuts to pieces H.Mcp 340. [OE *for-*+**cutte(n**]

fordo(o)(n *v.* **1.** kill A.Kn 1560; *refl.* B.Sh 1317; **fordide** *pa. sg.* LGW 2557. **2.** destroy B.ML 369, **fordo(n** *p.p.* TC 1.74, 525; disgrace, ruin F.Fkl 1562, H.Mcp 290, Pity 86. **3.** spoil Bo 2. m8. 13/19 (L *solvere*), obliterate, change TC 4.1681. [OE *fordōn, -dyde, -dōn*]

fordrye *see* **for** *prep.*

fordriven *p.p.* tossed about Bo 1. p3. 46/64. [OE *fordrifen*]

fordronke *ppl. adj.* very drunk C.Pard 674. [OE *fordruncen*]

fordwyned *p.p.* shrivelled RR 366. [from OE *fordwinan*]

foreyne *adj.* (only in Bo) **1.** alien Bo 1. p4. 83/115, 4. p3. 74/106. **2.** outside, foreign Bo 2. p5. 90/126, 3. p3. 53/70 (L *extrinsecus*) **3.** outer Bo 1. m2. 3 (L *externas*). **4.** legal, made in court Bo 3. p3. 48/63 (L *forenses*). [OF *forain*]

foreyne *n.* outer privy LGW 1962. [from prec.]

for(e)knowynge *see* **forknowinge.**

for(e)ward *adv.* forwards Astr 2.35. 5/7 *var*, *fro that tyme* ~ from then on 12. 3/4; *first and* ~ above all B.Mel 2431, 2684, first of all E.Mch 2187. [cf. OE *forþweard*]

forfered *ppl. adj.* extremely afraid F.Sq 527. [OE *for-* and **fere(n**]

forfeted *pa. sg.* sinned I.Pars 273. [OF *forfet* p.p.]

forgat, -gete(n *see* **foryete(n.**

forge(n *v. tr.* forge, fashion in a smithy PF 212; (fig.) invent I.Pars 610; *intr.* work at a forge C.Phs 14, I.Pars 554. [OF *forger*]

forgift *n.* forgiveness LGW 1853. [from **foryeve(n** and *gift* n. from ON]

forgo(o)n *v.* **1.** do without, lose D.WB 315, TC 3.1384; give up TC 2. 1330, 4.195; avoid E.Mch 2085. **forgoth** *pr. 3 sg.* TC 4.713, 5.63. **foryede** *pa.* TC 2.1330. **forgoon** *p.p.* B.Mel 2183. **2. forgo** *ppl. adj.* quite exhausted HF 115. [OE *forgān, -ēode, -gān*]

forkerveth *pr. 3 sg.* hews to pieces H.Mcp 340. [from OE *forċeorfan*, cf. **kerve(n)**
forknowinge *vbl. n.* foreknowledge Bo 5. p6. 194/272. [cf. next]
forknowinge *pr. p.* foreseeing TC 1.79. [from OE *fore*+**knowe(n)**
forleften *pa. pl.* left, withdrew from Bo 1. m3. 2 *var.* **forlaft** *p.p.* abandoned C.Phs 83. [OE *for*-+**leve(n)**
forleseth *pr. 3 sg.* loses I.Pars 789. **forlore/ -lorn** *p.p.* lost, forfeited TC 5.23, LGW 2663; wasted F.Fkl 1557; abandoned Bo 4. p3. 66/95. [from OE *forlēosan*, cf. **lese(n)**
forlete(n *v.* 1. leave, give up, abandon I.Pars 93, 119, Bo 1. m5. 21/30. **forleten** *p.p.* neglected, abandoned Bo 2. p4. 118/163, HF 694. 2. cease I.Pars 250; (with infin.) Bo 1. p5. 24/35, 3. p11. 50/68. 3. lose B.Pri 1848, C.Pard 864, Bo 1. m2. 2, 5. p6. 145/205; lack Bo 2. p5. 108/152. [OE *forlætan*]
forlive(n *v.* degenerate Bo 3. p6. 37/50. **forlived** *p.p.* degenerate, ignoble m6. 9/12. [OE *for*-+**live(n)**
forloyn *n.* recall (a horn call) BD 386. [OF *forloigne*]
forlong *see* **furlong.**
forlost *p.p.* utterly lost TC 3.280, 4.756. [from OE *forlosian*, cf. **loste**]
formaly *see* **formely.**
forme *n.* 1. shape Bo 3. p9. 1/2, 104/139, 4. p6. 50/72, LGW 1582, 1583; appearance Bo 4. p3. 63/90, p4. 4/5; body D.Fri 1471, Bo 3. p8. 26/35, LGW 1768; substance Bo 3. p11. 17/23, 47/63, TC 5.1854; plan, model Bo 4. p6. 72/83; archetype Bo 3. m9. 6/9; species Bo 5. m5. 10/15; embodiment A.Kn 2313. *pl.* created things LGW 2228; *save the* ~ keep up the appearance TC 2. 1243. 2. manner F.Sq 283, 337, TC 2.22, 4.78, 1579; style (in language) F.Sq 100. 3. customary or prescribed usage: *in* ~ correctly A.Prol 305, TC 2.41; *holde the* ~ preserve propriety TC 2. 1040. 4. conception Bo 5. p4. 116/167, 125/179; semblance F.Fkl 1161. 5. lair B.Sh 1294. [OF]
forme(n *v.* create C.Phs 12, Bo 3. m9. 9/12, ~ *to creature* create BD 716; shape Ven 14, RR 1189. **y)fo(u)rmed** *p.p.* modelled, mirrored TC 5.817; *han . .* ~ be endowed with TC 4.315. [OF *fo(u)rmer*]
forme-fader *n.* (or as two words) progenitor B.Mel 2293. [OE *forma* first+**fader**]
formel *n.* female (of birds) PF 371; ~ *egle* 373, 646. [OF adj.]
formely/formaly *adv.* correctly, logically TC 4.497; through their essential nature Bo 5. p4. 134/192 (L *formaliter*). [OF *formel* or from **forme**]
former *n.* creator C.Phs 19. [from **forme(n**]
former *adj. comp.* earlier, primeval FormA 2. **formest** *sup.* foremost, leading BD 890. [OE *forma* and *formesta* first]
forncast *p.p.* premeditated, planned B.NP 4407, I.Pars 448, TC 3.521. [OE *foran*+**caste(n)**]
forold *see* **for** *prep.*
forpampred† *p.p.* overindulged FormA 5. [OE *for*- and cf. WFlem *pamperen*]
forpyned *p.p.* tormented, suffering A.Prol 205, ~ *for/of* suffering through A.Kn

1453, LGW 2428; wasted RR 365. [from OE *for*-+*pīnian*]
fors/force *n.* 1. power A.Kn 2651, B.Mk 3237, violence A.Kn 1927, D.WB 888, authority Bo 3. p12. 99/135; *by* ~ perforce, of necessity A.Kn 2554; *of fyne* ~ by sheer necessity TC 5.421; *by* ~ *of* by virtue of H.Mcp 228. 2. *no* ~ *(of)* it does not matter (about) B.ML 285, D.Sum 2189, TC 2.1477, *is no* ~ C. Pard 303, *thereof no* ~ BD 1170; *do(o)n no* ~ *(of)* pay no attention (to), care nothing (about) B.NP 4131, D.Fri 1512, Bo 2. p4. 120/166, *make no* ~ *of* take no account of H.Mcp 68; *what* ~ what does it matter? E.Mch 1295, TC 2.378. [OF *force*]
forsake(n *v.* 1. abandon (person) B.Pri 1859, B.Mk 3431, D.WB 644, Bo 2. p1. 48/68; betray, be unfaithful to B.Mk 3220, TC 1.56, 4.15, LGW G. 265; desert Bo 4. p3. 15/21. 2. leave, give up (thing) I.Pars 693, Bo 2. p4. 2, LGW 2036; neglect Bo 2. p1. 30/42. 3. renounce B.Th 1984; disown, repudiate C.Phs 80, E.Mch 2299, I.Pars 994. 4. contradict, deny Bo 1. p4. 106/148, 2. p3. 51/74; ?ignore the fact Bo 3. p2. 75/107 (L *sequestrari*). **forso(o)k** *pa. sg.* B.Mk 3220, D.WB 649. **forsake(n** *p.p.* C.Phs 80. [OE *forsacan, -sōc, -sacen*]
forseid *p.p.* aforesaid B.Mel 2191 etc.; *always in prose except* PF 120. [OE *foresægd*]
forseinge *vbl. n.* foreseeing TC 4.989. [from OE *foresēon*]
forshapen *p.p.* transformed, metamorphosed TC 2.66. [OE *forscapen*]
forshright *p.p.* worn out with shrieking TC 4.1147. [OE *for*-+ stem found in *scrīċettan* screech]
forsleuthe(n *v.* waste (time) in idleness B.NP 4286; lose by sloth I.Pars 685 *var.* [OE *for*-+**slouthe** n.]
forsleweth *pr. 3 sg.* loses by delay I.Pars 685 *var.* [OE *forslǣwan*]
forsluggeth *pr. 3 sg.* neglects, spoils through sluggishness I.Pars 685. [OE *for*-+ Scand v. rel. to Sw dial. *slogga*]
forsongen *p.p.* worn out by singing RR 664. [OE *for*-+*p.p.* of **singe(n)**
forso(o)k *see* **forsake(n.**
forsothe *see* **so(o)th.**
forster *n.* forester A.Prol 117, BD 361. [OF *forestier*]
forstraught *p.p.* greatly agitated B.Sh 1295. [OE *for*-+-*straught* as in *distraught*, itself from **distract** infl. by **straught**]
forswering(e *vbl. n.* perjury C.Pard 657, HF 153. [from v. as next]
forswor *pa. sg.* (*refl.*) perjured himself HF 389. **forswor(n** *p.p. have* ~ (*goddes*) have sworn falsely to LGW 2522; *ben* ~ be perjured 2235, 2455. [OE *forswōr, -sworen* from *-swerian*]
forth *adv.* 1. onwards F.Fkl 964; (as command) Truth 18; *fro this* ~ from then on TC 1.484, 4.314; *so fer* ~ to that extent ABC 170 (see **ferforth**); *so* ~ so on D.Sum 1924, I.Pars 297. 2. *gon, riden* ~ go, ride on(wards) G.CY 1032, TC 2.688 (and with other verbs of motion); *dryven . .* ~ *a day* pass a day TC 5.628, *dryven* ~ *the world* pass the time B.Sh 1421. 3. *tellen, speken* ~ explain, tell more A.Kn 1336,

2816 (and with similar verbs). **4.** *fetten, clepen, bringen, putten* ~ fetch, call, bring, put out B.Sh 1483, PF 352, LGW 1835, put forth PF 603; *knit* ~ infer Bo 4. p2. 84/111. **5.** (with several other verbs for emphasis, usually of continuity) A.Kn 2820, E.Cl 1015, F.Fkl 1081, TC 5.194, Mars 148. [OE]

forthby *adv.* past TC 5.537 *var.* [forth+bi]

forth(e)re(n/furthere(n *v.* help, advance A.Kn 1137, TC 2.1368. [OE *fyrþrian* and *forþ*]

forthermo(o)r(e *adv.* moreover B.NP 4317; more A.Kn 2069. [**further**+mo(o)re]

fortherover *adv.* moreover C.Pard 648, I.Pars 207, Pity 85. [**further**+over]

forthest *see* **further** *adv.*

forthy *adv.* therefore, consequently A.Kn 1841, TC 1.232; *forwhy* . . ~ because . . therefore Bo 1. p6. 56–7/71–2; *nat* ~ nevertheless B.Mel 2165. [OE *for þȳ*]

forthinke(n *v.* displease, grieve E.Mch 1906, TC 2.1414; be displeased Bo 2. p4. 49/66.

forthoughte *pa. sg.* RR 1671. [OE *forþen-ćan* and *forþynćan*, *-þōhte*, *-þūhte*]

forthright *adv.* straight forward, directly F.Fkl 1503, RR 295. [from phr.]

forthward *adv.* forward B.ML 263, F.Fkl 1169, Astr 2.35.5/7 *var.* [OE *forþweard*]

forthwith *adv.* also I.Pars 419. [from phr.]

fortroden *p.p.* trodden down, trampled I.Pars 190, Bo 4. p1. 21/29. [from OE *fortredan*, see **trede(n**]

fortuit† *adj.* fortuitous Bo 5. p1. 58/83. [L *fortuïtus*]

fortunat *adj.* **1.** favoured by fortune, prosperous B.NP 3966, beneficent, happy E.Cl 422. **2.** propitious E.Mch 1970, Astr. 2.4.21/33. [L *fortūnātus*]

fortune *n.* **1.** Fortune, goddess of mutability A.Kn 915, 925, B.Mel 2640, B.Mk 3431, etc. BD 618, Bo 1. m5. 24/34, 2. p1. 12/16, etc., TC 1.138, 3.617, Fort 4, 8. **2.** lot (of an individual) A.Kn 2659, B.Mk 3823, B.NP 4189, *pl.* Bo 1. p4. 41/57, 2. m3. 16/19, 4. p6. 106/154; (individual's) good luck B.Mel 2749, *pl.* Bo 1. p4. 49/69. **3.** ?chance B.Sh 1428. [OF, L *fortūna*]

fortunel *adj.* governed by chance or Fortune Bo 5. m1. 10/14. [OF]

fortune(n *v.* **1.** control (someone's) destiny A.Kn 2377; find or place in a favourable position A.Prol 417; *wel* ~d successful Mars 180. **2.** befall BD 288. [OF *fortuner*]

fortunous *adj.* **1.** governed by Fortune Bo 2. p3. 59/86; fortuitous, accidental Bo 1. p6. 7/9, 10/13, 2. p6. 32/46, 5. p1. 52/74. **2.** transitory Bo 2. p4. 102/140, 124/172. [OF]

forwaked *ppl. adj.* worn out by lack of sleep B.ML 596, BD 126. [OE *for-*+**wake(n**]

forward *n.* agreement, promise A.Prol 829, A.Kn 1209, *as* ~ *is/was* in accordance with the agreement A.Kn 2619, B.ML 34; *hold(en* ~ TC 5.497, LGW 2500, *kepe* ~ A.Prol 852, *breke* ~ B.ML 40. [OE *foreweard*]

forward *see* **for(e)ward.**

forwelked *p.pl. adj.* wrinkled RR 361. [OE *for-*+**welked**]

forweped *ppl. adj.* worn out by weeping BD 126. [OE *for-*+**wepe(n**]

forwered *p.p.* worn out RR 235. [OE *forwerod*]

forwery *adj.* very weary PF 93. [OE *for-*+**wery**]

forwhy *adv.* and *conj.* why Bo 4. p2. 125/170, TC 3.1009, HF 20 *var*; because C.Pard 847, Bo 1. p1. 45/63, since Bo 2. p8. 25/36, 3. p10. 102/138, TC 3.477; consequently Bo 5. p4. 73/105, wherefore TC 2.12, 1238. [OE *for*+*hwī*]

forwiter *n.* foreknower Bo 5. p6. 210/295. [from v., see **forwo(o)t**]

forwiting *n.* foreknowledge B.NP 4433. [from infin. stem of next]

forwo(o)t *pr. 3 sg.* knows in advance B.NP 4424, 4438, TC 4.1071, HF 45. [OE *fore-witan*, pr. sg. *forewāt*]

forwrapped *p.p.* wrapped up C.Pard 718; concealed I.Pars 320. [OE *for-*+**wrappe(n**]

foryede *see* **forgo(o)n.**

foryelde *pr. subj. sg.* may (he) repay E.Cl 831, LGW 457. [OA *forġeldan*]

foryete(n/-geten *v.* **1.** forget A.Kn 3054, B.Mel 2602; ~ . . *minde/wit* lose (one's) memory, wits B.ML 527, LGW 1752. **2.** neglect B.NP 4144; ~ *to* omit to A.Kn 1882, 1914. **3.** *refl.* lack awareness of self Bo 1. p2. 15/22, 5. m3. 31/45. **foryeteth** *pr. 3 sg.* TC 2.375; forget RR 61. **forgat** *pa. 1, 3 sg.* A.Rv 4076, BD 790; **foryat** TC 5.1535. **forgete/-gate** 2 *sg.* LGW 540. **foryete(n** *p.p.* A.Kn 1914; **forgeten** A.Kn 3054, Scog 46. [OA *forġetan*, *-ġæt*, *-ġeten*, infl. by **gete(n**]

foryetelnesse *n.* forgetfulness I.Pars 827. [cf. OE *forġytelnes*]

foryetinge *vbl. n.* forgetfulness Bo 3. m11. 21/28.

foryeve(n/-yive *v.* **1.** *tr.* pardon, excuse I.Pars 301, TC 3.1129; (with dat. of person) A.Prol 743, E.Cl 526, LGW 1848. **2.** *intr.* be forgiving TC 5.1578, LGW 162. **forgaf** *pa. sg.* I.Pars 808; **foryaf** TC 3.1129. **foryeve/-gave** *pl.* LGW 1848. **foryeve(n** *p.p.* PF 82, **foryive(n** BD 877. [OA *forġefan*, see **yeve(n**]

foryifnesse/-yevenesse *n.* forgiveness B.Mel 2963, I.Pars 303, 987. [OE *forġif(e)nes*]

fostre(n *v.* **1.** foster, bring up A.Rv 3946, E.Cl 834; ~ *up* B.ML 275, C.Phs 219, *p.p.* in *povreliche yfostred up* brought up in poverty E.Cl 213; teach G.SN 539. **2.** cherish E.Cl 222, E.Mch 1387, H.Mcp 131, Fort 42. **3.** feed, nourish H.Mcp 165, 175, Bo 1. p2. 4/6; *p.p.* full grown RR 389. [OE *fōstrian*, cf. ON *fóstra*]

fostring *vbl. n.* nourishment D.Sum 1845.

fother *n.* load A.Prol 530, large amount A.Kn 1908. [OE]

foudre *n.* thunderbolt HF 535. [OF]

foul *n.* bird A.Prol 190, E.Cl 683, ~ *of ravyne* birds of prey PF 323, 527. [OE *fugol*]

foul *adj.* **1.** vile, bad, evil C.Pard 536, TC 1.213; painful TC 2.896, ?dim LGW 2240; ~ *or fair* all circumstances F.Sq 121; *for* ~ *ne fair* for anything that could be done B.ML 525, *neither* ~ *ne fair* neither good nor bad LGW 1818; ~ *feend* D.Fri 1610, G.CY 705. **2.** shameful B.NP 4087, D.Sum 2049, Anel 300, TC 4.275, Bo 3. p6. 7/9. **3.** sinful A.Prol 501, B.ML 925, D.Sum 1875, I.Pars 685, LGW 1380; dirty, squalid Bo 4. p3. 86/124. **4.** ugly, hideous D.WB 1063, E.Cl 1209, RR 159, 177, ~ *or fair* ugly or beautiful B.ML 764; ?savage B.Mk 3273. [OE *fūl*]

foule *adv.* **1.** badly A.Rv 4220, gravely D.Fri 1312; ~ *falle* (with dat.) may ill fortune come to H.Mcp 40, TC 4.462. **2.** shamefully D.WB 1069, I.Pars 815, TC 4.1467, 1577, LGW 1307. **3.** hideously RR 155. [OE *fūle*]

found, founde(n *see* **finde(n.**

founde *v.* try Anel 47, seek 241. [OE *fúndian*]

founde(n *v.* build, erect E.Cl 61, BD 922, PF 231, Bo 1. p5. 20/29, 2. m4. 1/2, TC 1.1065, HF 1981. **(y)founded** *p.p.* BD 922, **founden** Bo 3. p9. 147/199 *var.* [OF *fonder*]

foundred *pa. sg.* stumbled A.Kn 2687. [OF *fondrer*]

fourmed *see* **forme(n.**

fo(u)rneys *n.* (alchemist's) furnace A.Prol 559, G.CY 804; fire (under a cauldron) A.Prol 202; (fireplace of a) forge I.Pars 546. 554. [OF *fornais*]

fownes *n. pl.* fawns, young deer BD 429; (fig.) whelps, young desires TC 1.465 *var.* [OF]

fra *adv.* (nth.) fro: *til and* ~ to and fro A.Rv 4039. [ON *frā*]

frak(e)nes *n. pl.* freckles A.Kn 2169. [cf. ON *freknur*]

franchyse *n.* nobility B.Mk 3854, I.Pars 452; generosity, liberality E.Mch 1987, RR 955; delicacy, decency F.Fkl 1524. [OF]

frankeleyn *n.* franklin (landowner) A.Prol 331, F.Fkl 675. [AN *frraunclein*]

frape *n.* company TC 3.410. [OF *frap*]

fraught *p.p.* loaded B.ML 171. [from MDu *vrachten*]

fredom *n.* **1.** liberty Bo 1. p4. 37/52, TC 1.235. **2.** nobleness A.Prol 46, Mars 175, 294, TC. 2.161, LGW 1010. **3.** generosity B.ML 168, Anel 106, LGW 1127. [OE *frēodōm*]

free *n.* noble one CompL 104/98, TC 3.128. [next]

free *adj.* **1.** free A.Kn 1292, D.WB 936; unrestrained I.Pars 899; unrestricted B.Pri 1684, ~ *assent* A.Prol 852, ~ *chois* B.NP 4436, TC 4.971; ~ *wil* Bo 1. p4. 200/280. **2.** without pain I.Pars 272, Bo 3. p3. 22/30. **3.** (of rank) of free condition, not bondman B.Mel 2757, TC 1.840; noble G.SN 444; gracious, magnanimous E.Mch 2138, F.Sq 489. **4.** beautiful C.Phs 35, (? or gracious) A.Kn 2386, BD 484, TC 3.1522, 5.1362, 1390, 1471; **4.** generous B.Sh 1300, B.Mel 3076, B.NP 4104, F.Fkl 1622, TC 1.958, 5.823, LGW 2521; ~ . . *of dispence* A.Co 4387, B.Sh 1233. [OE *frēo*]

free *adv.* freely, totally F.Sq 541, TC 2.1121. [from prec.]

freend *n.* **1.** friend A.Prol 670, B.ML 269, *verray* ~ true friend D.WB 1204, E.Mch 1302, *grete* ~ close friend TC 2. 1403, *fulle* ~ intimate friend E.Mch 2066, TC 1.610, 1059; ~*es torn* friendly act C.Pard 815; (as address) D.Sum 1770, E.Mch 1400. **2.** lover F.Fkl 762, Anel 260, Mars 147, TC 2.803, ?5.343. **3.** relative, kinsman B.Mk 3461, I.Pars 1056, LGW 1827, ?1833, 1840. **4.** advocate, help: *ben* ~

D.Fri 1366, TC 2.1407, 1451, 1550, 1677, 5.128. [OE *frēond*, and ON *frǽndi* kinsman]

freendly *adj.* friendly G.CY 1302, favourable A.Kn 2680, F.Fkl 1467; propitious Astr 2.4. 31/48. [OE *frēondlić*]

freendly *adv.* in a friendly way A.Kn 1652, D.Sum 1849, favourably, kindly BD 852, TC 3.130 [OE *frēondlīce*]

fre(e)r(e *n.* friar, itinerant preacher A.Prol 208, 621. [OF]

freyne(n *v.* ask G.SN 433, TC 5.1227, importune B.Pri 1790. [OE *fregnan, frægn(i)an*]

frele *adj.* **1.** weak I.Pars 1078, vulnerable Bo 2. p6. 27/38. **2.** transitory Bo 2. p8. 16/23, 3. p10. 23/32. [OF]

frelenesse *n.* weakness, impermanence Bo 4. p2. 12/15. [from prec.]

freletee *n.* weakness, sinfulness C.Phs 78, E.Cl 1160, I.Pars 449, 477; lechery D.WB 92, 93. [OF *frailetē*]

frely *adv.* **1.** freely A.Kn 1207, 1849, totally LGW 683, willingly Bo 2. p2. 9/12, LGW 704. **2.** generously D.WB 150, LGW 1550, magnanimously F.Fkl 1604, G.SN 55. [from **free**]

frem(e)de *adj.* strange LGW 1046, foreign F.Sq 429; distant, reserved TC 2.248, ~ *and tame* wild and tame 3.529 *var.* [OE *fremede*]

frendschipe *n.* friendship A.Prol 428, TC 2.371, favour ? 240; *dide* ~ granted favour G.CY 1362. [OE *frēondscipe*]

frenesye *n.* madness D.Sum 2209, TC 1.727. [OF]

frenges *n. pl.* fringes D.Fri 1383, HF 1318. [OF]

fressh *adj.* **1.** fresh, new A.Prol 90, A.Kn 1511, B.Mk 3312, C.Pard 928. **2.** lovely, blooming A.Kn 1068, 1118, E.Mch 1782, F.Sq 384, TC 1.166. **3.** vigorous F.Sq 23, F.Fkl 1092, Anel 34, TC 2.636, 5.830; lusty B.Sh 1367, D.WB 508. **4.** gay, joyous TC 2.552, 3.611, RR 435; youthful F.Sq 622. [OE *fersc*]

fressh(e *adv.* recently, newly A.Prol 365, A.Kn 2832, B.Sh 1499; brightly, gaily A.Kn 1048, LGW 1207. [from prec.]

fresshe *v.* refresh RR 1513. [from adj. and OF *freschir*]

fresshly *adv.* joyously TC 5.390; ~ *newe* newly, starting afresh TC 4.457, anew 5.1010, unfailingly, with undiminished force BD 1228, TC 3.143, CompA 82. [from adj.]

fret *n.* ornament, net LGW 215, 225. [OF *fret(t)e*]

freto(n *v.* eat, devour A.Kn 2019, Bo 3. m2. 14/20; gnaw D.WB 561; (fig.) devour, annihilate Anel 12, 13; *made up* ~ caused to be consumed TC 5. 1470. **fret** *pr. 3 sg.* RR 387. **fre(e)ten** *pa. pl.* A.Kn 2068. **frete(n** *p.p.* B.ML 475, Bo 4. m7. 15/21; **yfreten** LGW 1951. [OE *fretan, frǣton, ǧe)freten*]

fretted *p.p.* ~ *ful of* thickly set with LGW 1117. [OF *fretē*]

fro *prep.* from A.Prol 44, Pity 89, (following obj.) B.Mk 3641; ~ *poynt to poynt* in all respects B.Mk 3652, PF 461; *be(n war* ~ beware of D.Sum 1994, LGW 473; ~ *me deed* dead to me TC 2.845; *wesh* . . ~ wash clear of B.ML 453, *putte us* ~ remove

from us G.SN 22; ~ *us-ward* away from us Astr 1.17.10/13 *var* (cf. **toward**). *adv.* in *to and* ~ A.Kn 1700, *see* **fra**. [ON *frá*]
from *prep.* from: *crouche* . . ~ A.Mil 3479, *blesse* . . ~ 3484, H.Mcp 321 bless against; ~ *Troilus* separated from Troilus TC 4.766; ~ . . *sighte* out of (one's) sight TC 5.635. [OE]
frote(n *v.* rub A.Mil 3747, TC 3.1115. [OF *froter*]
frothen *pr. pl.* foam (at mouth) A.Kn 1659. [cf. ON *fróða*]
frounce *n.* fold, crease Bo 1. p2. 20/28. [OF *fronce*]
frounced *p.p.* wrinkled RR 155, 365. [OF *froncir*]
frounceles *adj.* unwrinkled RR 860. [from n.]
frount *n.* countenance Bo 2. p8. 5/7. [OF *fro(u)nt*]
fructuous *adj.* fruitful, edifying I.Pars 73. [OF]
fruyt *n.* fruit (fig.) A.Kn 1282, E.Mch 1270, TC 1.385; offspring E.Cl 990; essence, essential part B.NP 4633, LGW 1160; result, outcome F.Sq 74; enjoyment D.WB 114. [OF *fruit*]
fruytesteres *n. pl.* fruit girls C.Pard 478. [OF *fruit*+OE fem. suff. *-estre*]
fugitif *adj.* fleeing (*of* 'from') HF 146. [OF]
fulfille(n *v.* **1.** fill (often in **fulfild** *ppl. adj.* full) A.Kn 940, C.Phs 3, B.ML 660, Bo 1. p4. 197/276, 2. p5. 20/27, m7. 5/7. **2.** satisfy (desire, appetite D.WB 1218, E.Cl 907, Bo 2. p5. 54/76, gratify F.Fkl 1372, Bo 3. m12. 30/42. **3.** execute, carry out, perform B.ML 284, B.Mel 2958, E.Cl 596; **fulfelle** consummate TC 3.510; accomplish I.Pars 19. **4.** ?equal, complete Bo 5. p6. 58/81 (L *implere atque exprimere*). [OE *fulfyllan*]
fulfillinge *vbl. n.* satisfaction Bo 2. p5. 58/81, 3. p7. 2/3.
full *adj.* **1.** full A.Kn 2279, B.Sh 1259; ~ *yeres* years of plenty Bo 1. m2. 17/25, ~ *conclusioun* firm conclusion LGW 2646; as *n.* in *the* ~ *of the mone* I.Pars 424, *at the/atte* ~ at the full F.Fkl 1069, hard A.Rv 4305, TC 1.209, completely 3.517, 534, in full E.Cl 749, indeed A.Rv 3936, *unto the* ~ without reserve TC 3.213. **2.** sated: ~ *to speke* sated with talking TC 3.1661. **3.** total, complete (belief, assent) G.SN 415, TC 3.436, Bo 2. p8. 30/43, *of* ~ *avysement* on full consideration B.ML 86; *his* ~ *entente* his firm intention C.Pard 849, ~ *blisfulnesse* true joy Bo 3. p9. 118/158; whole, entire in *ten dayes* ~ TC 5.239, ~ *a strete* 4.929. [OE]
full *adv.* quite, completely, very (with adjs.) A.Prol 119, B.NP 4449, BD 399, (with advs.) A.Kn 1356, TC 5.506, HF 1465; ~ *ofte tymes* B.Sh 1600, ~ *many a* D.Fri 1592, E.Mch 1584, LGW 2115, ~ *fewe* G.CY 1123; *so* ~ so utterly BD 583, completely (as intensive with v.) F.Fkl 1230, TC 1.378, LGW 1635; ~ *chosen* firmly chosen Mars 18. [OE]
fulliche *adv.* fully E.Cl 706, TC 1.316, HF 428. [OE *fullīce*]
fulsomnesse *n.* fullness, excess F.Sq 405. [from *full adj.*]
fume *n.* vapour B.NP 4114. [OF]

fumetere *n.* fumitory (herb) B.NP 4153. [OF *fumeterre*]
fumositee *n.* vapour, fume C.Pard 567, F.Sq 358. [OF]
fundacioun *n.* foundation: *of olde tyme of his* ~ since its building long ago LGW 739. [OF]
fundement *n.* **1.** foundation D.Sum 2103, HF 1132; (fig.) Bo 3. p11. 93/126. **2.** basis (for reasoning, etc.) Bo 4. p4. 155/220, 5. p1. 35/48. **3.** anus C.Pard 950. [OF *fundament*]
furial *adj.* torturing, fierce F.Sq 448. [OF, L *fūriālis*]
furlong *n.* furlong (an eighth of a mile) A.Rv 4166; **for-** race-track Bo 4. p3. 7/10; ~ *wey* time taken to walk a furlong, two or three minutes A.Mil 3637, A.Rv 4199, B.ML 557, E.Cl 516, HF 2064, LGW 307. [OE *furlăng*]
further *adv. comp.* further A.Rv 4117, 4222, Bo 4. p2. 120/163; more advanced E.Cl 712. **forthest** *sup.* Bo 4. p6. 86/123 *var.* Cf. **ferther**. [OE *furþor*]
furthere(n *see* **forth(e)re(n**.
fusible *adj.* capable of being fused G.CY 856. [OF]
fustian *n.* coarse cloth A.Prol 75. [OF *fustaigne*]

G

ga *see* **go(o)(n**.
gabbe(n *v.* gossip, chatter A.Mil 3510; talk foolishly, lie B.NP 4256, BD 1075, TC 3.301, 4.481; be wrong Bo 2. p5. 121/170. [ON *gabba*]
gabber(e *n.* idle talker I.Pars 89. [from prec.]
gadeling *v.* scoundrel, knave RR 938. [OE *gædeling*]
gadere(n *v.* **1.** gather, pick E.Mch 2231, Bo 3. m8. 3/4. **2.** assemble A.Prol 824, A.Kn 2183; summon Bo 1. p4. 5/7; attract Bo 2. p1. 1/2. **3.** deduce Bo 4. p2. 36/48, 157/214; collect Bo 3. m11. 4/5, ~ *togidre* draw (an argument) together Bo 2. p4. 103/141, 4. p3. 31/44. **4.** ?lead, guide Bo 4. m5. 4/5. [OE *gad(e)rian*]
gaderinge *vbl. n.* assembling B.Mel 2765.
gay *adj.* **1.** gay, joyful A.Mil 3339, D.WB 545, RR 32; wanton, amorous A.Mil 3769, D.WB 508, RR 83. **2.** finely dressed A.Prol 74, D.WB 236; or ? arrogant A.Rv 3926. **3.** fine, splendid A.Prol 111, H.Mcp 168, I.Pars 197, bright D.WB 344, RR 567. [OF]
gay *adv.* richly, handsomely A.Mil 3689. [from prec.]
gaylard/gaillard *adj.* gay, lively A.Mil 3336, A.Co 4367. [OF *gaillard*]
gayler *n.* jailer A.Kn 1064, LGW 1988. [OF *gaiolere*]
gayneth *pr. 3 sg.* avails A.Kn 1176, 1787, 2755. **gayned** *pa.* availed TC 1.352. [ON *gegna*]
gaytres/-ys *n.* ?buckthorn, ?honeysuckle B.NP 4155. [cf. OE *gāte-trēow*, perh. *-hris*]
gala(u)ntyne *n.* bread sauce Rosem 17, FormA 16. [OF]
gale(n *v.* exclaim D.WB 832; *subj. sg.* protest D.Fri 1336. [OE *galan* sing]

galianes/galiones *n. pl.* ?medical drinks (named after Galen, cf. **ipocras**) C.Pard 306.

galingale *n.* powdered root, spice A.Prol 381. [OF]

galle *n.* sore spot on skin D.WB 940. [OA *galla*]

galoche *n.* shoe F.Sq 555. [OF]

galping *ppl. adj.* yawning F.Sq 350, 354. [MDu *galpen*]

galwes *n. pl.* gallows B.Mk 3924, D.WB 658. [OA *galgan*]

gamed *pa. sg. impers.* pleased A.Prol 534. [cf. OE *gamenian*, and next]

game(n *n.* **1.** pleasure, joy BD 1220, TC 2.38, HF 1199. **2.** sport, entertainment A.Prol 853, A.Mil 3117, B.NP 3981, D.WB 648, HF 886; *make* ~ gambol, frisk A.Mil 3259, *make him* .. ~ *and glee* provide him with entertainment B.Th 2030; *hadde a* ~ was amused, entertained B.Mk 3740; *brek* .. *our* ~ spoil our entertainment B.Mk 3117; *pleyen thilke* ~ have sexual intercourse B.Mk 3478; *finde* ~ *in myn hood* find me a source of amusement TC 2. 1109-10, sim. HF 1810; *no* ~ no fun B.Sh 1480. **3.** joke, jest A.Kn 1806, A.Mil 3186, 3405, A.Co 4354, D.Fri 1279; *in my/his* ~ B.NP 4452, BD 238, G.CY 1326; see **agame, ernest. 4.** contest, game BD 618, 663; sport TC 1.868. **5.** trickery G.CY 1326, 1402, TC 3.1084. **6.** ?events TC 3.1494, *mannes* ~ manly conduct TC 3.1126. [OE *gamen*]

gan *see* **ginne(n.**

ganeth *pr. 3 sg.* yawns H.Mcp 35. [OE *gānian*]

gape(n *v.* gape A.Mil 3473 *var*, 3841 *var*, Bo 3. p3. 69/91; ~ *faste* opens his mouth wide LGW 2004; **gaping** *pr. p.* with mouth wide open A.Kn 2008, A.Mil 3444 *var*, B.NP 4232. [ON *gapa*; cf. **cape**]

gapinges *vbl. n. pl.* greedy desires Bo 2. m2. 11/15.

garde *see* **save garde.**

gardin-ward *see* **unto, toward.**

gargat *n.* throat B.NP 4525. [OF]

garleek *n.* garlic A.Prol 634. [OE *gārlēac*]

garnement *n.* garment Bo 1. p2. 19/28, RR 896. [OF]

garnere *see* **gerner.**

garnisoun *n.* garrison B.Mel 2217, 2538; protection 2527, 2529. [OF]

gas *see* **go(o)n.**

gastly *adj.* terrifying A.Kn 1984 [from *gast ppl. adj.*, OE *gǣstan* frighten]

gastnesse *n.* threat, terror Bo 3. p5. 19/26. [from *gast* as prec.]

gat *see* **gete(n.**

gate/yate *n.* gate, entry A.Kn 1415, I.Pars 714, PF 154, TC 2.617, 3.1725. [OE *ġeat*, A *gæt*; pl. *gatu*]

gat-tothed *adj.* with teeth set wide apart A.Prol 468, D.WB 603. [from ON *gat* opening]

gaude *n.* trick C.Pard 389, TC 2.351; *pl.* pranks I.Pars 651. [?AN deriv. of OF *gaudie*]

gaudé *adj.* ~ *grene* yellowish-green A.Kn 2079. [from OF *gaude* weld]

gauded *adj.* furnished with large beads (marking Paternosters) A.Prol 159. [from *gaud* n., cf. OF *gaudie*]

gaure(n *v.* ~ *on* stare at A.Mil 3827, B.Mk 3559, TC 2.1157. [?ON]

gea(u)nt/giaunt *n.* giant B.Th 1997, Bo 3, p12. 98/133, TC 5.838. [OF *jaiant*, OE *gigant*]

gebet *n.* gibbet HF 106. [OF *gibet*]

ge(e)re *n.*[1] **1.** armour A.Kn 1016, 2180, TC 2.635, 1012. **2.** clothes E.Cl 372, TC 4.1523. **3.** equipment A.Prol 365, utensils 352; belongings A.Rv 4016, B.ML 800. **4.** *pl.* ?calculations F.Fkl 1276. [ON *gervi*]

ge(e)re *n.*[2] behaviour A.Kn 1372; *in hir queynte* ~*s* in their wild fashion A.Kn 1531; *in no* ~ in no changeable fashion BD 1257. [?cf. MDu *gere*]

ge(e)ste *n.* **1.** tale (often in verse), story, history B.ML 1126, E.Mch 2284, F.Sq 211, TC 2.83; *in* ~ in verse B.Mel 2123. **2.** *pl.* deeds, exploits D.WB 642, TC 5.1511, HF 1434, 1515, 1737; *after his* ~ according to his exploits TC 2. 1349 *var*. [OF]

ge(e)ste *v.* tell tales in verse I.Pars 43. [from prec.]

ge(e)st(i)ours *n. pl.* story-tellers B.Th 2036, HF 1198. [from v.]

geeth *see* **go(o)n.**

gelde *v.* castrate B.Mk 3342. [ON *gelda*]

gendres *n. pl.* kinds HF 18. [OF]

generacioun *n.* procreation, reproduction D.WB 116, Bo 3. p11. 94/129, 125/173. [OF]

general *adj.* **1.** universal A.Kn 1663, 2969, B.ML 673, B.Mel 2239; comprehensive Astr 2.2.8/11; ~ *reule* rule without exceptions B.Mel 2255, Astr 1.6.5/7; *in* ~ usually Fort 56, 64, 72; *to ech in* ~ to everyone TC 3.1802. **2.** inclusive I.Pars 388; *in* ~ in general terms B.Mel 2423, TC 1.926, Truth 26, in all respects TC 5.822, in one body 1.163, without exception B.ML 417; total ABC 60; ?perfect BD 990. **3.** broad, general, unspecific F.Fkl 945, I.Pars 464; *in* ~ broadly A.Kn 2285. [OF]

generally *adv.* **1.** in general terms H.Mcp 328, I.Pars 608, 613, 619, 676. **2.** without exception Astr 1.21.13/17, 2.10.4/5, 11.3/4; everywhere D.WB 1037, TC 1.86. **3.** usually I.Pars 371, 1033. [from prec.]

gent *adj.* noble B.Th 1905; slender, delicate A.Mil 3234, RR 1032; fluent PF 558. [OF]

gent(e)rye *n.* **1.** noble birth or rank D.WB 1152, I.Pars 452 *var*, 461 (first two). **2.** nobility (of character, behaviour, etc.) D.WB 1146, I.Pars 461 (third); magnanimity LGW 394; *holden it a* ~ regard it as a sign of good breeding I.Pars 601. [OF]

gentil *adj.* **1.** noble, aristocratic A.Prol 72, A.Kn 952, D.WB 1153, E.Mch 1907, F.Sq 622, G.SN 425, I.Pars 961, Bo 3. p6. 27/36, LGW 1306. **2.** noble, gracious (of character and behaviour) A.Kn 1431, A.Mil 3171, D.WB 1157, Bo 3. p6. 31/42, TC 5. 1773, ~ *herte* refined, sensitive disposition A.Kn 1761, 1772, B.ML 660, E.Mch 1986, TC 3.5; superior (iron. of a person) A.Prol 647, 669, E.Mch 1995; friendly LGW 1090. **3.** refined, superior (animals and birds) F.Sq 195, PF 196, 337, 575, fine, delicate PF 373, RR 1016; ?solemn, holy D.WB 29, ?intricate RR 1081, ?feeble A.Mil 3360. [OF]

gentil(l)esse *n.* **1.** nobility, rank B.Mk 3441, D.WB 1109, I.Pars 585, Bo 3. p6. 24/32, 26/35; *fostre in* .. ~ bring up aristocratically E.Cl 593. **2.** nobility, graciousness, kindness A.Kn 920, D.WB 1163, Bo 3. p6. 32/44, TC 1.881, 2.160, 662, 3.1414/1400 *var*, Gent 1 *var*; *don* .. ~ behave nobly, be kind TC 3.882, *meneth* .. ~ intends kindness 1148; noble beauty, elegance F.Sq 426. [OF]

gentilly *adv.* honourably A.Kn 3104, F.Fkl 1608, courteously B.ML 1093, B.Sh 1471, TC 2.187; delicately, softly LGW 171. [from adj.]

gentilnesse *n.* nobility, graciousness Mars 175, TC 3. 1414/1400 *var*, Gent 1 *var*. [from adj.]

gentils *n. pl.* gentlefolk A.Mil 3113, C.Pard 323, D.WB 1209, E.Cl 480, Anel 67. [from adj.]

gentrice *n.* noble birth I.Pars 452 *var*. [OF *gentrise*]

geomancie *n.* divination by figures written on the ground I.Pars 605 *var*. [OF]

geometriens *n. pl.* geometricians Bo 3. p10. 98/133. [OF]

gerdone, gerdoun *see* **guer-**.

gerful *adj.* changeable A.Kn 1538, TC 4.286. [from **ge(e)re²**]

gery *adj.* changeable A.Kn 1536. [as prec.]

gerl *n.* girl A.Mil 3769. **girles** *pl.* young people A.Prol 664. [?]

germayns *adj. pl.* near of kin B.Mel 2558; see **cosin**. [OF]

gerner/garnere *n.* garner, granary A.Prol 593, Bo 1. p4. 54/75. [OF *gernier*]

gesse *v.* guess, suppose PF 602, Ven 10, imagine B.ML 622; *(as) I* ~ A.Prol 82, TC 1.996, LGW 419; *for to* ~ as an estimate A.Kn 2593. [?MLG, ult. rel. to **gete(n)**]

gest *n.* guest E.Cl 338, HF 288; lodger A.Mil 3188. [ON *gestr*]

get *see* **jet**.

gete(n *v.* **1.** get, win A.Kn 1512, B.ML 230, E.Cl 1210; preserve A.Kn 2755. **2.** beget B.ML 715, E.Mch 1437. **geteth** *pr. 3 sg.* A.Mil 3620; get I.Pars 828. **gat** *pa. sg.* A.Prol 703, TC 1.1077. **gete(n** *p.p.* A.Prol 291, B.Mel 2787, D.WB 1236; **ygeten** A.Mil 3564, B.Mel 2743. [ON *geta, gat, getinn*]

getinge *vbl. n.* getting, acquisition B.Mel 2814, Bo 3. p10. 102/138.

giaunt *see* **gea(u)nt**.

gyde *n.* guide A.Prol 804, B.ML 164, LGW 94; ruler G.SN 45. [OF]

gyde(n *v.* guide, direct B.ML 245, E.Cl 776, TC 1.183. **gydeth** *imper. pl.* B.Pri 1677. [OF]

gyderesse *n.* teacher, instructress Bo 4. p1. 6/8. [from prec.]

gyding *vbl. n.* guidance Bo 4. p1. 49/68, TC 5.643.

gye *v.* guide A.Kn 2786, Anel 6, HF 1093, BalCo 8; rule, direct A.Kn 1950, B.Sh 1286, E.Cl 75, I.Pars 13, TC 5.546, *refl.* conduct oneself LGW 2045; keep G.SN 136, 159. [OF *guier*]

gif *conj.* (nth.) if A.Rv 4181, 4190. [OE *gif*, assim. to *gif* v., nth. form of *yeve* give]

gigges *n. pl.* ?creaks or rapid movements HF 1942. [?OF *giguer* play the fiddle]

gigginge *n.* fitting (shields) with straps A.Kn 2504. [from *gige* n., OF *guige* strap]

gyle *n.* guile, deceit G.SN 195, BD 620, TC 1.719 *var*, RR 151; deception TC 3.777. [OF]

gilour *n.* trickster A.Rv 4321. [OF *guileor*]

gilt *n.* guilt A.Kn 1765, D.Fri 1612, PF 434, TC 5.1776; *in the* ~ guilty D.WB 387; *as in may* ~ by my fault F.Fkl 757; *withouten* ~ unjustly B.NP 4563, D.WB 244, F.Fkl 1039, Anel 298; offence D.WB 1096, TC 3.1177, LGW 1849, sins I.Pars 84, *pl.* B.Mel 3074, I.Pars 1043. [OE *gylt*]

gilte *adj.* golden (of hair) PF 267, LGW 230, 1315; gilded B.Mk 3554. [OE *ġe)gyld* p.p. of *gyldan*]

giltelees *adj.* guiltless, innocent A.Kn 1312, C.Pard 491, TC 2.328; **giltlees** B.ML 643, G.CY 1005. [OE *gyltléas*]

gilty *adj.* guilty A.Prol 660, C.Pard 429, I.Pars 580; **giltif** TC 3.1019, 1049. [OE *gyltiġ*; *-if* from OF]

gin *n.* contrivance F.Sq 322, G.CY 1165; means LGW 1784; *many a* ~ many tricks F.Sq 128; *pl.* snares, traps Bo 3. m8. 5, RR 1620. [from OF *engin*]

gingebreed *n.* preserved ginger B.Th 2044. [OF *gingembraz* infl. by **breed**]

gingere/gyngevre *n.* ginger RR 1369. [OF *gingivre*, OE *gingifer*]

ginglen *v.* jingle A.Prol 170. [imit.]

ginne *v.* **1.** begin (with obj.) TC 1.266; (with plain infin.) A.Kn 2798, 2805, TC 2.2, 5.1, 657, 1286, LGW 61; (with *(for)* to and infin.) A.Rv 3863, E.Mch 2329, TC 1.189, 218, 4.709, HF 2004. **2.** as *auxil.* of ingressive present, = does (with plain infin.) TC 4.12, 239 *var*, HF 1455; (with *to* and infin.) TC 2.849. **3.** as mere *auxil.* of past, = did (with plain infin.) A.Mil 3730, B.Mk 3383, E.Cl 535, TC 1.293, LGW 148, 292; (with *to* and infin.) A.Kn 1506, E.Cl 292, E.Mch 1929, G.SN 203, TC 2.1460, 5.1482, 1745. **gan** *pa. sg.* A.Rv 3863, E.Cl 292, HF 164. **gonne(n** *pl.* A.Kn 1658, G.SN 376, TC 2.150 *var*, 3.610, HF 944, 953; **gunne(n** TC 2.150 *var*, HF 1608, 1658. [OE *-ginnan*, cf. **biginne**]

gipoun *n.* tunic A.Prol 75, A.Kn 2120. [OF]

gipser *n.* purse A.Prol 357. [OF *gipsiere*]

girde(n *v.* cut, strike B.Mk 3736. [?]

girdilstede *n.* waist RR 826. [OE *gyrdel* + **stede¹**]

girles *see* **gerl**.

girt *pr. 3 sg.* girds Mars 100, LGW 1775. [OE *gyrdan*]

gyse *n.* manner, style A.Kn 1208, PF 399, RR 789; *at his ow(e)ne* ~ as he pleased A.Prol 663, A.Kn 1789; custom A.Kn 993, A.Rv 4126, TC 5.1650; usual way B.ML 790; plot TC 4.1370; *pl.* ways Bo 4. p6. 35/50. [OF]

giser *n.* liver Bo 3. m12. 29/42 (L *iecur*). [OF *gisier*]

gistes *n. pl.* casts of ? dice TC 2. 1349 *var*. [OF]

gyte *n.* gown A.Rv 3954, D.WB 559. [OF *guite*]

giterne *n.* cittern, a stringed instrument A.Mil 3333, C.Pard 466. [OF *guiterne*]

giterninge *vbl. n.* playing on the cittern A.Mil 3363. [from v. from prec.]

glad *adj.* **1.** glad, joyful A.Prol 811, B.ML

384; grateful B.Mk 3521, D.WB 222; ?heartfelt LGW 109; ?uncomplaining D.WB 1183. **2.** pleasing, happy (of time) B.ML 426, Mars 12, TC 1.951, 3.1646; ?fortunate Bo 1. m6. 16/23; ?pleasant BD 338. [OE *glæd*]

glade(n *v.* **1.** *tr.* make happy, cheer B.NP 4001, E.Cl 822, 1174, TC 2.1545, 4.1220; brighten E.Mch 2221; console, comfort A.Kn 2837, E.Cl 1107. **2.** *refl.* rejoice, be glad F.Sq 609, take comfort TC 5.1184. **3.** *intr.* **gladeth** *imper. pl.* rejoice Mars 1. [OE *gladian*]

glader *n.* gladdener A.Kn 2223. [from prec.]

gladly *adv.* **1.** willingly A.Prol 308, 803 var, C.Phs 173, **gladlier** *comp.* TC 5.1777; spontaneously I.Pars 612; *that ben ~ wise* who would like to be thought wise F.Sq 376. **2.** fittingly I.Pars 887, HF 1242; by preference LGW 770; usually, habitually B.NP 4414, F.Sq 224, I.Pars 675. [OE *glædlīce*]

gladsome *adj.* pleasing B.NP 3968. [from **glad**]

glareth *pr. 3 sg.* shines HF 272. **glaringe** *pr. p.* staring A.Prol 684. [cf. MDu *glaren*]

glase(n *v.* glaze BD 323; *his howve to ~* to mock, provide with a delusive protection, TC 5.469; cf. **howve.** [from *glas* n. OE *glæs*]

glasing *vbl. n.* glasswork BD 327.

gledy *adj.* glowing LGW 105. [from **gle(e)d(e)**]

glee *n.* music ABC 100, TC 2.1036; *pl.* musical instruments HF 1209, 1252; entertainment B.Th 2030, *see* **game(n.** [OE *glēo*]

gle(e)d(e *n.* glowing coal A.Kn 1997, I.Pars 548, TC 4.337, LGW 735. [OE *glēd*]

gleyre *n.* white (of egg) G.CY 806. [OF *glaire*]

glente *pa. pl.* glanced TC 4.1223. [ON; cf. Dan *glente*]

glewe *v.* glue, fasten HF 1761. **yglewed** *p.p.* F.Sq 182. [OF *gluer*]

glyde(n *v.* glide F.Sq 393, travel, go B.Th 2094, E.Mch 1887, Mars 53; *~ up* rise F.Sq 373, *~ in* flow into F.Fkl 1415, *~ thurgh* pierce A.Kn 1575, *~ doun* drop TC 4.1215. **glood** *pa. sg.* B.Th 2094, F.Sq 393. **gliden** *p.p.* E.Mch 1887. [OE *glīdan*, *glād*, *gliden*]

glimsing *n.* glimpse E.Mch 2383. [cf. MHG *glimsen*]

glorie *n.* **1.** renown B.Mk 3401, E.Mch 2243; *see* **veyn.** **2.** source or cause of honour or renown B.ML 851, B.Mk 3565; ?delight I.Pars 820 (Vulgate *gloria*), Bo 1. m1. 7/10. **3.** heavenly glory D.WB 490, I.Pars 719. [OF *gloire*, *glorie*]

glorifye(n *v.* **1.** *tr.* praise I.Pars 1037. **2.** *intr.* boast TC 3.186. **3.** *refl.* be puffed up, be proud TC 2.1593, HF 1134, (with *in*) take pride in I.Pars 405, 757, Bo 2. p5. 46/64, 3. p5. 23/32, (with *of*) p6. 28/37. [OF *glorefiier*]

glorious *adj.* **1.** illustrious B.Mk 3334, Bo 3. p2. 27/38. **2.** beautiful A.Kn 1955; splendid D.Sum 1793, E.Mch 1268. [OF]

glose *n.* **1.** gloss, interpretation D.Sum 1792, 1920, Bo 1. p4. 207/288, LGW 328; ?margin BD 333. **2.** specious interpretation: *withouten ~* truthfully F.Sq 166. [OF]

glose(n *v.* **1.** comment on, interpret B.Sh

1180, D.WB 119, TC 4.1410, LGW G. 254; *~ up and down* interpret differently D.WB 26. **2.** deceive B.Mk 3330, D.WB 509, use circumlocution E.Mch 2351; coax, induce TC 4.1471, Bo 2. p3. 45/64; flatter H.Mcp 34. [OF *gloser*]

glosinge *vbl. n.* interpretation D.Sum 1793.

glotonye *n.* gluttony C.Pard 482; *pl.* excesses 514. [OF]

glotoun *n.* glutton C.Pard 520. [OF]

gnawe(n *v.* **1.** gnaw, eat A.Kn 2507, TC 1.509; (fig.) corrode TC 4.621. **2.** *intr.* suffer TC 5.36. **gnow** *pa. sg.* B.Mk 3638. [OE *gnagan*, **gnōg*, *gnōgen*]

gniden *pa. pl.* crushed FormA 11em. [OE *gnidon* from *gnīdan*]

gnodded/knoddyd *pa. pl.* crushed FormA 11 var. [cf. OE *gnuddian*]

gnof *n.* churl A.Mil 3188. [cf. EFris *gnuffig* coarse]

gnow *see* **gnawe(n.**

gobet *n.* piece, fragment, lump A.Prol 696, Bo 5. p1. 51/73. [OF]

godsib *see* **gossip.**

goldes *n. pl.* marigolds A.Kn 1929. [OE *golde*]

goldlees *adj.* penniless B.Sh 1480. [from OE *gold* n.]

goldsmithry *n.* goldsmith's work A.Kn 2498. [from OE *goldsmiþ*]

golee *n.* mouthful PF 556. [OF]

golet *n.* gullet, throat. C.Pard 543. [OF]

goliardeys *n.* buffoon, joker A.Prol 560. [OF]

gomme *n.* gum LGW 121. [OF]

gonfanoun *n.* pennon RR 1201em. [OF]

gonge *n.* latrine I.Pars 885. [OE *gáng*]

gonne *n.* gun HF 1643, LGW 637. [?]

gonne(n, gunne(n *see* **ginne.**

good *n.* **1.** goodness, virtue B.Mel 2479, I.Pars 328, Bo 4. p3. 41/59. **2.** advantage, benefit B.Mel 2818, D.WB 231, F.Fkl 875, HF 1; *pl.* B.Mel 2752, I.Pars 312, Bo 3. p1. 36/48; good thing D.Sum 2281, BD 800, TC 2.97, *pl.* B.Mel 2605, I.Pars 452; good works I.Pars 231; *sovereyn ~* summum bonum Bo 2. p4. 104/143, m7. 2/3 etc. **3.** goods, property A.Prol 581, B.Sh 1433, G.CY 1376, PF 462, TC 3.1108, money B.Sh 1270, 1622. [OE *gōd*]

good *adj.* good, as *n. voc.* good friend TC 1.1017, 4.1660; as *adv.* well TC 1.119. [OE *gōd*]

goodly/-lich *adj.* pleasant B.NP 4010, LGW 1666; kind G.CY 1053, TC 2.1268; good-looking, comely F.Sq 623, TC 1.277; *as n. var.* TC 1.458, **goodlieste** *sup.* most excellent PF 375, TC 2.747, 880. [OE *gōdlīc*]

goodly *adv.* kindly, pleasantly A.Prol 803 var, TC 1.2606; sensibly B.Mel 2420, BD 529; well E.Mch 1935. [prec.]

goodliheed *n.* excellence TC 2.842, HF 274; comeliness BD 829; bounty BalCh 30. [from **goodly** adj.+OE suff. *-*hǣdu*]

goodman *n.* master of the house, householder C.Pard 361, LGW 1391. [**good**+**man**]

go(o)(n *v.* **1.** go A.Prol 12, A.Mil 3632, *~ (my) wey* 3133, 3607; *~ to the point* B.Sh 1503; *~ upon a daunce* dance D.WB 991; *~ ayen* fight Bo 3. p12. 77/103; *~ depper (in)* penetrate further G.SN 250, proceed further TC 2.485; ~ *aboute* encircle TC 3.1108; ~ *by dyverse tonges* spread in many languages Bo 2. m7. 8/11; ~ *fro the world die* D.WB 47; ~ *by the mone* be governed by the moon TC 5.377; ~ *nat aright* lose the way A.Rv 4254, ~ *amis* deviate Bo 3. m11. 11/15, get lost Bo 1. p5. 8/11; ~ *awey* A.Mil 3553, ~ *beforn* go in front E.Mch 2151, act first Bo 5. m4. 33/48, ~ *doun fall* A.Kn 2613, A.Rv 4307, ~ *forth* D.WB 1020, ~ *in* A.Kn 2602, LGW 640, ~ *of peel off* A.Mil 3811, ~ *up* A.Kn 2565, A.Mil 3431, ~ *up and doun* go about D.WB 878; *so fer ygoon* so far advanced F.Sq 538; *thikke as they may* ~ as many as could be A.Kn 2510, ~ *ytressed* wear hair in plaits TC 5.810, ~ *nigh wode* nearly go mad RR 263; ~ *ful ny the sothe* speak truly D.WB 931. **2.** walk A.Kn 3022, B.NP 4006, Bo 4. p2. 80/106, 5. m5. 8/12, p6. 136/192; ~ *upright* BD 622; ~ *or/ne ryde* walk (n)or ride, move A.Kn 968, 1351, B.Th 1995. **3.** depart, leave A.Mil 3570, A.Co 4412, B.Sh 1459, D.WB 171, F.Sq 293, TC 4.1276, ~ *fro* leave B.NP 4448; ~ *awey* pass away Bo 2. m3. 9/12; flee BD 540, TC 3.894. **4.** end A.Rv 3879, D.WB 477, 849, G.CY 907, 1425; pass (of time) B.ML 17, E.Mch 2140, PF 647 *var,* Bo 3. m9. 3/4, TC 5.1142; phrases with *p.p.:* ~ *sithen* ago A.Kn 1521, LGW 427; *nought* ~ *ful longe whyle* not long ago TC 2.507, ~ *is many a yere* many years ago B.ML 132. **5.** proceed (to) (with infin.) A.Kn 1838, A.Mil 3685, A.Rv 4250, D.WB 657, E.Mch 1923, TC 3.313, (with *and* and infin.) D.WB 137; ~ *to* pass to, turn to G.CY 1082, H.Mcp 237, I.Pars 603, TC 1.53, 3.1580, 1677; ~ *unto* read B.Mk 3515, devote oneself to A.Prol 286; ~ (*ther*) *about* occupy oneself (with) C.Phs 158, D.Fri 1530, TC 1.863, 1091, arrange the matter D.Sum 1837; ~ *a-begged* go begging F.Fkl 1580; ~ *a-blakeberied* be damned C.Pard 406; ~ *a-caterwawed* go serenading D.WB 354; *subj.* with *infin.* ~ *we .. let us .. F.Fkl 1217, TC 2.615, 5.402. **6.** fare, behave Bo 4. m3. 11/15; live D.WB 269, I.Pars 820; wander, haunt LGW 2069. **7.** play, sound B. NP 4042; work C.Pard 398. **8.** *lat* ~ allow to go TC 5.226, LGW 1213, allow to go free D.WB 1061, dismiss E.Mch 1596, forget TC 4.457. **9.** go (strengthening imper.) A.Kn 2760, A.Mil 3600, C.Phs 201, D.WB 838, TC 2.396. **go(o)st** *pr. 2 sg.* B.Pri 1668, HF 655. **go(o)th** *3 sg.* A.Kn 1071, A.Rv 4257; **ge(e)th** LGW 2145 (only). **go(o)th** *imper. pl.* F.Fkl 1488, Bo 4. m7. 44/63, **goth walketh** G.CY 1207. **go(o)n** *p.p.* B.ML 17, B.Sh 1522; **go** B.ML 1006, G.CY 907; **ygo(o)n** B.NP 4668, LGW 2206; **ygo** A.Prol 286, LGW 1193. Northern forms in *Reeve's Tale:* **gas** *pr. 3 sg.* A. 4037. **ga** *imper. sg.* 4102. **gan/geen** *p.p.* 4078. See **wende(n, yede.** [OE *gān, gǣþ, ǧe)gān*]

go(o)re *n.* flare A.Mil 3237; slash A.Mil 3322 *var;* gown, robe B.Th 1979. [OE *gāra*]

goos *n.* goose A.Mil 3317, PF 568. **gees** *pl.* B.NP 4581, E.Mch 2275. [OE *gōs, gēs*]

goosish *adj.* silly TC 3.584. [from prec.]

go(o)st, go(o)th *see* **go(o)n.**

go(o)st *n.* **1.** spirit A.Kn 2768, E.Cl 926, 972, TC 2.531, mind LGW 103. **2.** soul A.Mil 3646, B.ML 803, C.Phs 43, D.WB 97, TC 4.302, 5.1808; *yaf, yeldeth up the* ~ B.Pri 1862, LGW 886. **3.** spirit (after death) A.Prol 205, ABC 56. **4.** ghost B.Mk 3124, (iron.) H.Mcp 55, LGW 1295. **5.** evil spirit B.ML 404. **6.** the Holy Spirit B.Pri 1660, G.SN 328, I.Pars 250, ABC 93. [OE *gāst*]

go(o)stly *adj.* spiritual I.Pars 392, 962. [OE *gāstlič*]

go(o)stly *adv.* spiritually, mystically G.SN 109; ? with truth of spirit TC 5.1030. [OE *gāstlīče*]

gossip/godsib *n.* spiritual relative (of a sponsor at baptism in relation to child or its parents) I.Pars 908, a child of one's godfather 909; male spiritual relative D.WB 243; woman companion D.WB 529, 544. [OE *godsib*]

goter *n.* gutter, drain Bo 3. m3. -/2, TC 3.787, LGW 2705. [OF]

goune-clo(o)th *n.* cloth to make a gown of D.Sum 2247, 2252. [OF *goune*+*clo(o)th*]

gourde *n.* flask (in shape of gourd) H.Mcp 82. [OF]

governaille *n.* mastery, control E.Cl 1192; *pl.* means of control Bo 1. p6. 22/28. [OF]

governaunce *n.* **1.** rule, government B.Mk 3250, PF 387, LGW 1044. **2.** management, control A.Prol 281, B.NP 4055; guidance D.WB 1231, TC 2.467, 3.945. **3.** behaviour E.Mch 1603, H.Mcp 158, BalCh 2; self-control BD 1008, TC 2.1020. [OF]

governe *v.* **1.** govern A.Kn 1303, D.WB 219, Bo 2. m6. 12/17. **2.** control, regulate B.Sh 1451, Bo 5. m1. 12/18, TC 2.375; *refl.* B.Mel 2271, TC 3.475; ~ *and gye* control and guide B.Sh 1286, B.Mk 3587. **governeth** *imper. pl.* decide E.Cl 322. [OF]

governeresse *n.* ruler, mistress Pity 80, ABC 141. [OF]

governing *vbl. n.* government, control A.Prol 599, LGW 581; *pl.* looking after C.Phs 75.

governour *n.* master, director A.Prol 813; controller, ruler Bo 3. p11. 156/211. [OF *governeor*]

grace *n.* **1.** favour, good will A.Kn 1120, PF 421, TC 2.1070, respite C.Phs 240; *do* ~ behave graciously A.Kn 1874, be favourable (to) A.Kn 2322, B.Mel 3070, do (a) favour (to) C.Pard 737, LGW 451, allow TC 5.694, spare F.Sq 458; *of your* ~ in your kindness A.Kn 3080, E.Cl 864; *sauf, savinge your* ~ by your leave B.Mel 2878, 2736; *stonden in* (*hir*) ~ find favour with (her) A.Prol 88, A.Kn 1173, G.CY 1348, TC 2.714. *harde* ~ see **hard.** **2.** grace, divine benevolence A.Mil 3595, B.Pri 1793, I.Pars 48, PF 84, TC 1.933; act of grace A.Prol 573. **3.** graciousness G.SN 67, BD 1006, PF 319. **4.** fortune TC 1.907, 4.1233, 5.171; *goode* ~ TC 2.266; *sory* ~ misfortune D.WB 746, HF 1790, *with harde/sory* ~ bad luck to you C.Pard 717, D.Sum 2228 *var.* **5.** virtue, power RR 1099. **6.** *pl.* thanks B.Mel 2992. [OF]

gracelees *adj.* unlucky G.CY 1078; out of favour TC 1.781. [from prec.]

gracious *adj.* **1.** benevolent, merciful LGW 347. **2.** well-disposed TC 1.885. **3.** beautiful E.Cl 613. **4.** pleasing, attractive A.Mil 3693. [OF]
graciously *adv.* on favourable terms B.Sh 1534. [from prec.]
grame *n.* **1.** grief, pain G.CY 1403, TC 1.372, 4.529. **2.** harm Anel 276. **3.** anger, hatred TC 3.1028. [OE *grama*]
gramercy/grantmercy/graunt mercy *interj.* thank you B.Sh 1470, B.NP 4160, G.CY 1156, BD 560, TC 3.1305. [OF]
grapenel *n.* grapnel, grappling iron LGW 640. [AN]
graspe *v.* grope A.Rv 4293, TC 5.223, LGW 2186 *var.* [?OE **græpsan* or LG]
gra(u)nge *n.* barn, granary B.Sh 1256, HF 698; outlying farm A.Mil 3668. [OF]
graunt *n.* privilege A.Prol 252*a*; decree A.Kn 1306; permission TC 4.552; ~ *him made* granted him RR 851. [from next]
graunte(n *v.* **1.** grant, allow A.Prol 786, A.Kn 1828, B.Mel 3010, D.WB 904, TC 2.588; *God* ~ E.Mch 1792, TC 1.44, RR 42. **2.** consent B.ML 1093, C.Pard 327, TC 3.579, 5.949; assent LGW 2665. **3.** admit, agree B.Mel 2657, D.Fri 1535, Bo 2. p2. 9/12, HF 1618; ~ *wel* B.Mel 2451, D.WB 95, Bo 3. p9. 102/136; promise D.WB 1013. **grauntestow** *pr. 2 sg.* (with suffixed pron.) Bo 3. p11. -/41. [AN]
graunting *vbl. n.* assent: *in hir first* ~ as they are already agreed Bo 3. p11. 9/12 (L *quae paulo ante conclusa sunt*).
graunt mercy *see* **gramercy**.
grave(n *v.* **1.** engrave, carve C.Phs 15, TC 3.1462, HF 157, ~ *in* F.Fkl 830; (fig.) TC 2.1241. **2.** dig LGW 204, 678; bury E.Cl 681, F.Fkl 976, LGW 785. **grave(n** *p.p.* D.WB 1065, I.Pars 751; HF 473; **ygrave** A.Mil 3796, D.WB 496, TC 3.1499. [OE *grafan, ge)grafen*]
gre(e *n.[1]* favour, good will A.Kn 2733; *in* ~ kindly, favourably B.ML 259, E.Cl 1151, TC 2.529, Ven 73. [OF *gré*, L *grātum*]
gre(e *n.[2]* degree E.Mch 1375, LGW 1313 *var.* [OF *gré*, L *gradum*]
greef *see* **grief**.
gre(e)t *adj.* **1.** big A.Prol 559, C.Pard 877, TC 5.1469; coarse E.Mch 1422; ~ *and smale* of every size A.Mil 3178, C.Pard 659, everyone RR 1047; *many smale maken a* ~ I.Pars 362; *as n.* great part, substance PF 35, LGW 574. **2.** important, famous A.Kn 2032, TC 2.881, HF 1499; ~ *God* B.ML 334, B.Pri 1797. **3.** great, intense (of a quality) A.Prol 312, B.ML 528, BD 467; great, consummate (of a person) D.WB 1196, E.Mch 1501, I.Pars 593. **gretter** *comp.* A.Prol 197, B.ML 232, Mars 132; *more* ~ I.Pars 529 *var.* **grettest(e** *sup.* A.Prol 120, C.Pard 607, LGW 1050. [OE *grēat*, OA comp. **grēttra*]
gre(e)tnesse *n.* size BD 947; vastness Bo 2. p7. 19/26; enormity I.Pars 1004. [OF *grēatnesse*]
gre(e)ve(n *v.* **1.** *tr.* harm, injure A.Rv 4181, B.ML 352, B.Mel 2680, D.Fri 1490, TC 1.1001 *var*; *intr.* be harmful I.Pars 382; *nought ne* ~*th* does no harm TC 5.783. **2.** distress, vex A.Kn 917, B.Pri 1638, C.Phs 186, E.Cl 889, TC 2.237; *impers.* (with pron. obj.) E.Cl 647. **3.** *intr.* feel vexed,

take offence TC 1.343; *refl.* A.Rv 3859, D.Sum 1814, TC 3.1004, 4.603. [OF *grever*]
grey *adj.* grey A.Kn 1492, B.Th 1928, PF 335; (of eyes) ~ *as glas* A.Prol 152, A.Rv 3974, RR 546, 822; ~ *as goos* A.Mil 3317; *dappel/dappull* ~ dapple grey B.Th 2074, evid. the same as *pomely* ~ A.Prol 616; *as n.* greybeard TC 4.127. [OE *grǣg*]
greyn *n.* **1.** grain, corn A.Prol 596, C.Pard 374; cardamom seed A.Mil 3690, ~ *de Paradys* RR 1369; *in* ~ (dyed) scarlet (with an insect dye) B.Th 1917, F.Sq 511; ~ *of Portyngale* a crimson dye B.NP 4649. **2.** speck, small amount TC 3.1026; ?pearl B.Pri 1852, 1855. [OF]
greythe(n *v.* prepare B.Mk 3784, Bo 1. p4. 170/238; *refl.* A.Rv 4309; dress RR 584. [ON *greiða*]
grekissh *adj.* Greek Bo 1. p1. 21/29, 22/31, 4. m7. 7/9. [OE *grēcisc*]
grene *adj.* **1.** green A.Kn 1036, TC 4.1433; young, vigorous E.Cl 1173, TC 1.816; pale, sickly TC 4.1154, 5.243. **2.** *as n.* green leaves, grass A.Kn 1510, F.Sq 54, F.Fkl 1251, TC 4.770; green (grassy space) D.WB 998, F.Fkl 862, PF 328, LGW G. 50. [OE *grēne*]
grenehede *n.* rawness B.ML 163. [prec.+ OE suff. *-*hædu*]
grenning *pr. p. adj.* grinning, grimacing RR 156. [OE *grennian*]
grete *v.* greet B.Sh 1553, TC 3.1258, LGW 2299. **grette** *pa.* B.ML 1051, BD 503, TC 3.955, 5.293, LGW 116. **ygret** *p.p.* BD 517. [OE *grētan*]
grette *see* **grete**.
gretter, -est *see* **gre(e)t** *adj.*
grevaunce *n.* grievance, injury B.Mk 3703, I.Pars 660, hardship TC 1.647; *do* ~ injure B.Mel 2676. [OF]
greve *n.* grove B.NP 4013 *var*, TC 5.1144; spray, branch A.Kn 1507, LGW 227. Cf. **grove**. [OE *grǣfa*]
grevous *adj.* painful, oppressive B.Mel 2189, I.Pars 130, Bo 4. p4. 122/175; serious, grave A.Kn 1010, I.Pars 449, 884; difficult I.Pars 529; malicious I.Pars 641, RR 964; sorrowful Bo 1. p1. 61/85; grievous TC 4.904. [AN]
grevously *adv.* painfully B.Mel 2191, hard I.Pars 667, gravely LGW 369. [from prec.]
grief/greef *n.* trouble, distress B.Sh 1317, D.Sum 2174, G.CY 712, TC 2.1632; injury B.Mel 2735. [AN *gref*, OF *grief*]
gryl *adj.* horrible RR 73. [?OE **grylle*]
grinde *v.* grind (corn etc.) A.Rv 4032, D.WB 389, HF 1798; sharpen A.Kn 2140, B.Th 2073. **grint** *pr. 3 sg.* D.WB 389, HF 1798. **grounden** *p.p.* G.CY 760, 775; **ygrounde** A.Rv 3991, B.Th 2073. [OE *grindan, ge)grūnden*]
grinte *v. pa.* gnashed (*with*) D.Sum 2161 *var.* [?imit., based on prec.]
gripen *v.* grasp I.Pars 863, RR 204. [OE *grīpan*]
grys *adj.* grey A.Prol 194; *pomely* ~ dapple grey G.CY 559. [OF]
gris(e)ly *adj.* frightening, grim, hideous E.Mch 2233, F.Fkl 859, LGW 637; fearful: ~ *drede* I.Pars 177, 223, TC 4.155; terrible, horrible A.Kn 1363, B.Mk 3299, C.Pard 708, E.Mch 2233. [OE *grislīc*]

grislynesse n. hideousness, frightfulness I.Pars 864 var. [from prec.]
grobbe v. dig FormA 29. [? OE *grubbian*; cf. MDu *grobben*]
groyn n.¹ snout I.Pars 156. [OF]
groyn n.² grumble, complaint TC 1.349. [OF]
groyning vbl.n. grumbling, discontent A.Kn 2460. [from v. from OF *groignier*]
grom(e n. boy, lad HF 206, 1225, RR 200. [?]
grone(n v. groan B.NP 4076, TC 1.360, HF 338. [OE *grānian*]
gronte pa. groaned, cried out B.Mk 3899. [OE *grunnettan*]
grope v. 1. intr. grope, feel about A.Rv 4217, G.CY 1236, LGW 2186 var. 2. tr. test, examine A.Prol 644, D.Sum 1817. [OE *grāpian*]
grot n. particle, fragment D.Fri 1292. [OE]
grote n. groat, fourpenny piece B.NP 4148, C.Pard 376, TC 4.586. [MDu *groot*]
ground n. ground, floor B.ML 1153, B.NP 4371, LGW 827; (fig.) foundation E.Mch 1279, I.Pars 610, ABC 87, TC 3.982; soil TC 1.946; material A.Prol 453. [OE *grúnd*]
grounded ppl. adj. based TC 4.1672, **ygrounded** BD 921; instructed A.Prol 414. [from v. from prec.]
grounden see **grinde**.
grove n. grove, copse A.Kn 1478, B.NP 4013 var, 4406, C.Pard 762. [OE *gráf*]
growe(n v. intr. grow B.NP 4154, 4157, F.Sq 153; increase TC 3.1760, 5.1361; spring, arise D.WB 72. **growed** pa. D.WB 759; **grew** BD 157. **growe(n** p.p. TC 2.403, 872; (wel) **ygrowen** A.Rv 3973. [OE *grōwan, grēow, grōwen*]
grucche v. intr. grumble, complain A.Kn 3508, I.Pars 500, TC 1.255 var, 3.643. tr. complain of, resent E.Cl 354. [OF]
grucching vbl. n. grumbling D.WB 406, I.Pars 502. 509.
gruf adv. face down, flat A.Kn 949, B.Pri 1865, TC 4.912. [ON *á grúfu*]
gruwel n. gruel, soup: *casten the ~ in the fire* wreck everything TC 3.711. [OF *gruel*]
g(u)erdo(u)n n. reward B.Mk 3820, TC 1.818, RR 1526: *for alle ~s* ?despite temptations to the contrary B.Mel 2242. [OF]
g(u)erdone v. reward B.Mel 2465, I.Pars 283, TC 2.1295. [OF]
g(u)erdoning(e vbl. n. rewarding PF 455, TC 2.392.
guttes n. pl. guts, entrails B.Mk 3791, 3794. [OE *guttas*]

H

ha(a)f see **heve(n**.
haberdassher n. dealer in caps and small wares A.Prol 361. [? AF *hapertas*]
habergeoun see **ha(u)bergeoun**.
habit/abit n. 1. clothes B.Mk 3533, D.WB 342, TC 1.109. 2. bodily condition A.Kn 1378, Bo 1. p3. 33/46; disposition Bo 3. p1. 16/22. 3. constitution Bo 2. p1. 6/9. [OF]
habitacle n. small dwelling Bo 2. p7. 36/52; niche HF 1194. [OF]

habiten pr. pl. inhabit, live in RR 660. [OF *habiter*]
hab(o)unda(u)nt adj. abundant, plentiful B.NP 4115, I.Pars 913, Bo 4. p6. 253/337. [OF]
h)abounde v. abound, be full (with *in*, *of*) B.Mk 3938, E.Mch 1286, TC 2.159. [OF *abunder*]
haboundinge ppl. adj. abounding, overflowing ABC 135.
habundantly adv. abundantly B.ML 870. [from adj.]
h)abunda(u)nce n. abundance, plenty D.Sum 1723, TC 3.1042, Fort 29; fullness I.Pars 627; pl. Bo 2. p4. 10/14, 3. p3. 17/24. [OF]
hacches n. pl. deck planking LGW 648. [OE *hæcc*]
hackyng(e vbl. n. ?carving HF 1303 var. [from **hakke**]
hay n. hedge, TC 3.351, 5.1144 var, RR 54. [OE *heǧe*]
hayl interj. (of greeting) A.Mil 3579, D.Fri 1384, *al ~* A.Rv 4022. [ON *heill*]
hainselin n. man's short jacket I.Pars 422. [OF *hamselin*]
haire see **heyre**.
hait interj. (to a horse) gee up! D.Fri 1543, 1561. [?]
hakeney n. riding horse, hack G.CY 559, RR 1137. [prob. from place-name *Hackney*]
hakke v. hack, chop TC 2.1381; *~ and hewe* A.Kn 2865. [OE -*haccian*]
halde see **holde(n**.
hale v. pull ABC 68, Bo 3. m2. 22/32; attract PF 151. [OF *haler*]
half n. side PF 125 var, HF 1136, Bo 2. m6. 7/9; behalf BD 139, *on my ~* for my part TC 4.945; sake, *a Goddes ~* D.WB 50, BD 370. **halve** prep. TC 4.945. **halves** pl. A.Mil 3481. [OA]
half adj. half A.Prol 8, E.Mch 1300, D.WB 352; *~ goddys* demi-gods TC 4.1545, LGW 387; *~ word* quibble BD 1022. [OA]
half adv. half, partly F.Fkl 1511, G.SN 533, TC 2.67; *~ so* (with adj. and neg.) nearly A.Kn 1429, B.NP 4585, TC 5. 738; *correl. ~ horse, ~ man* Bo 4. m7. 21/30. [OA]
haliday/holiday n. (occas. as two words) holy day, festival of the Church A.Mil 3309, A.Rv 3952, I.Pars 667, Astr 1.11.1 var, LGW 35; festival of Cupid LGW 422. Cf. **ho(o)ly**. [OE *hāliğdæğ*]
halke n. corner, hiding-place G.SN 311, LGW 1780, RR 464; (*every*) *~ and herne* nook and cranny F.Fkl 1121. [OE *healoc*]
hals n. neck B.ML 73, PF 458; throat LGW G. 292. [OA *hals*]
halse/halsen v. beseech B.Pri 1835 var. [OA *halsian* and **halsnian*]
halt see **holde(n**.
halten v. limp TC 4.1457. **halt** pr. 3 sg. BD 622. [OA *haltian*]
halve see **half** n.
halvendel n. a half part, half TC 3.707, TC 5.335; adv. partly B.ML 713 var. [OA *halfan dǣl*]
halves see **half** n.
halwe n. saint B.ML 1060, G.CY 1244, I.Pars 902, apostle I.Pars 559, BD 831; shrine A.Prol 14, D.WB 657, LGW 1310. [OE *hālga*]

halwe(n v. consecrate, sanctify G.SN 551,
I.Pars 965; hold sacred TC 3.268, LGW
1871. [OE *hálgian*]
ham adv. (nth.) home A.Rv 4032. See
ho(o)m.
hameled p.p. mutilated, lame TC 2.964.
[from OE *hamelian*]
han see **have(n.**
hand see **hond.**
hande-brede n. handbreadth A.Mil 3811.
[OE *handbred*]
handwerk n. creatures, creation D.Fri 1562.
[OE *handġeweorc*]
hange(n/honge(n v. hang. **1.** (of an object)
tr. A.Kn 2410, A.Mil 3565, ~ (doun) the
heed BD 122, TC 2.689; intr. F.Sq 156,
Astr 2.23.27/29. **2.** (of a person) tr. and
intr. C.Phs 271, TC 1.833, LGW 264.
3. cover with hangings, adorn A.Kn 2568.
he(e)ng pa. sg. A.Prol 160, B.Pri 1824,
PF 282. **henge** pl. A.Prol 677, BD 174.
hanged p.p. A.Mil 3837, D.WB 658. [OE
hángian intr., *hōn, hēng, hángen* tr.]
hap n. **1.** chance B.Sh 1428, E.Mch 2057,
Bo 4. p6. 19/27; fortune LGW 1773, TC
1.896; good luck G.CY 1209, BD 1039;
bad luck TC 3.1246. **2.** chance event
BD 1279, Bo 5. p1. 64/92. [ON *happ*]
happe(n v. happen A.Prol 585, TC 2.29,
come about TC 4.1563. impers. (with
subject it) B.Mel 2196, 2676, H.Mcp 201,
TC 1.625, 5.991, (without expressed subject) B.NP 4177, D.WB 885, D.Sum 2027,
(with dat. of pers.) D.Fri 1401, C.Pard
606, PF 10. pr. subj. in ~ how ~ may whatever may happen TC 5.796. [from prec.]
happy adj. lucky TC 2.621, 1382; fortunate
B.Mel 2870. [from **hap**]
hard adj. **1.** hard (not soft) A.Prol 229,
C.Pard 541, TC 4.95. **2.** hard, difficult
D.Sum 1730, E.Cl 851, PF 2, Astr prol
17/23. **3.** cruel, severe, unyielding (of persons) D.Fri 1427, I.Pars 752, Bo 2. m1. 8/12;
unfortunate (of events) LGW 1056, Ven
47; ~ day F.Sq 499; ~ grace misfortune
PF 65, TC 1.713, ill will G.CY 1189, HF
1586. **harder** comp. TC 4.905, LGW 2554.
hardest sup. TC 2.729. [OE *heard*]
harde adv. firmly Bo 3. p11. 105/144;
violently A.Mil 3279, B.Sh 1393, TC
3.1531; with difficulty LGW 2483. [OE
hearde]
hardy adj. **1.** brave A.Kn 882, B.NP 4104,
Anel 36, hap helpeth ~ man LGW 1773,
cf. TC 4.601; bold, rash A.Rv 3957, B.Mk
3093, LGW 803. **2.** tough, enduring PF
176. [OF *hardi*]
hardily/hardely adv. assuredly A.Prol 156,
D.Sum 2285, BD 1043, TC 2.304; boldly
E.Mch 2273, RR 270. [from prec.]
hardiment n. daring TC 4.533. [OF]
hardinesse n. boldness, daring A.Kn 1948,
D.WB 612, I.Pars 460, TC 1.566; insolence I.Pars 437. [from **hardy**]
hardinge vbl. n. hardening, tempering F.Sq
243. [from v. from OE *heardian*]
hardnesse n. hardness, cruelty I.Pars 486,
Mars 232, TC 2.1245; hardship I.Pars
688. [from **hard**]
harye v. pull, drag I.Pars 171; ~ forth A.Kn
2726. **harwed** pa. despoiled, plundered,
in ~ Hell (of Christ) A.Mil 3512, D.Sum
2107. [OE *hergian*]

harlot n. rascal A.Prol 647, A.Rv 4268, I.Pars
624; servant, fellow D.Sum 1754; lecher
I.Pars 885. [OF]
harlotrye n. **1.** ribaldry, bawdy talk A.Mil
3145, 3184; pl. A.Prol 561. **2.** evil behaviour, wickedness D.Fri 1328; loose
living E.Mch 2262, I.Pars 902. [from prec.]
harm n. **1.** wrong, injury B.ML 836,
C.Pard 745, Mars 192, TC 3.861; misfortune B.ML 99; pl. evils B.Mel 3030,
TC 2.470, sins I.Pars 390. **2.** pain, grief
B.ML 1908, E.Mch 1908, BD 492, TC
5.417; pl. sufferings A.Kn 2229, pains
2232. **3.** disability I.Pars 624. **4.** a pity
A.Prol 385, B.Mel 2620, D.Sum 2015,
H.Mcp 201. [OE *hearm*]
harmful adj. capable of hurting BD 995.
[from prec.]
harmless adj. unharmed LGW 2664. [from
harm]
harneys n. **1.** armour A.Kn 1006, 1613.
2. harness I.Pars 433; (plough) ~ parts,
fittings A.Mil 3762. **3.** garnishing A.Kn
2896; (fig.) circumstances I.Pars 974. **4.**
equipment, gear D.WB 136. [OF *harneis*]
harneysed p.p. furnished with trimmings
A.Prol 114. [from prec.]
harre n. hinge A.Prol 550. [OE *heorra*]
harrow interj. cry of distress A.Mil 3286,
B.NP 4235, C.Pard 288. [OF *haro*]
harwed see **harye.**
hasard n. dice-playing C.Pard 465, 591.
[OF]
hasardour n. gambler C.Pard 596, 613,
I.Pars 580. [cf. prec.]
hasardrye n. gambling C.Pard 590, I.Pars
793. [from **hasard**]
haselwode n. **1.** hazel wood TC 5.1174.
as interj. (apparently of derision) 'fancy
that!' TC 5.505; ~s shaken TC 3.890. [OE
hæsel + wudu]
hast see **have(n.**
haste n. speed, urgency A.Mil 3545; in ~
A.Mil 3727, in alle ~ B.NP 4197, TC
3.1586, in ~ goodly TC 2.946, in wikked ~
B.Mel 2244. [OF]
haste v. refl. hurry A.Kn 2052, E.Mch 1406,
LGW 2456. [OF *haster*]
hastif adj. hasty, rash B.Mel 2553, TC
4.1567; eager E.Mch 1805; speedy, sudden
A.Mil 3545, B.Mel 2551. [OF]
hastifly adv. hurriedly B.ML 688, 1047.
[from prec.]
hastifnesse/hasty- n. rashness B.Mel 2311,
2323. [from **hastif**]
hastily adv. quickly A.Kn 1514, **hastilich**
E.Cl 911, F.Sq 430; soon, promptly
A.Kn 1714, B.Sh 1299, 1441, I.Pars 675,
TC 3.1442. [var. of **hastifly**]
hastou see **have(n).**
hat n. hat A.Prol 272, A.Mil 3122; by my ~
PF 589; ne..more than myn olde ~ TC
3.320. [OE *hæt*]
hate n. **1.** hatred A.Kn 1671, C.Phs 225,
BD 611; hadde in ~ hated B.Mk 3778.
2. object of hatred I.Pars 137. [OE *hete*,
modified by *hatian* v. and ON *hatr*]
hatte see **hote(n.**
ha(u)bergeoun n. sleeveless coat of mail:
worn by soldiers A.Prol 76, A.Kn 2119;
by penitents I.Pars 1052. [OF]
hauberk n. coat of mail A.Kn 2431, B.Th
2053, Mars 97. [OF *hauberc*]

haunt n. practice, skill A.Prol 447; usual place, district A.Prol 252c, B.Th 2001. [from next]

haunte(n v. practise habitually C.Pard 464, I.Pars 794, Bo 2. p6. 30/43; be continually in (a place) I.Pars 885. [OF *hanter*]

hauteyn adj. haughty, proud I.Pars 614, PF 262; noble LGW 1120; resonant C.Pard 330. [OF *hautain*]

have(n v. **1.** auxil. have A.Prol 18, A.Kn 2257, BD 271, TC 2.296. **2.** have, possess, enjoy A.Prol 224, B.NP 4110, D.Fri 1533, BD 172, TC 1.120; ~ *as lief, levere* see **leef;** ~ *good day* goodbye A.Kn 2740, B.NP 4287; *pr. subj.* in *so ~ I blis* B.ML 33, B.NP 4256, LGW 505; control, administer, in ~ *justise* C. Pard 587; enjoy sexually F.Fkl 1589, LGW 615. **3.** get, take A.Prol 255, A.Kn 2405, LGW 663; ~ *heer* E.Cl 567, G.CY 1187; ~ *heer my trouthe* take my word A.Kn 1610, D.WB 1013; *God ~ his soule* D.WB 530; *the devel ~* D.Fri 1547, TC 1.805. **4.** show, feel (emotion, etc.) ~ *compassioun (of)* A.Kn 1110, Mars 64, ~ *fere* D.WB 1022, ~ *mercy (on)* A.Kn 919, F.Fkl 978, TC 3.1173; ~ *merveyle* A.Mil 3423, ~ *patience* E.Mch 2369; ~ *pitee (of)* A.Kn 2225, (*on*) BD 715, LGW 1324, ~ *routh* A.Kn 2392, HF 2012. **5.** hold A.Kn 1448, TC 3.864; ~ *in (awe,* etc.) B.Mk 3749, F.Sq 700. **6.** *refl.* behave, conduct oneself B.Mel 2765. **7.** in phrases: ~ *at (the)* I attack you LGW 1383; ~ *do(n* stop, finish A.Mil 3728, E.Cl 149, PF 492; ~ *to do with* be concerned with LGW 2694, Mars 234; ~ *on hond* be engaged upon E.Mch 1686, Buk 30. **han** *infin.* A.Prol 752, D.WB 463, TC 1.349. **hast** *pr. 2 sg.* A.Mil 3567, HF 607, **hastou/-ow** (with suffixed pron.) B.ML 676, D.WB 800. **hath** *3 sg.* A.Mil 3353, HF 2052; **has** (nth.) A.Rv 4026, 4205. **have** *pl.* Pity 51, TC 5.466, HF 339; **han** B.Pri 1755, B.NP 4110. **haveth** *imper. pl.* B.ML 654, HF 325. **had(de** *pa. 1, 3 sg.* A.Kn 1577, 1597. **haddestow** *2 sg.* (with suffixed pron.) B.Mk 3136, TC 4.276. **hadde(n** *pl.* F.Fkl 1395, TC 3.864. **hadde** *subj.* B.Mk 3083, G.CY 1103. **had** *p.p.* A.Rv 4184, B.NP 4091. See also **nath.** [OE *habban, hæfþ/hafaþ, hæfde*]

having *vbl. n.* owning B.Mel 2739.

hawe n.[1] yard C.Pard 855; *chirche ~* churchyard I.Pars 801. [OE *haga*]

hawe n.[2] haw, fruit of hawthorn (as type of thing of no value) D.WB 659, TC 3.854. [OE *haga*]

hawebake n. baked haws, a mean dish B.ML 95. [from prec.+n. from OE *bacan*]

hawkes gen. hawk's TC 3.1496 var. [OE *hafoc*]

he pron. **1.** he *passim,* it F.Sq 49, G.CY 867, Astr 2.17.1. **2.** as *demons. pron.* this one A.Kn 2519, 2614–16, ~ *and ~* TC 2.1748; the one TC 1.237; one, a man D.WB 1170; as *demons. adj.* (with proper name) B.Mk 3863, B.NP 4584, E.Mch 1294. **3.** as *n.* man, in ~ *ne/or she* E.Mch 2290 var, TC 1.39, 5.1835, HF 1082. [OE *hē*]

Hebraik see **Ebraik.**

he(e)d/ (mainly prose) **heved** n. **1.** head A.Prol 272, B.Th 2060, C.Pard 743, TC 2.625; brain B.ML 1037, D.Sum 2208; (in

oath) *bi my(n ~* TC 4.593, HF 1875; *maugree his ~* see **maugree;** life, in *upon his ~* see **upon. 2.** transf. (of weapon) B.Th 2073; *beddes ~* A.Mil 3211, F.Sq 643, BD 1254, TC 2.1696, LGW 1334. **3.** source TC 2.844, Scog 43. **hed(d)es** *pl.* A.Kn 2180, F.Sq 203; **hevedes** B.Th 2032, G.SN 398 *var,* and prose. [OE *hēafod*]

he(e)de n. heed, notice: *take ~ (of, to)* pay attention (to) A.Prol 303, G.SN 435, TC 1.501, 4.852; (with *infin.*) take care D.WB 213, TC 5.1048; (with *cl.*) B.Mel 2635, D.Sum 1901; (absol.) TC 2.747, 5.903, HF 787. [from OE *hēdan* v.]

he(e)le n. health, well-being A.Kn 1271, B.Sh 1540, B.NP 4140, PF 128, TC 1.461; salvation I.Pars 1023; prosperity LGW 296. [OE *hǣlu*]

heele(n v. **1.** heal, restore to health A.Kn 1248, E.Mch 2372, F.Sq 641, BD 40, Bo 1. p1. 50/70. **2.** cure (*of* a disease) A.Kn 2706, TC 2.1315, 5.1049. **3.** cure (a disease, injury) C.Pard 366, F.Sq 471, I.Pars 998. [OE *hǣlan*]

he(e)p n. **1.** heap, pile A.Kn 944, G.CY 938, HF 2149; cf. **to-hepe. 2.** great number A.Prol 575, B.Pri 1687, BD 295, Astr 2.3.28/41. [OE *hēap*]

heer n. hair (human) A.Prol 589, A.Kn 2834, BD 456; single hair I.Pars 254, BD 855; *pl.* A.Kn 1388, B.Mk 3248; hair, fur (animal) G.CY 812, RR 228; *pl.* B.NP 4094, HF 1390. [OA *hēr*]

heer adv. **1.** here, in this place, to this place A.Kn 1643, D.Fri 1573, PF 57; now, at this point E.Cl 1090, TC 2.103; *have ~* take A.Kn 1610, TC 3.885; *lo ~!* D.Sum 2139, PF 568, TC 5.1849; ~ *and there* A.Rv 4217, TC 5.179. **2.** prefixed to prep. or adv. representing neut. pron. *it, this, that:* ~ **aboute** about this matter A.Mil 3562. ~ **after** after this, later E.Mch 1674, TC 5.990, ~ **afterward(es** TC 1.991, D.Fri 1515 var. ~ **agayns/ayeins** against this A.Kn 3039, I.Pars 668, in reply to that TC 2.1380. ~**by** by this E.Mch 1330, Bo 5. p6. 198/279, about this matter D.Sum 2204. ~**biforn/before** before this B.Mel 2450, BD 1136, Bo 3. p9. 39/51. ~**forth** beyond this D.WB 1001. ~**inne** in this G.CY 1292. ~**of** about this TC 2.108, LGW 1184, for this PF 502. ~**to** to this B.Mel 2481, in reply Bo 1. p4. 95/132, for this (matter) B.ML 243, BD 754. ~ **tofore** before this BD 189. ~**upon** then B.Sh 1331, E.Cl 190, in this matter TC 3.535. [OE *hēr*]

he(e)rdes n. hards, coarse part of flax RR 1233. [OE *heordan*]

he(e)re(n v. hear A.Prol 169, H.Mcp 115, TC 2.558, LGW 1; *as ye may/shal ~* A.Co 4364, E.Cl 91, TC 5.952, 1316; (*a*) *joye to ~* B.Th 1958, B.NP 4067, TC 3.217; *pitee to ~* A.Kn 2878, BD 107, HF 180; ~ *confessioun* A.Prol 221, I.Pars 1014; listen D.WB 856, I.Pars 69, TC 3.932. **herd** *p.p.* in *have ~ seye* have heard tell B.Pri 1721, B.Mk 3154, cf. F.Sq 603, TC 3.1659, *have ~ seyd* E.Cl 278, E.Mch 1637. [OA *hēran*]

heer-mele n. hair's breadth Astr 2.38.11/16. [**heer** n.+OE *mæl*]

he(e)st(e *n.* **1.** behest, command A.Kn 2532, C.Pard 641, D.WB 74; *doon at (one's)* ~ carry out (one's) command B.ML 382; commandment I.Pars 798. **2.** promise F.Fkl 1064, TC 5.355, 1208. [OE *hǣs*]

he(e)te *n.* heat C.Phs 38, Mars 88, HF 921; fever (love's fire) TC 1.420, 978, 4.511, [OE *hǣtu*]

heete *see* **hote(n.**

heeth *n.* heath, open land A.Prol 6, 606; heather A.Mil 3262. [OE *hǣþ*]

hef *see* **heve(n.**

hegge *n.* hedge B.NP 4408, I.Pars 870, TC 5.1144 *var*, RR 481. [OE *hecg*]

hey *n.* hay A.Mil 3262. *botel* ~ bundle of hay H.Mcp 14. [OA *hēg*]

heigh/hey/hye *adj.* **1.** high A.Mil 3384, D.WB 870, F.Sq 176, Astr 2.25.5/7; *on/an* ~ aloft A.Kn 1065, F.Fkl 849, HF 215, 1430; ~ *and/or low* A.Prol 817, B.ML 993, TC 3.27, *low and* ~ RR 841. **2.** in high place, rank: ~ *God/goddes* A.Kn 2349, C.Pard 640, D.Sum 1834, TC 3.1027; ~ *degree* B.Mk 3166, D.Fri 1300, ~ *estat* A.Prol 522, B.Mk 3647, E.Cl 923, I.Pars 152; *on* ~ *juyse* ? by solemn sentence B.ML 795. **3.** lofty, exalted TC 1.1084; ~ *sentence* A.Prol 306, E.Mch 1507, HF 1425*em*; ~ *service* A.Kn 2487, TC 3.1288; ~ *stile* E.Cl 18, F.Sq 106; extreme A.Kn 1798, 2913, B.ML 162, F.Fkl 1523, TC 3.897. [OE *hē(a)h*, *hē(a)g-*]

heighe/hye *adv.* **1.** high up A.Prol 271, F.Sq 267, HF 905; (fig.) at a high (social) level A.Rv 3981, B.Mk 3592. **2.** loud PF 499, HF 1599. [OE *hē(a)h*, *hēage*]

heighly *adv.* highly, liberally B.Mel 2462; strictly I.Pars 600, TC 2.1733. [OA *hēhlīce*]

heighnesse/hy- *n.* high rank I.Pars 190, 336. [OA *hēhnesse*]

heighte/highte *n.* height, altitude A.Kn 1890, Bo 1. p1. 3/4, Astr 1.1.2/3; high point, summit Bo 4. m1. 1/2, *the heye* ~ *of thinges* Bo 5. p6. 85/120 (L *excelso rerum cacumine*); (fig.) Bo 4. p6. 34/49; *upon* ~ high A.Kn 2919; *on* ~ aloud A.Kn 1784. [OA *hēhþu*]

heyne *n.*[1] mean wretch G.CY 1319. [? ON *hegna*]

heyne *n.*[2] hatred, malice G.CY 1317/19 *var*. [OF *hain*]

heinous *adj.* hateful TC 2.1617. [OF *haineux*]

heir(e/eyre *n.* legatee A.Rv 3978, Gent 15; successor B.Mk 3534, LGW 1819; son (to succeed) D.ML 766, E.Mch 1272. [OF *(h)eir*]

heyre/haire *n.* haircloth, *attrib.* in ~ *clowt* C.Pard 736; hair shirt G.SN 133, I.Pars 1052, RR 438. [OF]

heysugge *n.* hedge-sparrow PF 612. [OE *hęgesugge*; cf. **hay**]

heythen *see* **hethen.**

helde *v.*[1] *see* **holde(n.**

helde *v.*[2] pour, shed D.WB 272, Bo 2. m2. 1/2, HF 1686. [OA *héldan*]

hele *v.* hide, keep secret B.NP 4245, D.WB 950, BD 928. [OE *helan*]

helm *n.* helmet A.Kn 2676, Mars 99, TC 2.638. [OE]

helmed *adj.* equipped with a helmet B.Mk 3560, TC 2.593. [from prec.]

help(e *n.* **1.** help B.ML 101, ABC 12, Bo 1. p4. 188/263. **2.** helper, means of help B.Mel 2294, E.Mch 1328, PF 116, TC 1.1010, LGW 1616. [OE *help* and *helpe*]

helpe(n *v.* **1.** help, rescue A.Prol 18, A.Kn 1248 *var*, B.NP 4196, G.SN 57, TC 2.683 (*of* 'from'); *imper. sg.* as *exclam.* A.Mil 3815, A.Rv 4286, E.Mch 2366, TC 1.533, 4.1150. **2.** aid, assist B.Pri 1663, B.Mk 3858, TC 3.795, HF 1439; *intr.* A.Prol 258. *pr. subj.* in asseverations *as/so* ~ *me God* A.Kn 1127, A.Mil 3709, B.NP 4598, D.WB 201, BD 550. **3.** be of use (usu. with neg.) A.Kn 3033, B.NP 3992, Anel 293, TC 5.1183; *what* ~*th it?* A.Kn 2820, D.WB 316 *var*, TC 4.929. **helpeth** *imper. pl.* G.CY 1328, HF 521. **heelp/halp** *pa. sg.* A.Kn 1651 *var*, B.ML 920 *var*; **holpe** RR 1230. **holpe(n** *p.p.* A.Prol 18, E.Mch 2370, F.Fkl 1305. [OE *helpan*, *healp*, *holpen*]

hem *pron.* **1.** *acc.* them *passim*; (*refl.* with *v.*) themselves B.ML 1118, B.Sh 1443, G.SN 396, I.Pars 1063, TC 2.256. **2.** *dat.* to them D.WB 771, Bo 3. p3. 44/58, LGW 1865; ('dat. of interest') A.Rv 4010; for themselves F.Sq 56; (in impers. constr.) B.NP 4578, C.Pard 475, F.Sq 56, TC 2.1598, LGW 2603. [OE *heom*]

hemself *pron. pl.* themselves: *emph.* A.Kn 1254, B.ML 145; *refl.* D.WB 761, G.SN 510, TC 1.922. **hemselve(n** F.Fkl 1378, 1420, HF 1215, 2125. [prec.+**self**]

hemward *see* **toward.**

hen *n.* hen B.NP 4629; *not worth an* ~ D.WB 1112; *a pulled* ~ a trifle A.Prol 177. **hennes** *pl.* B.NP 4056, 4363. [OE *henn*]

hende *adj.* courteous, polite, gentle D.WB 628, D.Fri 1286, RR 285; (as ironically romantic epithet) A.Mil 3199, etc. [OE *ġehende*]

henne *adv.* hence, from here, away A.Kn 2356, C.Pard 687, TC 3.630; from now TC 4.1246. [OE *hionan*]

hennes/hens *adv.* hence, from here, away TC 3.1425, 5.653, *fro(m* ~ TC 5.607, from now HF 1284. [prec.+adv. *-es*]

hennesforth *adv.* henceforth, from now on F.Sq 658, TC 4.17, HF 782; *from* ~ I.Pars 1090, TC 5.895, RR 701. [**hennes**+**forth**]

hente(n *v.* **1.** seize, grasp A.Prol 698, A.Mil 3475, B.NP 4525, F.Fkl 1391; take B.ML 1144, D.Fri 1553, 1664, E.Cl 534; get A.Prol 299; raise A.Kn 957. **2.** catch A.Mil 3347, B.Pri 1760, B.Mk 3449, C.Pard 710, G.SN 536; take hold of D.WB 1252, TC 1.1045, (fig.) A.Kn 1300, TC 2.924, RR 1647. **3.** attach A.Kn 2638, A.Rv 4274. **hente** *pa. sg.* A.Prol 698, A.Mil 3475, B.NP 4525. **henten** *pl.* A.Kn 904. **hent** *p.p.* A.Kn 1581, B.NP 4249, D.Fri 1311; **yhent** C.Pard 868, G.SN 536. [OE *hentan*]

henter *n.* grabber Bo 1. p3. 57/81. [from prec.]

hepe *n.* rose-hip B.Th 1937. [OE *hēope*]

hepe(n *v.* increase, augment Bo 4. p5. 20/30, 5. p2. 28/40. *p.p.* accumulated TC 4.236. [OE *hēapian*]

heraud *n.* herald A.Kn 2533, HF 1321. [AN *heraut*]

heraude *v.* herald, sound praise of HF 1576. [OF *herauder*]

herbe/erbe *n.* plant Bo 3. p11. 66/90, TC

2.345; herb B.Th 1950; vegetable E.Cl 226; medicinal plant A.Kn 2713, B.NP 4139, TC 1.661, (in prov.) HF 290–1. [OF]

herbe yve n. (?) buck's-horn plantain B.NP 4156. [OF, perh. from *if* yew]

herbergage n. lodging A.Co 4329, B.ML 147, B.NP 4179, E.Cl 201. [OF]

herbergeours n. pl. harbingers, royal officials travelling in advance to find lodgings B.ML 997. [OF *herbergere*]

herberwe n. shelter, lodging A.Prol 765, I.Pars 1031; 'house', position in the zodiac F.Fkl 1035; harbour, port A.Prol 403. [OE *hereberg*]

herberwe v. give shelter, lodging B.ML 536 var, RR 491. [from prec.]

herberwynge vbl. n. giving lodging A.Co 4332.

herde/hierde n. shepherd A.Prol 603, TC 3.1235; (fig.) G.SN 192, TC 3.619. [OE *hi(e)rde/heorde*]

herdesse n. shepherdess TC 1.653. [from prec.]

her(e see hire.

her(e)myte n. hermit HF 659. [OF *h)ermite*, ML *heremita*]

Hereos/hereos n. sickness of lovers due to melancholy A.Kn 1374. [ML, blend of Gr *erōs* love and L (from Gr) *hēros* hero]

herie v. praise B.ML 1155, E.Cl 616, G.SN 47, TC 3.951; worship B.Mk 3419, LGW 786. **y)heried** p.p. B.ML 872, TC 2.973, 3.7, 1804. [OE *herian*]

heryinge vbl. n. praise B.Pri 1649, praising I.Pars 682; glory TC 3.48.

hering vbl. n. hearing, the sense of hearing I.Pars 207, Bo 2. p5. 20/28.

heritage n. heritage, inheritance B.ML 366, F.Fkl 1563, Pity 71, RR 201. [OF]

herke(n v. hear (with dir. obj.) B.ML 425, D.Fri 1656, LGW G. 139; (absol.) HF 613, 1030 var. **herketh** imper. pl. listen to D.Fri 1656, G.CY 1011. [OE *heorcian*; cf. next]

herkne(n v. **1.** (absol.) listen A.Prol 788, C.Pard 454, D.Fri 1551, TC 1.602, HF 725. **2.** hear, listen to (person) B.NP 4400, G.CY 927, I.Pars 1000, Bo 2. p1. 4/6. **3.** hear (thing, with n. obj. or cl.) A.Kn 2532, B.NP 4480, G.SN 261, TC 5.1812; (with *of*) E.Mch 1699, TC 1.164; attend to E.Cl 1141, **herkene** BD 752, (with *to*) B.Sh 1213, B.Th 2083. **herkneth** imper. pl. A.Prol 788, C.Pard 454. [OA *hercnian*]

herne n. nook, hiding place, G.CY 658, F.Fkl 1121 (see **halke**). [OE *hyrne*]

heroner n. falcon for flying at herons TC 4.413, *faukone* ~ LGW 1120. [OF *heironier*]

heronsewes n. pl. young herons F.Sq 68. [AN *herouncel*]

herse n. frame holding lights round a coffin, catafalque Pity 15, 36. [OF]

hert n. hart, stag A.Kn 1675, BD 351, LGW 1212. [OE *heorot*]

herte n. **1.** heart A.Kn 1079, C.Pard 655, TC 3.1371, LGW 1351; life F.Sq 566, G.CY 753, TC 3.1071; ~ *blod* life-blood A.Kn 2006, C.Pard 902, E.Mch 2347, I.Pars 154, TC 2.445; in phr. with *breke(n*, A.Kn 954, B.NP 4578, LGW 2347; in phr. with *breste(n* B.ML 697, D.WB 1103, E.Mch 2096; (in oaths) *Goddes* ~ A.Mil

3815, A.Rv 4087, C.Pard 651. **2.** the heart as the seat of love, affection A.Mil 3349, B.NP 4100, E.Mch 2145, Pity 14, TC 5.1517, RR 85; as endearment, *dere* ~ B.NP 4079, CompL 59, TC 2.871, *swete* ~ BD 206, Mars 215, TC 3.69; (of feeling) A.Prol 150, B.Pri 1745, TC 5.255, *of* ~ heartfelt B.NP 4493; (of anger) TC 3.110 var; (of pity) A.Kn 2371, B.ML 660, C.Phs 211, TC 3.904; *pitee renneth soone in gentil* ~ A.Kn 1761, E.Mch 1986, F.Sq 479, LGW 503; (of courage) A.Kn 2649, B.NP 4085, F.Fkl 1309, I.Pars 655; *mannes* ~ B.NP 4110, TC 3.1098, 4.154; *mouses* ~ D.WB 572, TC 3.736; (of loyalty) F.Sq 541, PF 355, TC 4.1417, LGW 1843; *don (one's)* ~ strive TC 5.115 var. **3.** mind, inner self A.Kn 1574, B.Mel 2334, D.WB 531, G.SN 245, TC 1.1070; nature B.NP 4029, E.Cl 723, E.Mch 1990, I.Pars 336; mood A.Kn 1513, B.Mel 2186, E.Mch 1244, F.Fkl 1136, BD 488; will, desire A.Kn 1876, B.Mel 2983, B.Mk 3932, E.Cl 214; soul B.ML 167. **herte** gen. in ~ *blod* C.Pard 902, E.Mch 2347, TC 2.445, ~ *roote* D.WB 471; **hertes** in ~ *reste* E.Cl 112, TC 3.1045, 4.581, LGW 519, ~ *lady* A.Kn 2776, CompL 55, TC 5.1390, ~ *lyf* F.Fkl 816, Anel 223, TC 2.1066. [OE *heorte*, gen. *heortan*]

hertelees adj. spiritless, cowardly B.NP 4098; dispirited TC 5.1594. [OE *heortlēas*]

hertely adj. cordial E.Cl 176, F.Sq 5, LGW 2124. [cf. next]

hertely adv. earnestly B.Mel 2242, B.NP 3983, TC 2.1277; sincerely TC 5.941; (I say, ask) cordially A.Prol 762, D.Sum 1801; exceedingly BD 85. [cf. OE *geheortlīce*]

herte-spoon n. hollow in breast-bone A.Kn 2606. [**herte** + OE *spōn* spoon]

het, hete see **hote(n**.

heterly adv. fiercely LGW 639. [OE *hetelīce* modified perh. after OE *biter*]

hethen adj. heathen B.ML 378, F.Fkl 1293; as n. A.Prol 66, B.Mk 3583. [OE *hǣþen*]

hethen/heythen adv. (nth.) from here A.Rv 4033. [ON *heðan*]

hethenesse n. heathen lands A.Prol 49, B.ML 1112. [from **hethen** adj.]

hething n. contempt: *drive til* ~ held up to mockery A.Rv 4110. [ON *hæðing*]

hette see **hote(n**.

hette pa. made hot PF 145. [OE *hætte*]

heved see **he(e)d**.

heve(n v. heave, lift A.Prol 550; raise: ~ *up eyen* I.Pars 986, TC 5.1159; *theron was to* ~ this called for hard work TC 2.1289. **ha(a)f** pa. A.Mil 3470; **hef** Bo 1. p1. 12/17. [OE *hebban*, *hōf*, *hafen*]

heven n. **1.** heaven (in Christian belief) A.Prol 519, B.Mk 3409, C.Pard 912, I.Pars 234, LGW 2; (as abode of pagan gods) TC 1.878, 3.590, HF 591; (fig.) (state of) bliss E.Mch 1647, F.Sq 558, TC 2.826, 3.1742. **2.** the heavens, sky A.Kn 2298, B.NP 4591, TC 3.626, LGW 1218, Astr 1.21.28/39; the stars and their disposition A.Kn 1090, E.Mch 1970; sphere TC 3.2, LGW 2236. **hevene** gen. sg. PF 72, TC 3.704, ~ *King* B.Sh 1583, B.NP 3986, D.WB 1181, HF 1084, ~ *Quene* ABC 24; **hevenes** G.SN 87

G.CY 1089, PF 58, TC 4.1594, HF 988. [OE *heofon*]
hevenish *adj.* celestial Mars 30, TC 5.1813, Astr 1.21.37/50. [OE *heofonisc*]
hevenishly *adv.* divinely A.Kn 1055 var. [from prec.]
hevenly/-lich *adj.* divine I.Pars 598, Truth 27; celestial Bo 1. m2. 6/9. [OE *heofonlić*]
hevenly *adv.* divinely A.Kn 1055 var; religiously E.Mch 1455 var. [OE *heofonlīće*]
hevy *adj.* **1.** heavy, laden H.Mcp 67, PF 380, Purse 7. **2.** serious, weighty B.Mel 2212, TC 1.651; hard Astr prol 33/46. **3.** sad, gloomy B.Mel 2899, Mars 12; *make ~ chere* look gravely upon (with pun, cf. **che(e)re**) Purse 4; indolent I.Pars 677. [OE *hefiġ*]
hevieth *pr. pl.* make heavy, dull Bo 5. m5. 11/15. **ihevyed** *p.p.* m5. 17/24. [OE *hefiġian*]
hevinesse *n.* **1.** sadness A.Kn 1454, BD 25, TC 1.24. **2.** heaviness, weight Bo 3. m9. 16/23, LGW 231. **3.** sluggishness I.Pars 686. [OE *hefiġnesse*]
hewe *n.[1]* **1.** colour B.ML 137, BD 497, FormA 18. **2.** complexion A.Prol 394, A.Mil 3255, BD 1214, LGW G. 162. **3.** appearance C.Pard 421, E.Mch 2063, F.Sq 508; *of ~* in appearance D.Fri 1622, E.Cl 377, PF 354, TC 4.743; *chaunge ~* grow pale or red (esp. in turn) TC 2.303, 3.1698, Ven 30; *hele and ~* health and looks TC 1.461, 5.1403, LGW 1159. **4.** false appearance, pretence C.Pard 421, E.Mch 2063, F.Sq 508. [OE *hiw*]
hewe *n.[2]* servant E.Mch 1785. [OE *hīwa*]
hewe(n *v.* chop A.Kn 1422, 2865; see **hakke**. [OE *hēawan*]
hid *ppl. adj.* hidden, secret B.ML 103, Bo 4. p6. 2, TC 1.530. [from next]
hyde(n *v.* hide B.Sh 1349, G.CY 1231, TC 4.496; *refl.* A.Kn 1481, B.Mk 3732, I.Pars 173; *~ conseil* keep a secret B.ML 777, D.WB 966, TC 4.1325; *~th to shewe hym* refrains from revealing himself I.Pars 394.
hidestow *pr. 2 sg.* (with suffixed pron.) D.WB 308. **hydeth** *3 sg.* I.Pars 113, **hit** F.Sq 512. **hid(de** *pa.* D.WB 745, E.Mch 1944, F.Sq 595. **hid** *p.p.* B.Mel 2274, I.Pars 115, TC 4.496; **yhid(de** G.SN 317, Bo 5. m4. 41/59; **yhed** BD 175. [OE *hȳdan*, *hȳdde*, *hȳdd*]
hider *adv.* hither, here A.Prol 672, B.NP 4000, RR 603. [OE]
hiderto *adv.* hitherto, up to this point Bo 3. p9. 1. [prec.+**to** prep.]
hiderward *adv.* in this direction B.Sh 1616, B.Mk 3159. [OE *hiderweard*]
hidous *adj.* hideous A.Kn 1978, RR 158, frightful A.Mil 3520, B.NP 4583. [AN]
hidously *adv.* horribly A.Kn 1701, HF 1599. [from prec.]
hye *n.* haste: *in ~* in haste A.Kn 2979, B.ML 209; quickly TC 2.88. [from next]
hye *v.* hurry A.Kn 2274, PF 193, TC 5.489; bring quickly F.Sq 291; *refl.* B.Sh 1400, BD 152, LGW 950. [OE *hīgian*]
hye *see* **heigh, heighe.**
hierde *see* **herde.**
hight(e *v. see* **hote(n.**
highte *n. see* **heighte.**
highteth *pr. 3 sg.* beautifies Bo 1. m2. 16/22. **yhight** *p.p.* adorned TC 5.541. [perh. developed from OE *hyht* hope, joy]

him *pron.* **1.** *acc.* him *passim*; *(refl.* with v.) himself A.Prol 87, A.Kn 1503, E.Mch 2234, F.Sq 355, TC 2.1463. **2.** *dat.* to him A.Mil 3290, E.Cl 559, for him A.Kn 1676; (in impers. constr.) A.Prol 486, 756, A.Kn 1385, B.Sh 1200, D.Sum 1956; *(refl.* with intr. v.) A.Kn 1691, TC 4.1163; for himself A.Prol 703, A.Mil 3620; *~ to purpos* see **purpos.** **3.** special uses: *~ and/or hire/here* man and/or woman B.ML 460, HF 1003; this man TC 3.34; (as demons. with proper name, cf. **he)** A.Kn 1210, B.ML 940, E.Mch 1368, 1734. [OE (dat.)]
himself *pron.* himself: *emph.* A.Rv 4321, LGW 1879; *refl.* A.Kn 1182, B.Mk 3212; he himself A.Prol 219, B.Th 2105, B.Mel 2649, LGW 1555; itself D.Sum 1968 *var*, I.Pars 778. **himselve(n** A.Prol 184, B.ML 44, B.Mk 3329, BD 419. [prec.+ **self**]
himward *see* **toward.**
hynde *n.* female (red) deer (corresp. to **hart)** BD 427, PF 195, Bo 3. m12. 7/9. [OE *hind*]
hindre *adj.* back, rear I.Pars 423, **hyndreste** *sup.* A.Prol 622. [cf. OE *hinder* adv.]
hindre *v.* hinder, impede A.Kn 1135, LGW 324, RR 1039. [OE *hindrian*]
hyne *n.* servant, peasant A.Prol 603, C.Pard 688. [OE *hīna* gen. pl.]
hynesse *see* **heighnesse.**
hir(e/her(e *pron.* **1.** *acc.* her A.Kn 1421, B.NP 4027, G.SN 534, TC 1.679; *(refl.* with v.) herself Anel 208. **2.** *dat.* to her E.Cl 843, E.Mch 2266, TC 3.570; (in impers. constr.) B.NP 4024, TC 1.985; *(refl.* with intr. v.) TC 2.812, LGW 810; *prep.* D.Sum 1993 *var.* **3.** special uses: *him and/or ~* see **him**; (as demons. with proper name) E.Mch 1734. [OE *hire* (dat.)]
hir(e *adj. poss.* her D.WB 901, TC 1.127. *pron.* gen. of her E.Mch 2334; *poss.* hers A.Mil 3407. [OE *hire*]
hir(e/her *adj. poss.* their A.Prol 368, B.NP 4486, C.Pard 291, HF 1505. *pron.* gen. of those B.Mel 2590. [OE *hira, heora*]
hyre *n.* payment, wages A.Prol 538, D.Sum 1973; reward D.WB 1008, PF 9, TC 1.334 (see **quyt(t)e(n)**); rent, in *sette to ~* farmed out A.Prol 507; ransom TC 4.506. [OE *hȳr*]
hir(e)s *pron. poss.* hers BD 1041, PF 588, TC 1.889. [**hir(e**+-*es* of n. gen.]
hirs *pron. pl. gen.* of those D.Sum 1926. *poss.* Bo 3. p11. 97/132. [**hir(e**+-*es* of n. gen.]
hirself *pron.* herself: *emph.* A.Mil 3543, B.Pri 1655; *refl.* B.NP 4019, TC 3.777, **hirselve(n** A.Rv 4142, B.NP 4558, TC 1.112. [**hir(e**+**self**]
his *pron.* gen. of him G.SN 138. *poss.* **1.** his *passim*; forming poss. with proper n. *Mars ~* Mars's LGW 2593. **2.** its A.Kn 1036, D.WB 1128, E.Cl 263, G.CY 1419, ABC 178, TC 2.42, 3.1038, Astr prol 71/98. [OE, masc. and neut.]
historial/estorial *adj.* historical C.Phs 156, LGW G. 307. [OF]
hit *see* **it.**
hiwed *adj.* in appearance, in colour B.NP 4059, BD 905, TC 2.1198. [from **hewe** n.]
hochepot *n.* hotch-potch, stew (fig.) B.Mel 2447. [OF]
hoker *n.* contempt A.Rv 3965. [OE *hōcor*

hokerly adv. scornfully I.Pars 584. [from prec.]

holde(n v. **1.** hold, grasp A.Kn 2894, B.Pri 1760, B.Mel 2516, TC 2.203, LGW 234; ~ up A.Prol 783, C.Pard 697, F.Fkl 1024, TC 2.974. **2.** keep A.Mil 3224, I.Pars 440, TC 3.29, maintain Bo 1. m4. 3/4; **helde** retain D.WB 272; detain D.Sum 1727; ~ (one's) pees keep quiet A.Kn 2668, B.NP 4625, G.CY 693, TC 4.455, ~ (one's) mouth/tonge B.Th 2081, H.Mcp 37, PF 521; ~ (oneself) stille B.Mel 2227, Bo 2. p3. 20/27, TC 4.532; ~ companye D.Fri 1521, F.Fkl 763, I.Pars 584, Mars 104, TC 2.1488; ~ covenant/forward/ trouthe A.Kn 2098, D.Fri 1525, TC 2.1084, LGW 2500, ~ (one's) day keep . . appointment D.WB 1024, TC 5.84; ~ . . wey take (a) road E.Cl 273, take a course, continue A.Kn 1506, B.ML 298; celebrate, observe A.Kn 2958, F.Sq 61, TC 1.161; obey D.WB 198; ~ in honde see hond; intr. in ~ with side with A.Kn 2517, A.Mil 3847. **3.** consider, believe B.NP 4628, D.WB 572, I.Pars 44, BD 36, TC 2.164. **4.** p.p. obliged, bound B.Mel 2893, D.WB 135, I.Pars 517, TC 2.241, 5.966. holdestow 2 sg. (with suffixed pron.) Bo 2. p1. 54/73. **holdeth** 3 sg. B.Mel 2335, E.Cl 1189; **halt** B.ML 721, F.Sq 61. holdeth imper. pl. A.Kn 1868, F.Fkl 1064. he(e)ld pa.sg. A.Prol 176, B.NP 4522, F.Fkl 916; hild RR 239. helde(n pl. B.Sh 1192, Bo 2. m5. 1/2. holde(n p.p. A.Prol 141, D.WB 523, TC 2.241; halde (nth.) A.Rv 4208; yholde HF 1286, LGW 1954. [OA háldan, héold, héoldon, ǧe)hálden]

holdinge vbl. n. maintaining I.Pars 437.

holiday see **haliday.**

holily adv. religiously D.Sum. 2286, E.Mch 1455; scrupulously Bo 3. p10. 48/66. [from **ho(o)ly**]

holynesse n. **1.** virtue A.Mil. 3180, B.ML 167, C.Pard 422, E.Mch 1628; chastity B.ML 713. **2.** piety, devotion A.Kn 1158, E.Mch 1253, TC 1.560; work of piety LGW 424. **3.** religion E.Mch 1708, LGW G. 296. [OE hálignes]

holm n. holm-oak, ilex A.Kn 2921. [altered from holn, OE holen holly]

holour n. lecher D.WB 254, I.Pars 626, paramour I.Pars 878. [OF holier]

holpe(n see **helpe(n.**

holt n. wood, coppice A.Prol 6, TC 3.351. [OE]

holwe adj. hollow G.CY 1265, HF 1035; emaciated A.Prol 289; (of eyes) sunken A.Kn 1363. [attrib. use of OE holh, *holw- hole]

homicyde n.[1] murderer B.NP 4414, E.Mch 1994, I.Pars 574. [OF from L homicida]

homicyde n.[2] murder C.Pard 644, D.Sum 2009. I.Pars 564. [OF from L homicidium]

hond/hand n. hand A.Prol 108, G.CY 1154, Astr 1.1.2; biforen ~ earlier G.CY 1317; in his ~ on a halter A.Rv 4115; in ~e in process, going on A.Rv 4035; bere(n on ~ accuse (falsely) B.ML 620, D.WB 226, Anel 158, Bo 1. p4. 180/252, TC 4.1404, deceive into thinking, convince (untruly) D.WB 232, 575; hold in ~ deceive, play with BD 1019, TC 2.477, 3.773; have in (one's) ~ have under control D.WB 211,

327; have on ~ be occupied with E.Mch 1686, TC 2.217, HF 1009; take(n on ~ undertake B.ML 348; of his/hir ~ in action A.Kn 2103, B.ML 579; his owne ~ by himself A.Mil 3624. [OE hánd]

honest adj. **1.** honourable A.Prol 246, E.Mch 2024; respectable D.WB 1183, I.Pars 1009; decent, suitable B.Sh 1239, C.Pard 328, E.Mch 2028. **2.** free from deceit, honest H.Mcp 75. [OF]

honestee n. honour B.Mk 3157, TC 2.706; virtue, chastity C.Phs 77, G.SN 89, TC 4.1576; decency, modesty B.Mk 3902, I.Pars 429 var; dignity D.Fri 1267. [OF]

honestetee/honestitee n. honour E.Cl 422; decency, modesty I.Pars 429; honesty Bo 1. p5. 33/49 var. [OF]

honestly adv. honourably A.Kn 1444, B.Sh 1434; fittingly E.Mch 2026; sincerely I.Pars 1046 var. [from **honest**]

honge see **hange(n.**

hony n. honey A.Kn 2908, B.Mel 2600, PF 354; attrib. sweet, eloquent Bo 2. p3. 7/9, 5. m2. 1. [OE huniǧ]

honour n. **1.** (the quality of) honour, A.Prol 46, B.Pri 1655, TC 2.161; in ~ of B.Pri 1854, F.Sq 113, TC 3.163, HF 1611. **2.** fame, reputation A.Kn 908, B.Sh 1611, D.Sum 2163; glory B.Mk 3401, HF 1793; good name TC 2.468; pl. signs of high standing C.Pard 617, Bo 2. p2. 21/29. **3.** respect H.Mcp 331, TC 1.152, LGW 149; show of respect B.Pri 1813, C.Pard 604; do ~ to A.Kn 997, B.ML 379, D.WB 299, PF 676. **4.** credit D.WB 1233, E.Cl 133. [AN]

honoure(n v. **1.** honour A.Kn 2716, I.Pars 408, TC 4.1524. **2.** worship B.ML 549, B.Mk 3753 var, I.Pars 708; celebrate D.Sum 1719, Mars 3. [OF]

hood n. hood A.Prol 103, A.Mil 3122, TC 2.1181; by myn ~! TC 5.1151, LGW 507; finde game in myn ~ laugh at me TC 2.1110, HF 1810: put in (someone's) ~ an ape make a fool of (him) B.Pri 1630; don thyn ~ put on your hat, 'call it a day' TC 2.954. [OE hód]

ho(o)l adj. **1.** whole, complete F.Fkl 1450, TC 1.961, BalCo 13; with ~ herte heartily A.Prol 533, BD 1224; as n. the whole amount A.Kn 3006; as adv. completely CompL 60/54, TC 1.1053. **2.** unharmed, undamaged B.Sh 1535, D.Fri 1370; ~ and sound B.ML 1150, B.Mel 2205, Bo 4. p1. 50/70. **3.** healthy, well D.Sum 2033, I.Pars 458, TC 2.1670; syke and ~ E.Mch 1289, ~ or syke I.Pars 961, HF 1270; cured C.Pard 357, D.WB 977, E.Mch 2007, F.Sq 161. [OE hál]

ho(o)ld n. **1.** possession B.NP 4064, D.WB 599, D.Fri 1607, E.Mch 1305 var; grasp F.Sq 167. **2.** stronghold, castle B.ML 507. [**holde(n** and ON hald]

ho(o)ly adj. **1.** sacred A.Prol 17, B.ML 451, E.Mch 1702, I.Pars 801, TC 3.1261; ~ chirche the Church A.Rv 3983, B.ML 675, D.Sum 2193, E.Mch 1662, I.Pars 93; ~ day Astr 1.11.1 var, see **haliday;** ~ Goost see **go(o)st;** ~ Trinitee B.Pri 1836; ~ writ the Bible A.Prol 739, C.Pard 483, D.Sum 1790, Buk 21; ~ houses religious houses D.Sum 1718. **2.** religious, devout A.Prol 178, A.Kn 2213, I.Pars 948; saintly

B.ML 692, 1129, C.Pard 635, D.WB 690, Bo 4. p6. 172/250. [OE *hālig*]

hoolly *adv.* wholly, completely A.Prol 599, BD 15, TC 1.366 RR 1163. [from **ho(o)l**]

hoolnesse *n.* wholeness Bo 4. p6. 127/184, 5. p4. 91/131. [from **ho(o)l**]

ho(o)lsom *adj.* wholesome, beneficial B.Mel 2285, PF 206, TC 1.947, 3.1746. [from **ho(o)l**]

ho(o)lsomnesse *n.* health B.Mel 2303. [from prec.]

ho(o)m *n.* **1.** home Truth 17; *at* ~ B.Mk 3128, D.Fri 1617, BD 77; *hous and* ~ H.Mcp 229. **2.** as *adv.* to (one's) home A.Prol 400, C.Pard 785, HF 655, **ham** (nth.) A.Rv. 4032. [OE *hām*]

ho(o)mcomynge *vbl. n.* home-coming, return A.Kn 884, B.ML 765, TC 5.503.

ho(o)mly *adj.* familiar, intimate, E.Mch 1785, 1792; simple, plain D.Sum 1843. [from **ho(o)m**]

ho(o)mly *adv.* familiarly G.CY 608, TC 2.1559, Bo 3. p12. 135/182; plainly A.Prol 328. [as prec.]

ho(o)mlinesse *n.* domesticity E.Cl 429; familiarity B.Mel 2876. [from adj.]

ho(o)mward *adv.* on the way home A.Prol 794, B.Pri 1734; towards home B.Pri 1739, TC 3.621. [OE *hāmweard*]

ho(o)r *adj.* grey, white (of hair) A.Rv 3878, D.Sum 2182; *old and* ~ E.Mch 1269, TC 5.1284; old E.Mch 1461, 1464; age, in *for* ~ RR 356 (see **for**). [OE *hār*]

ho(o)rd *n.* store A.Mil 3262, A.Co 4406, B.Sh 1274; hoard C.Pard 775; storehouse I.Pars 821; hoarding, avarice Truth 3. [OE]

ho(o)st/o(o)st *n.*[1] army A.Kn 874, B.Mk 3758, TC 1.80. [OF]

ho(o)st(e/ost(e *n.*[2] (only in CT) host, innkeeper, landlord A.Prol 747, F.Fkl 703, I.Pars 67. [OF]

hoot *adj.* hot A.Prol 394, A.Mil 3379, G.CY 956; fiery (to taste) E.Mch 1808, I.Pars 117; strong G.CY 887; passionate A.Prol 626, PF 246, violent A.Kn 1809; difficult E.Mch 2126; (of the humours) ruled by fire A.Prol 420, B.NP 4147, F.Sq 51, Astr 1.21.46/63. **hotter** *comp.* TC 1.449. [OE *hāt*]

hoot(e *adv.* passionately A.Prol 97, A.Kn 1737, B.ML 586. **hotter** *comp.* LGW 59. [from prec.]

hoote see **hote(n.**

hope *n.* hope, expectation A.Prol 88, D.WB 994, I.Pars 168; *good* ~ A.Kn 1878, F.Fkl 924, G.CY 678, TC 1.391, 5.348; *in* ~ *of* trusting in B.Mel 2630, *liljer of* hope B.NP 4594; *bitwixen* ~ *and drede* TC 5.630, 1207. [OE *hopa*]

hope(n *v.* hope A.Mil 3725, D.Fri 1414, TC 1.47; hope for I.Pars 94; expect, believe (a mainly northerly sense) A.Rv 4029; ~ *to God* devoutly wish E.Mch 1674, I.Pars 957, TC 2.1272. [OE *hopian*]

hoper/hopur *n.* hopper (in a mill) A.Rv 4036. [from next]

hoppe *v.* dance A.Rv 3876, A.Co 4375, TC 2.1107. [OE *hoppian*]

hoppestere *n.* dancer (mistakenly translating *bellatrici* as if *ballatrici*) A.Kn 2017. [OE]

horn *n.* **1.** horn (of animal) B.Mk 3296, Bo 4. m7. 34/49; snail's horn (fig.) *shrinke*

in ~ TC 1.300; horn (the material) B.NP 4589, D.Sum 1740, TC 2.642. **2.** (hunting) horn A.Prol 116, H.Mcp 90, BD 182; (drinking) horn A.Kn 2279, F.Fkl 1253; cornucopia Bo 2. m2. 2. **3.** point of a crescent moon TC 3.624. [OE]

horowe *n.* filth, *tunges* ~ slander Mars 206. [OE *horh*]

hors *n.* **1.** horse A.Prol 94, F.Sq 181, TC 1.223. **2.** (name of the wedge holding the 'pin' of an astrolabe) Astr 1.14.4/6. **hors** *pl.* A.Prol 74, B.Pri 1823, D.Fri 1547, BD 349, HF 952; **horses** I.Pars 434. [OE]

hors *adj.* hoarse BD 347, TC 4.1147. [ON **hārs, hāss*]

horsly† *adj.* like (a real) horse F.Sq 194. [from **hors** n.]

hose *n.* stocking, legging A.Rv 3933, G.CY 726, HF 1840. *pl.* **hosen** A.Prol 456, A.Rv 3955; B.Th 1923; **hoses** A.Mil 3319, I.Pars 423. [OE *hosa*]

hospitaliers *n. pl.* knights hospitallers I.Pars 891. [OF]

hostel *n.* lodging, inn (in phr. *bon* ~) HF 1022. [OF]

hostelrye *n.* inn A.Prol 23, G.CY 589, I.Pars 440; lodging A.Kn 2493, A.Mil 3203, B.NP 4184. [OF]

hostesse/o(o)stesse *n.* hostess Bo 4. m3. 16/21, LGW 2496. [OF]

hostileer *n.* innkeeper A.Prol 241, A.Co 4360, B.NP 4219; *pl.* inn servants I.Pars 440. [OF *hostelier*]

hote(n *v.* **1.** be called A.Prol 616, D.WB 144, F.Sq 30, HF 1580, TC 3.797. **2.** promise A.Kn 2398, 2472, B.ML 334, BD 1226, LGW 2502; assure B.ML 1132. **hoten** *infin.* D.WB 144, **hete** BD 1226, **hatte** RR 38. **heete** *pr. 1 sg.* B.ML 334. **hatte** *3 sg.* TC 3.797. *pl.* HF 1303 *var.* **highte** *sg.* I.Pars 51, HF 1580. **highten** *pl.* TC 1.788, LGW 423. **heete** *subj. sg.* A.Kn 2398. **highte** *pa.* A.Prol 616, A.Kn 860, A.Rv 4013, F.Sq 30; **het** BD 200, HF 1604; **hette** Mars 185. **hight** *p.p.* A.Kn 2472, B.NP 4039 *var*, D.WB 1024, E.Mch 1772; **ho(o)te(n** A.Rv 3941; **heet** (?*pa.*) B.NP 4039, F.Fkl 1388, TC 1.153. [OE *hātan, hēt/heht, hāten*]

hotte *n.* basket, pannier HF 1940*em*. [OF]

hound *n.* dog A.Prol 146, B.NP 4090, I.Pars 907; *a sleping* ~ *to wake* TC 3.764; hound (for hunting) A.Kn 1678, LGW 1121, BD 377. [OE *hŭnd*]

houndfissh *n.* dogfish E.Mch 1825. [**hound**+**fissh**]

houno† *n.* (word not certainly identified) *hors and ~ everybody* TC 4.210.

houre *n.* **1.** hour A.Mil 3519, B.Pri 1732, TC 1.456; ~ *equal* sixty minutes Astr 1.17.26/35, 2.8.2/3; ~ *inequal* one twelfth of the day or night A.Kn 2271, Astr 2.8.1/2, 12.16/22. **2.** time I.Pars 1051, TC 3.140, LGW 682; **3.** time of ascendancy of planets, deities A.Prol 416, A.Kn 2217, Astr 2.12.11/15. [AN]

hous *n.* **1.** house, home A.Prol 345, B.Sh 1221, E.Cl 871, TC 1.127, HF 663; *bless this* ~ A.Mil 3484; *change* ~ go elsewhere A.Kn 2809; ~ *and hoom* H.Mcp 229; ~ *to* ~ D.WB 547; *kepe* ~ E.Mch 1382; *come to* ~ *upon* become familiar with LGW 1546. **2.** household F.Sq 24, LGW 2619; family

C.Pard 649, D.WB 1153, Bo 2. m7. 9/12.
3. religious house A.Prol 252, B.Mk 3121,
G.CY 993. **4.** (astrol.) one-twelfth section
of the sky Astr 2.4.9/16, 36.2/3, 37.3/4,
TC 2.681; the influential position of a
planet or the sun in a sign of the zodiac
F.Sq 672. [OE *hūs*]
housbonde *n.* husband A.Kn 3081, D.WB
19, LGW 513. [OE *hūsbonda*]
housbondrye *n.* careful management,
economy A. Rv 4077, B.NP 4018, E.Mch
1296; household goods D.WB 288. [from
prec.]
housel *v.* administer Eucharist to I.Pars
1027. [from n., OE *hūsl*]
housholding *vbl. n.* (lavish) housekeeping,
extravagance RR 1132.
hove *v.* hover TC 3.1427; wait, linger TC
5.33, LGW 1196, BalCh 15*em.* [?]
how *adv.* how: ~ *that* A.Prol 642, A.Kn
1385, TC 4.75, howsoever, although I.Pars
710; ~ *sore that me smerte* however painful
to me it may be A.Kn 1394, TC 3.146,
1000; ~ *so (that)* although Bo 3. p2. 85/122,
5. p4. 139/200, TC 2.1271, however LGW
1984, 2293, ~ *so it be* TC 2.256. [OE *hū*]
how *interj.* ho, hi A.Mil 3437, 3577, B.Sh
1174 *var.* [?]
how-gates *adv.* (nth.) in what way, how
A.Rv 4037 *var.* [OE *hū*+ON *gata* way,
with adv. *-es*]
howped *pa. pl.* whooped B.NP 4590. [OE
hwōpan, OF *huper*]
howve *n.* hood (in prov. expressions meaning 'delude, hoodwink'): *sette his* ~ A.Rv
3911, *glase his* ~ TC 5.469, *maken him an* ~
TC 3.775, see **calle.** [OE *hūfe*]
humanitee *n.* kindness E.Cl 92. [OF]
humbleheed *n.* humble circumstances
B.Mk 3862 *var.* [*humble* adj., from OF,
+OE suff. *-*hǣdu*]
humblely/humbely *adv.* humbly TC
2.1257 *var*, 5.1354 *var*, LGW 156. [from
humble adj., from OF]
humblesse *n.* humility A.Kn 1781, I.Pars
481, Ven 18. [OF]
humour *n.* body fluid (supposed to determine health and temperament) A.Prol 421,
B.NP 4115, I.Pars 913. [AN (*h*)*umour*, OF
(*h*)*umor* from L]
hunte *n.* hunter, huntsman A.Kn 1678, 2628,
BD 345, 541. [OE *hunta*]
hurlest *pr. 2 sg.* thrust, force B.ML 297.
[? imit.; cf. LG *hurreln*]
hurtle(n *v.* attack Bo 2. p1. 19/27, LGW 638;
knock A.Kn 2616; (with *to*) dash (against)
Bo 5. m4. 36/52. [from OF *hurter* strike+
frequent. suff.]
hust *p.p.* hushed A.Kn 2981, TC 2.915,
LGW 2682; (as *interj.*) hush! A.Mil 3722.
[imit.]

I

i- = **j-** *see under* **j-**.
i-/y- *pref. in past participles, see also each verb.*
I/y *pron.* I; *h*)*it am* ~ see **it**; **ich** B.ML 39,
TC 1.678, 864, 5.40, **ik** (nth.) A.Rv 3867,
3888. Suffixed in *theech, theek*, see **thee** v.
[OE *ič*]
I *interj.* see **ei.**

vbake *p.p.* baked A.Rv 4312, LGW 709.
[OE *gebacen*]
ybedded *p.p.* put to bed TC 5.346. [OE
beddian]
ybenched *p.p.* provided with benches LGW
G.98. [see **benched**]
ybet *see* **be(e)te(n.**
yblent *see* **blende.**
icched *p.p.* itched A.Mil 3682. [OE *giččan*]
ich *see* **ech, I.**
yclad *see* **clothe(n.**
yclenched *p.p.* riveted A.Kn 1991. [OE
clenčan]
ycorve(n *see* **kerve(n.**
ydarted *p.p.* pierced TC 4.240. [v. from
dart(e]
idel *adj.* **1.** pointless, empty C.Pard 638,
worthless Bo 2. p5. 50/69; ~ *word(es)*
I.Pars 166, 647, Bo 5. p1. 27/37, LGW
767; *in* ~ in vain B.Mel 2494, C.Pard 642,
I.Pars 596, *on* ~ TC 1.955, 5.272. **2.** lazy
C.Phs 57, I. Pars 714, HF 1733, LGW
1700; at leisure A.Kn 2505, E.Cl 224,
Bo 3. m2. 10/15. [OE *idel*]
ydelly *adv.* in vain C.Pard 446. [OE *idellīče*]
idelnesse *n.* **1.** indolence A.Kn 1940,
G.SN 2, 17, I.Pars 714, (person.) RR 593.
2. inactivity B.ML 32, BD 602. [OE
idelnes(se]
ydight *see* **dighte(n.**
idolastre *n.* idolater B.Mk 3377, E.Mch
2298, I.Pars 749. [OF]
idole *n.* idol G.SN 269, BD 626, LGW 786.
[OF]
ydrawe *see* **drawe(n.**
idus *n.* ides (in Roman calendar) F.Sq 47.
[OF]
ye *see* **eye.**
yed/eyed *adj.* with eyes TC 4.1459. [from n.]
if *conj.* if A.Prol 145, D.Sum 1915; ~ *that*
C.Phs 189, BD 969, TC 5.1000, LGW
339; *but* ~ unless A.Prol 656, F.Fkl 912,
LGW 2071. **yif** Bo 1. p4. 3/4, LGW 2312
(and occas. in some MSS; also **3if**). [OE
gif]
yfeith *see* **feith.**
ifere *adv.* (mostly in TC, usu. at line-end)
together B.ML 394, TC 2.152, 1037,
3.273, LGW 903, RR 786; *all(e* ~ G.SN
380, TC 2.1477, 3.746, 4.1333, LGW 263.
[?from OE *gefēra* companion, in predic.
use]
yfinde *v.* find F.Sq 470, F.Fkl 1153, LGW
G. 415. [OE *gefindan*]
yfyned *p.p.* embellished RR 1696. [from v.
from **fyn**]
yfyred *p.p.* excited, impassioned LGW 1013.
[from v. from **fyr**]
ygo(o)(n *see* **go(o)n.**
ygret *see* **grete.**
ygrounde *see* **grinde.**
yhalowed *p.p.* chased with shouts BD 379.
[from OF *halloer*]
yharded *p.p.* hardened F.Sq 245, Bo 4. m5.
19/26. [from OE *heardian*]
yhed *see* **hyde(n.**
yhe(e)re *v.* hear A.Mil 3176, E.Mch 2154,
hear of TC 4.1313. [OA *gehēran*]
ihevyed *see* **hevieth.**
ik *see* **I.**
yknowe *v.* know, recognize D.Fri 1370 *var*,
F.Fkl 887, HF 1336. [OE *gecnāwan*]
ylaft *see* **le(e)ve(n** *v.*[1]

ile *n.* island B.ML 68, HF 416, LGW 1425 (Guido *insula*). [OF]

ylered *ppl. adj.* as *n. pl.* learned men TC 1.976 *var.* [from **le(e)re**]

il-hail *exclam.* bad luck! A.Rv 4089. [**il**(**le** + ON *heill*; cf. OIcel *illu heilli*]

ylyk(e/yliche *adj.* alike HF 1328, LGW 389, Astr 1.17.17/23; like A.Prol 592, A.Kn 1539. [OE *ġelīc*]

ylyke/yliche *adv.* alike, equally A.Kn 2526, D.Sum 2225, G.CY 1202, BD 9, LGW 56. [OE *ġelīce*]

ilke *adj.* same, very; *this* ~ A.Prol 64, G.SN 80, TC 3.507; *that* ~ A.Rv. 3872, Bo 2. p1. 8/11, RR 152; *that* ~ *same* the very same LGW 779. Cf. **thilk(e.** [OE *ilca*]

il(le *adj.* (nth.) bad A.Rv 4045, 4174, 4184. [ON *illr*]

illusion *n.* **1.** deception F.Fkl 1134, 1292; *doon* ~ *to* deceive G.CY 673. **2.** fancy TC 3.1041; apparition HF 493, TC 5.368. [OF]

ylor(e)n *see* **lese(n.**

ymaad *see* **make(n.**

image *n.* **1.** statue, carving A.Kn 1899, HF 121, RR 142; effigy B.Pri 1695, F.Fkl 1391, G.SN 509. **2.** figure (in astrology) A.Prol 418, Bo 4. m1. 15/22; HF 1269. **3.** likeness D.Fri 1642, Bo 3. m9. 22/32, 5. p6. 60/85; sense datum, impression Bo 5. m4. 4/6, 10/25. [OF]

imagerie *n.* carving HF 1190, 1304. [OF]

imaginacioun *n.* **1.** imagination (the faculty) Bo 3. p3. 2/3, 5. p4. 143/205, LGW 355. **2.** idea, fancy BD 14, A.Mil 3612; *vain* ~ wrong idea A.Kn 1094. **3.** scheming, plotting B.NP 4407. [OF]

imaginatyf *adj.* **1.** using mental images Bo 5. p4. 147/211. **2.** *ben* ~ speculate F.Fkl 1094. [OF]

imagine(n *v.* **1.** imagine, conceive TC 2.836, 4.1695. **2.** understand, deduce B.ML 889. **3.** fancy, imagine (something untrue) TC 5.617, 624. **4.** consider, wonder (about) E.Cl 598, TC 5.454. **5.** devise, plan I.Pars 447, TC 4.1626. **6.** suppose, take (to be) Bo 3. m11. 17/23, Astr 1.14.6/8, 21. 29/40. *p.p.* as *adj.* imaginary Astr 2.39.2. [OF *imaginer*]

imagining *vbl. n.* **1.** imagination, fancy LGW G. 331, Ven 36. **2.** plotting A.Kn 1995.

ymaked *see* **make(n.**

ymeynd *ppl. adj.* mingled A.Kn 2170. [OE *gemengd* from *mengan*]

ymel *prep.* (nth.) among A.Rv 4171. [ON *i milli*]

impacience/in- *n.* impatience B.Mel 2734, Bo 2. p1. 72/100; inability to endure I.Pars 276; resentment I.Pars 499. [OF]

impacient/in- *adj.* impatient, intolerant B.Mel 2730, I.Pars 401, Bo 2. p4. 72/99. [OF]

imparfit/in- *adj.* imperfect, incomplete Bo 3. p9. 16/22 *var*, p10. 39/55, Astr 1.18.3/4. Cf. **unparfit.** [OF *imparfait*]

ympe *n.* shoot B.Mk 3146. [OE *impa*]

imperie *n.* authority, rank Bo 2. p6. 8/12. [OF *emperie*]

impertinent *adj.* not pertinent, irrelevant E.Cl 54. [OF]

impetren *v.* entreat Bo 5. p3. 142/203. [OF *impetrer*]

implyeth/em- *pr. 3 sg.* enfolds Bo 5. m1. 10/14 (L *implicet*). [OF *emplier*]

ympne *n.* song, poem LGW 422. [OF *ymne*]

importable *adj.* unendurable, insupportable B.Mk 3792, E.Cl 1144. [OF]

imposicioun *n.* tax Bo 1. p4. 66/91. [OF]

impossible/in- *adj.* **1.** impossible B.Mel 2420, TC 1.783, HF 702. **2.** as *n.* impossible thing D.WB 688, F.Fkl 1009, LGW 1839, TC 3.525; as a problem in logic, L *impossibile*, D.Sum 2231. [OF]

impresse/en-/in- *v.* make a mark, impression E.Mch 1578, G.CY 1071; imprint Bo 5. m4. 31/45, WUnc 8; (fig.) TC 2.1371. [OF *em-/impresser*]

impressioun/in- *n.* mental impact F.Sq 371, TC 2.1238, HF 39; imprint A.Mil 3613, E.Mch 1978; image TC 1.298. [OF]

inclyn- see **enclyn-.**

inclinacioun *n.* bent, fancy D.WB 615. [OF]

inconstance *n.* fickleness D.Sum 1958. [OF]

inconvenient *n.* incongruity Bo 5. p3. 121/172.[OF]

incubus *n.* incubus (a lecherous demon) D.WB 880. [L]

Inde *adj.* from India Mars 246. [from n. from OF]

inde *adj.* (indigo) blue RR 67. [OF]

indignacioun *n.* disdain, insubordination I.Pars 402, Bo 1. p4. 74/102. [OF]

indulgence *n.* leniency B.Mel 2964; *of* ~ by permission D.WB 84. [OF]

induracioun *n.* hardening G.CY 855. [OF]

inequal *adj.* unequal, *houre* ~ one twelfth of day A.Kn 2271, Astr 2.36.2. *pl.* **houres** ~es Astr 2.8.1/2, 2.10.1. [L *inaequālis*]

infect *ppl. adj.* invalidated A.Prol 320; dimmed Bo 4. m5. 9/12. [L *infectum*; cf. next]

infecte/en- *v.* pollute, contaminate G.CY 889, 973, H.Mcp 39, LGW 2242. [L *infect-*, p.p. stem of *inficere*]

infe(e)re *adv.* together B.ML 328, D.WB 924, TC 2.1266 *var*, HF 250 *var.* [**in** + **fere** n.³, or **ifere** so analysed]

infermetee *n.* infirmity, weakness I.Pars 913, Bo 4. p2. 102/136. [OF]

infernal *adj.* from, of, the lower regions A.Kn 2684, TC 4.1543, LGW 1886; ~s *pl.* TC 5.368. [OF]

infinitee *n.* infinity Bo 5. p6. 22/31, 35/50. [OF]

infirme *adj.* feeble Bo 5. m2. 3/4. [L *infirmus*]

influence *n.* ethereal fluid, flow of energy E.Mch 1968; power exercised (by heavenly bodies) TC 3.618, Astr 1.21.44/61. [OF]

informacioun *n.* instruction, advice B.Mel 3060, Bo 2. p1. 22/31. [OF]

infortunat *adj.* unlucky, inauspicious B.ML 302, Astr 2.4.21/33. [L *infortūnātus*]

infortune *n.* misfortune TC 1.755 *var*; malevolent influence A.Kn 2021. [OF]

infortuned *ppl. adj.* afflicted, miserable TC 4.751. [OF *infortuner*]

infortuning *vbl. n.* making inauspicious Astr 2.4.27/42.

ingot *n.* mould (for metal) G.CY 818, 1233, 1314. [OF *lingot*]

inh(i)elde† *imper. pl.* pour in TC 3.44. [**in**(**ne** + **helde** v.²]

iniquitee *n.* **1.** injustice A.Kn 940, C.Phs 262. **2.** wickedness B.ML 453, B.NP 4405; wrongdoing, injury I.Pars 442, B.ML 358. [OF]

injure *n.* injury TC 3.1018. [OF]

inke *n.* ink TC 3.1693, LGW 2491; *pricke of* ~ ink-dot Astr 2.5.12/18, 38.14/21. [OF *enque*]

inknette† *pa. sg.* restrained TC 3.1088 *var.* [in(ne+knitte(n]

inly *adv.* **1.** inwardly TC 3.1606, deeply HF 31. **2.** wholly BD 276, TC 1.640 *var.* [OE *inlīče*]

inmest† *adv.* deep inside Bo 2. p4. 69/94 *var.* [cf. OE *innemest*]

inmid *prep.* in the middle of HF 923. [in(ne+midde]

inmoevableté *n.* immobility Bo 5. p6. 51/71 (L *immobilitate*). [from OF *movable*]

inmortal occ. sp. of *immortal* I.Pars 1078, TC 3.185. [L *immortālis*]

in(ne *n.* **1.** house A.Mil 3547, D.WB 350. **2.** inn B.NP 4216; lodging B.ML 1097, B.Pri 1632. [OE]

in(ne *prep.* **1.** in; **inne** at end of rel. cl.: A.Prol 41, B.ML 518, TC 2.6, 4.1268; with reference to B.Mel 2660. ~ *special* particularly A.Prol 444, TC 1.1055; ~ *general* A.Kn 2285, Fort 56; wearing LGW 405. **2.** into A.Rv 4094, B.Th 1962, G.SN 252, TC 4.467, 830; to I.Pars 175. **3.** on E.Mch 2137, I.Pars 773, TC 4. 1086. [OE]

inned *p.p.* lodged A.Kn 2192. [from n.]

innerest *adj. sup.* innermost Bo 4. p6. 82/117, 134/194. [OE *innera* inner]

innocent *n.* **1.** innocent, harmless person B.ML 618, Bo 1. m5. 26/37; simpleton G.CY 1076. **2.** young child, martyr B.Pri 1756. **innocentes/-tz** *pl.* Bo 1. p4. 143/198, B.ML 815, B.Pri 1798. [OF]

inobedience *n.* disobedience I.Pars 391. [OF]

inobedient *adj.* disobedient I.Pars 392. [OF]

inordinat *adj.* excessive I.Pars 414. [L *inordinātus*]

yno(u)gh *n.* **1.** enough A.Mil 3149, B.Sh 1409, C.Pard 962, E.Cl 365, F.Fkl 1619; *nat but* ~ quite enough G.CY 601; *have* ~ *to done* have difficulty H.Mcp 66. **2.** a great deal, plenty TC 1.881. **ynowe** *pl.* D.Sum 1681. [OE *ġenōh, ġenōge*]

yno(u)gh *adj.* (usu. following word qualified) **1.** enough, sufficient (quantity or number) A.Prol 373, A.Kn 1616, B.Sh 1624, E.Cl 792, TC 4.1266. **2.** abundant, plenty of A.Kn 2836, D.WB 332, PF 185, LGW 1284, **ynowe** *pl.* A.Mil 3178, B.Mel 2563, F.Sq 470, PF 233, TC 3.299, 4.107. [as prec.]

yno(u)gh *adv.* **1.** enough, sufficiently A.Kn 888, C.Pard 475, E.Mch 1560; *it oghte* ~ *suffyse* it should be enough B.Sh 1290, B.Mk 3648; *dere* ~ *a jane/leek/myte/risshe* dear enough at [a trivial price], valueless E.Cl 999, G.CY 795, TC 3.1161, 4.684; *dere* ~ *a myte* even to a slight extent LGW 741. **2.** exceedingly TC 4.134, copiously E.Mch 1781. **ynow(e** F.Fkl 708, G.CY 860, 945. [as the n.]

inp- see **imp-**.

inperfeccioun *n.* imperfection I.Pars 1007. [OF]

inplitable† *adj.* unreasonable Bo 1. p4. 59/82 *var* (L *inexplicabilis*). [from **plyte**]

inpudence *n.* shamelessness I.Pars 391. [L *impudentia*]

inpudent *adj.* shameless B.ML 309 *var*, I.Pars 397. [L *impudent-*]

inset *p.p.* implanted Bo 2. p3. 13/18. [OE *insettan*]

insight *n.* insight E.Cl 242; understanding, perception Bo 1. p6. 75/97; 5. m3. 11/15. [prob. Scand. or LG; cf. Sw *insiht*, Du *inzicht*]

inspired see **enspire**.

instable *adj.* changeable E.Mch 2057. [OF]

insta(u)nce *n.* **1.** request, urging E.Mch 1611, TC 2. 1411. **2.** instant time Bo 5. p6. 82/115. [OF]

instrument *n.* **1.** musical instrument A.Kn 1367, BD 314, TC 5.442. **2.** tool, mechanical device G.CY 1119, TC 1.631, Astr prol 10/13, 2.5.5/7; tool (fig.) B.ML 370, F.Sq 568, TC 1.10. **3.** = organ (of either sex) D.WB 132, 149. [OF]

interminable *adj.* (only Bo) endless, eternal; *life* ~ Bo 5. p6. 11/15, etc. [OF]

interrogacioun *n.* question, syllogism A.Mil 3194. [OF]

intervalle *n.* pause B.Mel 2724. [OF]

into *prep.* into A.Prol 23, C.Pard 539, BD 140; until B.Mel 2423, G.SN 552; to B.Mk 3157, H.Mcp 195; onto A.Mil 3471; ~ *shippes bord* on board ship A.Mil 3585; as far as C.Pard 722; towards F.Fkl 863. [OE]

intresse *n.* interest, concern Fort 71. [AN]

introduccioun *n.* preparation, first steps G.CY 1386. [OF]

introductorie *n.* introduction, text-book Astr prol 73/101. [LL *intrōductōrius*]

invocacioun *n.* invocation, supplication HF 67. [OF]

inward *adj.* interior Bo 3. m11. 3/45, Bo 5. m2. 4/5. [OE *inweard*]

inward *adv.* inwards A.Rv 4079, TC 2.1725, Astr 2.40.24/35; inwardly B.Mel 2835; privately TC 2.1732. [OE *inweard*]

inwardly *adv.* closely TC 2.264. [OE *inweardlīče*]

inwith *prep.* within, inside B.ML 797, E.Cl 870, TC 3.1499; in E.Mch 1394, 2342. [OE *in*+*wiþ*]

ypleynted *p.p.* filled with complaint TC 5.1597. [from v. from **pleynte**]

ipocras *n.* a cordial drink E.Mch 1807. [from **Ypocras** Hippocrates]

ypocrisie *n.* hypocrisy C.Pard 410, I.Pars 391. [OF]

yqueynt see **quenche(n**.

ire *n.* anger, bad temper A.Kn 940, D.Sum 1667, 1993 *var*, TC 1.793, wrath (as sin) I.Pars 388; *caught an* ~ got into an angry mood D.Sum 2003. [OF]

yreke *p.p.* raked over, covered A.Rv 3882. [cf. MDu *reken*]

iren *n.* iron A.Prol 500, PF 149, HF 1431. [OE]

irous *adj.* angry, irascible B.Mel 2315, D.Sum 2014, I.Pars 619. [AN]

irreguler *adj.* breaking the rules of (his) order I.Pars 782. [OF]

is *pr. 1 sg.* am A.Rv 4031, 4045, 4202. *2 sg.* art A.Rv 4089. (imitation of nth. dial., but second and third cases inaccurate because *is* not there used when pron. immediately precedes). [OE]

ysatled *p.p.* settled E.Mch 2405. [OE *sætlan*, rel. to *setlan*]

yse *n.* ice HF 1130. [OE *īs*]

yse(e *v.* see E.Mch 2402, BD 205, TC 2.1253, 4. 1048, LGW 15; ~ *upon* look upon TC 4.838. [OE *gesēon*]

ysene see **se(e)(n.**

yshore, yshorn see **shere.**

ysonge(n see **singe(n.**

ysounded *p.p.* sunk, penetrated TC 2.535. [OF *sonder*]

ysprad, yspred see **sprede(n.**

yspreynd see **springen** *v.*[2]

isse(n *v.* issue, come out TC 4.37, Bo 3. p12. 119/158. [OF *issir*]

issue *n.* result Bo 1. m6. 16/23, 5. p5. 72/104; outlet TC 5.205. [OF]

ystalled *p.p.* enthroned HF 1364. [OF *estaler*+*stall* n., OE *st(e)all*]

ystorve see **sterve(n.**

ystrengthed *p.p.* strengthened Bo 5. p6. 111/157. [from v. from **strengthe**]

yswonke see **swinke(n.**

it *pron.* it: (impers. subject) B.NP 4287, E.Cl 235, F.Fkl 1466, BD 190, Mars 263, Bo 5. p3. 67/93; (of time, etc.) A.Kn 2211, F.Sq 73, LGW 60; him E.Cl 679; they HF 1323, LGW 1506; ~ *am I* it is me BD 186, TC 1.588, 2.1311, 3.752, LGW 314; ~ *is* there is D.WB 63, D.Sum 1712, E.Cl 838, Bo 3. p9. 29/39, Truth 7. **hit** BD 186, 190, Mars 263, HF 377, 381, 1323, and *var* in LGW 1506, 1967, 2400, Truth 2, etc. [OE *hit*]

ythe(e *v.* prosper TC 4.439 *var*; cf. **thee(n.** [OE *gethēon*]

ythewed see **thewed.**

ythrongen see **thringe.**

ythrowe see **throwe(n.**

yto(o)ld see **telle(n.**

itself *pron.* itself I.Pars 490, 1042; **itselve** D.Sum 1968 *var*. [**it**+**self**]

yvel(e see **evel(e.**

ivy-leef *n.* ivy leaf: *pype(n in an* ~ whistle (for something) A.Kn 1838, TC 5.1433. [OE *ifig*+**leef**]

yvory/yvoire *n.* ivory B.Th 2066, BD 946. [OF]

ywar *adj.* aware TC 1.203 *var*, *to late* ~ 2.398. [OE *gewær*]

iwis *adv.* certainly, to be sure A.Mil 3277, BD 657, TC 2.239, HF 326, RR 44. [OE *gewis* adj.]

J

jade *n.* wretched horse, nag B.NP 4002. [?]

jagounce *n.* jacinth RR 1117*em*. [OF]

jakke *n.* (familiar form of man's name) ~ *of Dovere* ?kind of meat pie A.Co 4347; ~ *fool* A.Mil 3708. [AN]

jalous/jelous *adj.* **1.** jealous A.Kn 1329, C.Pard 367, PF 342. **2.** as *n.* jealous person Ven 62, TC 3.1168. **3.** furious A.Kn 2634. [OF *gelos*]

jalousye/jelousye *n.* jealousy A.Kn 1299, TC 2.753, Ven 33; ~ *of* zeal for I.Pars 539. [OF]

jambeux *n. pl.* leg armour B.Th 2065. [OF]

jane *n.* Genoese coin B.Th 1925, E.Cl 999 (see **yno(u)gh**). [OF *janne*]

jangle(n *v.* chatter B.ML 774, B.NP 4625, G.CY 1397 *var*, TC 2.666; dispute F.Sq 220. [OF *jangler*]

jangler *n.* chatterer A.Prol 560, H.Mcp 343, PF 457. [from prec.]

jangleresse *n.* chattering woman D.WB 638, E.Mch 2307. [OF]

janglerie *n.* tongue-wagging B.Mel 2274, TC 5.755. [OF]

jangles *n. pl.* chatter, gossip D.Fri 1407, I.Pars 650, HF 1960. [from v.]

jangling *vbl. n.* chatter H.Mcp 350, I.Pars 406; dispute F.Sq 257.

jangling *ppl. adj.* chattering PF 345, Bo 3. m2. 15/21. [from **jangle(n**]

jape *n.* **1.** trick A.Co 4338, B.Pri 1629, D.WB 242, F.Fkl 1271, TC 2.130, *made hir a fals* ~ played a deceitful trick on her HF 414; **2.** joke, jest A.Prol 705, A.Rv 4207, TC 1.911, 937, 3.408; foolishness B.NP 4281, D.Sum 1961, RR 12. [from next]

jape(n *v.* **1.** trick, deceive A.Kn 1729, TC 5.1134. **2.** joke, jest B.Th 1883, D.Fri 1513, TC 1.929, LGW 1699, mock TC 1.508. [? rel. to OF *japer* yelp and *gaber* mock]

japere *n.* jester, trickster I.Pars 89, 651, TC 2.340. [from prec.]

japerie *n.* joking, buffoonery E.Mch 1656, I.Pars 651. [from **jape(n**]

japeworthy *adj.* ridiculous Bo 5. p3. 94/132 (L *ridiculo*). [**jape**+**worthy**]

jargon *n.* chatter E.Mch 1848. [OF]

jargoning *n.* twittering RR 716. [from prec.]

jaspre *n.* jasper B.Mel 2297, TC 2.1229. [AN]

jaunyce *n.* jaundice RR 305. [OF]

jeet *n.* jet B.NP 4051. [OF *jaiet*]

jelous, jelousye see **jalous, jalousye.**

jet/get *n.* **1.** fashion, *of/in the newe* ~ A.Prol 682, A.Mil 3322 *var*. **2.** contrivance G.CY 1277. [OF].

jeupardies see **jupartye.**

jewel see **juwel.**

Jewerye *n.* Jewish quarter B.Pri 1679, 1741; Jewish people HF 1436. [AN]

jo *v.* come about, turn out TC 3.33. [?OF *joer*]

jocund *a.* cheerful, pleasant G.CY 596, Rosem 5. [OF]

jogelour *n.* conjurer, magician D.Fri 1467, F.Sq 219, HF 1259. [OF]

jogelrye *n.* conjuring trick F.Fkl 1265. [OF]

joye *n.* joy, happiness A.Kn 1028, G.CY 579, TC 5.615; *have* ~ *of* be pleased with B.Mel 2924; (in asseveration) *so have I* BD 1065, HF 1471, cf. TC 3.875; often in collocation with **blis(se:** A.Kn 1684, B.ML 409, B.NP 4256, 4356, D.WB 830, E.Mch 1771, F.Fkl 1099, Rosem 12. [OF]

joynant *adj.* adjacent, next A.Kn 1060. [OF *joignant*]

joynen/joignen *v.* **1.** join, unite G.SN 95, Bo 2. p6. 59/83, TC 3.1747; *refl.* associate with Bo 2. p6. 62/87, 4. p4. 139/196; bring together BD 393, TC 5.813. **2.** bring into conjunction TC 3.625, Astr 2.4.33/51. **ijoyned** *p.p.* Bo 2. p6. 59/83, 4. p1. 18/25. [OF *joign-*, stem of *joindre*]

joyning *vbl. n.* joint HF 1187.

joyning *ppl. adj.* adjoining LGW 1962. [from **joynen**]

joyntly *adv.* together Astr 2.11.9/13. [from OF *joint*]

joynture *n.* union Bo 2. p5. 32/45. [OF]

joly/jolif *adj.* **1.** merry, cheerful B.NP 4264, F.Sq 48, RR 109; ~ *as a pye* B.Sh 1399, D.WB 456; high-spirited, frisky A.Mil 3263, A.Rv 4154; fine, bright A.Mil 3316, A.Rv 3931. **2.** amorous, gallant A.Mil 3339, A.Rv 4232, C.Pard 453; ~ *wo* TC 2.1099, 1105, LGW 1192; ~ *Robin* (typical shepherd) TC 5.1174. **3.** pretty, handsome B.Sh 1613, D.WB 860, RR 829. [OF]

jolily *adv.* merrily A.Co 4370, B.Sh 1204. [from prec.]

jolinesse *n.* cheerfulness, enjoyment F.Sq 289; pleasure D.WB 926. [from **joly**]

jolitee *n.* **1.** pleasure F.Sq 344, I.Pars 1049, Bo 3. p7. 12/16, RR 52; ease A.Prol 680; sport A.Kn 1807; love, passion B.Th 2033. **2.** cheerfulness C.Pard 780, F.Sq 278; pleasantness H.Mcp 197. [cf. OF *joliveté*]

jompre/jumpere *v.* jumble TC 2.1037. ?**joinpred** *p.p.* TC 3. 1269 *var.* [?imit.]

jordan/jurdon *n.* flask, urinal C.Pard 305. [ML *jurdanus*]

jossa† *interj.* down here! A.Rv 4101. [?OF *jus ça*]

jouken *v.* lie up, lurk TC 5.409. [OF *jouquier*]

journee *n.* day's journey A.Kn 2738; day's work RR 579; journey E.Cl 783. [OF]

jowe *n.* jaw Bo 1. p4. 71/97, HF 1786. [?rel. to OE *ćeowan* chew]

jubbe *n.* jug, jar A.Mil 3628, B.Sh 1260. [?]

jubilee *n.* jubilee, fiftieth anniversary D.Sum 1862. [OF]

juge *n.*[1] judge A.Prol 814, C.Phs 123, PF 101; umpire A.Kn 1712. [OF]

juge *n.*[2] (apparently mistaken adoption of an OF *joug*, Vulg. *iugo*) yoke I. Pars 898.

jug(g)e(n *v.* judge, consider Bo 2. p7. 52/74, think TC 5.1203; give judgement PF 629; give judgement upon C.Phs 228, I.Pars 165, HF 357; discriminate TC 2.21. **juggestow** *pr. 2 sg.* (with suffixed pron.) Bo 3. p9. 143/193 *var.* **juggeth** *imper. pl.* TC 3.1312. [AN *juger*]

jug(g)ement *n.* judgement, decision A.Prol 778, C.Phs 198, Bo 4. p6. 165/240; opinion B.ML 1038, E.Cl 53, TC 4.1299; justice Bo 4. p4. 136/193. [OF]

juyse *n.* judgement, sentence A.Kn 1739, B.ML 795. [OF]

juparten *pr. pl.* endanger TC 4.1566. [v. from next]

jupartye *n.* **1.** danger TC 4.1386; *putte in* ~ risk F.Fkl 1495, TC 2.772, 3.868, 4.1512; balance of chances TC 2.465; betting G.CY 743. **2.** (chess) problem *pl.* **ieupardies** BD 666. [OF *jeu parti*]

jurdon *see* **jordan.**

just *adj.* **1.** just, fair B.NP 4240, Bo 5. p3. 114/161, TC 2.527; ~ *cause* good reason B.Mel 2256, TC 2.727. **2.** exact, true D.Sum 2090, HF 719; ~ *ascendant* Astr 2.4.44/65. [OF *juste*]

juste *n.* joust LGW 1115 *var*; *pl.* as *sg.* A.Kn 2720. [OF]

juste(n *v.* joust A.Prol 96, A.Kn 2604, LGW 1274; ~ *atte fan* tilt at the quintain H.Mcp 42. [OF *juster*]

justyce *n.* **1.** justice B.Mel 2598, Bo 1. p4. 85/117, HF 1820; condemnation ABC 142; redress B.NP 4230. **2.** judge A.Prol 314, D.WB 1028, I.Pars 571. [OF]

justing *vbl. n.* jousting LGW 1115 *var.*

justli *adv.* exactly Astr 1.17.14/18, 2.38. 20/28. [from **just**]

ju(w)el/jewel *n.* jewel A.Kn 2945, F.Sq 341, Mars 256 *var.* [AN]

K

kaynard *n.* fogey D.WB 235. [(?)AN; cf. F *cagnard*]

kakelinge *n.* cackling PF 562. [imit.]

kalendes *n. pl.* first day, beginning TC 2.7; day of reckoning TC 5.1634. [L *calendae*]

kan, kanst(ow *see* **conne.**

kaught(e, kecche *see* **cacche(n.**

kechil *n.* small cake; *Goddes* ~ an alms-cake D.Sum 1747. [OE *coećil*]

keen *n. pl.* kine, cows B.NP 4021. [from OE *cȳna*, gen. pl. of *cū* (with s-e vowel)]

ke(e)ne *adj.* **1.** sharp A.Prol 104, F.Sq 57, LGW 2654. **2.** bold B.Mk 3439; fierce E.Mch 1759, WUnc 6; cruel Fort 27. [OE *cēne*]

ke(e)p(e *n.* in *take* ~ (with *of* or cl.) take care, be concerned about A.Prol 398, take notice, attend to B.Mk 3757, C.Pard 352, 777, H.Mcp 310, I.Pars 597; (absol.) A.Prol 503, TC 1.486. [from next]

ke(e)pe(n *v.* **1.** keep, preserve B.Sh 1422, B.Mel 2831, TC 5.315, save D.WB 1056; *refl.* abstain (*fro*) C.Pard 562, E.Mch 1640; ~ *conseil* keep a secret B.Mel 2333, C.Pard 561, TC 1.992; ~ *tonge* H.Mcp 315, TC 3.294; *as gret a craft is* ~ *wel as winne* TC 3.1634. **2.** protect, guard B.Mel 2524, C.Phs 85, LGW 1995; ~ *fro* A.Kn 2302, B.ML 827, D.WB 906; ~ *(one's) name/ honour* TC 3.266 *var*, TC 5.1077, LGW 2587; *refl.* be on one's guard I.Pars 354. **3.** look after A.Prol 415, E.Mch 1343, Bo 3. m2. 4/5; ~ *hous* E.Mch 1382. **4.** observe, hold to F.Fkl 956, I.Pars 592, Bo 4. m6. 4/5, TC 3.419; ~ *trouthe* F.Fkl 1570, G.CY 1044. **5.** care (with infin.) A.Kn 2238, G.CY 1368, LGW 1032; (*of* 'for') B.Sh 1593. **6.** take care A.Prol 130, A.Rv 4101. **kepte** *pa.* A.Prol 442; **keped** LGW G. 294. **kept** *p.p.* A.Prol 276. [OE *cēpan, cēpte*]

kek† *int.* quack! PF 499, 594. [imit.]

kembe *v.* comb A.Kn 2143, HF 136, **kempt** *p.p.* RR 577. [OE *cemban*]

kempe *adj.* shaggy A.Kn 2134. [?ON]

ken *see* **kin.**

kene *adv.* keenly, sharply MercB 3, 13. [OE *cēne*, cf. **ke(e)ne**]

kenely *adv.* sharply HF 1725. [from **ke(e)ne**]

kenne *v.* perceive HF 498. **kend/kenned** *p.p.* known BD 787 *var.* [OE *cennan*]

keper(e *n.* supervisor E.Mch 1380; guardian A.Kn 2328; ~ *of the celle* prior A.Prol 172. [from **ke(e)pe(n**]

keping *vbl. n.* holding, watching A.Mil 3851, I.Pars 747, Fort 53; protection, care B.Mel 2216, 2829; preserving B.Mel 3034, I.Pars 571.

kerchief *n.* headscarf LGW 2202; ~ *of Valence* bedcover PF 272; see **coverchief.** [OF *cuevrechief*]

kers *n.* cress, valueless thing A.Mil 3756. [OE *cærs*]
kerve *v.* cut A.Kn 2013, B.Mk 3791, F.Sq 158, I.Pars 888, TC 2.325; carve A.Prol 100, D.Sum 2244, E.Mch 1773. **carf** *pa. sg.* A.Prol 100, B.Mk 3647, FormA 21. **corve(n** *p.p.* A.Mil 3318, PF 425; **ycorve(n** A.Kn 2013, B.Pri 1801. [OE *ċeorfan, ċearf, ġe)corfen*]
kervere *n.* carver A.Kn 1899. [from prec.]
kerving *vbl. n.* carving, sculpture A.Kn 1915, HF 1302.
kerving *ppl. adj.* cutting TC 1.631. [from v.]
kesse, keste *see* **kisse(n.**
kevere *see* **covere.**
kichene *n.* kitchen D.WB 869. [OE *cyċene*]
kyd(de *see* **kythe.**
kike *v.*[1] kick D.WB 941. [?ON]
kike *v.*[2] stare, gaze A.Mil 3445, 3841. [MDu *ki(e)ken*]
kimelin *n.* tub A.Mil 3548, 3621. [ML *cimiline, ciminile*]
kin *n.* **1.** family A.Rv 3942, E.Mch 2197, TC 1.90; *by your fader ~* (as *exclam.*) A.Rv 4038, B.NP 4158, H.Mcp 37, on your father's side B.Mk 3121; related, akin LGW 2244. **2.** kind, sort: *al* **ken** everyone BD 438; *som ~* of some kind B.ML 1137 var. **kinnes** *gen.* in *som ~* of some kind, some kind of B.ML 1137 var; see **alleskinnes, noskinnes. 3.** ?sex E.Mch 2197. [OE *cynn*]
kinde *n.* **1.** nature A.Kn 2451, Bo 3. m2. 32/46, HF 43; *of ~* by nature, naturally F.Sq 610, G.CY 659, Bo 2. p5. 110/155, TC 2.370; *(as) by wey of ~* in the natural course B.Pri 1840, B.Mel 2973; instinct B.NP 4386, LGW 2449; Nature F.Sq 469, PF 316, Bo 3. p7. 13/19, TC 1.238. **2.** family G.SN 121, D.WB 1101; species PF 174, 365; semen or its female analogue I.Pars 965. **3.** sort A.Kn 1401, Bo 2. p3. 24/35, *set in . . ~* classify G.CY 789; manner G.CY 981. [OE *ġecŷnde*]
kinde *adj.* **1.** kind A.Prol 647, E.Cl 602, LGW 921. **2.** natural TC 2.970, 4.768, HF 836. [OE *ġecŷnde*]
kindely *adj.* natural BD 778, HF 730. [OE *ġecŷndeliċ*]
kindely *adv.* **1.** naturally, by nature D.WB 402, I.Pars 492, Bo 4. p2. 69/91. **2.** kindly B.Sh 1543. [OE *ġecŷndelīċe*]
king *n.* king A.Prol 324, F.Sq 10, LGW 376; queen (bee) I.Pars 468; *hevene ~* God A.Mil 3464, B.Sh 1583, G.SN 542, HF 1084; *the ~es note* (name of a tune) A.Mil 3217; *~ of ~es* B.Mk 3357, D.Fri 1590; *Goal save the ~* Astr Prol 46/56. [OE *cyning*]
kinrede *n.* **1.** kindred, relations A.Kn 1286, B.Mel 2558, I.Pars 885; kinship I.Pars 206, 907. **2.** family A.Rv 3967, I.Pars 962; birth: *heigh ~* A.Kn 2790, F.Fkl 735; *noble ~* Bo 3. p6. 38/51, TC 5.979. [OE *cynræden*]
kirtel *n.* **1.** tunic A.Mil 3321, F.Fkl 1580. **2.** frock PF 235, RR 778. [OE *cyrtel*]
kisse(n *v.* kiss A.Mil 3284, E.Mch 2184, Mars 77; *intr.* kiss each other LGW 761; *been they kist* they have kissed each other B.ML 1074. **kesse** *infin.* E.Cl 1057. **kiste** *pa.* A.Mil 3305, TC 1.812; **keste** F.Sq 350, TC 3.1129, 1575; **kyssed** LGW 2208

var. **kist** *p.p.* A.Kn 1759, LGW 1337. [OE *cyssan*]
kythe *v.* show B.ML 636, G.CY 1054, TC 4.619; *~ on* (a person) show to D.Fri 1609, Mars 298; demonstrate HF 528, LGW 912; make known E.Mch 1943, LGW 1028; declare Anel 228. **kytheth** *imper. pl.* Mars 298. **kithed** *pa.* G.CY 1054; **kidde** TC 1.208. **kid** *p.p.* E.Mch 1943, LGW 1028, FormA 46. [OE *cŷpan, cŷdde*]
kitte *see* **cutte(n.**
knakke *n.* trick, wile A.Rv 4051 var, I.Pars 652, BD 1033. [?MDu *knak*]
knarre *n.* rugged fellow A.Prol 549. [cf. LG *knarre* crag]
knarry *adj.* gnarled A.Kn 1977. [from prec.]
knave *n.* **1.** servant A.Mil 3431, B.ML 474, LGW 1807; peasant D.WB 1190, I.Pars 188. **2.** villain D.WB 253, I.Pars 433. **3.** boy B.Sh 1500; *~ child* B.ML 715, E.Cl 444. [OE *cnafa*]
knavish *adj.* vulgar, low H.Mcp 205. [from prec.]
kneding-trogh *n.* kneading trough A.Mil 3548, 3620; **-tubbe** kneading tub A.Mil 3564. [from OE *cnēdan* + *trog*, and cf. MDu *tubbe*]
knee/knowe *n.* knee A.Prol 391, B.Pri 1719, TC 1.110, LGW 973; *falle on ~* kneel down TC 2.1202, *on ~s* A.Kn 1103, B.ML 1153, TC 3.1592, HF 1534; *sette (oneself) on (one's) ~* kneel D.Sum 2120, LGW 455, *on ~s* A.Mil 3723, F.Fkl 1025, TC 3.953, LGW 115, *sitte on ~(s* BD 106, LGW 2028. [OE *cnēo(w)*]
knele *v.* kneel A.Kn 897, I.Pars 991, TC 3.962. **kneleth** *imper. pl.* C.Pard 925, TC 3.965. **kneled** *pa.* A.Kn 897, LGW 295. **ykneled** *p.p.* A.Kn 1232. [OE *cnēowlian*]
knelinges *vbl. n. pl.* kneelings, going about on the knees I.Pars 1055.
knettinge *see* **knittinge.**
knyf *n.* knife, dagger A.Kn 1999. **knyves** pl. A.Prol 233. [LOE *cnīf* from ON]
knight *n.* **1.** knight A.Prol 42, C.Phs 2, TC 1.165; *~ in armes* G.CY 1347; *~ of the shire* member of Parliament A.Prol 356. **2.** champion E.Mch 1724, Anel 117; *Goddes ~* B.Mel 2848, G.SN 353, Bo 4. m1. 10/15; lover TC 2.871, 3.1309. [OE *cniht*]
knighthod/-hede *n.* knighthood A.Kn 2103, Mars 75, TC 5.1591; prowess B.Mk 3873. [OE *cnihthād*, and var. suff. *-*hǣdu]
knightly *adj.* gallant TC 2.628. [from **knight**]
knightly *adv.* bravely LGW 2089. [from **knight**]
knitte *v.* **1.** join, unite B.Sh 1230, F.Fkl 1230, PF 381, Bo 4. p6. 87/125; *refl.* (astrol.) be in conjunction B.ML 307. **2.** tie, fasten A.Rv 4083, TC 3.1734; *in ~* restrain TC 3.1088 var. **3.** (of brows) draw together A.Kn 1128; *~ up* sum up I.Pars 28, 47. **knette** *pa.* TC 3.1088 var. **knit** *p.p.* B.Mk 3224, LGW 89; **knet** PF 628, RR 1397; **yknet** TC 3.1734. [OE *cnyttan*; -*e-* forms s-e]
knittinge/knettinge *vbl. n.* joining, connection I.Pars 843, Bo 5. p1. 24/34.
knobbe *n.* lump, pimple A.Prol 633. [MLG]
knok *n.* knock, thump B.NP 4504. [from next]

knokke v. knock A.Mil 3432, C.Pard 730, RR 534. [OE *cnocian*]
knokkinge vbl. n. beating I.Pars 1055.
knoppe n. **1.** bud RR 1675, 1702. **2.** knob, stud RR 1080. [OE *cnop*]
knotte n. **1.** knot TC 3.1732; *love* ~ A.Prol 197. **2.** point (of story) F.Sq 401; difficulty, knub Bo 5. p3. 22/29; twist, catch I.Pars 494. [OE *cnotta*]
knotteles adj. without impediment, smoothly TC 5.769. [from prec.]
knowe see **knee**.
knoweleche/-liche n. knowledge I.Pars 75, Bo 4. m1. 11/14; acquaintance, friendship B.Sh 1220. [prob. from v.; see **knowlichen**]
knowe(n v. **1.** know A.Prol 240, G.CY 602, TC 4.289; ~ .. *fro* distinguish (from) D.WB 122, Fort 10. **2.** recognize, understand: A.Prol 382, Bo 1. p2. 8/11, TC 5.1404, HF 1452; acknowledge B.Mk 3812, G.SN 259; find out Astr 2.1.5/8.
knowestow pr. *2 sg.* (with suffixed pron.) A.Mil 3156, B.Mk 3414, Bo 1. p2. 8/11.
knew pa. *1, 3 sg.* A.Kn 1227, A.Prol 240.
knewe *2 sg.* Fort 21. **knewe(n** pl. A.Kn 3079, G.CY 1371 *var* (? *subj.*). **knewe** subj. sg. F.Sq 466, LGW 801. **knowe(n** p.p. A.Kn 1203, F.Sq 215, 280, Bo 1. m2. 6/8; **yknowe(n** A.Prol 423, F.Sq 256, BD 392. [OE *cnāwan, cnēow, ǧe)cnāwen*]
knowing vbl. n. knowledge B.Mk 3497, BD 538, HF 892; awareness Bo 5. p6. 77/108. pl. Bo 5. p5. 17/24.
knowleching vbl. n. knowledge G.CY 1432, BD 796, Bo 5. p5. 2. [from next but sense from n.]
knowlichen pr. pl. acknowledge B.Mel 2935. [EME *cnawlechien* from **knowe(n** + OE suff. *-lǣċan*]
konne(n, koude see **conne**.
konning see **conning**.
kultour see **culter**.

L

la(a)s n. **1.** net, snare A.Kn 1817, LGW 600, Ven 50. **2.** cord A.Prol 392, G.CY 574; (shoe) lace RR 843. [OF]
labbe n. tell-tale A.Mil 3509, TC 3.300 *var*. [from *labben* v., from LG]
labbing ppl. adj. blabbing E.Mch 2428. [as prec.]
label n. brass rule (on astrolabe) Astr 1.22.1/21.84, 2.3.8/12, etc. [OF]
laborous adj. laborious D.Fri 1428. [from next]
labour n. labour, hard work. A.Kn 2913, E.Cl 217, PF 93, exertion, effort B.Mk 3835; *do (one's)* ~ take pains A.Kn 2193, B.ML 381, B.Pri 1653, E.Mch 1765. [OF]
laboure(n v. **1.** intr. work, toil A.Prol 186, I.Pars 251; take pains TC 1.458, refl. 4.1009. **2.** work upon, ply B.Sh 1298. [OF *labourer*]
lacche n. snare RR 1624. [OF]
lace v. lace, fasten A.Mil 3267. [OF *lacier*]
lacerte n. muscle A.Kn 2753. [OF]
lache adj. slack, dull Bo 4. p3. 82/119. [OF]
lachesse n. laziness I.Pars 720. [OF]
lacinge vbl. n. fastening A.Kn 2504.

laddre n. ladder A.Mil 3624, Astr 1.12.3, RR 523. [OE *hlǣd(d)er*]
lade v. load TC 2.1544. [OE *hladan*]
ladel n. ladle, long spoon A.Kn 2020, H.Mcp 51. [OE *hlǣdel*]
lady n. **1.** lady A.Kn 912, E.Mch 2228, TC 1.166, LGW 283. **2.** mistress, ruler D.WB 1037, PF 639, TC 2.1714; ~ *of the house* D.Sum 220; *sovereign* ~ D.WB 1048, F.Fkl 1072, PF 416, TC 4.316; mistress (in love) A.Prol 88, D.WB 1230, TC 3.95. **3.** the Virgin Mary, *our* ~ B.ML 977, B.Pri 1700, C.Pard 308. **lady** gen. A.Prol 88, 695, TC 1.99, 2.32; **ladies/ladys** CompA 61, TC 5.675. [OE *hlǣfdiǧe*, gen. *-an*]
laft(e, laften see **le(e)ve(n** v.[1]
lay n.[1] song B.Th 1959, LGW 140, TC 2.921, RR 715; short romance for singing F.Fkl 710. [OF *lai*]
lay n.[2] belief, faith, religion B.ML 376, F.Sq 18, TC 1.340, 1001, LGW 336. [AN *lei* law]
laye(n see **leye(n**.
laynere n. lanyard, strap A.Kn 2504. [OF *laniere*]
lak n. **1.** fault, defect B.NP 4034, D.Sum 2139, BD 958, TC 2.1178, offence E.Mch 2199; blame LGW G. 298. **2.** want, lack E.Mch 2271, LSt 7, failure to perform D.Fri 1306. [cf. MLG *lak* fault, blame]
lake n.[1] pond D.WB 269, PF 313. [OE *lacu*]
lake n.[2] fine white linen B.Th 2048. [MDu *laken*]
lakke(n v. **1.** be missing, wanting A.Kn 2280, F.Fkl 1274, TC 4.945, (with dat. of pers.) A.Prol 756, F.Sq 16, F.Fkl 1186, BD 898, TC 4.1523; *ther* ~*th nothing* .. *that thou nart blind* your bodily eyes are totally blind G.SN 498. **2.** miss, do without D.Sum 2109, G.CY 672, Bo 4. p3. 4/5. **3.** find fault with, blame TC 1.189, RR 284. [from **lak**]
lakking vbl. n. stint RR 1147.
lamb n. lamb A.Mil 3704, C.Phs 102; (fig., = Christ) B.ML 459, B.Pri 1771; **lomb** B.ML 617, LGW 1798. [OE *lámb*]
lambic n. alembic TC 4.520. [OF *alembic*]
lambish adj. gentle, peaceable FormA 50. [from **lamb**]
lampe n. (?) vessel resembling a lamp G.CY 764. [OF]
langage n. **1.** words, speech A.Prol 211, A.Kn 2227, TC 3.1336, HF 861. **2.** language, tongue A.Co 4330, B.ML 516, F.Sq 100, Astr prol 40/57. [OF]
lange see **long** adj.[1]
lango(u)r n. distress B.Mk 3597, ABC 7, TC 5.268. [OF]
languiss(h)e(n/langw- v. languish, pine, grow weak E.Mch 1867, HF 2018, TC 3.241. [OF *languiss-* from *languir*]
languisshing vbl. n. languishing TC 1.529; faintness, debility I.Pars 913, Bo 4. p4. 209/292.
lap n. **1.** fold, edge, corner (of garment) G.SN 12, TC 2.448, Bo 1. p2. 19/27; wrapper E.Cl 585. **2.** lap A.Prol 686, B.Mk 3644, F.Sq 475. [OE *læppa*]
lappeth pr. *3 sg.* enfolds Mars 76. [from prec.]
large adj. **1.** large B.ML 190, HF 482; broad A.Prol 472, wide A.Kn 1956, B.Pri

1644; ample TC 1.109; *at (one's)* ~ (= OF *a sa* ~) free A.Kn 1283, 2288, D.WB 322; *pryme* ~ 9 a.m. F.Sq 360. **2.** liberal, generous I.Pars 465, B.Sh 1621, B.NP 4349, RR 1168; free (of speech) TC 5.804. [OF]

large *adv.* liberally A.Prol 734, ABC 174. [prec.]

largely *adv.* **1.** fully A.Kn 1908, 2738, I.Pars 532, TC 2.1707. **2.** freely B.Mel 2791, Bo 1. m6. 3/5, generously I.Pars 804. [from adj.]

largenesse *n.* generosity I.Pars 1051. [from adj.]

largesse *n.* **1.** generosity B.Sh 1212, TC 5.436, RR 1150. **2.** (an appeal) gift HF 1309. *fool* ~ see **fool**. [OF]

lasse/lesse *adj.* less A.Mil 3519, A.Co 4409, PF 201, TC 2.1532, 4.578; smaller B.Mel 2262, TC 2.470, 4.478, 5.618; ~ *and mo(o)re* all A.Kn 1756, *mo(o)re and* ~ B.ML 959, B.Mk 3433, C.Pard 939, D.WB 934, F.Fkl 1054. [OE *læssa*]

lasse/lesse *adv.* less B.Mel 2644, BD 994, TC 1.284, 4.616, LGW 333. [OE *læs*, and prec.]

last *n.* cartload: *a thousand* ~ *quad yeer a* thousand loads of bad years B.Pri 1628. [OE *hlæst*]

laste *adj. sup.* **1.** last A.Kn 2808, C.Phs 221, Bo 1. p4. 215/299; *Monday* ~ A.Mil 3430, *Aperill the* ~ TC 3.360; ~ *Jugement* B.Mel 3058; extreme Bo 3. m12. 40/58, furthest Bo 4. m1. 16/24 (L *extimum*). **2.** as *n.*: *atte/at the* ~ finally A.Prol 707, A.Kn 2826, D.WB 811, HF 496, Bo 2. p6. 85/119; *to my/the* ~ till death TC 1.537, 2.870, *in his* ~ *ende* I.Pars 94. [OE *lætost*]

laste *adv.* last B.NP 4015, I.Pars 1011, TC 5.565. [as prec.]

laste(n *v.* last, keep going A.Kn 2557, D.Sum 2012, LGW 693; extend: *as fer as* ~ *Itaille* to the furthest bounds of Italy E.Cl 266. **lasteth** *pr. 3 sg.* B.ML 499, TC 4.2; **last** E.Cl 266, PF 49, Bo 2. p4. 58/78, TC 4.588, LGW 2241. **laste** *pa.* B.Pri 1826, B.Mk 3508, TC 1.315, LGW 1239; **lasted** F.Fkl 806. [OE *læstan*]

lat, laten *see* **lete(n.**

lat(e)rede *adj.* tardy I.Pars 718. [OE *lætræde*]

lathe *n.* (nth.) barn A.Rv. 4088, HF 2140. [ON *hlaða*]

latis *n.* lattice, window TC 2.615. [OF]

latoun *n.* latten, brass A.Prol 699, B.Th 2067, F.Fkl 1245. [OF]

latter *adj. comp.* **1.** later, last D.WB 765 (see date), Bo 5. p6. 204/286; ~ *ende* last part, Bo 1. p5. 45/65, m6. 11/16; (prov.) *the* ~ *ende of joy is wo* B.NP 4395. [OE *lætra*]

latter *adv. comp.* more slowly I.Pars 971. [adv. use of prec.]

laude *n.* **1.** praise, honour B.Pri 1645, TC 3.1273, HF 1575, 1795; due, in *yeven him his* ~ D.Fri 1353. **2.** *pl.* early morning service (of the Church) A.Mil 3655. [OF]

laughe(n *v.* laugh A.Prol 474, D.WB 201, TC 1.514; smile E.Mch 1723. **lough** *pa. sg.* A.Mil 3114, D.WB 672, TC 1.1037. **lough(e** *pl.* A.Rv 3858, C.Pard 961; **laugheden** RR 863. **laughen** *p.p.* A.Rv 3855, **laughed** HF 409. [OA *hlæhhan, hlōh, hlōgon*]

launce *v.* buck, rear HF 946. [OF]

launcegay *n.* (kind of) lance B.Th 1942, 2011. [OF]

launcheth *pr. 3 sg.* pushes D.Sum 2145. [AN *launcher*]

launde *n.* glade, clearing A.Kn 1691, PF 302. [AN]

laure *n.* laurel-tree HF 1107. [OE *laur* from L]

laureat *p.p.* crowned with laurel B.Mk 3886. [L *laureātus*]

laurer *n.* laurel A.Kn 1027, E.Mch 2037, TC 3.542; ~-*crouned* laurel-crowned Anel 43, TC 5.1107. [OF *laurier*]

lauriol *n.* spurge laurel B.NP 4153. [OF *laureole*]

laus *see* **loos** *adj.*

lave(n *v.* draw, scoop up Bo 3. m12. 16/22; exhaust Bo 4. p6. 9/13. [OE *lafian*]

lavender *n.* laundress LGW 358. [OF *lavandiere*]

laverokke *n.* skylark RR 662. [OE *lāferce*]

lavour *n.* wash-basin D.WB 287. [OF]

lawe *n.* **1.** law A.Prol 577, B.Sh 1189, D.Sum 1889; *sergeant of the* ~ see **sergeaunt**, *man of* ~ lawyer B.ML 33, B.Mel 2485; *fader-in-*~ LGW 2272, *pl.* parents in law Bo 2. p3. 26/38; *sone-in-*~ B.Mk 3594, E.Cl 315; ~ *of kinde* instinctive behaviour BD 56, TC 1.238; *who shal yeve a lover any* ~? A.Kn 1164 (cf. Bo 3. m12. 37/52–3). **2.** faith, religion B.ML 237, 336, B.Pri 1754; *the olde* ~ the Old Testament I.Pars 837. **3.** custom D.WB 1089, TC 2.42. [OE *lagu*, from ON]

lawefully *adv.* according to law I.Pars 600, by law 593. [from prec.]

laxatif *n.* laxative, purging medicine A.Kn 2756, B.NP 4133. **laxatives** *pl.* B.NP 4152. [OF]

lazar *n.* leper A.Prol 242, 245. [L *Lazarus*]

leche *n.* doctor, healer A.Rv 3904, Bo 1. p4. 3/5, TC 1.857; *lyves* D.Sum 1892, BD 920; *soules* ~ C.Pard 916, ABC 134. [OE *læce*]

lechecraft *n.* medicine A.Kn 2745, TC 4.436. [OE *læcecræft*]

lecher(e *n.* healer Bo 4. p6. 148/216. [from *lechen* v. from **leche**]

lec(c)hour *n.* lecher B.Th 1935, D.Fri 1310, 1371, E.Mch 2257. [OF]

leden *n.* language F.Sq 435, 478. [OE]

leden *adj.* leaden G.CY 728. [from **leed**]

lede(n *v.* **1.** lead D.Sum 2026, Bo 3. p1. 24/33, PF 138; ~ *(one's) lyf* B.ML 1158, D.WB 94, F.Fkl 1552, TC 2.832; take TC 5.10, LGW 2021; conduct E.Cl 390. **2.** carry, bring A.Prol 530, B.ML 357, 442, TC 4.1514. **3.** govern B.ML 434; control TC 2.527. **ledeth** *pr. 3 sg.* PF 138, LGW 85; let B.Sh 1496 *var*, TC 2.882. **lad(de** *pa. sg.* A.Kn 1446, B.ML 442, B.Sh 1496 *var*, G.SN 374; **ledde** TC 3.59, LGW 2310. **ladde(n** *pl.* E.Cl 390, RR 1310; **ledde(n** G.SN 392, Bo 4. p4. 189/264. **lad** *p.p.* A.Kn 2620, B.ML 646, LGW 74; **led** TC 2.553; **ylad** A.Prol 530, Bo 5. p6. 41/59; **yled** Bo 5. p3. 123/175. [OE *lædan, lǣdde, ġelǣdd*]

ledere *n.* leader Bo 1. p3. 49/69, TC 4.1454. [from prec.]

leed *n.* **1.** lead G.SN 513, G.CY 828, HF 739. **2.** cauldron A.Prol 202. [OE *lēad*]

leef *n.* **1.** leaf B.Sh 1340, LGW 72, RR 905; petal LGW 228; (*quaken*) *lyk an aspen* ~ D.Sum 1667, LGW 2648; *light as* ~ *on lynde* E.Cl 1211. **2.** page A.Mil 3177, D.WB 635. *pl.* **leves** A.Kn 1496, BD 418, TC 4.225. [OE *lēaf*]

leef/lief *adj.* **1.** dear A.Kn 1136, C.Pard 731, E.Cl 479, TC 2.251; pleasing B.Sh 1349, TC 3.1619, 5.1738, desirable C.Pard 760; ~ *ne/or looth* anything B.Sh 1322, LGW 1639, *al be him looth or* ~ whether he likes it or not A.Kn 1837, sim. E.Mch 1961, H.Mcp 356; *have* ~ hold dear, love F.Sq 572, TC 3.864, 870; *hadde* (pa. subj.) *as* ~ would as soon D.Fri 1574. **2.** as *n.* dear one, love A.Mil 3792, B.NP 4069, D.WB 431, TC 4.611; desired object TC 4.1585. **3. lever(e** *comp.* preferable LGW 191, *have* ~ value more highly TC 4.570, prefer F.Fkl 1360, 1531, H.Mcp 170; (in impers. construction with *be* and dat. pron.) *him was* ~ he preferred A.Prol 293, *him had be* ~ he would have preferred A.Mil 3541, *me were* ~ I would rather A.Mil 3751, B.Sh 1372, C.Pard 615, TC 1.1034; (pers. with **hadde** (*pa. subj.*)) B.NP 4310, E.Mch 2163, F.Fkl 683, TC 2.1509. **levest** *sup.* in *me/hem were* ~ I/they would most like TC 2.189, HF 87. **le(e)ve** *wk. sg.* A.Kn 1136, C.Pard 731, TC 3.330. **le(e)ve** *pl.* F.Sq 341, TC 4.82. [OE *lēof*]

leef *see* **le(e)ve(n.**

leefful *see* **leveful.**

leefsel/levesel *n.* arbour A.Rv 4061; leafy bush (as an inn-sign) I.Pars 411. [OE *lēaf-sele*]

leek *n.* leek A.Prol 634, A.Rv 3879, RR 212; (as a worthless thing) G.CY 795 (see **yno(u)gh**), HF 1708, *nat worth a* ~ D.WB 572. [OE *lēac*]

le(e)n(e *v.*[1] **1.** lend A.Mil 3777, B.Sh 1376, G.CY 1024. **2.** give A.Kn 3082, Bo 4. p6. 151/219; grant LGW 2083; (fig.) ~ (*one's*) *ere* listen TC 1.725. **lente** *pa.* B.Sh 1544, G.CY 1050. **ylent** *p.p.* G.CY 1406. [OF *lēnan, lǣnde*]

leep(e *see* **lepe(n.**

le(e)re *n.* flesh, skin B.Th 2047. [OE *līra* and ON *lær*]

le(e)re *v.* **1.** learn B.ML 181, PF 25, HF 511. **2.** teach Anel 98, TC 2.97; *to* ~ to be taught, uninstructed TC 5.161. [OE *lǣran* teach]

lees *n.*[1] falsehood, lying LGW 1545; *without* ~ HF 1464, LGW 1022, 1128. [OE *lēas*]

lees *n.*[2] leash G.SN 19, *in o* ~ on one leash I.Pars 387; snare Anel 233. [OF]

lees *adj.* untrue RR 8. [OE *lēas*]

le(e)se *n.* (*prep.*) pasture TC 2.752, HF 1768. [OE *lǣs*]

le(e)st *adj. sup.* least, smallest A.Kn 1761, B.Sh 1236, BD 283; *atte* ~ at least A.Mil 3683, E.Cl 130; *atte* ~ *way* at any rate A.Kn 1121, F.Fkl 1417; *meste and* ~ everybody A.Kn 2198, TC 1.167. [OE *lǣst*]

le(e)st *adv. sup.* least B.Mk 3332, CompL 68, TC 1.516, RR 964. [OE *lǣst*]

leet *see* **lete(n.**

le(e)ve *n.* leave, permission A.Kn 1064, B.Mk 3136, D.WB 83, G.SN 483, LGW 1320; *by your* ~ A.Rv 3916, B.Sh 1550, TC 2.1634; *take* (*his*) ~ depart A.Kn 1217, B.NP 4288, TC 2.1721; *biside* (*one's*) ~

without (one's) consent TC 3.622, HF 2105. [OE *lēaf-*]

le(e)ve(n *v.*[1] **1.** leave A.Kn 1614, B.NP 4375, G.CY 1321, TC 4.87 var. **2.** leave alone TC 2.1008, (absol.) 5.1518; give up D.Sum 2089, F.Fkl 828, TC 4.896, forsake G.SN 287; *intr.* leave off, desist F.Sq 670, TC 1.686; refrain, omit (with infin.) A.Prol 492, B.Mk 3496, I.Pars 231. **3.** *intr.* remain BD 701, TC 2.735 var, Astr 2.10. 10/14. **le(e)f** *imper. sg.* D.Sum 2089, TC 4.852. **leveth** *pl.* B.Mel 2650, C.Pard 659. **lafte** *pa. sg.* A.Prol 492, B.Mk 3388; **lefte** E.Cl 656, F.Sq 670. **laften** *pl.* LGW 168. **y)laft** *p.p.* A.Kn 2016, G.CY 883, A.Kn 2746, TC 4.227; **y)left** BD 77, Mars 108, Bo 1. p4. 26/36: *alle thinges* ~ everything else left aside B.Mel 2831. [OE *lǣfan, lǣfde, ǧe)lǣfed*]

le(e)ve(n *v.*[2] believe B.Sh 1181, G.SN 213, PF 496, TC 1.342, 5.1637; trust TC 2.420; ~ *on* believe LGW G. 27; *to* ~ to be believed TC 3.308; *as I* ~ (asseveration) PF 875, LGW 1615. **le(e)vestow** *pr. 2 sg.* (with suffixed pron.) G.SN 212. **lef** *imper. sg.* TC 5.378 var. **leveth** *pl.* A.Kn 3088, B.Mel 2943. [OA *lēfan*]

lef *see* **le(e)ve(n** *v.*[1]

left(e *see* **le(e)ve(n** *v.*[1]; **lift.**

legende *n.* account of a saint's life B.NP 4311, G.SN 25, I.Pars 1088, (extended to 'Cupid's saints') B.ML 61, LGW 483, 2456; tale of suffering B.Sh 1335; story A.Mil 3141, D.WB 686, 742. [OF]

legge(n *see* **leye(n.**

ley, leigh *see* **lye(n** *v.*[2]

leye(n/laye(n *v.* **1.** lay A.Kn 2866, B.Pri 1852, D.Sum 1828, Purse 5, **legge(n** A.Mil 3269, A.Rv 3937; put by, store A.Mil 3262; ~ *adoun* subdue B.Mk 3289; ~ *on* attack, assail A.Rv 4229; ~*upon* spend on G.CY 783; ~ *hedes togeder* hold a discussion PF 554; ~ *hond to* take (your lot) A.Prol 841; ~ *hond upon* A.Rv 3937; ~ *the table* B.Sh 1442. **2.** *refl.* lie down A.Kn 1384, TC 2.515; *pass.* LGW 208. **3.** bet, wager A.Kn 1622, B.NP 4148, G.CY 611, TC 2.1505; *dar I* ~ TC 3.1605, HF 674; ~ *a rekening* lay odds Bo 2. p3. 48/70. **leyth/layth** *pr. 3 sg.* A.Rv 4021, 4229. **leyde(n** *pa.* A.Kn 1384, B.ML 213. **y)leyd** *p.p.* A.Prol 81, A.Mil 3568. [OE *lecgan, lǣgde, ǧe)lǣgd*]

leyser *n.* **1.** leisure, time A.Kn 1188, B.Mel 2219, C.Phs 238, BD 172; *at* ~ E.Cl 286, I.Pars 835, TC 3.516; *better* ~ more time D.WB 551, *at better* ~ at greater length TC 5.945, *by* (*good*) ~ with due deliberation B.Mel 2221, 2766. **2.** opportunity A.Mil 3293, TC 2.1369. [OF *leisir*]

leyt *n.* lightning flash I.Pars 839, Bo 1. m4. 8/11; flame I.Pars 954. [OE *lēget*]

lemaille *see* **lymaille.**

lemes *n.*[1] *pl. see* **lym.**

lemes *n.*[2] *pl.* flames B.NP 4120. [OE *lēoma*]

lemman *n.* sweetheart, A.Mil 3278, A.Rv 4240; lover B.ML 917, H.Mcp 204; mistress B.Th 1978, D.WB 722, 'wench' H.Mcp 220. [OE *lēofman*]

lendes *n. pl.* loins A.Mil 3237, 3304. [OE (pl.) *lendenu*]

lene *adj.* lean, thin A.Prol 287, A.NP 4003, MercB 28; feeble TC 2.132. [OE *hlǣne*]

lene v.² lean B.Mel 2638, LGW 179. [OE
hleonian]
lenesse n. leanness RR 307. [from adj.]
leng adv. comp. longer A.Rv 3872 var; see
ever. [OE]
lenger adj. comp. longer A.Prol 330, E.Cl
300, TC 2.292. **lengest** sup. TC 1.474.
[OE *lengra, lengest*]
lenger adv. comp. longer A.Kn 1576, B.ML
983, BD 656; A.Rv 3872 var, see ever.
longer Bo 2. m7. 19/27. **lengest** sup.
longest PF 549, Bo 4. p4. 36/50. [adj. and
re-formed on positive; and OE *lengest*]
lengthe n. length A.Kn 1970, TC 4.255, HF
1370; *on* ~ at full length TC 2.262; *upon*
~ after a long run BD 352; height A.Prol
83, B.ML 934. [OE *lengþu*]
leonesse/lyonesse n. lioness D.WB 637,
LGW 805, 817. [OF]
leonyn adj. lionlike B.Mk 3836. [OF *leonin*]
leos n. = Gr λεώς, people G.SN 103, 106.
leo(u)n/lyoun n. **1.** lion A.Kn 1598, B.NP
4369, D.Sum 1989, TC 1.1074. **2.** Leo
A.Kn 2462, F.Sq 265, TC 4.1592. [OF]
lepe(n v. **1.** leap, spring A.Kn 2687, D.WB
267, HF 2150. **2.** run hastily A.Co 4378,
TC 2.512, HF 1823. **leep** pa. A.Kn 2687,
E.Mch 2411, **lepe** TC 2.1637 var; **lepte**
TC 2.1637 var. [OE *hlēapan, hlēop*]
lered ppl. adj. learned (opp. **lewed**) C.Phs.
283, PF 46; as n. learned men TC 1.976
var. [from le(e)re]
lerne(n v. **1.** learn A.Prol 308, D.WB 921,
BD 1091, PF 1. **2.** teach G.CY 748, 844.
lerneth imper. pl. F.Fkl 777. [OE *leornian*]
lerninge vbl. n. **1.** learning A.Prol 300,
G.CY 842. **2.** instruction G.SN 184,
doctrine 353.
lese v. lose B.ML 225, G.SN 229, TC
3.832; ~ (*one's*) *lif* A.Kn 1290, B.NP 4332,
G.SN 321; ~ (*one's*) *hed* A.Kn 1215,
C.Phs 145; ~ *my name* F.Fkl 1362; ~ *no
time* B.ML 19. **leseth** imper. pl. B.ML 19.
lees pa. sg. HF 1414, LGW 945. **lor(e)n**
p.p. A.Mil 3536, B.Mk 3143, TC 1.373,
LGW 1048; **ylor(e)n** Bo 2. p8. 32/46,
LGW 26; **lore** BD 748, 1135. Cf. **loste**.
[OE *lēosan, lēas, ǧe)loren*]
lesing vbl. n.¹ losing, loss A.Kn 1707, I.Pars
1056, Bo 4. p6. 214/310, TC 3.830; *for* ~
for fear of losing B.Mk 3750. [from prec.]
lesing(e n.² **1.** lie, deceit A.Kn 1927, C.Pard
591, HF 676, 2123; deception HF 154;
make a ~ B.Mel 2257, G.SN 479. **2.**
lying I.Pars 593, 611. [OE *lēasung*]
lesse see **lasse**.
lessen v. intr. decrease TC 5.1438. [from
lesse]
lessoun n. **1.** lesson E.Cl 1193, Mars 33,
TC 3.51. **2.** reading, portion of Scriptures,
A.Prol 709. [OF *leçon*]
lest/list n. **1.** pleasure, delight A.Prol 132,
A.Kn 2984, TC 1.330, 3.1303. **2.** desire
BD 908, HF 287; wish, whim E.Cl 619;
will, what one wants D.WB 633. [from
list/lest]
lest(e see **list/lest**.
lete(n v. **1.** allow, let A.Prol 175, D.Sum
2232, E.Cl 539, TC 2.650, 4.200 var;
~ *alone* E.Cl 162. TC 1.1028, 2.1401;
~ *be* give up, let alone A.Prol 840, A.Mil
3285, D.Fri 1289, TC 1.701; ~ *flee* let
fly A.Mil 3806; ~ *go* D.WB 1061, E.Mch

2430, G.CY 1102; ~ *in* C.Pard 731, RR
700; ~ *out* A.Kn 1206; ~ *slyde* E.Cl 82,
F.Fkl 924, TC 5.351; release, in **laten**
blood A.Mil 3326, A.Co 4346. **2. lat**
imper. A.Prol 188, F.Fkl 1472, TC 2.1288;
often forming with infin. the equiv. of imper.
3 pers., B.Mk 3187, E.Mch 1892, G.CY 737,
TC 2.119, and 1 pers. pl. ~ *us* B.ML 170,
B.Sh 1413, B.Mel 2552, B.NP 4347,
C.Pard 883; esp. ~ *se* let(it)be seen A.Prol
831, A.Mil 3116, B.NP 4511. **3.** have, get
(something done) (fold. by infin. without
expressed subject, as **doo(n** 5) A.Kn 2731,
B.Mk 3349, C.Phs 208, D.Sum 2255,
LGW 676; sim. ~ *do(n* with infin. B.Mk
3342, C.Phs 173, F.Sq 45. **4.** leave D.WB
31, E.Mch 2217, G.SN 406, ABC 72;
leave off A.Rv 4214, abandon B.ML 325;
whoso wol han leef, he leef mot ~ TC
4.1585. **5.** consider Bo 2. p3. 18/25, p8.
23/33, TC 1.302. **leteth** pr. 3 sg. Bo 1.
p5. 24/34; **lat** TC 4.200 var. **leteth** imper.
pl. LGW 411. **leet** pa. sg. A.Kn 2731,
B.Mk 3349, Bo 3. m2. 24/35 var. **le(e)te** pl.
F.Fkl 1379, LGW 746. **lete(n** p.p. D.WB
767, HF 1934; **lat** E.Mch 1991 var;
yleten Bo 4. p4. 205/287. [OE. *lǣtan,
lēt, ǧe)lǣten*, ON *láta*]
lette n. delay E.Cl 300, TC 3.235, 4.41;
hindrance TC 1.361. [from v.]
lettegame n. spoilsport TC 3.527. [**lette(n**
+game(n.]
lette(n v. **1.** tr. prevent (with obj. person
or thing) TC 2.732, 4.1301; (with infin. of
thing prevented) A.Kn 1892, B.NP 4030,
F.Fkl 994, TC 2.94, 4.200 var; hinder,
obstruct A.Kn 889, E.Mch 1573, PF 151,
TC 3.545; interrupt B.Sh 1276; delay,
postpone B.NP 4274. **2.** intr. desist,
cease TC 2.1089; (with infin.) PF 439,
Bo 1. p4. 109/151; delay, wait B.ML
1117, B.NP 4224, D.WB 154, I.Pars
995; refrain (*of* 'from') A.Kn 1317.
letteth pr. 3 sg. E.Mch 1573; **let** PF 151,
Bo 3. p10. 110/149. **letteth** imper. pl.
TC 2.1136. **letted** pa. B.Mel 2591, E.Mch
1904; **lette** B.NP 4030, TC 2.1089. **let**
p.p. B.Mk 3788, TC 3.717. [OE *lettan,
lettede*]
lett(e)rure n. learning, literature B.Mk
3486, 3686, G.CY 846. [OF]
lettre/letter n. **1.** letter (epistle) B.ML 728,
TC 1.656, LGW 1354; pl. in sense of sg.
B.ML 736; writing BD 788; inscription
RR 1543. **2.** letter (of alphabet) F.Sq
101, TC 1.171, Astr 2.3.20/28; initial
letter I.Pars 43. [OF]
letuarie n. remedy A.Prol 426, C.Pard 307,
TC 5.741. [OF]
leve see **leef** adj.
leve v.³ allow LGW 2280; grant: *God* ~
B.Pri 1873, D.Fri 1644, TC 1.597, 2.1212,
3.56, 5.959. [OA *lēfan*]
leveful adj. allowed, permitted, legitimate
A.Rv 3912, D.WB 37, E.Mch 1448, G.SN
5, Bo 1. p3. 13/17; **leefful** I.Pars 41, 917,
leful TC 3. 1020 var. [from prec.]
levene n. lighting flash D.WB 276. [prob.
ON]
levere see **leef** adj.
leves see **leef** n.
levesel see **leefsel**.
lewed adj. **1.** ignorant B.ML 315, C.Pard

437, F.Sq 221; ~ *and nyce* ignorant and foolish G.CY 647, 925; simple, unlettered C.Phs 283, G.CY 787, I.Pars 508, HF 866; lay (not clerical) A.Prol 502. **2.** stupid, worthless E.Mch 2275, F.Fkl 1494, PF 616. **3.** lewd, lascivious A.Mil 3145, E.Mch 2149. **lewedest** *sup.* H.Mcp 184. [OE *lǣwede*]

lewedly *adv.* ignorantly B.ML 47, G.SN 430, H.Mcp 59; simply HF 866. [from prec.]

lewednesse *n.* ignorance, foolishness B.Mel 2111, F.Sq 223, Fort 68. [from **lewed**]

lyard *adj.* grey D.Fri 1563. [OF *liart*]

libel *n.* written declaration, statement of charge (in eccl. law) D.Fri 1595. [OF]

licence *n.* permission B.Mel 2200, D.WB 855, I.Pars 946; leave of absence B.Sh 1253. [OF]

licenciat *adj.* licenced to hear confessions A.Prol 220. [ML *licenciātus*]

liche *see* **lyk** *adj.*, **lyke** *adv.*

lichewake *n.* watch over the dead A.Kn 2958. [OE *līc* + *wacu*]

licour *n.* sap, moisture A.Prol 3; juice C.Pard 452, liquor TC 4.520. [OF]

lye *n.*[1] lie, deception TC 4.1407, HF 2129; *withouten (any)* ~ A.Kn 3015, D.WB 27, G.CY 599. [OE *lyge*]

lyes *n.*[2] *pl.* lees, dregs D.WB 302 (with pun on prec.), HF 2130. [OF *lie*]

lye *v.* blaze D.WB 1142. [from OA *lēg* n.]

lief *see* **leef** *adj.*

liege *see* **lige**.

lye(n/liggen *v.*[1] **1.** lie A.Kn 2205, E.Cl 379, TC 1.752, Astr 2.29.16/23; ~ *by* lie with, copulate with E.Mch 2394, TC 3.1428; ~ *in balance* TC 4.1560; ~ *upright* lie flat (on one's back) A.Rv 4194, B.Pri 1801, D.WB 578. **2.** remain, stay F.Fkl 1102, I.Pars 232, TC 5.1207, FormA 14; ~ *in await* B.NP 4415; ~ *in my power/ might* B.Sh 1456, D.WB 1011, A.Prol 538, LGW 690. **3.** lodge A.Prol 20, B.ML 887, D.Sum 1780. **liggen** *infin.* B.Th 2101. **list** *pr. 2 sg.* TC 2.991; **listow** TC 4.394. **lith** *3 sg.* A.Kn 1218, B.NP 4235, TC 2.465; **lyeth** BD 143 *var.* **liggen** *pl.* A.Kn 2205, B.NP 4415, TC 3.669. **liggeth** *imper. pl.* TC 3.948. **lay** *pa. sg.* A.Prol 20, B.Pri 1815, PF 95. **layen** *pl.* 3210; **leye** E.Cl 877. **laye** *subj.* TC 4.1560. **leyn** *p.p.* B.ML 887, E.Mch 2395; **ylayne** LGW 2410. [OE *licgan*, *læg*, *lǣgon*, *legen*]

lye(n *v.*[2] lie, tell lies D.WB 228, I.Pars 610, PF 629; *(if that) I shal/wol nat* ~ (asseveration) A.Prol 763, B.NP 4135, TC 3.880. **lixt** *pr. 2 sg.* D.Fri 1618, D.Sum 1761; **list** TC 1.797; **listow** (with suffixed pron.) H.Mcp 276, TC 4.394. **lyeth** *3 sg.* F.Sq 217, TC 4.834. **ley/leigh** *pa. sg.* TC 2.1077; **lyed** A.Prol 659. **lyeden** *pl.* Bo 1. p4. 180/252. [OE *lēogan*, *lēah*]

lyer *n.* liar B.Mel 2256, TC 3.309, 315. [from **lye(n** *v.*[2]]

lyf/lyve *n.* **1.** life A.Prol 71, D.WB 1222, G.SN 332, TC 1.95, HF 176; *on* ~ alive A.Kn 3039, D.Fri 1519, F.Sq 423, TC 2.138; *by my* ~! A.Rv 4024; *on peril of my* ~ (interj.) B.NP 4134, D.WB 1145, TC 4.113; *my/thy* (etc.) ~ during (one's) life D.WB 392, TC 2.205, 1056, Buk 19; *this* ~ life on earth A.Kn 3061, B.Mel 2803,

I.Pars 665; ~ *perdurable/interminable* eternal life I.Pars 246, Bo 5. p6. 29/41; *hertes* ~ own life F.Fkl 816, LGW 2278, (fig.) Anel 223, TC 2.1066, 3.1422; *bere* ~ be alive BD 64, TC 2.835; *brought of* ~ killed TC 5.1561; *lyves ende* death E.Cl 1036, TC 3.392; *lyves leche* saviour D.Sum 1892, BD 919. **2.** way of life B.Sh 1508, E.Mch 1663, LGW 1700; *lede (one's)* ~ see **lede(n**; *live (one's)* ~ C.Pard 780, D.WB 1179, E.Cl 487. **3.** age C.Phs 72. **4.** beloved I.Pars 948, BD 1038, Purse 12. **5.** biography B.Mk 3160, B.NP 4300, D.Sum 1980, TC 2.118; narrative A.Mil 3141. **lyves** *gen. sg.* D.WB 1257, PF 53, TC 5.1554. **lyves** *pl.* A.Kn 1718, D.WB 1261, F.Sq 233. See also **lyves** *adj.* [OE *līf*]

lyfly *adj.* lively Bo 4. p6. 15/22; bright, fresh Bo 1. p1. 5/7. [OE *līflic*]

lyfly *adv.* vividly A.Kn 2087, **lyvely** BD 905. [OE *līflīce*]

lyflode *n.* sustenance I.Pars 685. [OE *līflād*]

lift/left *adj.* left B.Mel 2502, Astr 1.6.2/3, RR 163; ~ *hand* left A.Kn 2953. [OE **lyft*, s-e *left*]

lige *adj.* **1.** liege, (feudal) superior, ~ *lord* C.Pard 337, F.Sq 111; ~ *lady* D.WB 1037. **2.** liege, inferior, ~ *man* E.Cl 310, LGW 379. **3.** as *n.* follower, subject B.Mk 3584, LGW 382. [OF]

ligeaunce *n.* allegiance B.ML 895. [AN]

ligge(n *see* **lye(n**.

light *n.* **1.** light A.Kn 1494, E.Cl 1124, PF 87, TC 5.543; (fig.) spiritual light B.Pri 1669, I.Pars 1037, Bo 3. m.10. 18/26; ~ *of eyen* sight ABC 105; *in his* ~ in his way A.Mil 3396. **2.** lamp TC 3.979. [OE *lēoht*, A *līht*]

light *adj.*[1] **1.** light (in weight) A.Kn 2120, PF 380, Bo 4. m6. 18/27, TC 5.1808; lightly clothed G.CY 568, WUnc 20; ~ *hond* Bo 4. m3. 23/32; *comp.* B.Mel 2690. **2.** cheerful A.Kn 1783, A.Mil 3671, TC 5.352; ~ *herte* G.SN 351, TC 5.684; frivolous HF 1096, LGW 1699, Astr prol 36/51. **3.** easy B.Mel 2230, BD 526, PF 553, TC 4.1570. [OE *lēoht*, *līht*]

light *adj.*[2] bright G.SN 381. [OE *lēoht/līht*]

lighte *adv.* brightly RR 1109; *comp.* HF 1289. [OE *lēohte*]

lighte(n *v.*[1] **1.** lighten, relieve (sorrow, etc.) TC 3.1082, HF 467; cheer, gladden (heart) B.Pri 1661, TC 5.634, *intr.* grow lighter, be cheered F.Sq 396. **2.** alight, descend F.Fkl 1183, 1248, HF 508, LGW 1713; arrive B.ML 786; cf. **alighte**. **lighte** *pa.* B.ML 786, 1104. [OE *līhtan*]

lighte(n *v.*[2] **1.** set light to I.Pars 1036. **2.** illuminate A.Kn 2426, F.Fkl 1050 *var*, ABC 74, TC 4.313, (fig.) brighten TC 1.293. **3.** *intr.* shine Bo 3. m11. 8/11, I.Pars 1037. **light** *p.p.* LGW 2506. [OE *līhtan*]

lighter *adv. comp.* more readily LGW 410. [from OE *lēohte*]

lightly *adv.* **1.** quickly A.Kn 1461, B.NP 4129; in light clothes F.Sq 390. **2.** cheerfully A.Kn 1870, carelessly I.Pars 1024; frivolously, heartlessly TC 2.668, 3.804. **3.** easily, readily A.Rv 4099, B.Mel 2777, H.Mcp 8, Astr 2.14.8/11. [OE *lēohtlīce*]

lightne v. illuminate, light up F.Fkl 1050 var, I.Pars 244, Bo 4. p4. 132/187. [from **light** adj.[2]]

lightnesse n.[1] **1.** levity I.Pars 379. **2.** agility A.Mil 3383. [from **light** adj.[1]]

lightnesse n.[2] brightness PF 263, Bo 1. m2. 7/9. [OE *lihtnes(se*]

lightsom adj. gay RR 936. [from **light** adj.[1]]

ligne see **lyne**.

lyk/liche adj. **1.** like (with obj.) A.Prol 259, A.Mil 3226, B.Th 1917, (following obj.) F.Sq 62; (with to) B.NP 4058, E.Cl 257, E.Mch 1786, I.Pars 888, BD 963; (absol.) TC 2.1040. **lik(k)er** comp. D.Sum 1925, TC 3.1028. **2.** similar, alike I.Pars 631, TC 2.44, LSt 5. **3.** likely HF 873, LGW 1068, RR 679. [OE *ge)lic̄*, ON *likr*]

lyke/liche adv. **1.** like A.Prol 590, A.Kn 2159, TC 5.1577, LGW 865; ~ as as if G.CY 576, PF 641, HF 1508. **2.** alike HF 10. [OE *ge-lic̄e*, and prec.]

lyke(n v. **1.** please (pers., with dat. obj. or (un)to) D.WB 625, CompL 127/121, TC 3.613, 5.133, 1737; (impers., with subject it and dat. of pers.) D.Fri 1278, TC 3.1302, HF 860, if it ~ yow/the if you please Bo 4. p7. 14/19, TC 4.101, LGW 319, RR 801; (without expressed subject, with dat. of pers.) A.Prol 777, B.ML 902, F.Fkl 1150, TC 1.829, 5.631, LGW 1672, (with dir. obj.) us ~th yow you please us E.Cl 106. **2.** like LGW 1076. [OE *lician*]

likerous adj. **1.** lecherous H.Mcp 189, FormA 57; wanton, lustful A.Mil 3244, D.WB 752. **2.** greedy C.Pard 540; eager F.Fkl 1119. [AN]

likerously adv. wantonly B.Mk 3747. [from prec.]

likerousnesse n. lecherousness D.WB 611, I.Pars 859; eagerness I.Pars 741; excessive relish of food, gluttony C.Phs 84, I.Pars 377. [from adj.]

lyking vbl. n. pleasure B.ML 767, C.Pard 455, D.WB 736, LGW 794.

lyking(e ppl. adj. pleasing B.Mel 2909, TC 1.309, RR 868; wel ~ thriving RR 1564. [from **lyke(n)**]

likker(e see **lyk**.

lyklihed n. likelihood, probability B.Pri 1786, E.Cl 448. [from *likly*, ON *likligr*, + OE suff. -*hǣdu*]

lykne v. liken, compare A.Prol 180, D.WB 369, BD 636, Bo 4. p3. 84/121. [from **lyk** adj.]

lyknesse n. **1.** resemblance I.Pars 212, HF 1070, Bo 2. p4. 32/44; parable A.Kn 2842. **2.** image I.Pars 544, Bo 3. pb. 66/85; shape, form LGW 1142, Bo 4. m7. 32/46. [OE *licnes(se*]

lym n.[1] **1.** mortar ~ and stoon F.Fkl 1149, G.CY 910, LGW 765. **2.** quick lime LGW 649, *unslekked* ~ G.CY 806. [OE *lim*]

lym n.[2] limb, any organ or part of the body BD 499. pl. A.Kn 2135, 2714, B.ML 772, TC 1.282, hir ~ or hir lives B.Mk 3284; (fig.) member I.Pars 136; **lemes** A.Rv 3886. [OE *lim*, pl. *limu/leomu*]

lymaille/lemaille n. (metal) filings G.CY 853, 1162. [OF]

lyme v. lime, catch with birdlime TC 1.353, D.WB 934 [from **lym** n.[1]]

lymere n. leash-hound BD 362, 365. [AN]

limite v. appoint B.Mel 2956. [OF *limiter*]

limitacioun n. district D.WB 877. [OF]

limitour n. limiter (friar licensed to beg within certain limits) A.Prol 209, D.WB 866, D.Fri 1265. [from OF *limiter*, v.]

lymrod n. limed stick B.Mk 3574. [from **lym** n.[1] in sense 'birdlime']

linage n. **1.** lineage, race A.Kn 1550, Bo 5. p3. 146/209; ancestry A.Kn 1829, A.Rv 4272, E.Cl 71, hey ~ E.Cl 991, E.Mch 1305 var; stock I.Pars 920; nobility B.Mk 3441; consanguinity LGW 2602; of ~ by birth B.Mel 2751. **2.** kindred, relations A.Kn 1110, B.ML 999, B.Mel 2192; family D.WB 1135. [OF]

lind n. lime-tree A.Kn 2922, E.Cl 1211, RR 1385. [OE]

lyne/ligne n. **1.** straight line, plumb-line E.Mch 2230, TC 1.1068, 2.1461, Astr prol 72/99, etc.; fishing line Mars 242; line of writing TC 2.1177; south ~ meridian I.Pars 2. **2.** descent, lineage A.Kn 1551, D.WB 1135, Purse 23. [OE *line*]

lyonesse see **leonesse**.

lyoun see **leoun**.

lipsed pa. lisped A.Prol 264. [OE *wlispian*]

lisse n. **1.** respite F.Fkl 1238, HF 220. **2.** comfort TC 3.343; joy TC 5.550. [OE *liss*]

lissen v. relieve BD 210, TC 1.1089; comfort TC 1.702, F.Fkl 1170. [OE *lissan*]

list n.[1] see **lest**.

list n.[2] ear D.WB 634. [OE *hlyst*]

list/lest v. **1.** impers. (with dat. of pers.) it pleases (me ~ = I please, like) A.Prol 750, B.ML 1048, F.Sq 123, PF 114, TC 2.223, 3.259, Rosem 23; me ~ ful/right vvele I have no wish A.Kn 1127, BD 239. **2.** pers. be pleased A.Mil 3176, B.Mk 3330, G.SN 30, TC 1.518, 3.1810, LGW 1884; like F.Fkl 689; wish B.Mel 2234. **lesteth** pr. 3 sg. LGW G.480. **listen** pl. TC 3.1810, LGW 575. **liste/leste** pa. A.Prol 102, B.Mk 3666, TC 3.1132. [OE *lystan*, -e- forms s-e]

listes n. pl. lists, enclosure for tournaments A.Prol 63, A.Kn 1713, etc., F.Sq 668. [OE *liste*]

listeth imper. pl. listen! B.Th 1902, 2023. [from OE *hlystan*]

listow see **lye(n** v.[2]

litarge n. litharge (lead monoxide) A.Prol 629, G.CY 775. [OF]

litargye n. lethargy, sleeping sickness Bo 1. p2. 14/20, TC 1.730. [ML *litargia*]

lite adv., adj., n. **1.** adv. little A.Kn 1723, G.CY 632, TC 1.826; ~ and ~ D.Sum 2235 var. **2.** adj. little, small A.Kn 1067, PF 64, TC 2.1646, Astr prol 20 var; grete/muche and ~ A.Prol 494, B.NP 4122, Anel 265. **3.** n. little B.ML 109, TC 5.176; a ~ A.Kn 1334, B.ML 352, BD 249, TC 2.254. [OE *lȳt* adj.]

litel adj., adv., n. **1.** adj. little A.Prol 87, B.ML 208, PF 57, TC 3.601; ~ of deficient in PF 513. **2.** adv. little A.Prol 438, B.Sh 1414, BD 401, TC 1.216; ~ and ~ B.Mel 2770. **3.** n. little, not much A.Kn 1779, B.Mk 3676, RR 179; short time A.Mil 3357, Bo 3. p1. 4/6, TC 4.690; short distance B.Mk 3599; a ~ somewhat B.Sh 1573, D.Fri 1446, Bo 1 p1. 32/45; into ~ nearly TC 4.884. [OE *lȳtel*]

litestere n. dyer FormA 17. [OE from ON *lita* v.+OE suff. *-estre*]
lith n. limb B.NP 4065, BD 953. [OE]
lith see **lye(n**.
lythe adj. easy, soft HF 118. [OE *līþe*]
lythe v. soothe TC 4.740 [OE *līþan*]
litherly adv. badly, ~ *biset his whyle* wasted his time A.Mil 3299. [OE *lȳþerlīce*]
lyvely see **lyfly** adv.
live(n v. live A.Prol 335, D.WB 111, PF 420, TC 4.447; be alive TC 4.1215; ~ *(one's) lyf* D.WB 1179; *while (I)* ~ for the rest of (my) life A.Kn 1295, D.Sum 2130, G.CY 736, TC 1.938; make a living C.Pard 445, D.Fri 1429; survive F.Fkl 679, BD 2, TC 4.758, LGW 1381. **livestow** *pr. 2 sg.* (with suffixed pron.) C.Pard 719. [OE *lifian*]
livere n.[1] liver (the organ) D.Sum 1839. [OE *lifer*]
livere n.[2] liver, *vertuous* ~ one who lives virtuously B.ML 1024. [from **live(n**]
liveree n. livery, uniform A.Prol 363. [AN]
lyves adj. living, ~ *creature* A.Kn 2395, E.Cl 903, TC 3.13, 4.252. [gen. sg. of *lyf*]
lyves see **lyf**.
livinge ppl. adj. as n.[1] living person: *fals* ~ evil liver I.Pars 640. [from **live(n**]
livinge n.[2] way of life C.Phs 107, I.Pars 596, Bo 1. m4. 2/2, TC 1.197; state of life G.SN 322; livelihood E.Cl 227; lifetime Anel 188. [from **live(n**]
lixt see **lye(n** v.[2]
lo- interj. **1.** look! A.Kn 1791, B.ML 925, D.Sum 1988, TC 1.514. **2.** Oh, Ah! A.Mil 3611, B.Mk 3326, E.Mch 1986, TC 1.205. [OE *lā*]
lode n. load A.Kn 2918. [OE *lād*]
lodemenage n. pilotage A.Prol 403. [from OE *lādmann*]
lodesmen n. pl. pilots LGW 1488 var. [from OE *lādmann*; see **lodman**]
lodesterre n. pole star A.Kn 2059; guiding star (fig.) TC 5.232, 1392. [OE *lād* way (see **lode**)+**sterre**]
lodman n. pilot LGW 1488 var. [OE *lādmann*]
lofte see **onlofte**.
logge n. lodging, shed B.NP 4043. [OF *loge*]
logged p.p. lodged B.NP 4186, 4188; **ylogged** 4181. [from OF *logier*]
logging n. lodging B.NP 4185. [from v. as prec.]
logh see **low(e**.
loke v. lock B.NP 4065, D.WB 317. **loken** p.p. B.NP 4065. [ON *loka*, OE *loc* n., *locen* p.p. of *lūcan*]
lokkes n. pl. locks (of hair) A.Prol 81, A.Mil 3374, Adam 3. [OE *loccas*]
loller n. Lollard B.Sh 1173, 1177. [var. of *Lollard*, from MDu]
lomb see **lamb**.
lond n. **1.** land A.Kn 2104, B.ML 903; countryside A.Rv 3988; *in* ~ to the country, away B.NP 4069, (as mere tag) B.Th 2077; *upon* ~ in the country A.Prol 702; earth (as element) A.Kn 2992; ground B.NP 4226. **2.** country, realm A.Prol 400, B.ML 604, F.Sq 9; (fig.) I.Pars 177. [OE *lánd*]
long adj.[1] long A.Prol 93, E.Mch 1602, TC 1.220; **lange** (nth.) A.Rv 4175; *al the* ~ *day*

A.Prol 354, G.CY 1221; *al the* ~ *night* A.Kn 2717, A.Rv 4235; lengthy PF 1, Bo 3. m11. 4/6. [OE *láng*]
long adj.[2] dependent (on), owing to (with *on*) G.CY 922, 930. [OE *geláng*]
longe adv. long, for a long time A.Prol 286, B.ML 378, B.Mk 3300, TC 2.1127; *as* ~ *as* Bo 3. p11. 38/52; ~ *agoon* B.Th 1899, Anel 150, LGW 443; *al the night* ~ Astr 2.12.25/35. [OE *lánge*]
longe(n v.[1] desire, yearn A.Prol 12, BD 83, TC 5.597, LGW 2260; (impers. with dat.) E.Mch 2332. [OE *lángian*]
longe(n v.[2] **1.** befit, suit (with *(un)to*) A.Rv 3885, F.Sq 16, LGW 151. **2.** belong D.Fri 1391, I.Pars 802, LGW 1963; (with *for* 'to') A.Mil 3209, F.Sq 39. [rel. to **long** adj.[2]]
longes n. pl. lungs A.Kn 2752. [OE *lungena*]
long-yherd adj. long-haired A.Mil 3738. [from **long** adj.+**heer**]
lo(o)ke(n v. **1.** intr. look, gaze A.Kn 1783, B.Th 1888, C.Pard 720, Truth 19; ~ *(up)on* A.Mil 3344, B.ML 937, BD 1217; tr. (with n. obj.) discern Bo 3. p12. 62/82 (*L cernenda*); (with cl.) see, try BD 537, TC 5.1113. **2.** intr. look, appear A.Prol 289, D.Sum 2173, G.CY 861, TC 1.206, RR 291. **3.** think, consider (*imper.*) A.Mil 3433, B.NP 4323, C.Pard 579, Bo 1. m7. 10/14, TC 3.316; ~ *how* however I.Pars 384, ~ *how that* just as I.Pars 548, 652, ~ *whan* whenever I.Pars 628, Astr 2.15.2, ~ *what* whatever F.Fkl 992, ~ *who that* whoever D.WB 1113, F.Fkl 771. **4.** make sure A.Mil 3549, B.Mel 2359, F.Fkl 1232.
lo(o)keth imper. pl. A.Kn 1798, G.CY 1329, TC 2.1135. [OE *lōcian*]
lo(o)king vbl. n. **1.** glance, gaze A.Kn 2171, I.Pars 853, Bo 1. p3. 4/5, LGW 1102; vision Bo 4. p4. 132/187; attention B.Mel 2332. **2.** appearance E.Cl 514, TC 1.173. **3.** (astr.) aspect A.Kn 2469, Mars 51.
lo(o)ne n. (prep.) loan B.Sh 1485, gift D.Sum 1861. [ON *lán*]
lo(o)re n. **1.** teaching, doctrine, A.Prol 527, B.NP 4160, TC 1.754; advice B.ML 342. **2.** learning B.ML 4, Anel 244, LGW 2450; knowledge E.Cl 788. [OE *lār*]
lo(o)s n.[1] praise, fame G.CY 1368, LGW 1514, RR 1161; reputation B.Mel 2834, 3036, HF 1620, etc.; rumour LGW 1424. **loses** pl. in *til hir* ~ in praise of them HF 1688. [OF *los*]
loos/laus adj. loose A.Rv. 4064, A.Co 4352, PF 570, Bo 4. p6. 93/133. [ON *lauss*]
lo(o)th adj. **1.** hateful, distasteful A.Mil 3393; (in impers. constr.) ~ *were hym* he would not like A.Prol 486, H.Mcp 145, sim. B.ML 91, E.Cl 364, F.Fkl 1599, TC 3.732; (pers.) loath, unwilling TC 3.369, **lo(o)thest** sup. F.Fkl 1313, TC 2.237. **lother** comp. LGW 191. Cf. **leef**. **2.** as adv. unwillingly TC 2.1234. [OE *lāþ*]
loothly adj. hideous D.WB 1100. [OE *lāþlić*]
loppe n. spider Astr 1.3.4/5, 19.2/3. [OE]
loppewebbe n. cobweb Astr 1.21.2/2. [prec.+OE *webb*]
lord n. **1.** ruler A.Prol 65, B.ML 575, E.Cl 64; master, employer A.Prol 601, A.Kn 3081, E.Cl 633, G.CY 718; great man, gentleman A.Prol 200, B.Pri 1680, TC

2.706. **2.** term of address, to a superior A.Kn 915, B.ML 883, E.Cl 106; to God B.ML 826, F.Fkl 876; (as title) ~ *God* B.Mel 3075, I.Pars 75; ~ (*Jesus*) *Crist* B.ML 811, D.WB 469, I.Pars 270; *our* ~ God/Christ B.Mel 2296, BD 690; *my* ~ B.Mel 2958, B.Mk 3114, D.Sum 2253; as *exclam.* C.Pard 840, BD 448, TC 1.330. [OE *hlǣford*]
lordeth *pr. 3 sg.* rules over Mars 166. [from prec.]
lordinges *n. pl.* lords, masters A.Prol 761, C.Pard 329, H.Mcp 309. [OE *hlǣfording*]
lordship(e *n.* **1.** power, authority A.Kn 1625, B.Mel 2271, F.Fkl 743, I.Pars 439, TC 3.1756, rule B.Mel 2706, rank E.Cl 797; office B.Mel 2666, Bo 3. p4. 3/4. **2.** ruler I.Pars 568; ruler of a feudal estate I.Pars 752, 757. **3.** favour, patronage A.Kn 1827, TC 2.1420, 3.76. [OE *hlǣfordscipe*]
lorel *n.* villain, scoundrel D.WB 273, Bo 1. p4. 222/308 (L *perditissimum*). [from *loren*, p.p. of **lese(n**]
lore, lor(e)n *see* **lese(n.**
los *n.¹ see* **lo(o)s.**
los *n.²* loss A.Kn 2543, BD 1139, TC 4.27; perdition D.WB 720. [prob. from **lost** *p.p.*, cf. **loste**]
losenge *n.* diamond shaped figure HF 1317, RR 893. [OF]
losengeour *n.* flatterer B.NP 4516, LGW 352, RR 1050. [OF]
losengerie *n.* flattery I.Pars 613. [OF]
loste *pa.* lost B.Mk 3360, D.WB 723, BD 75, TC 4.87 *var.* **losten** *pl.* A.Kn 936; B.NP 4562. **lost** *p.p.* A.Kn 2257, D.Sum 1997, TC 1.201; **ylost** G.CY 722, HF 183. [OE *losian*, pa. *losode*]
lothest *see* **lo(o)th.**
lotinge *pr. p.* lying concealed G.SN 186. [from OE **lotian*, rel. to *lutian*]
lough *see* **laughe(n, lowe.**
louke/lowke *n.* mate, accomplice A.Co 4415. [?]
loute(n *v.* bow B.Mk 3352, TC 3.683, HF 1704; bend RR 1554. [OE *lūtan*]
love *n.* love: *for Goddes* ~ for the love of God A.Mil 3172, 3838, B.NP 4133, 4144, D.WB 1060, G.CY 1176, TC 2.96; *for . . Cristes* ~ because of the love of Christ B.ML 565. ~**s** *gen.* in *at* ~ *reverence* in honour of love TC 3.1328/1405. *pl.* lovers TC 3.544, RR 1317. [OE *lufu*]
lovedayes *n. pl.* days for settling disputes by arbitration A.Prol 258, HF 695.
love-drinke *n.* aphrodisiac D.WB 754.
love-drury *n.* courtship D.Th 2085. [OF *druerie*]
lovely *adj.* amorous A.Mil 3342. [OE *luflič*]
love-lykinge *vbl. n.* romantic love B.Th 2040.
love-longinge *n.* desire A.Mil 3679, 3705; romantic love B.Th 1962. [from **love** + **longe(n** *v.¹*]
lovyere *n.* lover A.Prol 80. [from *love* v., OE *lufian*]
low(e/lo(u)gh *adj.* **1.** low (not high) A.Kn 1369, D.WB 1101, Bo 2. m7. 11/16; *heigh and/or* ~ everything, everyone A.Prol 817, H.Mcp 361, B.ML 993, 1142; ~ *and/or heigh* F.Fkl 1035, RR 841; ~ *degree* E.Cl 425, I.Pars 440, LGW 2081. **2.** low (not loud), soft A.Kn 2433. [ON *lágr*]

lowe *adv.* low BD 391, TC 3.683; humbly E.Mch 2013, LGW 2046; in a low voice F.Sq 216, RR 717, softly BD 304. [from prec.]
low(e)ly *adj.* humble A.Prol 99, Anel 142. [from **low(e** *adj.*]
low(e)ly *adv.* humbly B.Mel 2961, TC 2.1072, LGW 1626. [from **low(e** *adj.*]
lowenesse *n.* humility I.Pars 1080; low level Bo 5. m1. 11/16. [from **low(e** *adj.*]
lowke *see* **louke.**
luce *n.* pike (the fish) A.Prol 350. [OF]
lucre *n.* profit G.CY 1402; ~ *of vileynye* ill-gotten gain B.Pri 1681. [OF]
lufsom *adj.* lovely TC 5.465, 911. [OE *lufsum*]
lulleth *pr. 3 sg.* soothes B.ML 839. **lulled** *pa.* E.Cl 553. [imit.]
lunarie *n.* moon-wort, honesty G.CY 800. [ML *lunāria*]
lure *n.* bait (for hawk) D.Fri 1340, LGW 1371. [OF]
lure *v.* lure, entice D.WB 415. [from prec.]
lussheburghes *n. pl.* forged coin B.Mk 3152. [place name *Luxembourg*]
lust *n.* **1.** pleasure A.Prol 192, E.Mch 1643, TC 3.1819; interest F.Sq 402. **2.** desire, lust B.ML 925, I.Pars 845, Bo 4. p7. 66/92; wish F.Sq 6, BD 273, Anel 189. *pl.* A.Kn 3066, C.Pard 833, TC 5.592. Cf. **lest.** [OE]
lust *pr. 3 sg. impers.* (sometimes varying with **list/lest**) it pleases (with dat. of pers.) D.WB 78, 820, E.Cl 322, E.Mch 1344, H.Mcp 186. **lusteth** LGW 996 *var.* **lust(e** *pa.* G.CY 1235, BD 1019; ?*pers.* liked G.CY 1344. [from prec. on model of **list/lest**]
lusty *adj.* **1.** pleasant, cheerful A.Kn 2116, F.Sq 142, TC 2.1099. **2.** vigorous, gallant D.WB 553, E.Cl 1173, TC 5.402; gay: ~ *bacheler* A.Prol 80, D.WB 883, H.Mcp 107; brave: ~ *knight* A.Kn 2111, Anel 86, TC 4.1485. **lustier** *comp.* G.CY 1345. **lustieste** *sup.* LGW 716. [from **lust** *n.*]
lustihede *n.* vigour BD 27, LGW 1530; pleasure F.Sq 288, H.Mcp 274. [prec. + OE suff. -**hǣdu*]
lustily *adv.* cheerfully E.Mch 1802, Pity 36, TC 5.568; heartily A.Kn 1529, RR 747. [from **lusty**]
lustinesse *n.* pleasure A.Kn 1939, TC 3.177; vigour RR 1282. [from **lusty**]
luxure *n.* lust Bo 3. p7. 7/11. [OF]
luxurie *n.* lust B.ML 925, C.Pard 484, I.Pars 446. [OF]
luxurious *adj.* excessive Bo 1. p4. 224/312. [OF]

M

m' *see* **me.**
ma *adj.* (F) my ~ *dame* A.Rv 3956 *var*; (*par*) ~ *fay* (by) my faith B.Th 2010, TC 3.52.
maad *see* **make(n.**
ma(a)t *adj.* defeated A.Kn 955, B.ML 935; 'mate' (in chess) BD 660; exhausted, dejected Anel 176, TC 4.342. [OF *mat*]
madame *n.* madam, as title A.Prol 121,

B.NP 4348; as term of address B.NP 4160, TC 2.85, Rosem 1. [OF]
madde *v.* be mad, rage A.Mil 3156, 3559, Mars 253, TC 1.479. [from *mad* adj., OE *ġemǣdd*]
made *see* **make(n.**
magesté *n.* majesty (of God) A.Rv 4322 *var*, B.Mk 3358, D.WB 826; (of king) B.ML 1082, B.Mk 3862, Bo 1. p4. 105/146. [OF]
magicien *n.* magician, illusionist B.Mk 3397, F.Fkl 1184, HF 1260. [OF]
magik *n.* magic B.ML 214, F.Sq 218, F.Fkl 1295; ~ *naturel* magic not involving demonic powers, science A.Prol 416, F.Fkl 1125, HF 1266. [OF]
magistrat *n.* magistracy Bo 3. p4. 16/23. [L *magistrātus*]
magnanimitee *n.* courage G.SN 110, I.Pars 731. [OF]
magnificence *n.* splendour, grandeur B.ML 1000, E.Cl 815, glory B.Pri 1664, G.SN 50; the moral virtue of liberality with good taste I.Pars 736. [OF]
maheym/mayme *n.* maiming, bodily harm I.Pars 625. [OF]
may *n.* maiden B.ML 851, TC 5.1412. [OE *mǣġ*]
may *see* **mowe(n.**
mayde *n.* **1.** young girl A.Prol 69, C.Phs 7, E.Cl 2; ~ *child* girl B.Sh 1285, E.Cl 446; servant girl, maid A.Mil 3417, D.WB 241. **2.** unmarried girl, virgin A.Kn 1171, C.Phs 248, TC 2.880; virgin G.SN 48 *var*, Virgin B.ML 841, D.Sum 2202, ABC 49; male virgin D.WB 79. [as next]
mayden *n.* **1.** maiden, virgin, girl A.Kn 2305, E.Cl 210, G.SN 48 *var*, I.Pars 868, TC 2.83; lady-in-waiting A.Kn 2275. **maydens** *gen. sg.* as *adj.* maidenly C.Phs 55. **2.** virgin I.Pars 912. [OE *mæġden*]
maydenheed/-hod *n.* virginity A.Kn 2329, E.Cl 837, G.SN 126, LGW G. 294. [OE *mæġdenhād* and var. suff. -*hǣdu*]
maille *n.* mail-armour E.Cl 1202, TC 5.1559. [OF]
mayme *see* **maheym.**
mayntene *v.* maintain, uphold A.Kn 1441, E.Cl 1171, RR 1144. [OF *maintenir*]
maister *n.* master, boss A.Prol 261, B.Mk 3515, F.Fkl 1209; (as term of address) B.Pri 1627, D.Sum 1800; (as title) A.Mil 3437; (university degree of) Master D.Fri 1638, I.Pars 1043; *attrib.* chief A.Kn 2902, F.Sq 226 *var*, LGW 1965. **maistres** *gen.* F.Fkl 1220, 1302. *pl.* A.Prol 576. [OE *mæġester*, OF *maistre*]
maisterful *adj.* masterful TC 2.756. [from prec.]
mayst(ow *see* **mowen.**
maistresse *n.* **1.** mistress E.Cl 823, BD 797, Bo 1. p3. 6/8. **2.** governess, teacher C.Phs 72, F.Sq 344, Mars 33. [OF]
maistrye *n.* **1.** mastery, upper hand B.Mel 2248, D.WB 1236, I.Pars 927; charge, control B.Mk 3689, C.Phs 58, Fort 14; victory, B.Mk 3582; *for the* ~ extremely A.Prol 165. **2.** skill A.Mil 3383, HF 1094, RR 1208; master-stroke G.CY 1060. [OF]
make *n.* mate E.Mch 2080, H.Mcp 186, PF 310; marriage partner, husband D.WB 85, E.Cl 840, E.Mch 2214; wife E.Mch 1289; partner, opponent A.Kn 2556; match, equal HF 1172. [OE *maca*]

make(n *v.* **1.** make, create A.Prol 384, C.Pard 445, E.Mch 2029; ~ *avow* vow C.Pard 695, G.CY 865; ~ (*a*) *bed/couch* LGW 205, E.Cl 975; ~ *chere* see **che(e)re;** ~ *countenance* pretend B.Mel 2227; ~ *an ende* see **ende;** ~ *forward* plan A.Prol 33; ~ *melodie* A.Prol 9, A.Mil 3306, TC 3.187; ~ *mencioun* A.Kn 893, B.Mk 3311, PF 29, TC 5.1603; ~ *pees* B.Mel 2904; ~ *werre* A.Kn 1823, B.Mel 2240. **2.** make, cause (object) to be (qualified) A.Prol 184, B.NP 4359, Bo 3. p8. 44/61, TC 5.684; ~ *it strange* be awkward A.Rv 3980, F.Fkl 1223; ~ *it tough* make difficulties B.Sh 1569, BD 531, TC 2.1025. **3.** compose A.Prol 95, F.Fkl 710, TC 2.878, HF 622, LGW 417; *intr.* write B.ML 57. **4.** (causative, with obj. and infin.) make (with plain infin.) A.Prol 513, B.Mk 3316, E.Cl 13, TC 5.1126; (with *for* and infin.) A.Prol 427, A.Rv 3903, B.Mk 3294, TC 2.677; cause to be (with p.p.) HF 155; (with infin. without expressed subject, giving quasi-passive sense) B.Mk 3257. **made** *pa.* A.Prol 33, B.Mk 3546, PF 94; **maad** TC 1.251, RR 1192; **maked** A.Prol 526, B.NP 4378, C.Phs 147. **maden** *pl.* B.Mel 2208; **makeden** TC 4.121. **maked** *p.p.* A.Kn 1247, E.Cl 497, Bo 1. p1. 14/20 (and commonly in Bo); **maad** A.Prol 212, B.Mk 3607; **ymaad** B.ML 693, F.Sq 218, G.CY 1149; **ymaked** A.Kn 2065, C.Pard 545. [OE *macian, macode*]
makelees *adj.* matchless TC 1.172. [from **make** n.]
maker(e *n.* creator, maker D.WB 150, PF 199, Bo 1. m5. 1; author, composer I.Pars 1081, Bo 3. p6. 2/3. [from **make(n**]
makinge *vbl. n.* composition Adam 4; poetry TC 5.1789, LGW 74.
maladie *n.* illness I.Pars 1031, Bo 1. p1. 42/58; an illness, disease A.Prol 419, C.Pard 513. [OF]
malapert *adj.* presumptuous TC 3.87. [OF]
male *n.* bag A.Prol 694, C.Pard 920, I.Pars 26. [OF]
malefice *n.* black art, witchcraft I.Pars 341, Bo 1. p4. 196/275. [OF]
malencolie *see* **melancolye.**
malencolyk *adj.* melancholy A.Kn 1375. [from **melancolye**]
malgré *see* **maugree.**
maliso(u)n *n.* curse G.CY 1245, I.Pars 443, 903; cursing I.Pars 619. [OF]
malt *see* **melte.**
mal(e)talent *n.* ill-will, resentment RR 273, 330. [OF]
malvesye *n.* malmsey, a sweet wine B.Sh 1260. [OF, from Gr place-name *Malvasia*]
man *n.* **1.** man A.Kn 1169, D.WB 139, BD 931; servant, admirer TC 1.468; see **goodman.** **2.** human being A.Kn 1309, TC 3.10, FormA 10. Cf. **men. mannes** *gen.* E.Mch 1331, G.CY 812, TC 2.417. **men** *pl.* A.Prol 178, D.WB 326, LGW 1081; **mennes** *gen.* B.ML 202, BD 976. [OE]
manace *n.* menace, threat, threatening A.Kn 2003, B.Mk 3789, I.Pars 646. [OF]
manace *v.* threaten, menace E.Mch 1752, I.Pars 646, Bo 2. m4. 3/5. [OF]
manasinge *vbl. n.* threat A.Kn 2035.
manciple *see* **ma(u)nciple.**

mandement *n.* summons D.Fri 1284, 1346. [OF]

maner *n.* headquarters BD 1004. [OF *manoir*]

maner(e *n.* **1.** way, method E.Cl 818, F.Fkl 1425,|Bo 4. m6. 15/23, (uninfl. pl.) A.Mil 3328; *in this* ~ B.NP 4080, E.Cl 174, I.Pars 273, PF 533; *in no* ~ Bo 3. p10. 46/69. **2.** kind of A.Prol 71, B.Mk 3951, D.WB 451, F.Fkl 1433, TC 1.495; kind, mode I.Pars 681, 942, Bo 1. p6. 3/4, HF 1197. **3.** manners, behaviour A.Prol 140, F.Sq 546, BD 966, Pity 78; custom, habit C.Phs 120, *for the* ~ in accordance with convention TC 1.1021; *pl.* BD 1014, Bo 4. m3. 7/9. [OF]

manhede *n.* manhood, manliness A.Kn 1285, B.Mk 3861, H.Mcp 158; **manhod** A.Prol 756, TC 2.676, 4.1674, courage TC 4.529, 5.1476. [man+OE suff. -*hǣdu, -hād]

many/mony *adj.* many A.Kn 1521, BD 430, TC 5.1751; ~ *a* A.Prol 350, D.WB 399, TC 1.165; ~ *oon* many a one A.Prol 317, B.ML 929, G.CY 1391, HF 760; ~ *smale maken a greet* I.Pars 362; *as* ~ *heddes as* ~ *wittes there been* F.Sq 203. [OE maniǧ]

manye *n.* mania A.Kn 1374. [OF]

manifesten *v.* display Bo 2. p7. 31/43. [OF *manifester*]

manyfold *adj.* numerous Prov 1. [OA maniǧfáld]

manly *adv.* heroically A.Kn 987; nobly I.Pars 688. [OE mannlíće]

mannish *adj.* human B.Mel 2454; like a man TC 1.284; unwomanly B.ML 782; ~-*wood* man-mad E.Mch 1536, cf. HF 1747. [from **man**]

mansioun *n.* **1.** dwelling place, home A.Kn 1974, HF 754, 831. **2.** (astrol.) 'house' of planet F.Sq 50; daily position of moon F.Fkl 1130, 1285. Cf. **hous**. [OF]

mansuete *adj.* courteous TC 5. 194. [OF]

mansuetude *n.* meekness I.Pars 654. [OF]

mantelet *n.* short cloak, cape A.Kn 2163. [OF]

mappemounde *n.* map of the world Rosem 2. [OF]

mapul *n.* maple A.Kn 2923, RR 1384. [OE mæpel (trēow)]

marbel/marbul *n.* marble A.Kn 1893, TC 1.700; ~ *ston* B.Pri 1871, RR 1462. [OF]

marchal *n.*: ~ *in an/of his hall* master of ceremonies A.Prol 752, E.Mch 1930. [OF]

marchandise *n.* trade I.Pars 777, 780, Bo 2. m5. 15/22; merchandise, goods B.Sh 1539, (*pl.*) I.Pars 779 *var* [OF]

marchant *n.* merchant, businessman A.Prol 270, B.Sh 1191, FormA 22. [OF]

mareys *n.* marsh D.WB 970, Bo 2. p7. 26/36. [OF]

mary *n.* marrow C.Pard 542, Bo 3. p11. 84/114. [OE mearg]

mary-bones *n. pl.* marrow-bones A.Prol 380. [from prec.]

marineer *n.* mariner, sailor B.Pri 1627, Bo 4. m3. 16/22, LGW 2169. [AN]

mark/merk *n.*[1] mark, sign D.WB 619, I.Pars 98; fixed point LGW 784; image F.Fkl 880; sex D.WB 696. [OE mearc]

mark *n.*[2] mark (money of account, 13*s.* 4*d.*) C.Pard 390, G.CY 1026, 1030. [LOE *marc*]

marken *v.* **1.** mark, brand E.Cl 556, Bo 1. p4. 91/126, Astr 2.14.3. **2.** notice, consider Bo 3. p1. 33/44, HF 1103. [OE *mearcian*]

market-beter *n.* market-haunter A.Rv 3936. [LOE *market*, from L *mercātus* through Gmc,+agent n. from be(e)te(n[1]]

markis *n.* marquis E.Cl 64, 91, etc. [OF]

markisesse *n.* marchionesse E.Cl 283, 1014. [from prec.]

marle-pit *n.* clay-pit A.Mil 3460. [OF *marle+pit* from OE *pytt*]

martirdom *n.* martyrdom B.Pri 1800, G.SN 240; torment A.Kn 1460. [OE]

martyre *n.* martyrdom TC 4.818. [OF]

martireth *pr. 3 sg.* torments A.Kn 1562. [from *martir* n., from OE]

masculin *adj.* male Bo 2. p3. 28/40. [OF]

mase/maze *n.* maze, puzzle B.NP 4283, TC 5.468, LGW 2014. [from stem of next]

mased/mazed *ppl. adj.* bewildered, stupefied B.ML 526, 678, BD 12; stunned (with grief) Anel 322. [cf. **amased**]

maselyn *n.* maple-wood bowl B.Th 2042. [OF]

masonrye *n.* mason's work HF 1303, RR 302. [OF *maçonnerie*]

masse *n.* mass B.Sh 1413, D.Sum 1728, BD 928; *heighe* ~ E.Mch 1894; *to singe a fool a* ~ ?in using flattering words TC 3.88; ~ *peny* offering made at mass D.Sum 1749. [OE *mæsse*]

mast *n.*[1] (ship's) mast A.Mil 3264, BD 71, LGW 643. [OE *mæst*]

mast *n.*[2] nuts FormA 7, 37. [OE *mæst*]

masty *adj.* fattened (on mast) HF 1777. [from prec.]

mat(e *see* **maat.**

matere *n.* **1.** matter, affair A.Prol 727, D.Sum 2288, TC 1.1062; reason, cause B.Mel 2725, I.Pars 348. **2.** subject B.ML 322, C.Phs 104, TC 1.53. **3.** material, substance G.CY 770, I.Pars 137, Bo 1. m1. 2; matter (opp. form) TC 5.1322, LGW 1582. [OF]

material *n.* matter Bo 5. p4. 131/188. [OF, and LL *māteriāle*]

material *adj.* material, physical I.Pars 182, Bo 5. p1. 35/49. [as prec.]

matrimoi(g)ne *n.* matrimony A.Kn 3095, E.Mch 1573, I.Pars 882. [OF]

maugree/malgré *prep.* in spite of A.Kn 1607, B.Mk 3238, HF 461; ~ *(his) heed/even* in spite of all (he) could do A.Kn 1169, 2618, D.WB 887, LGW 2326, A.Kn 1796, D.WB 315. [OF]

maumet *n.* idol I.Pars 749, 860. [OF *mahumet*]

maumetrye *n.* Mahommedanism B.ML 236; idolatry I.Pars 750. [from prec.]

ma(u)nciple *n.* manciple, steward A.Prol 544, A.Rv 3993, H.Mcp 25. [OF]

mavis *n.* thrush RR 619, 665. [OF]

mawe *n.* belly, stomach B.ML 486, B.Sh 1190, B.Th 2013. [OE *maga*]

maze *pr. pl.* are bewildered E.Mch 2387. [prob. from **mased**]

mazednesse *n.* bewilderment E.Cl 1061. [from prec.]

me *pron.* **1.** *acc.* me *passim*; myself (*refl.* with *v.*) A.Kn 2363, C.Pard 330, TC 4.940. **2.** *dat.* to me A.Prol 39, A.Kn 1808,

D.WB 563, BD 8; for me E.Cl 153, LGW
46; (in impers. constr.) A.Kn 1646, B.ML
817, H.Mcp 23, BD 898, TC 4.1675.
(before vowels) **m/m'** TC 1.1050, 2.1401
(both var). [OE]
mede see **meeth.**
medewe n. meadow LGW G. 91, RR 128.
[OE *mǣdwe*, obl. of *mǣd*]
mediacioun n. means, help B.ML 234,
F.Sq 656; use Astr prol 8/11. [OF]
medicyne n. **1.** the science of medicine
TC 1.659. **2.** remedy E.Mch 2380, I.Pars
470, 591; healing ABC 78. **3.** pl. medi-
cines Bo 2. p1. 28/40; drugs, chemicals
F.Sq 244. [OF]
medle v. **1.** mix, mingle I.Pars 122, Bo 5.
p3. 76/107, LGW 874. **2.** muddle, confuse Bo 4. p5. 20/29. **3.** take part, occupy
oneself G.CY 1184; meddle, interfere
B.Mel 2731, G.CY 1424. [OF]
medlee adj. of mixed colour A.Prol 328.
[OF]
medling vbl. n. **1.** mixture Bo 1. p4.
179/251, RR 898. **2.** meddling, inter-
ference TC 4.167.
me(e)de n.[1] meadow A.Prol 89, D.WB 861,
LGW 41. [OE *mǣd*, A *mēd*]
me(e)de n.[2] **1.** reward A.Prol 770, Bo 4.
p3. 24/34, LGW 1662; to ~s as a reward
TC 2.1201; ~ of coroune corollary Bo 3.
p10. 102/137, 113/153 (F *loier de coroune*),
cf. 4. p3. 8/11. **2.** bribe A.Mil 3380,
bribery B.Mk 3579, C.Phs 133, I.Pars
167; (person.) PF 228. [OE *mēd*]
me(e)k(e adj. meek A.Prol 69, D.WB 434,
PF 341; ~ as a lamb E.Cl 538, G.SN 199.
meker comp. LGW 2198. **mekest** sup.
E.Mch 1552. [ON *miúkr*]
meke pr. subj. sg. refl. humble myself B.Mel
2873. [from prec.]
meel n. meal, repast B.ML 466, B.NP 4023,
D.Sum 1774. **meles** pl. BD 612. [OE *mǣl*]
meel-tyd n. mealtime TC 2.1556. [prec.+
tyd(e]
me(e)ne n. **1.** middle way I.Pars 833,
Bo 4. p7. 70/98; vertu is the ~ LGW 165.
2. medium, means: sg. E.Mch 1671, TC
5.104; pl. B.ML 480, D.Fri 1484, F.Fkl
884. **3.** go-between, conciliator A.Mil
3375, I.Pars 990. [from next]
me(e)ne adj. **1.** average TC 5.806; intermediate Bo 3. m9. 18/25. **2.** intervening
~ while(s) B.ML 668, G.CY 1262, TC
3.50. [AN *me(e)n*]
me(e)ne(n v. **1.** mean A.Prol 793, H.Mcp
73, TC 2.133; signify Mars 224, is to ~
signifies B.Mk 3941, HF 1104; portend
TC 1.552, 5.364. **2.** intend (with n. obj.)
TC 2.581, (with infin.) 5.1150; ~ wel A.Kn
2287, TC 3.337, 5.1104. **3.** say, assert
G.CY 1424, PF 4. **menestow** pr. 2 sg.
(with suffixed pron.) G.SN 309. **mente**
pa. sg., pl. A.Kn 2990, F.Fkl 981, TC
5.1693. LGW 309; **meneden** pl. Bo 5. p1.
33/46. **yment** p.p. HF 1742. [OE *mǣnan*,
mǣnde]
meest see **mo(o)st.**
me(e)te(n v.[1] meet (person) B.ML 1101,
Mars 138; ~ with G.CY 706, TC 5.1703;
~ yfere LGW 1643, B.ML 394, TC 2.152;
meet (together) A.Co 4383, TC 3.509,
LGW 148; wel (y)met D.Fri 1443, TC
2.586. **mette** pa. B.ML 559, TC 1.1075,

4.42, LGW 733. **metten** pl. HF 2092.
met p.p. A.Kn 1636, Mars 72; **ymet(te**
B.ML 1115, TC 2.586. [OE *mētan*, *mētte*]
me(e)te(n v.[2] dream B.Mk 3930, BD 118,
PF 108, TC 2.90, 3.1344/1330; impers.
(with dat. pron.) A.Mil 3684, B.NP 4084,
BD 276, TC 2.925, HF 119. **met** pr. 3 sg.
PF 104, 105. **mette** pa. B.NP 4223, PF 95,
HF 313. **met** p.p. B.NP 4116, 4445. [OE
mǣtan]
meeth/mede n. mead (the drink) A.Kn
2279, A.Mil 3261, B.Th 2042. [ON *mjǫ ðr*,
?W *medd*, OE *meodu*]
me(e)tre n. verse B.Mk 3171; pl. metrical
form B.ML 48, verses LGW 562. [OF]
megre adj. thin RR 218, 311. [OF]
meynee/meignee n. household, servants
A.Kn 1258, I.Pars 894, TC 1.127, RR 615;
following A.Co 4381, B.NP 4584; troop,
army B.Mk 3532, H.Mcp 228, LGW 1089;
company E.Mch 2436. [OF *mai(s)nee*]
meyntenaunce n. behaviour BD 834. [OF]
mekely adv. meekly, humbly B.ML 1079,
C.Pard 714, TC 2.16. [from **me(e)k(e** adj.]
melancolye/malen– n. melancholy, de-
pression B.NP 4123, BD 23, TC 5.360.
[OF]
melancolious adj. melancholy HF 30.
[from prec.]
mele n.[1] meal, flour A.Rv 3939, etc., D.Sum
1739. [OE *melu*]
mele n.[2] see **meel.**
melle see **mille.**
melodye n. melody, music A.Kn 872,
H.Mcp 114, PF 62; make(n ~ A.Prol 9,
G.SN 134, TC 5.462. [OF]
melte v. intr. melt TC 3.1445, 4.367,
CompA 28 var; tr. HF 1648. **malt** pa. TC
1.582, HF 922. **molte** p.p. TC 5.10, HF
1145. [OE *meltan*, *mealt*, *molten*]
membre n. **1.** limb BD 495, RR 1028;
member, organ D.WB 116, I.Pars 330;
privee ~s I.Pars 425. **2.** part, division
Bo 3. m9. 19/27, p10. 142/193, Astr prol
48/66. [OF]
memorie n. **1.** memory A.Kn 1906, G.SN
339, Bo 1. p6. 32/41; in ~ conscious A.Kn
2698. **2.** remembrance A.Mil 3112, LGW
1685; maken[¶]. . ~ remind B.Mk 3164;
memoire BD 945; see **drawe(n.** [OF]
men pron. indef. (with sg. v.) one, anyone
A.Prol 149, 232, A.Kn 2777, C.Pard 675,
G.SN 392, TC 4.866. **man** B.ML 43 var,
D.Sum 2002, 2054, F.Sq 553, BD 892.
[from **man** in reduced stress]
men see **man.**
mencioun n. mention, make ~ A.Kn 893,
E.Cl 1006, LGW 1228. [OF]
mendinants n. pl. mendicants D.Sum 1906,
1912. [OF]
menivere n. miniver (kind of fur) RR 227.
[OF]
mentes n. pl. plants of mint RR 731. [OE
minte]
mercy n. mercy A.Kn 918, I.Pars 94, TC
4.1149; mercy! have mercy A.Kn 2808,
D.WB 1048, TC 3.98; cry hem ~ ask them
for mercy B.Mel 2874; graunt ~ see
gramercy. [OF]
merciable adj. merciful B.Pri 1878, ABC 1,
LSt 17. [OF]
meridian n. meridian line (crossed by the
sun at noon) Astr 2.39.11/14, 14/18. [OF]

meridian *adj.* meridional, *altitude* ~ position of the sun at midday Astr prol 60/83, etc. [OF]

meridional *adj.* southerly, *angle* ~ due south F.Sq 263; *line* ~ (line crossed by the sun at midday) Astr 1.4.5/6, etc. [OF]

mery(e/miry(e/mury(e *adj.* **1.** merry, cheerful A.Prol 208, C.Pard 843, TC 3.952; *be* ~ cheer up A.Mil 3578, B.NP 4158; *make (us)* ~ C.Pard 883, G.CY 1195; ~ *as a papejay* B.Sh 1559; ~ *chere* (see **che(e)re**) A.Prol 857, B.NP 4651, TC 2.149; ~ *men* followers, companions in arms B.Th 2029. **merier/murier** *comp.* B.Th 2024, B.NP 4041. **2.** pleasant B.NP 4156, 4261, Bo 2. m4. 10/14, 3. p9. 56/74; tuneful A.Prol 235, B.NP 4041, RR 508. [OE *myriġe*]

merye/myrye/murye *adv.* happily A.Mil 3575, B.ML 126, E.Mch 2218, PF 592 *var.* **merier/murier** *comp.* B.NP 4460, E.Mch 2322. [OE *myriġe*]

meriely/myrily/murily *adv.* merrily, pleasantly A.Prol 714 *var*, B.Sh 1300, H.Mcp 138, RR 1329; **murierly** *comp.* A.Prol 714 *var.* [from **merye**]

merinesse/myri- *n.* enjoyment Bo 3. p2. 38/54. [from **merye**]

meryte *n.* **1.** deserts, reward C.Phs 277, Bo 1. p4. 176/246. **2.** merit, credit G.SN 33, I.Pars 1026, HF 669; moral quality Bo 4. p6. 201/291. **3.** *(pl.)* merits, rights and wrongs Bo 5. p2. 33/47, TC 4.965. [OF]

meritorie *adj.* meritorious I.Pars 831, 941. [OF]

merk *see* **mark.**

mermayden *n.* mermaid, siren Bo 1. p1. 49/68, RR 680, 682. [OE *mere* + **mayden**]

mersshy *adj.* marshy D.Sum 1710. [from OE *mersc*]

mervai(l)le/-veyle *n.* marvel, wonder B.ML 502, Bo 1. p4. 140/195, TC 1.476; *(have)* ~ *of* wonder at A.Mil 3423, F.Sq 87. [OF]

merveilen *v.* (only in Bo) marvel, wonder (with *on*, *of*) Bo 2. p5. 31/43, 4. p6. 145/211; (absol.) Bo 4. p1. 23/32; *refl.* Bo 4. p5. 13/20. [from prec.]

merveilinge *pr. p. adj.* wondering Bo 1. m3. 12/17. [from prec.]

merveillous *adj.* marvellous B.Pri 1643, G.CY 629, HF 459. [from **mervai(l)le**]

mes *n.* at good ~ at a fair range RR 1453. [OF]

meschaunce *see* **mischaunce.**

mescheef *see* **mischeef.**

mesel *n.* leper I.Pars 624. [OF]

meselrie *n.* leprosy I.Pars 625. [OF]

message *n.* **1.** message E.Cl 738, F.Sq 99, TC 4.812; *doo(n . .* ~ deliver (a) message B.ML 1087, G.SN 188, LGW 1486; errand TC 3.401, LGW 1486. **2.** messenger B.ML 144, 333. [OF]

messager *n.* messenger A.Kn 1491, BD 133, LGW 1091; harbinger B.ML 6; **messanger** HF 1568, 2128. [OF *messager*]

messaile = *me assaile* TC4. 1595 *var.*

messe *see* **masse.**

mest *see* **mo(o)st.**

mester *see* **mister.**

mesuage *n.* dwelling-house A.Rv 3979. [AN]

mesurable *adj.* moderate A.Prol 435,

C.Pard 515, F.Sq 362; modest I.Pars 936. [OF]

mesurably *adv.* moderately B.Mel 2795. [from prec.]

mesure *n.* **1.** measurement E.Cl 256, I.Pars 776, Bo 1. p1. 10/15, Astr 1.21. 17/23; *be it by met or by* ~ by whatever standard is applied I.Pars 799; *with* ~ in proportion B.Mk 3489. **2.** moderation B.Mel 2181, BD 881; *by* ~ in moderation, moderately I.Pars 465, RR 543; *out of* ~ immoderate(ly B.Mel 2607, 3038; *over* ~ immeasurably PF 300. [OF]

mesuren *v.* measure ABC 174, Bo 3. p2. 28/40, mete out I.Pars 776. [OF]

mesuring *vbl. n.* measure RR 1349. [from prec.]

met *n.* measuring I.Pars 799; *see* **mesure.** [OE *ġemet*]

mete *n.* **1.** food A.Prol 136, I.Pars 345, TC 1.485; ~ *and drinke* A.Prol 345, D.Sum 1875, LGW 2040. **2.** meal, dinner E.Mch 1921, TC 2.1462, LGW 1108; eating, table A.Prol 127, B.ML 1119, LGW 1602. [OE]

mete *adj.* meet, fitting A.Kn 1631, 2291, BD 316, LGW 1043; as *n.* equal BD 486. [OA *ġe-mēte*, WS -*mǣte*]

metely *adj.* well-proportioned RR 822. [from prec.]

meting *vbl. n.*[1] meeting TC 3. 1712, LGW 784. [from **me(e)te(n**[1])]

meting *vbl. n.*[2] dream BD 282. [from **me(e)te(n**[2])]

meve *see* **moeve(n.**

me-ward *see* **toward.**

mewe/muwe *n.* pen (for a hawk) F.Sq 643, 646, TC 3.1784; coop (for poultry) A.Prol 349; (fig.) hiding place, *in* ~ TC 1.381, 4.496. [OF *mue*]

mewet *see* **muwet.**

mychel *see* **muchel.**

mid *adj.*: ~ *pointe* middle BD 660. [OE *midd*]

midde *n.* middle Astr 2.14.1/2. [OE *midd*]

middel *n.* **1.** centre I.Pars 327, Bo 4. p6. 83/118. **2.** middle Astr 2.38.15/22; ~ *of the day* Astr 2.3.2/3, 2.25.10/15. [OE]

middeward *n.* middle G.CY 1190. [OE *middeward*]

might *n.* **1.** power, ability A.Prol 538, D.WB 1188, TC 1.33; potency A.Rv 3879, B.Mk 3136. **2.** strength A.Kn 3078, PF 149, TC 5.838; *do his* ~ exert himself A.Kn 960, E.Cl 1122; *over hir* ~ to excess C.Pard 468. *with al* (one's) ~ D.WB 899, TC 2.1552. [OE *miht*]

mighte(n *see* **muwe(n.**

mighty *adj.* **1.** mighty, powerful A.Kn 1708, Bo 1. p5. 53/77, TC 2.588; ~ *and riche* B.Mel 2157, RR 595. **2.** big A.Prol 108, TC 5.801. **3.** strong B.Mk 3325, Bo 4. p2. 60/79. [OE *mihtiġ*]

mightily *adv.* **1.** strongly A.Mil 3475, B.Mk 3517. **2.** greatly B.Mk 3782, TC 5.262. [from prec.]

mikel *adj.* much Anel 99, LGW 1175 *var*, 1677. Cf. **muchel** [ON *mikell*]

mile-wey *n.* time taken to walk a mile (c. 20 minutes) Astr 1.7.7/9, 16. 11/15. [*mile* from OE *mil* + **wey**]

milksop *n.* feeble fellow B.Mk 3100. [OA *milc* + **sop**]

mille/melle *n.* mill A.Rv 3923, E.Cl 1200, FormA 6; *who so first cometh to the ~ first grynt* D.WB 389. [OE *mylen*]
milnestones *n.pl.* millstones TC 2.1384. [OE *mylenstān*]
myn *poss.* **1.** *adj.* my (usu. before vowel or *h*-) A.Prol 782, 804, B.NP 4487, TC 3.375, LGW 147; (elsewhere, *pl.*) Bo 1. p1. 50/70. **2.** *pron.* mine A.Kn 2406, F.Sq 535, TC 1.21; *me and ~* B.Mel 3072; *of ~* B.Mk 3091. [OF *mīn*]
minde *n.* **1.** mind A.Kn 1402, D.Sum 2221, TC 3.1072; *have ~ (up)on* consider B.ML 908, Purse 26. **2.** senses B.ML 774, BD 511; *out of (one's) ~* B.Pri 1784, C.Pard 494, Mars 248, TC 4.917; consciousness HF 564. **3.** memory E.Mch 2390, Bo 2. p7. 60/87, TC 2.521; *forget hir ~* had lost her memory B.ML 527; *in ~* remembered F.Fkl 878. [OE *ġemўnd*]
myne *v.* mine TC 2.677, 4.471; undermine TC 3.767. [OF]
ministre *n.* servant G.SN 1, 411, G.CY 1300; officer B.NP 4232; *~ general* chief administrator A.Kn 1663. [OF]
ministreth *pr. 3 sg.* governs Bo 3. m6. 2/3. [OF]
minne *imper. sg.* bring to mind Scog 48. [ON *minna*]
minour *n.* miner A.Kn 2465. [OF]
minstralcye *n.* **1.** minstrelsy, playing of music, A.Kn 2197, E.Mch 1718, LGW 2615. **2.** musical instrument H.Mcp 113, 267. [OF]
minstrales *n. pl.* minstrels B.Th 2035, F.Sq 78, HF 1197. [OF]
mintinge *pr. p.* intending Bo 1. m2. 2/3. [from OE *myntan*]
minutes *n. pl.* **1.** minutes (angular measurement) Astr 1.8.8/11, 16.12/17, etc. **2.** minutes (of time) Astr 1.7.8/11. [OF]
miracle *n.* miracle, marvel A.Kn 2675, B.ML 477, F.Fkl 1056, HF 12; miraculous legend B.Th 1881; *pleyes of ~s* miracle plays D.WB 558. [OF]
myre *n.* mire, bog A.Prol 508, D.WB 972, I.Pars 419. [ON *mýrr*]
myry(e *see* **mery(e.**
myrily *see* **meriely.**
mirour *n.* **1.** mirror A.Kn 1399, F.Sq 82, RR 567; (fig.) TC 1.365. **2.** exemplar, paragon B.ML 166, F.Fkl 1454, BD 974. [OF]
mirre *n.* myrrh A.Kn 2938. [OE *myrra*]
mirthe *n.* mirth, pleasure, amusement A.Prol 759, B.NP 4347, E.Cl 1123; joy, gladness, E.Mch 1739, G.CY 1403, TC 3.715. [OE *myrġþ*]
mirtheles *adj.* mirthless, sad PF 592. [from prec.]
mis *adj.* amiss, wrong G.CY 999, TC 4.1267, 5.1426. [from **amis**]
misacounted *p.p.* miscalculated TC 5.1185. [from **account-**]
misaventure/misaunter *n.* misfortune, hard luck B.ML 616, Mars 140, TC 1.706. [OF]
misavise *pr. pl. refl.* act imprudently D.WB 230. [pref. *mis-+***avyse**]
misbileve *n.* suspicion G.CY 1213. [pref. *mis*+**bileve**]
misbeleved *adj.* faithless TC 3.838; as *n.* unbeliever ABC 146. [from prec.]

misboden *p.p.* threatened A.Kn 909. [OE from *misbēodan*]
misborne *p.p. refl.* misbehaved B.Mel 3067. [pref. *mis*+**bere(n**]
miscarie *v.* come to grief A.Prol 513. [pref. *mis*+**carie(n**]
mischaunce/mes- *n.* **1.** bad luck, disaster A.Co 4412, B.ML 914, TC 2.1019, HF 957; *with ~* bad luck to him D.Sum 2215. **2.** misadventure B.ML 610, B.NP 4531, TC 1.92, LGW 1826. **3.** misdoings C.Phs 80, F.Fkl 1292. [OF]
mischeef/mescheef *n.* misfortune, trouble A.Prol 493, E.Mch 1454, TC 1.755; *at ~* in distress A.Kn 2551; *doon ~* damage, harm A.Kn 1326, LGW 1261, 2331. [OF]
misconceyveth *pr. 3 sg.* misunderstands E.Mch 2410. [pref. *mis-*+**conceive**]
miscounting *vbl. n.* fiddling the accounts RR 196em. [pref. *mis-*+**counte**]
miscoveiting *vbl. n.* wrongful desire RR 196 var. [pref. *mis*+**coveite(n**]
misdede *n.* misdeed D.Fri 1664, I.Pars 281, 540. [OE *misdǣd*]
misdemen *v.* misjudge E.Mch 2410, HF 92, 97. [pref. *mis-*+**de(e)me(n**]
misdeparteth *pr. 3 sg.* divides wrongly B.ML 107. [pref. *mis-*+**departe(n**]
misdoer *n.* criminal B.Mel 2631, 2664. [from next]
misdoeth *pr. 3 sg.* ill-treats B.Mk 3112. **misdoon** *p.p.* done wrong I.Pars 85. [OE *misdōn*]
misdrawinges *n. pl.* pulling in different directions Bo 3. p12. 74/99. [from pref. *mis*+**drawe(n**]
myself *pron.* myself: *emph.* A.Prol 544, B.NP 4139, TC 2.1009; *refl.* B.NP 4617, TC 2.744; I myself D.WB 175. **myselve(n** A.Prol 803, E.Mch 1460, BD 34, TC 5.923. [**myn**+**self**]
misericorde *n.* mercy, pity B.Mel 2608, D.Sum 1910, I.Pars 804, TC 3.1177. *pl.* Bo 3. m12. 31/44. [OF]
misese *n.* discomfort I.Pars 177, 806; suffering I.Pars 194; injury Bo 1. p4. 48/66. [OF]
misesed *adj.* distressed I.Pars 806. [from prec.]
misfille *pa. subj.* it turned out badly: *impers.* (with dat.) A.Kn 2388. [pref. *mis-*+**falle(n**]
misforyaf *pa.* misgave TC 4.1426. [pref. *mis-*+**foryeve(n**]
misgyed *p.p. refl.* been misguided B.Mk 3723. [from pref. *mis-*+**gye**]
misgo(o)(n *p.p.* gone astray A.Rv 4218, 4252, I.Pars 80. [pref. *mis-*+**go(o)n**]
misgovernaunce *n.* misconduct B.Mk 3202. [pref. *mis-*+**governaunce**]
mishap *n.* misfortune B.Mk 3435. [pref. *mis-*+**hap**]
mishappe *v.* **1.** meet with bad luck B.Mel 2886; G.CY 944. **2.** *impers.* (with dat.) go wrong for A.Kn 1646. [pref. *mis-*+**happe(n**]
mishappy *adj.* unhappy B.Mel 2758. [pref. *mis-*+**happy**]
misknowinge *vbl. n.* ignorance Bo 3. m11. 18/24.
misknowinge *adj.* ignorant Bo 2. p8. 17/25. [from **knowe(n**]
mislay *pa.* lay wrong A.Mil 3647. [pref. *mis-*+**lye(n** v.[1]]

misledeth *pr. 3 sg.* lead astray Bo 3. p2. 17/24. **misledden** *pa. pl.* misconducted (themselves) TC 4.48. [OE *mislædan*]

misledinges *n. pl.* misdirections Bo 3. p8. 2/2.

misliketh *pr. 3 sg.* displeases LGW 1293. [OE *mislīcian*]

mislyved *adj.* wicked TC 4.330. [from pref. *mis-*+*lyf*]

mismetre *pr. subj. sg.* scan wrongly TC 5.1796. [from pref. *mis-*+OF *metre* n.]

missat *pa.* was out of place BD 941; misbecame RR 1194. [pref. *mis-*+*sitte(n)*]

misse *v.* **1.** *tr.* fail to find CompL 44, feel lack or absence of TC 3.445, 537; ~ *of* lack, feel want of B.Sh 1542, fail to find D.Fri 1416. **2.** fail, omit (with cl.) A.Mil 3679. **3.** *intr.* come to an end PF 40; come to grief TC 3.1624. [OE *missan*]

misseye *v.* **1.** say amiss E.Mch 2391, BD 528, *understood in* seye A.Mil 3139. **2.** speak ill of I.Pars 379, LGW 323. **misseyde** *pa.* LGW 440. **misseid** *p.p.* E.Mch 2391, RR 1260. [pref. *mis-*+*seye*]

misset *p.p.* misplaced BD 1210. [pref. *mis-*+*set(te)*]

misspeke *v.* speak wrongly A.Mil 3139, TC 1.934. **misspak** *pa.* TC 1.934. [pref. *mis-*+*speke(n)*]

mistaketh *pr. pl.* offend RR 1540. **mistake(n** *p.p.* done wrong BD 525, *refl.* B.Mel 2880, 3008. [pref. *mis-*+*take(n)*]

mister/mester *n.* **1.** trade A.Prol 613; occupation A.Kn 1340; *what* ~ *men* what kind of men A.Kn 1710; **2.** need RR 1426. [OF]

misterye *n.* ministry, office I.Pars 895, 900. [L *misterium*]

mistyde *v.* be unlucky B.Mel 2886. [OE *mistīdian*]

mistihede *n.* mystery Mars 224. [OE *mistiġ* +suff. -*hǣdu*]

mistily *adv.* obscurely G.CY 1394. [from OE *mistiġ*]

mistorneth *pr. 3 sg.* leads astray Bo 3. p3. 6/8; *p.p.* misled Bo 4. p2. 130/177. [pref. *mis-*+*torne(n)*]

mistrusten/-triste *v.* mistrust B.Mel 2949, C.Pard 369, TC 1.688. [pref. *mis-*+*truste(n)*]

misusen *v.* misuse, abuse G.CY 649, B.Mel 3040. [pref. *mis-*+*use(n)*]

miswanderinge *pr. p. adj.* erring, straying Bo 2. p8. 20/29, 3. p2. 16/23 (L *deuius*). [pref. *mis-*+OE *wandrian*]

misweyes *n. pl.* by-ways Bo 3. m11. 2, 5. p1, 14/20 (L both *deuns*). [pret. *mis-*+*wey*]

miswent *p.p.* gone wrong TC 1.633. [pref. *mis-*+*wende(n)*]

myte *n.*[1] mite, insect D.WB 560. [OE *mīte*]

myte *n.*[2] very small coin, 'bean' G.CY 1421, TC 3.832; *nat worth a* ~ A.Kn 1558, G.SN 511, G.CY 633; *rekke nat a* ~ G.CY 698, Mars 126; *dere ynough a* ~ see **yno(u)gh**. [OF]

miteyn *n.* mitten, glove C.Pard 372. [OF]

mixen/mixne *n.* dunghill I.Pars 911. [OE]

mo *adj., pron.* more (in number) A.Prol 576, C.Pard 891, D.Fri 1367, G.CY 675, HF 121; *withouten wordes* ~ A.Prol 808, C.Pard 678, TC 3.234, RR 641; others in addition D.WB 663, E.Cl 1039, CompL 62,

TC 1.613, 2.1274, 3.1514, 5.229; *withouten* ~ and nobody else A.Kn 2725, TC 4.1125, alone G.SN 207; *another* ~ A.Kn 2071, B.ML 978, TC 1.540; *othere* ~ B.Mk 3510, D.WB 894, E.Mch 1215, 2263; more (in quantity) TC 3.370. [OE *mā* adv.]

mo *adv.* more, any longer, again D.WB 864, TC 5.158, 1263; *reinforcing comp.* B.Sh 1603; see **evermo, nevermo**. [OE *mā*]

moche *see* **muchel**.

mocioun *n.* motion B.Mel 2429; inclination, desire TC 4.1291. [OF]

moder *n.* **1.** mother A.Mil 3795, C.Phs 119, PF 292; (fig.) source B.Mel 2754, C.Pard 591, I.Pars 710. **2.** principal plate (of astrolabe) Astr 1.3.1. **modres** *gen.* B.ML 786, G.CY 1243; **moder** Bo 2. p2. 11/16. [OE]

moeble *n.* property, movable goods TC 4.1380, 1460, 5.300; *pl.* E.Mch 1314, G.SN 540. [from next]

moeble *adj.* movable Astr 1.21.49/69. [OF]

moedes *n. pl.* modes Bo 2. p1. 32/45 (L *modos*).

moevable *adj.* **1.** mobile Bo 3. p12. 145/196, m12. 5/7; changeable Bo 4. p6. 45/65, 113/144. **2.** as *n.*: *first* ~ primum mobile Astr 1.17.31/37. [OF]

moevabletee *n.* mobility Bo 4. p6. 80/115. [OF]

moeve(n/meve(n *v.* **1.** move *intr.* PF 150, HF 825; *tr.* Bo 4. p6. 101/146. **2.** disturb Bo 1. m2. 12/17; (fig.) Bo 1. p4. 8/12. **3.** move, prompt B.ML 1136, I.Pars 128; urge (with *to* 'against') LGW G. 320; begin, provoke ~ *warre* B.Mel 2218; ~ *armes* Bo 2. m5. 18/26. [stem of OF *moveir*, AN *mover*]

moevere *n.* mover, cause (esp. God) A.Kn 2987, HF 81. [from prec.]

moevinge *vbl. n.* **1.** motion I.Pars 355, Bo 3. m9. 20/28, TC 1.285, stirring I.Pars 537; *pl.* impulses I.Pars 655, 915, Bo 2. m8. 14/21. **2.** *first* ~ primum mobile B.ML 295, Astr 1.17.27/36.

moysoun *n.* crop, growth RR 1677. [OF]

moiste *adj.* moist, wet A.Prol 420, PF 380, Bo 2. m6. 4/6; supple A.Prol 457; fresh B.Th 1954, C.Pard 315. [OF]

moisty *adj.* fresh H.Mcp 60. [from prec.]

mokre *v.* rake in, hoard TC 3.1375/1361, Bo 2. p5. 11/15. [prob. rel. to ON *moka* shovel muck, dung]

moleste *n.* trouble, distress Bo 3. p9. *var*/103, TC 4.880. [OF]

molestie *n.* trouble, distress Bo 3. p9. 77/*var*. [OF]

mollificacioun *n.* softening G.CY 854. [OF]

monche *v.* munch TC 1.914 *var*. [prob. imit.]

mone *n.*[1] moan, complaint TC 1.696, HF 362, LGW 2399; *make (his)* ~ complain A.Kn 1366, Mars 143, TC 5.250. [OE **mān*]

mone *n.*[2] moon A.Kn 2077, BD 824, HF 1531; position of the moon A.Prol 403. [OE *mōna*]

mon(e)th *n.* month A.Prol 92, D.WB 627, LGW 176, Astr 2.1.1/2. [OE *mōnaþ*]

mony *see* **many**.

monstre *n.* **1.** monster B.Mk 3302, BD 628, LGW 1928. **2.** monstrosity F.Fkl 1344, Bo 1. p4. 140/194. [OF]

montaigne n. mountain B.ML 24, B.Mk 3817, Bo 1. m7. 8/11. [OF]

mood n. mood C.Phs 126; anger A.Kn 1760. [OE mōd]

mo(o)re adj. greater B.Sh 1195, 1342, B.Mel 2322, TC 5.819, LGW 2331; the ~ part A.Kn 2824, A.Rv 3858, E.Mch 1231; more A.Prol 219, G.CY 919, BD 215, TC 2.406; ~ and lesse all B.ML 959, B.Mk 3433, C.Phs 53, TC 4.1544, lasse and ~ A.Kn 1756; as n. BD 744; anything further, in withoute(n ~ forthwith A.Kn 2316, G.SN 374, TC 2.1666, 3.973, 4.133. [OE māra]

mo(o)re adv. more A.Kn 1116, B.ML 280, B.NP 4517, C.Pard 879, TC 2.1471; with adj. or adv. forming comp. A.Prol 802, A.Mil 3247, B.Mk 3661, D.Sum 1870, I.Pars 1041, TC 3.1219, (reinforcing comp.) I.Pars 529 var; as n. in no ~ A.Mil 3707, CompL 82, TC 3.350; ~ and ~ A.Kn 2744, F.Fkl 964, TC 4.1345; the ~ BD 678, TC 1.406; the ~ .. the ~ D.WB 374, I.Pars 206, CompL 20; ever lenger the ~ B.Mel 2165, F.Sq 404, Pity 95, see **ever**. [adv. use of prec.]

moorne v. mourn D.WB 848, TC 5.793; yearn A.Mil 3704, B.Th 1933. [OE múrnan]

moorninge vbl. n. mourning, lament A.Kn 2968, B.ML 621, Bo 2. p1. 34/47.

mo(o)st/me(e)st adj. sup. greatest A.Prol 303, B.Mel 2225, D.WB 505, CompL 121, TC 3.417, 4.1532; pl. in ~e and leste all A.Kn 2198, F.Sq 300, TC 5.440, LGW 2303. [OE māst/mēest]

mo(o)st adv. most A.Kn 2767, D.WB 905, TC 1.1001 var, 2.247; mostly, chiefly A.Prol 561, E.Cl 932, TC 5.1780; with adj. or adv. forming sup. A.Kn 2203, E.Mch 1552, TC 1.231. [as prec.]

mo(o)t n. pl. blasts, (bugle-)calls BD 376. [OF]

mo(o)t v. 1. must A.Prol 232, B.Sh 1202, PF 408, TC 1.216, 4.17; ~ nede(s must necessarily A.Kn 1169, Bo 3. p10. 43/61, etc., TC 4.1353, HF 786, LGW 2698. 2. may (usu. subj.) A.Prol 832, B.NP 4490, E.Cl 557, G.CY 1225, TC 2.90; so ~ I thee as I hope to prosper B.Th 2007, D.WB 1215, TC 5.1160, so ~ I thrive A.Rv 4177, TC 2.135, HF 1329. pa. might E.Cl 550, LGW 1594, 2264. 3. pa. had to, was obliged to A.Prol 712, D.WB 440, TC 4.216. pa. in sense of pr. must A.Kn 1091, B.Sh 1370, B.Mel 2319, TC 3.1214, impers. in us ~ G.CY 946. **most** pr. 2 sg. B.ML 104, C.Phs 225, D.WB 340, **mostow** (with suffixed pron.) Bo 3. p11. 32/44. **mo(o)ten** pl. B.Mel 2560. **mo(o)te** subj. sg. A.Prol 832, TC 5.907. **moste** pa. sg., pl. A.Prol 712, B.Mk 3232, G.CY 1199, TC 3.1214; **mosten** pl. B.NP 4182, TC 2.894. **moste** subj. E.Cl 550; TC 1.1001 var. [OE mōt, 2 sg. mōst, pa. mōste]

moralitee n. morality A.Mil 3180, B.Mk 3687, I.Pars 1088; moral B.NP 4630; pl. moral qualities I.Pars 462. [OF]

mordre n. murder A.Kn 1256, B.NP 4243, RR 1136; ~ wol out B.Pri 1766, B.NP 4242. [OE morþor]

mordre v. murder B.NP 4415, D.WB 801, BD 724. [from prec.]

mordrer, -our/morthrer n. murderer B.NP 4416, E.Cl 732, PF 353. [from prec.]

mordring vbl. n. murdering A.Kn 2001.

mormal n. sore A.Prol 386. [OF mortmal]

morne n. ~ milk morning milk A.Prol 358, A.Mil 3236. Cf. **tomorwe**. [OE morgen]

morsel n. morsel, scrap A.Prol 128, I.Pars 633, tit-bit B.NP 4025; portion I.Pars 195. [OF]

mortal adj. 1. mortal (subject to death) E.Cl 1150, G.SN 438, Scog 5; earthly Bo 2. p4. 34/46, TC 3.18. 2. deadly A.Prol 61, PF 135, Pity 61; ~ enemy A.Kn 1553, 1794; ~ foo A.Kn 1590, 1736, LGW G. 248. [OF]

morter n. mortar FormA 15; (used as a float-wick lamp) TC 4.1245. [AN]

morthrer see **mordrer**.

mortifye/mortefie v. kill: 1. destroy, nullify I.Pars 233. 2. change chemically, transmute G.CY 1126, 1431. [OF mortifier]

mortreux n. pl. broths A.Prol 384. [OF]

morwe n. 1. morning B.NP 4420, E.Mch 1748, BD 1256, TC 3.1060; by the ~ in the morning A.Prol 334, B.Mk 3586, D.WB 755, TC 2.961; good ~ A.Mil 3580; eve and ~ all the time, incessantly A.Kn 2821, D.WB 152, TC 1.487; cf. **tyd**. 2. next day A.Kn 1629, B.ML 806, TC 4.1617. [OE morgen]

morweninge n. morning A.Kn 1062, F.Sq 397, LGW 1483; dawn Mars 26. [from prec.]

morwe-song n. morning words (with play on **evensong**) A.Prol 830. [morwe+song]

morwe-tyde n. (or as two words) morning, morning-hour B.NP 4206, E.Mch 2225, G.CY 588, I.Pars 708, RR 130. [morwe+tyd]

moste(n, mostow see **mo(o)t** v.

mote n. particle, speck (of dust) D.WB 868, (fig.) TC 3.1603. [OE mot]

motyf n. proposition, notion E.Mch 1491; hath caught a gret ~ was deeply moved B.ML 628. [OF]

motre v. mutter TC 2.541. [?imit.; cf. G. dial. muttern]

mottelee n. motley, varicoloured cloth A.Prol 271. [?AN from **mote**]

mo(u)ntance n. 1. amount TC 3.1732; length TC 2.1707, LGW 307. 2. value A.Kn 1570, C.Pard 863, H.Mcp 255. [OF]

mourdant n. chape, tag RR 1094. [OF]

mous n. mouse A.Prol 144, H.Mcp 177; dronke(n as a ~ A.Kn 1261, D.WB 246; ~es herte coward D.WB 572, TC 3.736. [OE mūs]

moustre n. pattern BD 912. [OF]

moveresse n. cause of quarrels RR 149em. [from **moeve(n**]

mowe n. grimace I.Pars 258, HF 1806, make a ~ TC 4.7. [OF]

mowe(n v. be able, have power; (in finite forms) may, might A.Prol 230, C.Pard 543, TC 1.253; can or/ne may E.Cl 816, TC 4.1164; coude or mighte B.Mk 3679; conne and mowen B.Mel 2933; might or may TC 3.1191; as auxil. of subj. equivalent, **mighte** (with plain infin.) A.Kn 2108, B. Mk 3626, TC 2.511, LGW 1833. **may** pr. 1, 3 sg. pl. A.Prol 230, A.Mil 3464, B.ML 126; **mayst** 2 sg. A.Mil 3528, H.Mcp 19,

TC 1.1052; **maystow** (with suffixed pron.) A.Kn 1236, TC 1.673; (**mayst thou** Mars 106, PF 163, TC 4.265 var, Astr 1.21.48/67 var). **mowe(n** pl. A.Kn 3066, G.SN 510, G.CY 909, Purse 25. **mowe** subj. 1 sg. BD 92, 2 sg. G.SN 300, HF 804, Bo 1. p6. 78/102. **mowen** pl. Bo 1. p5. 52/76, TC 4.1330. **mighte** pa. 1, 3 sg. A.Kn 1436, G.SN 250. **mightest** 2 sg. A.Kn 1655, RR 759; **mightestow** (with suffixed pron.) Bo 1. p3. 40/55, TC 4.262. **mighte(n** pl. A.Prol 169, B.ML 470, Mars 205, TC 2.1624. [OE mæg, late pl. mugon; mihte]

mowle(n v. go mouldy, moulder A.Rv 3870, B.ML 32. [EME muwle ? from ON *mugla]

muable n. mutable, changeable Bo 4. p6. 30/44, TC 3.822. [OF]

mucche v. munch, eat TC 1.914 var. [?rel. to **monche**]

muchel/muche/moche adj., n. **1.** adj. much A.Kn 2352, D.WB 811, 1079, BD 713, TC 2.1071; make ~ of E.Mch 2292; great: ~ and lyte all A.Prol 494, Anel 107; ~ or lyte HF 778; many G.CY 673, Bo 2. p5. 20/28. michel Astr 2.23.18/var. **2.** n. much A.Prol 467, I.Pars 1043, Bo 2. p8. 29/43, TC 2.1659. [OE myċel]

muchel/muche/moche adv. much, greatly A.Prol 132, B.Mel 2181, D.WB 347, TC 2.228, LGW 2525; to ~ too I.Pars 641; **mychel** Bo 3. p11. -/4 var. [as prec.]

mullok n. rubbish A.Rv 3873, G.CY 938, 940. [?rel. to OE myl dust]

multiplicacioun v. **1.** spreading HF 784, 820. **2.** making gold (by alchemy) G.CY 849. [OF]

multiplye v. **1.** multiply, increase B.Pri 1879, B.NP 4535, TC 1.486. **2.** increase gold (by transmutation) G.CY 669, 1479. [OF]

multiplying vbl. n. **1.** increase C.Pard 374. **2.** making gold (by alchemy) G.CY 1391.

mury(e, murier see **mery(e.**

murierly see **meriely.**

murily see **meriely.**

murmuracioun n. grumbling I.Pars 498. [OF]

murmure n. murmur, grumbling A.Kn 2459, E.Cl 628, I.Pars 503. [OF]

murmure v. murmur, grumble F.Sq 204, PF 520. [OF murmurer]

muscle n. mussel D.Sum 2100, Bo 5. p5. 21/30. [OE]

muse n. muse, poetic inspiration Bo 1. p5. 45/65, TC 2.9, Scog 38. [OF]

musen v. **1.** consider, TC 3.563; (with on) B.ML 1033. **2.** gaze HF 1287, RR 1527, [OF]

musicyens n. pl. musicians Bo 2. p6. 68/96. [OF]

muwe v. change TC 2.1258. [OF muer]

muwe see **mewe.**

muwet/mewet adj. mute TC 5.194. [OF muet]

N

n' see **ne.**

na see **no(o.**

na adv. no: ~ more A.Mil 3591 var, B.Sh 1242, LGW 506 var. [OE]

naan adj. (nth.) no A.Rv 4134 var, 4185 var; adv. none: ~ other A.Rv 4187 var. [OE nān]

nacioun n. nation A.Prol 53, HF 207; country B.ML 268; family, line D.WB 1068. [OF]

nadde see **nath.**

naddre/neddre n. adder E.Mch 1786, Bo 5. m5. 4/5, LGW 699. [OE nǣddre]

nadir n. diametrically opposite point Astr 2.6.1, 12.2, etc. [Arab]

nay adv. no (the general neg., regular in response to an open question) A.Kn 3064, C.Pard 442, D.Fri 1506, I.Pars 590, TC 1.770; (sometimes in emphatic contradiction) A.Mil 3792, D.WB 1067, D.Sum 1761, TC 2.128; seyn that ~ say no B.Mel 2573; it is no/na ~ there is no denying A.Rv 4183, B.Th 1956, B.NP 4242 var, E.Cl 817, BD 147; as exclam. B.NP 4623, E.Cl 421, G.CY 862, TC 2.128, 213. Cf. **no.** [ON nei]

nayl n. **1.** (finger-)nail BD 955, TC 2.1034; claw, talon A.Kn 2141, HF 542. **2.** nail A.Kn 2007, D.WB 769; snag A.Rv 3877; pl. instruments of Crucifixion I.Pars 259; exclam. in by ~es C.Pard 288, 651. [OE nægl]

naile v. nail, fasten A.Kn 2503, E.Cl 1184, I.Pars 258. [from prec.]

nayte v. disclaim I.Pars 1013; refuse Bo 1. m1. 16/22. [ON neyta]

nake v. lay bare Bo 4. m7. 45/65. [from **naked**]

naked adj. **1.** naked, nude A.Kn 1956, I.Pars 105, BD 125; ~ as a worm RR 454; belly ~ E.Mch 1326; unsheathed: ~ swerd F.Sq 84, 156; exposed: ~ erthe I.Pars. 345. **2.** deficient G.SN 486, BD 978; destitute Bo 4. p2. 125/170; unglossed, unadorned LGW 696, Astr prol 19/26. [OE nacod]

naker n. kettledrum A.Kn 2511. [OF nacre]

nale see **ale.**

nam[1] pr. 1 sg. am not (followed by neg.) A.Kn 2811, D.WB 148, LGW 989; ~ but am only, no more than A.Kn 1122, BD 1188, TC 4.957. **nart** 2 sg. G.SN 499, ABC 26, Bo 1. p5. 7/10. **nis** 3 sg. A.Kn 901, C.Phs 187, TC 1.203. **nas** pa. sg. A.Prol 251, G.CY 1344, TC 1.101; ~ but B.ML 938, B.NP 4307, TC 2.198. **nere** subj. A.Kn 875, E.Cl 405 var, H.Mcp 273; ~ that were it not that A.Kn 1600, B.ML 132, LGW 1920; ~ myn extorcioun were it not for his extortion D.Fri 1439, sim. B.NP 3984, G.CY 1362, ABC 24. **nere** pl. indic. A.Kn 1589. [OE nam, noart, nis, næs, næron/nēron]

nam[2] pa. took G.CY 1297. **nome** p.p. taken TC 5.190, LGW 822; **ynome** PF 38, LGW 2443, seized, captured TC 1.242; **nomen** TC 5.514, RR 394. (his, hir) wey ~ made (his, her, their) way TC 5.514, LGW 822, 1018, 1777. [OE nam, numen from niman]

name n. **1.** name A.Kn 1556, B.Th 1907. **2.** reputation D.WB 963, F.Sq 251, TC 5.1095, HF 346; good ~ A.Kn 3049, B.Mel 2815 (and freq.), TC 1.880. **3.** (divine) nature, power B.Pri 1643, H.Mcp 99, I.Pars 596, TC 1.878; a Goddes ~ A.Prol 854, C.Phs 250, H.Mcp 318. [OE nama]

namely/-lich(e *adv.* especially A.Kn 1268, C.Pard 563, TC 1.165, 743, LGW 545. [from **name**]
namo (or as two words) **1.** *adj.* no more A.Prol 101. *pron.* no one else A.Kn 1589, B.ML 695, D.WB 957; no others A.Prol 544, B.NP 4020. **2.** *adv.* never again F.Sq 573. [**na+mo**]
namo(o)re (or as two words) **1.** *adj.* no more E.Mch 2318, I.Pars 188. *pron.* A.Kn 974, B.ML 319, E.Cl 371, G.CY 651. **2.** *adv.* never again B.ML 1112. [**na+mo(o)re**]
napoplexie = ne apoplexie.
nappeth *pr. 3 sg.* sleeps, nods off, H.Mcp 9. [OE *hnappian*]
narette = ne ar(r)ette.
nart *see* **nam.**[1]
narwe *adj.* narrow, small A.Prol 625, B.NP 4012, LGW 740, **narwest** *sup.* Astr 1.18.4/5. [OE *nearu*]
narwe *adv.* closely A.Mil 3224, D.Sum 1803, TC 3.1734; carefully E.Mch 1988, Astr prol 51/72. [from prec.]
nas *see* **nam.**[1]
nat *adv.* not A.Prol 246, D.WB 9, BD 996; ~ *but* only A.Kn 2722, C.Pard 403, D.Sum 1728. [OE *nāht*]
natal *adj.* presiding over birthdays TC 3.150. [L *nātālis*]
nath *pr. 3 sg.* has not TC 5.1199; (auxil.) A.Kn 923 *var.* **nad(de** *pa.* G.CY 879; H.Mcp 51, BD 224 *var.*, LGW 278. **nadstow** *2 sg.* (with suffixed pron.) A.Rv 4088. See **have(n.** [OE *næþ, næfde*]
nathele(e)s *adv.* none the less A.Prol 35, C.Pard 303, BD 32, TC 1.19. [OE *nā þē lǣs*]
natif *adj.* natural, inborn TC 1.102. [OF]
nativitee *n.* birth B.Mk 3206, TC 2.685; astrological conditions at birth, horoscope Astr 2.4.1, 44/68. [OF]
nature *n.* **1.** nature as the controlling power of the world A.Kn 3007, C.Pard 295, E.Cl 902, F.Sq 487, F.Fkl 1345, I.Pars 527, BD 18, Bo 1. m2. 19/27, 3. p11. 90/123; natural force A.Kn 2758; (personified as a goddess) C.Phs 11, BD 871, PF 303. **2.** the natural course of things Bo 3. p3. 9/12, TC 1.105; *agains* ~ B.Mel 2776, I.Pars 865. **3.** inborn power I.Pars 450, Bo 3. p12. 76/103. **4.** instinct A.Prol 11, B.NP 4045, Bo 3. p11. 118/162. **5.** seed, generative fluid I.Pars 577. **6.** kind, character I.Pars 658, BD 631, Bo 3. p10. 67/92, TC 1.113. ~ *of resoun* rational being Bo 5. p2. 7/9 (L *rationalis natura*). [OF]
nature(e)l *adj.* natural A.Kn 2750, Bo 2. p6. 56/78, HF 28; normal I.Pars 647; ~ *day* twenty-four hours F.Sq 116, Mars 122, Astr 2.7.13/18; *magik* ~ see **magik.** [OF]
naught 1. *n.* nothing (in rhyme) A.Prol 756, H.Mcp 338, HF 994, *bringe to* ~ G.CY 1401, **no(u)ght** A.Prol 768, B.Mk 3616, D.WB 118, TC 1.444, 3.1136; (within line or in prose, form sometimes varying) A.Kn 2021, Bo 4. p2. 21/29, TC 1.544, (*al*) *for* ~ in vain, unavailing I.Pars 239, TC 3.1113, *as* ~ *ne were* as if it were nothing D.Fri 1549. **2.** *adv.* not, not at all: (in rhyme) **naught** A.Kn 2068, 2649, B.Pri 1701, D.WB 582, G.SN 269, **nought** B.NP 4437, G.CY 1302, BD 460, Anel 293, TC

2.575; (within line, sometimes var. **nat**) A.Prol 107, B.ML 830, C.Phs 14, PF 543, TC 2.46, 930. [OE *nā(wi)ht/nō(wi)ht*]
naxe = ne axe, *see* **aske(n.**
ne/n' *adv.* not (usu. with another neg.) A.Prol 70, E.Mch 2286, BD 1262. *conj.* nor B.Mk 3245, 3246, TC 2.15, LGW 1818; ~..~ neither..nor A.Mil 3110, B.Mel 2873, Scog 27. [OE]
nece *n.* niece D.WB 383, TC 1.975, etc.; applied loosely to a female relative or connection (cf. **cosin**) B.Sh 1290, 1553. [OF]
necessarie *adj.* **1.** necessary, needful B.Mel 2457, I.Pars 107, Bo 4. p1. 45/63. **2.** predetermined Bo 5. p3. 75/105, p6. 102/144, TC 4.1020; *pl.* ~s Bo 5. p4. 84/121. [AN, or L *necessarius*]
necessaries *n. pl.* necessities B.Mel 711, 871. [from prec.]
necessedent *pa. pl.* compelled Bo 3. m9. 5/7. [from **necessarie**]
necessitee *n.* **1.** necessity, predetermination B.NP 4435, Bo 5. p3. 27/36, etc., TC 4.1002, etc. **2.** need (compelling circumstances) B.Sh 1425, B.Mel 3048, I.Pars 571; *of* ~ B.NP 4182, E.Cl 94; *maken vertu of* ~ A.Kn 3042, F.Sq 593. [OF]
necligence *n.* negligence A.Kn 1881, E.Cl 661, LGW 537. [OF]
necligent *adj.* negligent, careless B.NP 4627, D.Sum 1816, PF 429. [OF]
necligently *adv.* negligently I.Pars 680. [from prec.]
neddre *see* **naddre.**
nede *n.* **1.** need, necessity B.ML 356, Bo 3. p9. 17/23, TC 2.1532; ~ *has na peer* A.Rv 4026; *for* ~s of necessity BD 1201. **2.** (predic. with *be*) necessary A.Prol 304, I.Pars 377, TC 3.46, 5.1858; *yow were* ~ you would need B.Sh 1299; *it is* (*moost*) ~ there is (greatest) need B.Mel 2238, 2432, I.Pars 929, *it is no* ~ E.Cl 461, BD 190, Bo 1. p4. 188/263, TC 3.466. **3.** extremity B.ML 658, E.Mch 1631, ABC 44; crisis B.Mk 3576; *frendes at* ~ Bo 3. p5. 47/65. **4.** business A.Mil 3632, B.Mel 2210, E.Mch 2019; *pl.* matters of business B.ML 174, B.Sh 1266, G.SN 178. [OA *nēd*]
nede *v.* **1.** need I.Pars 700. **2.** be necessary B.ML 871, I.Pars 927. **nedeth** *pr. 3 sg.* *impers.* (it) is necessary: (without expressed subject) A.Prol 462, A.Mil 3166, B.NP 4172, D.Sum 2097, TC 3.1676, (with subject *it*) A.Kn 1746, C.Pard 670, F.Fkl 1466, TC 2.1451, LGW 997, (with dat. of pers., as *hym* ~ he needs) B.Mel 2250, B.NP 4648, D.Fri 1275, D.Sum 2000, TC 2.11, 4.1344 *var.*; *what* ~ (*it, yow*, etc.) ? B.ML 232, D.Sum 1955, TC 2.497. **neded(e** *pa.* A.Rv 4020, B.NP 4024, C.Phs 106, D.WB 205; *subj.* in *us* ~ we should need TC 4.1344 *var.* [OE *nēodian*]
nede *adv.* necessarily TC 2.671, HF 724; *moot* ~ B.Mk 3697, BD 42, RR 1441. [from n.]
nedelees *adv.* unnecessarily E.Cl 455, I.Pars 698, TC 2.1527. [from **nede** n.]
nedely *adv.* of necessity, necessarily B.NP 4434, D.WB 968, TC 4.970. [from **nede**]
nedes *adv.* necessarily A.Kn 2324, I.Pars 317, TC 3.616; *moste* ~ B.Sh 1370, G.CY 1199, Bo 3. p11. 39/54; ~ *moot/moste* B.Sh 1561,

E.Cl 11, D.WB 1071, TC 3.1162. [gen. of **nede**]
nedes-cost *adv.* of necessity A.Kn 1477, LGW 2697. [from **nede**+ON *kostr*]
nedy *adj.* needy, poor B.Mel 2607, I.Pars 778, Bo 2. p2. 12/17. [from **nede**]
nedle *n.* needle G.SN 440, RR 97, 99. [OE *nædl*]
ne(e)dful *adj.* **1.** necessary B.Mel 2833. **2.** needy, necessitous B.ML 112, I.Pars 1032. [OA *nēdful*]
needfully *adv.* of necessity TC 4.1074. [from prec.]
neen *see* **no(o)n.**
ne(e)r *adv. comp.* nearer A.Prol 839, D.Fri 1549, F.Sq 1, TC 1.448; ~ *and* ~ A.Rv 4304, B.Pri 1710; *fer ne* ~ see **fer**; *never the* ~ no nearer success G.CY 721, PF 619; (in positive sense) near A.Kn 1439, *fer or* ~ TC 1.451. Cf. **ny.** [OE *nēar*, ON *nær*]
neet *n. pl.* cattle A.Prol 597. [OE *nēat* sg. and pl.]
neigh *see* **ny.**
neighebore *n.* neighbour A.Prol 535, D.WB 236, HF 649. [OA *nēhgebūr*]
nekke *n.* neck A.Prol 238, D.Fri 1574, TC 2.986; (fig.) life, safety A.Kn 1218, A.Rv 4009. [OE *hnecca*]
nekke-boon *n.* vertebrae B.Pri 1839; neck B.NP 4252; nape B.ML 669. [prec.+**bo(o)n**]
nempne(n *v.* name B.ML 507, E.Cl 609, I.Pars 598; tell F.Sq 318. [OE *nemnan*]
nere *see* **nam¹.**
nerf *n.* sinew TC 2.642. [OF]
nerkotikes *n.* narcotics, sedatives. A.Kn 1472, LGW 2670. [OF *narcotique*]
nethemast *adj. sup.* lowest Bo 1. p1. 25/36 var. [OE *niþemest*]
nether *adj. comp.* lower, bottom A.Mil 3852, D.WB 44b, Astr 1.12.6/8. **netherest** *sup.* Bo 1. p1. 20/28. Astr 1.4.2/3. [OE *neopera*]
netherdes *n. gen. sg.* cow-herd's B.Mel 2746. [**neet**+**herde**]
nevene *v.* name G.CY 821, HF 562, LGW 2237; *herde her name* ~ heard her name mentioned TC 1.876. [ON *nefna*]
never *adv.* never, not at all A.Prol 70, C.Pard 442, BD 1249, TC 2.277; ~ *so* (with adj. or adv., in concessions) however, no matter how A.Kn 1840, B.ML 355, D.WB 943, BD 912, TC 2.59; ~ *a* not a B.Sh 1593, BD 543; ~ *the* (with comp.) not at all (on this account) PF 619, TC 3.86, LGW 1363. [OE *næfre*]
nevermo *adv.* never again TC 3. 1440 var, HF 1926; **-mo(o)re** I.Pars 129, TC 1.938, LGW 2338. [prec.+**mo**, **mo(o)re**]
nevertheles *adv.* nevertheless, notwithstanding Anel 99, CompL 74. [use as sentence adv. of group, see **never**]
neverthemo *adv.* any more, either E.Mch 2089. [cf. prec.]
nevew *n.* nephew B.Mk 3594, LGW 2659; grandson HF 617, LGW 1440, 1442. [AN *nevu*]
newe *adj.* new A.Prol 176, D.WB 1244; fresh A.Kn 1037, C.Pard 839, LGW G. 161, RR 856; ~ *mone* A.Mil 3445; modern B.Pri 1764, I.Pars 721; *of* ~ newly, lately D.Fri 1342, for the first time G.CY 1043. [OE *nīwe*]
newe *adv.* newly, recently A.Mil 3221,

E.Cl 3, TC 5.650, LGW 1122; *al* ~ B.NP 4239, E.Mch 1826, afresh HF 506; ~ *and* ~ again and again C.Pard 929, TC 3.116; *ay* ~ constantly E.Mch 2204. [as prec.]
newe *v. tr.* renew Bo 4. p6. 104/150, TC 3.305. *intr.* BD 906. [from adj.]
newefangel *adj.* fond of novelty F.Sq 618, H.Mcp 193. [from **newe** adj.+OE **fangol* rel. to **fonge**]
new(e)fangelnesse *n.* fondness for novelty F.Sq 610, Anel 141, WUnc 1. [from prec.]
new(e)ly/-liche *adv.* newly, recently Bo 4. m3. 10/13, RR 1205. [from **newe** adj.]
next *adj. sup.* nearest B.Pri 1814, E.Mch 2201; *the* ~*e way* A.Kn 1413, B.ML 807, LGW 2481; next A.Mil 3554, B.Pri 1656, G.CY 951, TC 2.1273. as *adv.* next to G.SN 133, TC 1.950, HF 1486, Astr 1.9.1. [OA *nēhst*]
ny/neigh *adj.* near, close A.Mil 3392, B.Mel 2562, I.Pars 836. [OA *nēh*]
ny/nygh/neigh *adv.* **1.** nearly A.Co 4400, E.Mch 1775, Mars 89, Anel 14, TC 1.582; *wel* ~ very nearly A.Kn 1330, B.Mel 2233, D.Sum 2121, F.Fkl 1236, BD 3. **2.** close A.Prol 588, D.WB 178, Purse 19; closely B.Mel 2566. *prep.* near B.ML 550, TC 1.180, 2.68, LGW 316. Cf. **ne(e)r.** [OA *nēh*]
nyce *adj.* **1.** foolish A.Rv. 4282, B.NP 4505, TC 1.202, HF 207; ignorant D.WB 938, TC 1.625, RR 1257; ludicrous A.Rv 3855, TC 2.24. **2.** scrupulous A.Prol 398; particular (in detail) E.Mch 2434. [OF]
nycely *adv.* foolishly TC 5.1152. [from prec.]
nycetee *n.* foolishness G.SN 463, PF 572, RR 12; simplicity A.Rv 4046; pleasure, lust D.WB 412; scrupulosity TC 2.1288. [OF *niceté*]
nyfles *n. pl.* trifles, pretences D.Sum 1760. [?]
nigard *n.* miser B.NP 4105, TC 3.1379, RR 1175. [prob. ult. Scand.]
nigard *adj.* stingy RR 1172. [as prec.]
nigardye *n.* miserliness B.Sh 1362, Fort 53. [from prec.]
nigh *see* **ny.**
night *n.* night A.Prol 268, F.Fkl 1018, TC 3.1429, Astr 1.13.5/6, etc.; *have good* ~ TC 3.341, 420; *vulgar* ~ see **vulgar**; for phrases see **day**, and **anight**. [OE *niht*]
night-spel *n.* charm said at night A.Mil 3480. [prec.+OE *spell*, cf. **spelle**]
nigromancie *n.* necromancy I.Pars 605. [OF, altered from L *necromantia* by assoc. with *niger* black]
nigromanciens *n. pl.* necromancers I.Pars 603. [OF]
nil *pr. 1, 3 sg., pl.* **1.** will not D.WB 98, 941, BD 92, PF 222. **2.** am/is not willing E.Cl 646, G.CY 1463, TC 2.146. **nilt** *2 sg.* Bo 4. p2. 73/97; (with suffixed pron.) **niltow** TC 1.792, LGW 758. **nolde** *pa.* A.Kn 903, B.Th 2100, TC 1.150, LGW 1846. **noldestow** *2 sg.* (with pron.) TC 3.1264. Cf. **wil.** [OE *nyllan*, *nolde*]
nillinge *n.* refusing Bo 3. p11. 60/83; being unwilling Bo 5. p2. 14/20. [from prec.]
nyne *num. adj.* nine A.Prol 24, TC 3.598; *sustren* ~ Muses TC 3.1809; ~ *night* (cf. nine days' wonder) TC 4.588. [OE *nigon*]
nis *see* **nam¹.**
niste *see* **no(o)t.**

no *adv.* no, (in response to a negative question, confirming negation) no indeed C.Phs 237, F.Fkl 1000, H.Mcp 76, Bo 1. p6. 51/65, TC 1.773 (cf. 770), 2.502; (rejecting a neg. request) BD 720; as *exclam.* E.Cl 819. [OE *nā*]

noble *n.* (a gold coin worth 6*s.* 8*d.*) noble A.Mil 3256, C.Pard 907, HF 1315. [from adj., OF]

nobledest *pa. 2 sg.* didst ennoble G.SN 40. [from *noble* adj.]

nobley(e *n.* nobility (high rank) Bo 2. p3. 26/38; nobility (men of high rank) G.SN 449; high regard E.Cl 828, HF 1416; splendour F.Sq 77. [OF]

noblesse *n.* **1.** nobility, high rank D.WB 1167, E.Cl 468, Bo 2. m6; *your* ~ (term of address) B.Mel 2956. **2.** noble behaviour, character B.ML 185, Bo 3. p10. 157/215, TC 1.287, Gent 17; honour B.Mk 3208, Bo 3. p2. 26/37. **3.** splendour, magnificence B.ML 248, B.Mk 3438, E.Cl 782. [OF]

noght *see* **naught.**

noyous *adj.* troublesome B.Mel 2235 *var*, I.Pars 728 *var*, HF 574. [from **anoyous**]

noyse *n.* noise A.Kn 2492, PF 500, HF 783; sound H.Mcp 300; voice TC 4.374; disturbance B.Mel 2732. [OF]

noysen *pr. pl.* make a noise Bo 3. m6. 7/9. [from prec.]

nokked *adj.* notched RR 942. [from ME *nocke* notch, origin obsc.]

nolde *see* **nil.**

nombre(n *see* **no(u)mbre, no(u)mbre(n.**

nome(n *see* **nam².**

nones *n.* in *for the* ~ for the occasion, purpose A.Prol 379, A.Kn 879, 1423, B.Sh 1165, TC 1.561, LGW 295, on purpose D.Sum 2154; (sometimes with weakened meaning, almost as intensive tag) indeed, assuredly A.Prol 545, B.Mk 3132, LGW 1070 (all rhyming *bones*); *with the* ~ on (the) condition HF 2099, LGW 1540. [from misdivision of *for þen anes*, var. (with adv. *-s*) of *for þen ane*, OE **for þǣm ānum* for that one (thing, purpose); and OE *wiþ þǣm* (*þe*) on condition (that)]

nonne *n.* nun A.Prol 118, B.NP 3999, 4637. *pl. gen.* B.NP title *var*, **nonnes** B.NP 3999. [OE *nunne*]

nonnerye *n.* convent A.Rv 3946. [AN]

no(o) **1.** *adj.* no (before cons.; cf. next) A.Prol 70, B.NP 4110; **na** (nth.) A.Rv 4175, 4183. **2.** *adv.* no A.Mil 3716; not TC 3.578. [reduced from next, and OE *nā*]

no(o)n **1.** *adj.* no (before vowel or *h-*) A.Kn 1787, D.Sum 1990, TC 3.415; **naan** (nth.)/ **neen** (quasi-nth.) A.Rv 4185, 4187. **2.** *pron.* none A.Prol 524, D.WB 1122. **3.** *adv.* in *or* ~ or not D.Sum 2069, E.Mch 1741, F.Fkl 778, I.Pars 962. [OE *nān*]

no(o)t *pr. 1, 3 sg.* do not, does not know A.Prol 284, BD 29, TC 1.410, 5.1050; A.Kn 1263, C.Phs 284. **nost** *2 sg.* BD 1137, TC 4.642; **nostow** (with suffixed pron.) HF 1010. **niste** *pa.* A.Mil 3414, D.WB 996, F.Sq 634, HF 128, TC 1.96. [OE *nāt, nyste*]

nory *n.* pupil Bo 1. p3. 10/13, 3. p9. 119/159, p11. 160/217. [OF *nori*]

norice *n.* nurse B.NP 4305, F.Sq 347, I.Pars 550, Bo 1. p3. 4/6. [OF]

norice/norissen *v.* nourish A.Rv 3948, B.Mel 2784, Bo 3. m6. 9/13; foment B.Mel 2204. **y)norissed** *p.p.* brought up B.Mel 2635, 2701, E.Cl 399, TC 5.821. [OF *noriss-*, stem of *norir*]

norissing *vbl. n.* nourishment A.Prol 437, I.Pars 338, Bo 2. p3. 15/21, 4. p6. 25/36; growth to maturity A.Kn 3017; upbringing E.Cl 1040.

noriture *n.* nourishment TC 4.768, BalCh 27, RR 179*em.* [OF]

nortelrye† *n.* education A.Rv 3967. [irreg. formation on prec.]

northren *adj.* northern A.Kn 1987. [OE]

nosethirles *n. pl.* nostrils A.Prol 557, I.Pars 209. [OE *nosþyrl*]

noskinnes *quasi-adj.* of no kind HF 1794. [from OE *nānes cynnes* gen.; cf. **kin**]

nost, nostow *see* **no(o)t.**

notabilitee *n.* notable fact B.NP 4399. [OF]

notable *adj.* notorious B.Pri 1875, C.Phs 156; remarkable E.Mch 2241; noteworthy Astr prol 61/84. [OF]

note *n.*¹ **1.** tune A.Prol 235, B.Pri 1711, BD 472, PF 677; *by* ~ in unison TC 4.585. **2.** written mark Bo 5. m4. 13/19; token Bo 5. m3. 13/19. [OF]

note *n.*² business, job A.Rv 4068. [OE *notu*]

note *n.*³ nut RR 1360, 1377. [OE *hnutu*]

noteful *adj.* useful Bo 1. p1. 51/70, Astr prol 77/107. [from **note** n.²]

notemuge/-migge *n.* nutmeg B.Th 1953, RR 1361. [AN **nois mugue* adjusted to **note** n.³]

not-heed *n.* cropped head A.Prol 109. [**note** n.³+**he(e)d**]

nother *pron.* neither: *never* ~ LGW 192. Cf. **no(u)ther** [OE *nāþor/nōþer*]

nothing/no thing *adv.* not at all: often doubtful whether intended as one word or two, and editors differ, e.g. B.ML 575, 971, F.Fkl 1094, Anel 87, TC 1.137, 2.1473; rhythm suggests two in such as E.Cl 685, PF 470, LGW G. 78. See **thing.** [OE *nān þing*]

notifie *v.* proclaim B.ML 256; take note of TC 2.1591; indicate I.Pars 430, 437. [OF *notifier*]

nouchis *n. pl.* jewelled clasps E.Cl 382, HF 1350. Cf. **ouche.** [OF *nouche*]

nought *see* **naught.**

no(u)mbre *n.* number A.Prol 716, D.Sum 2261, Astr prol 2/3. [OF]

no(u)mbren *v.* number, count BD 439, Bo 4. p7. 14/20, TC 3.1269. [OF *nombrer*]

noun-power *n.* impotence, lack of power Bo 3. p5. 14/19. [AN *non poair*]

nouthe *adv.* now A.Prol 462, TC 1.985. [OE *nū+þā*]

no(u)ther *adv.* neither BD 342, 531, TC 4.771; *neither* ~ Bo 5. m3. 34/48. [OE *nā(w)þer, nō(w)þer*]

novelrye *n.* novelty F.Sq 619, TC 2.756, HF 686. [OF]

novys *n.* novice B.Mk 3129. [OF]

now *adv.* now: ~ *and* ~ at times F.Sq 430; ~ *or never* TC 4.101. See **as.** [OE *nū*]

nowher *adv.* nowhere A.Prol 251, F.Sq 14, TC 1.961. [OE *nō, nāhwǣr*]

O

o *adv.* ever: *for ay and* ∼ for ever and ever TC 2.1083. [OE *ā*]

o *see* **o(o)n, on, poynt.**

obeye *v.* obey (person or command) B.Mk 3354, E.Mch 1961, TC 5.167; ∼ *to*/*unto* B.Mel 2740, E.Cl 194, LGW 681, TC 3.1157; be subject to Astr 2.28.25/36. [OF *obéir*]

obeisa(u)nce *n.* **1.** obedience, submission A.Kn 2974, Mars 47: *do* ∼ (with dat. pron.) obey B.Mel 3045, E.Cl 24. **2.** *unto*/*at, in* . . ∼ under (one's) authority LGW 587, Pity 84. **3.** deference, respect E.Cl 230, LGW 1375; *pl.* signs of respect F.Sq 515, LGW 149, 1268. [OF]

obeisa(u)nt *adj.* obedient E.Cl 66, I.Pars 264, Bo 1. p4. 18/25. [OF]

obeising *adj.* compliant LGW 1266. [from *obeisen* v., OF *obéiss*-, stem of *obéir*]

object *ppl. adj.* presented Bo 5. p5. 3/4, 15/21. [L *obiectus*]

obligacioun *n.* bond LSt 2; surety B.Mel 2957. [OF]

observa(u)nce *n.* **1.** duty A.Kn 1316, E.Mch 1548, 1564; respectful attention, homage TC 3.970. *do* ∼ pay respect to Anel 218; take care I.Pars 747. **2.** observance, ceremony A.Kn 2264, TC 1.160, 198, 2.1345, 4.783, LGW 150, 1608; *do* . . ∼ perform a ceremony (in honour of sthg.) A.Kn 1045, 1500, TC 2.112. *pl.* attentions F.Sq 516, Anel 249; practices F.Fkl 1291, Astr 2.4.37/57; customs F.Fkl 956. [OF]

observe(n *v.* **1.** attend to I.Pars 303, Astr 2.4.3; (with infin.) take care I.Pars 429; practise, follow I.Pars 947. **2.** favour, countenance B.Pri 1821. [OF *observer*]

occasioun *n.* **1.** cause D.WB 740, I.Pars 338, LGW 994. **2.** opportunity C.Phs 66, I.Pars 511, 951. [OF]

occian *n.* ocean B.ML 505, Bo 4. m6. 9/14. [OF]

occident *n.* west B.ML 297. [OF]

occupye *v.* **1.** take up F.Sq 64, Bo 3. p1. 27/37, TC 5.1322, usurp Pity 90. **2.** take possession of B.ML 424, TC 4.836 [Prov 14:13 *extrema gaudii luctus occupat*]; inhabit Bo 4. p7. 69/96 (L *occupate*). **3.** busy (oneself) B.Mel 2786. [prob. AN = OF *occuper*]

octogamye† *n.* marrying eight times D.WB 33. [after OF *bigamie*]

of *prep.* **1.** of (in various relations of origin, possession, description, etc.) A.Prol 55, B.Mel 2264, F.Fkl 997, BD 5, TC 1.281; made of A.Prol 617; about, on the subject of A.Kn 2812, B.NP 4519; in A.Prol 250, B.NP 4040, F.Fkl 741; (of victory, power) over A.Kn 2246, B.Mel 2946, H.Mcp 128; (as indef. partitive, approaching sense 'some' or in neg. 'any') A.Prol 146, C.Pard 910, TC 2.396; ∼ *newe* newly, new D.Fri 1342, TC 2.20. **2.** by (of agent) A.Rv 3959, D.WB 661, I.Pars 279, LGW 1653, 2318; (of means) B.Pri 1669 *var*, ∼ *kinde* by nature F.Fkl 768, ∼ *right* TC 4.571; ∼ *your curteisye* A.Prol 725. **3.** from B.Mel 3063, D.WB 1153, TC 2.295, HF 807; because of A.Rv 4253, B.Th 2113, D.WB

636, TC 4.368, 607 *var* (see **ferd**); out of TC 2.683, 5. 1561; off TC 5.182. **4.** at (with *smile*, etc.) A.Mil 3524, A.Rv 4046, TC 2.1639. **5.** for (of thanks, excuse) B.Mk 3180, D.Sum 1868, F.Fkl 718, PF 421, TC 4.131, 279, LGW 2212; (of time) A.Mil 3415, D.Sum 2115; with (of pleasure) FormA 3; on (of pity) TC 2.1270, LGW 2421. **6.** about, with TC 2.389; *as* ∼ in regard to A.Prol 87, PF 299. [OE]

of(f) *adv.* off A.Prol 782, B.Mk 3762, C.Phs 226, TC 4.1173; *do* ∼ take off A.Kn 2676, BD 516; (v. omitted) B.Mk 3748, TC 4.1106; *com* ∼ come on, hurry up A.Mil 3728, PF 494, TC 2.310, 1738. [same as prec.]

offence *n.* **1.** harm, injury TC 4.199, FormA 19; *do* ∼ A.Kn 1083, D.Sum 2068, E.Cl 922. **2.** causing offence, wrong-doing B.Mel 3014, Bo 3. p4. 17/25, TC 1.556. **3.** feeling offended B.ML 1138. [OF]

offencioun ⋅ *n.* offence, crime Bo 1. p4. 200/281, damage, injury A.Kn 2416. [OF]

offend *v.* **1.** injure, ill-treat A.Kn 909, 3065. **2.** attack, assail A.Kn 2394, E.Mch 1756, TC 1.605. **3.** displease I.Pars 986, TC 2.244. [OF *ofendre*]

office *n.* **1.** duty B.Mel 2458, G.CY 924, PF 236; employment, position A.Prol 292, 1418, D.Fri 1428; place of business D.Fri 1577. **2.** function D.WB 127, Bo 1. p2. 2/3, TC 3.1436; *naturel* ∼ D.WB 1144, Bo 4. p2. 76/102, 85/113; service D.WB 1137; rites A.Kn 2863. **3.** *hous of* ∼ larder, store E.Cl 264. [OF]

officer *n.* **1.** official G.SN 368, Bo 1. p4. 69/95; administrator B.Sh 1255; lawyer A.Kn 1712, G.SN 497. **2.** servant A.Kn 2868, C.Pard 480, E.Cl 190. [AN]

offre(n *v.* offer, make offering (to a god or God) C.Pard 376, I.Pars 900, TC 5.306, LGW 932. [OF]

offring *vbl. n.* **1.** presenting alms at mass, offering A.Prol 450, I.Pars 407. **2.** alms A.Prol 489, D.Fri 1315. [OF]

ofshowve *v.* repel A.Rv 3912. [of(f)+OE *scūfan*; cf. **sho(o)f**]

oft(e *adv.* often B.ML 278, B.NP 4368, Bo 2. p6. 27/39, TC 4.1219; combining to form adv. phrases: ∼ *a day* many times a day, often A.Kn 1356, Adam 5; ∼ *sythes* many times A.Prol 485; ∼ *tyme(s* A.Prol 52, A.Kn 1312, TC 5.809; quasi-*adj.* (with vbl. n.) frequent I.Pars 233. **ofter** *comp.* B.NP 4618, E.Cl 620, TC 1.125. [OE]

often-tyme(s *adv.* A.Co 4390, D.WB 388, G.SN 14. [var. of **ofte tyme**, see prec.]

ofthowed *p.p.* thawed away HF 1143. [of(f)+OE *þāw*-, cf. *þawian*]

oght *see* **aught.**

oghte *v.* ought (with plain infin.) A.Prol 660, B.Mel 2806, TC 1.710; (with *to* and infin.) A.Prol 505, G.SN 6, Bo 5. p4. 118/169, RR 698; *impers.* (with dat. pron.) be right for B.ML 1097, B.Mel 2188, G.SN 14, I.Pars 1061, TC 1.649. [OE *āhte*, pa. subj. of *āgan*; see **owe**]

oynement *n.* ointment A.Prol 631, I.Pars 502, Rosem 7. [OF]

oynons *n. pl.* onions A.Prol 634. [OF]

oystre *n.* oyster A.Prol 182, D.Sum 2100, Bo 5. p5. 21/29. [OF]

olifaunts *n. pl.* elephants Bo 3. p8. 19/27. [OF]

oliveres *n. pl.* olive trees B.Mk 3226, RR 1314 *var*, 1381. [AN]
olmeris *n. pl.* elms RR 1314 *var*. [OF *ormiers*].
olofte *see* **onlofte.**
omelie *n.* homily I.Pars 1088. [OF]
on (occas. **an**) *prep.* **1.** on (of place, occasion, etc.) TC 1.714, A.Prol 12, E.Cl 81; ~ *a day* one day A.Prol 19, A.Kn 1668, E.Cl 86, ~ *a tyme* A.Kn 2388; ~ *heigh* high (up), above A.Kn 1065, A.Mil 3571, ~ *highte* A.Kn 2607, B.ML 12, ~ *lofte* B.ML 277, TC 1.138, 4.1221 (see also **onlofte**); in B.Sh 1408, B.NP 4388, D.WB 714, ~ *honde* in hand B.ML 348; ~ *even* in the evening E.Mch 1214, TC 1.487; (of trust, etc.) A.Prol 501, B.NP 4627, TC 5.383; ~ *hunting* a-hunting E.Cl 234, BD 355; ~ *ydel* in vain TC 1.955, 5.94; ~ *lyve* alive D.WB 5, E.Mch 1652, F.Fkl 932, BD 205, TC 4.1237; ~ *slepe* asleep LGW 209; o in ~ *point*, see **poynt**; ~ *alle thyng* above all BD 141. **2.** at E.Cl 413, BD 1217; ~ *reste* at rest, asleep F.Sq 379; ~ *to see* to look at A.Kn 1082, A.Mil 3247, LGW 2425; to B.NP 4233, F.Sq 374, TC 2.436; against A.Kn 2628, C.Pard 512, LGW 625. **3.** about: *think* ~ A.Mil 3478, *remember* ~ A.Kn 1501, B.NP 4223, E.Mch 1424, F.Fkl 786, TC 2.1197. **4.** for: *awaytinge* ~ A.Mil 3642, D.Fri 1376, F.Fkl 1299. **5.** by (means of) E.Mch 2163, of (illness) A.Rv 3993, (*a*)*long* ~ dependent on, because of G.CY 922, TC 3.783; *witnesse* ~ take as evidence B.Mk 3916, B.NP 4426, D.WB 951, D.Fri 1491. [OE]
on *adv.* on, forward TC 2.1341, 5.1011; *ley* ~ strike A.Kn 2558, A.Rv 4229, *sey* ~ speak out TC 2.314, *tell* ~ go on with your story A.Mil 3118, 3134, A.Co 4345. [OE]
oneden *pa. pl.* united, concentrated I.Pars 193. **oned** *p.p.* D.Sum 1968, Bo 4. p6. 51/74. [from **o(o)n**]
ones/onis *adv.* **1.** once D.WB 13, G.SN 312, TC 1.792, LGW 2301; *at* ~ at the same time A.Prol 765, TC 1.804, immediately TC 5.41, at **anes** (nth.) A.Rv 4074, see also **atones**; *al at* ~ TC 2.1383, 4.841, RR 710; *al* ~ in unison C.Pard 696; ~ *a ye(e)re* I.Pars 1026; ~ *for evere* once and for all Astr 2.3.6/8, 40/59. **2.** once on a particular occasion D.WB 543, E.Cl 1212d, TC 1.549; on any occasion B.Mel 2231, Bo 2. p1. 69/94, TC 4.1467. **3.** once, formerly A.Kn 1034, G.CY 748, Anel 245; ~ *on a tyme* A.Kn 2388. [OE *ānes*]
ongentil *see* **ungentel.**
onlofte *adv.* (varying with **o-/alofte**, sometimes as two words) above PF 683, TC 1.950, 4.1221, 5.8, 259; on high B.ML 277; high TC 5.348, HF 1726; in the air, sky PF 203, TC 3.670; continuing: *kepte* ~ sustained E.Cl 229; (fig.) up, to a position of advantage TC 1.922. [**on**+*loft*, cf. ON *á lopti*]
ook *n.* oak A.Kn 1702, PF 176, Bo 1. m6. 5/7; *grene* ~ *cerial* evergreen cerrial (Turkey) oak A.Kn 2290. [OE *āc*]
o(o)ld *adj.* **1.** old (of the age of people or things) A.Kn 1812, 1977, B.ML 560, C.Pard 713, TC 2.396; (with age defined) *of thritty winter* ~ B.Sh 1216, *of twelf*

monthe ~ B.Pri 1674, *seven night* ~ B.NP 4063; *or hit a furlong-way was* ~ HF 2064.
elder *comp.* B.Pri 1720, B.Mk 3450.
eldest *sup.* A.Kn 912, B.Mel 2345, F.Sq 30. **2.** as *n.*: the ~ *e* A.Kn 2449; *yonge and* ~(*e* all, everyone B.ML 417, 820, B.Mk 3351, F.Sq 88, TC 1.130, *as wel yonge as* ~*e* E.Cl 419, ~*e and yonge* HF 1233, *as wel* ~*e as yonge* D.Sum 1725. **3.** well-established, familiar A.Prol 174, B.Sh 1564, B.Mk 3281, E.Cl 13, TC 3.695; of long standing C.Pard 672, F.Fkl 1153, I.Pars 562; long B.Mel 2359; *of* ~ for a long time D.Fri 1615, E.Cl 964; past, former TC 4.415. **4.** ancient A.Kn 1163, B.ML 50, D.WB 857, E.Cl 1140, F.Sq 95. [OA *áld; eldra, éldest*]
o(o)n, before cons. usu. **o(o**, *num.* **1.** *adj.* one A.Prol 304, A.Kn 1953, 2725, B.NP 4385, G.SN 207, BD 184, Astr 1.10.16/22; single D.WB 573; united FormA 47, TC 2.1740; ~ *and* ~ one by one A.Prol 679; *many* ~ many a one A.Kn 2509, HF 1207; (ellipt.) ~ *of the clokke* Astr 2.3.52/76; *pron.* one A.Prol 148, B.Mk 3880, C.Pard 825, TC 1.350, LGW 1377; *that* ~ . . *that other* (*the toon* . . *the tothir*) (the) one . . the other D.WB 749, H.Mcp 222, PF 145, Bo 3. p11. 44/60, 4. p2. 58/76; (referring back) A.Rv 3915; (intensifying sup.) ~ *the faireste* (etc.) E.Cl 212, F.Fkl 734, CompL 89, TC 1.1081, 5.1056. **2.** *adj.* identical A.Kn 1012; the same, constant C.Pard 333, E.Cl 711, TC 2.37, 3.309; single, unmarried D.WB 66; alone, unique TC 3.782; *pron.* the same thing F.Sq 537; *after* ~ the same, consistent A.Prol 341, by the same standard A.Kn 1781; *at* ~ in agreement A.Rv 4197, TC 3.565 (cf. **ato(o)n**); *ever in* ~ continually A.Kn 1771, A.Rv 3880, B.Sh 1217, D.WB 209, TC 1.816. **3.** *pron. indef.* one B.NP 605, E.Mch 1552, (some)one A.Mil 3817, F.Sq 212, F.Fkl 1435, BD 47; see **many.** [OE *ān*]
oore *n.*[1] mercy A.Mil 3726. [OE *ār*]
oore *n.*[2] ore D.WB 1064. [OE *ōra*]
oores *n. pl.* oars Bo 2. m5. 14/20, LGW 2308. [OE *ār*]
oost, oostesse *see* **ho(o)st, hostesse.**
o(o)th *n.* oath A.Prol 120, C.Pard 472, TC 2.299. [OE *āþ*]
open-ers *n.* medlar A.Rv 3871. [OE *open*+*ers*]
open-heeded/heveded *adj.* bare-headed D.WB 645. [from OE *open*+*he(e)d*]
operacioun *n.* work, deed D.WB 1148; experiment F.Sq 130; effect F.Fkl 1290, Astr 1,21.44/61. [OF]
opie *n.* narcotic, opium A.Kn 1472, LGW 2670. [L *opium*]
opinioun *n.* **1.** opinion, belief A.Prol 183, Bo 1. p4. 210/294, (contrasted with 'stedefast knowinge') 5. p6. 110/156, TC 4.453. **2.** judgement B.NP 4425, PF 618, TC 1.347; *common* ~ C.Pard 601. [OF]
oppose(n *v.* lay to the charge of (a person) D.Fri 1597 *var*; object Bo 1. p5. 34/50 *var*. [OF *opposer*]
opposicioun *n.* opposite position (of sun and moon) F.Fkl 1057. [OF]
opposit *adj.* **1.** opposite (contrary in position) Astr 2.6.9/13. **2.** as *n.* opposite point A.Kn 1894, Astr 2.37.2. [OF]

oppresse v. **1.** distress B.Mel 2406, TC 3.1089, Bo 1. p2. 11/15; suppress G.SN 4, Fort 60. **2.** rape F.Fkl 1385, 1406, 1411, 1435. [OF *oppresser*]

oppressioun n. **1.** oppression, tyranny D.Sum 1990; wrong TC 2.1418. **2.** repression LGW 2592. **3.** rape D.WB 889, LGW 1868. [OF]

or conj.[1] or (else) A.Mil 3712, E.Mch 1388, TC 1.955; ~ . . ~ either . . or RR 261. [reduced form of ME *other*]

or conj.[2] before B.ML 289, BD 228, Bo 4. p4. 33/45, TC 1.56, 2.63, 3.202, 5.245; ~ *that* BD 1032, TC 1.5, 2.395, 5.44. [ONb *ār*]

or prep. before Bo 1. p2. 17/24, TC 2.245, 4.29, 1685 *var*, 5.164, LGW 2010. [as prec.]

oratorie n. chapel, shrine A.Kn 1905, 1917; private room (for prayer) D.WB 694. [AN]

ord n. point LGW 645; beginning, ~ *and ende* B.Mk 3911*em* (see **word**). [OE]

ordal n. ordeal TC 3.1046. [OE]

ordeyne v. establish, decree B.ML 415, I.Pars 229, Bo 3. p12. 53/70; appoint F.Sq 177; prepare G.CY 1277; set up A.Kn 2553. [OF]

orde(y)nour n. governor, ruler Bo 3. p12. 71/94. [AN]

ordenaunce/ordinaunce n. **1.** order, hierarchy I.Pars 260, PF 390, Bo 4. p6. 45/64 (L *dispositio*); good order E.Cl 961, I.Pars 177, Ven 38, δ; ~ in due order B.Mel 2303, TC 3.688. **2.** arrangement, decree A.Kn 3012, Bo 1. p4. 56/78, TC 5.1605; preparation, provision B.ML 250, F.Fkl 903, TC 3.535; plan B.ML 805, TC 2.510; divine dispensation I.Pars 922. **3.** command, disposal B.Mel 2915, BalCh 16; *in thyn* ~ B.ML 763. [OF]

ordenee adj. regular, well-ordered Bo 3. p12. 30/40 (L *dispositos*), 4. p1. 30/41, TC 1.892. [OF]

ordenely adv. conformably Bo 4. p6. 195/283 (L *disposite*). [from prec.]

ordina(a)t adj. orderly E.Mch 1284; ordered Bo 1. m4. 1/2. [L *ordinātus*]

ordinatly adv. in due order, properly I.Pars 1045. [from prec.]

ordinaunce see **ordenaunce**.

ordre n. **1.** order, arrangement I.Pars 217, Bo 4. p6. 32/45, 5. p1. 65/94, Fort 3; *naturel* ~ Bo 4. p2. 150/204; *(as) by* ~ in sequence B.Mk 3175, C.Pard 645, F. Sq 92, PF 400; *after the* ~ *of* according to B.Mel 2719. **2.** (religious) order A.Prol 214, D.Sum 2191, G.CY 998, I.Pars 891; ~s *four* (of friars) A.Prol 210; (transf.) TC 1.336; rank I.Pars 891; class Bo 1. p4. 112/155; ~ *of wedlok* E.Mch 1347. **3.** law A.Kn 3003, I.Pars 177, Bo 4. p6. 104/150. [OF]

ordred adj. in holy orders I.Pars 782, 894. [from prec.]

ordure n. **1.** filth, dirt I.Pars 157, mud Bo 1. m7. 6/9 (L *caeno*); excrement I.Pars 428, 885. **2.** defilement I.Pars 157, 851; rubbish, nonsense TC 5.385, I.Pars 715. [OF]

orfrays gold embroidery, braid RR 562, 869. [OF]

organs n. pl. organ G.SN 134; **orgon** (with pl. v.) B.NP 4041. [OF *organe*]

orient n. east (of the sky) A.Kn 1494; (of the world) B.Mk 3504, 3871. [OF]

original 1. adj. original: ~ *synne* I.Pars 333, 808. **2.** n. cause C.Pard 500; source LGW 1558. [OF]

orisonte/orizonte n. horizon E.Mch 1797, F.Fkl 1017, TC 5.276; (astron., the name given to a particular circle of the celestial sphere) Astr prol 7/9, 69/96, etc.; *right* ~ Astr 2.26.11/16. [OF]

oriso(u)n n. prayer A.Kn 2261, E.Mch 1706, I.Pars 1038. [OF]

orlo(g)ge n. clock B.NP 4044; (transf.) PF 350. [OF]

orphelin adj. orphaned Bo 2. p3. 21/30. [OF]

orpiment n. orpiment, yellow arsenic G.CY 759, 774. [OF]

osanne interj. hosanna (shout of praise) B.ML 642, G.SN 69. [LL *osanna*]

ost, ostesse see **ho(o)st, hostesse.**

ostelements n. pl. household goods Bo 2. p5. 85/119, 94/131. [OF]

other 1. adj. other A.Prol 113, C.Pard 614, PF 587, HF 585; *this* ~ *day* recently B.Sh 1543, BD 148, TC 2.507, yesterday TC 2.554; *this* ~ *night* last night BD 45; *every* ~ *day* TC 2.1166; ~ *thing* . . ~ *thing* one thing . . a different thing Bo 5. p6. 41/59; second RR 953. **2.** pron. other D.WB 482, LGW 717; the other A.Kn 1135, TC 3.977; *ech* . . ~ A.Kn 899, B.Mk 3468, E.Mch 2230, TC 5.1508; *everich* . . ~ A.Kn 1648, B.ML 1004, LGW 719; *everich* ~ each other F.Fkl 762; *oon and* ~ one and another A.Kn 2573; *that oon* . . *that* ~ see **o(o)n**; *o thing* . . ~ one thing . . another TC 4.1394; *noon* ~ nothing else A.Kn 1182, LGW 2323; *what* ~ what else TC 1.799. **othere** pl. others A.Kn 2885, B.Mk 3344, 3510, Bo 1.p.3. 24/33. **otheres** gen. sg. A.Kn 2734, D.Fri 1404, HF 2044, gen. pl. HF 2153 *var*. [OE *ōþer*]

otherweys adv. otherwise B.Mel 2255, E.Cl 1072, PF 654 *var*; ~ . . ~ in one way . . in another Bo 5. p4. 107/153. [prec.+ **wey**+gen. suff.]

otherwhyle/outherwhile adv. sometimes B.Mel 2733, Bo 2. p1. 78/107. [**other**+ **while**, infl. by **outher**]

otherwise adv. otherwise, in *noon* ~ in no other way I.Pars 572, PF 654 *var*. [**other**+ **wyse**]

ouche n. jewelled clasp D.WB 743. [from misdivision of *a nouche*; see **nouchis**]

ought see **aught.**

oule n.[1] owl B.NP 4282, TC 5.319. [OE *ūle*]

oules n.[2] pl. meat-hooks D.Sum 1730. [OE *āwol*]

ounce n. **1.** ounce G.CY 1121, etc. **2.** pl. G.CY 756, 776, RR 1118; little bits A.Prol 677. [OF *unce*]

ounded ppl. adj. wavy TC 4.743. [from OF *ondé*]

oundy adj. wavy HF 1386. [OF *ondé*]

ounding vbl. n. wavy ornament I.Pars 417. [from OF *onder*]

our adj. our, implying domestic association B.NP 4573; ~ *autour* LGW 1139. [OE *ūre*]

our(e pron. gen. of us A.Prol 799, 823, ABC 84; ours TC 4.539. **oures** B.Sh 1463, C.Pard 786. [OE *ūre*]

ourselven pron. ourselves TC 2.1331. [prec. +self]

out adv. **1.** out A.Prol 45, F.Fkl 1095, TC 2.1120; (v. of motion om.) TC 4.210, (al) mot ~ B.Sh 1350, D.WB 980, HF 2139, mordre wol ~ B.Pri 1766, B.NP 4242, 4247. **2.** ~ of as prep. without C.Pard 385, G.SN 46: ~ of doute A.Prol 487, B.ML 390, TC 1.152, ~ of drede Anel 303, PF 81, TC 1.775; ~ of charitee A.Prol 452, I.Pars 1043. **3.** interj. A.Mil 3286, B.NP 4570, E.Mch 2366. **4.** to the end TC 3.417; ~ and ~ altogether TC 2.739. [OE ūt]

outbreste v. burst out TC 4.237. [prec.+ **breste(n,** cf. OE ūtaberstan]

outcast ppl. adj. abject Bo 3. p4. 31/46, 4. p1. 37/51 (L abiectos); banished TC 5.615. [out+caste(n]

oute(n v. display D.WB 521, E.Mch 2438, G.CY 834. [OE ūtian]

outerly/outre-/-liche see utterly.

outfleynge vbl. n. flying out HF 1523. [out+ flee(n v.²]

outhees n. outcry (against a criminal) A.Kn 2012. [from OE ūt+hǣs]

outher conj. either A.Kn 1485, D.WB 259, E.Mch 2094, TC 2.416; or D.Sum 1828, TC 2.1351. Cf. eyther. [OE āwþer, ōwþer]

outherwhile see otherwhyle.

outlandish adj. foreign FormA 22. [OE ūtlendisc]

outrage n. **1.** excess, extravagance I.Pars 834, B.Mel 2726; luxury FormA 5. **2.** disorder, violence A.Kn 2012, B.Mel 2715, violent act B.Mel 2628. [OF]

outrageous adj. excessive B.Mel 2180, C.Pard 650; plentiful Bo 4. p6. 253/367; violent RR 174. [OF]

outrageously adv. to excess A.Rv 3998. [from prec.]

outraye(n/-reye v. break out E.Cl 643; go beyond the bounds Bo 3. p6. 37/50. [AN outreier]

outrance n. injury BalCh 26/25. [OF]

outrydere n. travelling official (of an abbey) A.Prol 166. [out+OE rīdere]

outstraughte pa. sg. stretched out RR 1515. [out+pa. of strecche(n]

out-take(n prep. except B.ML 277, RR 948. [p.p. of v. from out+take(n]

outtreste see utterest.

outward **1.** adj. external I.Pars 662. **2.** adv. outwardly, publicly E.Cl 424, I.Pars 298, RR 419, externally I.Pars 656, outside TC 2.1704. [OE ūtweard]

outwende v. come out HF 1645. [out+ wende(n]

over adj. upper A.Prol 133; **overest** sup. uppermost A.Prol 290. [OE ufera]

over adv. **1.** over, on: passe ~ leave that B.Pri 1633, B.NP 4452, BD 41. **2.** very, too B.Mel 2766, G.CY 955; ~ muchel B.Mel 2661; ~ greet G.CY 648, Bo 2. p4. 39/53; ~ lowe B.Mel 2655, Bo 3. m9. 17/23. [OE ofer]

over prep. **1.** over, above A.Kn 2029, C.Pard 712, F.Sq 411, TC 2.781; ~al see next. **2.** beyond D.Fri 1661, Anel 88, PF 300; ~bord B.ML 922; ~ see abroad B.NP 4257; more than C.Pard 687; in addition to A.Kn 1563, F.Sq 137, TC 1.386; ~ night the night before TC 2.1513, 1549. [OE ofer]

overal (or as two words) adv. everywhere A.Prol 216, 547, G.SN 507, PF 172, 284, Truth 4; in every way E.Cl 1048, E.Mch 2129. [prec.+al]

overbide v. survive D.WB 1260. [OE oferbīdan]

overblowe p.p. blown over, past LGW 1287. [over+blowe(n]

overcaste v. sadden A.Kn 1536. [over+ caste(n]

overcome(n v. **1.** overcome B.ML 264, BD 707, TC 1.243; defeat B.Mel 2282, LGW 2147, Bo 1. m1. 5/7. **2.** come over A.Kn 2800; happen TC 4.1069. [OE ofercuman]

overcomer n. conqueror Bo 1. m2. 9/13, 4. m7. 27/37. [from prec.]

overest see over adj.

overgilt adj. gold-embroidered RR 873. [OE ofergyld]

overgo(n v. pass away TC 1.846, 4.424; spread over Bo 2. p7. 26/37. [over+ go(o)(n]

overkervith pr. 3 sg. cuts across Astr 1.21.56/ 79, 2.26.23/35. [over+kerve(n]

overlad p.p. put upon, dominated B.Mk 3101. [from OE oferlǣdan]

overlade v. overload LGW 621. [over+ lade]

overlyeth pr. 3 sg. lies upon, overlays I.Pars 575. [over+lye(n]

overlowe adv. (or as two words) too low B.Mel 2655, Bo 3. m9. 17/23. [over+lowe]

overmacche v. defeat E.Mch 1220. [over+ ME macche from OE ġemæċċa n.]

overmast adj. sup. uppermost Bo 1. p1. 26/36 var. [from over adj.; cf. OE ufemest]

overraughte pa. reached over (to urge on) TC 5.1018. [over+reche]

overshake p.p. shaken off PF 681, etc. [over+shake]

overshote p.p. overrun BD 383. [over+ shete(n]

overskipte pa. passed over, omitted BD 1208. [over+skippe(n]

overslop(p)e n. top-coat, cassock G.CY 633. [OE oferslop]

oversprede v. spread over, cover E.Mch 1799. **oversprat** pr. 3 sg. TC 2.767. **overspradde** pa. A.Prol 678, A.Kn 2871, TC 2.769. [OE ofersprǣdan]

overspringe pr. subj. sg. rise above F.Fkl 1060. [over+springe(n v.¹]

overstreccheth pr. 3 sg. extends over Bo 2. p7. 27/38. [over+strecche(n]

overswimmen pr. pl. fly through Bo 5. m5. 5/7. [OE oferswimman]

overte adj. open HF 718. [OF]

overthrowe v. **1.** tr. overthrow, bring down, destroy B.Mk 3331, Bo 4. p6. 217/315. **2.** intr. be destroyed, collapse HF 1640. **overthrowe(n** p.p. destroyed, ruined TC 4.385, 5.1460, Bo 1. p4. 223/311. [over+throwe(n]

overthrowinge vbl. n. destruction B.Mel 2755; pl. Bo 2. m4. 11/15 (L ruinis).

overthrowinge adj. overwhelming Bo 1. m2. 1/2, headlong Bo 1. m6. 15/22 (L both praecipiti); strongly inclined Bo 4. p6. 207/300 (L praeceps). [from overthrowe]

overthwart adv. across TC 3.685, ~ and endelong in length and breadth, all over A.Kn 1991; askance BD 863, RR 292; prep. Astr 1.5.1; [over+ON þvert]

overwhelve v. overturn Bo 2. m3. 13/16. [**over**+OA *hwelfan*]

owe v. **1.** owe D.WB 425, D.Sum 2106, D.Fri 1615; (with *to*) ought B.Mel 2691, Bo 2. p5. 53/74; *him ~th* he ought LGW G. 360; cf. **oghte**. **2.** own C.Pard 361. [OE *āgan*]

ow(e)ne adj. (regularly with wk. ending in def. position) own A.Prol 213, C.Pard 704, BD 504, LGW 316; *myn ~ womman* independent TC 2.750; **awen** (nth.) A.Rv 4239. [OE *āgen-*]

owh interj. alas Bo 1. p6. 17/22, 4. p2. 1.

owher adv. anywhere A.Prol 653, BD 776, HF 478, LGW 1540. [OE *āhwǣr, ōhwǣr*]

P

pa v. kiss A.Mil 3709 var; see **ba.** [cf. **ba**]

pa(a)s n. **1.** step A.Kn 2217, TC 3.281, HF 1051, pl. B.ML 306; pace (as measure) Mars 121, Bo 1. p4. 173/242. **2.** pace, speed A.Kn 2901, C.Phs 164, LGW 284, RR 525; walking pace A.Prol 825, G.CY 575, *a ~* at walking pace A.Kn 2897, C.Pard 866, TC 2.627; *esily a ~* at an easy pace F.Sq 388; *a sory ~* with sad steps A.Mil 3741; *held his ~* (fig.) kept on his course TC 2.1349; *strong ~* difficult experience B.Mel 2635. **3.** passage, section (of a work) I.Pars 532. [OF]

pace see **passe(n.**

pacience n. patience B.Mel 2175, E.Cl 495, F.Fkl 773; *Jobes ~* D.WB 436; *take in ~* endure patiently A.Kn 1084, D.WB 1198; *took ~* kept his patience Bo 2. p7. 93/133. pl. I.Pars 662. [OF]

pacient n. patient A.Prol 415, 418, B.Mel 2202, TC 1.1090. [from *pacient* adj., from OF]

page n. **1.** boy A.Rv 3972; poor boy A.Kn 3030, D.Sum 2178, F.Fkl 692. **2.** page, serving boy A.Kn 1427, A.Mil 3376, LGW 2037. [OF]

pay n. pleasure; *to my ~* to my satisfaction PF 271, Ven 70, *more to ~* so as to give greater satisfaction PF 474. [OF *paie*, from next]

paye(n v. **1.** pay A.Prol 806, B.Sh 1380, F.Fkl 1568. **2.** p.p. satisfied D.WB 1185, BD 269, FormA 3; made favourable TC 2.682. **payde** pa. A.Prol 539, D.Fri 1617. **payed** p.p. B.Sh 1579, LGW 1125; **payd** BD 269; **ypayed** A.Kn 1802, B.Sh 1588, F.Fkl 1618. Cf. **apay(e)d** [OF *payer*]

payen adj. pagan A.Kn 2370 [OF]

payens n. pl. pagans B.ML 534, TC 5.1849, Astr 2.4.37/58. [OF]

pail(l)et n. pallet, shakedown TC 3.229. [AN]

payndemayn n. fine white bread B.Th 1915. [AN *pain demeine* = L *panis dominicus* 'lord's bread']

paisible see **pesible.**

pak n. pack, company LGW G. 299. [MLG]

palasye n. palsy, paralysis RR 1098. [OF *paralisie*]

paleys n.¹ palace A.Kn 2199, TC 5.540, HF 713; (astrol.) mansion Mars 54, 145. [OF]

paleys n.² see **palis.**

palestral adj. athletic TC 5.304. [Italian (Boccaccio), from L *palaestra*]

paleth v. makes pale Bo 2. m3. 2/3. [from OF *palir*]

palfrey n. riding-horse A.Prol 207, A.Rv 4075, LGW 1116. [OF *palefrei*]

palinge vbl. n. decorating with vertical stripes I.Pars 417. [from *pale* stake, OF *pal*]

palis/paleis n.² palisade Bo 1. p3. 56/78, p5. 22/32, p6. 28/36, 2. m4. 12/17. [OF]

palled ppl. adj. enfeebled H.Mcp 55. [from *palle* v., cf. **ap(p)alled**]

palmers n. pl. palmers, pilgrims to the Holy Land A.Prol 13. [AN]

palpable adj. solid, able to be touched HF 869. [LL *palpābilis*]

panade† n. poniard, dagger A.Rv 3929, 3960. [cf. OF *penarde*]

panier n. basket E.Mch 1568, HF 1939. [OF]

pan(ne n. **1.** dish A.Rv 3944, D.Fri 1614, G.CY 1210. **2.** skull, crown (of head) B.Mk 3142; (in asseveration) A.Kn 1165. [OE]

panter n. snare (for birds) LGW 131, RR 1621. [OF]

pape(e)r/papir n. paper G.CY 762, I.Pars 445, TC 5.1597; account-book A.Co 4404; *~-whit* LGW 1198. [AN]

papejay/popynjay n. parrot B.Sh 1559, E.Mch 2322, RR 81. [OF *papegai/papingai*]

par prep. (F, only in F phrases) by, by way of, for the sake of A.Mil 3839, A.Rv 4167, B.Sh 1205, B.Th 2010, 2081, C.Pard 606, D.Sum 2192. Cf. **paramour(s, pardee, parfay.**

paradys n. **1.** Paradise, Garden of Eden B.NP 4448, F.Fkl 912, I.Pars 325; *~ erthly* RR 648, *~ terrestre* E.Mch 1332. **2.** heaven B.Mel 2695, E.Mch 1964, HF 918. [OF]

parage n. birth, rank D.WB 250, 1120. [OF]

paraments/pare- n. pl. robes A.Kn 2501; tapestries LGW 1106; *chambre of ~* state room F.Sq 269. [OF]

paramour n.¹ mistress, concubine B.NP 4057, D.WB 454, 1372; lover TC 2.236. [as next]

paramour(s n.² love, love-making A.Mil 3354, 3756, A.Co 4372, B.Th 2033, E.Mch 1450; wenching A.Co 4392. [from next]

paramour(s adv. for love A.Kn 1155 (or as two words), B.Th 1933; with *love* amorously A.Kn 2112, TC 5.158, 332, LGW G. 260. [OF]

paraventure/per-, paraunter adv. perhaps A.Rv 3915, H.Mcp 71, BD 556, HF 304; by chance, as it happened E.Cl 234, TC 2.921. [OF]

par case see **per cas.**

parcel n. part F.Fkl 852, I.Pars 1006, Pity 106. [OF]

parchemin n. parchment Bo 5. m4. 9/12. [OF]

pardee interj. (by God) certainly, to be sure A.Prol 563, D.WB 200, TC 1.717, HF 134; **pardieux** TC 1.197. [OF]

pardoner n. pardoner, seller of indulgences A.Prol 543, C.Pard 318, HF 2127. [from next]

pardo(u)n 1. pardon, forgiveness B.Mel 2963, C.Pard 917, 926. **2.** papal indulgence A.Prol 687, C.Pard 920. [OF]

paregal adj. fully equal TC 5.840. [OF]

parements see **paraments.**

parentele *n.* kinship I.Pars 908. [OF]
parfay *interj.* by my faith, indeed A.Mil 3681, B.ML 1037, HF 938. [AN]
parfit *adj.* perfect, finished A.Prol 72, E.Mch 2383, PF 568, TC 1.104. [OF]
parfitly/-liche *adv.* perfectly D.WB 111, E.Mch 1834, Bo 3. m9. 12/16. [from prec.]
parfourne/-forme(n *v.* **1.** perform, carry out B.Mel 2256, E.Mch 2502, Bo 3. p3. 13/18, TC 3.417; express B.Pri 1646, 1797. **2.** fulfil B.Mk 3137, H.Mcp 190, I.Pars 981; ~ *up* complete D.Sum 2261. [OF]
parfourninge *vbl. n.* performance I.Pars 806.
parisshe *n.* parish A.Prol 449, *attrib.*: ~ *chirche* A.Mil 3307; ~ *clerk* A.Mil 3312, 3657; ~ *prest* B.Sh 1166, D.WB 532. [OF *paroisse*]
parisshens *n. pl.* parishioners A.Prol 482, 488. [OF *paroissiens*]
paritorie *n.* the herb pellitory G.CY 581 *var.* [AN *paritarie*]
parlement *n.* parliament, assembly A.Kn 3076, TC 4.143, 211; debate A.Kn 2970; decision A.Kn 1306; ~ *of Briddes* I.Pars 1086, ~ *of Foules* LGW 419. [OF]
parodie *n.* period, life TC 5.1548. [form of OF *periode*]
parsoners *n. pl.* partakers Bo 5. p5. 62/91 (L *participes*). [AN *parcener*]
part *n.* **1.** part (opp. whole) A.Kn 3006, F.Sq 40, Astr prol 74/102; *for the moore* ~ mostly A.Kn 2824, E.Mch 1231, TC 1.925; share A.Kn 1178, A.Co 4394, D.Sum 2225, TC 2.58; *an hondred* ~ a hundred times D.Sum 2062. **2.** side, party A.Kn 2185, Bo 1. p3. 25/35, TC 4. 1003; *for my* ~ LGW 912; *for thy* ~ TC 4.425; *have of my soule* ~ take the side of, protect, my soul A.Kn 2792. [OF]
parte(n *v.* **1.** depart C.Pard 649, 752, LGW 359, 1110. **2.** part A.Co 4362, TC 1.5; divide D.Sum 1967, I.Pars 8. **3.** share D.Fri 1534, Bo 1. p3.11/14, TC 1.589. [OF]
Parthes *n. pl.* Parthians C.Pard 622, Bo 2. p7. 45/64. [L *Parthi* from Gr]
party *adj.* in parts, variegated A.Kn 1053. [OF]
particuler *adj.* specialized E.Cl 35, F.Fkl 1122. [OF]
party(e *n.* **1.** part, division, A.Kn 3008, I.Pars 316, TC 2.394, Astr prol 19/25; part (of body) I.Pars 428, Bo 3. p10, 121/162; region (of the world) Bo 2. m6. 16/23. **2.** side B.Mel 2400, Bo 4. p3. 44/63, LGW G. 325; faction B.Mel 2204; partial judge A.Kn 2657. [OF]
parting *vbl. n.* departure B.ML 293, TC 3.1528.
partyng felawes *n. pl.* fellow-sharers I.Pars 637. [from **parte(n**]
partles *adj.* without a share Bo 4. p3. 27/39. [from **part**]
parvys *n.* forecourt (of St. Paul's, a meeting place of lawyers) A.Prol 310. [OF]
passant *adj.* leading A.Kn 2107. [OF]
passed *ppl. adj.* past TC 1.24, 3.1407; *time* ~ Bo 3. m2. 10/14, TC 5.746. [from next]
passe(n/pace *v.* **1.** *intr.* go, proceed A.Prol 36, B.Pri 1759, TC 2.80; pass by TC 5.1791 *var*; pass on A.Kn 1461, B.NP 4129; pass away, depart E.Cl 1092, I.Pars 458; ~

of pass over B.ML 205, F.Sq 288, LGW 1914, 2257; ~ *over* C.Pard 303, E.Mch 2115. **2.** *tr.* pass over TC 2.1595, 3.1576; endure B.Mel 2635. **3.** *intr.* go by, be finished A.Mil 3578, A.Rv 3879, B.Sh 1199, Bo 2. p1. 55/75, TC 5.1085; (of time) go by A.Rv 3889, B.ML 1143, B.Mk 3479, TC 5.681. **4.** *tr.* surpass A.Prol 574, B.NP 4501, E.Mch 1504, TC 4.1698, 5.838; exceed E.Mch 1417; go beyond B.Sh 1278, E.Mch 1252. **passed** *pa.* A.Prol 448, B.Pri 1738, TC 1.456; **paste** TC 2.398, 1260. **passed** *p.p.* TC 3.1628; **past** B.Mk 3479. [OF *passer*]
passing *ppl. adj.* extreme E.Mch 1225; excellent G.CY 614; transitory Bo 3. p8. 26/37. [from **passe(n**]
passioun *n.* **1.** suffering (esp. Christ's) A.Mil 3478, G.SN 26, I.Pars 275. **2.** emotion B.ML 1138, TC 4.705, LGW 259. [OF]
paste *see* **passe(n**.
pastee *n.* pasty, pie A.Co 4346. [OF]
patent *n.* letter of privilege A.Prol 315, C.Pard 337. [OF]
paternoster *n.* Lord's prayer I.Pars 508, 1039; as *interj.* A.Mil 3638; *develes* ~ muttered imprecations I.Pars 508. [L]
patrimoine *n.* patrimony I.Pars 790. [OF]
patron *n.*[1] pattern, model BD 910. [OF]
patro(u)n *n.*[2] patron, protector Mars 275, Anel 4. [OF]
paumes *n. pl.* palms TC 3.1114. [OF]
pax *n.* osculatory (used in the kiss of peace at Mass) I.Pars 407. [L]
pece *n.* piece I.Pars 356, PF 149. *pl.* fragments B.Sh 1326, TC 1.833; separate parts HF 1187. [AN]
pecok/pocok *n.* peacock A.Prol 104, PF 356, TC 1.210. [OE *pēa*, *pāwa + cocc*]
pecunial *adj.* monetary D.Fri 1314. [from L *pecūnia*]
pe(e)rt *adj.* forward, sprightly A.Rv 3950. [OF *apert*]
pees *n.* peace A.Prol 532, B.Mk 3524, PF 181, TC 4.1350; as *interj.* quiet B.ML 836, D.WB 850, PF 563, TC 3.1095; *hold (one's)* ~ keep quiet A.Kn 2668, C.Pard 462, PF 572. [OF]
peyne *n.* **1.** pain, suffering A.Kn 1319, C.Pard 511, TC 1.34; torment I.Pars 171 *var*; *dide* ~ tortured B.Mk 3794; *in the* ~ *under torture* A.Kn 1133, TC 1.674, 3.1502; *in her* ~*s* suffering TC 5.864; Passion B.Mel 2134; *of* ~ painful I.Pars 624. **2.** penalty, punishment D.Fri 1314, I.Pars 109, Bo 1. m5. 25/36; *up* ~ *of* under penalty of A.Kn 1707, D.Fri 1587, H.Mcp 86. **3.** endeavour, assiduity F.Sq 509; *do (one's)* ~ take trouble F.Fkl 730, H.Mcp 330, TC 2.475, 5.115 *var*. [OF]
peyne *v.* **1.** punish I.Pars 273. **2.** *refl.* take pains, make an effort A.Prol 139, B.NP 4495, C.Pard 330, PF 662, TC 5.75. [OF *peine*, pr. 3 sg. of *pener*]
peynted *ppl. adj.* deceptive TC 2.424. [from next]
peynte(n *v.* **1.** paint A.Kn 2087, C.Phs 34, TC 2.1041; smear LGW 875. **2.** adorn, beautify E.Mch 2062, I.Pars 610, 1022; disguise F.Sq 560. **peint** *p.p.* RR 1436. [OF *peindre*, p.p. *peint*]
peyntour *n.* painter TC 2.1041. [from prec.]

peynture n. painting C.Phs 33, Fort head, RR 142. [OF]

peyre n. pair A.Prol 473, D.WB 597, PF 595; (of armour, tablets) set A.Kn 2121, D.Sum 1741; (of beads) string, rosary A.Prol 159. [OF *paire*]

peytrel n. horse's breastplate G.CY 564, I.Pars 433. [AN]

pekke n. peck (a measure) A.Rv 4010. [AN]

pekke v. peck B.NP 4157. [form of *pick*, cf. **pike**]

pel n. peel, castle HF 1310. [OF]

pelet n. cannon-ball HF 1643. [OF *pelote*]

penant n. penitent B.Mk 3124. [OF]

penaunce n. **1.** penance (for sin) A.Prol 223, B.ML 991, I.Pars 105; do ~ I.Pars 104, LGW 479; self-abasement LGW 2077. **2.** suffering, misery B.ML 286, D.WB 727, TC 1.94; do ~ inflict pain (with indir. obj.) G. SN 530; disease Fort 36. [OF]

pencel n.[1] pencil, paintbrush A.Kn 2049. [OF]

pencel n.[2] pennon, streamer TC 5.1043. [AN]

peny n. **1.** penny C.Pard 376, D.Fri 1575, RR 246; for ~ ne for pound G.CY 707; masse ~ see **masse. 2.** money A.Rv 4119, pl. TC 3.1375/61; not a ~ F.Fkl 1616, RR 451. **pens** pl. C.Pard 376, 402, D.Fri 1576, 1599; **penyes** RR 189. [OE *pening*]

penible adj. ready to suffer B.Mk 3490; inured D.Sum 1846; anxious to please E.Cl 714. [OF]

penitauncer n. confessor who assigns a penance I.Pars 1008. [OF]

penitence n. **1.** penance I.Pars 102, 127; do ~ I.Pars 700, ABC 120. **2.** (being penitent) penitence I.Pars 81, 91. [OF]

penner n. pen-case E.Mch 1879. [ML *pennārium*]

pens see **peny.**

pensyf adj. sad F.Fkl 914 var. [OF]

peple n. **1.** people A.Prol 706, C.Phs 260, F.Sq 221, HF 360; common people, masses E.Cl 995, Bo 4. m5. 23/30 (L *uulgus*), TC 4. 183. **2.** army TC 1.73. **3.** nation B.ML 489; pl. Bo 2. m6. 10/14, FormA 2. **4.** subjects B.ML 942, B.Mel 2530, E.Cl 85; *Godes* ~ Jews B.Mk 3778, E.Mch 1367; ~ of God B.ML 942, E.Mch 1373. [OF]

per- see **par-.**

per/par cas, adv. by chance LGW 1967. [OF]

percely see **persly.**

perce(n v. pierce A.Prol 2, F.Sq 237, Astr 1.3.1/2; gaze through PF 331, TC 1.272. [OF]

perchaunce adv. (by chance) doubtless A.Prol 475. [OF]

percynge vbl. n. piercing B.Th 2052.

perdurable adj. (only in prose) eternal, everlasting B.Mel 2699, I.Pars 847, Bo 2. m3. 17/21; lyf ~ I.Pars 124, 184; imperishable Bo 1. p1. 15/21. pl. ~s I.Pars 811. [OF]

perdurabletee n. immortality Bo 2. p7. 63/91, 73/104. [OF]

perdurably adv. permanently Bo 3. p6. 23/31; eternally Bo 3. p11. 94/128, 142/193; **perdurablely** Bo 5. p4. 117/168 var. [from adj.]

pere n. equal A.Rv 4026, B.NP 4040, Purse 11. [OF]

pere-jonette n. early-ripening pear A.Mil 3248. [OE *pere*+OF *Jeannet* (as ripening by St. John's Day, 24 June)]

peril n. peril, danger A.Rv 3932, D.WB 89, TC 1.84; ~ of danger to D.WB 339; upon my ~ I assure you D.WB 561; up/on ~ of my lyf B.NP 4134, D.WB 1145, TC 4.113; up ~ of my soule B.NP 4134, E.Mch 2371. [OF]

perisse/perisshe v **1.** intr. perish C.Phs 99, I.Pars 254, Bo 2. p7. 7/9, 4. m4. 10/14. **2.** tr. destroy I.Pars 75, 579. [OF *périss-*, stem of *périr*]

perled adj. decorated (with pieces of) A.Mil 3251. [from OF *perle* pearl]

perpetuel n. perpetual, eternal I.Pars 137, Mars 47, Bo 5. p6. 70/98. [OF]

perpetuelly adv. for ever A.Kn 1024, G.SN 546, TC 3.1754. [from prec.]

perree/perrye n. jewellery A.Kn 2936, D.WB 344, LGW 1201. [OF *pierree, pierrerie*]

pers n. (Persian) blue A.Prol 439, 617. adj. RR 67. [OF]

perseverance n. continuance G.SN 443, TC 1.44; constancy BD 1007, BalCh 8. [OF]

persevere v. continue B.Mel 2454. C.Pard 497, TC 1.958. [OF *perseverer*]

perseveringe vbl. n. constancy G.SN 117.

persly/percely n. parsley A.Co 4350. [OE *petersilie*, OF *peresil*]

perso(u)n n.[1] person, individual B.Mk 3132, F.Sq 25, TC 2.168, 1487; any ~ anybody A.Prol 521, no ~ nobody B.Mel 2330; person, self I.Pars 519, 591; propre ~ own self B.Mel 2175, 2215, in (one's) propre ~ in person TC 2.1487, 4.83; with thy ~ yourself I.Pars 1032; Person, aspect of Godhead A.Kn 2725, G.SN 341. [OF]

perso(u)n n.[2] parson, parish priest A.Prol 478, A.Rv 3943, D.Fri 1313, D.Sum 2008, I.Pars 23. [AN, special use of prec.]

perspectives n. pl. optical glasses F.Sq 234 var. [OF]

pert see **pe(e)rt.**

pertinacie n. obstinacy I.Pars 391, 404. [from L *pertinācia*]

pertinent adj. suitable B.Mel 2204. [L *pertinent-*]

pervenke/-vynke n. periwinkle RR 903. [AN, from LL *pervinca*]

pesen n. pl. peas LGW 648. [OE *pisan*]

pesible/paisible adj. peaceful, calm Bo 1. p5. 2/3, FormA 1. [OF]

pestilence n. plague A.Kn 2469, C.Pard 679, (in curses) B.NP 4600, D.WB 1264; (fig.) curse, evil C.Phs 91, E.Mch 1793. [OF]

philosophical adj. fond of philosophy TC 5.1857. [prob. OF+*-al*]

philosophye n. philosophy A.Prol 295; alchemy G.CY 1058, 1139. [OF]

philosophre n. philosopher, learned writer B.ML 25, I.Pars 536, HF 758; alchemist, magician A.Prol 297, F.Fkl 1361, 1607, G.CY 837; ~s stoon G.CY 852; astrologer B.ML 310. [AN]

phisik n. medicine A.Prol 411, A.Kn 2760, TC 2.1038. [OF *phisique*]

phislyas n. ? medicine (by corruption of a misunderstood original, perh. Gr *physices* (Skeat)) B.Sh 1189 var.

pye n. magpie A.Rv 3950, E.Mch 1848, TC 3.527. [OF]

pietee n. pity TC 3.1033, 4.246, 731. [OF, var. of **pitee**]

piggesnye n. poppet A.Mil 3268. [OE *pigga* pig + eye]

pighte pa. 1. refl. pitched, landed A.Kn 2689. 2. pierced ABC 163. [OE *pihte* from *piccan*]

pyk n. pike (the fish) E.Mch 1419, TC 2.1041, Rosem 17. [from OE *pic* point]

pike v.[1] pick D.WB 44a, TC 2.1274, LGW 2467; pick over G.CY 941. [OE *pican*]

pike v.[2] peek, peep TC 3.60.[?] **pyked** adj. spiked, pointed D.Sum 1737 var. [prob. from ON *pík*]

pykepurs n. pickpocket, thief A.Kn 1998. [**pike** v.[1] + OE *purs*]

pikerel n. young pike E.Mch 1419. [from **pyk**]

pilche n. fur coat Prov 4. [OE *pylece*]

piled ppl. adj. hairless A.Prol 627; bald A.Rv 3935, 4306. [from v.]

pile(e)r n. pillar A.Kn 1993, BD 739, HF 1421; attrib. vine-prop PF 177. [AN]

pile(n v. plunder, rob D.Fri 1362, I.Pars 767, LGW 1262. [OE *pilian*]

pilgrim n. pilgrim A.Prol 26, A.Co 4349, TC 5.1577; traveller A.Kn 2848, HF 2122, Truth 18. [OF *pelegrin*]

pilours n. pl. robbers, scavengers A.Kn 1007, 1020, I.Pars 769. [from **pile(n**]

pilwe n. pillow E.Mch 2004, BD 254, TC 5.224. [OE *pylu*]

pilwe-beer n. pillow-case A.Prol 694. [see **bere** n.[2]]

piment n. spiced wine A.Mil 3378, Bo 2. m5. 6/9. [OF]

pin n.[1] pin, brooch A.Prol 196, 234; pin, bolt Astr 1.14.1/1, 2.38.5/8; peg F.Sq 127, 316; hangeth on a joly ~ is cheerfully tuned E.Mch 1516. [OE *pinn*]

pyn n.[2] pine (tree) Bo 2. m5. 13/18, RR 1379. [OE *pin*]

pinche(n v. 1. find fault A.Prol 326, H.Mcp 74, Fort 57; 2. pleat A.Prol 151. [ONF *pinchier*]

pyne n. suffering, misery A.Kn 1324, D.WB 787, TC 2.1165; torment: ~ of hell F.Sq 448, I.Pars 171 var; Passion: Goddes swete ~ B.Mel 2126, D.WB 385; harm PF 335. [OE *pin*]

pyne v. 1. tr. torture, torment A.Kn 1746, B.NP 4249, I.Pars 85. 2. intr. pine away, grieve Anel 205. [OE *pinian*]

pipe(n v. pipe, whistle A.Rv 3876, 3927, HF 1232; ~ in an ivy-leef see **ivy-leef**; squeak HF 785; pyping hot hissing A.Mil 3379. [OE *pipian*]

pyrie n. pear tree E.Mch 2217, 2325. [OE *pyrige*]

pissemyre n. ant D.Sum 1825. [from OF *pisser* + *mire* ant, prob. Scand]

pistel n. message D.WB 1021; epistle E.Cl 1154. [OE *pistol*]

pit/put n. pit A.Mil 3460, B.Pri 1761; helle ~ BD 171; ~ of helle I.Pars 170; TC 4.1540; grave E.Mch 1401, LGW 678. [OE *pytt*]

pit see **putte(n**.

pitaunce n. donation A.Prol 224. [OF]

pitee n. 1. pity, mercy A.Kn 920, B.ML 660, BD 97, Pity 1; han ~ (of) B.Mk 3231, Bo 4. p4. 187/257, LGW 1078; take(n ~ I.Pars 804; ~ renneth soone in gentil herte A.Kn 1761, E.Mch 1986, F.Sq 479, LGW 503. 2. sad (event) F.Fkl 1431, LGW 1976; it is ful gret ~ F.Fkl 1428; (it) ~ was Mars 135, TC 2.1577, HF 180. Cf. **pietee**. [OF *pité*]

pith n. vigour D.WB 475, RR 401. [OE *piþa*]

pitous adj. 1. piteous, sad A.Kn 955, B.NP 4213, RR 420; distressing E.Cl 1086, TC 3.918; pitiable C.Phs 166. 2. compassionate, tender-hearted A.Prol 143, A.Kn 953, Anel 9, merciful F.Sq 20, TC 4.949. 3. pious, devout I.Pars 1039. [OF]

pitously adv. 1. pitiably, wretchedly A.Kn 949, E.Cl 1082, TC 2.1076. 2. mercifully Pity 18, TC 5.1424. [from prec.]

place n. 1. place, residence A.Prol 607, D.Sum 1768; ? manor-house, ? marketplace B.Th 1910; lists A.Kn 2399. 2. rank, social position D.WB 1164. [OF]

plages n. pl. regions B.ML 543, Astr 1.5.8/11, 2.31.11/15. [OF]

plastres n. pl. plasters, dressings F.Sq 636. [OE]

plat adj. flat, certain A.Kn 1845; ~ swerd flat of the sword F.Sq 164; as n. F.Sq 162. [OF]

plat adv. flatly, bluntly C.Pard 648, TC 1.681; ~ and pleyn B.ML 886, B.Mk 3947; flat (on his face) B.Pri 1865. [from prec.]

plate n. plate (-armour) A.Kn 2121, B.Th 2055, FormA 49; (metal) sheeting I.Pars 433; sheet of metal Astr 1.3.1/2, 13.2. [OF]

plated adj. overlaid HF 1345. [from prec.]

platly adv. utterly I.Pars 485; directly, bluntly I.Pars 1022, TC 3.786; plainly TC 4.924. [from **plat** adj.]

pla(u)nte n. slip, cutting D.WB 763; slip of wood RR 929; plant F.Fkl 1032, TC 4.767. [OE and OF *plante*]

ple n. plea, appeal PF 485; lawsuit PF 101. [AN, = OF *plaid*]

plede/plete(n v. go to law TC 2.1468; dispute B.Mel 2559; reason Bo 2. p2.5/7. [OF *plaidier/plaitier*]

pleding(e/pletyng(e vbl. n. pleading I.Pars 166; argument BD 615, PF 495; lawsuit Bo 3. p3. 49/64.

pledoures n. pl. lawyers RR 198. [from **plede**]

plegges n. pl., pledges, sureties B.Mel 3018. [OF *plege*]

pley n. 1. play, sport PF 193; childes ~ E.Mch 1530; game E.Cl 10; games (funeral) A.Kn 2964, TC 5.1499. 2. amusement C.Pard 627, Mars 178; jest, joking A.Kn 1125, A.Mil 3773; sooth ~ quaad ~ a true jest is a bad jest A.Co 4357; in ernest or in ~ A.Kn 1125. 3. play: ~es of miracles D.WB 558. 4. performance BD 648; contrivance BD 570. [OE *plega*]

pleye(n v. 1. play, amuse oneself A.Kn 1127, A.Rv 4098, B.Mk 3666, TC 2.812, 5.1174, refl. A.Kn 1503, B.Sh 1527, F.Fkl 905, TC 5.431; play amorously A.Mil 3273, 3686, RR 1422; refl. E.Mch 1841, 2135; joke C.Pard 778, E.Mch 1389, BD 850. 2. play ((at) a game) F.Fkl 900, BD 51, TC 4.460, enjoy, take pleasure in B.Sh 1423; ((on) an instrument) A.Prol 236, A.Co 4396, H.Mcp 113, TC 3.614. 3. perform F.Fkl 1141. 4. act (the part of) A.Mil 3384, (fig.) TC 1.1074, 2.1240. [OE *plegan*]

pleying vbl. n. amusement A.Kn 1061, LGW 1469, RR105; love-play E.Mch 1854.

pleyn adj.¹ **1.** clear A.Kn 1487, B.Mk 3471, G.SN 284, LGW 328; as n. plain fact A.Kn 1091; open C.Phs 50, Anel 116; ~ sentence clear meaning PF 126. **2.** unadorned F.Fkl 720, in short and ~ briefly and simply E.Cl 577; sincere Anel 87; smooth RR 860 em. **3.** level with the ground H.Mcp 229. [OF plain]

pleyn adv.¹ plainly, clearly A.Prol 790, E.Cl 19, G.SN 360; plat and ~ see **plat** adv.; openly E.Cl 637, F.Sq 151. [from prec.]

pleyn adj.² complete, full A.Prol 315, 337, B.ML 324, E.Cl 926, G.SN 346; ~ felicitee ABC 13,T C 5.1818. [OF plein]

pleyn adv.² fully A.Prol 327. [from prec.]

pleyne(n v. **1.** complain A.Kn 1251, F.Fkl 1317, TC 1.409; ~ (up)on make complaint against C.Phs 167, D.Fri 1313, TC 3.1020; refl. D.WB 336, Bo 2. p2. 18/26. **2.** mourn, lament F.Fkl 819, PF 179, TC 5.985; wepe and ~ A.Kn 1320, B.Mk 3819, Pity 118; whinny Anel 157. [OF plaign-, stem of plaindre]

pleynesse n. level surface Bo 5. m4. 12/17. [from **pleyn** adj.¹]

pleyning(e vbl. n. lament I.Pars 84, BD 599, Bo 2. p2. 4/5.

pleynly/-liche adv.¹ clearly B.ML 894, G.CY 1057, Bo 3. p12. 17/21 (L planius); simply I.Pars 803, Bo 4. p2. 143/194 (L simpliciter), TC 2.1623; candidly, frankly A.Prol 727, E.Mch 1316, TC 1.395, 2.1126; distinctly TC 2.272 (perh. next), LGW 123; openly LGW 64. [from **pleyn** adj.¹]

pleynly adv.² fully A.Kn 1733, B.ML 880, I.Pars 304, 1017, Bo 1. p6. 54/69 (L plenissime). [from **pleyn** adj.²]

pleynte n. complaint B.ML 66, Bo 2. m2. 6/9, TC 1.408, 544; ~ of kinde (de planctu Naturae) PF 316. [OF]

plenere adj. full LGW 1607. [OF plener]

plentee n. plenty, abundance E.Cl 264, I.Pars 1080, Bo 3. p3. 37/48; (vitaille) greet ~ (food) in large quantities B.ML 443, C.Pard 811. [OF]

plentevous adj. plentiful A.Prol 344; fruitful, fertile Bo 1. p1. 40/55, m2. 17/24. [OF]

plentivously adv. abundantly, amply Bo 4. p6. 120/174. [from prec.]

plesa(u)nce n. **1.** pleasure, delight A.Kn 1571, D.WB 1232, TC 3.4; amusement F.Fkl 713; happiness A.Kn 2485; pleasing C.Pard 400, do (one) ~ give pleasure (to), try to please D.Sh 1381, D.WB 1736, E.Cl 1111, TC 3.971, give (one) the pleasure or satisfaction E.Mch 1612, sim. F.Fkl 1199, TC 5.314. **2.** desire E.Cl 305, PF 389, Rosem 22; will B.ML 762; do (someone's) ~ do as (someone) wishes B.NP 4056, E.Cl 658. **3.** pleasingness B.Mel 2369, H.Mcp 157, Anel 248; pleasantness Mars 238. [OF]

plesa(u)nt adj. pleasant A.Prol 138, B.Mel 2341, RR 1031; pleasing E.Mch 1621, G.CY 1014, I.Pars 850. [OF]

plese(n v. please A.Prol 610, E.Cl 665, TC 1.45, (with to of person) I.Pars 923. [OF plaisir]

plesinges vbl. n. pl. pleasures B.ML 711.

plete(n see **plede**; **pletyng(e** see **pledinge**.

plye v.¹ bend E.Cl 1169; shape E.Mch 1430. [OF plier]

plye v.² handle TC 1.732. [apheticfrom **applyen**]

plighte v. pledge: ~ (one's) trouthe give (one's) word, B.Sh 1388, C.Pard 702, D.WB 1009, TC 4.1610. **plighte** pa. sg. D.WB 1051, LGW 2466. **plighten** pl. F.Fkl 1328, LGW 778. **plight** p.p. C.Pard 702, Anel 227; yplight TC 3.782. [OE plihtan]

plighte pa. plucked TC 2.1120; pulled B.ML 15. **plight** p.p. B.Mk 3239, D.WB 790. [from OE *plyċċan, cf. **plukke**]

plyt n. position I.Pars 762, TC 2.74, 3.246, 1039; condition, state B.Mel 2338, E.Mch 2335, G.CY 952; plight Anel 297, PF 294, TC 2.1731, 1738. [AN, = ONF pleit fold]

plyte v. fold TC 2.1204; (fig.) turn over TC 2.697; pleat Bo 1. p2. 19/28. [cf. prec.]

plomet n. plummet Astr 2.23.26/39. [OF]

plom-rule n. plumb-rule Astr 2.38.6/9. [OF plomme+riule]

ploungen v. plunge, bathe (only in Bo, = mergere) Bo 1. p1. 55/76, 3. m8. 16/22, 4. m6. 10/15. [OF plungier]

ploungy adj. stormy Bo 1. m3. 6/8, 3. m1. 6/8. [from prec.]

plowmes n. pl. plums RR 1375. [OE plüme]

plukke v. pluck: ~ by the sleeve TC 4. 1403; ~ up cheer up G.CY 937. [LOE pluccian]

pocok see **pecok**.

poeplish† adj. vulgar TC 4.1677. [from **peple**]

poesye n. poetry TC 5.1790. [OF]

poetrye n. poetry, fiction E.Cl 33, TC 5.1855, HF 858; pl. poems F.Sq 206, HF 1478. [OF]

Poil(l)eys adj. Apulian F.Sq 195. [AN]

poyna(u)nt adj. **1.** pungent A.Prol 352, B.NP 4024. **2.** piercing I.Pars 130-2. [OF]

poynt n. **1.** point (sharp end) A.Prol 114, G.SN 440, LGW 1795 var, Astr 2.3.9/13; (of compass) Astr 2.5.7/10; (tagged) lace A.Mil 3322; (fig.) purpose, essence A.Prol 790, A.Kn 1501; to the ~ A.Kn 2965, B.Sh 1503, LGW 1634. **2.** spot Bo 4. m5. 2/3, Astr 1.18.12/16; full stop G.CY 1480; position I.Pars 921; mid ~ BD 660; in ~ to just about to B.ML 910, BD 13, ABC 48; o ~ ready TC 4.1153, 1638, 5.1285. **3.** detail B.Mel 2488, TC 1.891, 3.695 (or 'note of music'), LGW 2543; not a ~ TC 3.1509; fro ~ to ~ beginning to end A.Mk 3652, C.Phs 150, PF 461; at ~ devys to the last detail, carefully A.Mil 3689, F.Sq 560, HF 917; in good ~ healthy A.Prol 200, safe and well Bo 2. p4. 19/25 (L incolumis). [OF]

poynte v. **1.** describe in detail TC 3.497. **2.** stab RR 1058. [OF pointer]

pointel n. stylus, writing instrument D.Sum 1742, Bo 1. p1. 2/3. [OF]

poke n. bag: pigges in a ~ A.Rv 4278; money-bag A.Mil 3780. [ONF poque]

pokettes n. pl. little bags G.CY 808. [AN]

pokkes n. pl. pocks, pox C.Pard 358. [OE poccas]

pol n.¹ stick LGW 2202. [OE pāl]

pol n.² see **po(o)l**.

policye n. public business C.Pard 600. [OF]

polyve n. pulley F.Sq 184. [OF]

pollut *p.p.* polluted Bo 1. p4. 180/252. [L *pollūtus*]

pome garnettys *n. pl.* pomegranates RR 1356. [OF]

pomel *n.* knob, top A.Kn 2689. [OF]

pomely *adj.* dappled A.Prol 616, G.CY 559. [OF *pomelé*]

po(o)l *n.*² pole (of the sky) Bo 4. m5. 3/4, Astr 1.18.13/18, 2.26.23/34; ~ *artik* North Astr 1.14.6/8, 2.22.2/3; ~ *antartik* South Astr 2.25.7/9. [OF]

Po(o)pe-holy *adj.* as *n.* (sanctimonious) Hypocrisy RR 415 (F *Papelardie*). [*pope* from OE *pāpa*+**ho(o)ly**]

popelote† *n.* pet, sweetie A.Mil 3254. [OF]

popet *n.* pet B.Th 1891. [rel. to L *puppa* doll]

popynjay *see* **papejay.**

poplexie *n.* apoplexy B.NP 4031 *var.* [misdivision of **apoplexie**]

popped *pa. refl.* made up (her) face RR 1019. [OF *popiner*]

poppere *n.* little dagger A.Rv 3931. [OF]

poraille *n.* poor people, paupers, A.Prol 247. [OF *povraille*]

porcioun *n.* part Bo 2. p5. 41/57, Astr 2.4. 40/62, share Bo 3. p5. 16/22; quantity B.Sh 1246. [OF]

porisme *n.* corollary Bo 3. p10. 100/134. [L *porisma*]

porphurie/porfurie *n.* porphyry (slab) G.CY 775. [OF]

port *n.* bearing, manner A.Prol 69, PF 262, TC 1.1084. [OF]

portatif *adj.* portable Astr prol 52/73, 2.3.53/78. [OF]

porthors *n.* portas, portable breviary B.Sh 1321, 1325. [OF]

portreye/pur- *v.* draw A.Prol 96, BD 783; adorn with pictures RR 140; (fig.) picture to oneself, imagine E.Mch 1600, TC 5.716. [OF]

portreying *vbl. n.* painting A.Kn 1938.

portreiture *n.* painting, portrayal A.Kn 1968, 2036, BD 626, RR 172; *pl.* pictures A.Kn 1915, HF 125, RR 141. [OF]

pose *n.* cold in the head H.Mcp 62; *on the* ~ suffering from a cold A.Rv 4152. [OE (*ge)pos*]

pose *v.* suppose, put the case A.Kn 1162, Bo 4. p6. 132/192, TC 3.310, 571. [OF]

positive *adj.* (of law) enacted A.Kn 1167. [OF]

possessioun *n.* **1.** possession, act of possessing A.Kn 2242, F.Fkl 686, Bo 2. p5. 94/131. **2.** goods, things possessed (*sg.*) TC 2.1419, (*pl.*) B.Mel 2739, I.Pars 775. [OF]

possessioners *n. pl.* clerics with endowments D.Sum 1722. [from prec. (1)]

posseth *pr.* 3 *sg.* tosses LGW 2420. **possed** *p.p.* TC 1.415. [perh. modified from OF *pousser*]

possible *adj.* possible B.Sh 1222, LGW 1020; ~ *is* it is possible A.Kn 1240, B.ML 1031. [OF]

post *n.* post A.Prol 800; (fig.) prop, support A.Prol 214, TC 1.1000. [OE]

postum *n.* abscess Bo 3. p4. 9/12. [OF *apostume*]

potage *n.* broth B.Mk 3623, C.Pard 368. [OF]

potente *n.* staff D.Sum 1776, crutch TC 5.1222, RR 368. [OF *potence*]

potestat *n.* magistrate D.Sum 2017. [OF from L *potestāt-*]

pothecarie *see* **apot(h)ecarie.**

pouche *n.* pocket A.Rv 3931, HF 1349; moneybag A.Prol 368. [ONF]

poudre *n.* powder G.CY 760, 807; dust TC 5.309, HF 536. [OF]

poudre-marchant *n.* a sharp spice A.Prol 381.

pounage *n.* pig-food FormA 7. [OF *pasnage*]

poune *n.* pawn (in chess) BD 661. [OF]

pounsoned *ppl. adj.* pounced, ornamented with holes I.Pars 421. [OF *poinsonner*]

pounsoninge† *vbl. n.* pouncing, punching holes I.Pars 418.

pouped *pa., p.p.* puffed B.NP 4589, H.Mcp 90. [imit.]

poure *see* **povre.**

poure(n *v.* look closely, pore ((*up*)*on*) A.Prol 185, TC 2.1708, peer (*in*) G.CY 670, ~ *and prye* D.Sum 1738, (absol.) E.Mch 2112; (with cl.) strain to see HF 1121. [? OE *pūrian*]

pous *n.* pulse TC 3.1114. [OF]

poustee *n.* power Bo 4. p5. 9/12. [OF]

poverest *see* **povre.**

poverte *n.* poverty (rhyming with *herte, sherte*) B.ML 99, D.WB 1185, TC 4.1520; C.Pard 441, HF 88. **povertee** (rhyming with *bee*) BD 410. [OF]

povre/poure *adj.* poor: **1.** (indigent) A.Prol 225, B.NP 4011, E.Cl 1043, RR 61; as *n.pl., the* ~ D.WB 109, I.Pars 419, 708; as *n.* poverty Fort 2. **poverest** *sup.* C.Pard 449, E.Cl 205. **2.** miserable, unhappy LGW 1981. **3.** humble C.Phs 179. [OF]

povrely *adv.* like a poor person, poorly A.Kn 1412, E.Cl 213, RR 219; in a humble station A.Kn 1554. [from prec.]

practik *n.* practice D.WB 44d, 187; practical application Astr prol 51/70. [OF *practique*]

practisour *n.* practitioner A.Prol 422. [from v., OF *practiser*]

pray *see* **preye.**

praye *see* **preye(n.**

preambulacioun *n.* making a preamble D.WB 837. [from ML *preambulāre*]

precedent *adj.* previous Astr 2.32.3/4. [L]

precept *n.* command, ruling B.Mk 3247, D.WB 65. [OF]

preche *v.* preach A.Prol 481, C.Pard 329, TC 2.59. **precheth** *imper. pl.* E.Cl 12. [OF]

prechour *n.* preacher, advocate D.WB 165. [OF]

precious *adj.* **1.** precious, costly B.Mel 2830, D.WB 338, I.Pars 414; ~ *stone* jewel Bo 2. p5. 27/37, RR 1095. **2.** prized, dear E.Mch 1347, I.Pars 598, Bo 2. p1. 54/74; ~ *body* (of Christ) I.Pars 267; ~ *blood* I.Pars 132, ABC 59. **3.** dainty, fastidious, fussy D.WB 148, E.Mch 1962. [OF]

preciously *adv.* expensively D.WB 500. [from prec.]

predestinacioun *n.* foreordaining Bo 4. p6. 19/28. [OF]

predestinat *ppl. adj.* foreordained Bo 5. p2. 33/47 (L *praedestinata*).

predestinee *n.* predestination TC 4.966. [OF]

predicacioun *n.* preaching, sermon B.Sh 1176, C.Pard 345, D.Sum 2109. [OF] preef/preve/proeve *n.* **1.** proof D.Sum 2272, PF 497, LGW 28. **2.** test, trial E.Cl 787, G.CY 968, H.Mcp 75; ~ *of armes* test of prowess TC 1.470; *found at* ~ proved by trial TC 3.1002, 4.1659. **3.** experience B.NP 4173, LGW G. 528; *with yvel* ~ as *interj.* ill fortune to you! D.WB 247, *have ye good* ~ may you succeed G.CY 1379. [OF]

prees/presse *n.* **1.** (usu. **prees**) crowd B.ML 393, D.WB 522, TC 1.173, 2.1718, Truth 1; *put (forth) in* ~ thrust forward Scog 40, *refl.* PF 603, strive FormA 33; difficulty, stress B.Mk 3327. **2.** (usu. **presse**) press, device for pressing A.Prol 81; mould A.Prol 263. **3.** cupboard A.Mil 3212; (fig.) *leye on* ~ put away TC 1.559. [OF *presse*]

pre(e)sse(n/presen *v.* **1.** crowd, push forward A.Kn 2530, Pity 19, TC 1.446, LGW 642; hurry TC 2.1341. **2.** press, weigh down on LGW 1787, Bo 3. p11. 99/136. [OF]

pre(e)ve(n/proeve(n/prove(n *v.* **1.** prove A.Kn 3001, C.Phs 169, PF 534, TC 4.969, HF 707; ascertain, establish Astr 2.23. 25/37. **2.** approve Bo 5. p3. 19/25. **3.** test B.Mel 2627, E.Cl 1152, BD 552, TC 3.1048, LGW 9. **4.** prove true E.Mch 2425, TC 1.239; turn out A.Prol 547, G.CY 645; succeed G.CY 1212; *yvele* ~ be found wanting E.Cl 1000. [OF *prueve* and *prover*]

preferre *pr. subj. sg.* take precedence over D.WB 96. [OF *preferer*]

preye/pray *n.* prey A.Kn 2015, D.Fri 1455, TC 1.201; *pl.* D.Fri 1472. [OF]

preye(n/praye *v.* **1.** pray A.Prol 301, B.Pri 1877, D.Sum 1745, TC 1.48; ~ *to God* A.Rv 3918, B.ML 160, D.WB 826. **2.** beseech A.Prol 811, I.Pars 66, PF 543, TC 2.1451; *I* ~ *the/yow* A.Prol 725, B.NP 4083, TC 1.760; ~ (someone) *of* beg . . to do I.Pars 880. **3.** invite E.Cl 269. [OF]

preyere *n.* **1.** prayer (request) A.Kn 1204, H.Mcp 6, I.Pars 784, LGW 1141. **2.** prayer (act of praying) A.Mil 3587, I.Pars 1047; *pl.* devotions A.Prol 231, I.Pars 382; *sey his* ~ I.Pars 708. [OF]

preignant *adj.* cogent, telling TC 4.1179. [OF]

preying *vbl. n.* request TC 1.571, RR 1484.

preyneth *pr. 3 sg.* preens E.Mch 2011. [? rel. to OF *prẽon* pin]

preise(n *v.* **1.** praise B.Mel 2365, D.WB 294, TC 1.189, LGW 536; *to* ~ to be praised B.Mel 2706. **2.** appraise, value Bo 3. p11. 3/4, RR 1693. [OF *preisier*]

preiseres *n. pl.* praisers B.Mel 2367. [from prec.]

preisinge *vbl. n.* praising B.Mel 2209 (*of* 'for') Bo 1. p4. 159/221, TC 2.1589; glory (object of praise) I.Pars 949; *pl.* praises I.Pars 454, HF 635.

prelat *n.* church dignitary A.Prol 204, C.Pard 310. [OF]

prenostik *n.* omen Fort 54. [ML]

prente *n.* print D.WB 604. [OF]

prenten *v.* imprint TC 2.900. [from prec.]

prentis *n.* apprentice A.Co 4365, 4385, B.Sh 1490. [aphetic form of **apprentice**].

prentishood *n.* apprenticeship A.Co 4400. [prec.+ OE *-hād*]

presen *see* pre(e)sse(n.

presence *n.* **1.** presence (in space) A.Kn 927, G.CY 991, TC 5.233; *in* ~ in public E.Cl 1207; *in heigh* ~ before God B.ML 675. **2.** presentness (in time) Bo 5. p6. 53/74, 192/270. [OF]

present *n.* **1.** present time Bo 5. p6. 91/129. **2.** gift F.Sq 174, LGW 1935, RR 1192. [OF]

present *adj.* **1.** present E.Cl 80, Bo 1. p4. 141/195, TC 3.45; *this* ~ *life* I.Pars 186, 191, Bo 2. p4. 130/181. **2.** as *adv.* immediately A.Kn 1738, PF 423. [OF]

presentary *adj.* ever-present Bo 5. p6. 49/69, 73/103, 202/284 (L *praesentarius*).

presente *v.* present, offer C.Phs 256, LGW 1297, (as parliamentary term) PF 531. [OF]

presently *adv.* at the present time Bo 4. p6. 60/86, 5. p6. 78/109. [from adj.]

presse *see* prees; presse(n *see* pre(e)sse(n.

prest *n.* priest A.Prol 501, G.CY 840, I.Pars 318; *parish* ~ D.WB 532; (as term of address) *sire* ~ G.CY 1205, I.Pars 22; *sir parish* ~ B.Sh 1166. [OE *prẽost*]

prest *adj.* ready, prompt PF 307, TC 2.785, 5.800. [OF]

pretende *v.* aim TC 4.922. [OF *pretendre*]

pretorie *n.* Pretorian guard Bo 1. p4. 61/85. [OF]

preve *see* preef.

previdence *n.* foresight Bo 5. p6. 83/116 (L *praeuidentia*).

pricasour *n.* hard rider A.Prol 189. [from prik(k)en]

pridelees *adj.* without pride, unassuming E.Cl 930, CompL 26. [cf. next]

pride(n *v. refl.* (with *in*) feel proud (because of) I.Pars 456, 460. [from *pride* n., LOE *prýde*]

prye(n *v.* pry, peer D.Sum 1738, G.CY 668, TC 2.404; gaze A.Mil 3458; spy TC 2.1710. [?]

prighte *see* prik(k)e(n.

priking *vbl. n.* (hard) riding A.Kn 2599, B.Th 1965; tracking (a hare) by footprints A.Prol 191; (*pl.*) puncturings Bo 1. p1. 38/53.

prikke *n.* **1.** dot, speck, Bo 2. p7. 30/43, HF 907, Astr 2.5.12/18, 7.3/4; point, in *that* ~ B.ML 119, 1029. **2.** stab A.Kn 2606; sting I.Pars 468. *pl.* Bo 3. p5. 21/30 (L *aculeos*). [OE *prica*]

prik(k)e(n *v.* **1.** prick B.Mel 2516, E.Mch 1635; pierce A.Rv 4231; (fig.) incite, stimulate A.Prol 11, PF 389, TC 1.219, 4.633; goad, torment E.Cl 1038; *pr. 3 sg. impers.* is painful D.Fri 1594. **2.** spur, ride fast A.Kn 2678, B.Th 2001, G.CY 561, LGW 1213. **prighte** *pa.* F.Sq 418, ABC 163em. [OE *prician*]

prime *n.* time of day, usu. 9 a.m., A.Kn 2189, B.NP 4368, TC 2.992; ~ *of day* B.Sh 1396, B.Th 2015; ~ *large* past 9 o'clock F.Sq 360; *half way* ~ 7.30 a.m. A.Rv 3906; (transf.) beginning TC 1.157. [OE *prim*]

prymer *n.* school reading-book B.Pri 1707, 1731. [AN]

prymerole *n.* primrose, pretty little thing A.Mil 3268. [OF]

principal *adj.* principal A.Kn 1937, C.Pard 432, Astr 1.17.34/45; (following noun) A.Kn 1498, C.Phs 19, BD 1004; **principales, -x** *pl.* Astr 1.5.8/11, 2.31.11/15. [OF]

principles *n. pl.* natural disposition F.Sq 487, Bo 3. m11. 16/21. [AN var. of OF *principe*]

prys *n.* **1.** price A.Prol 815, Bo 1. p4. 56/78; value B.Mel 2286, D.WB 523, Bo 1. p5. 30/44; *of* ∼ excellent B.Th 2087. **2.** worth F.Fkl 911, RR 45; esteem D.WB 1152, F.Fkl 934, I.Pars 477, TC 1.375, 2.24, RR 300; praise Bo 3. p11. 5/6, TC 2.1585, fame, honour A.Kn 2241, reputation, renown A.Prol 67. **3.** prize A.Prol 237, LGW 298. [OF *pris*]

pryse *n.* booty, prey I.Pars 355. [OF *prise*]

priso(u)n *n.* prison A.Kn 1023; imprisonment A.Kn 2457, captivity B.Mk 3263, B.NP 4087. [AN *prisun*]

pryved *p.p.* exiled, shut out ABC 146 *var.* [from OF *priver*]

privee *n.* privy, latrine E.Mch 1954. [next]

prive(e *adj.* **1.** secret A.Kn 2460, B.Pri 1758, G.CY 1452, TC 3.787, 921; secretive A.Mil 3201; stealthy C.Pard 675. **2.** private E.Mch 1813, I.Pars 102, Bo 2. p3. 48/69; confidential, personally attending E.Cl 192, 519; ∼ *members* I.Pars 424. **3.** as *adv.* see **apert.** [OF]

prively *adv.* secretly, stealthily A.Prol 609, B.NP 4209,TC. 1.80, LGW 733; **privelich** TC 4.1601 *var.* [from **prive(e**]

privetee *n.* **1.** secrecy TC 3.283; confidence A.Co 4334, TC 2.1397; *in* ∼ secretly A.Mil 3623, B.Sh 1422, D.Sum 2143, *in hir* ∼ B.ML 548, in private E.Cl 249; *of* ∼ private A.Co 4388; secret D.WB 542. **2.** secrets, private affairs A.Kn 1411, A.Mil 3164 (pun on next sense), G.CY 1138, D.WB 531; private parts B.Mk 3905; *pl.* secret places Bo 2. p6. 29/41. [OF]

proces *n.* **1.** process, course A.Kn 2967, F.Sq 658, F.Fkl 829, *by* ∼ in course of time TC 4.418; ∼ *of time* B.Mel 2665, BD 1331; ∼ *of nature* F.Fkl 1345; proceedings, business TC 3.334; course of events B.Mk 3511. **2.** story TC 2.424, HF 251; discourse TC 2.268, 292; argument Bo 3. p10. 40/56; plea, suit TC 2.1615. [OF]

procu(ra)tour *n.* agent, lawyer D.Fri 1596 *var.* [OF]

procure *v.* bring about I.Pars 973. [OF *procurer*]

procuringe *vbl. n.* contriving I.Pars 784, 974.

proef, proeve(n *see* **preef, pre(e)ve(n.**

professioun *n.* taking of vows in a religious order B.Sh 1345, D.Sum 2135; vows D.Sum 1925. [OF]

profit *n.* profit, advantage A.Prol 249; *commune* ∼ see **com(m)une;** *to do(n (one's)* ∼ pursue, work for, one's profit B.Mel 2778, 2782. [OF]

profiteth *pr. 3 sg.* does good (*to*) Bo 2. p8. 8/12; is of advantage Bo 4. p7. 24/35, 26/38. [OF *profiter*]

profre *n.* offer E.Cl 154, LGW 2079, 2094 *var.* [AN]

profre *v.* proffer, offer E.Cl 848, G.CY 1123, LGW 1312; *refl.* LGW 405, press one's suit A.Mil 3289. **profrestow** *pr. 2 sg.* (with suffixed pron.) TC 3.1461. [AN *profrir*]

progressiouns *n. pl.* progressions Bo 4. p6. 30/43, 105/152; processes A.Kn 3013. [OF]

proheme/prohemye *n.* proem, prologue E.Cl 43 *var.* [OF]

prolaciouns *n. pl.* melodies Bo 2. p1. 32/45. [from L *prolation-*]

prolle *v.* search around G.CY 1412. [?]

pronounce *v.* state, declare C.Pard 335, G.CY 1299, PF 559, TC 4.213. [OF *pronuncier*]

pronouncere *n.* speaker Bo 2. p3. 39/56. [from prec.]

proporcionables *adj. pl.* proportional Bo 3. m9. 13/18. [OF]

proporcioneles *n. pl.* proportionate parts F.Fkl 1278. [OF]

propre *adj.* **1.** own A.Prol 540, B.Mk 3518, D.WB 159, I.Pars 1021, Bo 3. p4. 49/71; *in* ∼ as his own Bo 2. p2. 9/12; special D.WB 103, peculiar, characteristic F.Sq 610, Bo 2. p1. 38/53; usual TC 4.1152; ∼ *name* C.Pard 417, ∼ *nature* Bo 5. p5. 27/38, p6. 150/189, ∼ *kinde* F.Sq 610, 619, Bo 3. m2. 37/40, HF 43, ∼ *person* see **perso(u)n.** **2.** handsome A.Mil 3345, A.Co 4368, fine A.Rv 3972, C.Pard 309; real, true LGW G. 259. [OF]

proprely *adv.* appropriately A.Prol 729, A.Kn 2787, I.Pars 485; properly, correctly A.Kn 1459, D.WB 224, H.Mcp 209; *to speke* ∼ B.Mel 2429. [from prec.]

propretee *n.* **1.** nature, quality, peculiarity B.Mel 2363, B.NP 4142, Fort 69. **2.** ownership TC 4.392. [OF]

prospectives *n. pl.* magic glasses (?for foreseeing the future; but prob. an error for **perspectives,** see *OED*) F.Sq 234 *var.* [OF]

prospre *adj.* prosperous Bo 1. p4. 41/57. [OF]

prove(n *see* **pre(e)ve(n.**

proverbed *p.p.* spoken in a proverb TC 3.293. [from *proverbe* n. from OF]

provost *n.* chief magistrate B.Pri 1806, 1819; prefect, ruler Bo 1. p4. 43/59, 61/85. [OE *profost*]

provostrie *n.* praetorship Bo 3. p4. 56/81. [from prec.]

prow *n.* profit, advantage B.Sh 1598, B.NP 4140, TC 1.333, HF 579. [OF]

prowesse/pruesse *n.* bravery, valour TC 1.438, 2.660; excellence, virtue D.WB 1129 (= Dante's *probitate*), Bo 4. p3. 45/64, p4.201/281 (L *probitas*). [OF *proesce*]

Pruce *adj.* Prussian A.Kn 2122. [AN]

publisshen/pup- *v.* make known, spread abroad Bo 2. p7. -/44 (L *peruulganda*); *refl.* propagate themselves Bo 3. p11. 91/124 (L *propagentur*). **publiced/-lisshed** *p.p.* made public E.Cl 415, TC 5.1095 *var.* [from OF *publier,* infl. by vs. with stems in *-iss-* as **punysshe]**

pull *n.* bout of wrestling PF 164. [from next]

pulle(n *v.* **1.** pull A.Kn 1598, D.Sum 2069, LGW 2308. **2.** pluck A.Mil 3245, H.Mcp 304, TC 5.1546; ∼ *a finch* 'pluck a bird', i.e. copulate with a girl A.Prol 652. [OE *pullian*]

punysshe/punysche/punysse *v.* punish B.Mel 2631, Bo 1. p4. 171/239, TC 5.1095 *var,* 1707. [OF *puniss-,* stem of *punir*]

purchace(n *v.* **1.** get, acquire I.Pars 742, TC 2.713, 4.557, gain (for a consideration) I.Pars 1080; (absol.) buy, acquire possessions A.Prol 608. **2.** provide B.ML 873; ∼ *yow* (with *of* var) provide for yourself

TC 2.1125. **3.** bring about, effect B.Mel 2870, 2880c; BD 1122. [AN *purchacer*]
purchas *n.* takings, (ill-gotten) gains A.Prol 256, D.Fri 1451, 1530. [OF]
purchasour *n.* land-acquirer A.Prol 318. [AN]
pure *adj.* **1.** pure I.Pars 1046, BD 250, 259, Bo 4. p6. 36/52; chaste G.SN 48. **2.** very A.Kn 1279, BD 490, 1209, *the* ~ *deeth* death itself BD 583, TC 1.108 *var*, 4.1620, mere TC 1.285. [OF]
pure *adv.* purely BD 1010; *for* ~ *wood* simply out of anger RR 276; quite, completely BD 942 *var*. [as prec.]
pured *adj.* refined D.WB 143, F.Fkl 1560. [from v. from OF *purer*]
purely *adv.* simply, entirely BD 5, 843, HF 39. [from **pure**]
purfiled *ppl. adj.* embroidered A.Prol 193. [from OF *porfiler*]
purgacioun *n.* excretion D.WB 120. [OF]
purpos *n.* purpose A.Kn 2542, E.Cl 1078, TC 1.5; argument TC 2.897, 5.176; *to* ~ *to* the subject, point B.ML 170, H.Mcp 155, TC 3.330, 604, 5.1799; *it cam him to* ~ he decided F.Sq 606. [OF]
purpose(n *v.* intend B.Mel 2577, 3020, E.Cl 1067; propound, state Bo 4. p4. 55/75, 5. p6. 207/292; propose TC 4.1350. [OF]
purpre 1. *adj.* purple Bo 1. m6. 6/9, TC 4.869, LGW 654. **2.** *n.* purple colour Bo 2. m5. 11/15, 3. m8. 12/16; purple cloth I.Pars 933, RR 1071; *pl.* Bo 3. m4. 2/3. [OE *purpur(e,* OF *purpre*]
pursevauntes *n. pl.* pursuivants, heraldic assistants HF 1321. [OF]
pursue(n *v.* pursue I.Pars 355; persecute I.Pars 526; sue (to) B.Mel 2884; carry out Bo 4. p2. 65/86. [AN *pursuer*]
pursuit/-sute *n.* suit, petition D.WB 890; perseverance TC 2.959; continuing process TC 2.1744. [AN]
purtreye *see* **portreye.**
purtreyour *n.* painter A.Kn 1899 *var.* [AN]
purveiaunce/-veaunce/-viaunce *n.* **1.** providence, foresight A.Kn 1252, B.ML 483, F.Fkl 865, TC 2.527, 4.961; Bo 4. p6. 37/53, 150/218, 5. p3. 23/31, p6. 83/117, etc. (L all *prouidentia*). **2.** provision B.ML 247, D.WB 570, I.Pars 685, *unto his* ~ to provide for himself LGW 1561; prudence: *of my* ~ prudently D.WB 566. **3.** preparation A.Mil 3566, TC 3.533. [OF]
purveye(n *v.* **1.** foresee Bo 5. p3. 28/39, TC 4.1066. **2.** provide D.WB 917, *(of* 'with') 591, make provision TC 2.426. **3.** prepare B.Mel 2532, E.Cl 191, I.Pars 1003, TC 2.504. [AN *purveier*]
purveyinge *vbl. n.* foresight, providence TC 4.986, 1015.
put *see* **pit.**
put(e)rie *n.* prostitution I.Pars 886. [OF]
putours *n. pl.* procurers I.Pars 886. [AN]
putte(n *v.* **1.** put, place A.Kn 2363, B.Mk 3604, G.CY 762, TC 3.877; ~ *away* B.Mel 2184, Bo 3. m5. 6/8, turn away I.Pars 444; ~ *down* LSt 15; ~ *forth* G.SN 312, PF 603, Scog 40; ~ *in* commit, entrust, to B.Mel 2955, 3005; ~ *of* prevent Bo 1. p4. 42/58; ~ *on* impute to G.SN 455; ~ *out* B.Mk 3260, I.Pars 103, Bo 1. p5. 9/10; ~ *to* flight A.Kn 988, B.Mk 3532, TC 2.613. **2.** suppose B.Mel 2666, TC 1.783. **putteth**

pr. 3 sg. A.Mil 3802, B.Mel 2678; **put** B.Mel 2550, TC 4.1021, LGW 652. **putteth** *imper. pl.* A.Mil 3185. **putte** *pa. 1, 3 sg.* B.Pri 1630, D.WB. 68, BD 769. **puttest** *2 sg.* B.Mk 3875. **putten** *pl.* B.Mk 3260. **put** *p.p.* E.Cl 262. G.CY 761; **yput** G.CY 762, TC 3.275; **pit** (nth.) ARv. 4088. [OE **putian, pŷtan*]

Q

qua(a)d *adj.* bad B.Pri 1628; see **pley.** [MLG]
quake *v.* shake, tremble A.Mil 3614, D.Sum 1667, TC 1.871, LGW 2680. **quo(o)k** *pa. sg.* A.Kn 1576, TC 3.93, LGW 2317. **quaked** *p.p.* B.Mk 3831. [OE *cwacian,* pa. *cwacode*]
quakke *n.* in *on the* ~ with a frog in one's throat A.Rv 4152. [imit.]
qualm *n.*[1] plague A.Kn 2014, HF 1968; loss RR 357. [OA *cwalm*]
qualm† *n.*[2] croak TC 5.382. [imit.]
quappe *v.* throb, heave TC 3.57, LGW 865, 1767. [imit.]
quarter *n.* **1.** quarter B.ML 798, TC 5.880, Astr 1.7.3/5; ~ *night* nine o'clock A.Mil 3516; ~ *before day* 3 a.m. BD 198. **2.** 8 bushels (a quarter of a wagon-load) D.Sum 1963. [OF]
queynte† *n.* genitals (female) A.Mil 3276, D.WB 332, 444. [?modified form of ME *cunte,* ON *kunta,* after *queynte* adj.; *cunte* occurs from 13th cent., so could have been used if Chaucer had found it appropriate.]
queynt(e *adj.* strange, curious A.Kn 1531, D.WB 516 (?pun on n.), BD 1330, TC 1.411; ingenious A.Mil 3275, LGW 353; elaborate B.Sh 1189, HF 1925; skilfully contrived E.Mch 2061, F.Sq 234, TC 4.1629; elegant RR 65. [OF]
queynt(e *see* **quenche(n.**
queyntely,/-liche *adv.* cunningly, elaborately HF 1923, RR 569, 783. [from adj.]
queyntise *n.* artfulness I.Pars 733; finery I.Pars 932; adornment RR 840. [OF]
quelle *v.* kill B.NP 4580, C.Pard 854, G.CY 705; beat TC 4.46. [OE *cwellan*]
queme(n *v.* please, gratify TC 2.803, 5.695, Gent 20. [OE *cwēman*]
quenche(n *v.* **1.** *tr.* quench, extinguish A.Kn 2321, TC 3.846, 4.511. **2.** *intr.* go out A.Kn 2334, I.Pars 210. **queynte** *pa.* A.Kn 2334, 2337. **y)queynt** *p.p.* A.Kn 2321, A.Mil 3754, TC 4.313, 5.543. [OE -*cwencan, ocwencte*]
quene *n.* hussy, trollop H.Mcp 18. [OE *cwene*]
querele *n.* quarrel I.Pars 618; (law)suit Bo 3. p3. 49/64. [OF]
quern *n.* hand-mill B.Mk 3264, HF 1798, FormA 6. [OE *cweorn*]
questemongeres *n. pl.* jurymen, conductors of inquests I.Pars 796. [OF *queste*+ OE *mangere*]
questioun *n.* question: *holding hir* ~ debating A.Kn 2514; problem D.Sum 2223. [OF]
quik *adj.* **1.** alive A.Kn 1015, TC 2.52; lively I.Pars 658, Bo 4. p6. 15/23, **quikkest** *sup.* F.Fkl 1502; living TC 1.411; ~ *or/ne deed* F.Fkl 1336, BD 121, TC 3.79. **2.** quick A.Prol 306, F.Sq 194. [OE *cwic*]

quike(n *v.* **1.** quicken, revive: *tr.* G.SN 481; *intr.* I.Pars 235, TC 4.631. **2.** (of fire) *tr.* kindle F.Fkl 1050, I.Pars 628, keep alive TC 3.484; *intr.* revive A.Kn 2335, I.Pars 547, HF 2078. [OE *cwician*]

quiknesse *n.* liveliness BD 26. [from **quik**]

quinible *n.* high voice (a fifth above the treble) A.Mil 3332. [from L *quin(que* and OF *trible*, var. of *treble*]

quirboilly *n.* cuir-bouilli, hardened (boiled) leather B.Th 2065. [OF]

quisshin *n.* cushion TC 2.1229, 3.964. [OF *coissin*]

quistroun *n.* scullion RR 886. [OF]

quit *adj.* free, rid F.Fkl 1363, G.SN 448, PF 663, TC 1.529. [OF *quitte*]

quitly *adv.* freely, wholly A.Kn 1792. [from prec.]

quyt(t)e(n *v.* requite, pay, reward A.Prol 770, G.CY 1055, TC 4.1663, LGW 494; repay A.Mil 3119, D.WB 422, D.Fri 1292, G.CY 1025; *hir cost for to ~* pay her expenses B.Mk 3564; *~ (someone's) hire* repay D.WB 1008, PF 9, *~ his/hir while* B.ML 584, LGW 2227; pay (someone) out C.Pard 420, D.WB 483; pay off F.Fkl 1578; ransom A.Kn 1032; *refl.* do one's part F.Fkl 673. **quitte** *pa.* LGW 1918. **quit** *p.p.* F.Fkl 1534, TC 2.242; **yquit** F.Fkl 673. [OF *quit(t)er*]

quod *pa. sg.* said (*preceding subject*) A.Prol 788, B.NP 4099, BD 109, TC 1.551. [OE *cwæþ*]

quoniam *n.* genitals D.WB 608. [cf. **queynte**, perh. fanciful use of L *quoniam* suggested by F *con*]

quo(o)k *see* **quake**.

R

raa *n.* (nth.) roe (deer) A.Rv 4086. [OE *rā*]

rad(de *see* **rede(n**.

radevore *n.* ?tapestry LGW 2352. [prob. OF **ras de Vor*, a cloth of Lavaur (Tarn)]

rafles *n. pl.* game with three dice I.Pars 793. [OF]

rafte *see* **reve(n**.

rage *n.* **1.** frenzy, anger A.Kn 2011, B.NP 4556, TC 3.899; violent grief F.Fkl 836; (sexual) passion LGW 599, RR 1657. **2.** storm-blast A.Kn 1985; boiling Bo 1. m4. 4/5. [OF]

rage *v.* romp, sport (sexually) A.Prol 257, A.Mil 3273, A.Rv 3958. [OF]

ragerye *n.* lust, lechery D.WB 455, E.Mch 1847. [OF]

raked *p.p.* covered by raking B.Mel 3323. [from v. from OE *raca* n. and ON *raka* v.]

rakel *adj.* rash, hasty H.Mcp 278, 289, TC 1.1067, 3.429. [?]

rakelnesse *n.* rashness H.Mcp 283, Scog 16 *var.* [from prec.]

rake-stele *n.* rake-handle D.WB 949. [OE *raca* + **stele**]

raket *n.* ?a game like rackets, two players alternately striking a ball TC 4.460. [cf. F *raquette*]

raklet† *v.* behave rashly TC 3.1642. [from **rakel**]

rammish *adj.* like a ram, rank G.CY 887. [from OE *ramm*]

rampeth *pr. 3 sg.* rampages B.Mk 3094. [OF *ramper*]

rape *n.* haste Adam 7. [from ON *hrapa* v.]

rape *v.* in *~ and renne* seize and hold G.CY 1422. [AN *raper*]

rascaille *n.* rabble TC 5.1853. [OF]

rasour *n.* razor A.Kn 2417, HF 690, LGW 2654. [OF]

rated *p.p. ~ of* scolded for A.Mil 3463. [?rel. to **ar(r)ette**]

rathe *adv.* early A.Mil 3768, B.Sh 1289, TC 2. 1088; *late or ~* HF 2139. [OE *hraþe*]

rather *adj.* former Bo 2. p1. 8/10, p7. 89/127, TC 3.1337, 5.1799. [comp. from OE *hraþe* adj.]

rather *adv.* **1.** rather, sooner A.Prol 487, C.Pard 643, BD 240. *ever the ~ the more* Bo 2. m2. 14/19 (L *potius*). **2.** sooner, earlier E.Mch 2302, TC 1.865; *the ~* I.Pars 244, TC 1.835; *never the ~* no sooner BD 562. [OE *hraþor*]

raughte *see* **reche**.

raunsonynge *vbl. n.* ransoming, exacting payment I.Pars 753. [from v. from OF *ransouner*]

raunso(u)n *n.* ransom A.Kn 1024, 1176, I.Pars 225, *made his ~* paid his penalty D.WB 411. [OF]

ravyne *n.* rapine, greed PF 336, Bo 2. m2. 10/14; *pl.* robberies I.Pars 793; *foules of ~* birds of prey PF 323, 527. [OF]

ravinour *n.* plunderer, looter Bo 1. p3. 57/80, 4 p3. 73/105. [OF]

ravisshe(n *v.* **1.** seize Bo 1. p3. 25/34, TC 4.530, 637, abduct TC 5.895; draw (down) B.Pri 1659. **2.** carry away D.Sum 1676; (fig.) E.Mch 1750, F.Sq 547; enchant, persuade TC 4.1474, B.Mel 2923; *~d on* infatuated with E.Mch 1774. [OF *raviss-*, stem of *ravir*]

ravisshing *vbl. n.* abduction, rape TC 1.62, 4.548.

ravisshing *vbl. adj.* **1.** that carries away, violent Bo 1. m5. 3/4, 4. m6. 7/9. **2.** enchanting PF 198.

real *see* **royal**.

realme/reaume/re(a)me *n.* realm, kingdom B.ML 797, B.Sh 1306, Bo 2. p2. 61/85, LGW 1281. *pl.* B.NP 4326, Bo 3. p5. 7/10. [OF]

realtee *see* **royaltee**.

rebating *vbl. n.* abatement BalCh 23. [from *rebate* v., OF *rabattre*]

rebekke *n.* old dame (*lit.* fiddle) D.Fri 1573. Cf. **ribybe**. [OF *rebec*]

rebuked *p.p.* repulsed I.Pars 444. [AN *rebuker*]

recche/rekke(n *v.*[1] **1.** *intr.* reck, care (usu. with neg.) A.Kn 1398, D.WB 329, PF 606, TC 4.630; *~ of* F.Sq 71, BD 887, TC 1.797, 4.1447; *~ noght a bene* care not at all B.ML 94, B.NP 4004; *~ not a myte* G.CY 698, Anel 269. **2.** *impers.* (with dat. of pers.) D.WB 53, E.Mch 2276, Anel 182, LGW 365. **3.** *tr.* care about TC 4.630 *var.* **ro(u)ghte** *pa.* A.Mil 3772, PF 111, TC 4.667, LGW 605. [OE *reccan*[1], *rōhte*]

recche *v.*[2] *pr. subj. sg.* interpret B.NP 4086 *var.* [OE *reccan*[2]]

recchelees *adj.* heedless, reckless A.Prol 179 *var.*, E.Cl 488, HF 397; *~ of* negligent in securing B.ML 229. [OE *reċċelēas*]

reccheleesnesse *n.* recklessness, carelessness I.Pars 111, 611, Scog 16 *var.* [from prec.]

receit *n.* recipe, prescription G.CY 1353, 1366. [AN]

receyve(n *v.* receive B.ML 991, C.Pard 917; accept B.ML 259, E.Cl 1151, LGW 700; *p.p.* accepted, acceptable B.ML 307. [OF *receivre*]

rechased *p.p.* headed back BD 379. [*rechase* v., OF *rechasser*]

reche *v.* reach down, fetch BD 47. **raughte** *pa.* reached A.Prol 136, A.Kn 2915, A.Mil 3696, B.Th 1921; went TC 2.447; **reighte** reached HF 1374. [OE *rǣcan, rǣhte/rāhte*]

reclayme *v.* call back (a hawk), check H.Mcp 72. [OF *reclaimer*]

reclaiming *vbl. n.* enticement LGW 1371.

recom(m)aunde/-ende *v.* commend B.Mk 3909, G.SN 544; *refl.* commend oneself B.ML 278, TC 2.1070, 5.1323. [OF *recommander*, L *commendāre*]

reconciled *p.p.* restored, reconsecrated I.Pars 965. [from OF *reconcilier*]

reconforte *v.* comfort, encourage B.Mel 2850, TC 2.1672, 5.1395; *refl.* take heart A.Kn 2852. [OF]

reconissaunce *n.* recognizance, bond B.Sh 1520. [OF]

record *n.* reputation D.Sum 2049; testimony BD 934; *of ~* recorded D.Sum 2117. [OF]

recorde(n *v.* **1.** bring to mind, recall (to someone) A.Prol 829. **2.** remember TC 5.445, 718, *refl.* TC 3.1179; recall, call to mind Bo 3. m1. 34/46, p12. 2, LGW 1760; go over, repeat PF 609, TC 3.51. **3.** record B.Mel 2269; witness, confirm A.Kn 1745; tell LGW 2484. [OF *recorder*]

recours *n.* recourse B.Mel 2632; resort TC 2.1352; *wol have my ~* will return F.Sq 75. **recourses** *pl.* orbits Bo 1. m2. 9/12. [OF]

recovere(n *v.* regain, recover HF 354 (**rekever**), PF 688, TC 4.1283; get in return TC 3.181, 4.406; make up for B.ML 27. [AN]

recreaunt *adj.* cowardly, admitting defeat I.Pars 698, TC 1.814. [OF]

redeless *adj.* unresourceful Pity 27. [OE *rǣdlēas*]

redely *see* **redily.**

rede(n *v.*[1] read (aloud) A.Prol 709, B.Pri 1690, C.Phs 176, HF 722; read A.Prol 741, B.Mk 3770, BD 49; study F.Fkl 1120; *~ over* TC 2.1085 *var*; *~ on* D.WB 714, LGW 30; interpret B.NP 4086 *var*; *~ of* lecture on D.Fri 1518; tell E.Mch 1362. **redeth** *imper. pl.* B.Mk 3650, C.Pard 586, D.WB 1168. **redde** *pa. sg.* D.WB 714; **radde** PF 579. **redden** *pl.* TC 2.1706. **redde/radde** *pa.* TC 5.737. [same word as prec., senses diverging in ME]

reder *n.* reader PF 132, TC 5.270. [from **rede(n**[1]]

redy *adj.* ready (of persons or things) A.Prol 21, D.Fri 1321, TC 1.988, LGW 949; at hand BD 1256, Pity 104; *al ~* quite ready D.WB 854, E.Mch 1346, PF 213, 540; *~ tokene see* **token.** [cf. OE *ġerǣde*]

redily/redely *adv.* readily, soon A.Kn 2276, Bo 3. m2. 23/33, at once C.Pard 667; truly HF 130, 313. [from prec.]

redoutable *adj.* respected Bo 4. p5. 6/9 (L *reuerendus*). [OF]

redoute *v.* fear Bo 1. p3. 15/19, 2. p7. 44/64. [OF]

redoutinge *vbl. n.* reverence A.Kn 2050.

redresse *v.* **1.** redress, set right Mars 192, TC 3.1008, 5.139, Truth 8; redeem D.WB 696; correct ABC 129. **2.** restore F.Fkl 1436, Bo 4. p2. 99/131; *refl.* recover TC 2.969. **3.** *refl.* (with *in*) address oneself (to) I.Pars 1039. [OF]

re(e)d *n.*[1] **1.** advice B.Mk 3739, E.Mch 1668, PF 586, TC 5.428; adviser A.Prol 665. **2.** help A.Kn 1216, BD 587, TC 1.661. **3.** plan, course (of action) D.Sum 2030, BD 105, TC 2.1539; *to ~* as a plan TC 4.679. [OE *rǣd*, A *rēd*]

reed/rede *n.*[2] reed TC 2.1387, HF 1221. [OE *hrēod*]

re(e)d *adj.* **1.** red A.Prol 90, B.Sh 1301, BD 470; of gold (conventional epithet) B.Th 2059; *~ as rose* TC 2.1256, LGW 112, *rose ~* G.SN 254. **2.** as red material A.Prol 294, A.Rv 3954; red wine C.Pard 526, TC 3.1384/1370; the colour red LGW 533. [OE *rēad*]

reednesse *n.* redness, high colour G.CY 1097, 1100, Bo 1. p1. 53/74. [from prec.]

rees *n.* hurry, rush TC 4.350. [OE *rǣs*]

refect *adj.* restored Bo 4. p6. 257/344 (error) (L *refectus*).

refere *v. intr.* return TC 1.266; *~ to* apply to, concern G.CY 1083. [OF *referer*]

referre *v. tr.* (only in Bo, always rendering parts of L *referre*) refer, relate, bring back Bo 3. p2. 42/60, p10. 123/166, 136/185; apply 3. p6. 26/35, 4. p6. 38/54; attribute 1. p4. 17/24, 5. p6. 122/174. [L *referre*]

refreyde *v.* **1.** *tr.* cool: **refreyded** *p.p.* I.Pars 341, **refreyd** Rosem 21*em.* **2.** *intr.* grow cold TC 2.1343, 5.507, Rosem 21. [ONF *refreider*]

refreyne *v.* restrain, check I.Pars 294, 385; *refl.* I.Pars 382. [OF]

refreininge† *v.* refrain, burden RR 749. [from *refrein* n., OF]

refresshe(n *v.* refresh, renew the strength of Bo 4. p6. 257/344, LGW 1482; nourish D.WB 146; solace, comfort D.WB 38, D.Sum 1767; relieve LGW 1081. [OF *refreschier/-ir*]

refresshinge *vbl. n.* refreshment, renewal I.Pars 78, 220.

reft(e *see* **reve(n.**

refus *adj.* rejected TC 1.570. [OF]

refut *n.* refuge, (place of) safety B.ML 546, G.SN 75, ABC 33. [OF]

regal *adj.* royal Bo 1. p4. 85/117 (L *regiu*). [OF]

regalye *n.* royalty, rule Pity 65. [AN]

regals *n. pl.* princes LGW 2128. [OF]

regard *n.* in *at/in/(as)to ~ of* in comparison with I.Pars 399, 477, PF 58, Bo 4. m3. 25/34. Cf. **reward.** [OF]

regne *n.* **1.** kingdom, realm A.Kn 866, B.Mk 3380, E.Mch 2302, TC 3.29. **2.** reign, rule A.Kn 1624, I.Pars 702, B.Mk 3423. [OF]

regne(n *v.* reign B.Mk 3845, TC 4.790, 5.1864; prevail B.ML 776; *tr.* prevail in, dominate TC 2.379. [OF *reignier*]

reherce(n *v.* **1.** recount, relate A.Prol 732, F.Sq 298, Mars 162, TC 3.493; mention

I.Pars 910. **2.** repeat, go over A.Mil 3170, TC 2.572, 1029; *it nedeth nat* ~ F.Sq 599, F.Fkl 1466, BD 190, TC 2.917. [OF]

rehersaille *n.* enumeration G.CY 852. [from prec.]

rehersing *vbl. n.* recital A.Kn 1650, LGW 1185; *maken* ~ of repeat LGW 24.

reye *n.* rye D.Sum 1746. [OE *ryge*]

reyes *n. pl.* round dances HF 1236. [MHG, MDu *reie, rei*]

reighte *see* **reche.**

reyn *n.* rain A.Prol 492, TC 3.788; rainstorm B.Mk 3921, TC 3.626. *pl.* E.Mch 2140, HF 967. [OE *regn*]

reyne *n.* rein F.Sq 313, TC 5.90; *so large a* ~ so free a rein F.Fkl 755. [OF *reyne*]

reyne *v.* rain A.Kn 1535, TC 3.551, 1557; (of tears) TC 4.873, 5.1336. **ron** *pa. sg.* TC 3.640, 677; **reyned** 1557. [OE *regnian*; *ron* anal. pa. of *rinan*, orig.weak]

reynes *n. pl.* loins I.Pars 863. [OF *reins*]

reyse(n *v.*[1] **1.** raise D.WB 705, G.CY 861, BD 1278, exalt TC 2.1585; build up D.Sum 2102. **2.** rouse up TC 5.1471. **3.** collect D.Fri 1390. [ON *reisa*]

reised *v.*[2] *pa.* made a military expedition A.Prol 54. [MDu *reisen*]

rejoye *v. refl.* rejoice TC 5.395. [OF]

rejoys(s)e(n *v.* rejoice Bo 2. p7. 109/156, TC 2.1391, 5.1165; *refl.* E.Mch 1993, I.Pars 398, Bo 1. m5. 33/47. [OF *rejoiss-*, stem of *rejoir*]

rek(e)ne *v.* reckon, calculate A.Prol 401, BD 437, Astr 2.1.1; count A.Kn 1954, Bo 3. p2. 71/102; consider, adjudge B.ML 158, D.WB 367, I.Pars 617. **yrekened** *p.p.* D.WB 367, F.Sq 427. [OE *recenian*]

rek(e)ning *vbl. n.* reckoning, account A.Prol 600, I.Pars 648, Astr 2.22.10/14; *pl.* accounts A.Prol 760, HF 653.

rekever *see* **recovere(n.**

rekke *see* **recche.**

relayes *n. pl.* packs of fresh hounds BD 362. [OF]

relees *n.* release, remission ABC 3; *out of* ~ without ceasing G.SN 46. [OF]

rele(e)sse *v.* release, free B.Mk 3367, I.Pars 809; remit B.ML 1069; forgive F.Fkl 1613, I.Pars 309, 582. [OF *relesser*]

rele(e)ve *v.* relieve, help A.Rv 4182, ABC 6, LGW 128; restore I.Pars 945; cheer G.CY 872, TC 5.1042. [OF]

rele(e)ving *vbl. n.* remedy I.Pars 804, 805.

relente *v.* soften, melt G.CY 1278. [ML *relentāre* from *lentus*]

reles(s)ing(e *vbl. n.* release Bo 3. m12. 21/29; remission I.Pars 1026.

religioun *n.* religion G.SN 427, RR 429; religious life A.Prol 477; a religious order B.Mk 3134, G.CY 972. [OF]

religious *adj.* in a religious order B.Mk 3150, I.Pars 891, TC 2.759. [OF]

reme *see* **realme.**

remembre(n *v.* **1.** remember B.ML 1057, Bo 1. p6. 45/57, TC 3.1628, HF 64, (with *on*) A.Kn 1501, B.Pri 1703, (with *of*) I.Pars 702; *refl.* E.Cl 881, (with *upon*) B.Mel 2166, 2189, (with *of*) I.Pars 133, BD 717; *impers.* (with pron. obj.) TC 4.73, (with subject *it*) D.WB 469, Bo 3. p3. 21/29, TC 3.361. **remembreth** *imper. pl.* F.Fkl 1542, I.Pars 136, Bo 4. p2. 36/47. **2.** remind F.Fkl 1243. [OF]

remena(u)nt *n.* rest, remainder A.Prol 724, B.NP 4094, TC 4.1376, LGW 304. [OF]

remes *see* **realme.**

remeve(n/remo(e)ve(n *v.* remove, move away F.Fkl 993, TC 1.691, Astr 2.5.14/21.

remeveth *imper. pl.* G.CY 1008. Cf. **remuen.** [OF *remuev-*, stem of *removeir*]

remewe *see* **remue(n.**

remorde *v.* afflict Bo 4. p6. 182/265; afflict with remorse TC 4.1491. [OF *remordre*]

remounted *p.p.* restored, comforted Bo 3. p1. 6/8. [*remount* v. from OF *remonter*]

remuable *adj.* changeable TC 4.1682; able to move Bo 5. p5. 23/32 (L *mobilibus*). [OF]

remue(n/remewe *v.* move away, F.Sq 181, Bo 2. p6. 34/48, Astr 2.2.2/3 *var.* [OF]

ren *n.* run A.Rv 4079. [from **renne(n**]

renably *adv.* reasonably, fluently D.Fri 1509. [from OF *re(s)nable*]

rende *v.* **1.** *tr.* rend, tear B.Mel 2163 *var*, D.WB 635, Bo 1. m1. 3/4 (L *lacerae*), TC 4.1493, LGW 843*em*, RR 324*em*. **2.** *intr.* split B.NP 4291. **rent** *pr. 3 sg.* LGW 646. **rente** *pa.* B.NP 4291, TC 2.928, 4.744. **y)rent** *p.p.* B.ML 844, LGW 2613. [OE *réndan*]

rending *vbl. n.* tearing A.Kn 2834 *var.*

renegat *n.* renegade, villain B.ML 933; apostate LGW G. 401. [L *renegātus*]

reneye *v.* renounce, abjure B.ML 376, B.Mk 3751, G.SN 268, 448. [OF]

reneyinge *vbl. n.* denying I.Pars 793.

renewe *v.* do again Adam 5. [pref. *re-*+ **newe**]

renged *p.p.* arranged, set in rows RR 1380. [OF *renger*]

renges *n. pl.* ranks A.Kn 2594. [OF *renge*]

renne(n *v.*[1] **1.** run A.Rv 4065, B.NP 4373, D.WB 76, TC 3.964; hasten TC 1.1066, hurry A.Prol 509; (fig.) C.Phs 130; ~ *in* see **blame.** **2.** (of thought, etc.) ~ *in* come quickly into (mind, etc.) A.Kn 1402, see **pitee;** ~ *thurgh* E.Cl 214; *p.p.* advanced RR 320; ~ *biforn/toforn* run ahead of, anticipate Bo 4. p2. 96/127, 5. p6. 191/268 (L *praecurrit*). **3.** approach TC 2.1754; ~ *with/togidere* coincide Bo 5. p1. 62/90, p6. 211/297 (L *concurrit*). **4.** (of sound, etc.) run, spread, pass quickly A.Kn 1979, B.Mk 3303, PF 247, HF 1683, LGW 1423. **5.** run, flow A.Rv 4276, B.ML 661, E.Cl 1105, F.Sq 416, TC 4.1549; *pr.p.* as *adj.* Bo 2. m5. 12/17; (fig., of the tap of life) A.Rv 3890, 3893; HF 1651. *p.p.* clustered A.Kn 2165, interlaced RR 1396. **6.** (of astrolabe ring) move freely Astr 1.2.1; (of dice) ~*th for* runs in favour of B.ML 125; cut, slice LGW 641 *var.* **7.** continue, extend Astr 2.3.48/71; last LGW 1943. **ran** *pa. sg.* A.Kn 2185, A.Rv 4105; *pl.* B.NP 4571. **ronne(n** *pl.* A.Kn 2925, B.NP 4578. **ronne(n** *p.p.* B.ML 2, F.Sq 386, TC 2.1464; **yronne(n** A.Prol 8, A.Kn 2165, TC 2.907. [OE *rinnan, rann, *runnon*, *ge)runnen* and ON *renna*]

renne *v.*[2] hold; *rape and* ~ see **rape.** [form of OE *rǽnan*]

renner *n.* runner D.Fri 1283. [from **renne(n**]

renning *vbl. n.* running, run A.Prol 551.

renomed *ppl. adj.* renowned, famous Bo 2. p4. 59/81 *var*, 3. p2. 76/109. [from OF *renomé*]

renomee *n.* renown D.WB 1159, LGW 1513. [OF]

renoun *n.* renown, fame A.Prol 316, Pity 63, TC 1.481. [AN]

renovelances *n. pl.* renewals HF 693. [OF]

renovelle *v. tr.* renew B.Mel 3035, 3036. **renoveleth** *imper. pl.* Mars 19. *refl.* renew oneself Bo 3. p11. 91/124. *intr.* be renewed I.Pars 1027. [OF *reno(u)veler*]

rente *n.* income A.Prol 256, B.NP 4017, TC 4.85, revenue B.Mk 3572; salary Bo 3. p4. 57/83; tribute B.ML 1142, D.Sum 1821, BD 765; rent D.Fri 1390, I.Pars 886. [OF]

rente(n *v.* tear B.Mel 2163 var, LGW 843, RR 324. [var. of **rende** based on p.p.]

rentynge *vbl. n.* teasing A.Kn 2834 var.

repair *n.* resort, frequenting B.Sh 1211, D.WB 1224. [OF]

repaire *v.* return B.Sh 1516, C.Pard 878, F.Sq 589, HF 755; go, find a home TC 3.5; resort B.Mk 3885, B.NP 4410. [OF, from LL *repatriāre*]

repente(n *v.* repent B.Mel 2193, C.Pard 431; (with *of*) E.Mch 1663, I.Pars 300; (with direct obj.) LGW 339, (with infin.) LGW 2088, (with cl.) B.ML 378, E.Cl 860. *refl.* D.Fri 1629, H.Mcp 356, BD 1116. **repenteth** *imper. pl.* F.Fkl 1321. [OF *repentir*]

repleccioun *n.* repletion, surfeit B.NP 4027; *pl.* B.NP 4113. [OF]

repleet *ppl. adj.* filled (*of* 'with') B.NP 4147, C.Pard 489. [OF *replet-* or L *replētus*]

replicacioun *n.* reply A.Kn 1846, PF 536; folding together Bo 3. p12. 120/160. [OF]

reportour *n.* chairman, umpire A.Prol 814. [OF]

reprevable *adj.* reprehensible C.Pard 632, I.Pars 431; damaging LSt 24. [from next; cf. F *réprouvable*]

repreve *n.* reproof D.WB 16, E.Mch 2263, I.Pars 625; insult I.Pars 258; shame C.Pard 595, D.WB 84; reproach TC 2.419, *your* ~ reproach to you B.Mel 2413. [AN *repreove*, cf. next]

repreve *v.* reprove (with *of*) B.Mel 2893, I.Pars 625, LGW 1566; reproach D.WB 1207, F.Fkl 1537, TC 1.669; *to* ~ to be objected to B.Mel 2222. [OF *repruev-*, stem of *reprover*]

reprevinge *vbl. n.* reproach I.Pars 556, 628.

repugnen *v.* be contradictory or inconsistent Bo 5. p3. 5. [OF *repugner*]

requerable *adj.* desirable Bo 2. p6. 20/29. [OF]

requere(n/require(n *v.* **1.** ask, ask for, request D.WB 1010, TC 1.902, 3.483, (with *of* 'for') B.Mel 2873, (with direct obj. and dat. of person asked) TC 2.473; seek Bo 4. m1. 25/35; *to* ~ to be sought after Bo 3. p10. 166/227. **2.** require, call for, need E.Cl 430, Bo 3. p11. 135/185, TC 3.405. [OF *requer-, requier-*, stem of *requere*]

resalgar *n.* realgar (arsenic disulphide) G.CY 814. [Arab *rahj al-ghār*]

rescous *n.* rescue, help A.Kn 2643, TC 1.478, 3.1242. [OF]

rescowe *v.* rescue, save Bo 4. m5. 15/20, TC 3.857, LGW 515. [OF *rescou-*, stem of *rescoure*]

rescowing *vbl. n.* rescuing I.Pars 805.

rese *v.* shake A.Kn 1986. [OE *hrisian*]

resemblable *adj.* alike RR 985. [OF]

resemble *v.* be like (*to*) Bo 3. m7. 2/3; represent, typify D.WB 90. [OF *resembler*]

resign *v.* resign TC 1.432; abandon, renounce TC 3.25; consign B.ML 780. [OF *resigner*]

resolve *v.* flow out Bo 5. m1. 1; dissolve Bo 2. p7. 101/144; melt Bo 4. m5. 20/26; hold in solution Bo 1. m7. 6/9. [L *resolvere*]

resonable *adj.* rational, endowed with reason Bo 1. p6. 47/61, 5. p4. 138/199, B.NP 4244; reasonable, sensible D.WB 441, BD 534, TC 2.1135; suitable, sufficient B.Mk 3793, I.Pars 1051. *pl.* Bo 5. p6. 7/9. [OF]

resonab(le)ly *adv.* reasonably B.Mel 2456, I.Pars 273. [from prec.]

resoninge *vbl. n.* reasoning Bo 5. p5. 31/44 (L *ratiocinationi*), TC 4.1046. [from *reso(u)n* v., OF *raisoner*]

resoun *n.* reason, sense A.Prol 37, E.Mch 2369, I.Pars 266; *agayn* ~ irrational B.Mel 2725; *by* ~ sensibly G.CY 1199, HF 708, LGW 183, reasonably, fairly C.Pard 458; *of* ~ reasonable Bo 2. p5. 34/47, TC 2.366, rational I.Pars 537; (predic.) sensible B.Mel 2413, E.Mch 1768, *as is/was* ~ reasonably A.Prol 847, D.Sum 2277, F.Sq 296. **2.** reason, cause B.Mel 2169, F.Sq 406, Bo 3. p9. 12/16; *by* ~ *of* because of B.Mel 2213, I.Pars 801. **3.** argument A.Mil 3844, B.Mel 2426, Bo 3. p10. 40/56, TC 4.589. [OF]

resoune *v.* resound A.Kn 1278, F.Sq 413. [OF *resoner* infl. by **soun**]

respiten *v.* grant respite to F.Fkl 1582. [OF *respitier*]

resport† *n.* regard TC 4.86, 850. [OF]

rest(e *n.* **1.** rest, repose A.Kn 1003, 2490, E.Mch 1862, F.Sq 349, BD 245, PF 94; *go(n to* ~ A.Prol 820, F.Sq 364, TC 2.911, (transf., of sun) A.Prol 30, A.Mil 3422; *take* ~ B.ML 741; *pl.* times of repose TC 2.1722. **2.** peace, peace of mind, happiness Truth 10, B.Sh 1538, E.Cl 112, 160, F.Fkl 760; repose after death D.WB 501, E.Cl 30, TC 3.925. **3.** place of rest, abode PF 376; *sette at* ~ settle, fix TC 2.760. [OE *ræst/rest*]

reste(n *v.* **1.** rest A.Kn 2621, B.Sh 1299, F.Sq 126; (of time) stop RR 374; (of the sun) set E.Mch 2174; (of tongue) PF 514; *refl.* LGW 2168, RR 1347, 1455, (with *of*) cease (from) G.CY 869. **2.** remain, stay D.Sum 1736. **3.** *tr.* (fig.) lay, place for support TC 2.1326. [OE *ræstan/restan*]

restelees *adj.* finding no rest C.Pard 728, TC 1 1581; increasing Fort 70, [OE *restlēas*]

resting-whyles† *n. pl.* times of leisure, repose Bo 1. p4. 31/43 (L *inter secreta otia*). [*resting* vbl. n. + **while**]

restore *v.* **1.** return B.Mel 2300, TC 4.1347. **2.** repair, make good I.Pars 645, TC 1.1348. [OF *restorer*]

restreyne *v.* **1.** check, hold back (person) TC 1.676; *refl.* refrain B.Mk 3796, B.Mel 2682, TC 4.940. **2.** check, repress (desire, feeling) B.Mel 2282, 2622, I.Pars 916; (physical agent or force) B.Mk 3777, H.Mcp 329, TC 4.708, 872. **3.** restrict, confine Bo 2. p7. 57/83; Bo 1. m5. 11/16 (L *stringis breuiore mora*, = shorten)

restreyned *p.p. adj.* Bo 2. p8. 18/26. [OF *restreindre*]

resurreccioun *n.* resurrection, re-opening (of daisy) LGW 110 (only). [OF]

ret *see* **rede(n** v.²

retentif *adj.* retentive, in *the vertu* ~ the ability to retain I.Pars 913. [OF]

retenue *n.* suite E.Cl 270; *of* ~ in service A.Kn 2502; *at his* ~ at his service, command D.Fri 1355. [OF]

rethor *n.* rhetorician, master of eloquence B.NP 4397, F.Sq 38. [ML *rethor*, L *rhetor*]

rethorien *n.* orator, rhetorician Bo 2. p3. 39/55 (L *orator*), *pl.* Bo 2. p6. 69/97 (L *rhetores*). [OF]

rethorien *adj.* rhetorical Bo 2. p1. 29/41 (L *rhetoricae*). [as prec.]

rethorike *n.* **1.** rhetoric, the art of persuasion; its rules, F.Fkl 719, 726, HF 859; **Rethorice** (person.) Bo 2. p1. 31/43. **2.** eloquence E.Cl 32. [OF *rethorique*, L *rhetorica*/-*e*]

retourne *v. intr.* **1.** return (to a place or person) E.Cl 809, TC 3.1534, 4.1553, LGW 2017; (transf., of time) RR 382. **2.** go back, revert (to a topic) B.ML 986, E.Cl 597, Mars 211. **3.** revert (to a previous condition) B.Mel 3043. **4.** *tr., pr. p.* revolving, turning over TC 5. 1023. [OF *reto(u)rner*]

retourninge *vbl. n.* return, returning A.Kn 2095, Bo 3. m2. 28/41, I.Pars 176.

retracciouns *n. pl.* retractations, things to be withdrawn; (?) title of invented work (modelled on *Retractationes* of St. Augustine) [J. Norton-Smith, *Geoffrey Chaucer* (1974) p. 80 n.], I.Pars 1085. [from LL *retractiōnes*]

retreteth *pr. 3 sg.* reconsiders, treats again, Bo 5. m3. 36/52 (L *retractans*). [OF *re-traitier*]

retrograd *adj.* (of planets) 'moving in a direction contrary to the order of the signs, or from east to west' (*OED*) Astr 2.4.33/50, etc. [L *retrōgradus*]

reule *n.* **1.** rule, code of discipline of a religious order A.Prol 173. **2.** principle regulating procedure Astr prol 19/26, 1.6.5/7; rule, what is generally true B.Mel 2356, 2421, Fort 56, Astr 1.21.13/17; government I.Pars 217. **3.** revolving plate or rod on astrolabe Astr 1.1.4/5, 13.1. [OF]

reule(n *v.* **1.** control, guide, direct (person) TC 2.1377, Bo 1. p4. 153/213 (L *dirigebas*), *p.p.* controlled, governed A.Prol 816; *refl.* behave, conduct oneself E.Cl 327, TC 5.758. **2.** govern, control (events) A.Kn 1672, B.NP 4234; *p.p.* as *adj.* ?well-conducted, disciplined LGW 163. [OF *reuler*]

reuthe(- *see* **routhe(-.**

reve *n.* reeve, bailiff A.Prol 542, A.Mil 3144, A.Rv 3860; *chirche* ~ churchwarden D.Fri 1305. [OE *ġerḗfa*]

revel *n.* **1.** riotous merry-making, revelry A.Co 4402, E.Cl 392, *made* ~ A.Kn 2717; sport A.Mil 3652, pleasure B.NP 4393. **2.** festive occasion B.ML 353, Rosem 6; *pl.* C.Phs 65. [OF]

revelour *n.* reveller, disorderly liver, rake A.Co 4371, 4391, D.WB 453. [from *revel* v., OF *reveler*]

revelous *adj.* fond of revelry, convivial B.Sh 1194. [OF]

revelrye *n.* **1.** revelry, conviviality A.Rv 4005 *var.* **2.** RR 720 *var* ? = **reverdye** [from *revel* v.]

reve(n v. **1.** take away, remove B.Mk 3288, I.Pars 803, Fort 50; (with *fro, from*) G.SN 376, PF 86. **2.** despoil I.Pars 758; rob (someone *of* sthg.) A.Rv 4011, LGW 2325; steal, seize (sthg. *of* someone) B.Mk 3291, D.WB 888 *var*; take, esp. by force (with indir. obj. of person deprived) TC 1.188, 2.1659, 4.285, 468, LGW 1855. **rafte** *pa.* B.Mk 3288, LGW 1855; **refte** TC 1.484, HF 457. **yraft** *p.p.* A.Kn 2015, LGW 1572; **reft** Bo 1. m5. 17/24, LGW 2325. [OE *rēafian* (pa. *rēafode*)]

reverberacioun *n.* reverberation D.Sum 2234. [OF]

reverdye *n.* rejoicing, delight RR 720em (after the OF text). [OF]

reverence *n.* **1.** respect, deference, honour (to a person) A.Prol 141, B.Mel 2380, E.Cl 231, I.Pars 188; *thy* ~ the respect shown to you B.ML 116; *have/hold in* ~ B.NP 4403, TC 1.516, LGW 32; *don* ~ show respect or honour (to) A.Kn 2531, B.Pri 1705, D.WB 206, E.Cl 196, F.Fkl 1257, TC 4.69; *at the* ~ of out of respect for, in honour of, for the sake of G.SN 82, I.Pars 40, TC 3.40, 1328; *speketh* ~ speaks with respect E.Mch 2251. **2.** veneration, reverence B.Pri 1880, *in thy* ~ in veneration of you B.Pri 1663, *the* ~ *of God* the reverence due to God I.Pars 294. [OF]

reverence *v.* hold in high esteem G.CY 631. [from prec.]

reverent *adj.* **1.** worthy of respect, respected Bo 3. p4.2, p9.45/59; *pl.* ~s/z Bo 3. m4. 6/7. **2.** reverend Astr prol 61/85. [OF]

reverently *adv.* respectfully, in a reverent manner E.Cl 187, 952. [from prec.]

reverye *n.* **1.** wantonness, wildness A.Rv 4005 *var*; cf. **revelrye. 2.** ? delight RR 720; cf. **reverdye.** [OF]

revers *n.* opposite, contrary B.NP 4167, D.Sum 2056, Gent 6, Ven 32. [OF]

revesten *pr. 3 pl. refl.* clothe themselves anew TC 3.353. [OF *revestir*]

revoken v. **1.** recall to consciousness TC 3.1118. **2.** withdraw, retract I.Pars 1085. [L *revocāre* or OF *revoquer*]

revolucioun *n.* **1.** orbit Mars 30. **2.** The time in which a heavenly body completes a full circuit or course Astr 2.7.13/19. [OF]

reward *n.* regard, heed: *take* ~ *of/to* pay attention to B.Mel 2449, 2561, I.Pars 151, 435; *have* ~ *to* TC 2.1133, 5.1736, LGW 399, *at* 375; *havyng* ~ *to* considering PF 426. Cf. **regard.** [ONF, = OF *regard*]

rewde *see* **rude.**

rewe *n.* row, line A.Kn 2866, HF 1692, LGW G.285; *by* ~ in order D.WB 506. Cf. **arewe, rowe.** [OE *rǣw*, var. of **rāw*]

rewel-boon *n.* ivory (poss. of narwhal) B.Th 2068. [AN *roal/rohal*, prob. of Scand. origin, second element perh. *hval* whale]

rewe(n v. **1.** *intr.* repent, regret, feel sorrow A.Mil 3530, G.CY 729, TC 2.455, 5.1070. **2.** have pity on, feel pity for (with *up)on*) A.Kn 2233, B.ML 853, E.Cl 1050, E.Mch 1782, TC 1.460, 3.1770, 4.745. **3.** *tr.* do penance for G.CY 997; (with obj. *it*) regret TC 2.789, 1609. **4.** (with impers. subject *it* and dat. of pers.) fill with grief, cause to regret B.NP 4287, Anel 217, TC 4.1531; (without *it*) A.Mil 3462, E.Mch 2432. **reweth** *imper. pl.* F.Fkl 974, TC 4.1501. [OE *hrēowan*]

rewful *adj.* lamentable, sad LGW 1838, as *n.* sorrowful creature B.ML 854; **rewfulleste** *sup.* A.Kn 2886. [from *rew* n., OE *hrēow*]

rewfully *adv.* piteously, sorrowfully TC 3.65, 4.1691, 5.729. [from prec.]

rewliche *adj.* pitiable, pitiful Bo 2. p2. 43/60. [OE *hrēowlic̆*]

rewthe(- *see* **routhe(-.**

rial(- *see* **royal(-.**

riban *n.* ribbon. HF 1318. [OF]

ribaninges *n. pl.* ribbon-work, silk borders. RR 1077. [from prec.]

ribaudye *n.* **1.** debauchery, lasciviousness I.Pars 464 *var.* **2.** ribaldry, coarse or ribald jesting A.Rv 3866, C.Pard 324. [OF *ribau(l)die*]

ribawdrye *n.* debauchery, lasciviousness I.Pars 464 *var.* [OF *ribau(l)derie*]

ribybe *n.* (*lit.* rebeck, fiddle) an abusive term for an old woman D.Fri 1377. Cf. **rebekke.** [OF *rubebe, rebebe*]

ribible/ru- *n.* fiddle A.Mil 3331, A.Co 4396. [as prec.]

riche *adj.* **1.** wealthy A.Kn 1946, A.Mil 3188, Gent 13; abounding in wealth A.Kn 869; (transf., with *of*) abounding (in) A.Prol 311, 479; as *n.*: *sg.* rich man PF 103; *pl.* (without def. art.) rich people A.Prol 248; ~ *and povre* one and all I.Pars 461, LGW 388, TC 5.43. **2.** (of material objects) splendid, costly A.Prol 296, A.Kn 1911, B.ML 137, D.WB 345, fine, beautiful BD 1319, sumptuous, luxurious F.Sq 61, LGW 2302; precious E.Cl 1118; (of beauty) TC 5.818. **3.** (of colour) strong, deep RR 1188. [OE *rīce* and OF *riche*]

riche *adv.* splendidly A.Prol 609, HF 1327. [as prec.]

richely *adv.* richly, splendidly E.Cl 1130, LGW 1037; (with p.p.) A.Kn 1012, E.Cl 267, RR 578. [from adj.]

richesse *n.* riches, wealth A.Kn 1255, 1829, D.WB 257, E.Mch 2242, RR 1116; abundance TC 3.349; (person.) A.Kn 1926, 1947, PF 261, RR 1033, etc.; flower (of knighthood) Ven 12. **richesses** *pl.* (only in prose) B.Mel 2560, 2582, I.Pars 186, Bo 1. p3. 52/74. [OF *richesse*]

rideled *p p.* pleated, gathered in (at neck or waist) RR 1235, 1243. [from OF *rideler* fold]

ride(n *v.* **1.** *intr.* ride, go on horseback A.Prol 94, A.Kn 873, *infin.* = riding TC 2.1253; (with phrase of pace) A.Prol 825, ~ *a* (*softe*) *pas* A.Kn 2897, B.ML 399, TC 2.627, 5.61; set out A.Prol 855, TC 5.57; ~ *or go* (with variations) ride or walk, go, move A.Kn 1351, 2252, A.Rv 4238, C.Pard 748, D.Fri 1465; ~ *out* ride on an expedition A.Prol 45, on a tour of inspection B.Sh 1255; ~ *on* mount, copulate with B.NP 4358. **2.** (of ships) lie at anchor LGW 968. **3.** *tr.* ride on (one's way) A.Prol 856, D.Fri 1406, 1536. **rydestow** *pr. 2 sg.* (with suffixed pron.) D.Fri 1386. **rideth** *3 sg.* A.Kn 1691, B.ML 375; **rit** A.Kn 974, 981, TC 2.1284. **ro(o)d** *pa. sg.* A.Prol 169,

TC 2.627. **ride(n** *pl.* A.Prol 825, 856, C.Pard 968, TC 1.473. **riden** *p.p.* A.Prol 48, A.Kn 1503, TC 2.933, 5.68. [OE *rīdan; rīdeþ, rīt; rād, ridon; riden*]

ryding *vbl. n.* **1.** riding (horse) I.Pars 432; **2.** jousting or procession A.Co 4377.

riet *n.* the 'rete' or 'net' of an astrolabe, 'an open-work metal plate, affixed to an astrolabe, and serving to indicate the positions of the principal fixed stars' (*OED*) Astr 1.3.3/4, etc. [L *rete* net]

right *n.* **1.** justice, right A.Kn 3089, B.Mel 2569, C.Phs 174, Bo 1. p4. 39/54 (L *iure*), TC 3.1282; (with *do(n*) justice, just treatment D.WB 1049, TC 4.515, LGW 388; *have the* ~ be in the right BD 1282; *by* ~ with reason, justly B.ML 44, G.SN 103, Bo 2. p5. 33/46, TC 4.396, *by alle* ~ in all justice TC 2.763, 4.1280; *of* ~ rightfully, justifiably TC 3.984, 1795, 4.571, 5.1345. **2.** right, legal right, just claim B.Mk 3102, I.Pars 264, 758, Bo 2. p2. 18/25, LGW 606, 2133; *by* ~ D.Fri 1635, ABC 22; *of* ~ F.Fkl 1324; ~ *of holy chirche* the Church's blessing (on marriage) E.Mch 1662. **3.** jurisdiction Bo 2. p6. 23/33, 30/44 (L *ius*); prerogative, right Bo 2. p2. 16/23, 21/30 (L *mei iuris*); *of his* ~ in its own right Bo 1. m4. 13/19; *frendes* ~ privilege, prerogative TC 1.591. **4.** *pl.* rights I.Pars 802, HF 456; true reasons Bo 3. m11. 26/35 (L *recta*); laws Bo 4.m6. 12 (L *iura*); *at alle* ~ in all respects, fully A.Kn 1852, 2100. [OE *riht*]

right *adj.* **1.** straight TC 3.228, RR 1701; upright Bo 5. m5. 15/22 (L *recto* (*uultu*)); direct, straight (way) A.Kn 1263, 2739, B.ML 556, 1130, E.Cl 273, F.Fkl 1240; (fig.) I.Pars 80, ABC 75, Astr prol 29/40, Bo 5. p1. 15/21 (L *rectum iter*), morally right Bo 4. p4. 62/86; (astron.) perpendicular to the equator, ~ *assencioun* right ascension Astr 2.28.21/30, ~ *cercle* Astr 2.26.17/25. **2.** correct, proper, true I.Pars 218, 921, Bo 4. p4. 46/62 (L *recte estimas*); fitting, proper A.Kn 2718, Anel 224, Bo 4. m6. 32/47, TC 3.998. **3.** rightful, true Astr 1.2.3/4, TC 2.851, 4.308; true, own TC 2.1065, 3.1663, F.Fkl 1311, Mars 213, I.GW 1620, (following n.) TC 3.134, 981, 1472. **4.** right (hand, side) A.Kn 1959, B.Mel 2502, HF 322, LGW 942, RR 729. [OE *riht*]

right *adv.* **1.** directly, straight B.Sh 1503, F.Fkl 1390, LGW 738. **2.** exactly, just, wholly A.Prol 257, A. Rv 3917, E.Mch 1520, F.Sq 492, TC 2.1064, RR 1301, precisely TC 2.286, (with advs. of time) ~ *anon* A.Kn 965, HF 2027, ~ *now* just now A.Prol 767, A.Kn 2793, HF 1792, ~ *nouthe* TC 1.985, ~ *sone* LGW 2639, ~ *tho* D.WB 816, E.Cl 544, LGW 2721; (with preps. and advs. of place) ~ *at* A.Rv 4243, D.Fri 1537, TC 2.1248, ~ *by* close beside, A.Rv 4036, BD 163, ~ *in* F.Fkl 1394, 1502, BD 182; ~ *here* E.Cl 1090, ~ *there* A.Kn 2619, C.Pard 765, D.Sum 2068; ~ *as* just as (if) A.Prol 535, 661, D.WB 791, E.Mch 2000, PF 316, ~ *so* LGW 1555, TC 3.847, 4.1075, ~ *thus* E.Mch 1941, LGW 579; *intensive* very, (with advs.) B.Mel 2533, E.Cl 665, BD 755, (with adjs.) A.Prol 288, 762, D.WB 479, E.Cl 375, F.Fkl 933, prec. *a* A.Prol 857;

~ *ynough* C.Pard 962, F.Sq 470, G.CY 1018, ~ *that* that very thing BD 1307; (with neg.) at all, whatever A.Prol 756, B.Sh 1512, C.Phs 24, E.Cl 1011, TC 4.518, LGW 1325; *al* ~ exactly, indeed TC 1.99. Cf. **anon~, forth~, up~**. [OE *riht(e)*]

rightful *adj.* just, upright, righteous: (of persons) A.Kn 1719, B.ML 814, G.SN 389, I.Pars 236, Bo 1. m5. 29/42 (L *iustus*); (of actions) I.Pars 337, 501, ABC 132, PF 390, lawful I.Pars 744; rightful, orderly Bo 4. m6. 4/5; (of time) right, proper (? in her prime) RR 405 (F *en son droit aage*). [LOE *rihtful*]

rightfully *adv.* justly B.Mel 2575, I.Pars 571, Bo 4. m4. 13/17. [from prec.]

rightwis *adj.* righteous, just I.Pars 625, LGW 373, 905. [OE *rihtwis*]

rightwisnesse *n.* righteousness, justice C.Pard 637, D.Sum 1909, Fort 66, Gent 88. [OE *rihtwisnesse*]

rigour *n.* severity, harshness F.Fkl 775. [OF]

rym *n.* **1.** rhyme I.Pars 44, Ven 80. **2.** rhyming verse, verse BD 54, 463, LGW 66, D.WB 1127, TC 3.90; ~ *dogerel* doggerel verse B.Mel 2115. **3.** rhyming poem, tale in verse B.ML 96, B.Th 1899, B.Mel 2114, 2118. [OF *rime*]

ryme *v.* **1.** *intr.* compose (rhyming) verse B.Mel 2122, G.CY 1093, TC 1.532, Scog 35, HF 520. **2.** *tr.* recount in verse A.Kn 1459, compose in (rhyming) verse TC 2.10, PF 119, Scog 41. [OF *rimer*]

rymeyed† *p.p.* composed in rhyme F.Fkl 711. [from OF *rimeier*]

rymyng *vbl. n.* rhyming, verse-making B.ML 48, B.Mel 2120.

rinde *n.* bark TC 4.1139; hard skin, hide TC 2.642. [OE *rind*]

ring *n.* ring A.Mil 3794, D.WB 785, TC 3.885, Astr 1.1.1; (a mark round the eyes) TC 4.869; enclosed space (for performance), arena LGW 1887; *pl.* ringlets A.Kn 2165. [OE *hring*]

ringe *v.* **1.** *intr.* ring, resound A.Kn 2359, 2600, A.Mil 3655, TC 2.233, 3.1237; (fig.) A.Rv 3896, TC 3.1725; (of places) resound B.Pri 1803, BD 312, HF 1398. **2.** *tr.* ring (bell), sound C.Pard 331, (fig.) proclaim HF 1720; *my belle shal be ronge* my story shall be told TC 5.1062. **rong** *pa. sg.* A.Mil 3215, C.Pard 662. **ronge** *pl.* BD 1164. **ronge** *p.p.* TC 2.805, 5.1062; **yronge** HF 1655. [OE *hringan*, pa. *hringde*]

riot *n.* debauchery, wanton revelry A.Co 4392, C.Pard 465, D.WB 700, riotous conduct A. Co 4395. [OF *riote*]

riote *v.* revel, A.Co 4414. [OF *rioter*]

ryotour *n.* rake, one living in wanton debauchery C.Pard 661, 692, 716. [AN]

riotous *adj.* wanton, extravagant A.Co 4408, B.Mel 2277. [OF]

rype *adj.* ripe H.Mcp 83; mature A.Rv 3875, C.Phs 68; (fig.) mature, seasonable, wise E.Cl 220, 438. [OE *rīpe*]

rys *n.* spray, branch, twig A.Mil 3324, RR 1015. [OE *hrīs*]

rise(n *v.* **1.** rise, get up (from bed) A.Prol 33, A.Kn 1047; ~ *up, up* ~ A.Prol 823, E.Mch 2138; (from table) F.Sq 267, TC 2.1597; (from ground, etc.) TC 1.695, 4.1243; stand (up) B.Mel 2200, TC 2.1302, 3.594, (out of respect) B.Mk 3702, D.WB

1000; ~ *upon* rebel against B.Mk 3608, 3717. **2.** rise from death B.Mel 2265, I.Pars 160, TC 5.1844. **3.** rise (of heavenly bodies) A.Kn 2273, TC 3.1418, LGW 112. **4.** arise, begin C.Pard 567, TC 1.944, 5.1479, BD 70; be heard TC 1.85, LGW 1242. **5.** increase D.WB 1128; rise in position D.WB 1167. **6.** feel exalted TC 1.278. **riseth** *pr. 3 sg.* A.Kn 1493, C.Pard 567; **rist** A.Mil 3688, A.Rv. 4193, TC 1.944, *with refl. pron.* TC 2.812, 4.232, LGW 810. **riseth** *imper. pl.* I.Pars 160. **roos** *pa. sg.* A.Prol 823, A.Rv 4211, TC 1.85. **risen** *p.p.* A.Kn 1065, A.Mil 3798, B.Mel 2265. [OE *rīsan, rās, risen*]

rysing *vbl. n.*: ~ *of the sonne* sunrise Bo 1. m5. 10/15.

risshe *n.* rush RR 1701, (a thing of no value) TC 3.1161 (see **yno(u)gh**). [OE *risce*]

ryte *n.* rite, observance A.Kn 1902, 2284, 2370, TC 5.1849, Astr 2.4.37/58. [OF *rit* or L *rītus*]

ryve *v.* pierce, cleave C.Pard 828, TC 5.1560, LGW 661, 1351; thrust LGW 1793. **roof** *pa. sg.* HF 373, LGW 661, 1351. [ON *rifa*, pa. *reif*]

rive(e)r *n.* river A.Kn 3024, D.Sum 2080, E.Mch 2201, Bo 3. m10. 8/12; river-bank, river-meadow D.WB 884, (as place frequented for hawking) F.Fkl 1196, *for* ~ for hawking waterfowl TC 4.413, B.Th 1927. [OF *rivere*]

robbour *n.* robber B.Mk 3818, G.CY 659. [OF]

robe *n.* robe, gown A.Prol 296, B.Th 1924, G.SN 132. [OF]

roche *n.* rock F.Sq 500, TC 3.1497, HF 1116; *pl.* BD 156, HF 1035. Cf. **rokke**. [OF *roche*, var. of *ro(c)que*]

rode *n.¹* complexion A.Mil 3317, B.Th 1917. [OE *rudu*]

rode *n.²* cross TC 5.1860, HF 57; (swear) *by the* ~ BD 924; *by the* ~ (asseveration) BD 992, HF 2. [OE *rōd*]

rodebeem *n.* rood-beam, beam which supports the cross above the rood-screen in a church D.WB 496. [prec.+OE *bēam*]

rody *adj.* ruddy, fresh-complexioned BD 143, 905, F.Sq 385, RR 820; red, reddish, (of the sun) F.Sq 394, Bo 4. m6. 5/7, (of a wood) Bo 2. m3. 7/8 (L *inrubuit rosis*). [OE *rudiġ*]

roggeth *pr. 3 sg.* shakes LGW 2708. [? cf. Norw. dial. *rogga* drive on]

roghte *see* **recche**.

royal/real/rial *adj.* royal, regal B.NP 4366, 4374; (preceding n.) A.Kn 1829, B.ML 961, B.Th 2092, Pity 59, ABC 144, PF 330, ~ *blood* I.Pars 765, ~ *estat* F.Sq 26, ~ *habit* LGW 214, ~ *maiestee* Bo 1. p4. 105/146, ~ *palais* TC 3.1534; (following n.) *beest* ~ F.Sq 264, *blood* ~ A.Kn 1018, 1546, B.ML 657, B.Mk 3341, Anel 65, TC 1.435, 3.1800, *court* ~ A.Kn 1497, *estat* ~ TC 1.432, 4.1667; 5.1830, LGW 1036, *foul* ~ PF 394, *stok* ~ A.Kn 1551. **royales/reales** *pl.* B.Th 2038. **royaller** *comp.* B.ML 402 [OF *roial/real/rial*]

royalliche/-ly *adv.* royally, magnificently, splendidly A.Prol 378, A.Kn 1687, B.ML 968, E.Cl 421, 955, with pomp F.Sq 174 [from prec.]

royaltee *n.* royalty, royal splendour B.ML

418, 703, E.Cl 928; **realtee** sovereign
power Fort 60. [OF *roialté/realté*]
royleth *pr. 3 sg.* flows, rolls Bo 1. m7. 7/10
(L *uagatur*). [OF *roillier*]
roynet† *n.* roughness, scab RR 553. [OF
roigne]
roynous *adj.* rough RR 988. [AN]
rokes *n. gen. pl.* of rooks HF 1516. [OE *hrōc*]
roket *n.* rochet, cloak RR 1240, 1242. [ONF]
rokke *n.* rock F.Fkl 1061, BD 164, LGW
2195; rock F.Fkl 1073; *pl.* F.Fkl 859,
TC 2.1384, LGW 2193. Cf. **roche**. [OF
roke, *ro(c)que*]
rokken *v.* rock A.Rv 4157. [LOE *roccian*]
rolle *n.* roll C.Pard 911. [OF *ro(o)lle*]
rolle(n *v.* **1.** *tr.* revolve, turn over in the
mind Bo 3. m11.2/3 (L *in se reuoluat*), ~ *up
and doun* C.Pard 838, D.Sum 2217, TC
2.659, ~ *to and fro* TC 5.1313. *p.p.* talked
about TC 5.1061. **2.** *intr.* roll, turn over
and over A.Kn 2614, *pr. p.* A.Prol 201;
roule wander, roam D.WB 653. [OF
rol(l)er, *rouler*]
Romayn *n.* Roman B.Mk 3551, D.WB 647,
BD 1084; *pl.* B.ML 291, B.NP 4555; ref. to
St. Paul's *Epistle to the Romans* B.Mel
2178, 2630. [OF *Romain*]
Romayn *adj.* Roman B.ML 954; ~ *gestes*
stories of Roman history B.ML 1126,
D.WB 642, E.Mch 2284. [OF *romain*]
romaunce *n.* romance TC 3.980, (of Thebes)
TC 2.100, (Ovid's *Metamorphoses*) BD 48;
pl. B.Th 2038, 2087; in title *the ~ of the
Rose* RR 39, E.Mch 2032, BD 334, LGW
329. [OF *romanz*]
rombled *see* **rumbelen**.
rome(n *v.* walk, stroll, roam A.Kn 1119,
1528, B.Sh 1487, LGW 1497; make one's
way A.Mil 3694; ~ *to and fro* A.Kn 1099,
1113, TC 2.516; ~ *up and doun* A.Kn 1069,
1515, B.NP 4088, 4370, F.Fkl 1013, HF
140; (with refl. pron.) F.Fkl 843; go BD
443, LGW 1589. [?]
ron *see* **reyne**.
rond *see* **round**.
rone *n.* ?bush, thicket RR1674 (F *soz ciaus*).
[nth., cf. Norw. dial. *rune*]
ronges *n. pl.* rungs A.Mil 3625. [OE *hrung*]
roo *n.* roe PF 195; **roes** *pl.* BD 430, Bo 3.
m8. 6/8, RR 1401; **raa** (nth.) A. Rv 4086.
[OE *rā*]
roof *n.* roof A.Mil 3565, D.WB 778, BD 299;
rove *prep.* A.Mil 3837 *var*, HF 1948 *var*.
[OE *hrōf*]
roof *see* **ryve**.
roos *see* **rise(n**.
roost *n.* roast meat A.Prol 206. [OF *rost*]
ro(o)te *n.*[1] **1.** root (of plant or tree) A.Prol 2,
A.Mil 3206, I.Pars 113, Bo 3. p11. 82/112;
(rent up) *by the* ~ LGW 2613; *upon* ~
F.Sq 153; (fig.) *on* ~ firmly rooted TC
2.1378; *crop and* ~ the whole, everything
TC 5.1245, the perfection TC 2.348. **2.**
origin, source A.Prol 423, B.Mel 2399; (of
persons) B.ML 358, B.Pri 1655, G.CY
1069, TC 2.844, (as source of a lineage)
LGW 1368; (of qualities) B.Mel 2320,
3030, I.Pars 113, 388. **3.** foot (of a
mountain) E.Cl 58. **4.** basis, principle
Bo 3. m11. 29/40, 4. p4. 179/249; essential
part G.CY 1461; *herte* ~ bottom, depths of
the heart D.WB 471, LGW 1993, RR
1026. **5.** (astrol.) root, radix (number

assigned to a date, from which correspond-
ing quantities for other dates can be calculated) Astr 2.44.1; the 'epoch' of a nativity,
from which a computation may be made
B.ML 314, *pl.* F.Fkl 1276. [LOE *rōt*]
ropen *p.p.* reaped LGW 74. [strong p.p. not
recorded in OE; infin. *ripan*]
rore *n.* confusion, uproar TC 5.45. [MDu
roer]
rore *v.* roar, cry out loudly TC 4.241, 373,
B.NP 4078, (of thunder) LGW 1219; (of
a place) resound, echo A.Kn 2881. [OE
rārian]
roring *vbl. n.* loud lament E.Mch 2364.
rose *n.* rose C.Phs 33, TC 1.949; *gen.* A.Kn
1038; *attrib.* A.Kn 1961; *pl.* G.SN 220,
244, RR 1651; (in various allusive uses)
RR 856, PF 442, *as faire as is the* ~ LGW
613, *as fresh as is a* ~ D.WB 448, *red(e as* ~
B.Th 1916, TC 2.1256, LGW 112, *whyt as
lilie or* ~ RR 1015; in title of poem see
romaunce, as abbrev. for title LGW G.
344, 441, 470; (person.) name of character
RR 48. [OE *rose*]
rosen *adj.* **1.** made of roses RR 845. **2.**
rose-coloured, rosy (only in Bo, all but
first tr. L *roseus*) ~ *floures* Bo 2. m3. 7/9 (L
uernis inrubuit rosis); 1. m2. 16/23, 2. m3. 2,
m8. 4/6, 3. m1. 8/11. [OE *rosen*]
roser *n.* rose-bush RR 1651, 1659, I.Pars
858. [AN **roser*]
rosy *adj.* rose-coloured TC 2.1198, 3.1755,
5.278. [from **rose**]
roste *v.* roast A.Prol 383. **rosted** *pa. sg.*
A.Rv 4137; *p.p.* A.Prol 147, D.Sum 1841.
[OF *rostir*]
rote *n.*[2] rote, practice: *by* ~ by heart A.Prol
327, B.Pri 1712, 1735; C.Pard 332 (all
with *can*, *coude*). [?]
rote *n.*[3] a stringed instrument, perh. a kind
of fiddle A.Prol 236. [OF]
rotelees *adj.* rootless TC 4.770. [from **ro(o)te**
n.[1]]
roten *adj.* rotten A.Rv 3873, A.Co 4406,
G.SN 228, I.Pars 419, Anel 314, (fig.) A.Rv
3875; corrupt, filthy G.SN 17, I.Pars 139,
461. [ON *rotinn*]
roten-herted *adj.* rotten-hearted, thoroughly
corrupt I.Pars 689. [from prec.+**herte**]
rotie *pr. subj. 3 sg.* rot, make rotten A.Co
4407. [OE *rotian*]
rough *adj.* rough, hairy A.Mil 3738, D.Fri
1622, TC 1.948, RR 228. [OE *rūh*]
rouketh *pr. 3 sg.* cowers, huddles A.Kn 1308.
[cf. Norw. dial. *ruka* cower]
roule *see* **rolle(n**.
roum *n.* room, space LGW 1999; cf.
aroume [OE *rum*]
roum, *adj.* roomy, spacious A.Rv 4126,
large, wide Astr 1.2.2; **roumer** *comp.* A.Rv
4145. [OE *rūm*]
rouncy *n.* riding-horse; ? big horse, ? hackney, nag A.Prol 390. [OF *ronci*]
round *adj.* **1.** round, circular A.Kn 1889,
A.Rv 3934, F.Fkl 1228, G.SN 114, BD
946. **2.** (of limbs, breasts) round, well-
shaped, full A.Kn 2136, A.Rv 3975, BD
956, TC 3.1250, (of cheeks, lips) full, filled
out Rosem 4, A.Kn 2168; **rond** Astr 2.
38. 1 *var*, 3/4 *var*. [OF *ro(u)nd*]
round(e *adv.* round A.Prol 589; roundly,
resoundingly C.Pard 331; easily, with an
easy motion B.Th 2076. [from prec.]

rounded *pa. sg.* stood out in a rounded form A.Prol 263. [from adj.]

roundel *n.* **1.** roundel, a short lyric in which the opening line or lines recur in the middle and at the end A.Kn 1529, F.Fkl 948, PF 675, LGW 423. **2.** circle, ring HF 791, 798. [OF *rondel*]

roundes *n. pl.* circles, orbits Bo 3. m9. 21/29. (from adj. and/or F *rond*)

roundnesse *n.* roundness Bo 4. m1. 4/5 (L *globum*), 5. p4 101/145, 106/153 (*rotunditatem*). *pl.* orbits Bo 4. m6. 33/50 (*flexos . . . in orbes*). [from **round** adj.]

roune(n *v.* whisper **1.** *intr.* D.WB 241, G.CY 894, TC 3.568, 4.587. **2.** *tr.* D.WB 1021, D.Fri 1550, HF 2044; tell B.Th 2025. **3.** *tr.* call in a whisper HF 2107. [OE *rūnian*]

rouninges *vbl. n. pl.* whisperings, private conversations HF 1960.

route *n.* company, host, throng A.Prol 622, A.Kn 2153, B.ML 650, D.Sum 1695, TC 2.613, 5.65; *pl.* TC 2.620; large number RR 1667; flock RR 909. [AN *rute*, OF *route*]

route *v.*[1] snore A.Mil 3647, A.Rv 4167, BD 172. [OE *hrūtan*]

route *v.*[2] roar TC 3.743; rumble, boom HF 1038. [cf. Norw. *ruta*]

route *v.*[3] assemble, gather together B.ML 540. [OF *router*]

routhe *n.* **1.** pity, compassion, mercy TC 2.349, BD 97, F.Fkl 1520; *have* ~ A.Kn 2392, B.ML 654, E.Cl 579, F.Fkl 1261, TC 2.523; *caughte* ~ F.Fkl 1520; *for* ~ *out* of compassion, for pity's sake B.ML 529, E.Cl 893, F.Sq 438, TC 5.1099. **2.** distress, grief TC 5.1687; *make* ~ lament A.Rv 4200, LGW 669. **3.** a matter ·for sorrow, a pity BD 1310, TC 2.664, E.Mch 1908; ~ *for to see/here* A.Kn 914, B.ML 1052, E.Cl 562, F.Fkl 1349. [from **rewe(n]**

routhelees *adj.* ruthless, pitiless B.ML 863, Anel. 230, TC 2.346. [from prec.]

routing *vbl. n.*[1] snoring A.Rv 4166, 4214. [from **route** v.[1]]

routing *vbl. n.*[2] rumbling, whizzing HF 1933. [from **route** v.[2]]

rove *see* **roof.**

rowe *n.* row, line BD 975, HF 1451; *by* ~ in a row TC 2.970; (written) line HF 448; *pl.* rays, beams of light Mars 2. Cf. **arowe, rewe.** [? OE *rāw*, var. of *rǣw*]

rowe *adv.* roughly, angrily TC 1.206, G.CY 861. [OE *rūw-*, stem of *rūh* (see **rough**)+ adv. *-e*]

rowen *p.p.* rowed, moved on the water F.Fkl 1145; **rowed** rowed TC 1.969. [OE *rōwan*, p.p. *rōwen*]

roweres *n. pl.* rowers Bo 4. m3. 16/21. [from OE *rōwan*]

rubbe *v.* rub out Adam 6; rub A.Mil 3747, E.Mch 1827. [cf. LG *rubben*]

rubifying *ppl. adj.* reddening G.CY 797. [from *rubify*e v., OF *rubifier*]

rubriche *n.* rubric D.WB 346. [OF *rubrique*]

ruddok *n.* robin redbreast PF 349. [OE *rudduc*]

rude/rewde *adj.* ignorant A.Mil 3227, E.Mch 2351, rough, crude E.Cl 750, RR 752; (of language) lacking polish, plain, rude F.Fkl 718, Astr prol 31/43, unmannerly, discourteous B.NP 3998; of low birth, unrefined D.WB 1172; (of clothing) rough E.Mch 1798, coarse, poor E.Cl 916, 1012; (of scenery) rugged, wild H.Mcp 170. [OF *ru(i)de*]

rudeliche/-ly *adv.* coarsely, crudely A.Prol 734, roughly, uncared for E.Cl 380. [from prec.]

rudenesse *n.* roughness, uncouthness E.Cl 397, TC 4.1489, boorishness TC 4.1677. [from **rude**]

ruf invented alliterative word I.Pars 43.

rugged *adj.* rough, shaggy A.Kn 2883 var; see next. [cf. Sw. *rugga* roughen]

ruggy *adj.* rough, shaggy A.Kn 2883 var. [cf. Sw. *ruggig*]

ruyne *n.* ruin HF 1974; overthrowing, causing to fall B.Mel 2754, A.Kn 2463; (of person) ruin, downfall TC 4.387. [OF]

rum invented alliterative word I.Pars 43.

rumbel *n.* rumbling noise A.Kn 1979, murmuring, rumour E.Cl 997. [from next]

rumbelen *v.* rumble LGW 1218 var, HF 1026. **rombled** *pa.* murmured B.Mk 3725, made a rumbling noise (by groping) G.CY 1322. [? LG (cf. MDu *rommelen*), echoic]

rumblinge *n.* rumbling noise D.Sum 2233. [from prec.]

rumour *n.* rumour, general talk Bo 3. p6. 12/16 (L *rumore*); *pl.* (laudatory) remarks, fame Bo 2. p7. 81/116 (L *rumores*); (?) uproar, tumult TC 5.53. [OF]

rused *pa. sg.* made a detour (to escape from the hounds) BD 381. [OF *ruser*]

rusty *adj.* rusty A.Prol 618; looking like something rusted RR 159 (F *roilliee*). [OE *rūstiġ*]

S

sable *adj.* black Mars 284. [OF]

sachels *n. pl.* small bags Bo 1. p3. 53/75. [OF]

sacred *ppl. adj.* consecrated (to) I.Pars 801; dedicated, devout A.Kn 1921. [from v. from OF *sacrer*]

sacrement *n.* sacrament; *the* ~ *of the auter* the Eucharist I. Pars 582. [OF]

sacrifye *v.* offer sacrifice LGW 1348. [OF *sacrifier*]

sacrifyinge *vbl. n.* sacrifice Bo 4. m7. 9/12.

sacrifyse *n.* sacrifice A.Kn 2278, LGW 1350; *don* ~ A.Kn 1902, C.Pard 469, G.SN 392, TC 3.539, LGW 1310, *make* ~ BD 114. [OF]

sacrifyse *v.* sacrifice G.SN 365, TC 5.423. [from prec.]

sacrilege *n.* sacrilege I.Pars 801, Bo 1. p4. 181/253 *var* **sacrilegie** (L *sacrilegio*, MS. C gloss *sorcerie*), 184/257. [OF]

sad *adj.* **1.** stable, firm, steadfast, constant E.Cl 220, I.Pars 129, 310, Bo 1. m4.1, 2. p4. 54/73; unchanging E.Cl 602, unmoved E.Cl 693, 754; calm, settled G.SN 397; steadfastly devoted BalCo 9, H.Mcp 275; trustworthy B.ML 135, H.Mcp 258. **2.** serious, grave A.Kn 2985, E.Cl 237, 293, 1002, E.Mch 1399, BD 860, 918. **3.** sated, weary G.CY 877. **4.** sorrowful, sad RR 211 var. [OE *sæd*]

sad *adv.* firmly E.Cl 564 var.

sadly *adv.* **1.** firmly A.Kn 2602, D.Sum 2264; tightly E.Cl 1100; steadily Astr

2.29.13/17; steadfastly I.Pars 124. **2.**
gravely, soberly, discreetly B.Sh 1266,
B.Mel 2412. **3.** fully, deeply B.ML 743.
[from prec.]

sadnesse *n.* **1.** constancy E.Cl 452, firm-
ness Bo 4. p1. 42/59 (L *soliditate*). **2.**
seriousness, soberness E.Mch 1591, 1604,
CompL 26. [from **sad**]

saffron *v.* season: *to* ~ *with my predicacioun*
to season my preaching with C.Pard 345.
[from next]

saffroun *n.* saffron B.Th 1920. [OF *safran*,
ult. Arab]

say *see* **se(e)(n.**

sayl/seyl *n.* sail A.Prol 696, D.Sum 1688,
LGW 646; *coll. sg.* sails LGW 654. [OE
segl]

sayle(n *v.* sail B.ML 321, 440, TC 2.1; (fig.)
TC 1.606; (with obj.) ~ *his/hir cours* B.NP
4289, F.Fkl 851. *pr. p. adj.* moving by
means of sails, *the* ~ *fyr* PF 179. **yseyled**
p.p. B.NP 4289. [OE *segl(i)an*]

saylours/saillouris *n. pl.* dancers RR 770.
[OF *sailleor*]

sayn *see* **seye.**

sak *n.* **1.** sack, bag A.Rv 4017, E.Mch 2200.
2. robe of sackcloth RR 457. [OE *sacc*]

sake *n.* in phr. *for* (gen. or poss. adj.) ~ *out*
of consideration for, out of regard for
A.Prol 537, A.Kn 1317, D.Fri 1363, E.Cl
255, LGW 206. [OE *sacu*]

sakked *p.p.* put in sacks A.Rv 4070. [from
sak]

sal *n.* salt (only with qualifying word): ~
armoniak sal-ammoniac, ammonium
chloride G.CY 798, 824; ~ *peter* saltpetre
G.CY 808; ~ *preparat* prepared salt; ~
tartre salt of tartar, potassium carbonate
G.CY 810. [L]

sal *see* **shal.**

sale A.Rv 4187 *var see* **soule.**

salewe *see* **salue.**

salowe *adj.* sallow RR 355. [OE *salo*]

salte *adj.* salt (applied only to the sea and to
tears) B.ML 830; *after def. art.* B.ML 445,
1039; *pl.* B.Pri 1864, TC 4.814, 5.1374,
LGW 2284. [OA *salt*]

salue/saluwe/salewe *v.* salute, greet B.Pri
1723, B.Sh 1284, F.Fkl 1310, TC 2.1257.
[OF *saluer*]

saluing *vbl. n.* salutation, greeting A.Kn
1649, TC 2.1568.

salutacioun *n. pl.* greetings B.Sh 1198.
[OF]

sa(l)vacioun *n.* **1.** salvation (of the soul)
B.ML 283, D.Fri 1498; (in asseverations)
by my ~ D.Fri 1618, G.CY 848, H.Mcp 58,
God . . be my ~ D.WB 621, TC 2.381, 563.
2. preservation Bo 3. p11. 64/88 (L *tueri
salutem*); protection Bo 1. p4. 38/54 (L
pro tuendo), p4. 108/150; security, safety
B.Mel 2361, TC 1.464, 4.1382; saving
TC 2.486, *withoute any* ~ HF 208 without
saving any. **3.** cause of salvation, person
who saves G.SN 75, Mars 213. [OF
sauvacion/salv-]

salve *n.* salve, cure A.Kn 2712, TC 4.944.
[OA *salf-*]

salwes *n. pl.* willow-twigs, osiers D.WB 655.
[OA *salh, salg-*]

same *adj.* same, identical A.Kn 1740, 2873;
(of sthg. previously mentioned) A.Kn 2904,
A.Rv 3955; aforesaid B.Mel 2549, I.Pars

145; (with demons.) A.Kn 1784, A.Co
4405, B.Mk 3426, Bo 1. p4. 93/129, 3.
p10. 73/101 (*thilke* common in Bo); (with
o(n) B.Mel 2203, Bo 4. p2. 65/85. *pron.*:
that ~ the same person ABC 77; *the* ~ the
same thing B.Mel 2758, C.Pard 830, G.CY
1005. [ON *same*]

samit/samet *n.* samite (a rich silk fabric) TC
1.109, RR 836; a garment of samite RR
873. [OF *samit*]

samples *n. pl.* examples Astr2.40.4 *var.*
[OF *essample*]

sandes *see* **so(o)nd.**

sang *see* **singe(n, song.**

sangwyn *adj.* sanguine (of complexion:
characterized by ruddy colour and vigorous
disposition) A.Prol 333; ruddy, blood-red
A.Kn 2168. as *n.* cloth of blood-red colour
A.Prol 439. [OF *sanguin*]

sank *see* **sinke(n.**

sans/sanz *see* **sauns.**

sapience *n.* wisdom, understanding B.Pri
1662, E. Mch 1481; *pl.* kinds of intelligence,
faculties G.SN 338. [OF]

sarge *n.* serge A.Kn 2568. [OF *serge/sarge*]

sarpulers/sarpleris *n. pl.* canvas sacks Bo 1.
p3. 53/75. [AN *sarpler*]

Sarsinesshe/Sarsynesh *adj.* Saracen RR
1188*em.* [OF *Sarasinesche*]

sat *see* **sitte(n.**

satiry *n. pl.* satyrs TC 4.1544. [L *satyri*]

satisfaccioun *n.* satisfaction, restitution **1.**
(in eccl. sense) the third part of penance
I.Pars 87, 108, 1029. **2.** reparation, compensation (only in (?legal) phr.) *don* ~
Bo 4. p4. 172/240 (L *satisfacerem*). [OF]

sauf *adj.* safe, secure, safely kept B.ML 343,
D.WB 1015, G.CY 950; saved D.Fri 1500;
(in absol. constr., also **save**) ~ *your grace*
by your leave, with due respect B.Mel
2260, 2272, 2878, *myn honour* ~ without
prejudice to my honour TC 3.159. **vouche**
~ *see* **vouch-.** [OF]

sauf/save *prep.* except (for) A.Kn 1410,
D.WB 493, D.Sum 1707, E.Cl 508, G.CY
1006, TC 5.210. *conj.* except (that) E.Mch
2085, F.Fkl 944; ~ *that* D.Sum 2275, E.Cl
55. [from prec.]

saufly *adv.* safely, with safety B.NP 4398,
D.WB 878, E.Cl 870. [from **sauf** adj.]

saugh *see* **se(e)(n.**

saule *see* **soule.**

sauns/sans/sanz *prep.* without. Except for
Fort heading (in F) ~ *peinture*, only ~ *doute*
D.Sum 1838, ~ *faille* B.ML 501, HF 188,
429. [OF *sans/sanz*]

sauter *n.* psalter RR 431. [AN]

sautrye *n.* psaltery, dulcimer A.Prol 296,
A.Mil 3213, 3305, H.Mcp 268. [OF]

savacioun *see* **salvacioun.**

save *n.* (a decoction of) sage A.Kn 2713.
[L *salvia*]

save *see* **sauf.**

save(n *v.* save A.Mil 3533, C.Phs 261, TC
2.575, 3.1476, LGW 2001; spare, in ~ *or
spille* D.WB 493, E.Cl 503, LGW 1036,
sleen or ~ F.Fkl 975; preserve TC 2.1243,
4.159, 1376, LGW 447, protect TC 1.122;
keep C.Phs 200, (word) F.Fkl 1478; (theol.)
save I.Pars 286, 597, ABC 117; avoid
I.Pars 1047; (often in prayer or wish,
subj.) *God* ~ A.Kn 2563, 3108, A.Rv 4247,
C.Pard 304, D.Fri 1564, (as greeting) *God*

~ *you* D.Fri 1585, G.CY 583; (in asseverations) *so God me* ~ A.Mil 3281, B.Sh 1416, C.Pard 860, D.Sum 2112. **saveth** *imper. pl.* B.ML 229. [AN *sa(u)ver*]
save-garde *n.* safe-conduct TC 4.139. [OF *sauve-garde*]
saveour *n.* saviour I.Pars 285, Purse 16. [OF *sauveour*]
saveren *see* **savoure.**
savinge *n.* (?) saving, preservation, (?) safety Bo 3. p12. 75/100 (L *salus*). [from **save(n**]
saving(e *prep.* except A.Kn 2838, A.Rv 3971, TC 5.224; without prejudice or offence to: ~ *youre grace* B.Mel 2737, ~ *his honour* E.Mch 1766, ~ *hir worship* BD 1271. [pr. p. of **save(n**]
savory *adj.* pleasant, sweet TC 1.405. [OF *savouré*]
savoringe *vbl. n.* taste I.Pars 207, 959.
savorous *adj.* sweet, pleasant RR 84. [OF]
savour *n.* **1.** taste B.Mel 2348, Bo 3. m1. 4/6; (fig.) savour D.Sum 2196. **2.** smell D.Sum 2226, G.CY 887; perfume, scent G.SN 229, 243, I.Pars 636, PF 274, (fig.) G.SN 91. **3.** pleasure, pleasantness Fort 20, F.Sq 404; delight TC 2.269. [OF]
savoure *v.* **1.** *ntr.* taste D.WB 171, I.Pars 122. **2.** *tr.* relish, enjoy I.Pars 820 (*var* **saveren**), Truth 5. [OF *savourer*]
savoured *adj.* perfumed RR 547. [from **savour** n.]
savourly *adv.* with relish A.Mil 3735. [from **savour** n.]
saugh/sawgh, saw, sawe *see* **se(e)(n.**
sawcefleem *adj.* covered with pimples (from inflammation supposed to be caused by salt humours) A.Prol 625. [OF *sausefleme*]
sawe *n.* **1.** something said, saying, speech A.Kn 1526, TC 5.38; remark, word B.Mel 2925; discourse G.CY 691; *pl.* sayings TC 2.41, words 4.1395. **2.** traditional saying A.Kn 1163, B.Mel 2671, 3030, D.WB 660. [OE *sagu*]
scabbe *n.* **1.** scab RR 553. **2.** a skin disease in sheep C.Pard 358. [ON **skabbr* = OE *sceabb*]
scaffold *n.* scaffold, raised stand A.Kn 2533, raised platform or stage for plays A.Kn 3384. [AN **scaffaut,* OF *(e)schaffaut*]
scalded/y- *p.p.* scalded A.Kn 2020; burnt A.Mil 3853. [ONF *escalder*]
scale *n.* scale for measuring, a graduated line Astr 1.12.2, 4/6. [L *scala*]
scales *n. pl.* scales (of fish) PF 189. [OF *escale*]
scalle *n.* scall, a scaly disease of the skin Adam 3. [? ON *skalle*]
scalled *adj.* having the 'scall', scabby A.Prol 627. [from prec.]
scantitee *n.* scantiness I.Pars 431. [from **skant**]
scantnesse *n.* scantiness I.Pars 414, 420. [from **skant**]
scape(n *v.* escape A.Kn 1107, A.Rv 4087, TC 5.908. [ONF *escaper*]
scapinge *vbl. n.* escaping Bo 4. p4. 135/191.
scarlet *n.* scarlet stuff (a rich cloth, usually but not always of scarlet colour) A.Prol 456; ~ *in greyn* see **greyn.** *adj.* of scarlet colour D.WB 559; ~ *reed* B.NP 4351. [OF *escarlate*]
scarmishing *n.* skirmish LGW 1910. [from v., OF *eskermiss-* stem of *eskermir*]

scarmuch(e/scarmyche/skarmish *n.* skirmish TC 2.611, 934, 5.1508. [OF *escar(a)-muche,* and *eskermir* v.]
scars/skars *adj.* niggardly B.Mel 2789; scarce FormA 36. [ONF]
scarsetee/skarseté *n.* **1.** niggardliness B.Mel 2790. **2.** scarcity G.CY 1393; deficiency Ven 80. [ONF *escarceté*]
scarsly *adv.* **1.** parsimoniously A.Prol 583. **2.** scarcely, only just B.Sh 1418, B.Mk 3602, TC 2.43. [from **scars**]
scater/skatere *v.* scatter Bo 3. p9. 80/106 (L *profligat*), 3. m9. 31/43 (L *dissice*), G.CY 914. [?]
scathe *n.* harm, misfortune TC 4.207, *Polymites . . to* ~ to the harm of P . . . TC 5.938; matter for regret, a pity: *that was* ~ A.Prol 446, *were it* ~ E.Cl 1172. [ON *skaði*]
scatheles *adj.* harmless RR 1550. [from prec.]
science *n.* **1.** knowledge Bo 2. p7. 106/152, 5. p3. 73/103; knowledge, wisdom (of God) Bo 5. p5. 73/106, p6. 73/103, 201/283, (of gods)¡ HF 1091, D.WB 699, (human wisdom) I.Pars 229, 455; learning, knowledge A.Prol 316, B.Mk 3938 *var,* PF 25, TC 1.67, *pl.* B.Mel 2596. **2.** a particular branch of learning or knowledge F.Fkl 1122, Bo 1. p4. 12/17, a particular science or art F.Fkl 1139, G.CY 680, 732; (?) learned writing, human learning B.Pri 1666. [OF]
sclat/slate *n.* slate MercB 34, Astr 2.44. 38/54. [OF *esclate*]
sclaundre *n.* slander HF 1580, B.Sh 1373; disgrace, ill-repute E.Cl 722, 730, LGW 2231, Anel 275; scandal I.Pars 137. [AN *esclaundre*]
sclaundre *v.* slander G.CY 695, 998. [AN *esclandrer*]
sclave *n.* slave TC 3.391. [OF *esclave*]
sclendre/slendre *adj.* spare, slight A.Prol 587, E.Cl 1198, thin RR 858, slim E.Mch 1602; (of hair) thin, sparse B.Mk 3147; (of food) frugal B.NP 4023. [?]
scochouns *n. pl.* escutcheons RR 893. [AN *escuchon*]
scole *n.* **1.** school (for children) B.Pri 1685, 1688. **2.** the 'schools' of a medieval university B.NP 4427, D.WB 528, D.Sum 2186, E.Mch 1427, 1428. **3.** source of instruction, lesson TC 1.634. **4.** method, manner, fashion A.Prol 125, A.Mil 3329. [OE *scōl,* OF *escole*]
scole-matere *n.* subject-matter for scholastic debate D.Fri 1272. [prec.+ **matere**]
scoleye *v.* attend school, study A.Prol 302. [AF **escoleier*]
scoleiyng† *n.* schooling, training D.WB 44f *var.* [from prec.]
scoler *n.* scholar, student A.Prol 260, A.Mil 3190. [OE *scolere,* OF *escoler*]
scolering† *n.* ?young scholar D.WB 44f *var.* [from prec.]
scoleward *see* **toward.**
scomes *n. pl.* froth, lather Bo 4. m7. 39/56. [MDu, MLG *schūm*]
scorchith *pr. 3 sg.* scorches Bo 2. m6. 18/25 *var.* [?]
score *imper.* score, notch B.Sh 1606. [ON *skora*]
scorkleth *pr. 3 sg.* scorches, shrivels Bo

2. m6. 18/25 var. [rel. to *scorken* v., perh. from ON *skorpna*]

scorn n. scorn, derision TC 1.320, 335; *in* ~ scornfully, mockingly A.Rv 3915, C.Pard 623, TC 1.514; show of contempt, insult A.Mil 3388, taunt Anel 305; object of scorn A.Rv 4110. [OF *escarn*]

scorne(n v. **1.** *intr.* jeer TC 1.576 var. **2.** *tr.* scorn, ridicule, deride G.SN 506, TC 1.234, 576 var, jest at B.NP 4277, treat rudely TC 5. 982; hold in disdain, despise Bo 1. p3. 57/80, *pr. p.* 2. m4. 13/18. [OF *escarnir*]

scorner n. mocker B.Mel 2519, I.Pars 636; (of the pheasant) PF 357. [from prec.]

scorning vbl. n. scorn, mockery TC 1.105, I.Pars 635.

scorning adj. mocking PF 346. [from **scorne(n)**

scorpioun n. scorpion BD 636, I.Pars 854; (fig. of person) B.ML 404, (of tongue) H.Mcp 271; (astrol.) the zodiacal sign Scorpio HF 948, Astr 1.8.3/4. [OF *scorpion*]

scoure v. scour RR 540; scourge I.Pars 670 var. [? MDu, MLG *schuren*]

scourge n. scourge, whip B.Mk 3590, E.Cl 1157. [AN *escurge*]

scrippe n. bag, satchel (esp. of a pilgrim) D.Sum 1737, 1777, HF 2123. [OF *escrep(p)e*]

scripture n. writing, passage of writing LGW 1144, pl. writings A.Kn 2044; *in* ~ in writing, on record Bo 1. p4. 123/170; inscription TC 3.1369/1355. [L *scriptūra*]

scrit n. writing, written document E.Mch 1697, TC 2.1130. [OF *escrite*]

scriveyn n. scribe Adam 1. [OF *escrivain*]

scrivenish adv. like a professional scribe, in a formal hand TC 2.1026 (var **scryvenliche**). [from prec.]

seche(n see **seke(n**.

secree n. private or secret matter B.Mel 2331, B.Mk 3211, 3243, D.Fri 1341; (fig.) the most intimate part Bo 1. p4. 161/224; divine or natural mystery G.CY 1447 (i.e. the scientific book *Secreta Secretorum*). [OF *secré*]

secree adj. secret, hidden B.Sh 1320, C.Phs 143, D.Sum 1871, TC 1.744, 3.286; discreet, able to keep secrets B.NP 4105, D.WB 946, E.Mch 1909; private, secluded Bo 1. p4. 31/43 (L *inter secreta otia*). as adv. secretly F.Fkl. 1109. [as prec.]

secreenesse n. secrecy, secrets B.ML 773, TC 2. 843 var. [from prec.]

secrely adv. secretly B.Mel 2279, E.Cl 763, E.Mch 2006. [from **secree**]

secret adj. secret TC 2.1664; discreet TC 3.142, 478. [OF]

secte n. company, kind HF 1432, E.Cl 1171 (or ?sex); faith, religion F.Sq 17. [OF]

seculer adj. secular, belonging to the world, lay E. Mch 1251, 1322, I.Pars 961; as n. layman B.NP 4640. [OF]

sede v. bear seed Anel 306. [from **seed**]

see n.¹ sea A.Kn 2298, B.ML 68; *the Drye* ~ ? the Gobi Desert BD 1028, *the Grete* ~ the Mediterranean A.Prol 59, *the rede* ~ the Red Sea Bo 3. m3. 3/5; *fulle* ~ high tide Astr 2.46.3/4; (fig.) Bo 1. p3. 46/63. [OE *sǣ*]

see n.² seat TC 4.1023, HF 1210, 1251; throne HF 1361; seat of empire B.Mk 3339. [AN *se*]

seed n. seed, grain D.WB 71, 143, Bo 2. p1. 76/105; (fig.) ~ *of chastitee, grace, love, soth* G.SN 193, I.Pars 117, RR 1617, Bo 3. m11. 23/31; semen Bo 3. m6. 7/9 (L *germen*); offspring, progeny I.Pars 761, ABC 182. [OE *sǣd*]

seed-foul n. bird which lives on seeds PF 512, 576.

seel n.¹ seal B.ML 882, D.Sum 2128, TC 3.1462, (used in magic) F.Sq 131. [OF *seel*]

seel n.² bliss A.Rv 4239. [OE *sǣl*]

se(e)lden/seldom adv. seldom B.Mel 2594, LGW 35. [OE *séldan/séldum*]

seemlinesse n. comeliness, gracefulness LGW 1041. [from **semely** adj.]

se(e)(n v. **1.** see, look at A.Kn 1035, C.Pard 765, E.Cl 983, G.CY 1119; ~ *at eye* A.Kn 3016, G.CY 1059, ~ *with eye* B.ML 280, TC 2.301, 5.448; ~ *biforn* (of God, Providence) foresee A.Kn 1665, Bo 5. p3. 10/12 (L. *praeuiderit*); intr. see, have sight B.ML 551, E.Mch 1598, G.CY 1418; look B.NP 4621; (*for*) *to* ~ to look on A.Kn 2176, A.Mil 3202, TC 2.584, to be seen E. Mch 1466, F.Sq 366. **2.** perceive, understand A.Kn 1947, 3026, B.ML 938, E.Cl 599, LGW 668. **3.** observe from experience B.NP 4242, F.Sq 481, TC 3.1063. **4.** ascertain, find out; *lat* ~ (with indir. question) A.Prol 831, A.Rv 4125, D.WB 76, (absol.) TC 2.1430; (an attempt to remember) *lot me* ~ D.WB 585; show A.Kn 3083. **5.** keep watch over, *pr. subj.* in *God hym, etc.* ~ B.ML 156, C.Pard 715, D.Sum 2169, TC 2.85. **to sene** infl. infin. TC 1.454. **seest** pr. 2 sg. A.Kn 2232, **se(e)stow** (with suffixed pron.) HF 911. **seeth** 3 sg. B.ML 266. **se(e)(n** pl. A.Kn 1947, 2061. **seeth** imper. pl. I.Pars 77. **saugh** pa. 1, 3 sg. A.Prol 764, 850; **saw** TC 1.114; **say** B.NP 4304; **sey** B.ML 809; **scigh** A.Prol 1066; **sy** G.CY 1381 (last four in rhyme). **sawe** 2 sg. B.ML 848. **saugh** pl. G.CY 1106; **sawe** B.ML 218; **say** E.Cl 1114 (in rhyme); **seigh** TC 4.720 var; **seye(n** G.SN 110, TC 4.720 var, **seyn** B.Mel 2879 var; **sye(n** E.Mch 1804, TC 5.816 (in rhyme). **seye** p.p. D.WB 552; **seyn** B.Pri 1863; **yseye** HF 1367; **yseyn** TC 5. 448; **y)sene** as adj. visible, manifest, evident A.Kn 924, 2298, TC 1.700. [OE *sēon; sæh/seh, sēgon; seĝen,* and *ĝesēne* adj.]

se(e)te n. seat, throne A.Kn 2580, B.Mk 3715, I.Pars 162; dwelling-place, residence Bo 1. p5. 20/29 (L *sedem*), 2. m4. 2, (fig., of thought) Bo 1. p5. 28/41 (L *(mentis) sedem*); inmost part Bo 3. p11. 86/117. [ON *sæti*]

seeth see **sethe**.

sege n. **1.** seat, throne Bo 1. p4. 11/15 var, (fig., of the mind) Bo 1. p4. 183/256. **2.** siege A.Prol 56, B.Mk 3569, F.Sq 306, TC 2.84, LGW 1725. [OF]

sey, seye(n see **se(e)(n**.

seye/seyn/sayn v. **1.** say, speak, tell A.Prol 738, 779, 787; (absol.) speak A.Prol 761, 858, send a message TC 2.1344; ~ *on* speak TC 2.314; *herde* ~ heard tell HF 2053; *that was to* ~ what was to be said TC 4.1171; *shortly (for) to* ~ B.Mk 3235, 3545, TC 5.1009, *sooth(ly) to* ~ A.Prol 284, 468, BD 460, *ther is namoore to* ~ E.Cl 371, F.Sq 314, Pity 77; relate (a story)

A.Co 4364, B.ML 46, B.Mk 3160; ~ *forth*
tell on A.Rv 3905; quote, cite HF 289;
men seith people say, it is said A.Rv 4210,
PF 22, TC 2.724; cf. **misseye. 2.** *be* (*for*)
to ~ mean, signify A.Mil 3605, B.Pri
1713, B.Mk 3944, G.SN 87, 106; *this/that
is to* ~ A.Prol 181, 797, TC 3.74; *as who
saith* see **who. seist** *pr. 2 sg.* A.Kn 1605,
seystow (with suffixed pron.) A.Kn 1125.
seith *3 sg.* A.Prol 178, says (nth.) A.Rv
4180. **seye/seyn** *pl.* A.Kn 1198, A.Mil
3598, D.WB 123; **seggen/sygge(n** TC
4.194. **sey(e)th** *imper. pl.* A.Kn 1868,
B.Mel 2902, F.Fkl 1526, I.Pars 590. **seyde**
pa. A.Prol 70. **seyd** *p.p.* A. Prol. 305;
ysayd BD 270. [OE *secgan; sægde/segde;
ge)sægd/segd*]
seyl see **sayl.**
seyn see **se(e)(n.**
seynd see **senge.**
seynt(e *adj.* **1.** holy (in phr.) *for* ~ *charitee*
A.Kn 1721, B.NP 4510, D.Sum 2119, *for* ~
Trinitee D.Sum 1824. **2.** (prefixed to
names) Saint A.Prol 120, 173, 340, TC
3.705 *var;* ~ *idiot* TC 1.910. **3.** *n.* saint
C.Pard 949, D.WB 140, G.SN 553, LGW
1871. **seintes** *gen. pl.* B.ML 61, TC 2.118.
[OF *saint*]
seintuarie *n.* sanctuary I.Pars 781, Bo 1. p4.
88/122; sacred object, ?box which con-
tained relics C.Pard 953. [OF *saintuarie*]
seke see **syk.**
seke(n/seche(n *v.* **1.** *tr.* seek, look for
A.Kn 1200, B.Mk 3453, D.Sum 1955,
BD 1255; search for B.Pri 1780, C.Pard
694, FormA 30; try to discover G.CY 316,
Bo 1. m2. 11/16; seek out B.ML 718,
D.WB 909; search through, examine
B.ML 60, C.Pard 488, D.WB 919, TC
5.1855; investigate, pursue G.CY 1442.
2. go to, visit A.Prol 17, D.WB 657, F.Fkl
1077, LGW 1310; come to visit D.Fri
1411; approach ABC 114. **3.** (with infin.)
try Bo 4. m4. 6/10. **4.** *infin.* in passive
sense: *to* ~ not to be found, not at hand
G.CY 874; *not longe for to* ~ soon found
A.Prol 784. **5.** *intr.* seek, make a search
Ven 69, Astr 2.1.6/8; investigate Bo
1. p6. 19/25; ~ *after* look for A.Kn 1266,
Bo 2. p5. 55/77; *infin.* in concessive sense:
to ~ *up and down* even if one looked everywhere A.Kn 2587, A.Mil 3252. **6.** make
request (to) ABC 78. **7.** go, move HF
744. **8.** ~ *upon* harass, attack D.Fri 1494.
sekestow *pr. 2 sg.* (with suffixed pron.) TC
3.1455 *var.* **so(u)ghte** *pa. sg.* A.Kn 1200,
HF 185. **so(u)ghten** *pl.* TC 2.937, LGW
1515. **y)so(u)ght** *p.p.* B.Pri 1780, Pity 1,
TC 3.1317. [OE *sēcan, sōhte, ge)sōht*]
sekered see **sikered.**
seknesse see **siknesse.**
selde *adv.* seldom A.Kn 1539, D.WB 1128,
TC 2.168; *forming compd. adv.* in ~ *tyme*
seldom E.Cl 146 (cf. **ofte** *tyme*). [EME
selde, OE *séldor, séldost*]
seleth *pr. 3 sg.* seals B.ML 768. **seled** *p.p.*
B.ML 736, TC 4.293. [OF *seeler*]
self, usu. def. **selve** *adj.* same, self-same, very
A.Kn 2584, 2860, B.ML 115, F.Fkl 1394,
Bo 2. p2. 48/66, 5. p3. 67/94, TC 3.355,
4.1425, HF 1157; *us* **self** E.Cl 108, *us*
selve(n ourselves D.WB 812, I.Pars 349.
See **hemself, himself, hirself, itself,**

myself, ourselven, thyself, yourself.
[OE *self, selfa*]
sely *adj.* (some senses overlap) **1.** happy,
blessed TC 4.503, ?D.WB 132; holy B.ML
682; good B.Pri 1702. **2.** innocent,
harmless C.Pard 292, D.Sum 1983, E.Cl
948, LGW 2713; simple, hapless A.Mil
3404, 3614, E.Mch 2423, G.CY 1076,
TC 1.1191; pitiable, unfortunate, poor
D.WB 370, Mars 89, TC 1.871, 2.683,
5.1093; poor B.NP 4565, D.Sum 1906;
wretched A.Rv 3896; slight, trifling TC
1.338. [OE *gesælig*]
selily *adv.* happily Bo 2. p4. 64/87. [from
prec.]
selinesse *n.* happiness TC 3.813, 825, 831.
[from **sely**]
selle(n *v.* sell B.ML 140, D.Sum 2108, F.Fkl
1563, TC 3.1461; barter A.Prol 278; (*for*)
to ~ for sale C. Pard 564, D.WB 414; *he
fond neither to* ~ = he did not stop to trade
A.Mil 3821. **solde** *pa.* B.Mk 3255. *subj. sg.*
were to sell RR 452. **sold** *p.p.* A.Co 4347.
[OA *sellan, sálde, sáld*]
sel(l)y *adj.* wonderful HF 513. [OE *sellic*]
selve see **self.**
semblable *adj.* similar, like B.Mel 2475, Bo
3. m6. 1/2; (with *to*) B.Mel 2293, Bo 2. p5.
96/134; such-like, similar (resembling
something already mentioned) I.Pars 408,
417, 802, Bo 3. m9. 22/31, (following n.)
E.Mch 1500, Bo 3. m9. 9/13. [OF]
semblaunce *n.* appearance RR 145 (F
semblance), Bo 3. p10. 160/218 (L *similitu-
dine*), likeness RR 425; *into his* ~ in his
likeness Bo 4. p6. 248/361. [OF]
sembla(u)nt *n.* appearance, look LGW
1735, 2691, appearance, show E.Cl 928;
in hir ~ RR 863, *as by hir* ~ B.Mel 2195,
as it seemed, apparently; *by* ~ in appearance
RR 152 (F. *par semblant*), Bo 1. p1. 4/5;
make ~ have an expression B.Mel 2338,
assume an expression, feign, pretend (*of*)
B.Mel 2209, 2877, (*as though*) I.Pars 644.
[OF]
semely *adj.* seemly, comely A.Prol 751,
B.Th 1919, LGW 1603. **semelieste** *sup.*
H.Mcp 119. [ON *sœmiligr*]
semely *adv.* becomingly A.Prol 123, RR 748.
[ON *sœmiliga*]
semelihede *n.* comeliness, gracefulness RR
777, 1130. [from **semely** *adj.* + OE -*hædu*]
seme(n *v.* **1.** seem (to), appear (to) C.Phs
52, F.Sq 102, 394, G.CY 751, Gent 13,
RR 1011; look as if BD 866; appear (with
no sense of error or deception) Bo 3. m11.
18/25; *impers.* in *it* ~*eth/~ed* (*that/as*)
A.Kn 2662, F.Fkl 1296, TC 3.64; (with
dat.) *me* ~, *it* ~ *me*, etc. A.Prol 39, B.Mk
3361, F.Fkl 1023, Astr prol 34/48, TC
4.1424, Bo 2. p7. 63/91 *var.* **2.** think,
imagine D.Fri 1463, ? F.Sq 201, Bo 2. p7.
63/91 *var.* [ON *sœma*]
semy *adj.* thin, small A.Mil 3697 *var,* Rosem
11. [? OF *semé*]
semicope *n.* short cloak A.Prol 262. [pref.
semi + **cope**]
seming *n.* appearance TC 1.284; *as by* ~
to all appearance BD 944; *to my* ~ as it
appears to me B.Pri 1838. [from **seme(n**]
semisoun† *n.* slight sound A.Mil 3697 *var;*
cf. **semy.** [pref. *semi* + **soun;** cf. LL *semi-
sonus*]

senatorie *n.* the senatorial order Bo 3. p4. 57/83 (L *senatorii (census)*). [ML *senatorius* adj.]
senatour *n.* senator B.ML 961, LGW 584. ~**es** *gen. sg.* B.ML 981, 987; *pl.* B.Mk 3670, Bo 1. p4. 105/146; *gen. pl.* B.NP 4561. [OF *senateur*]
sencer *n.* censer A.Mil 3340. [OF *censier*]
sendal *n.* thin rich silk A.Prol 440. [OF *cendal*]
sende(n *v.* send A.Prol 426, B.ML 144, TC 4.894, LGW 1418; ~ *after* send for A.Kn 2762, B.ML 1047, TC 4.649, LGW 2267, ~ *for* A.Kn 2980, TC 2.1447; (of God, or gods) send, grant B.ML 766, 1160, E.Cl 206, esp. in *pr. subj.* D.WB 1258, 1264, G.CY 1481, TC 1.45, 3.705, 5.502. **sendeth** *pr. 3 sg.* F.Sq 113, TC 3.28; **sent** E.Cl 1151, Anel 194, Bo 5. p3. 116/165, TC 2.1123. **sendeth** *imper. pl.* C.Pard 614. **sende** *pa. sg.* A.Rv 4136, TC 2.1734, RR 1158; **sente** A.Mil 3378. **senten** *pl.* B.ML 136. **sente** *subj.* E.Mch 1665. **sent** *p.p.* A.Mil 3666, B.ML 268; **ysent** A.Kn 2870, B.ML 1041, Anel 113. [OE *séndan*, pa. *sende*]
sene *see* **se(e)(n.**
Senec(c)iens *n. pl.* followers of Seneca Bo 1. p3. 40/56. [OF]
senge *v.* singe D.WB 349. **seynd** *p.p.* broiled, grilled B.NP 4035. [OE *sencgan*]
sengle *adj.* single, unmarried E.Mch 1667, I.Pars 961. [OF *sengle*]
senglely *adv.* separately, severally Bo 3. p9. 101/134. [from prec.]
sens *n.* sense, meaning I.Pars 542. [OF]
sensibilitees *n. pl.* impressions, 'sensible species; the emanations from bodies, which were supposed to be the cause of sensation' (*OED*) Bo 5. m4. 5/7 (L *sensus et imagines*). [OF]
sensible *adj.* (only in Bo) **1.** perceptible by the senses Bo 5. p4. 131/188, 137/196, m4. 5/7, p5. 9/13, 33/47. **2.** having the faculty of sensation, capable of feeling Bo 5. p4.140/202. [OF]
sensinge *pr. p.* censing A.Mil 3341. [from OF *encenser*]
sensualitee *n.* (only in Pars) that part of man's nature concerned with the senses, man's animal instincts I.Pars 261, 265, 270. [OF]
sentement *n.* personal feeling, personal experience (of love) TC 2.13, 3.1797, LGW 69; passion, feeling TC 3.43; (sense of) feeling, sensation TC 4.1177. [OF]
sentence *n.* (senses sometimes overlap) **1.** meaning, sense B.ML 4355, G.SN 81, TC 1.393; drift, purport B.Mel 2136, C.Phs 177, I.Pars 58, PF 35, Bo 1. p6. 24/30 (L *sententiam*), TC 3.1327, *in this* ~ *with this meaning, in this sense* D.WB 1126; subject B.Pri 1753, D.Fri 1518, matter, material B.NP 3992, 4404. **2.** opinion B.Mel 2522, E.Cl 636, Bo 1. p6. 13/16, TC 4.1063, LGW 381; *heigh* ~ lofty judgement B.Mk 3938 *var.* **3.** saying of authority, maxim, dictum B.ML 113, 1139, B.Mel 2166, E.Mch 1307, Bo 1. p4. 19/27, TC 4.197; *heigh, best* ~ noble, weighty matter A.Prol 306, 798, E.Mch 1507; *pl.* doctrine I.Pars 77. **4.** decision, judgement, verdict A.Kn 2532, B.Mel

3026, C.Phs 172, G.SN 366, I.Pars 17, PF 383, Bo 1. p4. 171/239. [OF]
septemtrioun *n.* north B.Mk 3657. [L *septentrio*]
septentrional *adj.* northern Astr 2.40.31/45; *pl.* Astr 2.40.29/41. [L *septentriōnālis*]
sepulcre *n.* tomb D.WB 498. [OF]
sepulture *n.* burial LGW 2553, I.Pars 1031, mode of burial TC 5.299; burial-place, tomb TC 4.327, A.Kn 2854; (fig.) C.Pard 558, I.Pars 822. [OF]
serchen *v.* search out, penetrate B.Mel 2597; go about, haunt D.WB 867. [OF *cerchier*]
sereyns *n. pl.* sirens, mermaids RR 684. [OF *sereine*]
serement *n.* oath F.Fkl 1534 *var.* [OF]
sergeaunt *n.* sergeant, officer E.Cl 519, 524; *pl.* G.SN 361, Bo 3. p5. 27/37 (L *satellite*); ~ *of the Lawe* serjeant-at-law (member of a superior order of barristers) A.Prol 309. [OF *sergent*]
serie *n.* succession of points, process, argument A.Kn 3067. [L *series*]
Serien *adj.* Chinese Bo 2. m5. 9/13 *var* **Syrien.**
Seriens *n. pl.* 8/11. [from L *Sērēs*]
sermone *v.* preach, speak C.Pard 879. [AN *sarmuner*]
sermoning *vbl. n.* preaching A.Rv 3899, persuasive discourse, argument A.Kn 3091, discourse, talk A.Mil 3597, LGW 1184.
sermoun *n.* discourse, speech TC 2.965, 1299, 4.1282, LGW 2025, tale TC 2.1115; *pl.* writings B.ML 87; sermon B.Mel 2234, D.Sum 1789. [AN *sermun*]
serpent *n.* serpent B.Mk 3295, H.Mcp 109, TC 5.1497; (of the Garden of Eden) I.Pars 326; (fig.) (the devil) B.ML 361, B.Pri 1748, I.Pars 137, (of a wicked person) B.ML 360, (alluding to its proverbial guile and malignity) D.Sum 1994, 2001, F.Sq 512, (as symbol of jealousy) TC 3.837. [OF]
servage *n.* servitude, bondage (fig., of vice, sin) B.ML 368, I.Pars 276, 312, (of marriage) E.Cl 147; (feudal) allegiance, service E.Cl 482, (fig., of love) F.Fkl 794, BD 769. [OF]
serva(u)nt *n.* servant A.Prol 101, A.Kn 1421, B.ML 739, D.Fri 1501, I.Pars 150; (transf.) servant (of God, a god) A.Kn 2418, G.SN 419, I.Pars 630, (of Venus, Love) B.NP 4533, F.Fkl 937, PF 159, TC 1.48, 328, (of the servants of God, a title of the Pope) I.Pars 773 (echoed in TC 1.15); servant in love, professed lover A.Kn 1814, 2787, F.Fkl 793, Pity 60, TC 3.1487, 5.173. [OF]
servél *n.[1]* *pa. sg.* preserved, kept hidden F.Sq 521. [? OF *preserver* or L *servāre*]
serve(n *v.[2]* **1.** serve, attend A.Kn 1421, 1554, B.ML 531, E.Mch 1502, RR 696; serve, honour (God, a god) A.Kn 2330, G.SN 389, Bo 1. p4. 187/261, TC 5.143; serve (as a feudal lord, of wife's relation to husband) E.Cl 969, E.Mch 1291, I.Pars 932; be the servant of in love, be lover of A.Kn 1143, 3086, F.Fkl 731, PF 419, TC 1.817, 4.442. **2.** be useful, profit (with *to*) Bo 4. p6. 206/298 (L *famulari*); *intr.* serve, be of avail, be of use (*of* 'for') H.Mcp 339, TC 3.1136, 4.279, Astr 1.23.3/21.93. **3.** serve (with food) A.Prol 749, D.Sum 2279, set B.NP 4033, (fig.) D.Sum 1760.

4. treat, serve A.Kn 963, E.Cl 640, 641, LGW 2365, 2384. [OF *servir*]
servisable *adj.* ready to serve, willing A.Prol 99, E.Cl 979, E.Mch 1911, useful G.CY 1014. [OF]
servyse *n.* **1.** service, serving A.Prol 250, A.Kn 1415, G.CY 1065, I.Pars 443, *do(n* ~ be of service (to), do a service for B.Sh 1381, TC 1.82, be of use D.WB 101; servitude E.Cl 114; service (of God) I.Pars 314, 652, (of the devil) I.Pars 652, (of a god, Venus, etc.) A.Kn 2243, B.NP 4534, F.Sq 280, PF 284, TC 3.42. **2.** service in love, professed love F.Fkl 972, Mars 167, TC 3.161, 992, *do(n* ~ BD 1098, PF 478, TC 3.133, *your heyghe* ~ serving you in noble love TC 3.1288. **3.** religious service, office A.Prol 122, A.Kn 2887, D.Sum 1719, TC 1.164; (of bird-song) BD 302, RR 669; *do(n* ~ perform the service D. Sum 1897, (with *to*) worship G.SN 553. **4.** service at table A.Kn 2197, F.Sq 66. [OF]
servitour *n.* servant D.Sum 2185. [OF]
servitute *n.* servitude E.Cl 798, I.Pars 147. [OF]
sese *pr. subj. 3 sg.* seize PF 481. **sesed** *p.p.* caught Mars 240; put in possession (of) TC 3.445 var. [OF *seisir*]
sesoun *n.* season, time of year A.Prol 19, E.Mch 2049, TC 1.168; time of ripeness RR 1678; time HF 341. [OF]
sete(n *see* **sitte(n.**
setewale *see* **cetewale.**
sethe *v.* boil A.Prol 383. **seeth** *pa. sg.* E.Cl 227. **sode(n** *p.p.* I.Pars 900, 901. [OE *sēoþan, sēaþ, soden*]
sette(n *v.* **1.** set, place, put A.Prol 666, B.Mel 2160, E.Cl 290, H.Mcp 162, I.Pars 1036, TC 2.585; set (on fire) B.Mk 3223, TC 3.24, 4.126; (of eyes, look) cast, rest A.Kn 2984, B.ML 1053, E.Cl 233, Mars 247; place, put in position Astr 2.3.32/46; prepare, lay (table) E.Cl 975; spread, fix (net) B.Mel 2369; drive (sword) LGW 1795; array E.Cl 382; appoint Bo 4. p4. 168/235; stake (as at dice), risk TC 4.622; postulate, imagine TC 2.367, ~ *caas* put the case, suppose B.Mel 2681, 3041, TC 2.729; ~ *a-werk(e* set, put to work A.Co 4337, D.WB 215, ~ *in bokes* put in writing D.WB 129; ~ *doun* bring low BD 635; ~ *thereto* add Bo 2. p7. 34/48; ~ *up* raise, set up high TC 4.11; ~ (someone's) *cappe* see **cappe.** *p.p.* in *wel* ~ seemly BD 828. *intr.* in ~ *on* attack LGW 636. *pass.* be seated A.Kn 2528, C.Pard 392, TC 4.1175. *refl.* sit down A.Kn 1541, B.ML 329, C.Phs 207, C.Pard 663, E.Mch 2234, TC 2.600; *on knee(s* kneel A.Mil 3723, B.ML 638, D.Sum 2120, E.Cl 951, G.SN 396, TC 3.953. **2.** fix, ordain, establish (law) TC 3.36; set forth, arrange TC 3.334; fix (price) A.Prol 815, (place) A.Kn 1635, (time) A.Co 4383, E.Cl 774, Mars 52, TC 3.340; adjust, regulate (clock) Astr 2.3.45/66; fix, set (desire, intention, heart) on A.Prol 132, F.Fkl 812, B.Pri 1740, D.Fri 1374, LGW 1939, TC 4.1378, (heart at rest) TC 2.760. **3.** estimate, value, reckon: ~ *lyte of* TC 2.432; ~ *noght of, at noght* count as nothing E.Mch 2303, F.Fkl 821, TC 1.444; ~ *at no value* LGW 602. ~ *at, by, of* give for (in phrases comparing

objects of proverbially small value, usu. with neg.): **grote** TC 4.586, **hawe** D.WB 659, **kers** A.Mil 3756, **myte** TC 3.832, 900, **straw** B.NP 4280, **tare** A.Kn 1570, A.Rv 4000. **set** *pr. 3 sg.* D.Sum 1982, Pity 101, TC 3.832; **setteth** B.Mel 2369. **sette** *pa. sg.* TC 1.359. **sette(n** *pl.* TC 3.608, G.SN 396. **set** *p.p.* A.Prol 132, B.ML 440; **yset** A.Co 4337, E.Cl 409. [OE *settan, sette, ġe)sett*]
seur *adj.* sure B.Mel 2642, 2953. [OF *seüre, sure*]
seur *adv.* surely TC 3.1633, 4.421. [as prec.]
seureté/suretee *n.* safety, security D.WB 903, 911, FormA 46, safeguard C.Pard 937, security, freedom from anxiety Anel 215, TC 2.833, 3.1678, confidence I.Pars 735; surety, pledge A.Kn 1604, F.Sq 528. [OF *seürté/surté*]
seurly/surely *adv.* surely, soundly B.Sh 1465, B.Mel 2913. [from **seur** adj.]
sewe/suwe *v.* **1.** *tr.* follow B.Mel 2692, B.NP 4527, attend BalCo 12; pursue TC 1.379, Gent 4. **2.** *intr.* follow as a consequence, ensue B.Mel 2619, 2728 var, HF 840. [AN *suer, siwer*]
sewes *n. pl.* broths F.Sq 67. [OE *sēaw*]
sewing *adj.* similar, in proportion BD 959. [from **sewe**]
sexes *n. pl.* sexes, in *of sedes and of* ~ Bo 4. p6. 105/152 (L *fetuum seminumque*, F *sexes*; Robinson suggests ? var *sexuum*). [L *sexus*]
sexteyn *n.* sacristan B.Mk 3126, D.Sum 1859. [AN *segerstein/secrestein*]
shaar *n.* ploughshare A.Mil 3763. [OE *scear*]
shad(de *see* **shede.**
shadewy *adj.* shadowy, insubstantial Bo 3. p4. 40/58 (L *umbratiles*). [from **shadwe**]
shadowing *vbl. n.* shadow, shady place RR 1503. [from *shadow* v., OE *sceadwian*]
shadwe *n.* shadow B.ML 7, B.Sh 1199, RR 1411, (fig., of death) I.Pars 177, 211; shade BD 426; reflection RR 1520, 1529; ? shade, in ~ *or tabernacle of this lyf* Bo 2. p3. 55/80 (L *in hanc uitae scaenam*, F *en la cortine et en l'ombre*). **shadwes** *pl.* shadows, shade Bo 2. m5. 12/18 (L *umbra*); times of twilight Astr 2.16.10/14. [OE *scead(we*, obl. case of *sceadu*]
shadwed *p.p.* shadowed, shaded TC 2.821, RR 1511, **y~** A.Prol 607. [OE *sceadwian*]
shaft *n.* shaft (of arrow) A.Kn 1362, RR 973; *pl.* shafts (of arrows) PF 180, (of spears) A.Kn 2605. [OE *sceaft*]
shake *v.* shake A.Kn 1473, TC 1.869, HF 868, (one's head) B.Sh 1302, LGW 2344; *intr.* E.Mch 1849, shake out (in cleaning) E.Cl 978, quiver TC 3.890. **shook** *pa. sg.* A.Kn 2265, B.Mk 3274. **shoken** *pl.* RR 353. **shake** *p.p.* blown A.Prol 406; **yshaken** tremulous, sparkling Bo 1. m3. 11/15 (L *uibratus*). [OE *scacan, scōc, scacen*]
shal *v.* **1.** owe (with noun obj.) TC 3.791, 1649; be in duty bound F.Fkl 750. **2.** *auxil.* (of necessity or obligation) must, have to A.Prol 853, A.Kn 1732, 3014, 3030, B.ML 351, C.Pard 796, D.Fri 1636, E.Cl 38, G.CY 1358, TC 3.1474, 5.1085; (of duty) am/is to D.Fri 1353, G.SN 303, TC 2.1757, 3.1572, B.ML 996; (of destiny) B.ML 268, TC 4.126; (in commands) must, shall A.Prol 792, A.Kn 1391, TC 1.870,

PF 392; (expressing speaker's intention) A.Kn 2924, A.Rv 4087, C.Phs 129, PF 229, TC 2.754, LGW 694; (in prophecies) A.Mil 3517, C.Pard 365, E.Mch 1562, G.SN 241; (in proverbs or maxims) A.Mil 3186, C.Pard 649, D.WB 653, TC 5.791. **3.** *auxil.* (expressing futurity) shall, will A.Kn 2764, B.ML 98, B.Sh 1188, C.Pard 733, D.WB 177, E.Mch 1760, ABC 160, TC 4.771. **4.** (with ellipsis of infin.) A.Kn 1183, B.ML 1078, D.WB 507, F.Sq 598, TC 1.593, 4.1680, 5.833; (infin. of motion understood) B.ML 279, TC 4.210, 264, 1106. **shal** *pr. 1, 3 sg.* A.Prol 763, 792. **sal** *sg.* and *pl.* (nth.) A.Rv 4043, 4174. **shalt** *2 sg.* A.Kn 1153, **shaltow** (with suffixed pron.) A.Mil 3565, TC 1.803. **shal** *pl.* B.ML 329, TC 1.245, **shul** A.Kn 1821, A.Mil 3581, **shullen** A.Kn 3014, D.Fri 1331, E.Mch 1413, **shuln** B.Mel 2545, I.Pars 141. **sholde** *pa.* (*indic.* and *subj.*). **5.** ought to, should (in main cl.) A.Prol 184, A.Mil 3454, B.ML 44, D.WB 434, I.Pars 757, TC 5.1825; (in dependent cl.) A.Rv 3966, B.NP 4625, E.Cl 1146, Bo 1. m5. 25/36. **6.** (expressing indirect future) would A.Kn 689, 2662, B.ML 587, B.NP 4334, E.Cl 247; (of necessity) had to B.Mel 2849, E.Cl 515, I.Pars 282; (of destiny or intent) was to B.Mk 3891, B.NP 4332, E.Cl 261, TC 5.14, 32, was about to B.Pri 1848. **7.** (forming subjunctive equivalent, in concessions) should, were to C.Pard 451, TC 1.17, 3.81, 5.797; (in conditions) E.Cl 245, F.Sq 40, F.Fkl 931, would A.Prol 249; (in commands, etc.) A.Mil 3228, E.Mch 1707; (in comparisons) A.Kn 1980, TC 1.872; (of uncertified report) are said to TC 3.797. **8.** (conditional) would B.Mk 3627, C.Phs 145, D.Sum 1944, F.Fkl 775. **9.** (of repeated action) would TC 5.247, 256. **sholde** *1, 3 sg.* A.Prol 184, A.Kn 1380, **shulde** B.ML 247, Mars 251. **sholdestow** *2 sg.* (with suffixed pron.) H.Mcp 329, TC 5.351. [OE *sceal, scealt, sculon, scólde*]
shale *n.* shell HF 1281 [OE *scealu*]
shalmyes *n. pl.* shawms HF 1218. [OF *chalemel*]
shame *n.* **1.** shame A.Prol 503, D.WB 964, E.Cl 481, (person.) RR 980 (F *Honte*); dishonour, disgrace B.Mel 2636, B.Mk 3483, C.Phs 214, TC 1.107, LGW 1028; something dishonourable LGW 589; baseness, dishonourable act D.WB 1151. **2.** modesty D.WB 342, TC 2.1286, PF 444, 583, TC 2.645, LGW 535, confusion, embarrassment TC 1.867, 3.80, 1570. *for ~ of his degree* lest it should shame his condition F.Fkl 752; *for ~* (as adjuration) Anel 272, HF 557, *fy for ~* B.NP 4081, G.CY 1407; *do ~* inflict an injury, dishonour A.Kn 1555, 3050, E.Mch 2197, BD 1017, TC 2.763, 3.777; *have ~* be ashamed B.Mel 2966, suffer dishonour F.Fkl 1529; *it is/was a ~ (that/to)* it is/was dishonourable G.SN 505. **shames** *gen. sg.* TC 1.180, ~ *deth* shameful death, death of shame B.ML 819, E.Mch 2377. [OE *sc(e)amu*]
shame(n *v.* put to shame, bring disgrace upon F.Fkl 1164, 1565; *thee ~th pr. 3 sg.* *impers.* you are ashamed B.ML 101;

shamed *p.p.* ashamed TC 5.1727; brought to shame, HF 1634, **yshamed** HF 356. Cf. **ashamed**. [OE *sceamian*]
shamfast *adj.* modest, shy A.Kn 2055, C.Phs 55, LGW 1535, humble I.Pars 987; ashamed, dejected B.Mel 2236, RR 467, Bo 4. m7. 31/44 (L *pudibunda*). [OE *sceamfæst*]
shamfastnesse *n.* modesty A.Prol 840, C.Phs 55, ? humility, ? sense of shame I.Pars 985. [from prec.]
shap *n.* shape, form A.Kn 1889, B.Mk 3444, D.WB 258, G.SN 44, TC 5.473; sexual organs I.Pars 423. [OE *gesceap*]
shape(n *v.* **1.** create, fashion E.Cl 903, TC 4.252; build, cut out, shape B.Th 1890, D.WB 139, D.Fri 1463, Anel 357, TC 3.734, LGW 2014. **2.** arrange, bring about C.Pard 813, E.Mch 1632, TC 2.1363, 3.196, 4.652; devise, contrive A.Kn 2541, A.Mil 3403, B.ML 210, E.Cl 946, G.CY 1080, PF 502; provide E.Mch 1408; prepare E.Cl 198, 275; plan TC 1.207; appoint B.ML 253; assign, give LGW 2569. **3.** *refl.* set oneself, intend, prepare A.Prol 772, B.Mel 2995, E.Mch 2025, Bo 1. p4. 222/308 (L *imminentem*), TC 3.551, 5.1211, LGW 180; dispose oneself B.Mel 2307, 2989, address oneself Pity 20; make ready A.Prol 809; find means TC 4.925; intend, purpose C.Pard 874, F.Sq 214, LGW 1289; determine F.Fkl 809. **3.** destine, decree, ordain A.Kn 1225, B.Mk 3099, Anel 243, TC 3.1240, Scog 8; determine A.Kn 1108, B.ML 951; allot TC 2.282. **4.** *intr.* come to pass, happen TC 2.61. **shapeth** *imper. pl.* E.Mch 1408. **shoop** *pa. sg.* B.Sh 1244, TC 1.207. **shopen** *pl.* B.Mel 2995, F.Fkl 897. **shape(n** *p.p.* A.Kn 1108, 1225, B.Mk 3099, Anel 243; **yshape(n** A.Rv 4179, G.CY 1080, H.Mcp 43, TC 3.411. [OE *sc(i)eppan, scōp, scapen*]
shaply *adj.* likely, fit A.Prol 372, TC 4.1452. [from **shap**]
sharp *adj.* sharp A.Prol 114, E.Mch 1825, TC 1.632; piquant A.Prol 352; (fig.) keen I.Pars 453, PF 331, 565; harsh D.WB 14; painful I.Pars 131, TC 3.1625, 4.898. [OE *scearp*]
sharpe *adv.* sharply B.Th 2073; shrilly TC 1.729, HF 1202. [OE *scearpe*]
sharpeth *pr. 3 sg.* sharpens A.Mil 3763. [OA *scerpan*]
sharply *adv.* severely, harshly A.Prol 523, I.Pars 583; acutely, shrewdly E.Cl 1192. [from **sharp**]
sharpnesse *n.* sharpness, harshness (of Fortune) Bo 1. p4. 7/11. [from **sharp**]
shave *v.* A.Mil 3376 **shave(n** *p.p.* A.Prol 588, 690 var, E.Mch 1826, stripped clean of money Purse 19, **yshave** A.Prol 690 var, B.Sh 1499, B.Mk 3261. [OE *sceafan, scōf, sceafen*]
shaving *n.* shaving, thin slice G.CY 1239. [from **shave**]
shawe *n.* wood, thicket A.Co 4367, D.Fri 1386, TC 3.720. [OE *sceaga*]
she *pron.* she, abbr. **sh** TC 4.1212 var; used irregularly in obj. position TC 1.309; ~ .. ~ one woman .. another TC 2.1747. See **hir(e, hires,** and **he.** [prob. OE *hie*]
she-ape *n.* female ape I.Pars 424. [prec.+ **ape**]

shede v. **1.** shed B.Mk 3447; emit I.Pars 577; diffuse Bo 3. p11. 84/114 (L *diffundunt*). **shad** p.p. shed Bo 3. m7. 3/4, divided 4. p6. 90/128 (L *diffundi*), scattered 1. m1. 11/16 (L *funduntur*), **yshad** shed 2. m5. 17/24, scattered 3. m2. 20/29 (L *sparsus*). **2.** *intr.* pour, fall: **shadde** pa. B.Mk 3921. [OE *sc(e)ādan*]

sheef n. sheaf (of corn) LGW 190, 2579, (of arrows) A.Prol 104. **sheves** pl. HF 2140. [OE *scēaf*]

she(e)ne adj. bright A.Prol 115, F.Sq 53, F.Fkl 1045, TC 5.9, glistening, shining RR 127, 1512; fair, beautiful PF 299, (of persons) A.Kn 972, 1068, E.Mch 2328, Anel 38, HF 1536, LGW 1467. [OA *scēne*]

sheld n. shield A.Kn 2122, TC 2.640, 5.308; (transf.) protection, defence TC 2.201, 3.480, cover 2.1327; a French coin (*escu*) A.Prol 278, B.Sh 1521, 1542. [OA *scéld*]

shelde/shilde v. shield, protect TC 4.188, HF 88, *pr. subj.* in *God* ∼, protect, defend B.Th 2098, E.Mch 1787, forbid A.Mil 3427, B.Sh 1476, E.Cl 839, LGW 2082. [OE *scildan*, A *scéldan*]

shende v. **1.** destroy, ruin B.ML 927, D.WB 376, I.Pars 688, TC 1.972, 4.79, 1496, 5.893, spoil TC 2.590; harm RR 1400*em.* [? *intr.* be harmed (*OED*)], defile I.Pars 854, TC 4.1577; defeat LGW 652. **2.** disgrace, put to shame E.Mch 1320, TC 5.893, confound TC 3.1459 *var*; blame, reproach TC 5.1060, revile, scold B.Pri 1731. **shendeth** *pr. 3 sg.* B.ML 28, **shent** I.Pars 848, 854. **shente** pa. B.NP 4031. **shent** p.p. A.Kn 2754, TC 2.38, **yshent** D.Fri 1312. [OE *scéndan* put to shame]

shendshipe n. shame I.Pars 273. [p.p. of prec.+OE -*scipe*]

shene adv. brightly Mars 87. [OA *scēne*]

shepe see **shipe**.

shepne n. cowshed A.Kn 2000. **shipnes** pl. D.WB 871. [OE *scypen*]

shere n. pair of shears, scissors: *sg.* A.Kn 2417, B.Mk 3246; *pl.* D.WB 722, I.Pars 418. [OE *scērero* pl.+*scēar*]

shere v. cut B.Mk 3257. **shorn** p.p. shorn, shaven B.Mk 3142, TC 1.222; **yshore** TC 4.996; **yshorn** A.Prol 589. [OA *sceran*, p.p. *ʒe)scoren*]

shering-hokes n. pl. shearing-hooks (for cutting ropes of enemy ships) LGW 641. [from **shere**+OE *hōc*]

sherte n. shirt, smock B.Th 2049, B.Mk 3312, E.Mch 1852, I.Pars 197, TC 3.738; in *hire* ∼ in her night attire, i.e. without any rich garments, TC 4.96, *sin . . that shapen was my* ∼ since I was born LGW 2629, *erst than my* ∼ before I was born A.Kn 1566. [OE *scyrte*]

shete n. sheet A.Rv 4140, G.CY 879, TC 3.1056. [OA *scēte*]

shete(n v. shoot A.Rv 3928, I.Pars 714, LGW 635, RR 960, 989, 1341 *var*: **shette** p.p. RR 1341 *var*. [OE *scēotan*, p.p. *scoten*]

sheter n. *attrib.* fit for shooting (sense only here) PF 180. [from prec.]

shethe n. sheath B.Th 2066. TC 4.1185. [OE *scēaþ*]

shette(n v. shut, close D.WB 1141, G.SN 517, TC 3.749, close up (letter) TC 2.1090,

1226; clasp RR 1082; shut in TC 1.148, *refl.* TC 3.726; (transf.) shut fast (heart) B.ML 1056, TC 3.1086; enclose, limit Bo 5. p5. 74/107. **shette** pa. *sg.* A.Mil 3499, 3634, B.Sh 1275, TC 4.232. **shette(n** pl. B.Mk 3722, G.CY 1218, TC 1.148. **shet** p.p. A.Kn 2597, BD 335; **yshet(te** B.ML 560, B.Mel 2159, TC 3.1488 *var*. [OE *scyttan*, -*e*- s-e.]

sheves see **sheef**.

shewe(n v. **1.** *tr.* show, display A.Kn 2677, C.Pard 336, TC 2.110, ∼ *forth* C.Pard 347, D.Sum 1690, LSt 26, (a quality) A.Mil 3383, B.ML 1000, B.Mel 2465, E.Cl 495, Bo 3. p4. 6/8; display, grant (to) E.Cl 102, G.SN 161, TC 5.1714; reveal, show to D.Sum 1679, F.Fkl 1200, PF 168, TC 5.1447, (transf.) I.Pars 26, TC 4.1281; show forth, make manifest B.ML 477, B.Pri 1649; reveal (secret), confess B.Mel 2338, D.WB 283, D.Sum 1849, I.Pars 1000, allow to be seen E.Cl 922; set forth Astr prol 65/90, indicate Astr 1.20.3/4; expound Astr prol 19/25, I.Pars 873, explain B.Mel 2765, G.CY 1056, I.Pars 390, Bo 5. p4. 14/21 (L *patefacere*); demonstrate B.Mel 2285, B.NP 4543, Bo 2. p2. 7/10, 4. p4. 48/65; be proof, be a sign I.Pars 893; plead, argue B.Mel 2901, Bo 4. p2. 100/133; make known, express E.Cl 90, 762, PF 581, Bo 2. p3. 4/6 (L *proferas*), 3. m2. 1 (L *promere*), TC 1.33, 5.631; propose D.Sum 2219; perform TC 1.159; spread, enlarge Bo 2. p7. 47/67 (L *dilatare*). **2.** *intr.* appear, become evident B.Mel 2728 *var*, Bo 4. p2. 11/14, 5. p4. 100/144; seem B.Mel 2386, HF 281, *to* ∼ in appearance HF 1305; be seen RR 1113. *impers.* in *as (it)* ∼*th* as is seen, shown I.Pars 331, Astr 2.26.16/23, *pa.* I.Pars 696. *refl.* show oneself, appear I.Pars 173, Astr 2.34. 13/18. **shewinge** *pr. p.* as *adj.* evident, open to view Bo 2. m7. 3/4 (L *late patentes*), 4. p1. 8/11, p2. 93/124. **yshewed** p.p. TC 5.1251. [OE *scēawian*]

shifte v. provide, ordain D.WB 104, assign G.SN 278. [OE *sciftan*]

shilde see **shelde**.

shille adj. pl. shrill B.NP 4585 *var*. [OE *scyll*]

shimering vbl. n. glimmer A.Rv 4297. [from v., LOE *scymrian*]

shine n. shin A.Prol 386, A.Kn 1279. [OE *scinu*]

shyne(n v. shine A.Kn 2043, G.SN 254, G.CY 962, Bo 3. m1. 5/7, TC 3.768; (of person) B.Th 2034, Rosem 3; (fig.) TC 4.1575; (with subject *it*) be sunny A.Kn 1535, TC 4.299. **shynede** pa. *sg.* LGW 1119, 2194; **sho(o)n** A.Kn 1987, B.ML 11, E.Cl 1124, BD 336. **shoon/shone** pl. HF 507; **shynen** A.Kn 2043. [OE *scīnan*, *scān*, *scinon*]

shyninge vbl. n. shining, gleaming A.Mil 3255, Bo 1. p6. 78/102, 2. p5. 26/36, splendour, renown Bo 3. p4. 63/91.

shyninge ppl. adj. shining, resplendent Bo 4. m1. 13/19, 21/30, m2. 3/4. [from **shyne(n**)]

shynketh *pr. 3 sg.* pours out E.Mch 1722 *var*. [OE *scencan*; cf. **skinketh**]

ship n. ship TC 5.644; *to* ∼*(e)* aboard A.Mil 3540, B.ML 316, Anel 194, HF 420. [OE *scip*]

shipe/shepe *n.* hire, pay, reward I.Pars 568, Anel 193. [OE *scipe*]

shipman *n.* seaman, master of a ship A.Prol 388, A.Rv 3904, HF 2122. [OE *scipmann*]

shipnes *see* **shepne.**

shirreve *n.* sheriff A.Prol 359. [OE *scīrgerēfa*]

shiten *p.p.* defiled, filthy A.Prol 504. [OE *sciten*]

shitting *vbl. n.* shutting RR 1598. [from OE *scyttan*; cf. **shette(n**]

shivere *n.* slice D.Sum 1840. [from root of MLG *schive*, ? OE **scife*]

shiveren *pr. pl.* shiver, break A.Kn 2605. [from ME *shiver* n. splinter, of Gmc. origin.]

shod *p.p.* wearing shoes HF 98, RR 427, 842. [OE *scōd*]

shode *n.* crown of the head, temple A.Kn 2007; parting of the hair A.Mil 3316. [OE *scāda*]

sholder-/shulder-boon *n.* shoulder-blade C.Pard 350, I.Pars 603. [OE *sculdor+bo(o)n*]

shon *see* **shyne(n.**

shonde *n.* shame, disgrace B.Th 2098, HF 88. [OE *scánd*]

sho(o *n.* shoe A.Prol 253; *olde* ~ (fig.) something worn out D.WB 708; (in phr. with **wringe(n**) D.WB 492, E.Mch 1553. **shoos** *pl.* A.Prol 457, A.Mil 3267, 3318; **shoon** B.Th 1922, RR 843. [OE *scōh*, pl. *scōs*]

sho(o)f *pa. sg.* pushed, thrust PF 154, TC 3.487, RR 534, drove LGW 2412. **shove(n** *p.p.* driven Bo 2. p1. 75/103, advanced F.Fkl 1281, laid TC 3.1026, brought to notice LGW 1381; **yshove** carried about LGW 726. **sho(u)veth** *pr. 3 sg.* Bo 2. p1. 76/104. [OE *scūfan*, *scēaf*, *scofen*]

shoon *see* **shyne(n.**

short *adj.* short A.Prol 93, A.Kn 2510, D.WB 624; (of wit) A.Prol 746; quick B.Mel 2537; brief A.Kn 1476, A.Rv 4265, E.Cl 130, PF 1; *the* ~ *throte* i.e. the brief pleasure of swallowing C.Pard 517; brief, succinct (words, speech) A.Prol 306, TC 3.456; (in phrases = briefly) *in* ~ *and pleyn* E.Cl 577, *in* ~ TC 2.1219, 1266, 1405, 1493, *at* ~ *wordes* TC 2.956, 4.1658, LGW 2462. as *adv.* briefly TC 4.890, G.SN 360. [OE *sceort*]

shorte *adv.* with quick breaths TC 3.58. [from prec.]

shorte *v.* shorten A.Prol 791, D.WB 365, I.Pars 727, TC 5.96. [OE *sc(e)ortian*]

shortly *adv.* **1.** briefly, concisely (often in phr. as ~ *for to tellen/speken/seyn*) A.Prol 843, 985, A.Kn 1341, B.Mk 3235, E.Cl 141, TC 5.1009; in brief, to put it briefly A.Prol 30, B.ML 965, BD 434, TC 4.671. **2.** in short time, quickly A.Kn 1377, 1782, TC 3.1436, LGW 1785. [from **short** adj.]

short-sholdred *adj.* short in the upper arm A.Prol 549. [from **short**+OE *sculdor*]

shot *n.* arrow, missile A.Kn 2544, TC 2.58; the shooting of an arrow B.NP 4539. [OE *sc(e)ot*]

shot-windowe *n.* hinged window which can be opened or closed like a shutter A.Mil 3358, 3695. [? var. of *shut* shutter, from *shut* v.; see **shette(n**]

shour *n.* shower A.Prol 1, A.Mil 3520; assault, battle TC 4.47, *sharpe* ~*es* TC 1.470, 3.1064. [OE *scūr*]

shoutinge *vbl. n.* shouting, clamour A.Kn 2953, B.NP 4577, (of the noise of birds) PF 693. [from *shout* v., ? rel to **shete(n**]

sho(u)veth, shove(n *see* **sho(o)f.**

showving *vbl. n.* shoving, pushing H.Mcp 53. [see **sho(o)f**]

shredde *pa. 3 sg.* shredded, cut E.Cl 227. [OE *scrēadian*]

shrewe *n.* **1.** wicked, ill-disposed man, rascal, villain A.Rv 3907, C.Pard 819, D.WB 284, G.CY 995, Bo 3. p4. 19/28, (the devil) G.CY 917; (a malignant planet) Astr 2.4.33/52; (as term of abuse) wretch, scoundrel D.WB 291, 355; *pl.* B.Mel 2664, I.Pars 554, Bo 1. p3. 48/67, 4. p2. 7/9, etc. (esp. common in Bo, often for L *mali*, *improbi*). **2.** railing, scolding woman E.Mch 1222, 2428. [fig. use of OE *scrēawa*, shrew]

shrewe *v.* curse, beshrew B.NP 4616, D.WB 446, D.Fri 1442, D.Sum 2227. [from prec.]

shrewed *adj.* evil, wicked D.WB 54, D.Sum 2224, HF 275, LGW 1545. [**shrewe** n.+ suff. *-ed*]

shrewedly *adv.* harshly, cursedly D.Sum 2238. [from prec.]

shrewednesse *n.* wickedness B.Mel 2721, Bo 4. p3. 52/74, TC 2.858; malignancy, perversity D.WB 734; *pl.* wicked deeds I.Pars 442, Bo 4. p4. 24/44. [from **shrewed**]

shrichyng *vbl. n.* screeching TC 5.382 *var.* [cf. **shrighte**]

shrift(e *n.* confession D.Sum 1818, G.SN 277, I.Pars 87, BD 1114, LGW 745. [OE *scrift*]

shrifte-fadres *n. pl.* confessors D.Fri 1442. [from prec.+**fader**]

shrighte *pa.* shrieked A.Kn 2817, B.NP 4552, F.Sq 417. **shright** *p.p.* TC 5.320. [infin. *shriche*, EME, imit; cf. next]

shryked *pa. pl.* shrieked B.NP 4590 *var.* [cf. **skriked**]

shryking *vbl. n.* screeching TC 5.382 *var.* [rel. to MLG *schrempen* v. wrinkle]

shrimpes *n. pl.* small creatures B.Mk 3145. [rel. to MLG *schrempen* v. wrinkle]

shryned *p.p.* enshrined C.Pard 955, WUnc 15. [from *shryne* n., OE *scrīn*]

shrinke *v.* draw in TC 1.300. **shronk** *pa. sg.* shrank Bo 1. p1. 9/14. [OE *scrincan*, *scranc*, *scruncen*]

shryve(n *v.* **1.** confess (someone), hear the confession of D.Sum 2095; *refl.* make confession I.Pars 106, 129, 309, ? make one's last confession TC 2.440. **2.** reveal, expose TC 2.579. **shriven** *p.p.* D.Fri 1440, I.Pars 1008; **yshrive(n** A.Prol 226, C.Pard 380. [OE *scrifan*, *ge)scrifen*]

shroud *n.* robe RR 64 (F *robe*). [OE *scrūd*]

shrouded *p.p.* clad RR 55. [from prec.]

sy *see* **se(c)(n.**

sib *adj.* related, akin B.Mel 2565, 2566, RR 1199. [OE *sib(b)*]

sicamour *n.* sycamore HF 1278. [OF *sicamor*]

syde *n.* **1.** side (of a person) A.Prol 112, B.Th 2026, B.Mk 3804, B.NP 4357, F.Sq 84, TC 3.1248; *by* (*one's*) ~ beside B.NP 4382, E.Mch 1928; (of an object) *beddes* ~ B.NP 4269, E.Mch 1934, PF 98, TC 3.236, edge (of wood) B.NP 4601, D.WB 990, D.Fri 1380, BD 372, (harbour) B.NP 4261, (astrolabe) Astr 1.6.1, etc.; (of place or direction) E.Cl 57, E.Mch 2226, I.Pars 171,

PF 125, LGW 750, *on that other* ~ PF
293, TC 5.687, (fig.) hand A.Kn 1275,
1332, E.Mch 2097, TC 4.164, *on every* ~
everywhere, in all directions C.Phs 111,
E.Cl 81, I.Pars 714, TC 1.185, 4.1391,
5.699, *on eche* ~ D.WB 256. **2.** part, party
A.Kn 2733, E.Mch 1392, TC 4.1466; *on
either* ~ A.Kn 2553, B.ML 244; *as for/on
my* ~ for my part E.Mch 1410, G.SN 475.
[OE *side*]
sye *v.* sink down TC 5.182. [OE *sigan*]
sye(n *see* **se(e)(n.**
sight(e *n.* **1.** sight, something seen A.Kn
2116, A.Co 4379, B.ML 568, B.Mk 3677,
E.Cl 280, TC 1.294, *to* ~ in appearance
E.Cl 209, 682; *pl.* HF 2010. **2.** sight,
perception through the eyes A.Kn 1114,
1231, I.Pars 184, TC 2.702, look TC 2.669,
glimpse A.Mil 3443. **3.** vision, power of
sight B.ML 562, B.Mel 2891, D.Sum 2060,
E.Mch 2260, I.Pars 207, TC 4.312, *pl.*
Bo 1. m7. 6/8 (L *uisibus*), eyes Bo 1. p1.
58/80; glance I.Pars 853; (fig., of mind,
etc.) G.CY 1419, Bo 3. m11. 3/4, *pl.* Bo
3. m9. 30/43 (L *uisus*); (of God) B.Mel
3075, Bo 5. p6. 88/125, foresight, providence A.Kn 1672. **4.** seeing, range of
vision B.NP 4293, G.CY 916; (with *in, to*)
before (someone's) eyes B.ML 672, B.Pri
1658, E.Cl 1125, G.CY 1127, TC 4.941,
F.Fkl 1151, I.Pars 3; (with *from, out of*)
D.WB 956, TC 5.635, F.Sq 329, LGW
1001. [OE *sihþ, gesiht*]
sighte *see* **syke(n.**
signal *n.* sign, token TC 4.818, HF 459. [OF]
signe *n.* **1.** sign, gesture E.Mch 2150, 2209,
LGW 2367, motion A.Kn 2266. **2.** token,
indication TC 1.1164, B.Mel 2832, F.Sq
645, I.Pars 316, (of victory) TC 5.1652,
Anel 29, H.Mcp 127, (on the face) BD 917,
pl. symptoms C.Pard 891; figure, emblem
ABC 91; portent A.Mil 3683. **3.** (astrol.)
sign of the zodiac A.Kn 2462, B.NP 4384,
HF 949, LGW 2223, Astr prol 67/92,
etc. [OF]
signet *n.* signet-ring TC 2.1087. [OF]
signifiaunce *n.* signification, significance (of
dreams) TC 5.362, HF 17, meaning, pre-
diction RR 16, sign TC 5.1447. [OF]
significacioun *n.* signification, meaning
I.Pars 608, Bo 5. p1. 27/38; *pl.* indications
B.NP 4169. [OF]
significavit *n.* a form of writ, issued for the
arrest of an excommunicated person A.Prol
662. [L [the bishop] 'has certified']
syk/sigh *n.* sigh A.Kn 1117, F.Sq 498, PF
246, TC 2.145, 4.1527. [from **syke(n**]
syk/seke *adj.* sick, ill A.Kn 1600, A.Rv 3993,
B.NP 4027, PF 161, TC 2.1516; (heart)
BD 557, (sorrows) TC 3.1172. **syke** *def.*
D.Sum 1781, 2121, F.Fkl 1100, TC 2.1572,
pl. TC 3.1362/1348, as *n.* TC 3.61; **seke**
def. A.Prol 424 *var*, as *n. sg.* sick man PF
104, *pl.* A.Prol 18, 245, LGW 1203. [OE
sēoc]
syke(n *v.* sigh A.Kn 1540, E.Mch 2329, TC
1.192, 2.1573, 3.58; ~ *sore* A.Mil 3488,
B.Mk 3394, TC 1.751, 3.972, 4.1217.
sighte *pa.* B.ML 1035, TC 3.1080, 4.714,
5.715; **syked** A.Kn 2985, E.Cl 545. [OE
sīcan, -sāc]
siker *adj.* sure A.Kn 3049, B.NP 4353, F.Fkl
1139, BD 1149, certain G.CY 1047; secure

B.Mel 2511, I.Pars 93, LGW 2660, in
security Buk 28, safe G.CY 864, TC 3.921,
RR 1100; steady D.Sum 2069, dependable
B.Mel 2564. *comp.* more certain B.NP
4043. [OE *sicor*]
siker *adv.* surely D.WB 465, TC 2.991,
securely, uninterruptedly TC 3.1237.
[from prec.]
sikered/sekered *p.p.* betrothed LGW 2128.
[from adj.]
sikerly *adv.* certainly, assuredly, truly A.Prol
137, 154, B.Sh 1344, B.NP 3984, TC 2.520;
soundly TC 3.746. [from **siker**]
sikernesse *n.* security, safety B.Mk 3430,
E.Mch 1355, I.Pars 735, TC 2.843 *var*,
3.982; state of security TC 2.773, Bo 2.
p5. 133/188. [from **siker**]
sykinge *vbl. n.* sighing TC 1.724.
syklatoun *see* **ciclatoun.**
sikly *adj.* sick, ill TC 2.1528, 1543. [cf. ON
sjúkligr]
sikly *adv.* with ill will E.Cl 625. [from **syk**]
siknesse/sek- *n.* sickness, illness A.Kn 1256,
BD 36, TC 1.489, (of soul) I.Pars 458.
pl. Bo 3. p7. 3/4 *var*. [from **syk**]
silver *n.* silver A.Prol 115, G.CY 626, 826;
money A.Prol 232, 713, A.Rv 4135, G.CY
1018. [OE *siolfor*]
similitude *n.* likeness, a person like oneself
A.Mil 3228; likeness, counterpart F.Sq
480; figure, symbol Bo 3. p5. 18/25;
proposition G.SN 431. [OF]
symonials *n. pl.* simoniacs I.Pars 784. [OF
simonial]
symonye *n.* simony, trading in sacred things
D.Fri 1309, I.Pars 781. [OF *simonie*]
simphonye *n.* a kind of tabor B.Th 2005. [OF]
simple *adj.* simple A.Prol 119, B.NP 4016,
D.Sum 1789, TC 1.181, modest RR 1014,
TC 5.820, innocent BD 861, 918; simple,
single Bo 3. p9. 66/87 (L *simplex*), simple,
(considered) in itself B.NP 4435, Bo 5. p6.
127/179; *fee* ~ absolute possession (see
fee) A.Prol 319. [OF]
simplesse *n.* simplicity BalCh 15, (person.)
RR 954; simple character Bo 4. p6. 83/118.
[OF]
simplicite(e *n.* (only in Bo) simplicity,
simpleness of form Bo 3. p12. 121/162,
4. p6. 17/26, 34/49, etc. [OF]
sin *prep.* since, after, from A.Kn 1193, A.Mil
3665. *conj.* from the time that F.Sq 306,
I.Pars 1011, TC 5.873, ~ *that* A.Prol 601,
A.Rv 3890, TC 5.466, LGW 445; considering that, since A.Prol 853, A.Mil
3716, B.ML 56, TC 1.256, 4.332, 557; ~
that B.Mel 2118. [contraction of **sithen**]
singe(n *v.* sing A.Prol 236, A.Kn 2210, TC
2.825; (fig.) cry with pain D.Fri 1311,
1316; ~ *a masse* (obscure prov. phr.)
? talk nonsense, flatter TC 3.88. **sang**
pa. 1, 3 sg. B.Th 1961, E.Mch 1845, H.Mcp
243; **so(o)ng** A.Kn 1055, B.Pri 1736, BD
1158. **songe** *2 sg.* H.Mcp 294, Bo 1. p6.
14/18, 5. p3. 147/210. **songe(n** *pl.* D.WB
216, E.Mch 1735, LGW 139. **songe** *subj.
3 sg.* BD 929. **songe(n** *p.p.* A.Prol 266,
B.Pri 1851, HF 347, recited, told in verse
TC 5.1797; **ysonge(n** TC 5.1059, HF
1397, LGW G. 224. [OE *singan, sáng,
súngon, súngen*]
singers *n. pl.* singers, minstrels C.Pard 479.
[from prec.]

singing vbl. n. singing, song B.Pri 1747, B.NP 4489, pl. TC 3.1716.

singularitees n. pl. particulars, separate parts Bo 5. m3. 28/41, 33/47 (L singula). [OF singularité]

singuler adj. single, individual G.CY 997, I.Pars 300, particular Bo 2. p7. 39/56, 5. p6. 172/242, separate Bo 5. m3. 5/8; holding no office, private B.Mel 2625; special, pertaining to the individual (opp. common) HF 310; special Bo 2. p3. 31/45. [OF]

singulerly adv. singly Bo 4. p6. 49/71, 61/88. [from prec.]

sinke(n v. intr. sink, fall to the ground LGW 178, (into the ground) be swallowed up G.CY 912, go down (to hell) ABC 123; penetrate, enter TC 4.1494, (into heart, mind) A.Kn 951, TC 1.734, 2.650, 902, 3.1538, Anel 8; (fig., in flete or ~) fail, be in distress, see **flete(n**. tr. cause to sink F.Fkl 1073. **sank** pa. sg. I.Pars 839. **sonken** p.p. F.Fkl 892, 1269. [OE sincan, sanc, suncen]

sinne n. sin A.Prol 561, A.Mil 3146, I.Pars 331, etc. [OE synn]

sinne v. sin B.Mel 2720, C.Phs 138, I.Pars 96. [from prec.; cf. OE syngian]

sinwes n. pl. sinews I.Pars 690. [OE sin(e)we, obl. case of sinu]

sir(e n. **1.** form of address: sir, A.Kn 1715, B.ML 570, C.Pard 670, TC 2.957, good ~ B.NP 3957, E.Mch 2387, G.CY 1458; title of honour of a knight B.Th 1907, 2089; used before the Christian name of a priest B.NP 4010; used before a common noun A.Prol 837, A.Mil 3118, B.Sh 1166, B.NP 3982, C.Pard 943, D.WB 1001, E.Cl 1, (iron.) D.WB 242, 357, 365. pl. A.Rv 3909, C.Pard 366, D.WB 188, F.Fkl 716, TC 4.179. **2.** master (often in phr. lord and ~) A.Prol 355, G.CY 918, PF 12, husband D.WB 713. **3.** father A.Rv 4246 var, F.Mch 2265, TC 4.1455. [OF sire]

sis num. six (on dice) B.ML 125, B.Mk 3851. [OF]

sisoures n. pl. scissors HF 690. [OF cisoires]

site n. position, situation E.Cl 199, Bo 2. m4. 10/14, HF 1114, Astr 2.17. 25/36. [AN]

sith adv. then Anel 354, LGW 302; afterwards C.Pard 869, RR 1604 var. [OE siþþan]

sith conj. since A.Kn 930, B.ML 814, B.Mk 3268, E.Cl 556, TC 1.253; ~ that A.Mil 3231, B.Pri 1838, F.Fkl 1395, Mars 125. [as prec.]

sythe n.¹ scythe LGW 646. [OE siþe]

sithe n.² times with num. B.ML 733, 1155, Anel 222, TC 4.739, 5.472; many ~ RR 80; ofte ~ often, again and again A.Kn 1877, E.Cl 233, G.CY 1031. **sithes** pl. A,Prol 485, LGW G. 1. [OE siþ, gen. pl. siþa with num., instr. pl. siþum]

sithen/sitthe adv. afterwards A.Kn 2617, B.ML 58, 1121, TC 3.244, since then RR 1641; goon ~ a greet whyl/longe whyle/many yeres/many a day long ago LGW 427 var, TC 1.718, A.Kn 1521, F.Sq 536; then, next B.Sh 1238, B.Mk 3913, LGW 304. [OE siþþan]

sithen conj. since B.Mel 2947, TC 1.941, 2. 260, CompA 36, 51, ~ that A.Kn 2102, CompA 60. [as prec.]

sitte(n v. **1.** sit A.Prol 94, E.Mch 2217, TC 2.783, 3.1630, refl. A.Mil 3819; ~ doun

D.WB 838, E.Mch 1934, G.CY 1195, TC 2.213, ~ on knowe/knees kneel TC 2.1202 var, BD 106; remain, dwell TC 2.935, BD 1108; be placed Astr 2.1.3/4, 7.4/5. **2.** (of garment) suit, fit G.SN 132, RR 1239; (with dat.) affect (painfully) TC 3.240, 4.231, BD 1220; impers. (subject it) befit, suit B.Sh 1353, E.Mch 1277, 2315, TC 1.12, 246, 2.117, RR 750, yvel it sit it is unbecoming E.Cl 460. **sitteth** pr. 3 sg. A.Kn 1527, E.Cl 538; **sit** A.Kn 1599, 1800, B.ML 970, F.Fkl 1252, TC 4.1023, LGW 1201; **sitteth** imper. pl. TC 2.213. **sat** pa. sg. A.Prol 271, B.NP 4074; **seet** A.Kn 2075; **sete** BD 501. **sat(te** pl. C.Pard 664; **sate** BD 298; **sete(n** B.Mk 3734, F.Sq 92, BD 431, TC 2.1192, RR 714. **sat(t)e** subj. sg. TC 1.985 var, 2.117 var; **sete** ibid. em. **sete(n** p.p. A.Kn 1452, D.WB 420, TC 2.81. [OE sittan, sæt, OA sēton, seten]

sitting adj. suitable, fitting TC 4.437, Bo 1. p3. 13/17, RR 986. sup. PF 551. [from prec.]

sive n. sieve G.CY 940. [OE sife]

sixe num. six B.Sh 1364, F.Sq 391; (set the world) on ~ and sevene (dicing term) take a chance TC 4.622. [OE siex]

sixte num. sixth D.WB 45, F.Fkl 906, TC 5.1205. [OE sixta]

sixty num. sixty, sometimes a conventional expression of large number: TC 1.441, HF 1979, LGW G.273. [OE sixtiġ]

skant adj. niggardly ABC 175. [ON skammt]

skye n. cloud HF 1600; the ~ the sky F.Sq 503. [ON ský]

skile n. reason, cause, ground HF 726, (in phr. with is) reasonable B.ML 708, B.Mel 3000, TC 2.365, 3. 646; gret ~ good reason E.Cl 1152; reasonable claim LGW 1392; pl. reasons, arguments F.Sq 205, HF 867, PF 537, Bo 5. p3.52/72. [ON skil]

skilful adj. reasonable Anel 128, TC 2.392, 3.287, 938, LGW 385, discerning, discriminating B.ML 1038, G.SN 327, BD 534. [from prec.]

skilfully adv. reasonably, with reason G.SN 320, Mars 155, PF 634, TC 4.1265. [from prec.]

skilinge† vbl. n. reasoning Bo 4. p6. 97/140. [from skile v.]

skinketh pr. 3 sg. pours out E.Mch 1722 var. [MLG, MDu schenken; cf. **shynketh**]

skippe(n v. jump TC 1.218, dance A.Mil 3259, leap E.Mch 1672, hop Bo 3. m2. 18/27; go quickly, run I.Pars 361, pass quickly over LGW 622; there was no more to ~ there was no more skipping about TC 3.690. **skipte** pa. F.Fkl 1402. [? of MSw skuppa]

skriked pa. pl. shrieked B.NP 4590 var. [cf. ON skrækja]

slayn see **sle(e)(n**.

slake v. **1.** intr. decrease, abate F.Fkl 841, desist (from) E.Cl 705, relax effort C.Phs 82; fail TC 2.291; end E.Cl 137. **2.** tr. release Bo 3. m2. 12/17, relax, loosen Bo 2. m8. 11/16, 5. m1. 13/19; assuage, satisfy E.Cl 1107, LGW 2006, RR 317; diminish E.Cl 802. [OE slacian]

slak(ke adj. slow A.Kn 2901, slow, pliant Bo 3. m2. 1; loose E.Mch 1849, Bo 1. m1. 12; comp. (double) more dilatory B.Sh 1603. [OE slæc]

slaknesse n. idleness, sluggishness I.Pars 680. [from prec.]
slate see **sclat**.
slaughtre n. murder, killing A.Kn 2031, B.ML 956, I.Pars 103, to ~ of to the destruction of I.Pars 154. [ON *slahtr*]
slawe(n see **sle(e)(n**.
sledes n. pl. sledges, drags Bo 4. p1. 50/69 (L *vehiculis*). [MLG *sledde*]
sle(e)(n v. slay, kill A.Kn 1222, B.ML 940, C.Pard 491, D.Sum 2042, TC 5.46; (fig.) A.Kn 1567, D.Sum 1794, MercB 1, overcome with distress F.Sq 462, F.Fkl 893; destroy, extinguish Astr prol 46/64; destroy (the soul) B.Mel 2605. **slee** pr. 1 sg. as fut. B.Th 2002. **sleeth** 3 sg. B.Mel 2186. **slough** pa. sg. Anel 56, TC 5.1806; **slow** BD 727, HF 268, 956; **slowh** Bo 4. m7. 29/42. **slowen** pl. Bo 3. p5. 36/50. **slowe** subj. 2 sg. TC 4.506. **slayn** p.p. A.Prol 63, B.NP 4235; **yslayn** A.Kn 2708, HF 159; **slawe(n** E.Cl 544, TC 3.721, 4. 884; **yslawe** B.ML 484, C.Pard 856. [OE *slēan, slōh, slōgon, ġe)sleġen/ġe)slagen*]
sle(e)p n. sleep, slumber A.Kn 1361, F.Sq 347, TC 1.484, 3.1408, LGW 177; the dede ~ profound sleep, sleep of exhaustion A.Mil 3643, BD 127, TC 2.924; wolde han caught a ~ A.Rv 4227, took his ~ A.Kn 1390, fil on ~ HF 114, LGW 209; in ~ A.Kn 1384, B.NP 4124, TC 5.1447, 1715; to ~ E.Mch 1949, I.Pars 914. pl. A.Kn 1920, Bo 2. m5. 11/16. [OE *slǣp, A slēp*]
sleere n. slayer A.Kn 2005. [from v.]
sleigh see **sly**.
sleighte/slighte n. craft, cunning, trickery A.Prol 604, A.Rv 4011, G.CY 1227, I.Pars 166, TC 2.1512, LGW 1382; skill, skilfulness G.CY 867; adroitness, dexterity A.Kn 1948, A.Rv 4050, E.Cl 1102, LGW 2084; cunning trick, plan E.Mch 2131; pl. devices, tricks E.Mch 2421, G.CY 773, 976, plans TC 4.1451. [ON *slǣgð*]
sleyly see **slyly**.
slendre see **sclendre**.
slepe(n v. sleep A.Prol 10, B.Th 2100, E.Cl 14, F.Sq 381, TC 1.921; sleep in death I.Pars 193. **slepestow** pr. 2 sg. (with suffixed pron.) A.Rv 4169. **sleping(e** pr.p. causing sleep BD 162. **sleep** pa. sg. A.Prol 98, 397, B.ML 745, TC 2.925, HF 119 var. **slepe(n** pl. F.Sq 360, BD 166, 177. **slepte** pa. sg. A.Rv 4194, B.Mk 3809, E.Cl 224, HF 119 var. **slepte(n** pl. D.WB 770, TC 3.746, FormA 43. [OE *slǣpan, A slēpan; slēp, slēpon*]
slepy adj. sleepy, lethargic HF 75, 1783 var; inducing sleep A.Kn 1387. [from **sle(e)p**]
sleping n. sleep B.NP 4202, I.Pars 193, 575, BD 230, LGW 1333. [from prec.]
sleping-tyme n. time to sleep CompL 51. [prec.+**tyme**]
slewthe see **slouthe**.
sly/sleigh adj. skilful, clever F.Sq 672, BD 570, subtle, cunning TC 4.972, artfully contrived F.Sq 230, deceitful, wily B.NP 4405, D.Fri 1371, G.CY 655, TC 5.898; as n. sly one A.Mil 3392. **slyer** comp. D.Fri 1322. [ON *slǣgr*]
slyde(n v. slide, pass, go away E.Cl 82, F.Fkl 924, 1002, BD 567; pass (easily) Bo 3. p12. 142/190, 5. p2. 21/29, slip away

TC 5.769, (of time) TC 5.351. **slydeth** pr. 3 sg. Bo 3. p12. 142/190; **slit** G.CY 682, PF 3. [OE *slīdan*]
slider adj. slippery A.Kn 1264, LGW 648. [OE *slidor*]
slyding(e pr. p. adj. changeable, unstable TC 5.825, inconstant Bo 1. m5. 24/34, 4. m2. 9/14, slippery G.CY 732; flowing, gliding Bo 5. m1. 12/17. [from **slyde(n**]
slighte see **sleighte**.
slyk adj. such (nth, only in A.Rv) A.Rv 4130, 4170, 4171 var, 4173. [ON *slikr*]
slyk(e adj. sleek, glossy D.WB 351, RR 542. [OE *slice*]
slyly/sleyly adv. skilfully Astr 2.29. 13/18, 14/19, C.Pard 792, sagaciously A.Kn 1444; cleverly, cunningly D.Sum 1994, G.CY 1230, TC 2.462, 1185. [from **sly**]
slinge-stones n.pl. stones from a sling TC 2.941. [? MLG *slinge+***sto(o)n**]
slinke v. creep TC 3.1535. [OE *slincan*]
slippe v. pass, in lete ~ pass over, ignore LGW 623. [MLG *slippen*]
slitte(n v. pierce F.Fkl 1260, slit Bo 2. m6. 5/7. **slitte** pa. B.Mk 3674. [rel. to OE *slītan*]
slivere n. sliver, part TC 3.1013. [rel. to OE *slīfan* split]
slogardye n. slothfulness, laziness A.Kn 1042, C.Phs 57, G.SN 17. [from *slogard* n., cf. **sluggy**]
sloggy see **sluggy**.
slomber n. sleep A.Mil 3816. [from ME *slumeren* v.]
slombrestow pr. 2 sg. (with suffixed pron.) are you sleeping? TC 1.730. [ME *slumeren*, cf. MLG, MDu]
slombry adj. sleepy I.Pars 724. [from **slomber**]
slomeringe/slombringe vbl. n. slumber I.Pars 706, TC 2.67; pl. TC 5.246.
slong pa. 3 sg. threw, flung H.Mcp 306. [from ME *slingen*, prob. ON *slyngva, slǫng*]
slo(o n. sloe A.Mil 3246, RR 928. [OE *slā*]
sloppes n. pl. loose outer garments I.Pars 422. [cf. **overslop(p)e** and ON *sloppr*]
slough see **sle(e)(n**.
slouthe/slewthe n. sloth, sluggishness B.ML 530, F.Fkl 1232, G.SN 258, I.Pars 388, 686, TC 3.896. [EME *slāwð* from *slāw* adj.; OE *slǣwþ*]
slow/slough adj. slow LGW 840, RR 322, (in understanding) B.ML 315; sluggish B.Mel 2778, I.Pars 724, slothful D.Sum 1816, Bo 4. m7. 46/66, idle HF 1778. [OE *slāw*]
slow, slowe(n, slowh see **sle(e)(n**.
sluggy/sloggy adj. sluggish I.Pars 706 [rel. to *slug* v. prob. orig. Scand.; cf. Sw. dial. *slogga*]
sluttish adj. slovenly G.CY 636. [?]
smal adj. **1.** slender, slim A.Mil 3234, D.WB 261, E.Mch 1602, TC 3.1247, 4.744; narrow A.Prol 329, B.NP 4095; fine I.Pars 197; (of voice) high, treble A.Prol 688, A.Mil 3360. **2.** small, little A.Prol 9, B.Sh 1473, B.Pri 1726, D.Fri 1426, E.Cl 483, PF 353, TC 3.1462; humble E.Mch 1625; as n. in a ~ a little CompL 113/107. grete and ~ A.Mil 3178, 3208, A.Rv 4323, B.Sh 1214, C.Pard 659, ~ and grete A.Mil 3826. comp. Astr 2.38.6/8. sup. Astr prol 53/74. [OE *smæl, smal-*]

smal(e *adv.* little, *but* ~ but little D.WB 592, F.Sq 71, Astr prol 20/27; finely G.CY 760; (of voice) high Rosem 11; elegantly A.Mil 3320, D.WB 457. [from prec.]

smart *see* **smert.**

smatre *pr. pl. refl.* defile (themselves) I.Pars 857. [?]

smelle(n *v.* smell (*tr.* and *intr.*) B.Sh 1113, A.Mil 3691. **smelde** *pa.* HF 1685. [?]

smellinge *n.* sense of smell I.Pars 207, 959; odour G.CY 890. [from prec.]

smert *n.* pain, anguish A.Mil 3813, B.Mk 3796, G.CY 712, TC 5.417. [from next]

smert/smart *adj.* brisk RR 831, (of fire) G.CY 768; bitter, painful A.Kn 2225, F.Sq 480, F.Fkl 856, BD 507, 1107, TC 4.248, 5.1326. [LOE *smeart*]

smerte *adv.* sharply, painfully A.Prol 149, TC 4.243, sorely E.Cl 629. [from prec.]

smerte *v.* **1.** *tr.* hurt, pain F.Sq 564, Bo 2. p4. 4/6, TC 1.667; *impers.* (with obj. pron.) A.Prol 230, 534, A.Kn 1394, TC 3.146, 4.1186. **2.** feel pain, suffer D.Sum 2092, E.Cl 353, Mars 62, TC 1.1049, 3.1182, 4.1448, LGW 502. **smerteth** *pr. 3 sg.* TC 1.667; **smert** ABC 152. **smerte** *subj.* A.Prol 230, A.Kn 1394, TC 5.132. **smerte** *pa.* TC 2.930, 5.1224. *subj.* TC 4.1186, *pl.* B.Mk 3903. [OE *smeortan*]

smyle *v.* smile D.Fri 1446, TC 1.194, (*of* 'at') A.Rv 4046; smile on RR 1056. [? perh. Scand, cf. Sw *smila*, or MHG *smielen*]

smyler *n.* smiler, flatterer A.Kn 1999. [from prec.]

smyte(n *v.* smite, strike A.Kn 1220, A.Mil 3569, C.Phs 252, G.SN 528; ~ *of* cut off B.Mk 3881, C.Phs 226, TC 3.957; ~ *on* hit upon TC 1.273. **smyteth** *pr. 3 sg.* A.Kn 1709; smet A.Cl E.Cl 122. **smyteth** *imper. pl.* TC 3.1573. **smo(o)t** *pa. sg.* A.Prol 149, A.Rv 4275, HF 438. **smiten** *p.p.* BD 1323, TC 2.1145, LGW 2319; **ysmite** Bo 3. m7. 4/6. [OE *smītan, smāt, smiten*]

smith *n.* blacksmith A.Kn 2025, A.Mil 3761. [OE *smiþ*]

smithed *pa. sg.* forged A.Mil 3762. [OE *smiþode* from *smiþian*]

smitted *p.p.* besmirched, sullied TC 5.1545. [OE *smittod* from *smittian*]

smok *n.* shift, vest D.WB 783. [OE *smoc*]

smoking(e *pr. p. adj.* smoking Mars 120, smoky (with incense) A.Kn 2281. [from OE *smocian*]

smoklees *adj.* without a smock E.Cl 875. [from **smok**]

smoot *see* **smyte(n.**

smoterliche† *adj.* smirched in reputation A.Rv 3963. [cf. *smotry* grimy, in Lydgate]

smothe *adv.* smoothly A.Prol 676, TC 4.996. [from adj., OE *smōþ*]

snewed *pa.* snowed, abounded A.Prol 345. [from OE *snīwan*]

snibben *v.* reprove, chide A.Prol 523, A.Co 4401, F.Fkl 688. [Scand; cf. Dan *snibbe*]

snorteth *pr. 3 sg.* snorts, snores A.Rv 4163 *var*, B.ML 790 *var*. **snorted** *p.p.* (of the nose) turned up RR 157. [? imit.]

snow *n.* snow B.Mk 3942, TC 5.1176; (her.) white, argent B.Mk 3573; *pl.* snow-storms HF 967. [OE *snāw*]

snowed *p.p.* (of snow) fallen RR 558. [from prec.]

snowish *adj.* snowy, snow-white TC 3.1250. [from **snow**]

so *adv.* so A.Prol 11, 102, A.Mil 3386, B.ML 150, B.Mk 3139, D.WB 7, 825; in such a way, such TC 3.1579; as well, also A.Kn 1749; for that reason, accordingly TC 5.1233; (confirming preceding sentence) indeed TC 2.1284; (introd. wish or adjuration, with subj.) so A.Mil 3592, B.NP 4256, D.WB 830, BD 1065, TC 3.1470; ~*as* as well as, as far as Mars 161; *if (it)* ~ be/were if B.Pri 1640, F.Sq 109, H.Mcp 216, TC 5.696. [OE *swā*]

so *conj.* provided that TC 2.1162, 4.798, HF 423, LGW 1319; ~ *as* whereas Bo 4. p3. 25/36; ~ *that* provided that B.Pri 1638, C.Phs 186, D.WB 125, E.Mch 1357, HF 671. [as prec.]

sobre *adj.* grave, serious B.ML 97, E.Cl 366, BD 880, TC 3.237, Gent 9; temperate, abstemious E.Mch 1533; demure TC 5.820, LGW 2672. [OF]

sobrely *adv.* seriously, gravely B.Sh 1445, E.Cl 296, F.Fkl 1585, TC 3.359, 1588, modestly TC 2.648. [from prec.]

sobrenesse *n.* sobriety C.Pard 582, I.Pars 834. [from **sobre**]

socour *n.* succour, help A.Kn 918, B.ML 644, ABC 2, 168, LGW 1053, Fort 15; *do(on* ~ help Mars 292, LGW 1476; **socours** TC 2.1354, LGW 1341. [OF *sucurs/socours*]

socouren *v.* succour, aid TC 3.1264. [OF *succurre/succurir*]

sodein *adj.* (of actions, events) sudden, unforeseen B.ML 421, B.NP 3963, E.Cl 316, E.Mch 2057, TC 3.959, (death) F.Fkl 1010; (feelings) unpremeditated B.Mel 2324, I.Pars 541, TC 2.667; (of persons) forward, impetuous TC 5.1024, Bo 2. p3. 55/80. [AN *sodein*]

sode(i)nly/-liche *adv.* suddenly, without warning A.Kn 1118, 1530, D.WB 790, TC 1.209, 3.82; without delay, quickly C.Phs 131, E.Mch 1409; without premeditation B.Mel 2531, eagerly B.Mel 2199. [from prec.]

sode(n *see* **sethe.**

softe *adj.* soft A.Prol 153, B.NP 4357, TC 3.1247, (of voice) TC 5.636, LGW 745, gentle, mild D.Fri 1412, F.Fkl 907, PF 680; *a* ~ *pas* quietly, slowly A.Mil 3760, B.ML 399; lax, easy-going C.Phs 101, yielding, weak TC 1.137. [OE *sōfte*]

softe *adv.* softly A.Kn 2781, E.Cl 583, TC 3.566, on a soft bed 442; gently C.Phs 252, LGW 2708, tenderly B.ML 275, quietly TC 3.698, 1535, timidly BD 1212. [OE *sōfte*]

softely *adv.* softly, gently, tenderly B.Pri 1862, F.Sq 636, G.SN 408; (of voice) TC 5.506, LGW 2126; *a pas* ~ slowly, easily TC 2.627; quietly, unobtrusively A.Rv 4058, 4211, E.Mch 1954, TC 2.519, 1536; comfortably I.Pars 835. [from adj.]

softneth *pr. 3 sg.* assuages LGW 50. [from **softe** adj.]

soght(e *see* **seke(n.**

sojo(u)rne *v.* stay, dwell D.WB 987, E.Mch 1796, TC 5.483, 1350, continue, remain TC 5.213; delay LGW 2476, RR 381; stop TC 1.850. [OF *sorjurner*]

soken *n.* toll A.Rv 3987. [OE *sōcn*]

sokingly adv. gradually B.Mel 2766. [from soke v. soak, OE socian]

sol n. (alchem.) gold G.CY 826, 1440. [L]

solace v. comfort, refresh HF 2008, RR 613, 621. [OF solacier]

solas n. comfort, consolation TC 2.460, solace I.Pars 206, 740; respite B.Th 1972; pleasure, delight A.Prol 798, A.Mil 3200, B.Th 1904, B.NP 4393, F.Fkl 802, joy TC 1.31, 5.607. [OF]

soleyn adj. solitary BD 982, unmated PF 607, 614. [AN *solein]

solempne adj. festive, ceremonious F.Sq 111, BD 302; grand, imposing B.ML 387, F.Sq 61; of great dignity A.Prol 209; formal, public I.Pars 102. [OF]

solempnely adv. ceremoniously, with pomp B.ML 317, 399, F.Sq 179, gravely A.Prol 274. [from prec.]

solempnitee n. pomp, ceremony A.Kn 2702, D.WB 629, E.Mch 1709. [OF solempneté]

solitarie adj. solitary, alone A.Kn 1365; lonely Bo 1.p3. 7/10, Scog 46. [L solitārius]

somdel adv. somewhat, in some measure A.Prol 446, A.Kn 2170, A.Mil 3337, B.NP 4011, TC 1.1088. pron. something, part PF 112. [OE sum+dǣl, cf. next and **deel**]

som(e/sum adj. **1.** with sg. n. a certain, one A.Kn 1255, 1257, Bo 2. p4. 58/79, 65/89; some A.Prol 640, A.Mil 3452, BD 715, TC 1.33, 538; ~ tyme A.Kn 2474, 2621, B.ML 645, cf. **somtyme**; ~ day some day B.ML 1083, one day TC 1.136; ~ kynnes of some sort B.ML 1137 var; ~ certayn BD 119. **2.** with pl. n. **som** HF 1886, (men) B.ML 246, 1009, TC 2.47, (folk) A.Mil 3381; **somme** B.Mk 3317, (folk) B.Mel 2518. [OE sum]

som(e/sum pron. indef. **1.** sg. one TC 1.916, someone G.CY 995; ~ . . ~ one . . another A.Kn 3031, C.Pard 409, D.WB 104, G.CY 922–3 var; (with ordinal num.) with his tenthe ~ with or in his party of ten TC 2.1249; a part, portion TC 5.854, (with of) A.Mil 3175. **2.** pl. **som(m)e** B.Sh 1524, TC 4.995, (in apposition) the grettest of his lordes ~ LGW 1050; (with of) B.Mel 2139, 2195, F.Sq 225, G.SN 60, **som** BD 304, TC 2.1438; ~ . . ~ some . . others A.Kn 2516, D.WB 766–9, E.Mch 1471, G.CY 922–3 var, BD 174–6. al and ~ sg. altogether, the whole matter A.Kn 2761, D.WB 91, PF 650; alle and ~ pl. one and all A.Kn 2187, A.Mil 3136, B.ML 263, C.Pard 336, TC 4.1068; alle or ~ TC 1.240. [as prec.]

somer n. summer A.Prol 394, A.Kn 1337, G.CY 568, PF 680, LGW 170. **someres** gen. sg. B.ML 554, BD 821, **somers** LGW 142, ~ day TC 3.1061, ~ game summer entertainment D.WB 648. [OE sumor]

somer-sesoun n. season of summer E.Mch 2049; early summer, spring Bo 3. p8. 28/39 (L vernalium (florum), the firste ~ Bo 4. m6. 21/30 (L vere). [prec.+sesoun]

somme n. sum (of money) B.Sh 1376, 1407, F.Fkl 1220, TC 4.60, (of specified amount) G.CY 1364; total number, totality, perfection Bo 2. p4. 74/102, 3. p10. 158/216, 5. m3. 28/41; summary, epitome Bo 3. p8. 40/56; in ~ in a few words Bo 1. p4. 101/140; conclusion Bo 3. p12. 89/121 (L summa (rationum)); upshot, issue LGW 1559. [OF]

somnour n. summoner, apparitor, an officer who summoned delinquents before ecclesiastical courts A.Prol 543, D.Fri 1283, D.Sum 1665. [AN somenour]

somne/sompne v. summon, bring before the court D.Fri 1347, 1620; enjoin, call upon B.Mel 2652. [AN somon-, stem of somondre]

somonce n. summons D.Fri 1586. [OF]

somtyme adv. sometimes A.Kn 1668, A.Co 4402, B.Pri 1667, G.CY 949, TC 1.314, 747; at a certain time, at one time, formerly A.Prol 65, 85, D.WB 527; at some future time, some day A.Kn 1243, B.ML 110. [som(e+tyme]

somwhat n. something A.Rv 4203, B.Mel 2124, B.NP 3983, TC 1.672, 2.1309; in ~ to some extent I.Pars 246. [som(e+ what]

somwhat adv. to some extent, in some way, a little A.Prol 264, D.Fri 1571, E.Cl 579, TC 3.89, 5.634. [as prec]

sonde n. message B.ML 388, 1049, TC 3.492, 5.1372; messenger G.SN 525; sending, what is sent (by God), dispensation B.ML 760, 826, 902, I.Pars 625, gifts (of God) B.Sh 1409. [OE sånd/sönd]

sonded p.p. sanded TC 2.822. [from v. from so(o)nd]

sondry adj. various, different A.Prol 14, 25, D.Fri 1470, G.CY 791, TC 2.28, LGW 23. [OE syndriğ, infl. by sundor adj.]

sone n. son A.Prol 79, 336, TC 1.2, 2.102; (Christ) B.Pri 1656, 1670, G.SN 36, 417, ABC 125, 161; (of Eve) G.SN 62. [OE sunu]

song n. **1.** song, singing A.Kn 1492, A.Mil 3257, B.Pri 1726, B.NP 4501, TC 4.1433; (fig.) **sang** (nth.) A.Rv 4170. **2.** (a) song A.Prol 711, TC 2.883 BD 471, Anel 320, TC 5.633; poem B.Pri 1677. [OE sáng/sóng] cf. **even-song, morwe-song.**

sonne n. sun A.Prol 7, A.Kn 2273, B.NP 4388, F.Sq 48, TC 2.905, Astr prol 58/80, 2.1. rubr. (with fem. pron. hir); (fig.) ~ of excellence G.SN 52; under (the) ~ E.Cl 212, TC 2.174, 3.378. **sonne** gen. sg. A.Kn 1051, B.Mk 3944; **sonnes** TC 3.3, 5.664. [OE sunne]

sonnish adj. sun-like, golden TC 4.736, 816. [from prec.]

so(o)nd n. sand A.Mil 3748, B.ML 509, B.NP 4457. **sondes** pl. HF 691, **sandes** Bo 2. m2. 3/4. [OE sånd]

so(o)ne adv. soon, quickly A.Kn 1022, 1761, B.Pri 1702, B.Mel 2325, E.Mch 1986, TC 1.41; at once A.Mil 3446, B.ML 910, G.CY 1289, BD 195, TC 5.847; ~ after C.Phs 160, TC 2.1683, ~ hereafter TC 3.673, ~ therafter Bo 2. p6. 50/71 var, ~ after this A.Rv 4214, B.ML 407, E.Cl 1855, TC 3.1142, 1366, ~ after that D.Sum 1853, E.Mch 1805; ~ at eve/night this very evening/night TC 5.481, LGW 1637; as ~ as B.Pri 1778, B.NP 4215, C.Pard 609, as ~ as that B.Sh 1395, B.Mk 3473, as ~ as ever A.Rv 4292, B.Sh 1430, 1607, E.Cl 151, E.Mch 1913, TC 5.422, as ~ . . as B.Mel 2856, so ~ as C.Pard 806; how ~ that C.Phs 284, TC 3.112; to ~ C.Phs 68, 70, H.Mcp 285, TC 2.1291. **son(n)er** comp. Bo 4. p4. 28/38, RR 969; the ~ B.Mel 2640, TC 2.686. **sonest** sup. B.Mk 3716. [OE sóna]

so(o)ng, songe(n see **singe(n.**

so(o)r n. wound, pain A.Kn 2743, sore C.Pard 358; wound (of heart, mind, etc.), affliction A.Kn 1454, 2233, E.Mch 1243, Anel 242, TC 4.944; misery A.Kn 2849. [OE sār]

so(o)r adj. wounded, grieving, sad A.Kn 2695, 2804, F.Fkl 1571, Pity 2, TC 5.639; severe, bitter B.ML 758. [as prec.]

so(o)re adv. bitterly, sorely A.Prol 148, A.Mil 3488, B.Mk 3789, F.Fkl 1006, TC 1.751; grievously, painfully A.Prol 230, A.Kn 1115, E.Mch 1777, TC 1.490, LGW 2483; vigorously, violently A.Rv 4229, 4231; intensely, deeply A.Kn 2315, I.Pars 152; exceedingly F.Kn 2341, B.Mk 3395. **sorer** comp. LGW 502; **sorest** sup. PF 404. [OE sāre]

soot n. soot (i.e. something bitter) TC 3.1194. [OE sōt]

so(o)te adj. sweet, fresh, fragrant A.Prol 1, F.Sq 389, G.SN 91, I.Pars 636, RR 1425, TC 3.1231 var; cf. **swote.** [OE swōt]

so(o)th n. truth LGW 702, HF 1029; (with say, tell) A.Kn 1521, 1625, B.Mk 4615, E.Cl 855, TC 3.1212, 4.47, ~ to seyn A.Prol 284, B. ML 443, B.NP 4211, E.Mch 2082, TC 1.591; in ~ D.Sum 2010, TC 5.143, 371, HF 1057; for ~ in truth, indeed A.Prol 283, A.Kn 1460, A.Rv 3939, B.Th 1939, D.WB 46; (with indef. art.) truth, true saying, true thing B.Mk 3154, F.Sq 166, G.SN 477, TC 2.1137, 4.1407; (with def. art.) B.ML 1072, C.Pard 370, D.WB 931, G.CY 662, LGW 2114. pl. truths B.Mel 2367. [OE sōþ]

so(o)th adj. true A.Mil 3391, B.Mel 2136, C.Phs 157, E.Mch 1977, TC 3.619, PF 640, truthful F.Sq 21; as adv. truly C.Pard 636, TC 3.1357. **sother(e** comp. G.SN 214 var, Bo 3. p9. 102/137. [as prec.]

so(o)thfast adj. true Bo 2. p8. 11/16 (L uera), 5. m3. 4/5, TC 3.30, 4.870, 5.1860. [OE sōþfæst]

so(o)thfastly adv. truly Bo 3. p10. 26/37. [from prec.]

so(o)thfastnesse n. truth B.Mel 2365, B.NP 4518, E.Cl 796, G.SN 335, TC 4.1080, Truth 1; certainty I.Pars 380, as for no ~ because of uncertainty B.Mel 2595. [from so(o)thfast]

so(o)thly adv. truly, in truth A.Prol 117, A.Kn 1102, B.NP 4542, E.Mch 1477, I.Pars 122 (very common in Pars), TC 4.965; (with say, tell) A.Prol 468, A.Kn 1199, G.CY 1111, Pity 96, PF 270, TC 4.797. [from so(o)th adj.]

so(o)thnesse n. truth Bo 1. p6. 12/16, 5. m3. 33/47, in ~ in truth, in reality G.SN 261. [from so(o)th adj.]

sop n. sop, piece of bread dipped in wine, etc. A.Prol 334, E.Mch 1843. [OE sopp]

sope(e)r/souper n. supper A.Prol 748, A.Rv 4315, F.Sq 290, F.Fkl 1189, TC 2.947. [OF soper/super]

sophyme n. sophism, trick of logic E.Cl 5, F.Sq 554. [OF]

sophistrye n. cunning, trickery LGW 137. [OF]

sore v. soar, mount aloft F.Sq 123, TC 1.670, HF 499. [OF essorer]

sory adj. sad, sorrowful A.Kn 2004, D.WB 588, E.Mch 1244, H.Mcp 55, TC 1.14; sorry (with for) TC 5.140, 1098, (with of)

I.Pars 480, TC 5.1726; miserable B.ML 466, B.Sh 1307, ill C.Pard 876; lamentable, unlucky B.Th 1949, RR 1639. **sorier** comp. I.Pars 459. [OE sāriġ]

sort n.[1] kind, type A.Rv 4044, A.Co 4381, 4419; company B.ML 141. [OF sorte]

sort n.[2] fate, lot A.Prol 844, TC 2.1754, casting of lots, divination I.Pars 605, TC 1.76, 4.116, 4.1404. [OF]

sorted pa. assigned, allotted TC 5.1827. [OF sortir, assortir]

sorwe n. sorrow, grief A.Kn 951, B.ML 264, B.Mk 3588, G.CY 702, TC 1.1; (person.) BD 596, RR 301; distress, trouble A.Mil 3539; compassion F.Sq 422; make ~ grieve, mourn B.Mel 2171, D.WB 594, I.Pars 229, LGW 1248; bring to ~ harm, ruin B.NP 4419, C.Pard 848; (in imprecations) God (Jove) yeve me (etc.) ~ D.WB 151, TC 5.1525, 1781, with ~ with ill-luck to you D.WB 308. pl. A.Kn 3071, TC 1.54, HF 467. [OE sorh/sorg]

sorweful adj. sorrowful, grieving, melancholy A.Kn 1070, D.WB 986, F.Fkl 864, BD 14, TC 1.10, lamentable B.NP 4394, grim Bo 4. m2. 3/5 (L tristibus armis). **sorwefulleste** sup. E.Mch 2098, CompA 1. [OE sorhful]

sorwefully adv. sadly, sorrowfully A.Kn 2978, D.WB 913, E.Cl 914, F.Fkl 1590, TC 2.428. [from prec.]

sorwe(n v. sorrow, grieve A.Kn 2824, TC 4.394, 1106, (with for) I.Pars 296, 300. **sorwestow** pr. 2 sg. (with suffixed pron.) Bo 1. p6. 57/72. [OE sorgian]

sorwing vbl. n. sorrowing, sorrow BD 606.

soster see **suster.**

sote adv. sweetly LGW 2612. [OE swōte]

sotel, sotilly see **subtil(e, subtilly.**

sother(e see **so(o)th** adj.

soth-sawe n. true saying, truth HF 2089. pl. HF 676. [sooth + sawe]

sotted adj. besotted, foolish G.CY 1341. [? from sot v., cf. MDu sotten]

souded p.p. (lit. enlisted) confirmed, united B.Pri 1769. [OF souder]

sought(e see **seke(n.**

souke v. suck A.Rv 4157, B.Pri 1648, E.Cl 450; draw money (from) A.Co 4416: **souked** p.p. E.Cl 450. [OE sūcan str.]

soul adj. single, alone E.Mch 2080. [OF]

soule n. soul A.Prol 656, Bo 5. m4. 8/11, TC 5.1550; life D.Sum 1807, TC 2.1734; pl. living things PF 33; body and ~ D.Fri 1640, I.Pars 887, Bo 3. p11. 42/57, TC 4.1554. ~s gen. B.Pri 1650. In prayers and asseverations: God have thy ~ TC 2.1638, God on my ~ rewe A.Kn 1863, God my/his ~ blesse/save B.Mel 2112, B.NP 4485, D.WB 525, TC 3.102, Jupiter my ~ save LGW 1806, God yeve his ~ reste D.WB 501, E.Cl 30; by Goddes ~ A.Mil 3132, by my fader ~ A.Prol 781, B.Sh 1178, E.Mch 2393, up peril of my ~ B.NP 4134, E.Mch 2371. **saule** A.Rv 4187 var **sale,** 4263 (nth, only in A.Rv). [OE sāwol]

soulfre n. sulphur HF 1508. [AN sulf(e)re]

soun n. sound A.Prol 674, A.Kn 2881, A.Mil 3138, D.WB 974, H.Mcp 115, BD 162; noise, vaunt LGW 267. pl. A.Kn 2512, TC 5.1813. [AN]

sound adj. unhurt, in good health, whole B.Mel 2205, 2300, Bo 4. p1. 50/70, TC 3.1526, LGW 1619. [OE ġe)súnd]

sounde v. make sound, heal Anel 242, RR 966. [from prec.]

soune(n v. **1.** intr. sound, be heard Bo 2. p3. 12/17, make a sound TC 3.189, LGW 91, sound (like) TC 5.678; (with (in)to) tend to, incline to, be consonant with B.Mk 3157, F.Sq 517, I.Pars 1086, TC 1.1036, 3.1414, 4.1676. **2.** tr. sound (an instrument) A.Prol 565, F.Sq 270; utter TC 2.573; reproduce F.Sq 105; mean, signify Astr 1.21.38/52. **souninge(e** pr. p. in accord with A.Prol 275; ~ in tending to A.Prol 307, C.Phs 54; sounding RR 715, sonorous Bo 1. m2. 12/15. [OF soner]

souned in beste- ~ adj. of finest sound TC 2.1031. [from soun]

soupe(n v. sup, take supper A.Rv 4146, F.Sq 297, F.Fkl 1217, TC 2.944, 3.560. [OF soper/super]

souper see soper.

souple adj. pliant A.Prol 203, yielding B.Mk 3690. [OF]

sour adj. sour C.Pard 552; bitter, cruel Bo 1. p4. 58/81. [OE sūr]

sourdeth pr. 3 sg. rises, springs I.Pars 450, 475, 505. **sourden** pl. I.Pars 448, 865. [OF sourdre]

soure adv. sourly H.Mcp 32; bitterly B.Th 2012. [from adj.]

soures n. pl. bucks in their fourth year BD 429 [OF sor(e reddish-brown]

sours n. rising, upward flight D.Sum 1938, 1941, HF 544, 551; fountainhead, source E.Cl 49, (fig.) source, origin. TC 5.1591, Mars 174. [OF sors, source]

souter n. cobbler A.Rv 3904. [OE sūtere]

southren adj. southern I.Pars 42. [OE sūperne]

soutilte(e see subtiltee.

souvenaunce n. remembrance BalCh 13. [OF]

sovereyn n. ruler, lord, superior G.CY 590, ABC 69. pl. B.Mel 2628, 2664, I.Pars 392, 402. [OF so(u)verein]

sovereyn adj. supreme, most excellent A.Prol 67, B.ML 276, 1089, B.NP 4399; greatest A.Kn 1974, 2407, B.Mk 3339; highest B.Mel 2648, F.Fkl 1552; sovereign D.WB 1048, Bo 1. m5. 34/48 (L summos); lady ~ Mars 215, PF 422, LGW 94; ~ bountee B.Mel 2269, I.Pars 284, 368, ~ good Bo 2. p4. 104/142, 105/144 (common in Bo for L summum bonum); ~ signes superior signs (opp. to 'obedient' eastern signs) Astr 2.28.24/34. pl. supreme Bo 5. p2. 16/22. [as prec.]

sovereyn(e)tee n. sovereignty, supremacy, rule D.WB 1038, E.Cl 114, F.Fkl 751, I.Pars 774, TC 3.171. [OF so(u)vereineté]

sovereynly adv. royally B.Mel 2462; surpassingly, chiefly B.NP 4552, supremely Bo 3. p10. 91/123. [from adj.]

sowdan n. sultan B.ML 177, 186, 204. [OF soudan]

sowdanesse n. sultaness B.ML 358, 372. [from prec.]

sowe n. sow A.Prol 552, 556, A.Kn 2019, I.Pars 156. [OE sugu]

sowe v.¹ sew I.Pars 330; sew up TC 2.1201, 1204. **sowed** p.p. sewn A.Prol 685, G.CY 571. [OE si(o)wian]

sowe(n v.² sow (usu. fig.) B.Sh 1182, I.Pars

35, 642, Bo 3. m9. 24/35. **sowe(n** p.p. C.Pard 375, G.SN 194, TC 1.385, RR 1617; **ysowe(n** D.WB 71, spread HF 1488. [OE sāwan, ge)sāwen]

sowled p.p. endowed with a soul G.SN 329. [from soule]

space n. **1.** space of time A.Prol 87, A.Kn 1896, A.Mil 3596, TC 2.767, 5.942, ~ of time for E.Cl 103; time, opportunity A.Prol 35, C.Phs 239, G.SN 65, 355, TC 1.1064, 5.1704; respite TC 1.505; while A.Kn 2982, E.Cl 918, duration B.ML 577, 1014, F.Sq 116, PF 67; course A.Prol 176. **2.** extent A.Rv 4124, D.Sum 1692, TC 5.1630, LGW 307; area, expanse Bo 2. p7. 21/30, 65/94, 5. m5. 5/8; room PF 314, TC 1.714; space Astr 1.2.2/3; section Astr 1.20.3/4. [OF espace]

space v. walk TC 5.1791 var. [prec., or OF espacer]

spaynel n. spaniel D.WB 267. [OF espaignol]

spanne n. span (of the extended fingers, c. 9 inches) A.Prol 155. [OE spann]

span-newe adj. brand-new TC 3.1665. [adapted from ON spán-nýr, spánn 'chip']

spare v. refrain, hold back A.Prol 192, 737, B.Sh 1476, D.Fri 1328, 1543; refrain from TC 5.51, (with infin.) A.Kn 1396, I. Pars 996; nas ~d no linage no relationship was excluded LGW 2602; cease PF 699; restrain TC 5.204; spare, have mercy on D.WB 421, D.Fri 1325, E.Mch 2301, I.Pars 168, TC 1.435; refl. ? be reserved, haughty A.Rv 3966. **spareth** imper. pl. D.WB 186, D.Fri 1337, 1422. [OE sparian]

sparinge vbl. n. moderation, frugality I.Pars 835.

sparinge ppl. adj. sparing, frugal B.Mel 2789. [from spare]

sparkle n. (small) spark A.Rv 3885, B.Th 2095, Bo 3. p12. 102/140. [from spark n., OE spearca, ? by anal. with sparkle v., cf. MDu sparkelen]

sparre n. wooden beam A.Kn 990, 1076. [?MDu]

sparth n. battle-axe A.Kn 2520. [ON spar ða]

sparwe n. sparrow A.Prol 626, D.Sum 1804, **sparow** PF 351 var. [OE spearwa]

spece n. kind, sort I.Pars 407, 486, 491, species Bo 5. p4. 113/163, 123/176 (L species). **speces** pl. patterns A.Kn 3013; **spyces** I.Pars 83 var, 102 var. Cf. **especes**. [OF espece]

speche n. **1.** speaking, talk TC 2.497, 1291 var; withouten more/lenger ~ without more talk A.Prol 783, D.WB 1020, TC 5.388, briefly, in short TC 2.1421, 3.1510; fallen in ~ fall to talking F.Sq 238, F.Fkl 964, TC 2.1191, 5.107, 855; conversation TC 2.1600, rumour TC 3.584. **2.** power of speech A.Kn 2798, H.Mcp 48, TC 4.249, 1151; (manner of) speaking A.Mil 3338, B.Mel 2199, B.NP 3998, C.Pard 330, F.Fkl 718, TC 4.128; terminology G.CY 1443; discourse A.Prol 307, speech, plea PF 489; oratory TC 5.94 104. pl. agreements, compacts TC 3.510. **3.** speech (in general) HF 762, 781; language B.ML 519, TC 2.22. [OE sp(r)ǣč, A sp(r)ēč]

specheles adj. speechless TC 4.370, 1167. [OE spǣčlēas]

special adj. special I.Pars 894, HF 68;

distinctive, particular I.Pars 488, *the* ~
B.Mel 2545; *in* ~ especially, particularly
A.Prol 444, E.Cl 47, TC 1.260, 981. [OF
especial]
specially *adv.* especially B.ML 1081, D.Sum
1715, E.Cl 312, in particular A.Prol 15,
B.ML 183, D.WB 983, D.Sum 1921.
[from prec.]
spectacle *n.* eye-glass D.WB 1203. [OF]
speculacioun *n.* contemplation Bo 5. p2.
20/28. [OF]
spe(e)d *n.* success TC 1.17, 1043; *for
comune* ~ for the good of all PF 507; help
TC 2.9. [OE *spēd*]
spe(e)de(n *v.* **1.** *intr.* succeed, prosper
C.Phs 134, E.Mch 1632, TC 1.482, 774,
4.75. **2.** *tr.* assist, help B.Mk 3876, HF 78,
prosper, further, accomplish Bo 5. p2.
18/25, p5. 16/22, *p.p.* G.SN 357, PF 101;
pr. subj. in *God* ~ *me*, etc., A.Prol 769,
A.Kn 2558, B.Sh 1449, D.Sum 2205, TC
1.1041, *the devel* ~ *him* TC 4.630 *var*;
dispatch (a matter) Bo 5. p1. 2/3 (L *ex-
pedienda*), p4. 15/21 (L *expedire*); send
quickly, hasten A.Rv 4033. **3.** *refl.* make
haste A.Kn 1217, A.Mil 3562, B.Sh 1443,
D.Sum 1732, E.Mch 1927, PF 133, TC
4.220; *intr.* go quickly A.Mil 3649.
spedde *pa. sg.* F.Fkl 1262, TC 2.949,
LGW 200; *pl.* TC 2.26. **sped** *p.p.* A.Rv
4205, **speddc** *pl.* provided for TC 2.954;
ysped A.Rv 4220, Bo 5. p1. 2/3. [OE
spēdan]
spe(e)dful *adj.* efficacious, advantageous
B.ML 727, Bo 4. p4. 50/68, 5. p4. 18/25.
[from **spe(e)d**]
spe(e)dily *adv.* quickly B.Sh 1442, G.CY
1143. [from OE *spēdiġ*]
speke(n *v.* **1.** *intr.* speak A.Prol 636, B.Sh
1487, B.NP 4071; talk (together) TC
3.210; *(as) (for) to* ~ *of* with reference to
A.Prol 142, A.Kn 985, 2103, F.Sq 659,
TC 1.981; ~ *forth (of)* say more, go on
talking (about) A.Kn 2816, TC 5.853.
2. *tr.* speak, utter A.Prol 124, C.Pard 344,
TC 3.907; *(ensamples)* H.Mcp 187, *(re-
son(s)* A.Prol 274, TC 1.796; *(harm)*
D.WB 772; ~ *him* (etc.) *good/harm* speak
well/ill of him, etc. E.Mch 2017, 2310,
TC 2.786; (introd. direct quotation) B.ML
750, TC 5.1674. **spekestow** *pr. 2 sg.* (with
suffixed pron.) D.WB 837, G.SN 473.
speke *subj.* H.Mcp 324, I.Pars 911.
speketh *imper. pl.* A.Mil 3700, E.Cl 19.
(wel) speking *pr. p.* as *adj.* well-spoken
RR 1268. **spak** *pa. sg.* A.Kn 2296, A.Mil
3150, A.Rv 4022, LGW 97. **spe(e)ko(n** *pl.*
B.ML 2457, F.Sq 232, TC 5.432, 853,
BD 350; **spake(n** TC 1.565, 2.25, 5.516.
spake *subj.* TC 2.1119 *var*, **speke** *em.*
spoke(n *p.p.* A.Prol 31, C.Pard 589, TC
4.1233; **yspoke(n** A.Kn 2972, TC 4.1108.
[OE *sp(r)ecan*, *sp(r)æc*, *sp(r)ǣcon/sp(r)ēcon*,
ġe)sp(r)ecen]
speking *n.* speaking H.Mcp 335, I.Pars 111,
speech, oratory PF 488. [from prec.]
spelle *n.* *(prep. sg.)* story B.Th 2083. [OE
spel]
spence *n.* buttery D.Sum 1931. [OF *despence*]
spende(n *v.* spend A.Prol 806, A.Rv 4135,
D.Sum 1796, TC 4.1376, (fig.) expend
CompL 104, use up A.Prol 645, (absol.)
TC 3.1718, RR 1157; (of time) spend, pass

A.Mil 3219, E.Cl 391, LGW 482, 650,
waste (opportunity) TC 4.1612; (of
words) use (in vain) TC 4.702. **spente**
pa. sg. A.Prol 300. **spent** *p.p.* A.Prol 834,
LGW 1125; **spended** D.Sum 1950;
yspended Bo 5. p4. 15/22. [OE *spéndan*]
spending silver *n.* money to spend G.CY
1018. [*spending* vbl. n. + **silver**]
spere *n.*[1] spear A.Prol 114, A.Kn 2602,
Mars 101. [OE]
spere *n.*[2] sphere, orbit F.Fkl 1280, Mars 137,
TC 3.1495, 5.656, 1809, Scog 11; *pl.*
PF 59, Bo 1. m2. 9/13; globe Astr 1.17.
15/19, 2.26.1. [OF *espere*]
spered *p.p.* fastened, barred TC 5.531,
sperred *em.* (See *OED* spear v.[1]). [MDu
speren]
sperhauk/spar- *n.* sparrow-hawk B.Th
1957, B.NP 4647, PF 338, 569, TC 3.1192.
[OE *spearhafoc*]
spete *v.* spit TC 2.1617. **spette(n** *pa. pl.*
I.Pars 270. Cf. **spitte.** [OE *spǽtan*]
spewe *v.* vomit B.Mel 2607. [OE *spēowan*]
spewing *vbl. n.* vomit I.Pars 138.
spyce *n.* spice PF 206, E.Mch 1770. *pl.*
spiced cakes F.Sq 291, TC 5.852, LGW
1110. [OF *espice*]
spyced *p.p.* spiced A.Mil 3378; delicate,
over-particular A.Prol 526, *swete* ~ D.WB
435 see **swe(e)te.** [from *spice* v. from prec.]
spycery *n.* mixture of spices A.Kn 2935,
B.ML 136, B.Th 2043, C.Pard 544, LGW
675. [OF *espicerie*]
spyces *see* **spece.**
spye(n *v.* spy D.WB 357, G.SN 314, (with
of) A.Mil 3566, D.WB 316; spy out LGW
966; *pa.* watched F.Fkl 1506. [OF *espier*]
spille *v.* **1.** *tr.* kill LGW 1574, *p.p.* B.ML
857; destroy Pity 46, TC 5.588, (often
linked with **save(n,** *q.v.*) *p.p.* ruined, lost
D.WB 388, D.Fri 1611, H.Mcp 326, ABC
180; waste H.Mcp 153; spill I.Pars 965,
TC 5.880; shed I.Pars 571. **2.** *intr.* perish,
die A.Mil 3278, B.ML 587, 815, 910, (with
causative *doth*) CompL 14. **spillestow**
pr. 2 sg. (with suffixed pron.) Bo 1. p4. 3/4.
spilt *p.p.* B.ML 857, TC 4.263. [OE
spillan]
spinne *v.* spin B.Mk 3097, E.Cl 223. **span**
pa. sg. LGW 1762. **sponne** *pl.* TC 3.734.
[OE *spinnan, span, spunnon*]
spyr *n.* shoot TC 2.1335. [OE *spīr*]
spirit *n.* **1.** vital spirit, principle of life
Bo 1. m2. 13/18; one of three 'virtues'
controlling life TC 1.307, 3. 1088; vital force,
essence B.ML 943, HF 190, LGW G. 262,
pl. A.Kn 1369, I.Pars 629, BD 489. **2.**
spirit, immaterial element of a person A.Kn
2765, D.Sum 1845, E.Mch 1633, F.Fkl
727, I.Pars 126, 824, (opp. to *flesh*) 342,
BD 26, Pity 115, PF 92, TC 1.362, 3.1778,
4.711, 1620; *povre in* ~ (Matt. 5 : 3) D.Sum
1923; soul A.Kn 2809, B.ML 784, D.Sum
1677, E.Cl 1092, TC 1.423, 3.1351, 4.320,
1152, 1210. **3.** spiritual being (good or
evil) B.ML 783, F.Fkl 767, TC 3.808,
5.1212; ghost LGW 2066; *pl.* Bo 1. p4.
188/264, 4. p6. 66/94, 5. p2. 17/24, HF 41,
~ *of tempest* angels controlling winds (Rev.
7: 1–3) B.ML 491. **4.** alchemical substance G.CY 820, 822. [AN]
spiritually *adv.* in a spiritual sense I.Pars
441, 879. [from *spiritual* adj., L *spirituālis*]

spiritue(e)l see **espiritue(e)l.**
spitous adj. spiteful, malicious RR 979, inhospitable CompA 12. [AN despitous]
spitously adv. fiercely D.WB 223, vehemently A.Mil 3476. [from prec.]
spitte pr. 1 sg. spit C.Pard 421. **spitte(n** pa. pl. I.Pars 258, LGW 1433. Cf. **spete.** [OE (Nb) spittan]
spitting vbl. n. spittle I.Pars 258.
spore n. spur A.Prol 473, A.Kn 1704, 2603, TC 2.1427 var. [OE spora]
sporne/spurne v. kick, strike F.Sq 616, Truth 11; stumble, trip A.Rv 4280, TC 2.797. [OE spúrnan/spórnan]
spot n. defect, blemish E.Mch 2146; spot, tiny thing TC 5.1815. [? MDu spotte, LG spot]
spotted p.p. stained TC 4.1578. [spot v. from prec.]
spousaille n. marriage, wedding E.Cl 115, 180. [OF espousaille]
spouse n. spouse; husband B.Sh 1615, D.WB 433, G.SN 144; wife A.Kn 2222, E.Mch 2144; (fig.) bride I.Pars 948.
spouses gen. sg. TC 5.346. [OF spus/spuse]
spoused p.p. espoused, wedded E.Cl 3, 386. [OF espuser]
spray n. twig, shoot B.Th 1960. [?]
sprede(n v. **1.** tr. spread, cover, A.Kn 2903, Anel 40; spread (wings) LGW G. 168; disperse BD 874; extend, spread TC 2.54, Bo 2. m3. 1, (of word, honour, etc) B.Pri 1644, D.Sum 1822, Bo 2. m7. 7/10. **2.** intr. spread (wings) LGW G. 143, 236, (of heart) swell TC 1.278, 2.980; grow Mars 4, open TC 2.970, LGW 48, 173; extend (of honour) B.Pri 1767, E.Cl 418, 722. **spradde** pa. E.Cl 418. **sprad** p.p. A.Kn 2903, Bo 1. m3. 8/11, **spradde** pl. wide open TC 2.1422; **ysprad** B.Pri 1644; **yspred** A.Rv 4140. [OE sprædan]
spreynd see **springen** v.²
spring n. first beginning, dawn Astr 2.6.4/5; first growth RR 834; origin, source I.Pars 387 var; pl. springs (of water) HF 1984. [OE]
springe(n v.¹ spring, fly A.Kn 2607, HF 2079; spread (of fame) A.Kn 1437, Anel 74, LGW 719, 1054, (of smell) RR 1704; bound, leap A.Kn 1871, A.Mil 3282, D.Sum 1939, TC 4.239; (of water) rise, spring B.Mk 3234, Bo 5. m1. 1; (of day), rise, break A.Prol 822, A.Kn 2209, 2491, A.Mil 3674, F.Sq 346, (of sun) A.Kn 2522, B.NP 4068, (of horns of moon) TC 5.657; grow A.Kn 2173, (of vegetation) A.Kn 3018, B.Th 1950, B.NP 4392, F.Fkl 1147, LGW 38; (fig.) I.Pars 114, 388, (of love) TC 5.719; originate, proceed I.Pars 321, rise B.ML 889, issue I.Pars 761. **springing** pr. p. as adj. Bo 2. p5. 48/67. **sprang** pa. sg. B.Mk 3234, RR 1125; **sprong** FormA 31. **spronge(n** p.p. A.Kn 1437, B.Mel 2400; **yspronge** HF 2081, RR 718. [OE springan, sprang, sprúngen]
springen v.² sprinkle, scatter B.Sh/ML 1183; (fig.) B.ML 422, Bo 2. p4. 87/119. **spreynd** p.p. B.Pri 1830; **sprayned** Bo 2. p4. 87/119; **yspreynd** A.Kn 2169. [OE sprengan]
springers n. pl. sources, origins I.Pars 387 var. [from **springe(n** v.¹]
springes n. pl. dances HF 1235. [?rel. to OF espringuer, from Gmc.]

spring-flood n. spring tide, high tide F.Fkl 1070. [spring+flood]
springing vbl. n. beginning, source E.Cl 49, (fig.) I.Pars 322. [from **springe(n** v.¹]
spurne see **sporne.**
squaymous adj. squeamish A.Mil 3337. [AN escoymous]
squames n. pl. scales G.CY 759. [OF esquame]
squar(e adj. square FormA 24, RR 479; thick, solid A.Kn 1076, (of limbs) TC 5.801. [OF esquarré]
squyer n. squire A.Prol 79, A.Kn 1410, E.Mch 1772, F.Fkl 1609, TC 1.101. [OF esquier]
squiereth pr. 3 sg. escorts, attends D.WB 305. [from prec.]
squire n. square, implement for measuring D.Sum 2090, Astr 1.12.2/3. [OF esquire]
staat see **esta(a)t.**
stable adj. stable, abiding, unchanging A.Kn 3004, F.Fkl 871, I.Pars 182, Bo 2. m3. 18/23, TC 3.1751, firm, steadfast Bo 3. m10. 4/5, sure, certain E.Mch 1499, resolute, constant in affection D.WB 946, E.Cl 931, F.Sq 22, Mars 281, LGW 703, 1876. [OF (e)stable]
stabled p.p. established A.Kn 2995 var; **i)stabled** made secure E.Mch 2405 var. [OF establir]
stably/stably adv. unchangingly Bo 4. p6. 61/89, 79/113. [from adj.]
stableté n. stability Bo 4. p6. 113/164. [OF (e)stableté]
stablissheth pr. 3 sg. establishes Bo 4. p6. 34/49. **stablissed** p.p. A.Kn 2995 var. [aphetic from establisse(n)]
stadie† n. stadium, race-course Bo 4. p 3. 7/10. [L stadium]
staf n. staff A.Prol 495, A.Mil 3465, C.Pard 730, club D.WB 461, LGW 2000, stick (as type of thinness) A.Prol 592; shaft (of a cart) in **staves** gen. sg. in at the ~ ende at a distance Anel 184. **staves** pl. A.Kn 2510, B.Mk 4572. [OE stæf, pl. stafas]
staf-slinge n. sling with a handle B.Th 2019. [prec.+?MLG slinge]
stages n. pl. positions HF 122. [OF estage]
staire n. stairs, steps TC 2.813, 1705, (? on the side of Fortune's wheel) TC 1.215; degree Mars 129. **staires** gen. sg. TC 3.205. [OE stæger]
stak pa. sg. tr. pinned TC 3.1372; intr. was fastened RR 458. Cf. **stiken.** [OE *stecan, *stæc]
stakereth pr. 3 sg. staggers LGW 2687. [ON stakra]
stal see **stele(n.**
stale adj. (of ale) which has stood and become clear B.Th 1954. [?]
stalke n. stalk A.Kn 1036, TC 2.968, stem, trunk I.Pars 114; piece of straw A.Rv 3919; upright of a ladder A.Mil 3625. [? dim. of stale, OE stalu]
stalke v. walk stealthily, softly A.Kn 1479, A.Mil 3648, LGW 1781, creep up TC 2. 519; (with refl. pron.) E.Cl 525. [OE *stealcian]
stamin n. coarse cloth of worsted I.Pars 1052, LGW 2360. [OF estamin]
stampe pr. pl. pound in a mortar C.Pard 538; stamp with feet HF 2154. [? OE *stampian]

stande *see* **stonde(n.**
stank *n.* lake, pool I.Pars 841. [OF *estanc*]
stape(n *ppl. adj.* advanced B.NP 4011 *var*, E.Mch 1514. [OE *stapen*, p.p. of *steppan*]
stare *n.* starling PF 348. [OE *stær*]
starf *see* **sterve(n.**
stark *adj.* violent, severe B.Mk 3560; strong, powerful E.Mch 1458, HF 545. [OE *stearc*]
startlinge *pr. p.* prancing A.Kn 1502 *var*, LGW 1204. [OE *steartlian*]
stat *see* **esta(a)t.**
statly *see* **estatlich.**
statue *n.* image A.Kn 975. [OF]
stature *n.* stature, height A.Prol 83, TC 1. 281, 5.806, Astr 2. 43. 11/15; build, form E.Cl 257, BD 828, LGW 2446, RR 828; shape, form PF 366. [OF]
statut *n.* statute, decree A.Prol 327, D.WB 198, PF 387, Scog 1. *pl.* rules Astr prol 73/101. [OF]
staunchen *v.* allay, satisfy Bo 3. p3. 66/87, 3. m3. 2/3. *p.p.* Bo 2. p2. 34/47. [from AN equiv. of OF *estanchier*]
stede *n.*[1] place HF 731, 829; *in ~ of* instead of A.Prol 231, A.Kn 2140, B.Mk 3308, LGW 231, 534, RR 481; *stant in no ~ is* of no avail B.Mel 2280. [OE]
stede *n.*[2] steed A.Kn 2157, B.Th 1941, F.Sq 81, TC 1.1073, 3.1703. [OE *stēda*]
sted(e)fast/stidefast *adj.* steadfast, resolute B.Mel 2564, B.NP 4558, E.Cl 564, G.SN 382, I.Pars 305, Fort 17. [OE *defæst*]
sted(e)fastly/stide- *adv.* steadfastly, firmly B.Mel 2701, D.WB 947, E.Cl 1094. [from prec.]
sted(e)fastnesse/stid(e)- *n.* steadfastness, constancy E.Cl 699, E.Mch 2063, Anel 81, Bo 2. p2. 35/49, LSt 14, 21. [OE *stedefæstnes*]
steel/stiel *n.* steel A.Kn 1983, TC 2.593, RR 946; (fig.) CompL 62/56, TC 4.325, HF 683; *trewe as (any) ~* E.Mch 2426, PF 395, TC 5.831, LGW 334, 2582. [OA *stēle*, WS *style*]
steer *n.* steer, bullock A.Kn 2149. [OE *stēor*]
ste(e)re/styere *n.*[1] helm, rudder B.ML 833, Bo 3. p12. 55/74, HF 437, LGW. 2416, *in ~ astern* TC 5.641. [OE *stēor*]
ste(e)re *n.*[2] helmsman, pilot, guide B.ML 448, TC 3.1291, Purse 12. [OE *stēora*]
ste(e)re *v.* steer, control TC 2.4, 4.282; *p.p.* LGW 935. [OE *stēoran*]
ste(e)relees *adj.* without a rudder, rudderless B. ML 439, TC 1.416. [from **stere** n.[1]]
steyen *see* **stye(n.**
stele *n.* handle, end A.Mil 3785. [OE *stela*]
stele(n *v.* **1.** *tr.* and *absol.* steal A.Prol 562, A.Rv 3997, 4246, B.ML 105, RR 190; carry off, abduct C.Phs 184, TC 5.48; (fig.) I.Pars 790. **2.** *intr.* go secretly, quietly A.Mil 3786, B.Mk 3763, TC 1.81, 5.752, *refl.* C.Pard 610; *~ away* TC 4.1503, 1529, 5.702, HF 418, LGW 779, 796, (of hunted animal) BD 381, *~ his wey* LGW 2174; (with *on*) BD 654. **stal** *pa. sg.* LGW 796, 1327. **stole(n** *p.p.* A.Kn 2627, B.ML 744, TC 3.1451, LGW 2154; **stoln** A.Rv 4111 *var*, 4183. [OE *stelan, stæl, stolen*]
steling *vbl. n.* stealing, bringing stealthily I.Pars 800.

stellifye *v.* make into a star HF 586, 1002, LGW 525. [OF *stellifier*]
stemed *pa.* glowed A.Prol 202. [from OA *stēman* emit vapour]
stente(n *see* **stinte(n.**
stepe *adj. pl.* projecting, glaring A.Prol 201, 753. [OE *stēap*]
steppes *n. pl.* footprints Bo 5. m5. 7/10, TC 5.1791, LGW 829, 2209; traces, vestiges Bo 1. p3. 33/45 (L *vestigia*). [OE *stepe*]
stere, steringe *see* **stire(n, stiringe.**
sterlinges *n. pl.* silver pennies, sterling coins C.Pard 907, HF 1315. [? LOE *steorling* from **sterre**]
sterne/stierne *adj.* stern, cruel A.Kn 2154, 2441, I.Pars 170, TC 4.94, 1184; strong, violent A.Kn 2610, TC 3.743. [OE *styrne*]
sternelich/-ly *adv.* sternly LGW 239, grimly HF 1498, violently TC 3.677 *var*. [from prec.]
sterre *n.* star. A.Prol 268, A.Kn 2037, 2061, HF 599, Bo 1. m5. 1/2; (fig.) (of the Virgin Mary) B.ML 852, (of a lady) TC 5.638; *pl. ~s* seven planets BD 824; *gen. pl.* E.Cl 1124, HF 997. [OE *steorra*]
sterry *adj.* starry Bo 2. m2. 5/7, PF 43. [from prec.]
stert *n.* start TC 5.254, *at a ~* at a bound A.Kn 1705. [from next]
sterte(n *v.* **1.** *intr.* leap, jump A.Kn 952, LGW 697; bound, spring A.Kn 2684, A.Mil 3736, TC 3.1497, LGW 864, 1350, prance A.Kn 1502 *var, refl.* A.Kn 1579; awake suddenly A.Kn 1044, A.Mil 3816, E.Cl 1060; (fig.) go suddenly LGW 660; go quickly, hurry D.WB 573, TC 2.1094, rush TC 4.242, *~ in* rush in E.Mch 2153, slip quickly in TC 2.1634; move away TC 3.949, depart 4.93; (of blood, tears) burst out LGW 851, 1301; advance B.ML 4 *var*. **2.** *tr.* rouse, start (a hare) HF 681. **stert** *pr. 3 sg.* HF 681. **sterte** *pa. sg.* A.Kn 1579 *var*, TC 4.1411; **stirte** A.Kn 1579 *var*, H.Mcp 303. **sterten** *pl.* B.Mel 2225. **stert** *p.p.* (with *had*) E.Cl 1060; **ystert** B.ML 4 *var*; (with *ben*) **stirt** F.Fkl 1377. [? OE *steortian, *styrtan*]
sterve(n *v.* die A.Kn 1249, B.Pri 1819, C.Pard 865, PF 420, TC 1.17, (*for hunger*, etc.) B.Mk 3645, C.Pard 451, LGW 1277. **starf** *pa. sg.* B.Mk 3817, TC 2.449. **storven** *pl.* C.Pard 888. **ystorve** *p.p.* A.Kn 2014. [OE *steorfan, stearf, sturfon, storfen*]
stevene *n.*[1] voice A.Kn 2562, B.NP 4481, HF 561, LGW 2328; speech, language F.Sq 150; talk, rumour TC 3.1723; sound BD 307; noise, din LGW 1219. [OE *stefn* (f.)]
stevene *n.*[2] appointed time, appointment (with **sette(n**) A.Kn 1524, A.Co 4383, Mars 52. [OE *stefn* (m.)]
stewe *n.*[1] small (heated) room, room with a fireplace TC 3.601, 698; brothel HF 26.
stewes/stywes *pl.* C.Pard 465, **styves** D.Fri 1332. [OF *estuve*]
stewe/stuwe *n.*[2] fishpond A.Prol 350. [OF *estui*]
stibo(u)rn *adj.* stubborn D.WB 456, 637. [?]
stidefast *see* **sted(e)fast.**
stye(n/steyen *v.* ascend, mount Bo 3. m9. 28/39, 4. p6. 258/375. [OE *stīgan*]
stierne *see* **sterne.**

stif *adj.* strong A.Prol 673, RR 115, bold RR 1270, hard, firm D.Sum 2267. [OE *stif*]
stifly *adv.* strongly D.WB 380. [from prec.]
stiken *v.* **1.** pierce, stab B.Mk 3897, F.Fkl 1476. **2.** stick *tr.* Astr 2.38.5/7, fix B.Th 2097; stick *intr.* B.ML 509, TC 1.297, 3.1105. **stiking** *pr.p.* piercing C.Phs 211.
stiked *p.p.* stabbed B.ML 430, *a ~ swyn* a stuck pig C.Pard 556; fastened LGW G. 161 *var.*; **ystiked** A.Kn 1565. [OE *stician*]
stikinge *vbl. n.* fixing, setting I.Pars 954.
stikke *n.* stick, piece of wood G.CY 1265, ABC 90, RR 926, branch, twig BD 423; *pl.* palings B.NP 4038. [OE *sticca*]
style *n.*[1] stile B.Th 1988, C.Pard 712, F.Sq 106 (with play on next). [OE *stiġel*]
style *n.*[2] style E.Cl 18, 41, 1148, F.Sq 105. [OF *style*]
stillatorie *n.* still, vessel for distillation G.CY 580. [ML *stillatorium*]
stille *adj.* silent A.Kn 2535, D.WB 1034, PF 511, TC 2.953; motionless, in *let be ~* leave alone B.NP 4633, E.Cl 891. [OE]
stille *adv.* quietly A.Kn 1003, A.Mil 3420, E. Cl 525, 1077; without moving D.Sum 2200, Anel 54; *as ~ as (any) stoon* A.Mil 3472, E.Mch 1818, F.Sq 171, TC 2.600, 3.699, 5.1729, LGW 310; continually, always B.ML 720, C.Pard 725. [OE *stille*]
stille *v.* silence, quieten B.Mel 2704, TC 2.230; reduce B.Mel 2677. [OE *stillan*]
stillenesse *n.* silence Bo 2. p1. 2, 4/5. [from **stille** *adj.*]
stinge *v.* sting, bite B.ML 406, D. Sum 1995, C.Pard 413, E.Mch 2059, LGW 699, pierce 1729. **stongen** *p.p.* A.Kn 1079; **ystonge** C.Pard 355. [OE *stingan, ġe)stúngen*]
stink *n.* stench B.Mk 3810, D.Sum 2274, I.Pars 209, ABC 56. [*from* next]
stinke(n *v.* stink G.CY 886. **stank** *pa. · sg.* B.Mk 3807, HF 1654. [OE *stincan, stanc*]
stinte(n/stente(n *v.* **1.** *intr.* cease, leave off A.Kn 2811, G.CY 883, TC 3.1234, Ven 61; (with *of*) A.Kn 903, B.Pri 1747, B.Mel 2164, E.Cl 703, TC 2.1361, cease speaking of A.Kn 1334, 2093, B.ML 953, F.Fkl 814, TC 1.1086, 2.687; (with infin.) B.Mel 2559, E.Cl 972, I.Pars 90; refrain, forbear B.Mk 3925; (of process, condition, etc.) come to an end B.ML 413, D.WB 732, LGW 1240; stop, rest BD 154, TC 1.273, LGW 294, stay TC 2.1729. **2.** *tr.* restrain, stop A.Mil 3144, B.NP 4347, RR 1441; cause to cease, bring to an end A.Kn 2348, 2450, 2732, E.Cl 747, ABC 63, assuage, quench (grief, etc.) TC 2.383, 5.686. **stinteth** *imper. pl.* TC 2.1729. **stint(e** *pa. sg.* A. Kn 2421 *var*; **stente** TC 1.736. **stinte(n** *pl.* LGW 294 *var*, TC 2.103 *var*; **stente(n** TC 1.60, 2.103 *var*. **stint** *p.p.* A.Kn 2421 *var*, TC 3.1106; **stent** A.Kn 1368; **ystint** D.WB 390; **stinted** A.Kn 2968. [OE *styntan*]
stintinge *vbl. n.* ceasing, end Bo 2. m7. 23/32.
stire(n/stere *v.* **1.** *tr.* stir (coals) G.CY 1278; (fig.) disturb, stir TC 1.228; excite, provoke B.Mel 2318, 2696, C.Pard 346, I.Pars 446; bring forward (reasons) Bo 3. p12. 148/200, propose TC 4.1451, discuss TC 3.1643. **2.** *intr.* move HF 567, 817; *pr. p.* moving HF 478, stirring A.Mil 3673, TC 3.692, 1236. [OE *styrian*]

stiringe/steringe *vbl. n.* stirring, motion HF 800; moving, exciting I.Pars 355, *pl.* I.Pars 655.
stiropes *n. pl.* stirrups B.Sh 1163, D.Sum 1665. [OE *stiġrāp*]
stirt(e *see* **sterte(n.**
stith *n.* anvil A.Kn 2026. [ON *steði*]
styves *see* **stewe.**
styward *n.* steward A.Prol 579, B.ML 914, F.Sq 291. [OE *stiweard*]
stywes *see* **stewe.**
Stoiciens *n. pl.* Stoics Bo1. p3. 24/33, etc., 5. m4. 4/6. [OF]
stok *n.* stump, block Astr 2.38.4/5, *pl.* logs A.Kn 2934, trunks, tree-stumps Bo 5. m1. 9/12, *by ~es and by stones* (orig. of idols) TC 3.589; line of descent, race A.Kn 1551, source Gent 1, 8. [OE *stoc*]
stoke *v.* stab, thrust A.Kn 2546. [? OF *estoquier*]
stokked *p.p.* fastened in the stocks, imprisoned TC 3.380. [from **stok**]
stole *n.* stool, chair D.WB 288, frame LGW 2352. [OE *stōl*]
stomak *n.* stomach TC 1.787, Bo 3. m12. 29/41 (*~ or the giser* = L *iecur*); appetite D.Sum 1847; ?feeling D.Fri 1441. [OF *estomac*]
stomblen *pr. pl.* stumble A.Kn 2613. [?ON **stumla*]
stonde(n/stande *v.* **1.** stand A.Rv 4036, B.ML 1050, B.NP 4497, TC 1.292, LGW 1499, (fig.) (in lady's eyes) TC 1.428; remain standing B.Mk 3458, *tr.* resist, endure PF 164; stand still (command to horse) A.Rv 4101; take up a position (*~ at defence*) E.Cl 1195, be placed TC 3.247; remain, be (in a condition) B.Mk 3165, TC 2.712, (*grace, love*) A.Prol 88, A.Kn 1173, E.Cl 1091, E.Mch 1590, TC 2.714, 5.171, (*drede*) B.ML 657, B.Sh 1427, (*disjoynt*) B.Sh 1601, TC 3.496, 5.1619. **2.** (of things) stand, be situated A.Rv 3923, B.Mk 3509, Rag.GSN 173, TC 2.1146, be set Astr 2.34. 9/13; *~ writen* PF 155, *~ formed* TC 5.817; (of heaven, planets) be placed A.Kn 1090, Astr 2.29.5/6; be set in view (as a prize) B.Th 1931; (of circumstances) be TC 3.923, 4.161, *impers.* with *it*, (often with *so, thus*) A.Kn 1322, B.Sh 1447, B.Mel 2999, C.Pard 645, F.Sq 576, TC 3.785, *~ with* (someone) A.Mil 3426, B.Sh 1269, TC 1.602; remain TC 3.851, remain unchanged E.Mch 2314; *~ in stede* (of argument) B. Mel 2280 see **stede** *n.*[1]; *let ~* let be B.Sh 1410; (of wind) be set (in a quarter) TC 1.418; stick fast D.Fri 1541. **3.** in phrases: *~ ther-agayn* oppose D.Fri 1488; *~ at* abide by (judgement) A.Prol 778, B.ML 36; *~ bifore* stand before, be brought into the presence of B.ML 618, D.Sum 2065; *~ by* support, maintain B.ML 345, B.Mk 3102, D.WB 1015; *~ for (naught)* be considered (useless) TC 4.312 (? pun, represent zeros), Bo 4. p2. 21/29; *~ in* be wearing TC 2.534, consist of E.Mch 2022, I.Pars 451, 958, Truth 10, Bo 2. p4. 102/140; *~ on* be grounded on I.Pars 107; *~ (un)to* be faithful to TC 5. 1679, submit to, obey I.Pars 60, 483, PF 546, endure, put up with A.Mil 3830. **stondeth** *pr. 3 sg.* A.Kn 1639, TC 2.1146; **stant** F. Sq 171, BD 156, TC 2.1188;

stont TC 3.1562 var. **stondeth** imper. pl.
E.Cl 1195, I.Pars 77. **stood** pa. sg. A.Prol
354, TC 1.172. **sto(o)de(n** pl. B.ML 176,
E.Mch 1105, 1715. **stode** subj. sg. TC
1.1039 var. **stonden** p.p. E.Mch 1494,
BD 975, HF 1928; **ystonde** TC 5.1612.
[OE stándan, stōd, stōdon, ģe)stánden]
sto(o)n n.. stone, piece of stone A.Kn 1888,
A.Rv 4280, F.Fkl 993, over stile and ~
B.Th 1988; in comparisons: blind E.Mch
2156, cold BD 123, dead BD 1300, Pity 16,
dumb A. Prol 774, hard E.Mch 1990, still
A.Mil 3472, see **stille**; jar C.Pard 347;
testicle B.NP 4638; (fig.) rock (of security)
TC 2.843; precious stone, gem E.Cl 1118,
TC 3.891, pl. A.Kn 2146, Bo 3. m3. 3/5,
LGW 2224; (alchem.) G.CY 852, 1452.
[OE stān]
sto(o)r n. stock A.Prol 598, C.Pard 365,
store D.Sum 2159, in ~ in reserve E.Cl 17;
kepte . . to his ~ took for his own use LGW
2337; telle of (it) no ~ set no value on
B.NP 4344, D.WB 203. [from OF estor]
sto(o)re adj. bold, brazen E.Mch 2367.
[LOE stōr from ON]
stope ppl. adj. advanced B.NP 4011 var. See
stape(n.
stoppen v. stop TC 2.804. **stopped** p.p.
plugged G.CY 1163, 1268. [OE (for)-
stoppian]
store v. store, furnish B.Sh 1463. [from OF
estorer]
storial adj. historical A.Mil 3179, LGW 702.
[OF historial]
storie n. history, legend (of saint, etc.) A.Prol
709, B.Pri 1653, G.SN 83; history, narrative E.Mch 1366; tale, story A.Mil 3111,
B.Mk 3900, F.Sq 655, Anel 10, TC 5.585;
(as) the ~ telleth, etc. C.Phs 161, 258, F.Sq
655, H.Mcp 128, TC 5.1037, 1051, 1651,
HF 406; pl. histories, stories A.Kn 859,
2155, C.Pard 488, E.Mch 2232, TC 3.297,
books of history TC 5.1044. [AN estorie]
stot n. horse A.Prol 615; term of abuse for a
woman (in nth. dial. = heifer) D.Fri. 1630
[OE]
stounde n. time, while, short time B.ML
1021, E.Cl 1098, TC 1.1086, 3.1695, PF
142 var, LGW 949; a litel ~ TC 4.594 var;
in a ~ at a time, once A.Rv 3992, upon a ~
at one time TC 4.625; harde ~ hard time,
time of pain Anel 238; pl. seasons TC 3.
1752; by ~ in turn Bo 4. m6. 17/25 (L
uicibus). [OE stúnd]
stoundemele adv. hour by hour, gradually
TC 5.674. [OE stundmǣlum]
stoupe v. stoop E.Mch 2348, G.CY 1311;
bend, strain D.Sum 1560 var. **stoupeth**
imper. pl. G.CY 1327. **stouping** pr. p.
drooping TC 2.968, adj. bent E.Mch 1738.
[OE stūpian]
stour n. battle RR 1270; pl. B.Mk 3560. [AN
estur]
stourdy see **sturdy**.
stout(e adj. strong A.Prol 545, TC 5.1454;
bold A.Kn 2154, TC 5.1493, LGW 627.
[OF estout]
strake v. go, proceed BD 1312 [? from Gmc.;
cf. NFris straake]
strangle v. strangle I.Pars 441; worry to
death I.Pars 768; choke, kill A.Kn 2018;
kill (by sword) Bo 1. p4. 169/237 (L
iugulare gladio). [OF estrangler]

strangling vbl. n. strangling A.Kn 2458,
I.Pars 1006, worrying, killing LGW 807.
straught, straughte(n see **strecche(n,
streight.**
stra(u)nge adj. **1.** foreign A.Prol 13, 464,
A.Kn 2718, B.ML 178, 268, not of one's
own kin E.Cl 138, E.Mch 1440; external,
not inherent D.WB 1161, not its own Astr
2. 19. 5/6. **2.** unknown, unfamiliar B.Mel
2733, Astr 2. 17 rubr., unusual, exceptional, strange F.Sq 67, Anel 202, TC
2.24, 5.120, 860; unfriendly RR 1065,
distant B.Sh 1453, PF 584, TC 5.1632;
made it ~ made difficulties, was reluctant
A.Rv 3980, F.Fkl 1223. **3.** as n. a stranger
TC 2.1660; pl. strangers TC 2.411. comp.
TC 4.388, 5.130. Cf. **estraunge**. [OF
estrange]
straungely adv. distantly, coldly TC 5.955,
? as if she were a stranger TC 2.1423.
[from prec.]
straungenesse n. strangeness I.Pars 414;
coldness, aloofness B.Sh 1576. [from
straunge]
straunger n. stranger LGW 1075, Bo 2. m5.
13/19; pl. foreigners Bo 1. p 3. 39/55, P4.
47/65. [OF estrangier]
straw see **stree.**
strawen/strowe v. strew LGW 207, G.
101. **strawe** pr. subj. 2 sg. F. Sq 613.
strawed p.p. strewn I.Pars 198; **ystrawed**
BD 628 var. [OE stre(o)wian]
strecche(n v. **1.** tr. extend, stretch B.NP
4498, C.Pard 395; long ~ stretch out at full
length TC 4.1163, longe ~ (of hair) extend
at length RR 1021; extend, increase Bo
2. m8. 7/11 (L tendere). refl. rise to full
height HF 1373. **2.** (fig.) intr. be adequate,
suffice TC 2.341; extend, reach G.SN 469,
G.CY 1087, Anel 341, Bo 2. p7. 40/57.
refl. B.Mel 3015, TC 1.903. **streighte** pa.
sg. HF 1373. **straughte(n** pl. A.Kn 2916,
RR 1021. **streight(e** p.p. outstretched
TC 4.1163, opened Bo 3. p1. 3/4; **straught**
stretched out Bo 5. m5. 2/3; **strecched**
Bo 5. p6. 22/31. Cf. **stre(i)ght**. [OE
streċċan, strehte/strǣhte]
stree/straw n. straw A.Kn 2918, 2933, A.Mil
3748, TC 2.1745, 4.184, (as type of something of little value) B.Mel 2526, B.NP
4280, I.Pars 601, BD 671; as interj. (expressing contempt) E.Mch 1567, F.Fkl
695, G.CY 925; **strees** pl. BD 718. [OE
strēaw]
stre(e)m n. stream, river A.Prol 464, B.ML
23, PF 138, LGW 2508, (fig., of life) A.Rv
3895; current A.Prol 402; stream, flow (of
blood) A.Kn 2610, A.Rv 4276; ray, beam
(of light) A.Kn 1495, C.Phs 38, E.Mch
2220, BD 338, Mars 83, Astr 1.13.3/4, (of
lady's eyes) TC 1.305, 3.129. [OE strēam]
streen n. strain, stock E.Cl 157. [OE strēon]
stre(i)ght adj. straight A.Mil 3316, BD 942,
957, TC 3.1247; the ~e wey the direct way
A.Kn 1690. **straighter** comp. more spread
out RR 119. [p.p. of **strecche(n**]
stre(i)ght adv. straight, directly A.Prol 671,
E.Mch 1436, TC 1.606, 2.1461; immediately, straightway TC 1.53, 2.599 var,
4.1243, HF 1992, **straught** TC 2.599 var;
~ amorwe early in the morning, first thing
TC 3.552. [as prec.]
streyne v. clasp tightly, press E.Mch 1753,

TC 3.1205, hold, confine RR 1471, constrict, grip TC 3.1071, restrain, hold together Astr 1.14.4/6; constrain B.NP 4434, E.Cl 144, LGW 2684, Mars 220; press, strain Bo 1. m6. 9/13, (a liquid) C.Pard 538. [OF *estraindre*]

streit adj. narrow A.Kn 1984, A.Rv 4122, Bo 3. m2. 16/27, Astr 1.22.2/21.85; secret, retired Bo 3. p2. 2/3, 3. m9. 28/40 (L *augustam* taken as *angustam*); strict, rigorous A.Prol 174; limited, small D.Fri 1426, inadequate B.NP 4179, scanty RR 457; his ~e swerd his drawn sword (= L *stricta*) B.NP 4547. [OF *estreit*]

streite adv. tightly A.Prol 457, closely TC 4.1689; strictly, securely E.Mch 2129, LGW 723. [as prec.]

streitnes n. narrowness Astr 1.21.34/46. [from *streit*]

stremeden pa. pl. streamed TC 4.247. [from v. from stre(e)m]

streng n. string D.Sum 2067, TC 1.732, 2. 1033, PF 197. [OE]

strenger, -est see strong.

strengest-feythed adj. strongest in faith TC 1.1007. [strong+feith]

strengthe n. strength A.Prol 84, BD 421, TC 2.260, power 5.1490, HF 1980; fortitude I.Pars 728, Bo 1. p4. 5/7; force BD 351; (person.) A.Kn 1948. pl. sources of strength B.Mk 3248, forces Bo 2. m4. 6/9. [OE *strengþu*]

strepe(n v. strip E.Mch 2200; refl. E.Cl 894, E.Mch 1958; (someone of, out of, clothing) A.Kn 1006, E.Cl 863; ~ of take off A.Rv 4063. [OA *strēpan*]

strete n. street, road A.Kn 2902, B.ML 1103, F.Fkl 1502, TC 2.1248; by wey and eek by ~ everywhere C.Pard 694; Watlinge ~ the Milky Way HF 939. [OE strǣt, A strēt]

stryf n. strife, quarrel, contention A.Kn 1187, B.ML 200, E.Mch 1475, G.CY 931; maken ~ quarrel D.Sum 2000, TC 5.341; took ~ contended Bo 1. p4. 61/85 (certamen . . . suscepi), LGW 595. [OF *estrif*]

stryk n. stroke, mark Astr 1.9. 3/4, 2.12. 12/17. [OE strica]

strike n. hank (of flax) A.Prol 676. [from next]

stryken v. strike D.Fri 1364; stroke F.Sq 165 var. **stryked** pa. pl. went, ran B.Pri 1864 var. **strike** p.p. struck MercB 35; **ystrike** MercB 34. [OE strīcan, stricen]

stryve(n v. strive, struggle PF 606, Fort 30; ~ with B.Mel 2671, D.Sum 1986, H.Mcp 79, I.Pars 664, TC 3.38, contend A.Kn 1177, Bo 2. p2. 5/7, vie A.Kn 1038; ~ ayein/agayn(s struggle against, oppose A.Kn 3040, E.Cl 170, I.Pars 561, TC 4.175, 5.166. **stryf** imper. sg. Bo 2. p2. 5/7. **stryvinge** pr. p. Bo 4. m6. 16/24, as adj. contentious Bo 2. p7. 87/124. **stroof** pa. sg. TC 5.819. **stryven** p.p. Bo 1. p3. 18/24. [OF *estriver*]

stryving vbl. n. striving, strife B.Mel 2674, C.Pard 550.

stroyer n. destroyer PF 360. [from destroye(n]

strond n. shore B.ML 825, 864, LGW 1498, 2189; pl. HF 148, Bo 4. m5. 18/23, countries A.Prol 13, Bo 2. m5. 15/21. [OE stránd]

strong adj. strong, (of persons) A.Prol 239, TC 5.830; ~ of freendes having powerful friends C.Phs 4, 135; (of things) A.Kn 1056, 1451, B.Mk 3561, TC 5.1486, (of drink, etc.) strong, powerful A.Prol 635, 750, C.Pard 867, I.Pars 823, LGW 2670, (of breath) B.ML 772, (of voice) B.NP 4494, (of heart) E.Cl 806; (of God, providence) powerful A.Kn 2373, Bo 4. p6. 242/352; (of pain) severe A.Kn 1338, 2771, TC 5.864, LGW 569, (of cold) RR 72; difficult B.Mel 2635; thoroughgoing, downright C.Pard 789, E.Mch 2367; (of witness) powerful H.Mcp 284. **stronger** comp. B.Mel 2538, **strenger** B.Mel 2410, C.Pard 825. **strongest** sup. B.Mel 2527, **strengest** TC 1.243. [OE stráng, strengra, stréngest]

stronge adv. strongly RR 944, firmly PF 231, securely RR 241. [OE stránge]

strongly adv. violently I.Pars 951, securely B.ML 577, firmly, powerfully B.Mel 2421, Bo 3. p11. 2. [from strong]

stroof see stryve(n.

stro(o)k n. stroke, blow A.Kn 1701, D.WB 636, E.Cl 812, TC 2.1382; at o~ in a single moment Bo 5. p6. 195/275 (L uno ictu). [OE *strāc]

strouted pa. stuck out A.Mil 3315. [OE strūtian]

strowe see strawen.

stubbes n. pl. stumps A.Kn 1978. [OE stubb]

stubbel-goos n. goose fed on stubble, fatted goose A.Co 4351. [AN stuble+goos]

studie n. 1. study, learning A.Prol 303, 438, LGW G. 39, studying F.Fkl 1124. 2. study, library F.Fkl 1207, 1214, HF 633; school, place of learning Bo 1. p1. 47/66. 3. state of meditation, reverie A.Kn 1530, TC 2.1180; (in Bo, repr. various senses of L studium) inclination, desire Bo 4. p2. 38/50, p3. 84/121, zeal, enthusiasm 1. m1. 2/3, devotion 3. m2. 18/26, pursuit, endeavour 3. p2. 4/6, 58/83. [OF estudie]

studie(n v. study A.Prol 184, D.Sum 1819, E.Cl 8; give heed I.Pars 1090, deliberate, take thought (in perplexity) E.Cl 5, E.Mch 1955. **studieth** imper. pl. A.Prol 841. [OF estudier]

stuffed p.p. filled E.Cl 264. [?OF estoffer]

sturdy/stourdy. adj. stern, cruel, harsh E.Cl 698, 1049, Bo 3. m2. 8/11; ?furious D.Sum 2162; firm, strong TC 2.1380; strongly built D.Sum 1754. [OF estourdi]

sturdily/sturdely adv. resolutely, boldly A.Mil 3434, Mars 82. [from prec.]

sturdinesse n. sternness, harshness E.Cl 700. [from sturdy]

suasioun n. persuasiveness Bo 2. p1. 29/41. [OF]

subdekne n. subdeacon I.Pars 891. [AN subdiakene]

subgit/subget n. 1. subject, subordinate B.Mel 2528, I.Pars 467; servant D.Sum 1990, TC 2.828. 2. substance Bo 5. p1. 35/49 (L de materiali subiecto). [OF su(b)get]

subgit/-get adj. subject I.Pars 264, Bo 5. m4. 17/24, TC 5.1790; **subgetes** pl. I.Pars 634. [as prec.]

subjeccio(u)n n. subjection, submission B.ML 270, (with of 'to') I.Pars 276, in ~

under dominion, control B.Mk 3656, Mars 32; suggestion I.Pars 351. [OF *subjection*]

sublymatories *n. pl.* vessels used for sublimation G.CY 793. [ML *sublīmātorium*]

sublymed *p.p.* sublimated G.CY 774. [OF *sublimer*]

sublyming *vbl. n.* sublimation G.CY 770. [as prec.]

submissioun *n.* submissiveness B.Mel 3013. [OF]

submitte *v.* **1.** *intr.* submit B.ML 35, Bo 2. p5. 104/145; *refl.* B.Mel 3011. **2.** *tr.* subject, bring under control Bo 1. p4. 167/233 (L *submitteret*), Bo 5. p1. 27/*var.* **summitted** *p.p.* Bo 4. p6. 92/132, 5. p1. /38 *var*, submitted Bo 3. p10. 10/13 (L *(rei) subiectae*). [L *submittere*]

substance *n.* **1.** substance, essence Bo 3. p10. 74/102, 177/242, essential quality, existing *per se* C.Pard 539, Bo 3. p9. 63/83, TC 4.1505; substantial existence ABC 87. **2.** substance, material HF 768; *the ∼ is in me* the point (of this saying) touches me B.NP 3993; the majority TC 4.217. **3.** means, wealth A.Prol 489, B.Mel 2189, I.Pars 848, LGW 1560; supply, provision TC 4.1513. [OF]

subtil(e/sotil/sotel *adj.* ethereal TC 1.305; thin A.Kn 2030, delicately woven A.Kn 1054, PF 272; cleverly devised HF 1188; (of argument, etc.) subtle, intricate, ingenious B.ML 213, 888, E.Cl 459, TC 2. 257, Astr prol 38/53; (of persons) skilful, clever C.Phs 141, LGW 672, (transf.) A.Kn 2049, Bo 3. m2. 1 (L *arguto*), RR 688; ingenious, cunning A.Mil 3275, E.Mch 1427, F.Fkl 1141, LGW 1556, 2559, (of look) sly F.Sq 285. [OF *soutil/subtil*]

subtilitee *n.* subtlety, craft, secret knowledge G.CY 620, 1247, skill, ingenuity G.CY 1371 *var*; *pl.* tricks E.Mch 2421; excessive subtlety, nicety (in argument) HF 855 *var.* [OF]

subtilly/sotilly *adv.* cleverly F.Fkl 1284, subtly B.Mel 2501, skilfully D.WB 499, F.Sq 222, G.SN 80, RR 772, 1119, craftily, cunningly A.Prol 610, B.ML 746, B.Mk 3314, E.Mch 2003, insidiously C.Pard 565, treacherously D.Sum 1995. [from adj.]

subtiltee/soutilte(e *n.* acuteness, perspicacity D.Sum 2290, skill, cleverness B.NP 4509, G.CY 1371 *var*, Ven 77, cunning, guile B.Mk 3569, D.Fri 1420, F.Sq 140, TC 5.1254, 1782, LGW 2546; cunning device, trick D.WB 576, G.CY 844; (excessive) subtlety, nicety (in argument) HF 855 *var.* [OF *soutilté* altered after adj.]

succede *v.* succeed B.Mk 3572, E.Cl 632, 1135; follow Astr 2.12.24/33, 29/40. [OF *succeder*]

succedent/succident *n.* (astrol.) a succedent house (the 2nd, 5th, 8th and 11th, which are about to follow the most important houses) Astr 2. 4. 30/46. [L *succēdentem*]

successioun *n.* succession: *by ∼(s* in succession, successively, A.Kn 3014, Bo 5. p6. 66/92. [OF]

sucre/sugre *n.* sugar B.Th 2046, F.Sq 614; = sweet TC 3.1194. [OF *sucre*]

sucred *p.p.* sweetened, softened TC 2.384. [from prec.]

suffisa(u)nce *n.* sufficient supply PF 637, sufficiency A.Prol 490, B.Mel 2841, D.Sum 1843, ?wealth BD 703; ability Ven 17; satisfaction, contentment B.NP 4029, Bo 3. p3. 38/50, TC 5.763, (person.) I.Pars 833, source of satisfaction, fulfilment of desire BD 1038, TC 3.1309, 4.1640. [OF]

suffisa(u)nt *adj.* sufficient, adequate A.Kn 1631, A.Mil 3551, B.ML 243, E.Cl 960; satisfactory D.WB 910; capable, able C.Pard 932, LGW 1067, 2524. [OF]

suffisa(u)ntly *adv.* sufficiently, adequately B.Mel 2492, Bo 4. p6. 9/14, Astr prol 27/38. [from prec.]

suffyse *v.* **1.** suffice, be adequate A.Rv 4125, B.Mk 3648, C.Pard 434, TC 3.335, be able Bo 5. p1. 15/21, allow, admit B.ML 1099, BD 902, 1094; (with *(un)to*) B.Sh 1436, B.Mel 2572, E.Cl 740, E.Mch 1999, (with *for*) A.Kn 1233; ∼ *unto* ?be satisfied with, be content Truth 2. **2.** *impers.* (*it*) *suffiseth* it is enough B.Sh 1242, D.Sum 1903, (with dat. pron.) A.Mil 3559, D.WB 1235, HF 1876, LGW 573, Rosem 15, Ven 54. [OF *suffis-*, stem of *suffire*]

suffrable *adj.* patient D.WB 442. [OF]

suffraunce *n.* patience, long-suffering B.Mel 2479, E.Cl 1162, I.Pars 654, 730; receptiveness, receptivity (glossing *passioun* = L *passio*) Bo 5. m4. 33/47, p5. 5/7; permission F.Fkl 788, I.Pars 625. [AN]

suffraunt *adj.* long-suffering, patient BD 1010, as *n.* (the) patient man TC 4.1584. [AN pr. p.]

suffre(n *v.* **1.** suffer, permit, allow (something to be done, to happen) A.Prol 649, D.WB 412, E.Mch 2044, TC 3.154, 1467, Bo 1. m5. 24/34. **2.** undergo, endure B.Mel 2175, 2961, E.Cl 670, G.SN 490, I.Pars 665, Bo 2. p1. 67/92 (L *toleres*), suffer, experience Bo 4. m3. 22/30, submit patiently to I.Pars 660, be obedient to Bo 1. m5. 3/5 ((*legemque*) *pati*), be the object of, receive Bo 5. m4. 16/24, 31/44 (L *impressas patitur notas*). **3.** *intr.* endure, suffer B.Mel 2407, 2670, F.Fkl 777, I.Pars 660; ∼ *to the tyde* ?be patient until the right time, ?yield to the season TC 1.954. **suff(e)reth** *imper. pl.* D.Sum 1671, TC 4.1204. [AN *suffrir*]

suggestioun *n.* prompting to evil, temptation I.Pars 331, 355; imputation B.Mk 3607. [AN]

sugre *see* **sucre.**

suyte/sute *n.* fashion, pattern A.Kn 2873, A.Mil 3242, BD 261. [AN *siute*]

sukkenye *n.* smock, frock RR 1232. [OF *soucanie*]

superfice/superficie *n.* surface Bo 3. p8. 32/45, Astr 1.21.19/26, 26/36. [OF]

superfluitee *n.* superfluity, excess A.Prol 436, B.NP 4117, C.Pard 471. [OF]

supersticious *adj.* based on false belief F.Fkl 1272. [OF]

supplicacio(u)n *n.* prayer Bo 5. p3. 140/200; petition Purse 26. [OF]

supplien *v.* supplicate, entreat Bo 3. p8. 8/10. [OF *supplier*]

supportacioun *n.* support B.Mel 2332. [OF]

suppose *v.* suppose, believe B.Mel 2128, C.Pard 889, D.Sum 1791, E.Cl 347, TC

4.1408, conceive, imagine D.WB 786, expect B.Mel 2593, B.Mk 3332. [OF *sup(p)oser*]

supposinge *vbl. n.* supposition, imagining E.Cl 1041, G.CY 873.

supprysed/surprised *p.p.* surprised, violently affected B.Mel 2924, TC 3.1184. [AN *supris(e*, OF *surprise*, p.p. of *surprendre*]

surcote *n.* surcoat, outer coat A.Prol 617. [OF *surcot*]

surement *n.* assurance, pledge F.Fkl 1534 *var.* [AN from *assurement*]

suretee *see* **seureté**.

surfeet *n.* surfeit I.Pars 913. [OF *surfait*]

surgien *n.* surgeon B.Mel 2195, 2201. [AN]

surmounten *v.* surpass, exceed Bo 4. m1. 1, TC 3.1038, LGW G. 111, LGW 123, (with *of*) surpass (in) BD 826. [AN *surmunter*]

surplus *n.* difference over and above TC 4.60. [OF]

surquidrie *n.* presumption, arrogance, haughtiness I.Pars 403, 1067, TC 1.213. [OF *s(o)urcuiderie*]

Surrien *adj.* Syrian B.ML 153, etc. as *n.* B.ML 394, 963. [OF from L *Suria/Syria*]

sursanure *n.* a wound healed outwardly, but not inwardly F.Fkl 1113. [OF *sur-sanure*]

surveyance *n.* superintendence C.Phs 95. [OF **surve(i)ance*]

suspecioun *n.* suspicion B.ML 681, B.NP 4222, G.CY 686, H.Mcp 288, (with *of*) B.Sh 1512, TC 5.1647, LGW 1290, *take* ~ TC 2.561. [AN]

suspecious *adj.* exciting suspicion, ominous E.Cl 540. [OF]

suspect *n.* suspicion: *be in* ~ *of* suspect E.Cl 905; *have* ~ *of* C.Phs 263; *have in* ~ B.Mel 2385, 2387, 2498. [L *suspectus*]

suspect *adj.* exciting suspicion, ominous E.Cl 541, 542. [as prec.]

sustene *v.* 1. hold up A.Kn 1993; support I.Pars 439, TC 2.1686, Pity 111, ABC 22, sustain, keep B.ML 160; bear, withstand, B.ML 847, B.Pri 1673, E.Mch 1760, TC 4.795, 5.242; endure B.Mel 2654. 2. *intr.* hold oneself upright Anel 177; *refl.* F.Fkl 861. [OF *sustenir*]

suster (**soster** A.Mil 3486) *n.* sister A.Kn 871, B.Mk 3672, E.Cl 589, TC 2.69, HF 367; *gen. sg.* uninfl. LGW 2365. **sustres** *pl.* B.NP 4057, 4458, (Muses) Anel 16; **sustren** A.Kn 1019, TC 5.1227, LGW 979, (Fates) TC 3.733, 5.3, (Muses) TC 3.1809, HF 1401. [OE *s(w)ustor*, *swostor*, gen. unchanged; LWS pl. *swustru*]

sute *see* **suyte**.

suwe *see* **sewe**.

swa *adv.* so (nth.) A.Rv 4030, 4040, 4239. [OE *swā*]

swayn *n.* servant A.Rv 4027, youth, man B.Th 1914. [ON *sveinn*]

swal *see* **swelle**.

swalowe/swolwe/swelwe *v.* swallow B.Mel 2808, E.Cl 1188, H.Mcp 36, I.Pars 731, HF 1036. [OE *swelgan*, p.p. *swolgen*]

swalwe *n.* swallow A.Mil 3258, PF 353, TC 2.64. [OE *swealwe*]

swappe *n.* blow, stroke HF 543. [from next]

swappe *v.* strike E.Cl 586, G.SN 366. **swapte** *pa.* dashed, struck TC 4.245, fell E.Cl 1099. [prob. echoic]

swatte *see* **swete** *v.*

swe(e)te *adj.* 1. sweet (of taste) A.Mil 3206, A.Co 4373, D.WB 459, (of smell) A.Prol 5, A.Kn 2427, TC 1.949, (of sound) B.NP 4069, H.Mcp 300, BD 307, RR 89; pleasing, delightful (of words, etc.) A.Prol 265, B.Mel 2304, D.WB 734, E.Cl 32, Bo 5. m2. 2. 2. precious, dear A.Kn 2254, 2780, A.Mil 3698, 3767, B.Pri 1846, BD 108, TC 3.98, 5.228, (as term of affectionate address) F.Fkl 978, BD 204, TC 1.533, 3.1163. **swetter** *comp.* RR 622, 768. [OE *swēte*, comp. *swēt(t)ra*]

swe(e)te *adv.* sweetly A.Mil 3305, 3691, D.Sum 1804, LGW 761; ~ *spyced* bland D.WB 435. [as prec.]

sweigh *n.* motion, momentum B.ML 296, Bo 1. m5. 3/4, 2. p1. 81/112, TC 2.1383. [?rel. to ON *sveigja* bend]

sweynte† *ppl. adj.* wearied, slothful HF 1783 *var.* [p.p. of *swenchen*, OE *swencan*]

swelle *v.* swell A.Kn 2743, 2752, C.Pard 354, E.Mch 2306. **swal** *pa. sg.* swelled (up) B.Pri 1750, D.WB 967. **swollen** *p.p.* swollen I.Pars 423, (with sorrow) TC 5.201, (with pride) E.Cl 950. [OE *swellan*, *a swall*, *swollen*]

sweller† *n.* inflater Bo 3. p6. 5/6. [from prec.]

swellinge *vbl. n.* swelling Bo 1. p5. 51/75, ~ *of herte* inflation by pride I.Pars 391, 398.

swelte *v.* die (only in extended senses in Ch.): be overcome (by emotion, heat), faint Mars 128, 216, TC 3.347, swelter, melt A.Mil 3703. **swelte** *pa. sg.* A.Kn 1356, E.Mch 1776. [OE *sweltan*, pa. *swealt*]

swelwe *see* **swalowe**.

swepe *v.* sweep E.Cl 978, G.CY 936. **ysweped** *p.p.* G.CY 938. [ME *swepe* replacing OE *swāpan*, cf. **swipian*, ON *svipa*]

swerd *n.* sword A.Prol 112, A.Kn 1706, B.ML 64, H.Mcp 340, TC 2.203; (fig.) A.Kn 1575, TC 5.1591, (sorrow) Anel 212, 270, (winter) F.Sq 57, LGW 127. [OE *sweord*]

swere(n *v.* swear A.Kn 1821, A.Mil 3502, B.Sh 1325, LGW 666, affirm, assert A.Prol 454, BD 684, TC 3.269; ~ *sooth* I.Pars 593, ~ *thy trouthe* BD 753; *intr.* curse, utter profane oaths B.Sh 1171, C.Pard 287, I.Pars 591. **swereth** *imper. pl.* I.Pars 591. **swo(o)r** *pa. 1, 3 sg.* A.Kn 959, D.WB 397. **swore** *2 sg.* LGW 1378. **swore(n** *pl.* B.ML 344, E.Cl 496. **swore** *p.p.* A.Prol 810, E.Cl 403; **yswore** F.Sq 325, LGW 1285; **sworn** A.Kn 1666, *although we hadde it* ~ *though we had sworn the contrary* A.Kn 1089, sim. D.WB 640, G.CY 681, TC 4.976, 5.283; as *adj.* in ~ *brother* A.Kn 1147, 1161, C.Pard 808, D.Fri 1405, HF 2101; **ysworn** A.Kn 1132, TC 2.570. [OE *swerian*, *swōr*, *swōron*, *ge)sworen*]

swete *n.* sweetness PF 161. [from **swe(e)te** *adj.*]

swete *v.* sweat A.Mil 3702, G.CY 579, 1186, TC 2.943, 1533; *tr.* G.SN 522. **swatte** *pa. sg.* B.Th 1966, G.CY 560. [OE *swǣtan*]

swetely *adv.* sweetly A.Mil 3215, BD 849, kindly A.Prol 221, patiently I.Pars 656. [from **swe(e)te** *adj.*]

swety *adj.* sweaty FormA 28. [from n. from **swete** v.]

swetnesse n. sweetness (of taste) TC 1.638, 3.179, (of smell) LGW 120, (of sound) BD 297, Mars 179, PF 198, RR 719; delight, pleasure B.Mel 2348, Bo 2. p3. 7/9; gentleness, graciousness B.Pri 1745, I.Pars 1053 var, ABC 51. [OE]

sweven n. dream, vision B.Mk 3930, B.NP 4086, BD 119, 279, HF 3, PF 115, TC 5.358, RR 3, (associated with **dre(e)m**) B.NP 4111, 4113, RR 28, *bothe ~ and dreem* B.NP 4361, (apparently distinguished from *dreem*) HF 9. [OE *swefn*]

swevening n. dream RR 1, 26. [from prec.]

swich adj. such (+noun, without art.) A.Prol 247, A.Rv 4272, C.Pard 400, H.Mcp 171, such a(n TC 5.1831, LGW 1975; (+indef. art. and n.) A.Prol 360, B.Pri 1629, B.Mk 3580, B.NP 4067, PF 14, such and such A.Co 4384, F.Fkl 1326, TC 3.1159, LGW 2605, ~ *a man* so-and-so TC 2.1699; (predic.) TC 2.742, 4.390; ~ *it is* . . this is what it is (to be).. A.Rv 4318, B.NP 4626, PF 570; (referring to previous adj.) A.Prol 313, 485; (with dependent rel.) such .. as, those .. who, ~ *as* B.Mel 2201, 2523, B.NP 4018, TC 5.899, LGW 43, ~ .. ~ B.Mk 3604; ~ .. *as* of the kind (that) A.Prol 684, B.Mk 3209, E.Cl 886, F.Fkl 743, ~ .. *as that* those .. that G.CY 719; (fold. by *that*-cl.) A.Kn 862, (by cl. without *that*) G.CY 1402, (by *so*+cl.) BD 28; (with indef. pron.) *othere* ~ G.CY 795, ~ *othere* G.SN 512, Bo 2. p2. 21/29, ~ *another* A.Kn 1907, B.ML 159, *non* ~ F.Sq 41, ~ *oon* F.Sq 231, Mars 183, TC 1.369, 521; (with numerals) B.ML 550, TC 2.126, 182, *mo (floures)* ~ *seven* seven times as many BD 408; ~ *manere (peple, etc.)* such B.Mel 2503, D.WB 451, 1127, I.Pars 103, *in* ~ (*a*) *manere* B.Mel 2617, 2789, E.Mch 2153, F.Sq 508, TC 1.291, 4.1182, LGW 166, *in* ~ (*a*) *wyse* B.ML 153, B.Mel 2762, B.Mk 3609, TC 1.992, 4.833, RR 473. [OE *swelč/swilč*]

swilk adj. (nth.) such A.Rv 4171 var. [nth form of OE *swilc*]

swimme v. swim LGW 2450, float A.Mil 3550, 3575, (fig.) be immersed, abound in D.Sum 1926. **swommen** pa. pl. were filled with swimming things PF 188. [OE *swimman*, pa. pl. *swummon*]

swyn n. swine, pig B.ML 745, C.Pard 556, *tusked* ~ boar F.Fkl 1254; (as term of abuse) D.WB 460, H.Mcp 40. **swyn** pl. A.Prol 598, Bo 4. m3. 18/24, HF 1777. [OE *swin*, sg. and pl.]

swynes-heed† n. (term of abuse) swinish fellow A.Rv 4262. [prec.+**he(e)d**]

swink n. labour, toil A.Prol 188, 540, A.Rv 4353, G.CY 730. [OE *swinc*]

swinke(n v. **1.** intr. toil, labour A.Prol 186, A.Mil 3491, C.Pard 874, D.WB 202, TC 5.272, LGW 2041. **2.** tr. gain by labour, work for G.SN 21, cause to labour, overwork HF 16. **swonken** p.p. A.Rv 4235; **yswonke** H.Mcp 18. [OE *swincan, ǧe)swuncen*]

swinker n. labourer, toiler A.Prol 531. [from prec.]

swire n. neck, throat RR 325. [OE *swira*]

swythe adv. quickly B.ML 730, C.Pard 796, PF 503, TC 4.737, HF 538; *as* ~ as quickly as possible, at once B.ML 637, G.CY 936, 1309, PF 623, LGW 913. [OE *swiþe*]

swyve v. tr. lie with, copulate with A.Rv 4178, 4266, H.Mcp 256. intr. fornicate A.Co 4422. **swyved** pa. E.Mch 2378. p.p. A.Mil 3850, A.Rv 4317. [OE *swifan* str. v., move]

swogh see **swo(u)gh.**

swolow n. gulf LGW 1104. [OE *ǧeswelg*+ **swalowe** v.]

swolwe see **swalowe.**

swonken see **swinke(n.**

swoor see **swere(n.**

swoot n. sweat G.CY 578. [OE *swāt*]

swo(o)te adj. sweet A.Kn 2860, A.Mil 3205, PF 296 var, TC 3.1231 var, LGW 118, 173, RR 60. Cf. **so(o)te, swete.** [OE *swōt*]

swor, swore, sworen see **swere(n.**

swote adv. sweetly TC 1.158. [OE *swōte*]

swo(u)gh n.[1] sound, noise as of wind A.Kn 1979, PF 247, HF 1031, 1941; sigh, groan A.Mil 3619. [from OE *swōgan*]

swo(u)gh/swow n.[2] swoon, faint, D.WB 799, E.Cl 1100, F.Sq 476, TC 3.1120, Pity 16; **swow** anguish BD 215. [? from **aswown(e]**

swowne n. swoon; (*fil*) *in* ~ (fell) in a swoon F.Fkl 1080. [from **aswown(e]**

swowne/swoune v. swoon, faint B.ML 1058, E.Mch 1776, F.Sq 430, TC 2.574, LGW 872. **swowneth** imper. pl. TC 3.1190. [?from next]

swowning n. swooning, fainting C.Phs 246, E.Cl. 1080, 1087, [?formed on OE *ǧeswogen* p.p., cf. **aswown(e** and **swowne** n.]

T

t = **to**, -o elided before infin. beginning with vowel, as **taffraye** E.Cl 455, **tareste** F.Fkl 1370.

taa see **take(n.**

ta(a)s n. heap A.Kn 1005, 1009, 1020. [OF *tas*]

tabard n. loose upper garment A.Prol 541; herald's coat, as an inn-sign A.Prol 20, 719. [OF *tabart*]

tabernacle n. canopied niche in wall HF 123, 1190; (?) canopied scaffold serving as theatre Bo 2. p3. 56/81 (*shadwe* or ~ = L *scaenam*) [OF]

table n. **1.** (dining) table A.Prol 100, B.Sh 1442, C.Pard 490, TC 5.437, *at* ~ BD 646, at board, lodging G.CY 1015; ~ *dormaunt* permanent side-table A.Prol 353. **2.** (writing) tablet BD 780, Bo 5. m4. 13/18, pl. D.Sum 1741, Astr 2.40. 19/26; tablet (for inscription) A.Kn 1305, HF 142, table (of the Law) C.Pard 639. **3.** pl. tables (for calculation) F.Fkl 1273, Astr prol 56/78. **4.** plate Astr 1. 14. 2/3, 2. 21. 4/5. **5.** pl. the game of tables, backgammon F.Fkl 900, I.Pars 793, BD 51. [OF]

tabour n. tabor, small drum D.Sum 2268. [OF]

tabouren pr. pl. drum, din LGW 354. [from prec.]

tache n. defect, blemish WUnc 18. **tecches** pl. defects, faults TC 3.935, qualities, characteristics HF 1778. [OF *teche/tache*]

taffata n. taffeta A.Prol 440. [OF *taffetas* or ML *taffata*]

tayl *n.* tail A.Rv 4164, B.Mk 3222, B.NP 4093, D.Sum 1687, E.Mch 2060; *top and* ~ beginning and end HF 880; (with punning ref. to genitals) A.Rv 3878, D.WB 466. [OE *tægel*]

tail(l)ages *n. pl.* taxes I.Pars 567, 752. [OF]

taille *n.* tally, account scored on wood B.Sh 1606 (with pun on **tayl**), *by* ~ on credit A.Prol 570. [OF]

takel *n.* archery-gear, arrows A.Prol 106. [cf. MLG *takel*]

take(n *v.* **1.** take A.Kn 2781, TC 3.1359; catch B.Mel 2223, D.Fri 1472; take on, adopt B.Mel 2691; seize B.NP 4126, TC 2.289, (of desire, fever) BD 273, TC 2.1520; understand, infer A.Kn 2266; catch (a blow), strike D.WB 792; undertake (journey) A.Prol 34, LGW 1450; ~ *on hem/hym* put on TC 1.918; ~ **cure, he(e)de, ke(e)p(e), pitee** see the nouns. **2.** receive, accept A.Kn 1186, 2226, B.ML 351, D.WB 1224, TC 5.581; accept as lover C.Pard 371; perceive B.NP 4630; *is not taken of* does not apply to D.WB 77; ~ *it (in desdeyn, in pacience, wel, agrief, for the beste,* etc.) A.Prol 789, A.Kn 1084, 3043, B.NP 4083, TC 5.1606; ~ *for* consider, esteem D.WB 1116. **3.** give, hand over, present B.Sh 1594, BD 48, TC 2.1147, 1318, LGW 1135, 2372; entrust I.Pars 880; ~ *agayn* give back G.CY 1034, H.Mcp 91. **4.** *refl.* betake oneself, go B.Th 1985, I.Pars 842. **5.** *intr.* attach oneself to D.WB 31. **6.** *intr.* come to pass TC 4.1562. **taa** *infin.* (nth.) A.Rv 4129, 4130. **takestow** *pr. 2 sg.* (with suffixed pron.) G.SN 435. **takth/tath** *3 sg.* B.ML 728. **taketh** *imper. pl.* TC 1.232. **to(o)k** *pa. sg.* A.Prol 303, PF 695. **to(o)ke(n** *pl.* A.Rv 4309, B.Mel 2713. **take(n** *p.p.* A.Kn 1866, TC 3.1144; **ytake(n** B.ML 348, B.Mel 2604. [LOE *tacan* from ON *taka*, *tók*, re-formed after OE cl. VI]

tald *see* **telle(n**.

tale *n.* **1.** tale, story A.Kn 3126, B.ML 46; long story E.Cl 383; often with **telle(n** A.Prol 731, 831, etc., (give) account (of) A.Prol 330; account, something said I.Pars 46; esteem, regard, see **telle(n**. **2.** discourse, talk TC 2.218, 267, 3.1403, something to say BD 536, *took first the* ~ began to speak TC 2.1605; *pl.* stories TC 4.671; conversation, talk TC 2.149, 498, 1566, 4.702, 5.178, *after* ~ after all this talk TC 3.224. [OE *talu*]

tale(n *v.* tell tales A.Prol 772; speak, talk I.Pars 378, TC 3.231, 1235. [OE *talian*]

talent *n.* inclination, desire B.ML 1137, C.Pard 540, I.Pars 228, TC 3.145, LGW 1771. [OF]

taling *vbl. n.* tale-telling B.Sh 1624.

talking *vbl. n.* talk, discourse B.NP 3980, G.CY 684. [from *talken*, ME formation from **tale(n]**

talle *adj.* ?ready to obey, docile, meek; ?quick, prompt Mars 38. [OE *ġetæl* prompt]

tapicer *n.* weaver of tapestry A.Prol 362. [AN]

tapite *v.* cover with tapestry BD 260. [from *tapit* n., OE *teped* and LL *tapētum*]

tappe *n.* spigot, plug stopping the opening of a cask A.Rv 3892; the opening so stopped A.Rv 3890, 3893. [OE *tæppa*]

tappestere *n.* (female) tapster, barmaid A.Prol 241, A.Mil 3336. [OE *tæppestre*]

tare *n.* tare, seed of vetch (taken as insignificant) A.Kn 1570, A.Rv 4000, A.Rv 4056. [?]

targe *n.* shield A.Prol 471, A.Kn 975, Anel 33; (fig.) defence ABC 176. [OF]

tarie(n *v.* **1.** *tr.* delay, detain B.Mk 3463, E.Mch 1696, F.Sq 73; postpone F.Sq 402; ~ *(forth) the day/time* waste time A.Kn 2820, A.Rv 3905, TC 2.1739. **2.** *intr.* delay, wait B.NP 4260, C.Pard 851, PF 415, TC 5.1610. [?]

taryinge *vbl. n.* tarrying, delay A.Prol 821, B.Pri 1807, PF 468, TC 1.2.1642.

tartre *n.* tartar G.CY 813, *oille of* ~ A.Prol 630. [OF]

tasseled *p.p.* tasselled, fringed A.Mil 3251, RR 1079. [from *tassel* n. from OF]

tast *n.* taste, relish (*of* 'for') PF 160. [OF]

taste *v.* try, test LGW 1993; taste Bo 3. p1. 20/28; feel G.SN 503. [OF *taster*]

tastinge *vbl. n.* (sense of) taste I.Pars 959.

tath *see* **take(n**.

taverner *n.* inn-keeper C.Pard 685, 707. [AN]

tecches *see* **tache**.

teche(n *v.* teach, instruct A.Prol 308, B.Sh 1180, G.SN 343, H.Mcp 132, TC 1.698; tell B.ML 133, D.WB 1019, 1050, show TC 5.1016, RR 518; direct (to), B.NP 4139, D.Fri 1326. **techeth** *imper. pl.* TC 3.1293. **taughte** *pa.* A.Prol 497. **taught** *p.p.* B.ML 224; **ytaught** A.Prol 127, B.Pri 1699. [OE *tǣċan, tǣhte/tēhte]*

teyne *n.* thin metal rod or plate G.CY 1225, 1240, 1332. [ON *teinn* twig, rod]

telle(n *v.* **1.** tell, recount, relate A.Prol 38, B.Sh 1185, TC 1.1, LGW 1; ~ *forth* A.Kn 1354, C.Pard 341, TC 1.260, ~ *on* A.Mil 3134, A.Co 4345, F.Fkl 702, TC 2.1195; ~ *(a) tale* A.Prol 731, 735, etc. **2.** count I.Pars 390; enumerate G.CY 799, BD 440; ~ *of* account, esteem B.Mk 3676, ~ *no/litel tale of* PF 326, B.NP 4308, *no store/deyntee of* B.NP 4344, D.WB 203, 208. **telleth** *imper. 3 sg.*) BD 73, HF 426. **telleth** *imper. pl.* A.Mil 3118. **tolde** *pa. sg.* HF 1380. **tolde(n** *pl.* A.Mil 3184, D.Fri 1358. **to(o)ld** *p.p.* A.Prol 715, B.ML 56; **yto(o)ld** A.Mil 3109, LGW 1592; **tald** (nth.) A.Rv 4207. [OA *tellan, tālde, ġe)táld*]

temen *v.* bring, in ~ *us on bere* cause us to die HF 1744. [OA *tēman*]

temper *n.* humour, mood RR 346. [from v., see **tempreth**]

tempest (*thee*) *imper. sg. refl.* distress yourself Truth 8. *pr. subj. 2 sg.* Bo 2. p4. 50/68. [OF *tempester*]

tempestous *adj.* tempestuous, stormy TC 2.5. [AN]

temple *n.* temple A.Kn 1918, B.Mk 3386, TC 4.947, (fig.) ABC 145; Inn of Court A.Prol 567. [OE *tempel* and OF *temple*]

temporal/-el *adj.* temporal B.ML 107, D.WB 1132, I.Pars 243, TC 4.1061. **temporel(e)s** *pl.* B.Mel 2188, I.Pars 685. [L *temporālis*, OF *temporel*]

tempreth *pr. 3 sg.* blends G.CY 901. **tem-pred(e** *pa.* tempered, hardened PF 214, tuned, brought into harmony Bo 3. m12. 14/19. *p.p.* blended G.CY 926. [OE *temprian*]

temps *n.* tense G.CY 875. [OF]
tempte *v.* test, try E.Cl 452, 620, 735; tempt D.Fri 1661, I.Pars 332. [OF *tempter*]
tendeth *pr. 3 sg.* tends Bo 1. p6. 30/39 (L *tendat*); **tenden** *pr. pl.* proceed, hasten Bo 3. p11. 158/213 (L *festinent*). [OF *tendre*]
tene *n.* vexation, ill-will A.Kn 3106, ABC 3, TC 1.814, 4.1605; affliction, trouble Anel 140, TC 2.61, 5.240, HF 387. [OE *tēona*]
tenour *n.* tenor, purport LGW 929. [OF]
tenthe *adj.* tenth TC 2.1249 *see* **som(e.** [from OA *tēn*]
tentifly *adv.* attentively, carefully E.Cl 334. [from OF *tentif*]
tercel *adj.* male (of falcon, eagle) PF 393, 449, **tercels** *pl.* PF 540; as *n.* PF 405, 415. [OF]
tercelet *n.* male falcon F.Sq 504, 648, PF 529, 596. [AN]
terciane *adj.* tertian; *fevere* ~ a fever in which paroxysms recur every third day B.NP 4149. [L (*febris*) *tertiana*]
tere *v.* tear B.Sh 1326, RR 325. **torn** *p.p.* TC 4.1482, LGW 2103. [OE *teran*, *toren*]
tery *adj.* tearful TC 4.821. [from OE *tēar*]
terins *n. pl.* siskins RR 665. [OF]
terme *n.* **1.** time, space of time, period A.Kn 3028, BD 79; (*to*) ~ *of* (*one's*) *lyf* as long as (one) lives A.Kn 1029, D.WB 644, D.Fri 1331, G.CY 1479, I.Pars 966; appointed time TC 5.696, 1209, LGW 2499. **2.** goal, end Bo 3. m9. 35/48; border, bound Bo 2. m8. 8/11, 3. m12. 40/57 (L *terminos*); term, part of the zodiac F.Fkl 1288. **3.** term, expression, technical term A.Prol 639, B.Sh 1189, E.Mch 1569, F.Fkl 1266, TC 2.1038, HF 857; *in* ~ in technical language C.Pard 311; *pl.* formal expressions E.Cl 16, works, language A.Rv 3917, *in* ~ in set legal phraseology A.Prol 323. [OF]
terme-day *n.* appointed day BD 730. [prec. +**day**]
termyne *v.* determine, set down in definite terms PF 530. [OF *terminer*]
terrestre *adj.* earthly E.Mch 1332. [OF]
terve *pr. subj. sg.* flay, skin G.CY 1274 *var.* **terved** *p.p.* G.CY 1171 *var.* [?OE **tyrfan* rel. to *turf*]
testament *n.* testament, will D.WB 424, D.Fri 1305. [L *testamentum*]
testers *n. pl.* head-pieces, casques A.Kn 2499. [OF *testiere*]
testes *n. pl.* vessels for treating metals G.CY 818. [OF *test*]
testif *adj.* headstrong A.Rv 4004, TC 5.802. [AN]
tete *n.* teat A.Mil 3704. [OF]
textue(e)l *adj.* well-versed in 'texts', well-read, learned H.Mcp 235, 316, I.Pars 57. [AN]
th = **the**, -*e* elided before noun beginning with vowel, as **tharivaile** HF 451, **their** D.Sum 1939.
thair *adj. poss.* (nth.) their A.Rv 4172. [ON *þeira*]
thakketh *pr. 3 sg.* pats D.Fri 1559. **thakked** *p.p.* A.Mil 3304. [OE *þaccian*]
thalighte *see* **alighte.**
than/then *conj.* than A.Prol 219, B.NP 4535, G.CY 1410, TC 1.532. [OE *þanne/þænne*]

than in *er* ~ see **er** conj.
thank/thonk *n.* goodwill, favour, gratitude I.Pars 1035, TC 3.441, 1777; expression of gratitude, thanks E.Mch 1801, TC 1.1015, 1060, 3.643, *his* ~ the thanks to him LGW 452. **thankes** *gen., adv.* in *his/hir/my* ~ willingly, of (..) free will A.Kn 1626, 2107, 2114, D.WB 272, I.Pars 1069, RR 1321. *have/get* ~ be thanked, have the merit TC 1.21, 803; *can* ~ see **conne.** [OE *þanc/þonc*]
thanke(n/thonke(n *v.* thank A.Kn 1876, TC 3.1664, (with indirect obj. of person, direct of thing) TC 2.155, Fort 51, (with *of* 'for') B.ML 1113. *p.p.* in ~*d be* (*God*, etc.) A.Kn 925, B.ML 686, D.WB 5. [OE *þancian/þoncian*]
thankinges *vbl. n. pl.* thanks B.Mel 2994.
than(ne *adv.* then A.Prol 12, B.NP 4616, D.WB 1062, E.Mch 1327, TC 5.1427, LGW 1018; next PF 324; ~ *at erst*(*e* see **er** adv. **thenne** TC 1.409, 2.1553. [OE *þanne/þænne*]
thar *pr. 3 sg. impers.* it is necessary: (with dat. pron.) *the/him* ~ you/he need, must D.WB 329, 336, D.Fri 1365, H.Mcp 352, Bo 2. p3. 62 *em*, 3. p11. 71/96, A.Rv 4320, BD 256, ABC 76, TC 2.1661; (with dependent cl.) B.Mel 2258; (with infin.) Bo 2. p3. 62/90. **thurfte** *pa. subj. sg.* in *yow* ~ *never have* you would never need to have TC 3.572 *em*; **thurste** TC 3.572 *var*; **thurfe** RR 1089 *em*, 1324 *em*; **durst** RR 1089, 1324. [OE *þearf*, *þurfon*, *þorfte*; ME pa. confused with forms of **durre**]
that *def. art.* the, in ~ *oon*, ~ *other* A.Kn 1013–14, 2045, B.NP 4186–8, D.WB 749, D.Sum 2021; ~ *ilke* A.Kn 3033, D.WB 1076. [OE *þæt* neut.]
that *conj.* so that B.ML 1052, B.NP 4048, Mars 135; in such a way that TC 1.807; as quickly as B.ML 1036; as well as F.Fkl 1262; in that Bo 3. p4. 32/46; (added to other conjs.); *if* ~ A.Prol 399, B.Sh 1379, BD 969, *for* ~ because A.Kn 2068, TC 4.998, *though* ~ A.Prol 68, *whan* ~ A.Prol 1, B.NP 4554; (after interrogs. and rels.) A.Kn 1568, 2482, B.Mk 3205, B.NP 4130, F.Sq 401, TC 1.5, 2.36, 5.149; introd. exclamation B.Mk 3619, E.Mch 2338. [OE *þæt(te*]
that *pron. rel.* that, which, who A.Prol 10, 146, B.ML 1109, B.Sh 1417, E.Mch 1462, TC 1.15, etc.; whom BD 979; by whom TC 2.189; ~ .. *they* who TC 2.172–3; (elliptical, incorporating antecedent) that which, what A.Kn 1425, B.Sh 1379, G.CY 642, TC 5.187. [OE *þæt*]
tho *def. art. the;* with abstract *n.* ~ *deeth* A.Prol 605, A.Kn 1220, B.Mel 3003, PF 588, TC 4.739. [LOE *þe*]
the *adv.* by so much, the ~ *bet* by so much the better BD 668, TC 1.481, ~ *las/lesse* by so much the less BD 675, TC 1.974. [OE *þē*]
theatre *n.* theatre Bo 1. p1. 35/49; amphitheatre A.Kn 1885, 1901, 2091. [OF]
thedom/-dam *n.* success; *yvel* ~ bad luck B.Sh 1595. [from **thee(n**+OE suff. -*dōm*]
thee *pron. 2 sg.* **1.** *acc.* you *passim*; (refl. with *v.*) yourself A.Mil 3728, C.Pard 966, D.WB 336, G.CY 1295, HF 627. **2.** *dat.* to you A.Kn 1083, B.ML 836, B.Sh 1620,

D.Sum 1946; (in impers. constr.) B.NP 4643, D.WB 318, 336, F.Fkl 1589, TC 2.1394, 3.264. [OE *þē*]

theef *n.* thief, robber A.Mil 3791, H.Mcp 224; wretch, villain TC 1.870, 3.1098, esp. *false* ~ C.Pard 759, D.WB 800, D.Fri 1338, H.Mcp 292, BD 650, HF 1779, LGW 2330. **theves** *gen. sg.* thievish LGW 465. *pl.* C.Pard 789, D.WB 1194. [OE *þēof*]

theefly *adv.* stealthily, furtively LGW 1781. [from prec.]

thee(n *v.* prosper, thrive G.CY 641; (esp. in asseverations) *so mote I* ~ B.Th 2007, B.NP 4166, (with suffixed pron.) *so* **theech** C.Pard 947, G.CY 929, *so* **theek** A.Rv 3865; *lat him never* ~ B.NP 4622, sim. TC 4.439 *var.* [OE *þēon*]

theme *n.* text, topic C.Pard 333, 425. [L *thema*]

thenke(n/thinke(n *v.* think A.Kn 1606, D.WB 201, TC 2.1506; intend A.Rv 4223, I.Pars 671, MercB 28; imagine A.Mil 3253, G.SN 215, I.Pars 949; think of TC 1.476; comprehend Bo 5. p4. 11/15 (L *cogitari*), 12/17; believe HF 1879; ~ (*up*)*on* remember B.ML 1096, BD 100; ~ *hereby* think of this D.Sum 2204. **thenche** *infin.* A.Mil 3253. **thinkestow** *pr. 2 sg.* (with suffixed pron.) TC 2.1373. **thenketh** *imper. pl.* C.Phs 75, E.Cl 116, TC 1.26, 5.1840. **tho(u)ghte** *pa.* A.Kn 984, TC 1.276. **tho(u)ght** *p.p.* TC 4.554. [OE *þencan, þōhte*]

then(ne *see* **than(ne.**

thenne *see* **thinne.**

thenne *adv.* thence, away D.WB 1141. [OE *þanon(e* app. infl. by **henne**]

thennes *adv.* from there, away B.ML 510, F.Sq 326, TC 3.1145, 5.885; absent TC 4.695; *fro(m* ~ B.ML 308, TC 5.1814; *fro* ~ *that* from the place which G.SN 66, from the place to which B.ML 1043. [prec. + adv. *-es*]

theorik *n.* theory Astr prol 75/103; theoretical account 63/88. [OF *theorique*]

ther *adv.* **1.** there A.Mil 3790, 3823; then G.CY 1480; ~ *bisyde* F.Fkl 902; *now here now* ~ TC 4.240, *here and* ~ LGW 2516; (unemphatic, preceding v.) A.Prol 118, 208; (introd. wish, curse or blessing) A.Kn 2815, D.Fri 1561, E.Mch 1308, TC 3.947, 1437, 5.1525. **2.** *conj.* and *rel.* where A.Kn 1618, B.ML 469, TC 2.333, in which G.SN 332, whereas A.Kn 1272, G.CY 724, whereby D.WB 128, wherever A.Mil 3702, D.WB 237, if D.Fri 1366, since LGW 1625; ~ *as* where A.Prol 34, 249, E.Mch 1382, F.Sq 267, wherever A.Kn 2984, whereas D.WB 1177. **3.** prefixed to prep. or adv., representing neut. pron. *it, that, this*: ~**aboute** around it A.Kn 937, on it G.CY 832, *is* ~ intends HF 597, *go* ~ occupy (oneself) with it D.Sum 1837. ~**after** for it D.WB 518, afterwards BD 66. ~**agayn(s** against that D.Fri 1488, in that situation I.Pars 665, in reply to that TC 2.369. ~**by** by/from/through this A.Mil 3693, D.WB 20, G.CY 740, *lyve* ~ live on this C.Pard 445, *come* ~ find this/it D.WB 984, F.Fkl 1115. ~**biforn** in advance, beforehand A.Kn 2034, B.ML 197, C.Pard 624, previously A.Rv 3997. ~**fro**

from there HF 736, 838, 895, from that TC 1.627. ~**in** in that B.ML 218, F.Sq 322, TC 3.695; inside, within A.Mil 3551, B.Th 1945, B.Mk 3573, TC 4.785. ~**of** about that A.Prol 462, A.Mil 3783, TC 4.1277; through that I.Pars 314, TC 5.374; (to result) from that A.Kn 2990; ~ *bifalle(n/folwe(n* result from that B.Mel 2230, 2579, ~ (*I do*) *no fors* (I think) that does not matter E.Mch 2430, G.CY 1019, BD 542, *in trust* ~ relying on what it may bring G.CY 876. ~**on** about that B.ML 1033, F.Sq 3, TC 2.1197; concerning, as for that 1289; ~ . . *lak* lack of that E.Mch 2346. ~**out** outside B.Mk 3362, G.CY 1136. ~**to** to it/that B.Mel 2395, G.CY 738, 744; for it/that A.Kn 2109, H.Mcp 43, TC 1.1064; about it/that BD 1250; also A.Prol 153, 289, 499, BD 1006, TC 2.377; ~ *able* suitable for it BD 779; *as many yeres as* ~ *may be multiplyed* however many times those years may be multiplied Bo 2. p7. 72/103. ~**upon** immediately A.Prol 819, over this A.Mil 3323; ~ . . *radde* read it PF 20. ~**whyle** whilst, during the time that TC 3.538; *allas* ~ alas for that time ABC 54 *var.* ~**whyles** when Bo 5. p6. 159/224. ~**with** with it/that A.Prol 678, A.Mil 3777, E.Cl 887, by it/that TC 1.243; because of that B.NP 4066, TC 1.274; thereupon A.Kn 1299, B.Mk 3620, TC 1.278; also B.Mk 3489, F.Sq 194, H.Mcp 123; moreover H.Mcp 136, BD 978, Mars 241; at the same time I.Pars 10, PF 201, Bo 3. p12. 127/170. ~**withal** with it/that TC 3.1330/1407; thereupon B.Mel 2196, TC 3.1350/1336; besides, moreover A.Mil 3233, B.Mk 3612, Anel 86; at the same time A.Mil 3788; then LGW 864. [OE *þǣr*]

thewed *ppl. adj.* (with prec. *wel*) instructed in manners and morals Mars 180, RR 1008. **ythewed** PF 47, Bo 4. p6. 164/239. [from v. from OE *þēaw*; see next]

thewes *n. pl.* personal qualities (mental and moral) E.Cl 409, G.SN 101, HF 1834; (without qualif.) good qualities HF 1851. [OE *þēaw*]

thikke *adj.* **1.** thick A.Kn 2605, PF 273, sturdy A.Prol 549, A.Rv 3973, strong, stout A.Kn 1056; *thurgh* ~ *and* (*thurgh*) *thenne* everywhere A.Rv 4066. **2.** thickly grown A.Kn 1579, BD 399; opaque HF 908; close packed A.Kn 2612. **3.** frequent Bo 4. m5. 12/16, numerous D.WB 868. [OE *þicce*]

thikke *adv.* thickly, closely (grown) RR 1396, 1419; frequently TC 2.456, LGW 655; *as* ~ *of nouchis* as thickly with jewels HF 1350; ~ *sterred* thick with stars Astr 2.23.1/2. [OE *þicce*]

thikke-herd *adj.* thick-haired A.Kn 2518. [from **thikke** adj.+**heer**]

thilk(e *adj. demons.* that (same), the A.Prol 182, B.Mel 2258, F.Sq 607, ~ *same night* that very same night B.Mk 3426; ~ *same* Bo 4. p4. 87/121, 158/224, 4. p6. 103/149. [**the** art.+**ilke**]

thin *poss.* **1.** *adj.* your (before vowel or *h-*) A.Kn 1139, F.Fkl 1091, **thy** (before cons.) C.Pard 304, TC 1.524. **2.** *pron.* yours A.Kn 1235, TC 3.1458; *oon of* ~ one of your subjects A.Kn 2381. [OE *þīn*]

thing *n.* **1.** thing A.Prol 175, A.Kn 1260, matter A.Kn 2707, B.Sh 1467, F.Sq 337, cause I.Pars 255, 283; conclusion Bo 2. p6. 85/119; *pl.* questions Bo 5. p1. 12/16; *for any* ~ at any cost A.Prol 276; *som maner* ~ something D.WB 405; *wonder* ~ wondrous speech F.Fkl 1175, wondrous story B.NP 4327, wondrous event G.CY 1106, TC 1.621; *it is open* ~ it is manifest Bo 4. p6. 71/101. **2.** event C.Phs 156; *pl.* deeds LGW 1274, *doon a* ~ act B.NP 4434, *pl.* in *do my* ~ persist in my habits 4279; *dide hir* ~ performed her rites A.Kn 2293; *his* ~ *seyd* read his Breviary B.Sh 1281; *werk* . . *thy* ~ act B.Mel 2193; *fulfild this* ~ carried out this instruction E.Cl 596; *make a* ~ draw up a document A.Prol 325. **3.** object A.Rv 4302, TC 2.908; *sg.* and *pl.* possession(s, belongings B.Sh 1407, E.Cl 504, 652, G.SN 540, I.Pars 877, 880, Bo 2. p2. 19/27; presents D.WB 221; *comune* ~(*s* commonwealth Bo 1. p4. 19/27-8 (L *res publicas*), 2. p7. 14/19. **4.** sexual organs D.WB 121. **5.** creature E.Mch 1429, H.Mcp 190, BD 12, PF 326, TC 1.103, RR 336, 361. **6.** speech F.Sq 434, I.Pars 495, TC 1.1022; tale E.Cl 15, *pl.* words Bo 1. p5. 2, accusations 34/50; prayers D.WB 876; *wommanisshe* ~ feminine prattle TC 4.694; *newe* ~ news HF 1887 *em*; *make* ~ write literary works LGW 430. *no* ~ *nothing* editors differ in division—rhythm suggests two words in A.Mil 3598, B.Mk 3628, D.Sum 2181, LGW 1853, etc.; cf. **nothing** *adv.* (Normal pl. **thinges**, but occas. **thing**: *more* ~ TC 4.543, LGW 11, *other* ~ BD 349; perh. G.SN 540. In *alle* ~ usu. indeterminate: A.Kn 3036, B.ML 277, F.Sq 15, 260 *var*, BD 141, TC 1.237; but *sg.* TC 3.696 and in *alle* ~ *hath tyme* D.Fri 1475, TC 3.855.) [OE *þing* sg. and pl.]

thinke *v.* (with dat.) seem TC 1.405; *impers.* A.Kn 1867, C.Pard 801, F.Sq 406, PF 548, TC 5.120; (with subject *it*) A.Prol 37, B.NP 3968, F.Fkl 1398, LGW 984; (in mixed constr., logical subject in obl. case) TC 2.25. **tho(u)ghte** *pa.* A.Prol 385, B.ML 697, B.NP 4578, F.Sq 527, BD 50, TC 1.294. [OE *þyncan, þūhte*]

thinke(n *see* **thenke(n.**

thinne *adj.* **1.** thin Astr 1.3.2/3; sparse A.Prol 679; little, weak E.Mch 1682, G.CY 741; frugal FormA 36; fainter Bo 1. p6. 76/99. **thenne** A.Rv 4066. **2.** attenuated Bo 2. m7. 14/20, 3. p3. 2/3, tenuous p12. 60/79, 5. m3. 11/16. [OE *þynne*]

thirlcth *pr. 3 sg.* pierces Anel 211. **thirled** *p.p.* pierced A.Kn 2710, Anel 350, TC 2.642. [OE *þyrlian*]

this *adj. demons.* this B.Pri 1860, C.Pard 786; ~ *day* today D.Sum 1808; *al* ~ *fourtenight* for a fortnight A.Kn 929; ~ *day fyfty wykes* a year hence A.Kn 1850; *on* ~ *same* upon the lady (that I spoke of) BD 1035; with proper name TC 1.113, 2.939, 1339. **thise** *pl.* A.Prol 701, B.ML 59, C.Pard 839; **these** HF 11, LGW 19. [OE *þes, þis*; pl. *þās*]

this *pron. demons.* this B.Pri 1718, TC 1.621; that, in ~ *is to seyn* B.Pri 1690, F.Sq 175; *after* ~ TC 2.1674; *er* ~ before now TC 3.498, *by* ~ by this time TC 3.793; *right*

with ~ at that very moment HF 1689; *other* ~ *or that* of one kind or another HF 1888; as abbr. of 'this is' B.NP 4247, E.Cl 56, F.Fkl 889, TC 3.635, 936, ~ *al and som* this is the upshot A.Kn 2761, PF 650, TC 2.363, 4.1193, 1274, ~ *is* treated as monosyllable A.Kn 1091, D.WB 91, F.Fkl 1606 *var*, PF 620. [OE *þis*]

thyself *pron.* yourself: *emph.* TC 1.717, 2.1316; *refl.* B.Mel 2250, TC 2.1000, 4.620; you yourself TC 3.369. **thyselve(n** A.Kn 1174, I.Pars 517. [OE *þin* + **self**]

tho *adj. demons. pl.* those A.Kn 1123, B.NP 4141, TC 4.193, 5.733, Astr 1.8.4/6. [OE *þā*]

tho *pron. demons. pl.* those A.Kn 2351, D.WB 595, TC 1.931, 1085, LGW 153. [OE *þā*]

tho *adv.* then A.Kn 993, TC 1.1058, LGW 1830; *er* ~ before that time TC 5.448, LGW 1062. [OE *þā*]

thoght *see* **tho(u)ght.**

thoghte *see* **thenke(n, thinke.**

thoghtful *adj.* pensive, grave E.Cl 295; moody I.Pars 677. [from **tho(u)ght**]

tholed *p.p.* suffered D.Fri 1546. [OE *þolod* from *þolian*]

Tholosan *n.* man of Toulouse (applied wrongly to Statius) HF 1460. [L *Tolōsānus*]

thombe *n.* thumb A.Prol 563, F.Sq 83. [OE *þūma*]

thonder *n.* thunder A.Prol 492, D.WB 732. [OE *þunor*]

thonder-dent/dynt *n.* thunderstroke A.Mil 3807, D.WB 276, TC 5.1505. [prec.+ **dint**]

thonderer *n.* thunderer Bo 4. m6. 2. [from **thondre** *v.*]

thonder-leit *n.* thunderbolt I.Pars 839, Bo 1. m4. 8/11 *var* **-light.** [**thonder**+OE *leget*]

thondre *subj. sg.* should roar Bo 2. m4. 11/15. [OE *þunrian*]

thunderinge *pr. p.* resounding A.Kn 2174. [OE *þunrian*]

thorpes *see* **thro(o)p.**

thou/thow *pron. 2 sg.* thou, you C.Phs 318, D.Fri 1396; suffixed to v. **artow** D.Fri 1392, **crydestow** A.Kn 1083, **dostow** D.Sum 1954, **thenkestow** TC 4.849. [OE *þū*]

tho(u)ght *n.* **1.** thought, idea G.CY 1071, BD 4, TC 2.745, 771, 809; mind B.Pri 1794, BD 706, 789, Bo 1. m2. 1, 5. m3. 8/12; thinking Bo 1. p5. 28/42, comprehension Bo 5. m2. 8/12, p3. 104/147, rational power Bo 1. p5. 49/76; *skilful* ~ power of reason G.SN 327; intention Bo 4. p6. 52/75, 91/131 (L *mente*); desire E.Mch 2359, TC 1.442; ~ *and/ne werk/dede* A.Prol 479, G.CY 1275, 1303, TC 3.1053, 4.981, LGW 2542. **2.** anxiety B.Pri 1779, PF 89, TC 3.1139, sorrow, grief F.Fkl 822, 1084, TC 1.579. [OE *ge)þōht*]

thoughte *see* **thenke(n, thinke.**

thral *n.* slave, servant B.Mk 3343, C.Phs 183, D.WB 155, F.Fkl 769; ~ *and bonde* D.Fri 1660; *his* ~ *to whom* in the power of whomsoever H.Mcp 357. [OE *þrǣl*]

thral *adj.* captive, subject, enslaved A.Kn 1552, I.Pars 148, Truth 23, ~ *to* Bo 3. m5. 6/7, p8. 15/21; ~ *and bonde* B.Mel 2751; *gentil or* ~ well-born or bond I.Pars 961. [from prec.]

thraldom *n.* slavery I.Pars 142, 748 *var,* 772; servitude B.ML 286, 338, TC 2.856. [from prec.+OE suff. *-dōm*]
thralle(n *v.* imprison TC 2.773, subject 1.235, enslave RR 882. [from the n.]
threpe *pr. pl.* affirm to be G.CY 826. [OE *þrēapian* rebuke]
thres(s)hfold *n.* threshold E.Cl 288. [OE *þerscold*]
threste(n *v.* **1.** *tr.* and *intr.* push, thrust A.Kn 2612, E.Mch 2003, Bo 2. p5. 100/140, TC 3.1574; cram Bo 2. p5. 59/83; ~ *in* throng in C.Phs 260. **2.** *tr.* oppress, trouble TC 4.254. **thraste** *pa. sg.* TC 2.1155; **threste** 4.254. **thraste** *pl.* C.Phs 260. [OE *þrǣstan*]
threte(n *v.* threaten, menace I.Pars 646, TC 4.909, rebuke LGW 754. [OE *þrēatian*]
threting *vbl. n.* threats G.CY 698.
threw *see* **throwe(n.**
thrid(de *adj.* third A.Kn 1463, TC 2.56; *the* ~ *day* the day after the next B.Sh 1265; *the* ~ *hevenes lord* Mars (the planet) Mars 29. [OE *þridda*]
thrye *adv.* thrice TC 2.89, 463, 1285. [OE *þrīga*]
thryes *adv.* thrice A.Prol 63, A.Kn 2952. [from prec.+adv. *-es*]
thrift *n.* profit, success G.CY 739, 1425; *by my* ~ if I succeed, upon my word A.Rv 4049, TC 2.1483, 3.871, 4.1630, HF 1847; *good* ~ good luck TC 2.582, 847, 1687, 3.947; *yvel* ~ bad luck HF 1786. [ON]
thrifty *adj.* **1.** profitable, advantageous B.ML 138, frugal B.Sh 1416. **2.** suitable, rewarding B.ML 46, fine B.Sh 1165; respectable, decent D.WB 238, successful E.Mch 1912, worthy Anel 197; *sup.* most admirable TC 1.1081, worthiest 2.737; *in* ~ *wyse* admiringly TC 1.275. [from prec.]
thriftily *adv.* carefully A.Prol 105, properly A.Mil 3131, becomingly TC 3.211, ? encouragingly F.Fkl 1174; *werken* ~ arrange things fittingly A.Mil 3131. [from prec.]
thringe *v.* press (in) TC 4.66. **thringing** *pr. p.* crowding, assembling RR 656. **throng** *pa. sg.* thrust, pressed E.Mch 2353, hastened Anel 55. **ythrongen** *p.p.* pressed, restricted Bo 2. p7. 32/46. [OE *þringan, þráng, geþrúngen*]
thriste *v.* press upon Bo 4. m7. 41/58. **thrist** *p.p.* in ~ *thyself into* plunged into Bo 4. p4. 142/200. [ON *prýsta*]
thrittene *num.* thirteen D.Sum 2259. [OA *þrēotēne*]
thritty *num.* thirty B.Sh 1216, B.NP 4380. [OE *þrĭt(t)ig*]
thryve(n *v.* **1.** prosper B.Sh 1418, G.CY 1212, TC 2.1607; succeed G.CY 1411, 1478; flourish Bo 3. m4. 3/4, 5. m4. 19/27, TC 1.966; recover D.Sum 1944; *so moot I* ~ as I may be saved A.Mil 3675, A.Rv 4177, TC 2.135, sim. D.Sum 1764, TC 2.120; *yvel* ~ fare badly RR 1067. **2. thryvinge** *pr. p.* ? active Bo 5. m4. 15/21 (L *uigens*). **throf** *pa. sg.* Bo 3. m4. 3/4. [ON *þrifa-sk*]
throng *see* **thringe.**
thro(o)p *n.* hamlet, village E.Cl 199, 208, I.Pars 12; **thorpes** *pl.* PF 350. [OE *þrop*]
throte *n.* throat A.Kn 2013, B.ML 600, (of voice) A.Mil 3218, BD 320, RR 507; gullet B.NP 4025, C.Pard 517, 527. [OE *þrote*]

throte-bolle *n.* 'throat-bowl', Adam's apple A.Rv 4273. [OE *þrotbolla*]
throwe *n.* space of time D.Sum 1815, TC 4.384; *but a* ~ for just a short time B.ML 953, E.Cl 450, *in a* ~ in an instant Pity 86, LGW 866, *withinne a* ~ within a short time TC 5.1461, LGW 1286; *many a* ~ often G.CY 941. [OE *þrāg*]
throwe(n *v.* **1.** (physical) throw B.ML 85, I.Pars 863, TC 3.1418, HF 789; *p.p.* imprisoned LGW 1960, ~ *yfere* join RR 786. **2.** (fig.) cast (eyes, etc.) TC 2.971, 3.184, 4.1159, 5.929, ~ *out of* reject from E.Cl 453; ~ *adoun* reduce to poverty Bo 3. p5. 34/46; ~ *fro* deprive of Pity 89. **threw** *pa. sg.* B.ML 85. **y)throwe** *p.p.* G.CY 940, LGW 1960; **throwen** TC 4.1159. [OE *þrāwan, þrēow, ge)þrāwen*]
throwes *n. pl.* torments TC 5.206, 1201. [?]
thrustel *n.* thrush, song-thrush B.Th 1963, PF 364, RR 665. [OE *þrostle*]
thrustelcok *n.* male song-thrush B.Th 1959. [from prec.]
thundringe *vbl. n.* thunder HF 1040. [from thondre]
thurfte *see* **thar.**
thurgh *prep.* **1.** through (direction) A.Kn 1075, A.Rv 4066, PF 500. **2.** throughout E.Mch 1466, F.Fkl 1452, LGW 1867. **3.** by means of B.ML 290, F.Fkl 1295, G.CY 743, TC 1.39. **4.** because of B.ML 22, 542, G.SN 325, Bo 3. p11. 118/163, LGW 1361. [OE *þurh*]
thurghdarted *p.p.* transfixed TC 1.325. [thurgh+*darte(n* v., cf. **ydarted**]
thurghgirt *p.p.* pierced through A.Kn 1010. [thurgh+ME *girde(n* of obsc. origin]
thurghout *prep.* throughout A.Kn 1432, F.Sq 46; across B.ML 464, 490, 506; through (direction) A.Kn 1096, B.NP 4408, TC 3.601, right through LGW 1793; ~ *hire herte* out of her heart TC 5.769. [thurgh+out]
thurghpassen *v.* pierce Bo 4. m3. 32/45. [thurgh+*passe(n*]
thurghshoten *p.p.* shot through, pierced TC 1.325. [thurgh+p.p. of **shete(n**]
thurrok *n.* bilge of a ship I.Pars 363, (fig.) 715. [OE *þurruc*]
thurst *n.* thirst B.ML 100, RR 1507. [OE *þurst*]
thurst *pr. 1 sg.* am thirsty TC 1.406. **thursteth** *3 sg.* longs TC 5.1406, LGW 103. **thursted** *hym, pa. impers.* he was thirsty B.Mk 3229. [OE *þyrstan*]
thurste, thurte *see* **thar.**
thwyte *pr. pl.* carve, whittle HF 1938. **thwiten** *p.p.* carved RR 933. [OE *þwitan, þwiten*]
thwitel *n.* knife A.Rv 3933. [from prec.]
tyd(e *n.* **1.** tide (of sea) A.Prol 401, B.ML 1134, B.NP 4294; *of al a* ~ ? despite the tide, during a whole tide B.ML 510. **2.** time TC 2.1739, LGW 2010, time of occurrence TC 4.1077; *in every* ~ at all times HF 1951; *in that* ~ at that period LGW G. 304; *in the morwe* ~ tomorrow morning B.NP 4206, *agayn the even* ~ towards evening 4262 (also as compounds); season: *ageyn this . . someres* ~ in anticipation of summertime F.Sq 142. **3.** occasion TC 5.700; *on a* ~ on one occasion Mars 51.

4. propitious time B.NP 4286, RR 1452; *to the* ~ till the time of success TC 1.954. **5.** hour Astr 2. 3. 10/14, 5. 9/12, 18/27; *pl.* hours Bo 1. m5. 13/19 (L *horas*); *at o* ~ at the same hour LGW 783. **6.** ? day; or ? *of a* ~ in time B.ML 798. [OE *tīd*]

tyde(n *v.* **1.** (with dat. pron.) happen to, befall B.ML 337, Mars 202. **2.** happen Bo 2. p5. 105/148 var. **tydeth** *pr. 3 sg.* Mars 202; **tit** TC 1.333; **tydes** A.Rv 4175. **tid** *p.p.* TC 1.907, 2.224. [OE *tīdan, tiden*]

tidif *n.* (a small bird) LGW 154. **tydyves** *pl.* F.Sq 648 var. [?]

tyding *n.* event B.ML 726; piece of news E.Cl 901, TC 2.951, HF 648; report LGW 1424. *pl.* news, stories B.ML 129, H.Mcp 360, HF 1027. [LOE *tīdung* and ON *tiðendi*]

tikel *adj.* uncertain A.Mil 3428. [? cf. **tikleth**]

tikelnesse *n.* insecurity Truth 3. [from prec.]

tikleth *pr. 3 sg.* pleases greatly D.WB 471. **tikled** *pa. sg.* either *impers.* it gratified, or with var. *I*, pleased D.WB 395. [?]

tilien *v.* till, cultivate B.Mel 2780. [OE *tilian*]

tilyere *n.* tiller Bo 5. p1. 55/78. [from prec.]

tilyinge *vbl. n.* tilling Bo 5. p1. 50/72.

til(1 *conj.* until A.Prol 698, D.WB 283, F.Sq 290, ~ *that* A.Kn 983, B.Mk 3748. [as next]

til(1 *prep.* **1.** until A.Kn 1621, D.Sum 2012, TC 2.1521, 1651; ~ *now late* ? recently BD 203. **2.** to A.Prol 180, A.Mil 3400, C.Pard 697. **3.** into A.Kn 2062, A.Mil 3390. **4.** *adv.* in ~ *and fra* (nth.) to and fro A.Rv 4039. [ONb and ON *til*]

timbestere *n.* female tambourine player RR 769. [from OF *timbrer* v.]

tyme *n.* **1.** time A.Prol 44, A.Kn 3018; *ofte* ~ often A.Prol 52, B.Pri 1719, ~*s* A.Kn 1312; *som* ~ at some time A.Kn 2474, E.Mch 1862 (cf. **somtyme**; *(a) longe* ~ (for) a long time A.Kn 1573, B.ML 979; *up)on a* ~ (a (once) upon a time A.Kn 2388, once B.Mk 3887, F.Sq 624; *for the mene* ~ meantime B.Sh 1277, *of olde* ~ in that former time B.ML 50; *longe* ~ *agoon* long ago C.Pard 436, TC 5.1325, *of* ~ *yoore* for a long time F.Fkl 963; ~ *comynge* future B.Mel 2213, E.Cl 79, I.Pars 735, Bo 2. p4. 41/56; *in any* ~ at any time Bo 2. p5. 5/7; *in good* ~ fortunately, appropriately G.CY 1048. **2.** occasion B.NP 4203, 4367, 4644, TC 5.97. **3.** due time, right moment, opportunity (often with *poss.*) B.Mel 2918, 3022, E.Mch 2001, F.Fkl 1034, 1308, TC 2.1193, 1721, 3.518; *hath (his)* ~ has due season, a right time D.Fri 1475, E.Cl 6, E.Mch 1972, TC 2.989; *be* ~ be the right time A.Mil 3672, Bo 1. p2. 1; time of death I.Pars 727; leisure A.Prol 35, A.Mil 3219; *by* ~(*s* in good time I.Pars 363, TC 4.1105, early, soon TC 2.1093, LGW 452, in a short time G.CY 913, cf. **bitymes**; *in* ~ *and space* as opportunity offered G.SN 355. **4.** lifetime, age Pity 31, HF 1249, reign A.Prol 324, F.Sq 13, LGW 2444; period of time, in *dryve(n (forth/away) the* ~ TC 2.983, 5.680. **5.** hour E.Cl 902, TC 5.221, Astr 2. 3. rubr., point in time 11. 7/10; *pl.* seasons TC 5.376. **6.** temporal world

(opp. to eternity) Bo 5. p6. 13/18, 35/50; *by* ~*s* in time Bo 4. p6. 53/77 (L *temporibus*) **7.** passage of time RR 381, 388, 391, *pl.* Bo 3. m9. 2/4, sorts of time RR 380; *chaunginge of* ~ passing of time Bo 3. p4. 67/97. [OE *tīma*]

tymely *adj./adv.* early I.Pars 1066 var. [OE *tīmlīce*]

tyne *n.* barrel Rosem 9. [OF]

tipet *n.* dangling point (of hood) A.Prol 233, A.Rv 3953, HF 1841. [? AN from *tip* n., ON *typpi*]

tyren *v.* tear, rend Bo 3. m12. 30/43, TC 1.787. [OF *tirer*]

titeringe *vbl. n.* hesitation, vacillation TC 2.1744. [from v. from ON *titra* shake]

tytheres *n. pl.* tithe-payers: *smale* ~ payers of less than the due tithes D.Fri 1312. [from v. from OE *tēogoþian*]

tytled *p.p.* dedicated I.Pars 894. [from OF *titler*]

titlelees *adj.* without title, usurping H.Mcp 223. [from n. from OF *title*]

to *n.* toe A.Kn 2726. **toos** *pl.* B.NP 4370, 4521; **toon** 4052, HF 2028. [OE *tā*, pl. *tān*]

to *prep.* **1.** to (often of direction) B.ML 316, B.Sh 1503, HF 1; ~ *reste* gone to rest A.Prol 30, *him* ~ *fete/fote* at his feet B.ML 1104, LGW 1314; ~ *grounde* on the ground B.NP 4371, ~ *his hond* at hand E.Cl 66; *appetyt* ~ appetite for E.Mch 2336; *nede* ~ need of I.Pars 527; ~ *love* ot Jove A.Kn 2222; against B.Mel 3074. **2.** as far as A.Prol 391, B.Th 1921. **3.** (before indirect obj.) A.Prol 673, B.Mk 3420, *lyk* ~ BD 963; *lyketh* ~ pleases G.CY 1469, *lakketh* ~ G.SN 498; *delicat* ~ *sighte* delicate to see E.Cl 682, *felawe* ~ companion to D.Sum 2086; (following obj.) G.CY 1449 (separated from obj.) E.Mch 1459, 1611. **4.** as (of persons, indicating position) ~ *wife* A.Kn 1289, E.Cl 793, 840, BD 716, LGW 1304; ~ *borwe* as a pledge A.Kn 1622, F.Fkl 1234; ~ *wedde* A.Kn 1218; ~ *my supposinge* as I believe E.Cl 1041; *as* ~ *my jugement* E.Cl 53, *as* ~ *my doom* in my opinion F.Sq 677, PF 480, TC 1.100. [OE *tō*]

to- *pref.* expressing separation, destruction, etc. [OE *tō-*]

tobete *v.* beat severely G.SN 405. [OE *tōbēatan*]

tobreke *v.* **1.** *intr.* break (apart), shatter A.Rv 3918 var, G.CY 907, HF 779, Bo 3. m9. 31/44. **2.** **tobroke(n** *p.p.* broken (to pieces) A.Rv 4277, D.WB 277, Scog 1. [OE *tōbrecan, -broçen*]

tobrᴇsᴛᴇ *v.* **1.** *tr.* break to pieces, shatter A.Kn 2611, 2691. **2.** *intr.* be shattered TC 2.608. **tobrosten** *p.p.* A.Kn 2691, 2757. [OE *tōberstan, tōborsten*]

tocleve *v.* split asunder TC 5.613. [OE *tōclēofan*]

todassched *p.p.* shattered TC 2.640. **todasshte** *pa. sg.* ? clawed (herself) RR 337. [**to-**+ME *daschen*, prob. imit.]

todrawen *v.* **1.** pull Bo 1. p5. 48/70 (L *distrahunt*). **todrowen** *pa. pl.* p3. 27/38. **2.** allure, attract Bo 4. m3. 30/43 (L *detrahunt*). [**to-**+**drawe**(n]

todriven *p.p.* scattered LGW 1280. [OE *tōdrīfen*]

toforn adv. before, ahead Bo 5. p6. 191/268. [as next]

toforn prep. before F.Sq 268; (postponed) God ~ in God's sight (I swear) TC 1.1049, 2.431, 992; goth ~ precedes Bo 5. p5. 6/8. **tofore** TC 2.1409. [OE tōforan]

togedre(s see **togider.**

toght adj. taut D.Sum 2267. [? rel. to OE tēon draw, p.p. togen]

togider/togidre(s/toged(e)res adv. **1.** together A.Prol 824, B.Mk 3222, BD 809, TC 4.1322; ymet ~ met one another A.Kn 2624, love hem ~ love one another I.Pars 203; foldest .. ~ dost interweave Bo 3. p12. 120/160; comprehendeth ~ embraces simultaneously Bo 5. p6. 28/40. **2.** likewise Bo 3. p11. 6/7. [OE tōgædere]

togo p.p. scattered LGW 653. [OE tōgān]

togreve v. harm, injure TC 1.1001 var. [to-+gre(e)ve(n]

tohangen v. hang HF 1782 var. [to-+OE hangian]

to-hepe adv. together TC 3.1764, LGW 2009, Astr 1.14.5/6. [to prep.+he(e)p]

tohewen pr. pl. hack to pieces A.Kn 2609. p.p. B.ML 437, TC 2.638. [OE tōhēawan, -hēawen]

token n. token, sign B.Sh 1549, HF 911 (MSS), LGW 1275; by redy ~ B.Sh 1580 in ready money, in cash. [OE tāc(e)n]

tokening n. sign, proof G.CY 1153, TC 4.779. [OE tācnung]

tokneth pr. 3 sg. marks, distinguishes Bo 1. m6. 12/17. [from OE tācnian]

tolle(n v.¹ take toll A.Prol 562. [from OE toll n.]

tollen v.² see **tulle.**

Tol(l)etanes adj. pl. of Toledo F.Fkl 1273. [OF]

tombesteres n. dancing girls C.Pard 477. [OE tumbere+fem. suff. -estre]

tomelte v. melt utterly, disappear TC 3.348. [to-+OE meltan]

tomorwe adv. tomorrow A.Prol 780, D.Sum 2012, TC 1.861. **tomorn** D.WB 1245, D.Fri 1588 (only). [OE tō morgen(ne]

tonge n. **1.** tongue A.Mil 3692, C.Pard 356; (of a bell) A.Rv 3896. **2.** speech, what one says H.Mcp 319, Scog 21; language (national) B.Mk 3497, F.Fkl 711, Bo 2. p7. 35/50, TC 2.14, 5.1794; eloquence B.ML 899, B.Mk 3336, E.Mch 1341, skill in speaking TC 5.1796; kepe ~ control the tongue or ? preserve secrecy TC 3.294; light of ~ loose tongued LGW 1699; of ~ large loose tongued TC 5.804. [OE túnge]

tonged adj. in trewer ~ more gracious in speech BD 927. [from **trew(e**+prec.]

tonight adv. tonight (this night) A.Rv 4253, (the night to come) B.Sh 1468, D.Fri 1636, E.Mch 2253, TC 5.1169, LGW 1710; last night B.NP 4116, C.Pard 673. [OE tōniht]

tonne n. cask A.Rv 3894, E.Cl 215; of another ~ in another vein LGW 195, cf. D.WB 170. [OE tunne]

tonne-greet adj. as thick as a barrel A.Kn 1994. [prec.+**greet**]

to(o adv. too, very B.ML 420, BD 796, TC 2.398, LGW 2597, Astr 2.25. 20/29; also TC 1. 540 var. [OE tō]

to(o)k see **take(n.**

tool n. weapon B.NP 4106. **toles** pl. tools TC 1.632. [OE tōl]

to(o)n see **o(o)n.**

to(o)rd n. turd C.Pard 955. [OE]

tooth n. appetite, taste D.WB 449. [OE tōþ]

top n. top LGW 738, head A.Prol 590, ~ and tail beginning and end HF 880; hair C.Phs 255. [OE top(þ]

torace pr. subj. pl. may tear to pieces E.Cl 572. [to-+race(n, ME var. of rase(n, OF raser]

torende v. **1.** tear to pieces B.Mk 3215, C.Phs 102, PF 432; tear (hair) LGW 2188. **2.** (fig.) afflict Bo 5. m3. 1/1; afflict TC 4.341, refl. afflict themselves, suffer 2.790; wound Bo 4. p6. 224/325. **torente** pa. B.Mk 3215, TC 4.341. **torent** p.p. C.Phs 102. [OE tōréndan]

toret(s see **turet.**

torment/tur- n. **1.** torture B.Pri 1818, B.Mk 3779, TC 1.8, 4.1698; (fig.) A.Kn 2228. **2.** suffering A.Kn 1298, B.ML 845, F.Fkl 1101, TC 5.654, RR 274. [OF]

tormente(n/tur- v. **1.** torture B.ML 885, I.Pars 183. **2.** torment, harass A.Kn 1314, Bo 1. m5. 39/54, TC 4.634, LGW 871. [OF to(u)rmenter]

tormentyse† n. torment B.Mk 3707. [cf. OF torment]

tormentour n. tormentor B.ML 818, G.SN 373. [OF]

tormentrye n. torture D.WB 251. [OF tourmenterie]

torn n. turn, service, in frendes ~ C.Pard 815. [AN *torn/turn and next]

torne(n/turne(n v. **1.** tr. turn, revolve BD 643, Bo 2. p2. 37/51, Astr 2. 14. 2, 27. 3/5; turn (on lathe) A.Rv 3928; throw (dice) A.Kn 1238; move, spur on LGW 1205; ~ aboute turn back TC 5.85; ~ up-so-down turn upside down I.Pars 495; intr. ~ to turn against I.Pars 625; it goth to ~ ayein to himself it returns to itself Bo 3. m9. 21/29-30. **2.** tr. deflect Bo 3. p1. 36/48 (L flexeris), overcome Bo 2. m6. 20/28 (L uertere); change B.Mel 2257; convert I.Pars 772; overthrow B.NP 4593, intr. ~ on depend on TC 2.1347. **3.** intr. go, travel A.Kn 1327, 2454, TC 5.482; refl. turn away F.Fkl 1011, turn round TC 4.855, LGW 144; ~ ageyn return E.Cl 872, TC 3.1516, LGW 2200, 2205, revert (to) B.NP 4564, Bo 4. p4. 125/178. **4.** toss sleeplessly BD 256, TC 1.196, 5.211, ~ to and fro D.WB 1085. **5.** bring about Bo 1. m5. 24/34; ~ (in)to transform, change into tr. G.CY 1403, H.Mcp 100, BD 599; intr. TC 2.90, 3.179, be reduced to TC 4.119, 5.309; vary Bo 2. m3. 14/17. **5.** direct Bo 3. p6. 179/253; ~ in direct towards Bo 3. p2. 34/49; ~ thyself to apply yourself to Bo 3. p6. 181/256 (L te conuerteris); **turned** (for) to applied to, directed towards A.Mil 3192, BD 795. **turneth** imper. pl. B.NP 4599. [OE túrnian, týrnan, AN turner]

torning vbl. n. turning round Bo 5. p4. 62/89; falling TC 1.856; bend, corner HF 182, (? dance) movement RR 761.

tortuous n. oblique B.ML 302, Astr 2. 28. 19/27. [AN]

toscatered p.p. dispersed D.Sum 1969. [to-+OE *scaterian]

toshake p.p. shaken to pieces LGW 962, 1765. [OE tōscacen]

toshivered *p.p.* broken into splinters PF 493. [**to-**+*shiver* v., cf. MDu *scheveren*]
toshrede *pr. pl.* cut to pieces A.Kn 2609. [**to-**+OE *scrēadian*]
toslitered *p.p.* slashed with cuts RR 840. [frequentative, rel. to OE *tōslitan*]
tosterte *v.* burst TC 2.980. [**to-**+*sterte(n*]
tostoupe *v.* ? strain D.Sum 1560 var. [**to-**+ stoupe]
toswinke *pr. pl.* toil C.Pard 519 var. [**to-**+ swinke(n]
totelere *n. attrib.* tale-bearing LGW 353. [from *tutel* v. whisper, cf. MDu *tūte*]
totere *pr. pl.* tear in pieces C.Pard 474. **totar** *pa. sg.* B.Mk 3801. **totore**/ **-torn** *p.p.* torn in pieces Bo 3. m2. 13/19, tattered G.CY 635, PF 110, defaced TC 4.358, dishevelled RR 327. [OE *tōteran*]
tother *see* **other.**
toty *adj.* dizzy A.Rv 4253. [?]
totrede *v.* trample under foot I.Pars 864. [OE *tōtredan*]
touche *vbl. n.* touching, fingering TC 5.443. [OF]
touche(n *v.* **1.** touch, feel A.Rv 3932, I.Pars 327, TC 2.1033; trim (with a file) PF 216 var; embrace, have sexual intercourse with D.WB 87, G.SN 156; reach A.Kn 2561, HF 1375; affect RR 1026 *em.* **2.** concern A.Mil 3179, 3494, ~ *to* B.Mel 2489; deal with D.Fri 1271, I.Pars 957, PF 285; involve TC 1.1033; *intr.* suit, fit TC 2.1662. [OF *tuchier*]
touching(e *vbl. n.* touch (sense of) I.Pars 207, 210, Bo 5. p4. 102/147, 104/150; (act of) I.Pars 854; handling Bo 1. p5. 54/78.
touchinge *pr. p.* as *prep.* concerning, on the subject of B.Mel 2345, D.Sum 1988, 2290, TC 2.1023. [**touche(n** v. 2]
tough *adj.* **1.** tough, strong A.Kn 1992. **2.** make(n it ~ perform vigorously B.Sh 1569, be pressing TC 3.87, 5.101; create difficulty BD 531; ? show off, put on a performance TC 2.1025. [OE *tōh*]
to(u)mbling *ppl. adj.* changing, fading Bo 2. m3. 16/19; perishable, transient p4. 110/ 151, 3. p9. 124/165 (L *caducis*, *-a* in all). [from v., cf. OE *tūmbian*]
toun *n.* town, city C.Pard 570, LGW 257, ? farm B.NP 4138, I.Pars 898, townspeople TC 2.378; ~ *and tour* in its entirety E.Mch 2172, *at every ~es* ende at the entrance to every town D.Fri 1285; *prep.* phrases without art.: *at* ~ at Sittingbourne D.Sum 2294, *in* ~ in the town TC 3.188, 4.588, among men B.Th 1983; *into* ~ into the town TC 2.1111, *of* ~ belonging to the town A.Mil 3380, *out of* ~ out of the town D.Fri 1571, F Fkl 1351, TC 4.331, away from the town 3.570, *to* ~ to the town B.Th 2028. [OE *tūn*]
tour *n.* tower A.Kn 1030; (astrol.) mansion Mars 113. [LOE *tūr*, OF *tour*]
tourettes *see* **turet.**
t(o)urneying(e *vbl. n.* tournament A.Kn 2557, 2720, RR 1206, 1407. [from OF *torneier*]
toute *n.* buttocks A.Mil 3812, 3853. [?]
tow *n.* flax; see **distaf.** [MLG *touw*]
towayl *n.* towel B.Mk 3935, cloth RR 161. [OF *toaille*]
toward *prep.* to A.Prol 27, B.ML 1148, Bo 2. p5. 18/25; for E.Cl 778; near LGW 1965; on the way to B.Mk 3216; (divided)

to me-ward to me Bo 1. m1. 19/28, TC 4.1666; *to us-ward* B.Mel 2938, Astr 1.17.40/54; *to yow-ward* Bo 5. p6. 99/140, *to him-ward* Bo 5. p6. 99/140, 108/154, *to hem-ward* Bo 2. p5. 27/38), *to scole-ward* B.Pri 1739, *to Scotland-ward* B.ML 718, sim. E.Cl 51, F.Fkl 1505. [OE *tōweard*, *tō* .. *weard*; cf. **fro**]
towonde *pa. sg.* flew apart Mars 102. [prob. for *towond*, **to-**+*winde(n*]
to-ye(e)re *adv.* this year D.WB 168, TC 3.241, HF 84. [**to** prep.+*yeer*]
trace/tras *n.* track, footprint Bo 5. m5. 3/4, 7/10, (fig.) example Gent 3; group, procession LGW 285. [OF]
trace *pr. pl.* go, tread PF 54. [OF *tracier*]
tragedien *n.* writer of tragedy Bo 3. p6. 2. [OF]
trayed *pa.* betrayed HF 390 var, LGW 2486. [OF *trair*]
trays *n.* traces A.Kn 2139, TC 1.222. [OF, pl. of *trait*]
traysen *v.* betray TC 4.438, HF 390 var. [OF *traiss-*, stem of *trair*]
trayteresse *n.* treacherous, deceitful woman BD 620, 813. [OF *traitresse*]
traitorie *n.* treachery B.ML 781. [from next]
traitour *n.* traitor A.Kn 1130; deceiver TC 4.5. [OF]
traytours *adj.* treacherous C.Pard 896. [OF *traitos* modified by prec.]
translate *v.* **1.** translate LGW 370. **2.** transfer (*into* 'to') Bo 2. p5. 15/21 (L *translata*). **3.** transform E.Cl 385. [L *translātus* and OF *translater*]
transmewe(n *see* **transmuwe(n.**
transmutacioun *n.* change, mutability A.Kn 2839, Fort 1; *pl.* changes HF 1969. [OF]
transmuwe(n *v.* transform TC 4.467; *p.p.* reduced 830. [OF *transmuer*]
transporte *v.* bring, lead Bo 3. p4. 26/38, p9. 15/20; ~ *upon al* extend to all, implicate all in Bo 1. p4. 155/215 (L *transferre*). [OF *transporter*]
trapped *p.p.* furnished with trappings A.Kn 2157, 2890. [from n., F. *drap*]
trappures *n. pl.* trappings A.Kn 2499. [OF **trapeure*]
travail(l)e *n.* effort A.Kn 2406, I.Pars 735, TC 5.184, 1852; *do* ~ take pains E.Cl 1210; *han* ~ take trouble TC 2.1437; labour B.Mel 2526, G.CY 781, BD 602, Bo 4. m7. 20/28; suffering A.Mil 3646, I.Pars 455, TC 1.372; difficulty TC 2.3; *pl.* sufferings I.Pars 256, 730. [OF *travail*, *-e* forms from next]
travaile(n *v.* **1.** make an effort, toil D.Fri 1365, I.Pars 652, Bo 4. p4. 169/154; ~ *to* strive to Bo 2. p1. 18/25. **2.** work, labour I.Pars 667, 723. **3.** suffer I.Pars 985, Bo 4. p6. 171/248. **4.** journey RR 370. **5.** travailinge *pr.p.* in childbirth A.Kn 2083. **6.** ytraveiled *p.p.* ? laboured over Bo 5. p3. 30/41. [OF *travaillier*]
travailling *vbl. n.* toiling I.Pars 257.
trave *n.* wooden frame A.Mil 3282. [OF]
travers *n.* curtain, screen E.Mch 1817, TC 3.674. [OF]
trecherye *n.* treachery, trickery B.NP 4520, G.CY 1069. [OF]
trechoures *n. pl.* deceivers RR 197. [OF]
tredefoul *n.* 'bird-treader', lecher B.Mk 3135, B.NP 4641. [from next+**foul**]

trede(n v. **1.** tread, walk A.Kn 3022. **tret** pr. 3 sg. D.Sum 2002, TC 2.347. **troden** pa. pl. HF 2153. p.p. stepped C.Pard 712. **2. trad** pa. sg. copulated with B.NP 4368. [OE tredan, træd, trædon, treden]
treding vbl. n. copulation B.Mk 3145.
tre(e n. tree A.Kn 2062; Cross A.Mil 3767, B.ML 456; gallows C.Phs 271; wood D.WB 101, E.Cl 558, TC 2.47, RR 948. [OE trēo(w]
tregetour n. magician, illusionist F.Fkl 1141, 1143, HF 1260. [OF]
treye adj. three C.Pard 653. [OF trei(s]
trench n. walk, path F.Sq 392. [OF trenche]
trenden v. turn Bo 3. m11. 2/3. [OE tréndan]
trentals n. pl. sets of thirty masses for the dead D.Sum 1717, 1724. [ML trentāle]
tresorere n. treasurer ABC 107, Purse 18. [AN]
tresorie n. treasury I.Pars 893, HF 524. [OF]
treso(u)r n. treasure, wealth B.ML 442, D.WB 204, Mars 256 var, LGW 1652; (fig.) LGW 2628. [OF]
trespace(n v. **1.** commit an offence TC 3.1175; ~ to offend against B.Mk 3093, C.Pard 416, E.Mch 1828, I.Pars 992, RR 1036; ~ ageyns (a command) B.Mk 3754; ~ unto injure B.Mel 3067. **2.** intr. commit sin B.Mel 2609, I.Pars 1012, ~ to sin against B.Mel 3074; tr. commit (sins) B.Mel 3075. [OF trespasser]
trespas n. offence A.Kn 1764, C.Phs 242, HF 428, LGW 408; injury B.Mel 2547, B.NP 4610; sin B.Mk 3370, C.Pard 904, F.Fkl 1366, I.Pars 1012, 1016; crime Bo 1. p4. 178/248. [OF]
trespassinge vbl. n. offence LGW 155.
trespassours n. pl. offenders B.Mel 2548, 2622. [OF]
tresse n. plait, braid A.Kn 1049, pl. hair C.Phs 37, as evere I mote brouke my ~ as long as I may keep my hair E.Mch 2308. [OF]
tresse v. **1.** (of a person) dress hair of, in tresses or plaits RR 599, TC 5.810. **2.** (of hair) arrange in tresses D.WB 344, RR 779. [OF trecier]
tretable adj. amenable I.Pars 658, BD 923, docile LGW 411, reasonable BD 533. [OF traitable]
tretee n. treaty A.Kn 1288. B.Mk 3865, C.Pard 619, agreement E.Mch 1692; in ~ into discussion F.Fkl 1219. [AN]
trete(n v. **1.** treat, behave towards I.Pars 582, TC 5.134. **2.** tell, describe TC 1.742, LGW 575, 1692; summarize PF 34; ~ of speak about, discuss C.Pard 521, F.Sq 220, Bo 3. p11. 111/153, p12. 150/202, HF 54. **3.** ~ of negotiate B.Mel 2988, TC 1.975, 4.1346. **4.** hirselven .. ~ behave TC 4.813; ~ of folye behave improperly C.Phs 64. [OF tretier]
tretis/-ice n. **1.** treaty B.ML 233, TC 4.670; negotiation E.Cl 331, TC 4.64, 136. **2.** treatise B.Mel 2147, 2153, I.Pars 957, 1081, Astr prol 4/5, 15/20. **3.** document TC 2.1697. [AN tretiz]
tretys adj. well-proportioned RR 932, shapely A.Prol 152, RR 1016, 1216. [OF]
trewe/truwe n. truce TC 3.1779, 4.58/57, 1312; time of truce 1314, pl. 5.401. [OE trēowa/trūwa]

trew(e adj. **1.** true B.Mel 2929, E.Cl 855; genuine F.Sq 465, Bo 5. m4. 28/41 (L ueris), FormA 20; proper I.Pars 920. **2.** good A.Kn 1326, B.Mel 3061; honest F.Sq 537, G.CY 969, 1039, TC 2.828; impartial A.Kn 1864, 2657, B.NP 4240; wise A.Mil 3529; skilled A.Mil 3781, diligent A.Prol 531. **3.** real, faithful Bo 2. p8. 25/36 (L fidelium), loyal, steadfast B.Sh 1397, D.WB 1221, E.Mch 2285, F.Fkl 1424, 1539, TC 4.1610, LGW 444, PF 479; (as) .. ~ as (any) steel E.Mch 2426, PF 395, TC 5.831, LGW 334; as n. Anel 105, pl. the faithful B.ML 456. **4.** unfailing Bo 2. m5. 2/3 (L fidelibus). [OE trēowe]
trewely adv. **1.** truly, indeed A.Prol 707, BD 33, TC 5.19. **2.** loyally CompL 99/93, TC 2.493, 5.174. **3.** accurately Astr 2. 18 rubr.; honestly A.Rv 4133; truthfully, from the heart A.Prol 481, I.Pars 1045; ful ~ fully HF 1661; wel and ~ F.Fkl 1588; **treweliche** TC 1.246, 4.1415, 5.380. [from prec.]
trewe-love n. herb Paris A.Mil 3692. [trew(e + love]
triacle n. remedy, medicine B.ML 479, C.Pard 314. [OF]
tryce v. pull B.Mk 3715. [MDu trisen hoist]
trye adj. choice B.Th 2046. [OF trie n. choice]
trille v. **1.** tr. turn F.Sq 316, 321. **2.** intr. roll, run D.Sum 1864 var. [cf. Sw trilla]
tryne adj. triple G.SN 45, TC 5.1866 var. [OF]
trip(e n. small piece D.Sum 1747. [?]
trippe(n v. dance A.Mil 3328, prance F.Sq 312. [OF trip(p)er]
trist see trust.
triste n. hunting station TC 2.1534. [OF]
triste(n see truste(n.
Troyanisshe adj. Trojan HF 201. [from L Troiānus]
tromp(e n. trumpet PF 344, LGW 635. pl. A.Kn 2671 var. [OF, cf. **trumpe(n**]
trompours n. pl. trumpeters A.Kn 2671 var. [OF]
tronchoun n. spear shaft A.Kn 2615. [OF]
trone n. throne B.Mk 3333, 3950; in ~ enthroned A.Kn 2529, TC 4.1086. [OF]
trot n. in riden .. ~ ride at a trot G.CY 575. [OF]
trotte v. trot D.WB 838; go, exist E.Mch 1538. [OF troter]
troublable† n. disturbing Bo 4. m2. 7/10 (L turbida). [from **trouble(n**]
trouble adj. disturbed E.Cl 465, H.Mcp 279, I.Pars 537, confused 824; anxious CompL 133/127, turbulent Bo 1. m7. 2 (L turbidus); turbid I.Pars 816. [OF]
trouble(n v. **1.** trouble, disturb D.WB 363, I.Pars 544, 677, 740, Bo 2. m4. 10/15 (L miscens), Bo 4. m5. 22/29 (L turbant); p.p. confused Bo 5. p3. 4. **2.** afflict B.Mel 2191, G.SN 72, harm Bo 5. p2. 27/38 (L turbantur), p.p. diseased B.Mel 2891. **3.** change Bo 5. p6. 107/152 (L perturbat). [OF trubler]
troubly adj. cloudy, obscuring Bo 4. m5. 24/32 (L nubilus). [from n., OF truble]
troublinges vbl. n. pl., disturbances Bo 4. m2. 8/11.
trouth(e n. **1.** loyalty, constancy A.Prol 46, A.Kn 2789, B.Mk 3578, (esp. constancy in

love) E.Cl 794, TC 1.584, 691, 3.1229, LGW 1255; troth, pledged faith F.Fkl 998, *by my* ~ A.Prol 763, BD 1309, *upon my* ~ A.Kn 1855, *plighte* . . ~ pledge B.Sh 1388, have heer my ~ here is my pledge D.WB 1013, *breke* . . ~ break faith F.Fkl 1519; *holde* . . ~ keep faith D.Fri 1525, *kepe* . . ~ F.Fkl 1570. **2.** veracity, truthfulness F.Sq 508, I.Pars 349, what is true, truth B.Mel 2393, G.SN 238, 259, G.CY 1285, I.Pars 401, MercB 10, Bo 3. m11. 12/16, 4. m1. 11/16; the truth I.Pars 593; *of ful sad* ~ unshakably true Bo 5. p6. 119/169; *in* ~ truthfully I.Pars 592; *to the* ~ exactly Astr 2. 17. rubr.; *after the* ~ accurately 2. 34. 9/13. **3.** righteousness Truth 7, 14, ? A.Co 4397; *mente* ~ had honourable intentions TC 2.665; *fortheren* ~ advance virtue TC 5.1707. [OE *trēowþ*]
trowe(n v. **1.** believe (a thing, n. or pron. obj. or cl.) A.Kn 1520, A.Mil 3416, B.Mel 2364, TC 4.383; (occas. a person) BD 544, TC 4.1547; ~ *in*/*on* (person or thing) G.SN 171, 378, TC 5.383, LGW G. 21; think, judge (with *that*-cl.) A.Kn 2101, B.ML 222, Bo 2. p3. 56/81, 5. p4. 56/80, p5. 59/86. **2.** trust D.Fri 1557, TC 2.956 *var*, 5.327, ~ *on* trust in TC 5.736, Bo 2. m3. 16/20. **3.** ? obey D.Sum 1985. **4.** (*as*) *I* ~ (expletive) I think, imagine A.Prol 155, 524, B.ML 354, TC 1.640. **trowestow** *pr. 2 sg.* (with suffixed pron.) Bo 1. p3. 16/22, 4. p2. 91/121, p4. 169/236. **troweth** *imper. pl.* B.Mel 2701. [OE *trēow(i)an*]
trufles n. pl. idle jests I.Pars 715. [OF]
trumpe(n v. blow a trumpet HF 1243, 1250. [OF *tromper*; cf. **tromp(e**]
trust/trist n. **1.** trust, reliance TC 3.941, 1305; assured faith HF 1971; *in* ~ *of* in reliance on I.Pars 738, Truth 9, through reliance on B.Mel 2840, *in* ~ *therof* through reliance on it G.CY 876. **2.** loyalty, fidelity TC 3.403, 5.1259, ? friendship or ? confidence in him 4.1382. **3.** what they relied on, object of faith TC 1.154. [OE *tryst*, ON *traust* n., *treysta* v.]
truste(n/triste(n v. **1.** trust, rely on B.Mk 3422, G.SN 163, TC 3.1227, ~ *to* B.Mel 2300, 2374, TC 1.601, 2.491, LGW 333, 1256; ~ *in*/(*up)on* A.Prol 501, E.Cl 149, 159, TC 2.956 *var*, 3.587; *brotel for to* ~ too unreliable to trust I.Pars 473, LGW 1885; (with refl. pron.) have confidence B.Mel 2836. **2.** ~ *on*/*in* believe in truth of B.NP 4627, TC 5.1709. **3. truste(th)** *imper.* in ~ (*me*) (*wel*) believe me (emphasizing or otiose) A.Kn 2182, D.ML 1040, D.WD 118, D.Sum 1869, E.Mch 1561, TC 2.1245, RR 170. [OE **trystan*, ON *treysta*]
truwe see **trewe.**
tuel/tuwel 1. chimney-pipe HF 1649. **2.** anus D.Sum 2148. [OF]
tukked *p.p.* girded A.Prol 621; **ytukked** (*up*) tucked up D.Sum 1737, LGW 982. [OE *tūcian*]
tulle v. lure, attract A.Rv 4134, **tollen** Bo 2. p7. 11/15. [cf. OE *for-tyllan* seduce]
turet/toret n. **1.** eye (in which the ring of the astrolabe turns) Astr 1. 2. 1. **2. tourettes** *pl.* swivels (rings on dogs' collars) A.Kn 2152. [OF *toret*]
Turkeys adj. Turkish A.Kn 2895. [AN]
turne(n see **torne(n.**

turtel n. turtle-dove A.Mil 3706, E.Mch 2080, PF 355. [OE *turtla*/*-le*]
tuwel see **tuel.**
twa num. two (nth.) A.Rv 4129. [OE]
twey(e num. two A.Prol 704, 792. [OE *twēgen*]
tweyfo(o)ld adj. double G.CY 566. [OE *twif(e)ald* infl. by prec.]
twyes adv. twice A.Co 4348, TC 3.98. [LOE *twiȝes*]
twighte *pa. sg.* pulled TC 4.1185. **twight** *p.p.* pulled D.Fri 1563, (fig.) torn, distracted TC 4.572. [? OE **twiht(e* from **twiċċan*]
twyne v. twist, spin TC 5.7. [cf. OE *twin* n. twine]
twinkled *pa.* twinkled A.Prol 267. *p.p.* winked Bo 2. p3. 49/71. [OE *twinclian*]
twinne(n v. **1.** *intr.* part, leave one another TC 3.1711, 4.904, 1270, *tr.* *be(n* (**y**)**twinned** be separated TC 4.476, 5.679; go, proceed A.Prol 835. **2.** with *prep.* separate (from a person) ~ *from* TC 4.758, 5.339, LGW 2032; depart (from a thing) ~ *from* C.Pard 430, Anel 102, ~ *out of* B.ML 517, B.Mk 3195, F.Sq 577. [OE *twinn* adj.]
twinninge *vbl. n.* separation TC 4.1303.
twist(e n. branch E.Mch 2349, F.Sq 442; tendril TC 3.1230. [? from next]
twiste v. twist (fig.) wring, hurt F.Sq 566, TC 4.1129. *pa.* wrung (hand) E.Mch 2005, (heart) TC 4.254, tormented D.WB 494, *subj.* would constrain TC 3.1769.
twist *p.p.* warped HF 775. [?]
twitereth *pr. 3 sg.* chirps Bo 3. m2. 21/30. [imit.]
Tyrene adj. Tyrrhenian, Tuscan Bo 3. m8. 7/9. [L *Tyrrhēnus*]

U

umbreyde *pa. sg.* reproached LGW 1671 *var.* [var. of **upbreyde**]
un- *pref.* expressing (1) negation, (2) reversal, deprivation. [OE *un-*]
unable adj. unfit, weak G.CY 1131, LSt 10. [cf. OF *inhabile*]
unagreable adj. miserable Bo 1. m1. 20/29 (L *ingratas*). [from **agreable**]
unapt adj. unfitted or ? undisposed TC 1.978. [from L *aptus*]
unaraced *ppl. adj.* untorn, unobliterated Bo 4. p1. 35/48 *var* (L *inconuulsa*). [from **arace**]
unarmed *p.p.* relieved of armour F.Sq 173. [from **armen**]
unassayed *ppl. adj.* untried, not experienced Bo 2. p4. 69/94. [from **assaye(n**]
unavysed *ppl. adj.* without consideration, thoughtless H.Mcp 280, unpremeditated I.Pars 449, unaware TC 1.378. [from **avysed**]
unbinde(n v. **1.** untie, undo B.Mel 2973, Bo 1. p6. 75/106, 3. m2. 5/7, TC 3.1732; dissolve I.Pars 511; *p.p.* broken Bo 4. p6. 107/156. **2.** free, release I.Pars 1072, *p.p.* free E.Mch 1226, Bo 5. p4. 39/55, ~ *fro*/*of* I.Pars 277, PF 523, *p.p.* Bo 1. m5. 20/29, 5. p6. 209/293; *refl.* Bo 3. m12.2. **unbounde** *p.p.* B.Mel 2973, E.Mch 1226. [OE *unbindan*]
unbityde† v. fail to take place Bo 5. p4.

24/35, p6. 116/164, 117/166. [from **bitide(n**]

unbodie v. leave the body TC 5.1550. [from body]

unbrent ppl. adj. unburnt, unconsumed B.Pri 1658, **unbrende** pl. HF 173. [from **brenne(n**]

unbroyden ppl. adj. unbraided, loose TC 4.817. [from OE *brogden*, p.p. of *breġdan*; cf. **broided**]

unbuxumnesse n. disobedience BalCh 26. [from **buxumnesse**]

uncircumscript adj. boundless TC 5.1865. [from L *circumscrīptus*; cf. **circumscrive**]

unclose(n v. open LGW 65, 111, 117. [from **clo(o)s**]

unclothede pa. sg. divested (fig.) Bo 4. m7. 7/11. [from **clothe(n**]

uncommitted ppl. adj. not delegated (to the one who exercises it) PF 518. [from **committe**]

uncouple v. let loose (hounds); (absol., fig.) ~ *on* pursue, attack B.Mk 3692. [from *couplen* v., see **coupled**]

uncoupling vbl. n. unleashing BD 377.

uncouth adj. strange Bo 2. p1. 35/49, unfamiliar TC 2.151; marvellous 3.1797, wondrous HF 1279, 2010; striking, exotic A.Kn 2497, F.Sq 284; ~ *to* alien to Bo 2. p2. 35/49 (L *alienam*). [OE *uncūþ*]

uncouthly adv. strikingly RR 584. [from prec.]

uncovenable adj. unseemly I.Pars 431, 631; unfit, venal Bo 4. p6. 208/301. [from **covenable**]

uncurteisly adv. coarsely E.Mch 2363. [from **curteis**]

undefouled ppl. adj. undefiled Bo 2. p4. 17/22. [from **defoule(n**]

undepartable adj. inseparable, permanent Bo 4. p3. 39/56. [from OF *departable*]

under adv. below BD 426, TC 1.923, underneath 3.1571, HF 805. [OE]

under prep. under A.Prol 105, A.Rv 4061; below A.Kn 1981, HF 1919, LGW G. 234, 1471; close by (a wood) D.WB 990, D.Fri 1380; through D.Fri 1386, Bo 5. m5. 9/13; under cover of B.ML 360, 406, F.Sq 507, 509; because of TC 1.180; by means of Astr prol 19/26; in addition to H.Mcp 198; with, in the midst of Bo 2. p3. 36/52, 37/53, in accordance with B.ML 223, CompL 30/26; ~ *my gore* within my robe B.Th 1979; ~ *wede* in his dress 2107; ~ *hewe/colour* of on the pretext of C.Pard 421, D.WB 399, F.Sq 508, E.Mch 2063; ~ (*your*) *yerde* see **yerd(e**; ~ *signes* under the influence of . . signs Astr 1. 21. 43/60; *putte(n* ~ *hem* subdue to themselves Bo 1. m5. 33/47; ~ (*the*) *hevene* on earth G.SN 215, I.Pars 287. [OE]

undergrowe ppl. adj. of short stature A.Prol 156. [**under**+p.p. of **growe(n**]

undermeles n. pl. (early) afternoons D.WB 875. [OE *undernmǣl*; cf. next]

undern n. midmorning E.Cl 260, 981, B.NP 4412. [OE; the time designated varied at different periods]

underno(o)m pa. sg. perceived G.SN 243.

undernome p.p. reproved (with *of*) I.Pars 401. [OE *undernam/-*nōm, -numen*]

underpyghte pa. filled up B.ML 789. [**under**+**pighte**]

underput p.p. subjected Bo 1. p6. 67/87. [**under**+**putte(n**]

underspore† v. push underneath A.Mil 3465. [**under**+?**spore**]

understonde(n v. understand A.Kn 3016, C.Pard 646, E.Mch 1685, believe B.Sh 1358, BD 1261, TC 5.887; interpret Bo 4. p4. 64/88, 5. p4. 64/92; ~ *wel* grasp, recognize B.Mel 2527, E.Cl 344; ~ *in/of* interpret with reference to B.Mel 2275, 2660. **understandestow** pr. *2 sg.* (with suffixed pron.) Bo 4. p4. 103/145. **understondeth** imper. pl. G.CY 1165, I.Pars 541. **understood** pa. sg. TC 1.493, 5.1642. **understoden** pl. Bo 5. p1. 33/46, 61/88. **understonde(n** p.p. B.ML 520, Bo 2. p1. 6/7. [OE *understándan, -stód, -stódon, -stánden*]

undertake(n v. **1.** undertake I.Pars 691, 732, Bo 4. p2. 20/27, TC 2.807, LGW G. 71, 1452; *wys to* ~ wise in his enterprises A.Prol 405. **2.** declare, affirm A.Prol 288, D.WB 592; *I dar this fully* ~ I solemnly declare TC 3.338. **undertook** pa. sg. LGW 1452. **undertake** p.p. G. 71. [**under**+**take(n**]

undevocioun n. lack of zeal I.Pars 723. [from **devocioun**]

undigne adj. unworthy (*to* 'of') E.Cl 359, I.Pars 791. [from **digne**]

undiscomfited pp. adj. undisturbed Bo 1. m4. 3/5. [from **disconfite**]

undiscreet adj. undiscerning E.Cl 996. [from **discreet**]

undo(n v. **1.** undo TC 4.352, RR 1280; (absol.) open up (the door) A.Mil 3765. **2.** explain BD 899, RR 9. [OE]

undoutous adj. undoubting Bo 5. p1. 20/28. [from **doutous**]

uneschewably adv. inevitably Bo 5. p3. 86/120. [from next]

uneschuable adj. inevitable Bo 5. p1. 66/95. [from **eschewe(n**]

unespied ppl. adj. undetected TC 4.1457. [from **espye(n**]

unethe see **unnethe(s**.

unfamous adj. forgotten HF 1146. [from *famous* adj., from AN]

unfeyned ppl. adj. unfeigned, true G.SN 434. [from **feyne(n**]

unfestlich† adj. jaded, unfestive F.Sq 366. [from **fe(e)stlich**]

unfolde(n v. **1.** open (letter) TC 2.1702. **2.** expand Bo 4. p6. 53/77, 92/131; ~ *by* expanded into 85/122. **3.** explain Bo 4. p6. 244/334. **4.** deploy, perform Bo 4. m5. 5/7 (L *explicet*). [from **folde**]

unfoldinge vbl. n. expansion Bo 4. p6. 51/73. [from **folde**]

ungentel/ongentil adj. lowly (not of noble birth) Bo 2. p4. 59/80; vile, depraved Bo 3. m6. 9 *var*/13. [from **gentil**]

ungiltif adj. guiltless TC 3.1018. [from **giltif**, see **gilty**]

ungrobbed ppl. adj. not dug round FormA 14. [from *grobbe* v., cf. MDu *grobben*]

unhap n. misfortune, bad luck TC 1.552, 2.456, HF 89, Scog 29. [ON *úhapp*]

unhappy adj. unfortunate G.CY 1084, unlucky B.ML 306, ill-fated, wretched TC 4.1341. [from prec.]

unhappily adv. unluckily TC 1.666, 5.937. [from prec.]

unhardy adj. timid A.Rv 4210. [from **hardy**]

unhe(e)le n. misfortune C.Phs 116. [OE *unhǽlu*]
unholsom adj. corrupt TC 4.330. [from ho(o)lsom]
unhoped ppl. adj. unexpected Bo 4. p6. 162/236. [from hope(n)]
universal/-el adj. complete I.Pars 292; comprehensive Bo 5. p4. 113/162; pl. -s Bo 5. p4. 122/176. [OF]
universe n. in in ~ universally TC 3.36. [OF; = It in *universo*]
universel n. ? generalization Bo 5. p4. 137/197. [OF]
universitee n. totality, universal nature Bo 5. p4. 115/165. [OF]
unjoined p.p. separated Bo 5. p3. 147/211, split, undone m3. 1/2. [from joynen]
unkind(e adj. **1.** unnatural B.ML 88, C.Pard 903, PF 358, TC 3.1438 var. **2.** cruel I.Pars 970, TC 4.266, 1440, 1652, HF 284, LGW 857, 1261, 2716. [OE *uncýnde*]
unkindely adj. unnatural I.Pars 577. [OE *ungecyndelic̄*]
unkindely adv. unnaturally C.Pard 485, I.Pars 154, cruelly TC 1.617, HF 295. [OE *ungecyndelīce*]
unkindenesse n. cruelty, Anel 292, LGW 153; unnatural behaviour B.ML 1057. [from adj.]
unknitten v. untie Bo 5. p3. 22/29. [OE *uncnyttan*]
unknowe ppl. adj. unknown A.Prol 126, A.Kn 1406, F.Sq 246. [OE *un(ge)cnāwen*]
unknowing(e adj. ignorant Bo 4. p6. 154/224. [from knowe(n)]
unkonninge n. ignorance B.Mel 3066; lack of skill I.Pars 1082. [see next]
unkonning(e adj. unskilful TC 5.1139, RR 686; ignorant A.Kn 2393, Bo 1. p1. 43/60, p3. 35/48, 5. m3. 25/36. [from conning]
unkorven ppl. adj. unpruned FormA 14. [from corven, pp. of kerve(n)]
unlaced ppl. adj. disentangled Bo 3. p12. 118/157. [from lacen v., OF *lacier*]
unleveful adj. **1.** impermissible, unlawful I.Pars 593, 777. **2.** ? deceitful Bo 2. p1. 40/56 (L *falsae inlecebris felicitatis*). [from leveful, 2 perh. infl. by OE *ungelēafful* unbelieving]
unlyk adj. unlike B.NP 4094. adv. ~ that different(ly) from what TC 2.1656. [OE *ungelic̄* and OE *ŭlīkr*]
unlykly adj. unsuitable E.Mch 2180, unlikely CompL 95/89. [prec. and ON *ŭlı̄kligr*]
unlyklinesse n. unsuitableness I.C 1.10. [from prec.]
unloven v. cease to love TC 5.1698. [from loven, OE *lufian*]
unlust n. weariness, disinclination I.Pars 680. [OE]
unmanhod n. unmanly deed: don ~ behave in a cowardly way TC 1.824. [from manhod]
unmeke adj. proud Bo 4. m7. 27/38; haughty RR 590. [from me(e)k(e; cf. ON *ŭmjūkr*]
unmerie adj. gloomy HF 74. [OE *unmyrge*]
unmesurable adj. excessive, intemperate I.Pars 813, 818; enormous B.ML 934. [from mesurable]

unmete adj. unsuitable CompL 75/69; incompetent RR 752. inferior 990. [OE *unmǽte*]
unmighty adj. powerless Bo 1. m4. 12/16, 4. p2. 95/126, 186/256; unable, incapable (with infin.) TC 2.858. [OE *unmihtig*]
unmoevable adj. immovable, unalterable Bo 4. p6. 72/102, 109/157, 5. p6. 49/69. [from moevable]
unmoevabletee n. stability Bo 4. p6. 89/128. [from moevabletee]
unneste imper. sg. come forth, leave the nest TC 4.305. [from nest n., OE]
unnethe(s adv. with difficulty A.Mil 3121, D.WB 198, I.Pars 92, 623, BD 712, Bo 5. p6. 120/169, TC 2.4, 5.35, HF 900, LGW 959; scarcely B.ML 1050, Mars 128, TC 3.1034; wel ~ scarcely B.Mk 3611, E.Cl 892, TC 1.354, HF 2041; (with neg.) ~ .. noon scarcely any G.CY 1390, LGW G. 33, no man ~ I.Pars 910. [OE *unēape*]
unordred adj. not in holy orders, lay I.Pars 961. [from ordred]
unparfit adj. imperfect Bo 3. p9. 16/22 var. Cf. **imparfit**. [from parfit]
unparigal adj. unequal Bo 3. p1. 8/11. [from paregal]
unpitous/-pietous adj. afflicted, cruel Bo 1. m1. 20/28 (L *impia*). [from pitous]
unpleyte(n v. unfold, explain Bo 2. p8. 7/10; expand, move Bo 5. m4. 15/22. [from *pleyten* v., OF *pleit* n. fold]
unpreyed ppl. adj. unsolicited TC 4.513. [from preye(n)]
unprofitable adj. useless Bo 1. p1. 43/60, 45/63; valueless p3. 53/75. [from *profitable*, OF]
unpurveyed ppl. adj. unprovided for, neglected Bo 2. p1. 14/20. [from purveye(n)]
unraced ppl. adj. untorn, unaltered Bo 4. p1. 35/48 var (L *inconuulsa*). [from race v., form of arace]
unremeved ppl. adj. without being moved Astr 2.46. 23/33. [from remeve(n)]
unreprovable adj. without reproach LGW 691. [from *reprovable*, var. of reprevable]
unreste n. trouble, disturbance D.Fri 1495, E.Cl 719, Bo 4. p6. 123/178; sorrow, pain TC 4.879, 5.1567, 1604, LGW 1339; distress D.WB 1104. [from rest(e]
unresty adj. restless, unquiet TC 5.1355. [from prec.]
unright n. harm D.WB 1093; offence, dishonour TC 2.453, wrong 4.550. [OE *unriht*]
unright adv. wrongly TC 5.661. [OE *unrihte*]
unrightful adj. unjust Bo 1. p3. 21/28, unrightoous Bo 4. m4. 9/13, wicked, evil I.GW 1771. [OE *unrihtful*]
unsad adj. unstable, unreliable E.Cl 995. [OE *unsæd*]
unsavory adj. displeasing I.Pars 510, 723. [from savory]
unscience n. lack of knowledge Bo 5. p3. 72/101 (L *scientia non est*). [from science]
unsely adj. unhappy Bo 4. p4. 15/20, 37/51, 65/89, 81/112; unsuccessful A.Rv 4210; unfortunate TC 1.35. [OE *unsǽliḡ*]
unselinesse n. unhappiness Bo 4. p4. 39/54, 81/113, pl. types of unhappiness 23/32. [OE *unsǽliḡnesse*]
unset ppl. adj. unappointed, unexpected A.Kn 1524. [from sette(n)]

unshethe v. unsheathe, draw TC 4.776. [from v. from OE *scēap*]
unshette *pa. sg.* unlocked E.Mch 2047. **unshette** *ppl. adj.* unlocked HF 1953. [from **shette(n)**]
unshewed *ppl. adj.* unconfessed I.Pars 999. [from **shewe(n)**]
unsittinge *pr. p. adj.* unfitting TC 2.307. [from **sitte(n)**]
unskilful *adj.* foolish TC 1.790. [from **skilful**]
unskilfully *adv.* unreasonably Bo 1. p4. 144/199; inappropriately Bo 3. p6. 2. [from prec.]
unslekked *ppl. adj.* unslaked G.CY 806. [from *slekke* var. of *sleche*, OE *sleċċan*; cf. **slake**]
unsoft(e *adj.* rough E.Mch 1824; painful HF 36. [OE *unsōfte* adv.]
unsolempne *adj.* uncelebrated Bo 1. p3. 42/58 (L *incelebris*). [from **solempne**]
unsowen *pr. pl.* undo I.Pars 622. [from **sowe** v.[1]]
unspeedful *adj.* unfruitful, unsuccessful Bo 5. p6. 214/302. [from **spe(e)dful**]
unstaunchable *adj.* inexhaustible Bo 2. p7. 78/112 (L *inexhausta*). [from **staunchen**]
unstaunched *ppl. adj.* insatiable Bo 2. p6. 73/103. [as prec.]
unstedefastnesse *n.* frailty I.Pars 584. [from **sted(e)fastnesse**]
unstra(u)nge† *adj.* well-known Astr 2.17. *rubr.* [from **stra(u)nge**]
unsufferable *adj.* intolerable Bo 2. p1. 14/19, 3. p7. 3/5. [from OF *suffrable*]
unswelle decrease (in sorrow) TC 4.1146, 5.214. [from **swelle**]
unswete *adj.* bitter HF 72. [OE *unswēte*]
unteyd *ppl. adj.* free TC 2.752. [from OE *untigan*, A -*tēgan]
unthank *n.* injury, ill-luck A.Rv 4082; ill-will, hostility TC 5.699. [OE *unþanc*]
unthrift *n.* nonsense, foolishness TC 4.431. [from **thrift**]
unthrifty *adj.* profitless TC 4.1530. [from prec.]
unthriftily *adv.* poorly G.CY 893. [from prec.]
until *prep.* until B.ML 1070, BD 41; to A.Mil 3761, TC 1.354. [ON **und* up to + **til(l**]
untyme *n.* *in* ~ at the wrong times I.Pars 1051. [OE *untīma*]
unto *prep.* to A.Prol 71, C.Pard 482, (following obj.) G.CY 898; until A.Kn 2412, B.ML 765, B.Sh 1419, D.WB 507, Astr 1. 8. 6/8; for B.Mel 2771, C.Pard 522, TC 2.1193; *sayn* ~ (*this tale*) say about (this story) B.NP 4236; *deserve* .. ~ *yow* deserve from you G.CY 1352; ~ *the gardinward* towards the garden A.Mil 3572, cf. **toward.** *conj.* until PF 647. [*un-* as **until** + **to**]
untold *ppl. adj.* unconfessed I.Pars 1010; uncounted A.Mil 3780. [OE *untēald*, A -*tāld]
untressed *ppl. adj.* loose A.Kn 2289, unarranged E.Cl 379. [from **tresse** v.]
untretable *adj.* inexorable Bo 2. p8. 2. [from **tretable**]
untrew(e *adj.* unfaithful, faithless E.Mch 2203, F.Fkl 984, H.Mcp 188, Anel 274, LGW 1573; treacherous B.Mk 3218, E.Cl

995, E.Mch 1786; untrustworthy G.CY 1042; false TC 3.306. [OE *untrēowe*]
untrewe *adv.* falsely, untruthfully A.Prol 735. [from prec.]
untriste *adj.* distrustful TC 3.839. [from *trist* adj., rel. to ON *traustr* and **trust**]
untrouthe *n.* faithlessness, infidelity E.Mch 2241, TC 3.984, 5.1098, HF 384; treachery B.ML 687. [OE *untrēowþ*]
untrust *n.* distrust E.Mch 2206. [from **trust**]
unusage† *n.* want of use Bo 2. p7. 38/55. [from **usage**]
unwar *adj.* unaware TC 1.304; unexpected B.ML 427, B.Mk 3954, Bo 2. p2. 50/69; unforeseen Bo 5. p1. 54/77, 64/92. [OE *unwær*]
unwar *adv.* unexpectedly F.Fkl 1356, TC 1.549; heedlessly I.Pars 885. [from prec.]
unwarly *adv.* unexpectedly Bo 1. m1. 9/13. [from adj.]
unwe(e)lde *adj.* feeble A.Rv 3886, RR 359. [from OA *wélde*]
unwe(e)ldy *adj.* unwieldy H.Mcp 55. [from **weldy**]
unwemmed *ppl. adj.* spotless B.ML 924, ABC 91; untouched, sound Bo 5. p6. 207/291. [OE]
unwened *ppl. adj.* unexpected Bo 4. p6. 162/236. [from **wene(n)**]
unwist *ppl. adj.* **1.** unknown (with *of* 'to') A.Kn 2977, TC 2.1294, 3.603, LGW 1653; unsuspected TC 2.1509. **2.** unaware TC 1.93, 2.1400. [from **wist** *p.p.* of **wite(n)**]
unwit *n.* folly G.CY 1085, stupidity Mars 271. [from **wit**; cf. ON *úvit*]
unwiting *see* unwot.
unwitingly *adv.* unknowingly C.Pard 486. [from next]
unwot *pr. 3 sg.* fails to know Bo 5. p6. 112/159; **unwiting** *of* (*this*) *pr. p.* not knowing (this) F.Fkl 936, G.CY 1320. [from **wite(n)**]
unwrye v. uncover TC1.858. [from **wrye(n**[1]]
unyolden *ppl. adj.* not having surrendered A.Kn 2642, 2724. [from *p.p.* of **yelde(n)**]
up *adv.* **1.** up A.Prol 783, A.Kn 2273, B.ML 487; upwards D.Sum 1938; out of bed LGW 47; open A.Mil 3801, TC 2.615; ~ *and doun* everywhere A.Kn 2054, see **doun**; *now* ~ *now doun* upwards and downwards A.Kn 1533, in all directions LGW 2420; ~ *-so-doun* topsy-turvy I.Pars 495, Bo 5. p.3. 60/84; *turne(n* ~ *-so-doun* turn upside down, to the opposite A.Kn 1377, G.CY 625, LSt 5, overthrow I.Pars 260, 263. **2.** forming phrs. with verbs: *armed* ~ completely armed A.Kn 1852; *drinken* ~ TC 3.1035; *y)fostred* ~ brought up, reared B.ML 275, E.Cl 213; *knytte* ~ put together I.Pars 28; *maken* ~ set up A.Kn 1884; *pekke* ~ B.NP 4157; *plukke* ~ G.CY 937; *trussed* ~ A.Prol 681; *yeven* ~ yield, surrender A.Kn 2427 var, B.Pri 1862, E.Mch 2312. **3.** (with v. understood) mounts TC 1.1073; as *imper.* lift up HF 1021. [OE]
up *prep.* upon Astr 2. 1. 2, ~ *peyne of* on pain of A.Kn 1707, 2543, ~ *peril of* on pain of (losing) B.NP 4134, D.Sum 2271; ~ *poynt to* on the point of TC 4.1153 var. [from prec.]
upbounde *p.p.* arranged TC 3.517 var. [**up** + **binde**]

upbreyde v. reproach TC 5.1710; subj. sg. Anel 118. pa. LGW 1671 var. [OE up-breġdan, -bræġd]
upcaste pa. sg. threw ashore B.ML 906 var.
upcasteth imper. pl. turn upwards TC 5.1838 var. [up+caste(n)
updrow pa. sg. raised LGW 1459 var. [up+drawe(n)
upenbossed p.p. adj. embossed LGW 1200 var. [up+enbossed]
uphaf pa. sg. lifted up A.Kn 2428. [cf. OE uphóf, see heve(n)
uphepinge vbl. n. accumulation Bo 2. p3. 31/45. [up+hepe(n)
upon prep. **1.** (of place) on TC 2.918, in A.Mil 3359, 3440, D.WB 991; at B.Sh 1314, Bo 4. p1. 17/23; to (following.obj.) LGW 1946; **2.** (of time) ~ a day (etc.) one day A.Kn 1414, B.ML 594, LGW 631, in one day A.Prol 703; after I.Pars 126, TC 3.549. **3.** (of various relations) against A.Kn 2629, BD 1023; about HF 972, TC 5.735, in respect of TC 4.993; in addition to Bo 3. p10. 98/132; on pain of (losing) A.Kn 1344, D.WB 1016; by means of, with I.Pars 267; (in asseverations) by (my trouthe, etc.) A.Kn 1855, A.Mil 3502, B.Mk 3125. ~ cas by chance A.Mil 3661; ~ a fire on fire TC 4.126; ~ lyve alive TC 2.1030; ~ lond in the country A.Prol 702; ~the viritoot ? aotir A.Mil 3770; crye ~ beseech A.Rv 4006; enamoured ~ in love with LGW 1610; wayte ~ wait for HF 342; wardeyns ~ protection for D.WB 1216. [up+on]
upon adv. on; wered ~ wore D.WB 559, hadde ~ had on A.Prol 617, D.Fri 1382. [from prec.]
uppe adv. in an open position F.Sq 615.
upper comp. higher HF 884, 961, Astr 2.12.13/18. [OE up, uppe]
uppcreste adj. sup. top one, uppermost Bo 1. p1. 26/36 var. [formed on adj. upper, from prec.; cf. MDu upperst]
up-plight see plighte.
upreysed p.p. raised LGW 1163 var. [up+reyse(n)
upright adj. perpendicular Bo 5. m5. 12/18, Astr 2 38. 5/8, straight A.Mil 3264, RR 1702. [OE upriht]
upright(e adv. **1.** perpendicularly A.Kn 1387, Astr 2. 28. 23/33, 38. 7/10. **2.** upwards D.Sum 2266; on (one's) back A.Rv 4194, B.Pri 1801; gaping ~ with open mouth, face upwards A.Kn 2008, A.Mil 3444 var, B.NP 4232, C.Pard 674. [OE uprihte]
upryseth pr. 3 sg. rises B.Sh 1241, LGW 49; **uprist** Mars 4, TC 4.1443, LGW 1188 [up+rise(n)
upriste n. (prep.) rising (of sun) A.Kn 1051. [up+-rist rising, as in OE ærist]
upspringe v. rise Mars 14. **upsprong** pa. sg. grew up FormA 10. [up+springe(n)
upsterte/-stirte pa. leapt up A.Kn 1080, D.WB 794; arose TC 4.183; (fig.) A.Kn 1299 [all treated as two words by most edd. except Skeat]. [up+sterte(n)
uptaken p.p. lifted B.Pri 1812 var. [up+take(n)
upyaf pa. sg. yielded, exuded A.Kn 2427 var. [up+yeve(n)
upyolden p.p. given up A.Kn 3052 var. [up+yelde(n)

us pron. **1.** acc. us passim; men in general ABC 95; (refl. with v.) ourselves A.Prol 721, B.Mel 3011, E.Mch 1841, TC 5.402; see self. **2.** dat. to us A.Prol 747, TC 2.96; for us A.Rv 4132, B.Pri 1669; (in impers. constr.) A.Prol 750, 785, C.Pard 512, 801, D.Fri 1275, TC 2.783. [OE ūs]
usage n. **1.** custom D.Sum 2278, TC 1.150; habit RR 293, habits I.Pars 139, of old ~ from long habit B.Sh 1564; of ~ of habit, habitual C.Pard 899, I.Pars 448; of verray ~ from pure habit I.Pars 601; (as) [is] ~ (as) [is] the custom B.ML 998, D.WB 589, E.Mch 1706, LGW 2617; hadde . . in ~ had the habit B.Pri 1696. **2.** practice I.Pars 690, Bo 2. p5. 16/22, 4. p6. 186/270; craft, skill A.Prol 110; use, experience Bo 4. p6. 213/309; long experience A.Kn 2448; to his ~ for his enjoyment LGW 2337; customary speech Bo 4. p7. 22/32 (L usu). [OF]
usance n. custom PF 674, LGW 586, 1476, RR 683; opinioun of ~s usual opinion Bo 3. p4. 64/93. [OF]
usaunt adj. accustomed A.Rv 3940, ~ to addicted to I.Pars 821. [AN]
use(n v. **1.** use, employ D.WB 137, 149, Bo 1. m5. 33/46, 2. p1. 12/16, TC 2.1038; practise G.CY 729; spend B.Mel 2743, 2764, 2788, 2838; enjoy A.Kn 2385, I.Pars 375, Bo 3. p4. 3/4, 41/60, m7. 2; obey B.ML 44; follow Bo 1. m2. 8/12; p.p. trodden BD 401; familiar Bo 1. m5. 10/14, 3. p12. 36/47; worn D.WB 562. **2.** accustom I.Pars 245, p.p. accustomed G.CY 666; **3.** be accustomed, used (with infin.) BD 1013, TC 3.1023, 4.182, 681, LGW 364, 787; pr.p. in the habit D.WB 777. [OF user]
usinge vbl. n. practising I.Pars 465.
usure n. usury B.Pri 1681, D.Fri 1309, RR 185. [ML ūsūria]
usurpe pr. 1 sg. claim falsely Astr prol 42/59. [OF usurper]
usward see fro, toward.
utt(e)rest/outtreste adj. sup. **1.** utmost Bo 4. p3. 50/72, 52/73; supreme E.Cl 787. **2.** outmost, furthest Bo 1. p1. 60/83, 3. p12. 142/191, 4. p6. 85/121, ? remote Bo 3. p10. 21/29 (L extrema); first Bo 2. m6. 11/15. [OE ūttra comp. from ūt]
utterly/outerly/outrely, -liche adv. utterly A.Kn 1563, B.NP 4419, Bo 2. p2. 19/26; completely B.Mel 2943, D.WB 664, E.Cl 639, I.Pars 234, TC 1.382; entirely C.Pard 849, TC 3.1486, 4.955, LGW 626; fully I.Pars 390; extremely E.Cl 335; finally BD 1244; absolutely A.Prol 237, Bo 5. p4. 13/19; plainly, directly A.Kn 1164, D.Mel 2210, Bo 4. p7. 3/4; with the utmost force E.Cl 768. [see prec.; out- forms after OF outrement]

V

vacacioun n. leisure, spare time D.WB 683. [OF]
vache n. cow Truth 22 var. [OF]
valance n.[1] fine cloth PF 272. [F Valence]
valance n.[2] sign of the zodiac opposite to a planet's mansion (= L detrimentum) Mars 145. [OF faillance]

vane n. weather-vane E.Cl 996; **fan** quintain H.Mcp 42. [OE *fana*]
vanishe v. vanish D.WB 996, G.SN 216; waste away C.Pard 732. [OF *evaniss*-, stem of *evanir*]
vanisshinge vbl. n. made a ~ disappeared A.Kn 2360.
vanitee n. folly A.Mil 3835, D.Sum 2208, frivolity E.Cl 250, TC 4.729; idle tale 703; triviality, worthlessness Bo 2. p7. 86/122 (L *leuitate*); pl. vain things B.NP 4281, I.Pars 1085. [OF]
variaunce n. variation E.Cl 710, I.Pars 427; infidelity, fickleness TC 5.1670; mutability Fort 45. [OF]
variaunt adj. slippery, treacherous G.CY 1175; pl. **-s** changing Bo 1. m5. 15/21. [OF]
varie(n v. vary B.Mel 2144; be changed TC 2.1621; of *trouthe* ~ deviate from truth HF 807; alternate Bo 2. m8. 1; pr. 3 sg. is variation Astr 2. 15. 5/6. **varyinge** pr. p. unstable BD 802. [OF *varier*]
vasselage n. prowess A.Kn 3054, (iron.) LGW 1667. [OF]
vavasour n. sub-vassal, landholder (immed. below baron) A.Prol 360. [OF]
veyn adj. false A.Kn 1094, Bo 3. p10. 8/11; fruitless I.Pars 876, empty Bo 3. p6. 25/33; ~e *glorie* empty pride A.Kn 2240, C.Pard 411, I.Pars 391, Bo 2. p7. 88/121 (L *superbam gloriam*); worthless G.SN 497, Bo 5. p5. 37/54, TC 3.817; pretentious Bo 4. m2. 1; imperfect, feeble Bo 3. p10. 24/32; *in* ~ fruitlessly, in vain B.NP 3989, H.Mcp 150, TC 4.314, 5.1373, worthless G.SN 285; *take in* ~ wrongly swear by I.Pars 588. [OF]
veyne n. vein A.Kn 2747; (of plants) A.Prol 3; *every* ~ (fig.) every part PF 425, every corner TC 4.943, 5.417. [OF]
venerian adj. devoted to Venus D.WB 609. [L *venerius*]
venerye n. hunting A.Kn 2308, A.Prol 166 (pun on homonym = sexual activity unlikely, because that word unrecorded until much later). [OF]
vengeaunce n. revenge B.Mel 2626, 2632, D.Sum 2004, retribution B.ML 923; punishment A.Kn 2066, 3506, ABC 176; *do(n* ~ take revenge B.Mel 2199, 2218, punish A.Kn 2461; *take* ~ *of* (= on) B.Mel 2632. [OF]
venge(n v. **1.** refl. revenge oneself B.Mel 2471, 2542, TC 5.1468 var. **2.** avenge (crime, etc.) B.Mel 2561, 2648, 2659, (person) 2649. [OF *vengier*]
venim n. **1.** venom, poison A.Kn 2754, B.Mk 3321; (fig.) B.ML 891, C.Pard 421, E.Mch 2061, LGW 2593; pl. B.NP 4345 var; pains, torments Bo 4. m2. 7/10. **2.** dye Bo 2. m5. 8/11. [OF]
venimous adj. poisonous B.Mk 3295, B.NP 4345 var, I.Pars 576; (fig.) corrupt, evil B.Mk 3767, Bo 2. m6. 22/31. [OF]
venquisshe(n v. vanquish, overcome B.ML 291, F.Fkl 774, B.Mel 2529, ? surpass B.Mel 2280, 2284. [OF *venquis*, pa. of *veintre*]
ventusinge vbl. n. cupping A.Kn 2747. [from OF *ventouser*]
ver n. spring TC 1.157. [OF]
verdegrees n. a greenish pigment G.CY 790. [OF *vert de Grece*]

verdit/voirdit n. verdict A.Prol 787, PF 503. [AN]
verye n. (word used in charm) ? evil spirit A.Mil 3485. [? corruption of OE *we(a)rg felon*]
verifie v. show to be true, substantiate G.CY 1068. [OF *verifier*]
vermyne n. pests, rats C.Pard 858, E.Cl 1095, insects, vermin TC 3.381. [OF]
vernage n. an Italian wine B.Sh 1261, E.Mch 1807. [OF]
vernisshed p.p. made shine A.Rv 4149. [OF *verniss(i)er*]
verray adj. **1.** true, genuine A.Prol 72, 338 var, 422, A.Kn 1551, B.ML 167, C.Pard 576, Bo 3. p3. 4/5, p9. 132/177, TC 3.825; due, just RR 1627. **2.** loyal, faithful A.Mil 3609, E.Cl 343, TC 3.141, 4.302 var, LGW 1686, Bo 2. p8. 33/48. **3.** pure, sheer A.Kn 1748, D.WB 488, F.Fkl 860, 1027, TC 4.357; *by* ~ *force* by main force B.Mk 3237. **4.** simple, exact (of truth) A.Rv 3924, B.Mel 2393, F.Sq 166; truthful, *in* ~ *and sooth* Bo 4. p2. 187/258, *sothfast or* ~ Bo 5. m3. 4/5-6. **5.** real, veritable B.NP 4081, 4600, D.WB 253, TC 1.202, LGW G. 259; (as intensive, equiv. to 'even') B.NP 4575. **6.** exact Astr 1. 18. 13/16, due 1. 17. 14/18. **7.** as adv., truly I.Pars 87, 292, HF 1079. [AN *verrai*]
verraily adv. truly A.Prol 338 var, B.Mk 3774, E.Mch 1311; exactly Astr 2.5.19/27, 26. 19/28. [from prec.]
verrayment adv. truly B.Th 1903. [AN]
verre n. glass TC 2.867. [OF]
vers n. verse B.Pri 1712, line HF 1098. pl. unchanged verses B.Mel 2297, PF 124, Bo 1. m1. 1/2, TC 1.7. [OF]
versified p.p. put into verse B.Mk 3168. [from OF *versifier*]
versifiour n. writer of verse, poet B.Mel 2783. [OF]
vertu(e n. **1.** power A.Kn 2249, HF 526, 550, RR 1087; (vitalizing) power A.Prol 4, (divine) power B.Pri 1661, HF 1101, TC 3. 1766; magic power F.Sq 146, 157, RR 1644; physical strength RR 1208, ? B.Mel 2846, ? talents A.Kn 1436; ~ *naturel* inherent power, ability I.Pars 453; *in/by* ~ *of* through the power of B.Pri 1836, D.WB 616, I.Pars 340, 917, Bo 4. p6. 68/97, *through the* ~ *of* because of the value of TC 3.1288. **2.** (moral) excellence A.Prol 307, B.ML 363, 1156, I.Pars 544, Bo 4. p7. 62/87 (L *uirtus*), TC 2. 844; (a) virtue F.Fkl 773, H.Mcp 332, I.Pars 197, 311, TC 3.294; ethics F.Fkl 689; (mental or physical) excellence PF 376, TC 1.429, 438, LGW 54, (an) excellence Pity 50, TC 1. 1085; *make(n* ~ *of necessitee* make the best of what must be F.Sq 593, TC 4.1586; ~ *plese* satisfy (the requirements of) virtue E.Cl 216. [OF]
vertulees adj. without power TC 2.344. [from prec.]
vertuous adj. virtuous TC 1.898; effective A.Prol 251; powerful RR 1096. [OF]
vese/veze n. rush, blast A.Kn 1985. [from v. from OE *fēsian*]
vessel n. vessel TC 5.311; coll. plate B.Mk 3338, 3494, I.Pars 446. [AN]
viage n. **1.** journey A.Prol 723, 792, B.NP

4274, travelling A.Prol 77. **2.** enterprise B.ML 259, B.Sh 1561, TC 2.1061, 3.732; *doo(n* ~ undertake business TC 2.75. [OF *veage*]

vicaire *n.* deputy PF 379, regent ABC 140; ~ general principal agent C.Phs 20; vicar D.Sum 2008. [OF]

vicary *n.* vicar (orig. deputy to a rector) I.Pars 22. [L *vicārius*]

vice *n.* vice B.Mk 3713, TC 1.252; fault D.Fri 1578, TC 1.987; defect D.WB 955, F.Sq 101. [OF]

victor *adj.* victor's PF 182. [OF n.]

victorie *n.* victory A.Kn 2433, B.Mel 2378, TC 5.586; triumph A.Kn 872, B.ML 967. [AN]

vigile *n.* wake TC 5.305. [OF]

vigilyes *n. pl.* evening services A.Prol 377, D.WB 556. [L *vigilia*]

vileinye *n.* **1.** shame, dishonour A.Kn 2729, E.Mch 2310, TC 1.1033; *do(o)n* .. ~ bring disgrace E.Mch 1791, 2261, Bo 3. p4. 12/17, rape F.Fkl 1404, LGW 1823, act dishonourably D.WB 1151; *lucre of* ~ shameful lucre B.Pri 1681, *him to* ~ to his dishonour H.Mcp 260. **2.** injury B.NP 4477, *do(o)n* .. ~ do an injury A.Rv 4191, B.Mel 2547, 2595. **3.** evil, vice I.Pars 852, HF 96; lust, lechery G.SN 156, 231, I.Pars 857, 880, 940; *do(o)n* ~ commit sin D.WB 962, 1138. **4.** boorishness A.Prol 726, 740; ignoble condition I.Pars 143. **5.** discourteous, offensive words A.Prol 70, C.Pard 740, D.WB 34, 53, E.Mch 2303; *doon him .. a* ~ speak the shameful truth about him LGW 2333; *with* ~ with blasphemous words C.Pard 898. **6.** (person.) ? Hostility RR 166, 169, 977. [OF]

vileins *adj.* evil D.WB 1158, I.Pars 631, 652, 715, LGW 1824 *var*; depraved H.Mcp 183; discourteous D.Fri 1268; lecherous I.Pars 854. [OF]

vileinsly *adv.* shamefully I.Pars 154, RR 1498, cruelly I.Pars 279. [from prec.]

vinolent *adj.* full of wine D.WB 467, D.Sum 1931. [L *vinolentus*]

violes *n. pl.* phials G.CY 793. [OF *fiole*]

virelayes *n. pl.* lyrics (in stanzas linked by rhyme) F.Fkl 948, LGW 423. [OF]

viritoot† *n.* in *upon the* ~ astir A.Mil 3770. [? cf. OF *virer* turn]

viritrate† *n* (term of abuse) hag, crone D.Fri 1582. [cf. *trot* n. hag; first element perh. as prec.]

visage *n.* **1.** face A.Prol 109, TC 4.862; demeanour I.Pars 430; *in* ~ in appearance E.Cl 711. **2.** (fig.) *with two* ~s with two meanings TC 5 899; intent, concern 1838. [OF]

visage *v.* put a bold face on E.Mch 2273. [from prec.]

visitaciouns *n. pl.* visits D.WB 555. [AN]

vitaile(n *v.* provide with victuals A.Mil 3627, B.ML 869, LGW 1093. [OF *vitailler*]

vitaille *n.* victuals, provisions A.Prol 248, B.ML 443, E.Cl 59. [OF]

vitaillers *n. pl.* victuallers A.Co 4366. [OF]

vitremyte† *n.* ? woman's light head-dress B.Mk 3562. [?]

void *adj.* destitute Bo 2. p5. 127/180; empty, free TC 2.173, LGW 167; (astrol.) solitary Mars 114. [OF]

voydé *n.* spiced wine, nightcap TC 3.674. [AN]

voide(n *v.* **1.** expel A.Kn 2751, drive out E.Cl 910, remove F.Sq 188, F.Fkl 1150, 1159, ? 1195. **voydeth** *imper. pl.* dismiss G.CY 1136 *var*. **2.** empty (house) E.Mch 1815, LGW 2625. **3.** leave E.Cl 806, Bo 1. p4. 90/124. **4.** *intr.* depart TC 2.912, 3.232. **5.** frustrate, invalidate Bo 5. p6. 173/244. [OF *voider*]

voirdit *see* **verdit.**

vois *n.* **1.** voice A.Prol 688, TC 1.111; sound, name Bo 5. p1. 26/37, 28/39; *with o* ~ together, unanimously TC 2.955, G.SN 420, LGW 296; (fig.) inspiration TC 3.45. **2.** report B.ML 155, 169; (favourable) opinion, praise E.Mch 1592, TC 3.1723; judgement TC 4.195; plea PF 545. [OF]

volage *adj.* wanton H.Mcp 239; foolish RR 1284. [OF]

volatyl *n.* birds, fowl B.Sh 1262. [OF]

voltor *n.* vulture Bo 3. m12. 29/41. **volturis** *pl.* TC 1.788. [AN *vultur*, OF *voltour*]

volupeer *n.* nightcap A.Mil 3241, A.Rv 4303. [AN *volupier*]

vouche-sauf (or as two words) *v.* **1.** agree, grant (with cl. or infin.) A.Prol 807, 812, G.CY 1246; condescend ABC 27, F.Fkl 1071, TC 5.1341. **2.** *intr.* agree B.Pri 1641, E.Cl 306, F.Fkl 1334, I.Pars 52, TC 5.922; allow Astr prol 78/107; be content TC 2.1183. **3.** confer, bestow Anel 254. **vouche-sauf** *subj. sg.* E.Cl 306, F.Fkl 1071. **voucheth sauf** *imper. pl.* E.Cl 885, F.Fkl 1043. [OF *voucher*+**sauf**]

vulgar *adj.* in *day* ~ (astrol.) natural (as opposed to artificial) day Astr 2.9. rubr. [L *vulgaris*]

vulgarly *adv.* ? in a practical way TC 4.1513. [from prec.]

W

waast *n.* waist B.Th 1890. [? OE *wæst* rel. to **wexe(n**]

waat *see* **wite(n.**

wacche *n.* sentinel B.Mel 2216. [OE *wæćće*]

wachet *n.* light-blue colour A.Mil 3321, *var* **waget.** [OF]

wade(n *v.* **1.** *tr.* pass, cross D.Sum 2084. **2.** *intr.* go, reach B.Mk 3684; ~ *in* pass into TC 2.150, ~ *out of* move on from E.Mch 1684. [OE *wadan*]

wafereres *n. pl.* cake sellers C.Pard 479. [AN *wafrer*]

wafres *n. pl.* wafers, cakes A.Mil 3379. [AN]

wagges *pr. 3 sg.* (nth.) shakes A.Rv 4039. [formed on OE *wagian*]

wagging *vbl. n.* waving, movement TC 2.1745.

way *see* **wey.**

wayk *adj.* weak B.ML 932, Anel 341, diminished Bo 1. p6. 76/99. **weyker** *comp.* B.Mel 2673. [ON *veikr*]

wayken *v.* lessen TC 4.1144. [from prec.]

wail(l)e(n *v.* *intr.* wail, lament A.Kn 931, F.Fkl 1116, TC 5.211 *var.* *tr.* bewail I.Pars 178, TC 1.755 *var.* [ON *veila*]

waymente(n *v.* lament I.Pars 230. [OF *waimenter*]

waymenting(e vbl. n. lamenting A.Kn 902, I.Pars 85, lamentation RR 510.

wayn n. cart, carriage Bo 4. m1. 22/32, m5. 4/6. [OE wæġ(e)n]

wayte(n v. **1.** tr. observe F.Sq 129, Astr 2.23.4/5; (with obj. cl.) watch TC 1.190, notice Astr 2.27.2/3, 34.6/8. imper. in ~ what whatever D.WB 517, cf. lo(o)ke(n. **2.** intr. watch A.Mil 3295, F.Sq 88, Astr 2.38.8/12; take care A.Prol 571. **3.** tr. await A.Mil 3302, B.NP 4413, F.Sq 444; watch for F.Fkl 1263; (with obj. cl. or infin.) watch one's opportunity A.Kn 1222, B.Mk 3331, watch B.ML 593, lie in wait B.ML 582; watch to see E.Cl 708; expect B.ML 246, I.Pars 403, TC 3.491, ~ when E.Mch 2096. **4.** intr. wait A.Kn 929; ~ after wait for, expect B.ML 467, E.Mch 1303, desire A.Prol 525; ~ (up)on wait for A.Mil 3642, HF 342, watch for D.Fri 1376, set hope on TC 3.534. **5.** attend LGW 1269, ~ on TC 5.24. [ONF wait(i)er]

waiting vbl. n. watching H.Mcp 252.

wake(n v. **1.** tr. waken (person) B.Sh 1187, TC 3.764, Scog 38. `2.` intr. remain awake A.Mil 3672, E.Mch 1856, TC 3.341, 1560; keep watch or vigil D.Sum 1847, F.Fkl 819, I.Pars 1048, BD 977, Anel 293, TC 1.921; ~ or wynke wake or sleep PF 7 var, 482. **3.** wake up A.Kn 1393, B.ML 806, E.Mch 2397, LGW 1787. **waketh** imper. pl. D.Fri 1654, I.Pars 1048. **wo(o)k** pa. sg. A.Kn 1393, LGW 1787. **wakned** p.p. B.NP 4199; **waked** BD 294, 977. [OE wæcnan, wōc; wacian, wacode]

wake-pleyes n. pl. funeral games A.Kn 2960. [OE *wacu+plega]

waker adj. vigilant PF 358. [OE wacor]

waking vbl. n. period of wakefulness B.ML 22; keeping vigil I.Pars 1048; pl. vigils I.Pars 257, 1038.

wakinge ppl. adj. watchful Bo 4. m7. 24/34. [from v.]

walk n. walking A.Kn 1069, B.ML 559, TC 1.190. [from next]

walke(n v. **1.** walk, go A.Kn 1052, B.Sh 1280; roam A.Kn 2309, B.Pri 1752, D.WB 873. **walketh** imper. pl. in goth ~ forth go out G.CY 1207. **walked** p.p. in was go ~ had walked, gone D.Sum 1778, BD 387. **2.** exist, live C.Pard 530; dwell A.Kn 1283. **welk** pa. sg. PF 297, TC 2.517, 5.1235; **walked** sg. and pl. A.Mil 3458, D.WB 564. [OE wealcan roll, wēolc]

walsh-note n. walnut HF 1281. [MDu walsch-not]

walwe v. **1.** wallow, roll A.Rv 4278, D.WB 1085, writhe TC 1.699, 5.211 var, LGW 1166, ~and winde twist and turn D.WB 1102. **walwed** p.p. steeped (in) Rosem 17, 18. **2.** surge A.Mil 3616, disturb Bo 1. m7. 3, ~ up surge up Bo 2. p6. 6/9. [OE wealwian]

wan adj. **1.** pale, sickly, in pale and ~ A.Mil 3828, TC 2.551, 4.235; unhealthy G.CY 728. **2.** dark A.Kn 2456. [OE wann dark, gloomy]

wan see **winne(n.**

wandring n. wandering, erring A.Prol 467. [from OE wandrian]

wanges n. pl. (nth.) molars A.Rv 4030. [OE wáng cheek]

wang-tooth n. molar B.Mk 3234. [OE wáng-tōþ]

wane/wanie v. wane, decrease A.Kn 2078, E.Cl 998, HF 2115. [OE wanian]

wanhope n. despair A.Kn 1249, I.Pars 693, 731. [OE wan- privative pref.+**hope**]

wante(n v. **1.** lack, be without B.Mel 2216, Bo 2. p5. 32/45, 5. p6. 112/159, TC 4. 1568; do not know PF 287; be free from Bo 5. p3. 80/113. **2.** be lacking B.Mel 2238, I.Pars 514, Pity 76; (with dat. pron.) him wanted he lacked B.Mel 2236. [ON vanta]

wanting vbl. n. lack, absence G.SN 100; for ~ of because she could not have A.Kn 2665.

wantoun adj. jovial A.Prol 208; amorous E.Mch 1846; unchaste E.Cl 236. [OE wan- privative pref.+togen p.p. of tēon]

wantounly adv. amorously B.Sh 1571. [from prec.]

wantownesse n. lasciviousness B.ML 31; for his ~ ? out of caprice, affectation A.Prol 264. [from adj.]

wantrust n. distrust H.Mcp 281, TC 1.794. [OE wan- privative pref.+**trust**]

war adj. **1.** prudent A.Prol 309, B.Sh 1555, cautious Bo 2. m4. 1, knowing, informed A.Mil 3604. **2.** be(n ~ be aware A.Prol 157, A.Kn 896, TC 2.275, 3.1702, 5.533, HF 496, 1407; be(n ~ of be aware of, notice B.Mel 2579, BD 445, 515. **3.** be(n ~ beware A.Kn 1218, B.Mk 3923, often imper. be/beth ~ B.Mk 3330, C.Phs 97, 278, D.WB 906, D.Sum 2074; be(n ~ by beware by the example of D.WB 180, F.Sq 490, TC 1.203, 635, ~ from D.Sum 1993, I.Pars 628. [OE wær]

waraunt n. in drawe to ~ cite in support RR 6. [ONF warant]

waraunte v. warrant, avow A.Mil 3791, RR 930; **warente** protect C.Pard 338. [ONF warantir]

warde n. (prep.) guardianship: in our ~ in our keeping C.Phs 201, under my ~ in my charge I.Pars 880; on ~ (give) into his charge BD 248. [OE weard]

wardecors n. bodyguard D.WB 359. [AN]

wardein n. master A.Rv 3999, 4006, &c.; guardian TC 3.665, 5.1177; pl. D.WB 1216, LGW 753. [ONF]

warderere† interj. look out behind A.Rv 4101. [AN *ware derere]

wardrobe n. privy B.Pri 1762. [ONF warderobe]

war(e imper. sg. and pl. beware of D.Sum 1903; ~ fro 1994; take care that B.NP 4146. refl. beware B.Th 1889, I.Pars 797, 1053; ~ fro beware of C.Pard 905. [OE warian]

ware n. wares, goods B.ML 140, B.Sh 1246, D.WB 522, FormA 22. [OE waru]

warente see **waraunte.**

wariangles n. pl. shrikes, butcher-birds D.Fri 1408. [? OE *weargincel]

warie(n v. curse B.ML 372, TC 2.1619, 5.1378. [OA wærgan]

warisoun n. requital RR 1537. [ONF]

warisshe(n v. **1.** tr. cure B.Mel 2207, 2467, F.Fkl 856, 1138, BD 1104; save C.Pard 906; treat I.Pars 998. **2.** intr. recover B.Mel 2172. [ONF wariss-, stem of warir]

warisshinge vbl. n. curing, healing B.Mel 2205.

warly *adv.* cautiously, prudently TC 3.454. [OE *wærlīce*]

warne(n *v.*[1] **1.** warn A.Mil 3583, B.ML 16; forewarn B.NP 4422, HF 46, 51; *hit is ~d me* I am forewarned LGW 2658. **2.** inform E.Cl 1073, G.CY 590, PF 45, HF 893, 1068; advise E.Mch 1383, 1415. **3.** invite B.Mel 2652. [OE *war(e)nian*]

warne(n *v.*[2] *see* **werne(n.**

warnestore(n *v.* defend, fortify B.Mel 2487, 2521, Bo 1. p3. 55/77. [from ONF *warnesture* n.]

warnestoring(e *n.* fortifying B.Mel 2535, fortification 2525. [from prec.]

warning(e *vbl. n.* information G.CY 593; *at my ~* when I tell you TC 3.195.

warping/werpyng *n. for ~ to* prevent bending Astr 2.38.1. [from OE *weorpan*]

wasshe(n *v.* wash B.ML 356, TC 4.646. **wes(s)h** *pa. sg.* A.Kn 2283, B.ML 453. **wesshen** *pl.* TC 2.1184. **wasshe(n** *p.p.* A.Mil 3311, C.Pard 353, steeped Bo 4. m6. 8/12. [OE *wæscan*, **wēosc, -wæscen*]

wast *n.* waste, extravagance B.Sh 1609, C.Pard 593, D.WB 500, I.Pars 813. [ONF]

waste *adj.* ruined A.Kn 1331. [ONF *wast(e)*]

wastel-breed *n.* cake-bread A.Prol 147. [ONF + **breed**]

waste(n *v.* **1.** *tr.* waste, spend extravagantly B.Mel 2796, E.Mch 1343; *~ of* A.Co 4416; lose G.CY 1422; idle away PF 283; destroy A.Kn 3020, I.Pars 848; consume TC 2.393. **2.** *intr.* decay A.Kn 3023; pass (of time) LGW 2678; decrease, pass away B.ML 20, *~ . . awey* D.Sum 2235; diminish TC 2.348. [ONF *waster*]

wasting(e *vbl. n.* waste, spoiling B.Mel 2582.

wat *see* **wite(n.**

watering *n.* watering place A.Prol 826. [from v., OE *wæterian*]

wawe *n.* wave B.ML 508, TC 2.1, LGW 865. [? OE **wagu*]

waxe(n *see* **wexe(n.**

we *pron.* (authorial) I.Pars 619, 639, B.Mk 3487, TC 3.219, LGW 17; men (in general) A.Kn 3022, 3027, E.Cl 118, G.CY 957, 960, LGW 2580. [OE]

webbe *n.* weaver A.Prol 362. [OE *webba*]

wedde *n.* in *to ~* as a pledge A.Kn 1218, B.Sh 1613. [OE *wedd*]

wedde(n **1.** *tr.* marry, espouse A.Mil 3228, D.WB 166. **2.** give (daughter) in marriage TC 5.863. **3.** (absol.) marry, get married A.Mil 3229, D.WB 50; *refl.* D.WB 85, E.Cl 151. [OE *weddian*]

weder *n.* weather D.Sum 2253; bad weather TC 2.2, 3.676, *pl.* storms PF 681, 686, [OE]

wedes *n.*[1] *pl.* weeds TC 1.946. [OE *wēod*]

we(e)de *n.*[2] clothing A.Kn 1006, B.Th 2107 (see **under**), E.Cl 863, TC 1.177, 3.1431. [OE *wǣde*]

we(e)l *adj.* **1.** fortunate PF 611; stable, favourable BD 643; stable A.Kn 926; *al is ~* TC 3.528, 652; *make it ~* make it as you wish 710. **2.** *~ was him/hem* happy was/were he/they A.Kn 2109, B.NP 4066, TC 3.231; *~ is/was him* he is/was fortunate TC 1.350, 3.612. See **worthe(n.**

we(e)l *adv.* **1.** quite, about (with numbers) A.Prol 24, A.Mil 3637, F.Sq 383; (with adjs. and advs.) very A.Prol 614, A.Kn 1330, 2342, much A.Kn 1429, A.Mil 3711, A.Co 4406, B.NP 4043; *~ unnethes*

scarcely F.Fkl 736, TC 1.354; *as ~ as* as well as A.Kn 1777, E.Mch 2356, 2384, as much as . . (so much) B.Mel 2809; both . . and A.Prol 49, A.Kn 2733, *never so ~* (with subj. v.) however virtuously I.Pars 511, *~ the lasse* much less Bo 4. p5. 19/28, TC 4.616. **2.** (with vs.) (emphasizing probability) A.Prol 369, A.Kn 1405, 2250, B.Mel 2115, F.Fkl 957, 1156; (with **oghte**, emphasizing obligation) certainly A.Prol 505, A.Kn 1249, LGW 27, 1957. **3.** (with vs.) fittingly A.Prol 87, 512, A.Kn 2154, D.WB 509, PF 589, *it sit ~ to be so* it is fittingly so TC 1.246. **4.** (with vs. shading into intensive) carefully A.Prol 279, virtuously A.Kn 2287, readily B.Mel 2451, clearly PF 600; (more vaguely) indeed A.Kn 924, 1262, 1627, G.CY 1059, BD 1002, *dar ~ seyn/telle* dare swear A.Kn 1886, B.ML 783; *wot ~* realize TC 4.1261. **5.** *interj.* H.Mcp 25, 104. [OE *wēl*]

we(e)lde(n *v.* rule, control B.Mk 3200, 3452, 3855; possess D.WB 271; move with ease D.Sum 1947; wield LGW 2000. **welte** *pa. sg.* B.Mk 3200; **we(e)lded** 3855. [OA *wēldan* (orig. causative)]

weeldinge *vbl. n.* control, power B.Mel 2800.

weeply† *adj.* sad Bo 1. p1. 2/3, pathetic Bo 3. m12. 4/6. [from n. from **wepe(n**]

we(e)re *pa. a sg.* wert, were B.Mk 3850. *subj. sg.* A.Prol 737, D.WB 1107, E.Cl 168, H.Mcp 347, TC 2.1013. [OE *wǣre*, A *wēre*]

weet/wete *adj.* wet A.Rv 4107, TC 5.1690. [OE *wǣt*]

weex *see* **wexe(n.**

wey/way *n.* **1.** path, road A.Kn 897, 1264, C.Pard 761, Bo 4. p2. 120/163, (fig.) G.SN 92, *pl.* B.Mel 2308; journey A.Prol 791, Bo 4. m1. 23/33; route A.Rv 4020, 4078, BD 382, *every ~* in all directions G.SN 108; with verbs *ride(n/go(n (forth) (one's) ~* A. Prol 856, A.Mil 3601, 3712, B.Mk 3108, D.Fri 1536; *holde his ~* keep on A.Kn 1506, E.Mch 1932; *take (one's) ~* set out, go A.Prol 34, A.Kn 1482; *goon besydes in the ~* turn aside from an obstacle G.CY 1416; *failed of thy ~* lost your way Bo 1. p5. 8/11; *stondest now in ~* are likely TC 3.247; *by the ~* en route A.Prol 467, 806, 834, *goth by the ~* travels D.WB 1193, *a (twenty) devel ~* by the name of the (twenty) devil(s) A.Mil 3134, 3713, A.Rv 4257, D.Sum 2242, G.CY 782, to destruction LGW 2177; *in that ~* along that road I.Pars 78; *in (Caunterbury* ~ *on* the way to Canterbury H.Mcp 3; *by ~ and . . by strete* along paths and roads, everywhere C.Pard 694. **2.** time (needed to walk a distance), *furlong ~* D.Sum 1692, Anel 328, TC 4.1237, LGW 307, 841, *mile ~* B.Sh 1466, Astr 1.16.11/15; *half ~ pryme* halfway through prime (7.30 a.m.) A.Rv 3906. **3.** means B.ML 1084, B.Mk 3470, Bo 5. p6. 65/91, method Anel 283, TC 4.1366; *by ~ of* in accordance with B.ML 219, B.Pri 1840, I.Pars 707; *by no ~ / no maner ~* by no means B.ML 1084, I.Pars 134, RR 1532; *every ~* from everywhere G.SN 108; *non other mene ~es newe* no alternative intermediate way Anel 286; *at the leste ~*

at least A.Kn 1121, A.Mil 3680, F.Fkl
1417, G.CY 676; ? cause, occasion TC
2.777 var. **4. weyes** adv. gen. in on other
~ by another means D.Sum 2211 var,
non other ~ by no other method C.Pard
412, by al ~ in every respect BD 1271, in
any ~ at all Bo 5. p1. 7/10. [OE weġ]
wey adv. away in do ~ see **do(o)(n** A.Mil
3287, G.SN 487, TC 2.110; (absol.) let
it alone TC 2.893. [from **aweye**, OE on
weġ]
weye(n v. weigh B.Mk 3776. **weyed** pa. sg.
G.CY 1298, **weyeden** pl. A.Prol 454.
[OE wegan, wæġ, wæġon]
weyere n. equaller (L equator) Astr 1.17.
15/21. [from prec.]
weyght see **wight** n.[2]
weylaway interj. alas! A.Kn 938, A. Rv 4113.
[OE weġ lā weġ]
weyve(n v. **1.** neglect B.Mel 2256, TC
2.284, 4.602 var; abandon, relinquish
B.Mel 2406, D.WB 1176, H.Mcp 178,
I.Pars 33, Anel 294, Bo 1. m7. 11/16. **2.**
avoid TC 2.1050, turn aside I.Pars 353; ~
fro(m deviate from E.Mch 1483, turn from
2424. **3.** remove B.ML 308. [AN weyver]
welde n.[1] weld (plant) FormA 17. [OE
*wéalde]
welde n.[2] control RR 395; **wolde** possession
RR 451. [OE ġewéald, A. -wáld]
weldy adj. vigorous, active TC 2.636. [from
prec.]
wele n. joy A.Kn 1272, E.Cl 842, BD 603, in
her ~ happy A.Kn 2673; good fortune
TC 4.482, 483; prosperity B.ML 122,
175, D.Sum 1723, E.Cl 474; success C.Phs
115, I.Pars 484. [OE wela]
weleful adj. happy B.Mel 2507, Bo 1. m1.
8/11, 22/31, 2. p3. 52/76, p4. 71/96, 85/118,
m8. 17/25, 4. p4. 136/192; fortunate Bo 1.
m1. 13/18, 2. m1. 12/17, p3. 26/37, p4.
7/9, 3. p7. 19/26; successful Bo 1. p6.
59/76; secure Bo 2. m4. 12/17; blessed
B.ML 451. [from prec.]
welefulnesse n. happiness Bo 1. p3. 23/32,
3. p1. 26/35 (L felicitatem). [from prec.]
welfare n. welfare B.Sh 1529; safety F.Fkl
838, benefit A.Kn 3063; happiness BD
582, 1040, TC 4.228, 5.1359. [**we(e)l**+
fare(n]
wel-faringe ppl. adj. handsome B.Mk 3132,
BD 452; **beste** ~ sup. F.Fkl 932. [**we(e)l**+
fare(n]
welken n. sky, heavens B.Mk 3921, TC 3.
551. [OE weolcen]
welke(n v. languish Bo 4. p7. 66/92. p.p.
withered C.Pard 738, D.WB 277. [cf.
MDu welken]
well(e n. well A.Kn 1533, E.Cl 276; spring
B.Th 2105, B.Mk 3234, F.Fkl 898; (fig.)
source B.ML 323, B.Pri 1846, D.WB 107,
F.Sq 505, Bo 3. m9. 29/41, 4. m6. 28/41,
TC 5.1330. [OA wella]
welle(n v. well, gush TC 4.709, 5.215. [OA
wellan]
welmeth pr. 3 sg. gushes RR 1561. [? OA
*welman]
wel-willy adj. benevolent TC 3.1257. [cf.
Sw välvillig]
wem n. hurt F.Sq 121; blemish RR 930.
[OE wem(m]
wemmelees adj. stainless G.SN 47. [from
prec.]

wenche n. girl, lass (somewhat derogatory)
A.Mil 3254, A.Rv 3973, 4178, A.Co 4374,
H.Mcp 215, HF 206; servant-girl A.Mil
3631; concubine B.Mk 3417, mistress
C.Pard 453; prostitute, whore D.WB 393,
D.Fri 1355, 1359, E.Mch 2202, H.Mcp 220.
[OE wenċel]
wende(n v. **1.** go G.CY 970, BD 67, refl.
E.Mch 1779, G.CY 1110, TC 2.812, ~
forth A.Kn 2360, ~ (forth) his wey B.Mk
3724, B.NP 4288, D.WB 918, D.Sum 1734;
~ to and fro swing vigorously A.Kn 1700;
~ aboute turn round HF 1868, ~ aright
succeed A.Mil 3405, ~ forby pass by
B.Pri 1792, turn or ~ turn or go on Anel
187; ryde or ~/~ or ride walk or ride B.Pri
1683, TC 1.473; reach D.Sum 2273; is
went is advanced F.Sq 567. **2.** depart
B.Pri 1730, PF 492, TC 3.208, 5.546, disappear, pass away A.Kn 3025. **3.** live
I.Pars 143, TC 5.1574; dress G.CY 1017;
~ in dress in A.Mil 3319, B.Mk 3533; how
so I ~ however I fare CompA 78. **wendeth**
pr. 3 sg. D.WB 918; **went** TC 2.36. **went(e**
pa. sg. A.Prol 78, A.Rv 4159. **wente(n** pl.
A.Kn 999, B.ML 997, **wentestow** 2 sg.
(with suffixed pron.) A.Mil 3486. **went** p.p.
A.Mil 3665. [OE wéndan, pa. wende]
wende(n pa. of **wene(n.**
wending vbl. n. departing Bo 2. p1. 70/96,
departure TC 4.1344 var, 1436, 1630.
wene n. in withouten (any)~ without doubt
TC 4.1593, RR 574, 732. [OE wēn]
wene(n v. **1.** think, imagine A.Rv 4048,
C.Pard 349, Bo 2. m7. 2/2, 3. p10. 51/70,
TC 1.489; think themselves A.Kn 1804;
judge Bo 3. m4. 9/12. **wende** pa. (with
infin.) in ~ konne thought he knew TC
3.83; ~ for to dye thought she would die
TC 2.1169, LGW 1913, ~ han loren
thought he had lost LGW 1048, ~ have
seyn thought I saw E.Mch 2393. **wened**
(to) p.p. understood (by) Bo 4. p7. 16/22,
45/63. **2.** expect A.Rv 4320, E.Mch 1280,
Anel 124, Bo 2. m7. 19/26, TC 1.217,
4.1650; nat to ~ not to be expected Bo 3.
p2. 72/103. **wenestow** pr. 2 sg. (with
suffixed pron.) D.WB 311. **3.** intend
B.Mel 2233, TC 4.88. [OE wēnan]
wening(e vbl. n. belief Bo 5. p6. 41/58, understanding TC 4. 992.
wente n. **1.** path BD 398, HF 182, passage
TC 3.787. **2.** turn; **make(n mani a** ~ turn
many times TC 2.815, 5.605, 1194, toss
many times TC 2.63. [from **wende(n]**
wepe(n v. weep A.Rv 4248, TC 4.369; ~ in
weep over B.Mel 2167. **we(e)p** pa. sg.
B.ML 606 var, D.WB 588, E.Cl 545, Anel
138, LGW 846, 873, 2706; **wept(e** A.Prol
148 var, D.WB 592 var, TC 2.562, 3.64.
wepen pl. B.ML 820; **wepten** TC 5.1822.
wopen p.p. F.Sq 523, TC 1.941 var,
5.724 var, Bo 1. p5. 42/60 var; **wepen**
TC 1.941 var, 5.724 var; **wept** E.Mch
1544, LGW 2077. [OE wēpan, wēop,
wēopon, wōpen]
wepinge vbl. n. lamentation: in ~ at a time
of mourning B.Mel 2235.
werche(n/werke(n/wirche(n/worken v.
(-ch forms usu. in rhyme) **1.** intr. work,
toil A.Mil 3664, E.Mch 1833, I.Pars 251;
act A.Mil 3527, B.Mel 2245, E.Cl 463,
TC 1.1071; contrive TC 2.1401, RR 1164;

perform good deeds, do good D.Sum 2114,
G.SN 65; ~ *with it softe* treat it gently
TC 3.1638; do needlework LGW 2351.
2. *tr.* perform, do A.Mil 3308, B.ML 994,
B.Mel 2193, C.Pard 487, F.Fkl 872, TC
5.861, Astr prol 50/70, execute Bo 4. m7.
1/2, fulfil H.Mcp 239. **3.** cause A.Kn
2072, B.NP 4128, BD 815, TC 3.1354/1340,
5.1236, achieve LGW 1696; bring it about
(that) E.Mch 1692. **4.** make, create B.Mel
2296, D.WB 117, G.SN 326, TC 2.577;
weave, work LGW 1721; one. *p.p.*:
fashioned A.Prol 196, A.Kn 1012, G.SN
27, HF 1173; formed PF 418; born BD
90; worked, depicted A.Kn 1919, BD 327;
woven RR 1195, embroidered 836; written
B.ML 747, composed LGW 372; experienced RR 86. **werketh** *pr. 3 sg.*
B.Mel 2386; **worcheth** BD 815. **werk**
imper. sg. B.Mel 2193; **wirk** E.Mch 1485.
werketh *pl.* TC 3.943. **wro(u)ghte(n** *pa.*
E.Cl 1152, E.Mch 1692. **wroghtestow**
2 sg. (with suffixed pron.) B.Mk 3583.
y)wro(u)ght *p.p.* A.Prol 196, 367. [OE
wyrčan/wirčan; worhte, wrohte]
were *n.*[1] weir, PF 138, fish-trap TC 3.35.
[OE *wer*]
were *n.*[2] state of perplexity, confusion HF
979, state of distress LGW 2686; *withouten* ~ without doubt BD 1295. [? rel. to
werre]
were *v.*[1] defend A.Kn 2550. [OE *werian*]
were(n *v.*[2] wear B.Mk 3562, E.Cl 886, RR
234; ~ *(up)on* D.WB 559, 1018. **were**
pr. pl. A.Kn 2948. *subj. sg.* Gent 7. **wered(e**
pa. A.Prol 75, 564, 680, A.Kn 1388, A.Mil
3235. **wered** *p.p.* B.Mk 3315, 3663. [OE
werian, pa. *werede*]
wery *adj.* weary B.Th 1968, TC 4.302 *var*,
tired of blows Bo 4. m5. 12/16; (with infin.)
~ *for to speke* tired of speaking B.ML 1071,
nys nat ~ *for to love* never tires of loving
E.Mch 1291; in phr. with p.p. with pref.
for-: ~ **forwaked**, ~ **forgo**, ~ **forsongen**.
[OE *wērig*]
werk/work *n.* **1.** work, task A.Mil 3311,
Bo 3. p11. 125/172, LGW 891; labour
C.Phs 224; *a*~ to work A.Co 4337. **2.** deed
A.Prol 479, B.ML 930, B.Mel 2410, deeds
E.Cl 28, 107, *pl.* deeds G.SN 112, 384, *pl.
gen.* B.Mk 3286; behaviour, conduct TC
1.265, LGW 89; practice B.ML 930, *pl.*
BD 801. **3.** suffering F.Fkl 1106, TC
4.852. **4.** business TC 2.960, 3.735, device,
plan TC 3.697; *pl.* affairs Bo 1. m5. 23/33,
3. p12. 95/130, matters HF 54. **5.** creation, piece of work F.Fkl 872, 873, Bo 1.
p6. 11/15, 2 p15 41/58, LGW 2230, *pl.*
PF 374; composition Astr prol 43/60;
writing, story G.SN 77, 84, TC 2.16, LGW
96, *pl.* pictures BD 784. **6.** craftsmanship
B.Th 2054, HF 127, Astr 1.19.2/3. [OE
weorc, A *werc*]
werke(n *see* **werche(n.**
werker/worcher *n.* doer B.Mk 3576,
D.Sum 1937, Mars 261. [from v.; see
werche(n]
werkes *pr. pl.* (nth.) ache A.Rv 4030. [OE
wærcan, ON *verkja*]
werkinge(e/wirking/worching *vbl. n.* **1.**
action, deeds B.Mel 2590, G.SN 116, G.CY
1311, 1367, I.Pars 111, Bo 3. p11. 68/93;
(devilish) practices B.Mel 2786; contri-

vances G.CY 622. **2.** behaviour E.Cl 495;
typical behaviour D.WB 698. **3.** performance, operation G.CY 780, I.Pars 109,
PF 5, Bo 3. p11. 18/24; effect I.Pars 240;
function I.Pars 250; *beginnere of* ~ source
of creation (L *operante principio*) Bo 5. p1.
34/47; movements HF 1944. **4.** calcula-
tions F.Fkl 1280, Astr 2.7.11/15.
werne(n/warne(n *v.* refuse ABC 11 *var*,
TC 3.12, 149; forbid D.WB 333; ~*d wel
and faire* refused firmly HF 1539; ~ *me*
turn me away RR 636, *from hir* . . . ~*d be*
be prohibited to her 442. [OE *wéarnian*]
werpyng *see* **warping.**
werre *n.* war A.Prol 47, A.Kn 1287, battle
D.WB 390, conflict TC 5.234; (fig.) *holden*
~ *with* contest against A.Kn 2236. [ONF]
werre *adv.* worse BD 616. [ON *verri* adj.]
werreye(n *v.* make war against, attack A.Kn
1544, F.Sq 10, I.Pars 401, 487, TC 5.584;
~ *(up)on* make war on A.Kn 1484, B.Mk
3522. [ONF *werreier*]
werreyour *n.* warrior LGW 597. [ONF
werreieor]
wers/worse *adj. comp.* more difficult I.Pars
998; *leng the* ~ the worse the older it is
A.Rv 3872; as *n.* worse pain TC 3.1074,
4.840. [OE *wyrs*]
werte *n.* wart A.Prol 555. [OE *wearte*]
wesele *n.* weasel A.Mil 3234, B.Mel 2515.
[OE *wesule*]
weste(n *v.* draw towards the west PF 266,
LGW 61, 197. [from OE *west* adv.]
westre(n *v.* draw towards the west TC 2.906.
[from OE *west* adv. + frequentative suff.
-er]
wete(n *v.*[1] wet Bo 1. m1. 4/6, bathe TC 3.1115.
ywet *p.p.* (of 'whistle') A.Rv 4155. [OE
wætan]
weten *v.*[2] *see* **wite(n.**
weve(n *v.* **1.** weave Bo 1. p1. 15/22, p3.
29/40; interweave LGW 2364, ~ *in* Bo 1.
p1. 21/29, ~ *to and fro* LGW 2358. **2.**
(fig.) contrive (for) Bo 3. p12. 117/156,
4. p6. 27/38, perform 70/100. **waf** *pa. sg.*
LGW 2364. **y)wove(n** *p.p.* Bo 1. p1.
15/22, 4. p6. 70/100. [OE *wefan, wæf,
ġe)wefen*]
wex *n.* wax A.Prol 675, E.Mch 1430, G.CY
1164. [OE *weax*]
wexe(n/waxe(n *v.* **1.** wax, increase C.Phs
23, D.WB 28. **2.** grow E.Mch 1462, BD
415, PF 206, Bo 3. p11. 72/98, RR 1367;
develop Bo 5. p1. 37/51; ~ *up* grow up
Bo 1. p6. 74/96. **3.** become A.Kn 3024,
B.NP 3966, PF 207, TC 2.1578, 5.618; ~ *I
wood* may I go mad G.CY 1377; turn into
B.Th 1914, C.Phs 71, G.CY 1122, TC
3.727; ~ *in a were* become troubled HF
979. **we(e)x** *pa. sg.* A.Kn 1362, A.Rv 4234
var, B.ML 563, B.Sh 1301 *var*; **wax** A.Rv
4234 *var*, B.Sh 1301 *var*. **wex** *pl.* B.Mk
3365 *var*, LGW 727 *var*, **wexe** B.Mk 3365
em, wexen BD 489; **woxen** Bo 3. m12. 25/35.
waxen *p.p.* BD 414; **wexe** HF 1146 *var*;
woxe(n E.Mch 1762, HF 1146 *var*;
ywaxe(n BD 1275, TC 5.708; **ywoxen**
E.Mch 1462. [OE *weaxan, wēox, wēoxon,
ġe)weaxen*]
wha *see* **who.**
whan/when *adv.*, *conj.* when A.Prol 780,
A.Kn 2805, C.Pard 489; after TC 4.587,
5.990, LGW 2149; since TC 1.404, LGW

836; until B.ML 593; ~ *that* when A.Prol
1, B.Pri 1848, whenever Anel 93; ~ *so that*
whenever F.Fkl 1005; ~ *that ever* whenever
D.WB 45. *interrog.* C.Pard 733, PF 495.
rel. on the occasion on which B.Mel 2630;
~ ... *than* when B.Mk 3955; ~ *tyme is*
in due time LGW 281. [OE *hwanne,
hwænne*]
what *adj.* and *pron.* **1.** *interrog.* what, what
kind of B.Th 1885, H.Mcp 247; why A.Prol
184, A.Kn 1307, B.ML 56, D.WB 329,
D.Fri 1543, TC 5.946; who TC 1.765,
862; *wite ye* ~ do you know what I shall
do? HF 1618, do you know what else?
1784; ~ *thogh* what matter if . . ? B.NP
4003, E.Mch 2293. **2.** *indef.* whatever
B.Th 2064, D.Sum 1735, Anel 203, *wayte* ~
whatever D.WB 517; whichever E.Cl 10,
165, F.Sq 160, whosoever TC 1.679. ~ *so*
whatever A.Prol 522, A.Mil 3843, however
G.CY 965; ~ *man so* whoever F.Sq 157, ~
so ever whatever Bo 4. p7. 48/66–7, whosoever E.Mch 1832. as *n.* in adv. phr. *a
litel* ~ slightly Bo 4. p6. 6/9. **3.** ~ *for* . .
and (for) on account partly of . . and partly
of, what with . . and with A.Kn 1453, A.Rv
3967, F.Sq 397, sim. B.ML 21–2. **4.** as
exclam. C.Pard 439, D.WB 311, ~ . . *a*
what a . . TC 2.464; ~ *me is wo* how sad
I am HF 300. **5.** as *conj.* as much as TC
4.35. **6.** as *rel.* which HF 282. [OE *hwæt*]
wheelen/whielen *v.* wheel, turn TC 1.139.
[from n., OE *hwēol*]
wheither *see* **whether.**
whelkes *n. pl.* pimples A.Prol 632. [OE
hwylca]
whelp *n.* cub A.Kn 2627; pup BD 389; *pl.*
cubs Bo 4. p3. 78/113, ? dogs B.NP 4122.
[OE *hwelp*]
when *see* **whan.**
whennes *adv.* whence C.Pard 335, G.SN
247, *fro(m* ~ B.Mel 2400, I.Pars 136, *of* ~
G.SN 432–3. [**when**+ adv. *-es*]
wher *conj.* whether A.Kn 1101, B.Mel 2123,
TC 2.1263; ~ *so* B.ML 294, 917, G.SN
153, TC 1.270. [OE *hwæþer*]
wher(e *adv., conj.* **1.** where A.Prol 421,
B.Sh 1514, wherever Anel 133, ~ *that
(ever)* wherever A.Kn 1207, G.CY 733,
H.Mcp 96. *interrog.* B.Mk 3727, G.SN 216,
TC 3.1397/83. *rel.* where B.Pri 1785,
1796, ~ *that* G.CY 918, when D.WB 704.
~ *as conj.* where B.Pri 1695, whereas B.Mel
2443, Astr 2.5.2/3, when B.Mel 2734, because B.ML 647; *rel.* C.Phs 64, to which
Astr 2.16.4/6; ~ *so conj.* wherever H.Mcp
361, BD 614, 977, Pity 102, TC 5.1797.
2. prefixed to *prep.* (cf. **ther**): ~**fore**
wherefore E.Cl 879; why TC 1.311, for
any reason C.Phs 216; ~*for that* why BD
1034, 1088, PF 17, because of whom B.Mel
2559; ~**fro** from which TC 1.436; ~**in** in
which E.Cl 376; ~**of** from what D.WB 72,
I.Pars 450, of what G.CY 1148, TC 4.641,
for what H.Mcp 339, RR 703, *rel.* (anything) of which Bo 2. p5. 130/185, (a
thing) of which G.CY 1035; ~**on** on what
TC 2.691, *rel.* (anything) on which 5.1199;
~**on** *it was long* what it resulted from G.CY
930; ~**through** through which BD 120; ~
to why G.CY 640, TC 1.409; ~**with** with
what D.WB 131, *rel.* (sthg.) with which
D.Sum 1718, Bo 2. p3. 3/4, TC 1.942,

4.1371, the wherewithal A.Prol 302. [OE
hwǣr]
whether *pron.* whichever (of two) A.Kn
1856, D.WB 1227, Bo 4. p2. 70/92; *the* ~
which one D.WB 1234. *conj.* whether B.Mel
2339, TC 1.132; (introd. direct question)
A.Kn 1125, D.Sum 2069, Bo 1. p6. 6/7,
TC 5.735. [OE *hwæþer*]
whetston/wheston *n.* whetstone TC 1.631
var. [OE *hwetstān*]
why *adv.* why A.Kn 2990; to cause this
CompL 108; what HF 52; ~ *that* A.Prol
717; as *n.* reason TC 2.777 *var*; *rel.* in
cause ~ the reason was/what was the
reason? A.Rv 4144, E.Mch 2435; *exclam.*
A.Mil 3285, TC 1.1025. [OE *hwȳ/hwī*]
which *adj. interrog.* which, what A.Prol 40,
F.Fkl 1622, of what kind B.Mel 2552,
B.Mk 3769; ~ . . *that* whichever A.Prol
796. *rel.* (of things and people) D.Sum
2029, to whom H.Mcp 307; ~ *that* which
B.Mk 3196, who(m) B.ML 461, C.Phs 221,
D.WB 537, TC 4.176; (with repeated n.)
D.WB 363, 993, BD 893, *at* ~ *day* on that
same day TC 4.50; *the* ~ which B.Th
2154, TC 5.391, LGW 1612; *exclam.* ~ (*a*)
what a A.Kn 2675; E.Cl 1086, F.Fkl 1442,
BD 734, 859, TC 1.803. [OE *hwilc*]
while *n.* time A.Mil 3299, *a* ~ for a time
E.Mch 2405, G.CY 986, 1184; *al thilke* ~
during that time I.Pars 553, *any* ~ to any
degree H.Mcp 195, *every* ~ constantly TC
1.328, (*with)in a* (*litel*) ~ in a short time
F.Sq 590, BD 378, TC 2.1683; *in this* ~
at the same time TC 3.776, *longe* ~ for a
long time HF 1484 *var*, *or hit were longe* ~
before long LGW 1571, *in/for the/this*
meene ~ meanwhile B.ML 546, Bo 5. p5.
8/12, Astr 2.7.15/21–2, with *pl.* B.ML
668; *litel* ~ for a short time B.ML 1132,
no ~ not for even a short time B.Mk 3538,
D.WB 255, *to longe* ~ for too long LGW
1003, *gon sithen longe* ~ for a long time
past TC 1.718, *gon is a grete* ~ long ago
LGW 427, *not gon ful longe* ~ recently
TC 2.507; *in lasse* ~ sooner C.Pard 865,
outher ~ . . *outher* ~ at one time . . at
another Bo 2. p1. 77–8/107, Bo 3. p12.
119/158; *quyte* (*one's*) ~ pay (one) out
B.ML 584, LGW 2227, RR 1542; *nought
worth the* ~ TC 5.882; *alas/weylawey the* ~
alas for the time (when that happened)
E.Cl 251, BD 619, TC 3.1078. [OE *hwīl*]
while *adv., conj.* while A.Kn 2462, G.SN
134, ~ *that* A.Kn 1360, E.Cl 166. [OE
þā hwile þe, from prec.]
whyle(e)r *adv.* before, a while ago G.CY
1328. [from prec.+ **er** adv.]
whiles *conj.* while F.Fkl 1118, G.CY 1137,
(*the*) ~ *that* G.CY 1188, BD 151. [OE
hwīl+ adv. *-es*]
whilk *adj.* nth. form of **which** A.Rv 4078.
whilom *adv.* once, formerly A.Prol 795, A.Kn
859, B.Mk 3266. [OE *hwīlum* at times]
whippeltree *n.* ? cornel-tree A.Kn 2923.
[cf. MLG *wipul-bôm*]
whyt *adj.* white: *the* ~ *and rede* white and red
wine C.Pard 526, 562, ? TC 3.1384/1370
(or perh. silver and gold). [OE *hwit*]
who *pron.* **1.** *interrog.* who G.CY 599, ~
that A.Kn 2962, **whom** G.SN 304, **whos**
TC 4.973. **2.** *indef.* whoever A.Mil 3152,
TC 3.49, **whom** whomsoever PF 114,

622, TC 1.189, 2.1717, (no matter) to whom 3.1194; *as ~ seith* as if to say BD 559, as one might say Bo 5. m3. 21/31, TC 1.1011; he who BD 32, LGW 1366, *~ that* TC 3.1019 *var,* if anyone RR 1295. **3.** *rel.* **whom** (of people) D.Fri 1491, PF 278, (of things) Bo 5. p6. 29/41, 30/42, LGW 83; **whos** (of people) B.ML 642, *the ~* TC 5.1359, (of things) Bo 2. p5. 102/144. **wha** (nth.) A.Rv 4173. [OE *hwā, hwām, hwæs*]

whoso *pron. indef.* whoever, whosoever, if anyone A.Prol 644, A.Kn 3045, B.Mel 2619, D.WB 349, E.Mch 1582; for anyone who A.Prol 741, B.ML 195; *~ that* E.Mch 2016; **whomso** whosoever TC 5.145. [OE *swā hwā swā*]

wide *adv.* widely, far D.Fri 1524, E.Cl 722, TC 1.384, LGW 978, RR 1704. [OE *wide*]

widewher *adv.* far and wide B.ML 136, TC 3.404. [prec.+**wher(e)**]

widwe *n.* widow B.NP 4011, TC 1.97. [OE *widewe*]

widwehod *n.* widowhood I.Pars 916; **widwehed** LGW G. 295. [OE *widewanhād, -*hǣdu*]

wyf *n.* woman A.Prol 445, C.Phs 71, D.WB 998, E.Mch 2285, TC 3.106, 1296; wife A.Kn 932, A.Mil 3589, B.ML 533, B.NP 4553, D.WB 144, 378; mistress of a household G.CY 1015, *to* **wif/wyve** as wife A.Kn 1289, 1860; **wyves** *gen. sg.* B.Pri 1631, B.Mk 3102, E.Cl 599, 1170, E.Mch 1239, LGW 2151. *pl.* A.Prol 234, B.Mk 3149, D.WB 36, TC 2.119. [OE *wīf*]

wyfho(o)d *n.* womanliness, chastity LGW 253, 545, 691, 2587, wifely loyalty B.ML 76, E.Cl 699, E.Mch 2190, F.Fkl 1451, LGW 1687; marriage D.WB 149. [OE *wīfhād*]

wyflees *adj.* unmarried E.Mch 1236, 1248. [OE *wīflēas*]

wight *n.*[1] **1.** creature, person, man A.Prol 280, B.Sh 1511, TC 1.13, 2.195; *every maner ~* every person A.Kn 1875, *no maner ~* (in neg. context) anyone A.Prol 71, Mars 116. **2.** time, distance: *a lite ~* for a short time A.Rv 4283; *a litel ~* to a slight degree TC 5.926, 927. **3.** *pl.* unearthly creatures A.Mil 3479. [OE *wiht*]

wight *n.*[2]**/weyght** weight A.Kn 2145, F.Fkl 1560, G.CY 1226, *of ~* by weight A.Kn 2520, heavy TC 2.1385; burden B.Pri 1673, G.SN 73; solemnity Bo 4. p1. 3, importance p6. 21/31, 255/370. (*wight* in rhyme except G.CY 1226; *weyght* there and in D.Pri and Bo). [OE *wiht* and ON **weht*]

wight *adj.* active, nimble A.Rv 4086, B.Mk 3457. [ON *vígt*]

wike/wouke *n.* week A.Kn 1850, C.Pard 362, TC 4.1278, 5.492. [OE *wicu/wucu*]

wiket *n.* wicket-gate E.Mch 2045, HF 477. [OF]

wikke *adj.* **1.** bad, evil A.Kn 1580, B.Mel 2247, 2264, TC 1.403; malign A.Kn 1087; cruel G.SN 524; malicious B.NP 4613, I.Pars 493; depraved Bo 5. p3. 122/174. **2.** noxious TC 1.946; difficult B.ML 118; sour (taste) Bo 3. m1. 5/6; poor, debased (metal) HF 1346; foul RR 925; excessive Fort 55. **3.** as *n.* evil state TC 3.1074, 4.840. [OE *wicca* n. wizard]

wikked *adj.* wicked, bad B.ML 994, TC 1.93; cruel A.Rv 4201, Bo 3. m10. 2, malicious H.Mcp 320, 351, I.Pars 494, Mars 6, TC 1.39; dangerous I.Pars 729, horrible B.Mk 3806; evil, harmful Bo 4. m3. 17/23, malign Astr 2.4.22/37; unfavourable HF 1620; indicating evil BD 917. [OE *wicca*+adj. suffix *-ed*]

wikkedly *adv.* wickedly E.Cl 723, maliciously I.Pars 644. [from prec.]

wil/wol *v.* **1.** wish, desire (sthg.) E.Mch 1421, Anel 244, Bo 1. p4. 108/149; (with infin.) A.Prol 27, A.Kn 2519, Ven 11, are willing to B.Mel 2669; (with cl.) B.Pri 1843, D.Fri 1447, E.Cl 347; (with v. (*go, do,* etc.) understood) A.Rv 4040, B.Sh 1551, B.NP 4477, D.Fri 1387, E.Mch 2264, F,Fkl 778, TC 4.1628, want to send B.ML 738, will do so G.CY 986, *~ out* must come out B.NP 4242; *~ of* desire TC 2.396; *whoso ~ preye* whoever wants to pray (well) D.Sum 1879. **2.** require, demand TC 3.988, LGW 952. **3.** *auxil.* (with infin.) am/is accustomed to A.Prol 636, 638, B.Mel 2515, B.Mk 3695, C.Pard 413, 572, D.WB 1184. **4.** *auxil.* (expressing futurity) will A.Rv 4250, C.Pard 462, D.Sum 1835, PF 494, Bo 5. p6. 121/172 (L *respondebo*), 4. p4. 23/32. **5.** *intr.* want to, wish B.ML 917, E.Cl 361, Bo 2. p4. 89/123, 4. p7. 23/33, TC 4.264, LGW 2106, permit H.Mcp 28; *whoso ~* whosoever pleases D.WB 119. **6.** **wold(e** *condit.* and indirect *fut.* should/would like to B.Sh 1182, TC 1.716, Bo 3. p10. 168/231 (L *uelit*); were about to A.Mil 3606; *~ han* (with p.p.) often in sense 'wanted in vain to': A.Kn 1759, A.Rv 4227, D.WB 798; *~* (with *han* and p.p. understood) would have done TC 1.125; *~ that* wished in vain that D.Sum 2122; *~ wene* would · probably think G.CY 1088. **7.** **wold(e** *fayn* (with infin.) very much want to B.Mel 2468, B.Sh 1482, B.NP 4488, *~ fayn han hyed* would have liked to hasten TC 3.655. **8.** **wold(e** *subj.* if only it might be that B.ML 161; *~ God* if only God would grant (that) B.Mk 3626, D.WB 1103, F.Fkl 891, 976, BD 814, TC 1.459, *ne ~ God* God forbid F.Fkl 756. **wilt** *pr. 2 sg.* A.Kn 1595, ABC 181; **wolt** D.Fri 1402; (with suffixed pron.) **wiltow** A.Kn 1156, **woltow** 1544, G.SN 307. **wol(l)(e)(n** *pr. pl.* A.Kn 2221, B.ML 468, B.Mel 2561. **wolde** *pa. 1, 3 sg.* D.WB 639, 641. **woldest** *2 sg.* A.Kn 1142. **wolde(n** *pl.* A.Prol 27, B.ML 144. **wold** *p.p.* B.Mel 2190, LGW 1209. [OE *willan/wyllan; wolde; ... mæl*]

wilde *adj.* **1.** wild (of animals) A.Rv 4065, F.Fkl 1190; (of places) A.Kn 2309, B.Th 1993; fierce (of sea, etc.) A.Mil 3517, B.ML 468; *~ fyr* inextinguishable or fiercely burning fire D.WB 373, (of flaming spirits on dishes) I.Pars 445, (fig.) erysipelas A.Rv 4172. **2.** (of people) violent, passionate TC 2.116; lecherous A.Mil 3225, unrestrained RR 1284; *~ or tame* passionate or not B.Mk 3481. [OE]

wildely *adv.* heedlessly BD 875. [from prec.]

wildnesse *n.* wilderness FormA 34. [from adj.]

wyle *n.* cunning plan, stratagem, trick A.Mil 3403, A.Rv 4047, BD 673, LGW 1439;

guile, subtlety TC 3.1077, deceit 1.719 *var*, 2.271; skill PF 215 *var*. *pl*. cunning Bo 4.p3. 78/112, *with his* ~ craftily LGW 2294. [? ON *wihl, vél*]

wilful *adj*. voluntary D.WB 1179, Bo 3. p11. 112/153 (L *voluntariis*); self-willed, perverse TC 3.935. [OE *wilful* implied in *wilfullīċe*]

wilfulhed *n*. arrogance LGW G. 355. [prec. + OE suff. -*hǣdu*]

wilfully *adv*. willingly, voluntarily B.Mel 2612, C.Pard 441; deliberately I.Pars 576, purposely B.NP 4557, TC 2.284; perversely B.Mel 2426, B.NP 4286, 4622, Bo 4. p2. 133/181, obstinately I.Pars 586. [LOE *wilfullīċe*]

wilfulnesse *n*. wilfulness, perversity A.Kn 3057, TC 1.793, LSt 6; impetuousness B.Mel 2553, 2572; obstinate desire 2551. [from **wilful**]

wil(l)/wille *n*. 1. wish, desire A.Kn 1317, B.Mel 2716, F.Fkl 704, TC 4.639 *var*; *if (it) be (thy)* ~ if you please/agree A.Kn 1104, A.Mil 3361, E.Cl 326, *pl*. TC 4.107; *han* ~ wish B.Mel 2622; *as it is Goddes* ~ as God wishes C.Pard 726, *as by (my) owen* ~ with (my) agreement C.Pard 619, voluntarily I.Pars 732; *after thy* ~ as you wish ABC 143; *agayn (hir)* ~ against (her) wishes F.Fkl 748; *at (thy)* ~ in (your) power A.Kn 2387, D.WB 897, Anel 196, TC 5.587, as you wish Bo 1. p6. 4/5; *of thy free* ~ voluntarily Bo 1. p4. 200/280; *of hir* ~ easily Bo 3. p4. 66/95; *with her free* ~ willingly Bo 2. m1. 10/14, sim. p6. 71/100; *with full yvel* ~ list him he is most unwilling TC 5.1637; *with hertely* ~ wholeheartedly E.Cl 176; *good* ~ favour TC 2.1209; ~ *of herte* desire I.Pars 1039. 2. sexual desire A.Rv 3877, 3880, 3887, E.Mch 2134, RR 1531; *have* . . ~ satisfy desire A.Mil 3277, B.ML 588. 3. (object of) desire A.Kn 2669, Bo 4. p5. 24/36. 4. intention B.Mel 2339, E.Cl 294, Bo 4. p2. 18/24, 19/26; decision A.Kn 1845, 2560, B.Mel 2446, C.Phs 175, ABC 57, TC 3.623; injunction I.Pars 889; *doon his* ~ carry out his intention B.Mel 2908, E.Cl 539. 5. (faculty of) volition or choice A.Kn 3078, E.Cl 716, F.Sq 568, PF 417; Bo 3. p11. 119/163, 121/167, 4. p2. 37/49, *free* ~ freedom of choice Bo 4. p6. 20/29, 5. p2. 2/3 (L *libertas arbitrii*). 6. *with evene* ~ with a placid mind Bo 2. p1. 67/92 (L *aequo animo*). [OE *willa, ġewill*]

willing *vbl. n*. desire, volition E.Cl 319, Bo 3. p11. 60/82, 5. p2. 14/19; *pl*. wills Bo 5. p6. 208/293.

wilne(n *v*. desire A.Kn 2114, 2564, F.Sq 120, BD 1262. [OE *wilnian*]

wilning(e *vbl. n*. wishing Bo 3. p11. 60/82 *var*, *pl*. desires 117/161.

wimpel *n*. wimple, a head-dress covering chin and neck A.Prol 151, LGW 888. [LOE *wimpel*]

wimpleth *pr. 3 sg. refl*. conceals herself Bo 2. p1. 43/59. **ywimpled** *p.p*. covered with a wimple A.Prol 470, LGW 797. [from prec.]

wyn *n*. wine B.ML 743, C.Pard 566, F.Fkl 782, TC 5.852; ~ *ape* ape-wine (enlivening) H.Mcp 44. [OE *win*]

wind *n*. wind (fig.) empty fame Bo 2. m7. 19/27. (L *aura*). [OE]

windas *n*. windlass F.Sq 184. [AN *windas*]

winde(n *v*. 1. *tr*. wind, wrap up E.Cl 583, (fig.) enwrap G.SN 42, Rosem 18; embrace TC 3.1232; involve, entangle G.CY 980. 2. turn, in ~ *up and doun* revolve in the mind TC 2.601, 3.1541; lead LGW 85. 3. *intr*. bend TC 1.257; twist D.WB 1102; turn, go TC 3.1440, LGW 818, 2253; *pr. p*. changing Bo 2. p8. 17/24 *var*. **wynt** *pr. 3 sg*. LGW 85. **wond** *pa. sg*. LGW 2253. **ywounde** *p.p*. Rosem 18. [OE *windan, wánd, ġewúnden*]

wyndy *adj*. changeable as wind Bo 2. p8. 17/24 *var*. [OE *windiġ*]

windinge *vbl. n*. coiling I.Pars 417.

wind-melle *n*. windmill HF 1280. [wind + mille]

windre† *v*. trim, embellish RR 1020, *p.p*. 1018*em* (F *guignie*). [cf. OF *guingnier* deck, adorn]

winke(n *v*. 1. close the eyes TC 3.1537; ~ *with* . . *ye* close the eyes B.NP 4620; *wake or* ~ wake or sleep Pity 109, PF 482. 2. ~ *on* glance invitingly at F.Sq 348; *loke or* ~ ? open or close his eyes TC 1.301. [OE *wincian*]

winne(n *v*. 1. win, gain A.Kn 2258, TC 1.698; win over A.Mil 3381; *for al this world to* ~ though all the world were the reward D.WB 961, TC 1.504; *time is wonne* time will be gained TC 2.1743; *p.p*. acquired, begotten LGW 2564. 2. conquer A.Kn 864, F.Sq 214, attack D.Sum 2082. 3. *intr*. win gain, profit A.Prol 427, C.Pard 403, I.Pars 637; win the prize D.WB 414. 4. ~ *on* get the better of A.Prol 594, TC 1.390; ~ *to* succeed in bringing Anel 20, succeed in reaching LGW 2427. **wan** *pa. sg* A.Prol 442, BD 267, LGW 1922. *pl*. F.Fkl 1401. **wonne(n** *p.p*. A.Prol 59, A.Kn 877; **ywonne** TC 4.1315. [OE *winnan, wann, ġe)wonnen*]

winning(e *vbl. n*. 1. gain, profit A.Prol 275, D.WB 416, D.Fri 1478 *var*, HF 1972, RR 187, 205; *pl*. B.ML 127, HF 1965. 2. obtaining TC 1.199.

winsinge *ppl. adj*. skittish A.Mil 3263. [from v. from OF *guencir*]

winter *n*. 1. winter B.Mel 2783, E.Mch 2140, F.Sq 57. **winters** *sg. gen*. TC 57. **winter(e)s** *pl*. Astr 2.26.14/20. 2. **winter** *pl*. for (specified number of) years B.Mk 3249, D.Fri 1651, F.Sq 43, TC 1.811; *many a* ~ *beforn* many years before B.ML 197; *a thritty* (etc.) ~ thirty years (old) B.Sh 1216, D.WB 600; *this(e twenty* ~ for the last twenty years PF 473; *many (a)* **wintres** *space* for many years B.ML 577. [OE *winter*, pl. *winter, -tru*]

wirche(n, wirk see **werche(n**.

wirking/-ynge see **werking(e, workinge**.

wys *adj*. wise, prudent A.Rv 4054, E.Mch 1569, TC 1.1052, 2.158; discreet D.WB 229, TC 3.482, 947, 5.820; *the* ~ the wise man A.Mil 3598, B.ML 113, *pl*. G.CY 1067; *make it* ~ hesitate, delay for discussion A.Prol 785. [OE *wis*]

wis *adv*. certainly, surely TC 2.474, 887, 4.903, HF 1819; (in asseverations, cf. **wisly**) A.Kn 2786, B.NP 4598, D.WB 621, F.Fkl 1470, TC 2.381, HF 576. [OE *ġe-wiss*]

wisdom n. wisdom A.Prol 575, B.NP 4162; a wise thing, sensible course A.Kn 3041, TC 3.882 var. [OE]

wyse n. manner, way A.Kn 2370, B.Mk 3890; in this ~ in this way A.Kn 1446, as follows I.Pars 76, in what ~ how A.Kn 1843, in swich ~ in such a manner B.ML 153, in alle/every (maner) ~ at all costs B.Sh 1251, in all respects B.Sh 1435, G.SN 496, ? above all B.Sh 1536; (many a) sondri ~ in many ways B.Mel 2430, in different ways D.WB 102, pl. TC 1.159; in no maner ~ by any means D.Sum 1898; in his beste ~ as best he could F.Fkl 731; the pure ~ of the mere manner of TC 1.285. Cf. **carole-wyse**. [OE wise]

wys(e)ly adv. wisely, sagely A.Kn 2851; sensibly TC 1.205, 5.1291; prudently B.Sh 1450, discreetly C.Pard 792, E.Cl 952. [OE wislīce]

wisly adv. certainly, firmly F.Fkl 789, TC 3.1653; for certain A.Rv 3994, E.Mch 2114; (in asseverations) so/as ~ as certainly A.Kn 1863, B.Mel 2112, PF 117, TC 2.1230, 4.90. [OE wislīce]

wisse(n v. 1. tr. guide, inform D.WB 1008, instruct D.Fri 1415, ABC 155, HF 491, 2024; so God me ~ as God may be my guide D.Sum 1858. 2. intr. give instruction PF 74. 3. thyselven ~ manage your own affairs TC 1.622. [OE wissian]

wist(e see **wite(n.**

wit n. 1. mind, reason B.ML 609, D.WB 1095, F.Sq 336, BD 992, HF 1175, out of his ~ out of his mind, insane A.Kn 1456, B.Mk 3728, F.Fkl 1027; pl. mind A.Mil 3559, minds B.ML 202, TC 2.271; make his ~ thinne drive him to madness G.CY 741. 2. understanding, judgement, intelligence A.Kn 2195, C.Pard 778, E.Mch 2245, H.Mcp 279, TC 2.662; wisdom B.Mel 2702, E.Cl 428, I.Pars 1081, PF 591; as to (my) ~ as I understand it D.WB 41, F.Fkl 875, PF 547; as fer as I have ~ to the best of my ability F.Fkl 985, TC 3.997; emforth my ~ as far as I am able TC 2.243, 997; **wittes** gen. sg. in ~ ende TC 3.931. 3. cleverness, ingenuity A.Rv 3901, D.WB 400, 426, Bo 2. p3. 40/57, ? character p4. 33/44 (L ingenii), TC 3.135; persuasive power 2.1672; pl. clever devices D.Fri 1479. 4. skill, talent A.Prol 746, E.Mch 1682, I.Pars 48, BD 898, TC 3.1311; cunning TC 5.1782; pl. talents F.Fkl 706. 5. (physical) senses Bo 5. p5. 5/7, 18/26, 30/43, (L sensus); pl. Bo 5. m5. 11/16, p6. 170/249; fine ~ B.Mel 2614, I.Pars 207, 959. 6. opinion TC 5.758, pl. B.Sq 203, intent TC 4.1104, LGW 1420. 7. (piece of) wisdom C.Pard 326, (piece of) cleverness E.Cl 459. [OE ge)witt]

wyte n. blame, reproach G.CY 953, TC 2.1648, 3.739; yow to ~ a reproach to you RR 1541. [OE wīte]

wite(n/weten v.¹ 1. know A.Prol 740, F.Sq 399, TC 3.465, expect A.Prol 224; ~ of know about A.Kn 1525, 1809, B.Sh 1529, ~ of thee know from thee Bo 4. p5. 17/26; it were for to ~ it is to be asked Bo 3. p10. 119/159–60; do you ~ let you know TC 2.1635; ~ wel know with certainty TC 4.600, 5.1084, realize A.Rv 4255. 2. y)wist p.p. known G.SN 282, made public

TC 1.513, 3.404, 4.1560, HF 351, recognized TC 1.321, 3.431. **wo(o)t** pr. 1, 3 sg. A.Prol 389, A.Kn 1262; var. (nth.) A.Rv 4086. **wo(o)st** 2 sg. A.Kn 1174, **wostow** 2304. **wite(n** pl. A.Kn 1260, TC 4.198; **wo(o)t** A.Prol 740. **witeth** imper. pl. CompL 96/90. **wiste** pa. 3 sg. E.Mch 2006. **wistest** 2 sg. A.Kn 1156 var, **wistestow** TC 3.1644. **wiste** pl. F.Fkl 1491. **wiste** subj. B.Pri 1638, C.Pard 513, F.Fkl 968. **wist** p.p. Bo 5. p3. 102/144, **ywist** m3. 24/34. [OE witan, wāt, witon; wiste]

wyte(n v.² 1. blame, reproach B.ML 108, E.Mch 2177, Mars 270, Anel 110; ~ of blame for I.Pars 1016, TC 1.825, 2.385. 2. blame on, attribute to A.Mil 3140, B.Mk 3636, TC 3.63, 5.1335; refl. impute to (oneself) TC 2.1000. [OE witan]

with prep. (mostly in modern senses, also as follows) by A.Kn 2018, B.ML 475, B.Sh 1295, B.Pri 1875, B.Mel 2733, E.Mch 1819, LGW 1430; ~ a ren at a run A.Rv 4079; in (circumstances) I.Pars 86; ~ that as for what E.Mch 1499 var. [OE wiþ blended with senses of mid]

withal(le adv. moreover A.Kn 2661, B.Mk 3314, also, as well D.WB 156, F.Fkl 687, HF 212, 1528, 2141, indeed A.Prol 127, 283, 751, LGW 812, 1603; ? therewith BD 1205. [prec.+al]

withdrawe(n v. withdraw I.Pars 143, 449, 802; withhold D.WB 617, I.Pars 377; remove, refrain from I.Pars 951; ? subdue G.CY 1423, hold back, restrain Bo 1. m5. 39/55, 2. p2. 17/23; pull back Bo 4. m6. 30/45; is . . ~ fro has refrained from TC 4.886. **withdrow(gh** pa. sg. Bo 3. p2. 1/2. **withdrawe(n** p.p. Bo 1. p1. 42/59, TC 4.886. [OE wiþ-+**drawe(n**]

withdrawinge vbl. n. withholding I.Pars 568.

withholde(n v. 1. retain, keep I.Pars 744, Bo 3. p10. 159/218, preserve Bo 4. p6. 247/360, 249/362; p.p. employed B.Mel 2202, retained (legally) LGW 192. 2. restrain B.Mk 3186, Bo 2. p1. 57/79, m2. 12/17, p4. 89/122; p.p. ensnared Bo 4. p3. 85/123, detained G.SN 345. 3. refl. refrain RR 723. [OE wiþ-+**holde(n** v.]

withinforth adv. inside Bo 5. p5. 9/13. [next+**forth**]

within(ne adv. inside D.WB 943; ~ and withoute A.Mil 3240, PF 244. [OE wiþinnan]

within(ne prep. within (place) A.Kn 1300, (following obj.) TC 4.1615; (of time) ~ a while within a short time A.Kn 1437, HF 413; ~ the thridde morwe within three days BD 214. [as prec.]

withouteforth adv. outside I.Pars 172, Bo 5. m4. 17/25, 41/57, on the outside Bo 3. m11. 19/27; from outside Bo 5. p4. 109/157, 132/190. [next+**forth**]

withoute(n adv. outside A.Kn 1888, A.Mil 3482, B.NP 4038, Bo 3. m11. 17/23, 4. p3. 64/92, TC 2.611, from outside, outwardly F.Fkl 1111; within and . . ~ PF 244; of ~ from another place TC 1. 270. [OE wiþūtan]

withoute(n prep. without A.Prol 343, BD 943; ~ drede doubtless B.ML 29, ~ any more without more ado A.Kn 1541, and no more A.Rv 3970; ~ (other companye) leave

aside A.Prol 461; see **excepcioun**; ~
paramours leaving aside lovers TC 2.236.
[as prec.]
withseye(n v. **1.** deny A.Kn 1140, Bo 3.
p10. 45/64; refuse LGW 367; renounce
G.SN 447, 457. **2.** contradict A.Prol 805,
~ *to* Bo 5. p1. 32/45; oppose I.Pars 507,
TC 4.215. [OE *wiþsecgan*; cf. **seye**]
withstonde(n v. **1.** *tr.* resist D.Fri 1497,
1659, I.Pars 353, 733, 821; (physically) resist Bo 3. p8. 31/43; avoid G.SN 14; become opaque to Bo 1. m7. 5/7. **2.** *tr.*
oppose Bo 3. p10. 81/111, p12. 79/107, TC
4.160, 1298, LGW 1183; refute TC 1.1008.
3. *intr.* offer opposition I.Pars 729, TC
2.202; ~ (*to*) become opaque to, obstruct
Bo 5. m2. 6/8 (L *resistunt*), 7/10 (L *obstat*).
withsto(o)d *pa. sg.* Bo 1. p4, 56/78, LGW
1183. **withsto(o)de** *subj. sg.* TC 4.552.
withstonde(n *p.p.* I.Pars 953, TC 1.253,
LGW 1186. [OE *wiþstándan, -stód,
-stánden*]
withstondinge *vbl. n.* resisting I.Pars 455, *in*
~ *that* by preventing that Bo 3. p11. 106/
145.
witing *vbl. n.* discovery A.Kn 1611, knowledge B.NP 4439, D.WB 649, E.Cl 492,
Bo 5. p3. 81/114; *to my* ~ to the best of my
knowledge TC 2.236, RR 397. [from
wite(n)]
witingly *adv.* knowingly, wilfully I.Pars 401,
579, 721. [from pr. p. of **wite(n)**]
witnesfully *adv.* publicly, openly Bo 4. p5.
7/10 (L *testatius*). [from next]
witnesse n. **1.** testimony, evidence B.ML
629, C.Phs 169, 186, H.Mcp 284, Anel
298, *in* ~ as proof ABC 143; *fals* ~ I.Pars
796; ~ *on* (take) as testimony B.Mk 3916,
B.NP 4426, C.Pard 634, D.WB 951, (take)
as evidence G.SN 277. **2.** *bere(n* ~ give
testimony B.ML 626, B.Mel 2824, F.Fkl
1367; *tak . . to* ~ call on . . as my witness
C.Pard 483, TC 3.260. [OE *witnes*]
witnesse(n v. **1.** *intr.* testify, bear witness
B.Mel 2649, G.CY 1067, I.Pars 842, 1036.
2. *tr.* give evidence of, bear witness to I.Pars
594; *p.p.* attested Bo 5. p6. 31/44. [from
prec.]
witnessing n. testimony C.Phs 194, *berth the*
~ gives evidence in support LGW 299;
fals ~ false testimony I.Pars 796. [from
prec.]
witterly *adv.* plainly, indeed LGW 2606 var.
[cf. MSw *vitterliga*]
wyve v. marry E.Cl 140, 173. [OE *wīfian*]
wivere n. snake TC 3.1010. [OF *wyvre*]
wlatsom *adj.* nauseating B.Mk 3814;
heinous B.NP 4243. [from OE *wlætta*
nausea]
woful *adj.* sorrowful, sad (people) A.Kn
1063, TC 4.365; (time) B.ML 261; (words)
TC 1.7, 2.573; unfortunate Mars 106; as
n. the wretched B.ML 850. **wofulleste**
sup. TC 4.303. [from **wo(o)**]
wol, wolde *see* **wil.**
wolde *see* **welde**².
wolle n. wool A.Mil 3249, RR 238. [OE
wull]
wombe n. **1.** belly A.Rv 4290, B.Mk 3627,
C.Pard 522; stomach D.Sum 1888. **2.**
womb B.Mk 3674, E.Cl 877, 887, E.Mch
2414, Bo 2. p2. 11/16. **3.** cavity in astrolabe Astr 1.3.2/3, 6.6/8, etc. [OE *wámb*]

womman n. woman B.NP 4356; **wommen**
pl. B.Th 1984, maids BD 124, TC 3.688,
766. [OE *wífmann, wimman*, pl. *-menn*]
wommanhede n. womanhood B.ML 851,
G.CY 1346, *your* ~ (address) TC 3.1302;
womanliness, virtue, A.Kn 1748, E.Cl 239,
1075, Anel 299, TC 3.1740, 5.473, ?
feminine wiles 4.1462. [prec.+OE suff.
*-*hǽdu]
wom(m)anly *adv.* pleasingly BD 850, TC
2.1668, 5.577. [from n.]
womman(n)ishe *adj.* feminine, typical of
women TC 4.694. [from n.]
wonde v. desist LGW 1187. [OE *wándian*]
wonder n. **1.** marvel, cause of amazement
B.ML 408, B.Pri 1863; *no* ~ A.Prol 502,
641, *what* ~ B.ML 267; *gret* ~ Anel 148,
litel ~ D.WB 1102; wonderfulness HF
533; *pl.* miracles G.SN 359. **2.** amazement E.Cl 1058, Pity 29, feeling of amazement HF 607, expression of amazement
F.Sq 257; *han* ~ be amazed B.ML 1016,
TC 5.981, BD 1. [OE *wundor*]
wonder *adj.* amazing, marvellous, strange
B.NP 4268, F.Fkl 1175, Anel 333, TC
1.419, LGW 291. [from prec., orig. in
compds.]
wonder *adv.* marvellously, amazingly G.CY
1035, BD 443, TC 1.288, HF 114. [as
prec.]
wonderful *adj.* **1.** amazing, wonderful,
B.ML 477, PF 5, Bo 3. p12. 121/161, HF
62, strange RR 290. **2.** difficult Bo 4. p4.
43/59, 54/73. [LOE *wunderful*]
wonderly/-liche *adv.* amazingly HF 1173,
1327; exceptionally A.Prol 84, TC 3.678;
arrestingly TC 1.729. [OE *wunderlíče*]
wondre(n v. **1.** be amazed G.SN 245,
G.CY 603, TC 3.753, 5.162; ~ (*up)on* be
amazed at F.Sq 236, Bo 3. p8. 24/34, 38/53,
express amazement at B.Pri 1805, think
about F.Fkl 1514. **wondreth** *imper. pl.*
TC 3.753. **2.** be curious, want to know
A.Kn 1445, E.Cl 1019, G.SN 246, G.CY
569, TC 4.647; ~ *on* want to know about
TC 3.32; speculate HF 583. [OE *wundrian*]
wondryng *vbl. n.* amazement F.Sq 305, 308;
cause for amazement TC 2.35, CompA 50.
wone n. habit, custom LGW 2449; *is the* ~
is the custom LGW 714, 1744, 2131; *be(n*
his/hir ~ to be his/her habit, practice A.Prol
335, B.Pri 1694, HF 76. [OE *ġewuna*]
wone(n v. **1.** live, dwell A.Prol 388, G.SN
38, *p.p.* dwelt B.NP 4406, I.Pars 345.
2. *p.p.* wont, rarely woned, as *adj.* accustomed I.Pars 823, Bo 4. p4. 130/183;
in the habit of B.Sh 1564, C.Phs 162;
than he was ~ than he was accustomed to
TC 5.619; *ben* ~ *to* be accustomed to
(sthg.) E.Cl 339, RR 576, (with infin.) be
accustomed to (do . .) A.Kn 1195, H.Mcp
129, BD 150, TC 1.183, 5.277, HF 113;
as hit . . . hath be ~ *yore* as was formerly the
custom LGW 2353. [OE *wunian, ġewunod*]
wonger n. pillow B.Th 2102. [OE *wángere*]
woning n. dwelling A.Prol 606, ABC 145.
[from v.; cf. OE *wunung*]
wo(o n. **1.** woe, sorrow, misery A.Kn 919,
1582, E.Cl 643, TC 1.34, *do(n/werke(n*
(*ful*) ~ cause (much) sorrow, misery A.Kn
2624, B.Mk 3583, D.WB 384, D.Fri 1491,
TC 2.1360, 4.487, CompA 18; *allas for* ~
alas! TC 2.409. **2.** *me (etc.) is (so)* ~ I am

(so) unhappy, I grieve (so much) B.ML 817, BD 566, 573, TC 1.356, 3.1698, LGW G. 60; *wher me be ~* whether I am unhappy TC 3.66; *were us ~ alyve* we should be grieved to live E.Cl 139; *~ was* (with n.) was unhappy A.Prol 351, B.ML 757, D.WB 913; *hire herte was ful ~* her heart was very sad E.Cl 753; *~ worth* (with n.) a curse on TC 2.344, 345. **3.** lamentation, noise of grief TC 5.1509, LGW 2379, *make(n ~* lament A.Kn 900, B.NP 4566, TC 4.855, 5.1052. [OE *wā*]

wood *adj.* **1.** mad A.Prol 184, D.WB 232, TC 1.499, 3.398, HF 202. **2.** madly angry, furious A.Kn 1329, A.Mil 3394, D.WB 313, D.Sum 2152, Bo 4. m7. 16/22, fiercely violent A.Kn 2631, E.Mch 1536, Mars 123; fierce Bo 1. m4. 10/14, p4. 8/12, 2. p6. 41/58, 3. m2. 13/19; *for pure ~* out of sheer rage RR 276. **3.** senseless G.SN 450, CompL 90/84. **4.** tumultuous Bo 1. p3. 55/77; raving p5. 45/65 (L *saeuientis*); wild Bo 3. m4. 1/2 (L *saeuientis*); *is ten so ~* becomes ten times as violent LGW 736. [OE *wōd*]

woodeth *pr. 3 sg.* rages, rants G.SN 467; *~ into* fiercely seeks Bo 4. p4. 5/7 (L *saeuit*). **wooden** *pl.* rage Bo 4. m3. 34/47. [from prec.]

woodly *adv.* fiercely A.Kn 1301, passionately LGW 1752. [from adj.]

woodnesse *n.* **1.** madness A.Kn 2011, A.Mil 3452, C.Pard 496, TC 3.794, 1382; folly B.Mel 2671. **2.** fierceness Bo 2. m5. 18/26 (L *furor*), 4. m2. 4/6 (L *rabie*); violence Bo 2. m6. 20/28, *pl.* violence m4. 13/18. **3.** passion, infatuation TC 4.238; ? agony Bo 3. m12. 27/39. [OE *wōdnesse*]

wook *see* **wake(n.**

woon *n.* **1.** resource, help TC 4.1181. **2.** abundance BD 475, LGW 1652, 2161, RR 1673. **3.** dwelling, retreat HF 1166, *pl.* D.Sum 2105; place B.Th 1991. [ON *ván* hope, expectation]

woost, woot *see* **wite(n.**

worcheth *see* **werche(n.**

worching *see* **werking(e.**

word *n.* **1.** word, saying A.Prol 738, B.Mel 2303, language Bo 4. p7. 17/25, axiom A.Co 4405, assertion E.Cl 541; decree A.Kn 1109, 1304; *with that ~* at that, then A.Kn 1112, A.Rv 4248, C.Phs 232, TC 2.91, LGW 578; *at a/o ~* in brief B.Mel 2119, G.CY 1360; *~ for ~* tit for tat D.WB 422; *~ and ende* beginning and end, all B.Mk 3911, TC 2.1495, 3.702, 5.1669, cf. **ord;** *good ~* approval TC 5.1081, 1622, *wikked ~* slander I.Pars 520, insult 660; *pl. hadde the ~* was spokesman I.Pars 67, *in fewe ~es* briefly F.Fkl 1525; *withouten ~es mo* G.CY 1255, TC 2.1405, 3.234, 4.219, 500. **2.** teaching D.Sum 1937, G.SN 330, preaching 404, 416; *pl.* lesson A.Prol 498; prophecy I.Pars 281, gospel 588; advice B.Mel 2447. **3.** promise, vow E.Mch 2314, TC 4.1550, 5.994, LGW 2519, Gent 9, LSt 2, ? testimony BD 933. [OE]

worken *see* **werche(n.**

working *see* **werking(e.**

workinge/wirkynge *ppl. adj.* *~ corage* active spirit Bo 5. p5. 6/8. [from v., see **werche(n]**

world *n.* **1.** world, earth A.Kn 901, B.Mk 3828, Bo 3. m2. 4/5; life, existence A.Kn 2777, B.ML 1144, B.Sh 1426, B.Mel 3074, D.WB 47; *for al the ~* in all respects A.Kn 1372, BD 825, for any price TC 5.1697; *for al this ~ to winne* see **winne(n;** *the newe ~* the new fashion A.Prol 176; *~es blis* B.NP 4390, *~es* welfare BD 1040, *~es* joy earthly delight BalCo 12. **2.** secular life, world of the flesh A.Rv 3876, D.Sum 1876, PF 66; *my ~* my fleshly joy D.WB 473; *what maner ~* what kind of business D.Sum 2171, *dryve forth the ~* pass our lives, carry on our business B.Sh 1421. **3.** mankind A.Kn 1666, B.Mk 3472, 3831, B.NP 4535, TC 1.211; *this ~ of prees* thronging humanity B.Mk 3327; *al this ~* everyone ABC 2. **worldes** *gen.* B.Mk 3828, *pl.* TC 3.1490. [OE *w(e)orold*, gen. *-e*]

worldly *adj.* **1.** on earth, mortal B.Mk 3201, E.Cl 826, TC 4.881. **2.** earthly, temporal A.Kn 2849, B.ML 422, B.NP 4396, E.Mch 2055, I.Pars 1085, TC 3.820; material E.Cl 719. **3.** of the world, regular D.WB 684; secular D.WB 1033, E.Mch 1390. worldly A.Prol 292; carnal D.WB 1218. [OE *woruldlic*]

worly *adj.* worthy, excellent B.Th 2107 *var.* [OE *weorplic/wurp-*]

worm *n.* **1.** worm PF 326, LGW 318; *~ foul* worm-eating bird PF 505; *naked as a ~* entirely naked RR 454; *lyk a ~* naked E.Cl 880; *pl.* F.Sq 617, H.Mcp 171. **2.** *pl.* maggots B.Mel 2187, B.Mk 3806, D.WB 560, I.Pars 198, 210, 864; (fig.) *the ~ of conscience* the gnawing pang of conscience C.Phs 280. **3.** snake C.Pard 355. [OE *wyrm/wurm*]

worse *see* **wers.**

worship *n.* **1.** worship, honour (given) A.Kn 1904, 1912, B.Pri 1844, C.Phs 26, Bo 5. p6. 222/312 *var.* **2.** honour (earned), dignity B.Sh 1203, B.Mel 2675, LGW 659; reputation, renown F.Fkl 811, 962, G.CY 632, BD 1230, 1271; *seyn ~* speak honourably BD 1032; *with ~* honourably B.Mel 3032. [OE *weorpscipe/wurp-*]

worshipful *adj.* **1.** worthy of honour A.Kn 1435, B.Mk 3488, G.CY 992, I.Pars 598; *the ~* RR 797. **2.** honoured B.Mel 2955, E.Cl 401, Bo 3. p4. 44/63, 4. m1. 18/27. [from prec.]

wort *n.*[1] unfermented beer G.CY 813. [OE *wyrt*]

wortes *n.*[2] *pl.* cabbages B.NP 4411, 4464, E.Cl 226. [OE *wyrt* plant]

worth *n.* value: *in ~* as valuable, favourably BalCo 16. [OE *weorp/wurp*]

worth *adj.* **1.** worth, equivalent to B.Sh 1196; (often object of little value: leek, fly, mite) A.Prol 182, A.Kn 1558, D.WB 572, H.Mcp 254; *noght ~ to make it wys* not worth debating about A.Prol 785; *~ his olde sho* anything at all D.WB 708; *~ a bene* at all E.Mch 1854. **2.** valuable Bo 2. p5. 8/11, 3. p10. 70/96, TC 2.866, 3.14; worthy H.Mcp 200. [OE *weorp/wurp*]

worthe(n *v.* **1.** be, become: *~ with* dwell, remain with TC 5.329; pass Mars 248. **yworthe** *p.p.* become, reduced to BD 579; **worth** *pr. 3 sg.* *~ upon* gets upon B.Th 1941; **worth** *up(on imper. sg.* climb up Bo 2. p2. 39/54, get upon TC 2.1011. **2.** *pr. 3 sg.*

in _wo_ ~ a curse on/it is ill for TC 2.344-7, 4.763 _var_; _wel_ ~ _of dremes_ . . . _thise olde wyves_ dreams are all very well for old women. TC 5.379. [OE _weorþan/wurþan_; p.p. _worden_]

worthy _adj._ **1.** deserving, worthy, respectable (often iron. esp. in Prol.) A.Prol 269, 279, 283, 360, 459, noble, honourable B.Mk 3565, 3580, H.Mcp 111, PF 395, TC 1.226, RR 255; worthy of B.Mel 2967, D.Sum 1973, I.Pars 271, ABC 23; ~ _to_ worthy of Bo 4. m7. 50/72; _is_ ~ (with infin.) deserves I.Pars 273; ? fine B.Sh 1210; ? handsome RR 1268; _more_ ~ ? preferable TC 2.1328. **2.** distinguished A.Prol 43, A.Kn 1001, 1025, E.Cl 65, of rank D.Sum 2279, E.Cl 156. **3.** strong B.ML 579, B.Mk 3439, F.Fkl 1092, brave TC 5.1561, 1766, 1770. **4.** fitting B.NP 4433, I.Pars 785, Bo 3. p12. 99/136, 100/137, 4. p1. 16/23, HF 1669, LGW 317, equal 612; effective HF 727. **5.** valuable Bo 2. p4. 106/146, 3. p10. 36/51. [from n.]

worthily _adv._ fittingly A.Kn 2737, nobly, bravely TC 2.186, in a fit state I.Pars 385, deservedly E.Cl 1022. [from prec.]

wost-, wot _see_ **wite(n.**

wouke/wowke _see_ **wike.**

wounde _n._ **1.** wound B.Mk 3790; _dethes_ ~ stroke of death TC 3.1697, _by_ ~ _of thought_ by injury to the mind Bo 4. m3. 34/48. **2.** plague I.Pars 593; _ten_ ~_es (of Egipte)_ ten plagues BD 1207. **wounde** _gen._ HF 374. [OE _wúnd_]

wowe(n _v._ woo A.Mil 3372, B.ML 589, TC 5.791. [OE _wógian_]

wowing _n._ courtship LGW 1553. [from prec.]

woxe(n _see_ **wexe(n.**

wrak _n._ wreck B.ML 513. [cf. MDu _wrak_]

wrang _see_ **wrong.**

wrappe(n _v._ **1.** wrap C.Pard 736, cover F.Sq 636. **2.** conceal F.Sq 507, Bo 2. p5. 118/167. **3.** entwine F.Fkl 1356, involve Bo 4. p3. 2/2; ~ _hem in_ habituate themselves to I.Pars 586. **4.** ? embrace Bo 5. m1. 10/14; ~ _him in_ submits to Astr prol 5/6. [?]

wrappinge _n._ covering I.Pars 423. [from prec.]

wrastle(n _v._ wrestle A.Rv 3928, B.Mk 3456; (fig.) ~ _agayn_ struggle against I.Pars 729, Bo 4. p2. 131/179. [OE *_wrǽstlian_]

wrastling _vbl. n._ wrestling A.Prol 548, B.Th 1930.

wrathe/wreththe _v._ anger, enrage H.Mcp 80, BD 1151, TC 3.174; _refl._ become angry I.Pars 1013. [from next]

wrat(t)h(e/wreththe _n._ anger B.Mel 2314, TC 3.110 _var_; _pl._ Bo 4. m7. 37/52; ? distress BD 605; ? displeasure 877; ? hostility Anel 51. [OE _wrǽþþu_]

wraw _adj._ angry H.Mcp 46, ? peevish, perverse I.Pars 677 _var._ [?]

wrawnesse _n._ ? perverseness, peevishness I.Pars 680. [from prec.]

wrecche _n._ **1.** miserable creature A.Kn 931, TC 1.708, 3.933; ~ _of_ ~_s_ most miserable of all TC 4.271. **2.** despicable creature D.Sum 2063, G.CY 1158, TC 1.777; villain C.Pard 892, TC 5.705; sinner I.Pars 967, Bo 4. p2. 115/155. **3.** miser B.Mel 2793, ? TC 1.889. **4.** exile

G.SN 58, outcast Bo 1. p5. 4/6. **5.** pauper D.Fri 1609, I.Pars 471. [OE _wrecća_]

wrecche _adj._ miserable, unhappy F.Fkl 1020, I.Pars 214, ? _pl._ Bo 4. p4. 15/20 (L _infeliciores_). [from prec.]

wrecched _adj._ **1.** miserable, unhappy B.ML 274, Bo 2. m1. 8/11, p4. 80/110, LGW G. 414, Fort 25; oppressed Bo 4. m1. 29/42. **2.** despicable B.Mel 3074, I.Pars 173, TC 5.1817, 1851, LGW 900; shabby, threadbare E.Cl 850; sinful I.Pars 185, horrible 425, Bo 4. m7. 9/13; weak Bo 2. p4. 90/124; bad Bo 1. p7. 41/58; cowardly TC 3.736. [from n.]

wrecchedly _adv._ miserably B.Mk 3167, 3772; in a vile fashion D.Sum 2054. [from prec.]

wrecchednesse _n._ **1.** misery A.Rv 3897, D.WB 716, Bo 1. m1. 4/5, TC 3.381. **2.** evildoing F.Fkl 1271, offence, crime 1523, vile conduct TC 3.1787; rubbish I.Pars 34, 605; vileness PF 601, stupidity TC 2.286, sinfulness LSt 13. **3.** miserable food H.Mcp 171. [from adj.]

wreche _n._ vengeance B.Mk 3403, 3793, 3805, TC 5.890, LGW 1892, Scog 30; punishment B.ML 679; torment TC 2.784. [OE _wrǽč_]

wreen _see_ **wryen**[1].

wreye _v._ reveal A.Mil 3503, 3507, F.Fkl 944, **wrye** Mars 91; betray TC 3.284. [OE _wrégan_ accuse]

wreigh _see_ **wryen**[1].

wreke(n _v._ **1.** avenge B.Mel 2563, TC 1.62; ~ (_up)on_ A.Kn 961; _refl._: ~ _him_ avenge himself C.Pard 857, ~ _him of_ avenge himself for RR 1523; _yourself upon yourself yow_ ~ F.Sq 454. **2.** (with obj. _ire_) give vent to, gratify B.Mk 3787, TC 5.589, LGW G. 324; (with obj. _sorwe(s)_) make up for TC 3.905. **wrak** _pa. sg._ TC 5.1468 _var._ **wreke(n** _p.p._ D.WB 809, F.Fkl 784; **wroken** TC 1.88, 207; **ywroke** 5.589. [OE _wrecan_, _wrǽc_, _wrecen_]

wreker _n._ avenger PF 361, ~ _out of thyself_ no avenger other than thyself Bo 4. p4. 141/199. [from prec.]

wrekinge _vbl. n._ avenging Bo 4. m7. 3/4.

wrenches _n. pl._ tricks G.CY 1081. [OE _wrenč_]

wreste _v._ constrain, force TC 4.1427. [OE _wrǽstan_]

wreththe _see_ **wrat(t)h(e.**

wrye _see_ **wreye.**

wrye(n _v._[1] **1.** cover A.Kn 2904, D.Sum 1827, E.Cl 887, TC 2.539, 3.1056, LGW 735, RR 912; **wreen** RR 56; ~ _yow_ cover yourself TC 2.380. **2.** conceal BD 628, TC 3.620, 4.1654; ~ _himself_ dissemble TC 1.329. **wry** _imper sg._ LGW 735 _var._ **wreigh** _pa. sg._ TC 3.1056. **wrye(n** _p.p._ LGW 1201, RR 912; **ywrye(n** A.Kn 2904, BD 628. [OE _wrēon_, _wráh_, _ge)wrigen_]

wrye(n _v._[2] go, turn BD 627, TC 2.906; ~ _a-weyward_ turn away H.Mcp 262; ~ _faste (awey)_ twist rapidly away A.Mil 3283. **ywryen** _p.p._ sped on TC 3.1451. [OE _wrígian_]

wright(e _n._ workman A.Prol 614, A.Mil 3143, creator D.WB 117 _var._ [OE _wyrhta_]

wringe(n _v._ **1.** wring hands E.Cl 1212; ~ _hondes/fingres_ B.ML 606, TC 4.738, 1171. **2.** pinch, hurt TC 3.1531; (of shoes, in

proverbial phr.) D.WB 492, E.Mch 1553.
3. extract moisture from B.Th 1966; ~ *out*
squeeze through (hole) HF 2110. **wrong**
pa. sg. D.WB 492. *p.p.* TC 4.1171. [OE
wringan, wráng, wrúngen]
write(n *v.* write A.Prol 96; (fig.) signal, spell
out A.Rv 3869; *was doon ther* ~ had been
depicted there RR 413; inscribe B.ML
191. **writ** *pr. 3 sg.* B.Mk 3516, D.WB 709,
Bo 2. p7. 41/59 (L *significat*), TC 1.394;
writeth B.ML 77. **writeth** *imper. pl.*
TC 5.1399. **wro(o)t** *pa. sg.* E.Mch 2032,
TC 1.655. **writen** *pl.* F.Sq 551, TC 3.1199,
(? *pr.*) HF 1504. **write** *subj. 1 sg.* B.Mk
3843. **write(n** *p.p.* A.Prol 161, B.ML 195;
ywrite(n B.NP 4632, B.ML 191. [OE
wrítan, wrát, writon, ge)writen]
wrythe(n *v. tr.* encircle RR 160; *intr.* twist
TC 3.1231; ~ *awey* turn aside TC 4.9; ~
awey in be diverted to Bo 5. p3. 15/20; ~
out shoot out, breathe forth Bo 1. m4. 7/9
(L *torquet*); ~ *out fro* wriggle out of, escape
from TC 4.986. **wrytheth** *pr. 3 sg.* Bo 1.
m4. 7/9; **wryth** TC 3.1231. **ywrithen** *p.p.*
RR 160. [OE *wríþan, gewriþen*]
wrything *vbl. n.* turning F.Sq 127.
wroght(e *see* **werche(n.**
wroken *see* **wreke(n.**
wrong *n.* injury C.Phs 174; insult G.SN 489;
error G.SN 443; *receyveth* ~ is ill used TC
2.1679. [from next]
wrong *adj.* wrongful B.ML 681, ~ *conceit*
misapprehension G.CY 1214; *al* ~ (you
are) quite wrong TC 5.1161. [LOE *wráng*
from ON **wrang-*]
wrong *adv.* amiss, astray A.Kn 1267,
wrang (nth.) A.Rv 4252; wrongly Bo 2.
p1. 36/51; unfittingly BD 951. [from prec.]
wrong *see* **wringe(n.**
wrongful *adj.* wrongful, unjust I.Pars 567,
Bo 4. p5. 18/27; erroneous Bo 2. p1. 71/98,
5. p6. 41/58; insincere I.Pars 613. [from n.]
wrongfully *adv.* wrongfully, unlawfully Bo
1. p4. 73/101; erroneously G.SN 442, Bo 5.
p6. 36/51; sinfully I.Pars 336; uninten-
tionally I.Pars 620. [from prec.]
wroteth *pr. 3 sg.* grubs, pokes about I.Pars
157. [OE *wrótan*]
wroth *adj.* angry A.Prol 451, B.Mk 3153,
fierce I.Pars 170; hostile Bo 4. p4. 189/263,
at odds A.Co 4398, E.Cl 437, BD 582, at
war D.WB 1239. [OE *wráþ*]
wrothly *adv.* ? sadly Bo 1. p1. 52/73 (L
maestior). [from prec.]
wrought(e *see* **werche(n.**

Y

y- vocalic *see* **i-.**
ya *see* **ye** adv.
yaf *see* **yeve(n.**
yare *adj.* ready, prepared LGW 2270. [OE
ȝearu]
yate *see* **gate.**
yave(n *see* **yeve(n.**
ye *adv.* yes (in response to an open question)
A.Mil 3719, D.WB 1105, D.Fri 1392,
G.SN 212, TC 1.775; (as exclam. of con-
firmation, and various shades of scepticism)
indeed, to be sure A.Mil 3455, A.Rv 4268,

C.Pard 692, F.Fkl 1472, TC 3.890, **ya**
B.NP 4644; even D.Sum 1726. Cf **yis**. [OE
ȝé]
ye *pron. 2 pl. nom.* (often as polite form to one
person) you A.Prol 780, A.Kn 1567; *as* ~
as you (do) D.WB 1088; *save only* ~ except
you E.Cl 508. Cf. **yow**. [OE *ȝé*]
yeddinges *n. pl.* songs A.Prol 237. [OA
ȝedding]
yede *pa. sg.* went G.CY 1141, TC 5.843, RR
1033; poured G.CY 1281. **yeden** *pl.* went
TC 2.936. [OE *ȝe-ēode*]
yeer *n.* **1.** year A.Prol 347, A.Kn 1458,
season G.SN 246, Bo 4. m6. 20/29; *a* ~ for
a year A.Kn 1426, B.NP 4246; *the* ~in the
year Astr 2.1.4/6, 3.11/15; *this* ~ during
this year A.Prol 764, C.Pard 686; *so many
a* ~ for so many years A.Kn 3086; *as many
a* ~ *as* for as many years as A.Rv 3889; ~ *by*
~ year after year A.Kn 1203, C.Pard 389;
from ~ *to* ~ year after year A.Kn 1443,
LGW 1926; *of half* ~ *age* six months old
A.Rv 3971; *after tymes of the* ~ according
to the time of year TC 5.376; *of ferne* ~ of
yesteryear TC 5.1176. **yeres** *gen. sg.*
D.WB 916. **2. yeer** *pl.* in [*num.*] ~ for-
years A.Kn 1446, D.Sum 1860, F.Fkl
1582; B.Pri 1628; [*num.*] ~ *of age* —years
old A.Prol 601, D.WB 4, E.Mch 1421; *but
of a twenty* ~ and thre only twenty-three
years old LGW 2075; *of fyve and twenty* ~
his age I caste I guess his age at twenty-five
years A.Kn 2172; *this* [*num.*] ~ for the
last—years BD 37. **3. ye(e)res** *pl.* years
Bo 1. m2. 17/25, harvests Bo 2. p1. 77/106;
for years B.ML 463; ~[*num.*] for—years
B.NP 4406, F.Fkl 1062, TC 2.1298; *gon
sithen many* ~ many years ago A.Kn 1521;
a certein ~ after a certain number of years
B.Mk 3367; *in certeyn* ~ space after the
passing of some years PF 67; *by lengthe of
certeyn* ~ in the course of some years A.Kn
2967; *myne olde* ~ my old age A.Rv 3869.
[OE *ȝéar*, sg. and pl.]
yelde(n/yilde(n *v.* **1.** give C.Phs 189, E.Cl
843; pay D.Sum 1821; repay B.Mel 2482,
E.Mch 1452, I.Pars 370; give back Bo 3.
m12. 21/30, TC 4.347; give off Bo 4. m6.
20/29; ~ *up* give up A.Kn 3052 *var*, TC
1.801, LGW 886; ~ *ayein* repay Bo 3. p4.
37/54; *God* ~ *yow* may God reward you!
D.Sum 1772, TC 1.1055; ~ *acountes* give
a reckoning I.Pars 378; ~ *preyeres* utter
prayers Bo 5. p6. 217/306; ~ .. *dette* (of
bodi) D.WB 130, etc., see **dette.** **2.** yield,
surrender D.WB 912; *refl.* submit TC
3.1208, **volden** *p.p.* in *þe(n* ~ given in TC
3.1211, as *adj.* submissive Q6. **yeldeth**
pr. 3 sg. I.Pars 370, **ylldeth** Bo 4. m6.
20/29 *var*, **yelt** TC 1.385. **yeldeth** *imper.
pl.* B.Mel 2482, TC 3.1208. **yelde** *subj. sg.*
D.Sum 1772, TC 1.1055. **yolde(n** *p.p.*
A.Kn 3052 *var*, TC 3.1211. [OA *ȝéldan*,
p.p. *ȝólden*]
yeld(e)halle *n.* guildhall A.Prol 370. [OA
ȝéld+hall]
yelle *see* **yolle.**
yelow/yelwe *adj.* yellow A.Kn 2132, PF
186; sallow RR 310. [OE *ȝeolu*]
yelpe *v.* boast A.Kn 2238, TC 3.307. [OA
ȝelpan]
yeman *n.* **1.** yeoman, retainer A.Prol 101,
pl. A.Kn 2509; servant G.CY 562, 587, etc.

2. official D.Fri 1380, 1387, etc. [from yong+man]
yemanly adv. handsomely, as befits a yeoman A.Prol 106. [from prec.]
yemanrye n. freeholder status A.Rv 3949. [from yeman+OF -erie]
yerd n. garden, enclosure B.NP 4037, 4089, D.Sum 1798, TC 2.820, RR 492em; pen B.NP 4187. [OE géard]
yerd(e n. **1.** rod (for punishing) A.Prol 149, I.Pars 670, 671, pl. 1055; staff (weapon) TC 2.1427, (fig.) scourge 154. **2.** wand, staff A.Kn 1387; under (your) ~ subject to (your) authority B.Sh 1287, E.Cl 22, PF 640, TC 3.137. **3.** bough, sapling Bo 3. m2. 22/32, TC 1.257. **4.** yard (measure) A.Kn 1050. [OA gérd]
yerne adj. lively A.Mil 3257. [OE géorn]
yerne adv. briskly C.Pard 398, eagerly D.WB 993, quickly PF 3; as ~ soon, quickly TC 3.151, 4.112, 4.201, HF 910; late or ~ later or soon, ever TC 3.376. [OE géorne]
yerne(n v. desire BD 1092, seek TC 3. 152; what is to ~ what is to be desired 4.198. [OA gérnan]
yesternight adv. last night TC 5.221. [OE geostran+night]
yet adv. **1.** besides, also A.Prol 612, A.Kn 2005, E.Mch 2429, indeed (for emphasis) I.Pars 338, TC 2.588. **2.** always C.Pard 425, F.Fkl 688, still TC 1.239, even now B.NP 4096, as ~ still E.Cl 120, just yet HF 599, even so TC 5.105; ~ today even now F.Fkl 1473, ~ tomorwe hereafter TC 5.1526, never ~ never hitherto A.Prol 70, F.Sq 423. **3.** nevertheless D.WB 479, HF 421. [OE giet]
yeten v. shed Bo 1. m7. 1/2. [OE géotan]
yeve(n/yive(n v. **1.** give: ~ acountes of answer for I.Pars 253, ~ rekening 253; ~ acquitance dismiss A.Co 4411; ~ advertence take heed HF 709; ~ audience listen PF 308; ~ charge give orders E.Cl 193; ~ credence believe B.Mel 2944; ~ ensaumple set an example A.Prol 496, 505, B.Mel 2692; ~ leve give leave D.WB 83; ~ penaunce impose penance A.Prol 223; ~ signal of manifest TC 4.818; ~ his herte / hemself devote himself/themselves I.Pars 368, 906; ~ nat a pulled hen/a leek care not at all A.Prol 177, HF 1708; yaf in hir thought vouchsafed to put in her mind B.Pri 1794. ~ up utter E.Mch 2364, ~ it up yield E.Mch 2312. **2.** exude PF 274; ~ up give off A.Kn 2427 var. **3.** grant, promise Bo 4. p6. 1/2 (L tui muneris sit). **4.** intr. give A.Prol 227, I.Pars 810, TC 3.1719. yif imper. sg. D.Sum 1963, TC 1.1042. yeveth pl. B.Mel 2944. yeve subj. sg. E.Cl 30, F.Fkl 679, LGW G. 333; yive BD 683. yaf pa. sg. A.Prol 177, TC 2.651; gaf RR 757. yaf pl. A.Prol 302, yave(n TC 2.1323, 4.710; yeven HF 1708 (? pr.). yave subj. sg. TC 2.977. yeve(n p.p. C.Pard 449, D.WB 771; (y)yive(n F.Fkl 1450, TC 3.1611, LGW 1281. [OE gifan, A géfan; géaf/gæf; géafon/géfon; gifen/géfen].
yever/yiver n. giver I.Pars 791, LGW 2228. [from prec.]

yevynge vbl. n. giving, proclaiming B.Mel 2222.
yexeth pr. 3 sg. belches A.Rv 4151. [OE geocsian]
yif see if, yeve(n.
yift(e n. gift A.Kn 2735, D.WB 39, E.Mch 1312. [ON gift and yeve(n]
yis adv. yes (usu. differing from ye in emphasizing affirmative): (in response to a negative question) A.Mil 3369, F.Fkl 1367, I.Pars 560, Bo 3. p10. 129/174, TC 2.1424; (contradicting a negative) BD 1309, TC 2.278, HF 706; (emphasizing) B.NP 4006, D.WB 856. [OE gése/gíse]
yiver see yever.
yolde(n see yelde(n.
yolle/yelle pr. pl. cry out A.Kn 2672; yelleden pa. pl. screeched B.NP 4579 var. [OA gellan, pa. pl. gullon]
yond adv. yonder, over there F.Fkl 1326, TC 5.1162. [OE geond]
yonder adj. over there, yonder TC 2.1237, the/that/tho ~ A.Kn 1119, TC 2.1188, 5.575, 580, 610. [from next]
yonder adv. over, there B.ML 1018, TC 2.1146, 3.663, 5.565, 568, 669; HF 936, 1064, 1070; ~ doun down there 912 var. [rel. to yond, first in ME]
yong adj. young A.Prol 79, 213, immature B.NP 4505, BD 1095, early (in its course) A.Prol 7, F.Sq 385, fresh F.Sq 54, ? blooming A.Kn 2386; ~ or/and old (etc.) see o(o)ld; of so ~ age at such an early age E.Cl 241, BD 793, ful ~ of age very young G.SN 128; ~ folk B.Mel 2435, 2542; ~ thyng young creature E.Mch 1429. [OE geong]
yo(o)re adv. formerly B.ML 174, 984, for a long time 272, Pity 93; ful ~ long ago A.Rv 3897, ABC 150, Anel 243, for a long time A.Rv 4230, PF 476; ful ~ ago(n long ago A.Kn 1813, A.Mil 3537, for a long time E.Mch 1637; so ~ (ago) so much earlier E.Mch 2116, for so long Pity 1; of ~ (ago) formerly TC 4.719, 5.1734, LGW G. 13, (who lived) long ago A.Kn 1941. Cf. tyme. [OE geára]
youling n. lamentation A.Kn 1278. [imit.; cf. ON gaula]
your(e pron. gen. of you: ~ bother love the love of you two TC 4.168, in ~ despit in scorn of you B.Pri 1753; yours G.CY 1248, TC 2.256. youres C.Pard 672, F.Sq 597, TC 1.423. Cf. ye, yow. [OE ēower]
yourself pron. yourself: emph. C.Pard 742, TC 3.909; refl. B.Sh 1317, B.Mel 2170. yourselve(n D.WB 1327, BD 724, TC 2.131; yourselves E.Mch 1506. [prec.+ self]
yow/you pron. 2 pl. obj. you (often as polite form to one person) **1.** acc. passim; (refl. with v.) B.Th 1889, B.Mel 2189; yourselves B.ML 37. **2.** dat. to you A.Prol 34, B.Sh 1378, C.Pard 904, PF 645; refl. for yourself E.Cl 130; (in impers. constr.) A.Kn 1847, F.Fkl 1215, TC 2.1183, 3.939, LGW G. 245. ye (after prep., in weak stress) TC 1. 5. [OE ēow]
yowward see toward.

SELECT LIST OF PROPER NAMES

[This list gives mainly names spelt in abnormal or unfamiliar ways, and some others needing identification.]

Absolon Absalom **1.** son of King David LGW 249, 539. **2.** the parish clerk A.Mil 3313, etc.

Achademicis the Academy of Plato Bo 1. p1. 48/67 (L *Academicis studiis*).

Achate(e Achates, friend of Aeneas HF 226; **Achates** LGW 964, etc.

Achelous a river in Greece, personified Bo 4. m7. 30/43. **Achelois** gen. B.Mk 3296.

Achemenie Persia, but extended to include Armenia Bo 5. m1. 2/3. [from L *Achaemenes*, eponymous founder of Persian royal house]

Achille Achilles TC 5.1806; **Achilles** B.ML 198, B.NP 4338, F.Sq 239, TC 2.416, HF 398.

A(d)mete Admetus, husband of Alcestis TC 1.664.

Adoon/Adoun Adonis, loved by Aphrodite A.Kn 2224, TC 3.721.

Adrian(e Ariadne B.ML 67, HF 407, LGW 268, 1969, etc.

Af(f)rik(e Africa B.NP 4314, PF 37, Bo 2. p6. 50/70. **Auffrike** HF 1339, **Auffrikes** gen. 431.

Af(f)rican Scipio Africanus Major PF 41, 44, etc.; *the* ~ BD 287.

Agameno(u)n Agamemnon Bo 4. m7. 1, TC 3.382.

Agaton Agathon, a Greek tragic poet of 5th c. B.C. LGW 526.

Albin ?Decius Albinus Bo 1. p4. 73/101, 156/217.

Alceste Alcestis B.ML 75, F.Fkl 1442, TC 5.1778, LGW G. 209, etc.

Alcion/Alcyone Alcyone B.ML 57, BD 65, 145, etc.

Aleyn Alanus de Insulis PF 316.

Alete Alecto, one of the Furies TC 4.24.

Alexander Alexander of Macedonia, 'the Great' HF 1413, ~ **Macedo** 915; **Alisaundre** B.Mk 3821, H.Mcp 226, BD 1060.

Alfonce *see* **Piers.**

Algezir Algeciras, in Spain A.Prol 57.

Alhabor Sirius, the dog-star Astr 2.3.30/43.

Alisa(u)ndre Alexandria A.Prol 51, B.Mk 3582, G.CY 975, BD 1026.

Alisaundre *see* **Alexander.**

Alkabucius Alchabitius, an Arabian astronomer Astr 1.8.9/13.

Almageste 1. a major astronomical treatise by Ptolemy D.WB 183, 325. **2.** a textbook of astrology A.Mil 3208.

Almena Alcmena, mother of Hercules TC 3.1428.

Alocen Alhazen, an Arabian mathematician F.Sq 232.

Amete *see* **A(d)mete.**

Amphiorax Amphiaraus, one of the Seven against Thebes D.WB 741, Anel 57, TC 2.105, 5.1500.

Amphioun Amphion, King of Thebes A.Kn 1546, E.Mch 1716, H.Mcp 116,

Anaxogore Anaxagoras Bo 1. p3. 38/53.

Anne 1. St. Anne, mother of the Virgin B.ML 641, D.Fri 1613, G.SN 70. **2.** Anna, sister of Dido HF 367, LGW 1168, etc.

Anteclaudian *Anticlaudianus*, a poem by Alanus de Insulis HF 986.

Antecrist Antichrist I.Pars 788.

Antheus Antaeus B.Mk 3298, Bo 4. m7. 35/51.

Antilegius Antilochus (error for Archilochus) BD 1069.

Ant(h)iochus 1. King of Antioch in the legend of Apollonius of Tyre B.ML 82. **2.** Antiochus Epiphanes, King of Syria 175–164 B.C. B.Mk 3765.

Antonius 1. Mark Antony A.Kn 2032, LGW 588, etc., **Antony** LGW 625, etc. **2.** Antoninus, Roman emperor (Caracalla) Bo 3. p5. 35/49.

Apennyn the Apennines E.Cl 45.

Aquarius/Aquarie a sign of the zodiac Astr 1.8.3/4, 2.6.12/17.

Aquilon Aquilo, the north wind Bo 1. m6. 8/11, 2. m3. 12/15.

Arabie Arabia F.Sq 110 var **Arabe**, BD 982.

Archimoris gen. of Archemorus (or Opheltes), infant son of Hypsipyle TC 5.1499.

Arcture/Arctour the constellation Boötes Bo 4. m5. 1/2; **Arcturus** the star α Boötis Bo 1. m5. 19/27.

Arge Argos TC 5.805, 934. **Argon** LGW 2682.

Argonauticon a poem by Valerius Flaccus LGW 1457.

Argus 1. a mythical monster with a hundred eyes A.Kn 1390, D.WB 358, E.Mch 2111, TC 4.1459. **2.** the builder of the ship *Argo* LGW 1453. **3.** Algus, inventor of Arabic numerals (Al-Khwārizmī) BD 435.

Aries the Ram, a sign of the zodiac F.Sq 51, F.Fkl 1282, Astr 1.8.2/3, 17.12/16, etc. **Ariete** TC 4.1592, 5.1190.

Arionis harpe Arion's harp, the constellation Lyra HF 1005.

Armorik(e Armorica, Brittany B.Mk 3578, F.Fkl 729.

Arnold of the Newe Toun Arnaldus de Villanova (prob. Villeneuve-Loubet near Nice) G.CY 1428.

Arpies the Harpies B.Mk 3290, Bo 4. m7. 23/33.

Arthemesie Artemisia, wife of Mausolus F.Fkl 1451.

Ascaphilo Ascalaphus TC 5.319.

Asie 1. Asia HF 1339. **2.** Asia Minor B.Pri 1678.

Assuer(e/Assuerus Ahasuerus B.Mel 2291, E.Mch 1374, 1745.

Athalus Attalus III of Pergamum BD 663.

Athamante Athamas, king in Thessaly, driven mad by Juno TC 4.1539.

Atiteris HF 1227, unidentified.
Atlantes gen. Atlas's HF 1007 var **Athalantes**; ~ doughtres the constellation of the Pleiades.
At(t)hala(u)nte Atalanta A.Kn 2070, PF 286.
Attheon Actaeon A.Kn 2065, 2303.
Attropos Atropos, the Fate TC 4.1208, 1546.
Auffrike see **Af(f)rik(e.**
Augustin St. Augustine B.Mel 2807, B.NP 4431, I.Pars 97, etc. **Austin** A.Prol 187, B.Sh 1449, B.Pri 1631, LGW 1690.
Aurora 1. goddess of dawn LGW 774. **2.** a Latin metrical version of parts of the Bible by Petrus de Riga of Rheims BD 1169.
Averrois Averroes, an Arabian physician A.Prol 433.
Avicen Avicenna, an Arabian philosopher and physician A.Prol 432, C.Pard 889.

Babiloyne/-loigne Babylon B.Mk 3339, D.Sum 2082, BD 1061, LGW 706.
Bachus Bacchus PF 275, Bo 1. m6. 10/15; **Bacus** C.Phs 58, E.Mch 1722, TC 5. 208, gen. LGW 2376.
Baldeswelle Bawdeswell, Norfolk A.Prol 620.
Ballenus Belinous or Belenos, a disciple of Hermes Trismegistus HF 1273.
Balthasar Belshazzar B.Mk 3373, 3395.
Barbarie heathendom F.Fkl 1452.
Basilie, Seint St. Basil I.Pars 221.
Bayard a name for a horse A.Rv 4115, G.CY 1413, TC 1.218. [OF, = 'bay']
Belmarye a Moorish state in north Africa A.Prol 57, A.Kn 2630.
Benedight Benedict A.Mil 3483; **Beneit** A.Prol 173.
Bernard 1. St. Bernard of Clairvaux G.SN 30, I.Pars 130, 166, etc., prob. LGW 16. **2.** Bernard Gordon, professor of medicine at Montpellier A.Prol 434.
Bilyea Bilia F.Fkl 1455.
Blee Blean forest G.CY 556, H.Mcp 3.
Boece Boethius B.NP 4432, D.WB 1168, I.Pars 1088, Bo 1. p4. 56/78, Adam 2, LGW 425.
Boloigne 1. Boulogne A.Prol 465. **2.** Bologna E.Cl 589, 686, etc.
Book of Decrees the Decretum by Gratian B.Mel 2594.
Boreas/Borias the north wind Bo 1. m/3. 8/12, m5. 17/24.
Briseida Briseis HF 398, **Brixseyde** B.ML 71.
Britayne/Bretaigne 1. Brittany A.Prol 409, F.Fkl 729, 992, etc. **2.** Britain F.Fkl 810, RR 1199.
Bromeholm Bromholm (Priory), Norfolk A.Rv 4286.
Brugges Bruges B.Sh 1245, etc., B.Th 1923.
Brutes gen. of Brutus, legendary Trojan founder of Britain Purse 22.
Burdeux Bordeaux C.Pard 571; from ~ward from Bordeaux A.Prol 397, cf. **toward.**
Burgoyne Burgundy RR 554.
Busirides Busiris Bo 2. p6. 47/66, **Busirus** B.Mk 3293.

Cadme Cadmus A.Kn 1546, **Cadmus** 1547.
Caym Cain I.Pars 1015.
Calidoine Calydon TC 5.805, 934.

Calipsa Calypso HF 1272.
Calistopee Callisto A.Kn 2056; **Calyxte** PF 286.
Calkas Calchas TC 1.66, 71, etc.
Cal(l)iope Calliope, chief of the Muses Bo 3. m12. 16/23, TC 3.45, HF 1400.
Cambinskan, correctly **Cambyuskan** Genghis Khan F.Sq 12, etc.
Campai(g)ne Campania in Italy Bo 1. p4. 61/84.
Campaneus Capaneus, one of the Seven against Thebes Anel 59; **Cap(p)aneus** A.Kn 932, TC 5. 1504.
Canace(e 1. B.ML 78, LGW G. 219. **2.** F.Sq 33, etc.
Cane Cana D.WB 11.
Canios followers of Julius Canius or Canus Bo 1. p3. 40/56.
Cantebrigge/-bregge Cambridge A.Rv 3921, 3990.
Capitolie Capitol B.Mk 3893.
Caribdis the whirlpool Charybdis TC 5.644.
Carrenar(e Kara Nor (Black Lake) east of the Gobi Desert BD 1029.
Cartage Carthage A.Prol 404, B.NP 4555, F.Fkl 1400, BD 732, PF 44, LGW 1000.
Cassidor(i)e/-dorus Cassiodorus B.Mel 2386, 2538, 2628, etc.
Cataloigne Catalonia HF 1248.
Cato(u)n 1. Cato of Utica Bo 2. m7. 14/19, 4. p6. 161/234. **2.** Dionysius Cato, supposed author of Distichs A.Mil 3227, B.Mel 2371, 2406, etc., B.NP 4130, E.Mch 1377, G.CY 688.
Cecil(i)e, Seint(e St. Cecilia G.SN 28, 85, etc., LGW 426.
Cedasus Scedasus of Leuctra in Boeotia F.Fkl 1428.
Ceys/Seys Ceyx, husband of Alcyone B.ML 57, BD 63, 75, etc.
Cenobia/-e Zenobia, queen of Palmyra B.Mk 3437, 3545.
Cesar 1. Julius Astr 1.10.7/10. **2.** Octavius LGW 592, 595, 663; Augustus Astr 1.10.7/10. **3.** Gaius (Caligula) Bo 1. p4. 132/183.
Cesiphus see **Sesiphus.**
Chaldey(e Chaldea B.Mk 3347.
Charles gen. of Charlemagne B.Mk 3577.
Chepe Cheapside in London A.Prol 754, A.Co 4377, C.Pard 564, H.Mcp 24.
Chorus 1. Corus or Caurus, the north-west wind Bo 1. m3. 5/7, 4. m5. 17/23. **2.** a sea-god (otherwise unknown) LGW 2422.
Cibella Cybele LGW 531.
Cipioun see **Scipioun.**
Cylenius Cyllenius, Mercury (born on Mt. Cyllene) Mars 144, gen. 113.
Cypre Cyprus B.Mk 3581.
Cipryde Venus PF 277, TC 4.1216 var, 5.208; **Cipris** TC 3.725, HF 518.
Circes Circe A.Kn 1944, Bo 4. m3. 24/32, HF 1272.
Circo the Circus Bo 2. p3. 41/59.
Cirrea Cirra, near Delphi Anel 17.
Cithe/Cithia see **Scithia.**
Citherea Cytherea, Venus A.Kn 2215, PF 113, TC 3.1255.
Cithero see **Marcus Tullius.**
Cithero(u)n Cithaeron A.Kn 1936, 2223.
Cleo Clio, the muse of history TC 2.8.
Cleopat(a)ras/-patre Cleopatra PF 291, LGW 259, 582, etc.

Clitemistra/Clitermystra Clytemnestra D.WB 737.
Colatyne Collatinus, husband of Lucretia LGW 1705, etc.
Colcos Colchis LGW 1425, etc.
Coloigne Cologne A.Prol 466.
Constantyn Constantinus Afer of Carthage A.Prol 433, E.Mch 1810.
Corinne prob. Corinna, a poetess of Tanagra, elder contemporary of Pindar Anel 21.
Cresus Croesus A.Kn 1946, B.Mk 3917, B.NP 4328, Bo 2. p2. 42/58, HF 105.
Crisippus Chrysippus, mentioned by Jerome D.WB 677.
Cristofre an image of St. Christopher on a brooch A.Prol 115.
Cupide Cupid, son of Venus A.Kn 1623, B.ML 61, PF 212, TC 3. 1808, 4. 1216 var, 5.582; **Cupido** A.Kn 1963, TC 3.461, HF 137, LGW 1140.
Cutberd, Seint St. Cuthbert A.Rv 4127.

Dalida Delilah B.Mk 3253, BD 738, WUnc 16.
Damascien Johannes Damascenus, an Arabian physician A.Prol 433.
Damasie, Seint Pope Damasus I I.Pars 788.
Damassene adj. as n. Damascus B.Mk 3197.
Danao Danaus LGW 2563, etc.
Dane Daphne A.Kn 2062, TC 3.726.
Dant Dante B.Mk 3651, D.WB 1126, D.Fri 1520, **Dante** LGW 360, **Daunte** HF 450.
Dantes gen. D.WB 1127.
Dares (Frigius) Dares Phrygius, supposed author of an account of the Trojan War BD 1070, TC 1.146, 5.1771, HF 1467.
Dedalus Daedalus BD 570, Bo 3. p12. 118/156, HF 919.
Deiscorides Dioscorides, a Greek physician A.Prol 430.
Delphyn the constellation Delphin, the Dolphin HF 1006.
Delphos Delphi F.Fkl 1077, TC 4.1411.
Demopho(u)n Demophon, loved by Phyllis B.ML 65, BD 728, HF 388, LGW 264, 2398, etc.
Depeford Deptford A.Rv 3906.
Diane Diana A.Kn 1682, 1912, etc., PF 281, TC 3.731.
Dianira/-e Deianira, wife of Hercules B.ML 66, B.Mk 3310, D.WB 725, HF 402.
Dyte Dictys Cretensis, supposed author of an account of the Trojan War TC 1.146.
Drye See the Gobi Desert BD 1028.

Eacides gen. of Aeacides, sc. Achilles, grandson of Aeacus HF 1206.
Ecclesiaste Ecclesiasticus B.NP 4319, D.WB 651.
Echo/Ecquo/Ekko Echo, a nymph F.Fkl 951, BD 735, RR 1474.
Eclympasteyr(e ?Enclimpostair BD 167.
Ector Hector A.Kn 2832, B.ML 198, B.NP 4332, BD 328, TC 1.110, etc.
Ecuba Hecuba TC 5.12.
Edippus Oedipus TC 2.102, 4.300.
Egeus Aegeus A.Kn 2838, LGW 1944.
Egiste(s Aegyptus LGW 2570, 2600.
Elcanor HF 516 unidentified: ?Helcana.
Eleaticis the school of Elea (Velia), headed by Zeno Bo 1. p1. 48/66 (L Eleaticis .. studiis).

Eleyne 1. Helen of Troy B.ML 70, E.Mch 1754, BD 331, PF 291, TC 1.62, etc., LGW 254. 2. St. Helen C.Pard 951.
Elicon(e Helicon Anel 17, TC 3.1809, HF 522.
Elie Elijah D.Sum 1890, 2116, HF 588.
Elise(e Elisha D.Sum 2116.
Elisos Elysium TC 4.790.
Emelward in to ~ towards Emilia E.Cl 51; see **toward.**
Eneas/Enee Aeneas B.ML 64, BD 733, TC 2.1474, HF 165, etc., LGW 927, etc.
Eneid Aeneid LGW 928. **Eneidos** (sc. Aeneidos liber) B.NP 4549, HF 378.
En(n)ok Enoch D.Sum 2116 var, HF 588.
Ennopye Oenopia, later Aegina LGW 2155.
Enone Oenone HF 399 var; cf. TC 1.654.
Eolus Aeolus, god of winds HF 203, 1571, etc.
Epist(el)les Ovid's Heroides B.ML 55, LGW 1465.
Ercules Hercules A.Kn 1943, B.ML 200, Bo 2. p6. 49/68, HF 402, LGW 515, etc.
Eriphilem Eriphyle D.WB 743.
Ermony Armenia Anel 72.
Erro Hero B.ML 69; cf. LGW 263.
Erudice Eurydice Bo 3. m12. 41/59 var, TC 4.791.
Esculapius Aesculapius, god of medicine A.Prol 429.
Eson Aeson LGW 1398, 1402.
Ester/Hester Esther B.Mel 2291, E.Mch 1371, BD 987, LGW 250.
Ethyocles Eteocles TC 5.1489, 1507.
Ethna Etna Bo 2. m5. 23/32.
Euripidis Euripides Bo 3. p7. 18/25.
Eurip(p)e Euripus, a strait between Boeotia and Euboea Bo 2. m1. 3.
Europe Europa TC 3.722.
Eva Eve B.ML 368, D.WB 715; **Eve** E.Mch 1329, G.SN 62, I.Pars 325.
Ezekias/Ezechiel Hezekiah I.Pars 983 var; **Ezechie** I.Pars 135.

Femenye the country of the Amazons A.Kn 866, 877.
Ferrare Ferrara E.Cl 51.
Finistere Cape Finisterre in north-west Spain A.Prol 408.
Flaundres Flanders A.Prol 86, B.Sh 1389, B.Th 1909, C.Pard 463; to ~ward towards Flanders B.Sh 1490, cf. **toward.**
Flegiton/Flegetoun Phlegethon TC 3.1600.
Fryse Friesland Buk 23, RR 1093.

Galathee Galatea F.Fkl 1110.
Galgopheye Gargaphia in Boeotia A.Kn 2626.
Galice Galicia in Spain A.Prol 466.
Galien 1. Galen the physician A.Prol 431, I.Pars 831, BD 572. 2. the emperor Gallienus B.Mk 3526.
Gatesden John of Gaddesden, physician A.Prol 434.
Gaufred/Gaufride 1. Geoffrey of Monmouth HF 1470. 2. Geoffrey of Vinsauf B.NP 4537.
Gaunt Ghent A.Prol 448, RR 574.
Gazan Gaza B.Mk 3237.
Geminis the zodiacal sign Gemini E.Mch 2222, Astr 2.3. 24/34, etc.
Genilo(u)n Ganelon, betrayer of Roland B.Sh 1384, B. Mk 3579, B.NP 4417, BD 1121.

Germeynes *gen.* of Germanicus Bo 1. p4. 132/183.

Gernade Granada A.Prol 56.

Gerounde the Gironde F.Fkl 1222.

Gilbertyn Gilbertus Anglicus, a medical writer A.Prol 434.

Gyle, Seint St. Giles G.CY 1185, HF 1183.

Gysen the tributary of the Tigris called Gyndes by Herodotus, now Diała or Kerkah D.Sum 2080.

Glascurion Glasgerion HF 1208.

Golias Goliath B.ML 934.

Gootlond the island of Gotland A.Prol 408.

Habradate Abradates, King of the Susi F.Fkl 1414.

Hayles Hailes Abbey in Gloucestershire C.Pard 652.

Haly Hali, an Arabian physician A.Prol 431.

Helie Eli I.Pars 897.

Helowys Héloïse, wife of Abelard D.WB 677.

Hemonides the son of Haemon TC 5.1492.

Herines Erinyes, the Furies TC 4.22. **Herenus** *gen.* Pity 92.

Hermes Hermes Trismegistus G.CY 1434. *gen.* HF 1273.

Hermion Hermione B.ML 66.

Herodes Herod A.Mil 3384, C.Pard 488. *pl.* B.Pri 1764.

Hesperus the evening star Bo 1. m5. 8/11, etc.

Hester *see* Ester.

Hierse Herse, daughter of Cecrops, loved by Mercury TC 3.729.

Hogge Hodge, nickname for Roger A.Co 4336.

Hugelyn Ugolino of Pisa B.Mk 3597.

Ydra/-e Hydra Bo 4. p6. 13/19, m7. 29/42.

Ilio(u)n Ilion, the citadel of Troy B.ML 289, B.NP 4546, BD 1248, HF 158, LGW 936.

Imeneus Hymenaeus, god of marriage TC 3.1258.

Inde India A.Kn 2156, C.Pard 722, D.WB 824, D.Sum 1980, BD 889, TC 5.971.

Innocent Pope Innocent III B.Mel 2758, LGW G. 415.

Ypermistra/-e Hypermnestra, daughter of Danaus B.ML 75, LGW 268, 2575, etc.

Ypocras Hippocrates A.Prol 431, BD 572; *cf.* Glossary.

Ipolita Hippolyte A.Kn 868, etc., Anel 36.

Ipomedon Hippomedon, one of the Seven against Thebes Anel 58, TC 5.1502.

Isaye Isaiah I.Pars 198, 210, 281, HF 514.

Isaude/Isoude Isolde PF 290, HF 1796, LGW 254.

Isidis Isis HF 1844.

Isidre Isidore I.Pars 89, 551.

Isiphile(e Hypsipyle B.ML 67, HF 400, LGW 266, 1395, etc.

Isope Aesop B.Mel 2374.

Itacus the Ithacan, Ulysses Bo 4. m7. 13/18.

Itail(l)e Italy B.ML 441, B.Mk 3650, E.Cl 33, E.Mch 1511, HF 147, LGW 952.

Iulo Iulus (*alias* Ascanius) HF 177.

Jaconitos Jaconites LGW 1590.

Jakke Straw Jack Straw, leader of the Peasants' Revolt 1381 B.NP 4584.

Jame, Seint 1. St. James B.Mel 2309, 2707, E.Cl 1154, I.Pars 348; in oaths A.Rv 4264,

B.Sh 1545, D.WB 312, D.Fri 1443, HF 885. 2. the shrine of Santiago at Compostela in northern Spain A.Prol 466.

Jan(e)kin Jenkin (diminutive of *John*), Johnny B.Sh 1172, D.WB 303, etc., D.Sum 2288.

Jepte Jephthah C.Phs 240.

Jeremye Jeremiah C.Pard 635, I.Pars 76, 592.

J(h)esus Syrak Jesus son of Sirach B.Mel 2185, etc.; *cf.* E.Mch 2250.

John (Seint) 1. St. John the Evangelist B.Pri 1772, D.Fri 1647, I.Pars 216, 349, etc.; in oaths B.ML 18, 1019, C.Pard 752, D.WB 164, D.Sum 1800, **Johan** BD 1319. 2. St. John the Baptist C.Pard 491. 3. St. John Chrysostom I.Pars 109.

Jonas Jonah B.ML 486.

Jonathas Jonathan LGW 251.

Jove Jove, Jupiter A.Kn 2222, TC 3.722, LGW 525; the planet Jupiter TC 3.625; **Joves/Jovis** TC 2.1607, 3.15, 5.2, 1525, HF 219, etc. **Joves/Jovis** *gen.* E.Mch 2224, TC 1.878, 3.3, 150, 4.1337. Cf. **Jup(p)iter.**

Jubaltar(e Gibraltar B.ML 947.

Judas 1. Iscariot D.Fri 1350, C.CY 1003, I.Pars 502, etc. 2. Maccabeus B.Mel 2848.

Judicum the Book of Judges B.Mk 3236.

Julius Julius Caesar A.Kn 2031, B.ML 199, B.Mk 3863, etc., HF 1502.

Jup(p)iter A.Kn 2442, G.SN 364, TC 2. 233, HF 215, FormA 57; the planet Astr 2. 12. 17/24. Cf. **Jove.**

Kenulphus Cenwulf B.NP 4301.

Laborintus the Labyrinth HF 1921.

Lacidomie Lacedaemon C.Pard 605, F.Fkl 1380.

Ladomea/Laodomya/La(u)domia Laodamia B.ML 71, F.Fkl 1445, LGW 263.

Lame(a)do(u)n Laomedon BD 329, TC 4. 124.

Lamek Lamech BD 1162, Anel 150; **Lameth** D.WB 54, F.Sq 550.

Latona Diana, the moon TC 5.655 (Diana, as Latona's daughter, was sometimes called *Latonia*).

Lavyne 1. Lavinium HF 148. 2. Lavinia BD 331, LGW 257, 1331, **Lavyna** HF 458.

Lemno(u)n Lemnos LGW 1463.

Lenne, N. Nicholas of Lynn Astr prol 62/86.

Leo the zodiacal sign Astr 1.8.2/3, etc.; **Leo(u)n/Lyo(u)n** F.Sq 265, F.Fkl 1058, TC 4. 32, 1592, 5.1019, Astr 2.25.28/40.

Lepe a town in the south-west of Spain, near the Portuguese frontier north of Jerez C.Pard 563, 570.

Lete Lethe HF 71.

Lettow Lithuania A.Prol 54.

Lia Leah (symbol of active life) G.SN 96, 98.

Libeux Libeaus Desconus (The Fair Unknown) B.Th 2090.

Libie Libya Bo 4. m7. 36/52, HF 488, LGW 959, 992.

Lyde Lydia B.Mk 3917, B.NP 4328, HF 105.

Lyeys Ayas in Armenia A.Prol 58.

Ligurge Lycurgus A.Kn 2129, 2644. **Ligurgus** *gen.* LGW 2425.

Lyma error for *Livia* D.WB 747, 750.

Lymote prob. Elymas HF 1274.

Linian Giovanni da Legnano, a jurist of Bologna E.Cl 34.

Lino Lynceus LGW 2569, etc.

Loy, Seint(e St. Eligius A.Prol 120, D.Fri 1564.
Longius usu. Longinus ABC 163.
Lo(o)th Lot C.Pard 485.
Loreyne Lorraine RR 766.
Lucye/Lucya Lucia (Lucilia), wife of Lucretius D.WB 747.
Lucifer 1. Satan B.Mk 3189, I.Pars 788. **2.** the morning star Bo 1. m5. 11/16, 3. m1. 6/9, 4. m6. 11/17, TC 3.1417.
Lucina a name of Diana A.Kn 2085, F.Fkl 1045, TC 4.1591; the moon TC 5.655em.
Lucresse/Lucrece Lucretia B.ML 63, F.Fkl 1405, BD 1082, LGW 257, etc.
Lumbardye Lombardy B.Mk 3590, E.Cl 46, E.Mch 1245, F.Sq 193.

Macedo the Macedonian HF 915.
Macedoyne Macedonia B.Mk 3846, F.Fkl 1435, BD 1062.
Machabee 1. Judas Maccabeus B.Mel 2849. **2.** the books of the Maccabees B.Mk 3769, 3845.
Macrobes/Macrobeus/Macrobie Macrobius B.NP 4313, BD 284, PF 111, RR 7.
Madrian perh. St. Mathurin B.Mk 3082.
Mahoun/Makomete Mahomet B.ML 224, 333, 336, 340.
Malin/Malkin/Malle Molly **1.** A.Rv 4236, **2.** B.ML 30, **3.** B.NP 4574, **4.** B.NP 4021.
Marcia Marsyas [wrongly made fem.] HF 1229.
Marcia Catoun Marcia, daughter of Cato of Utica LGW 252.
Marcian Martianus Capella of Carthage, a satirist of the 5th c. E.Mch 1732, HF 985.
Marcus Tullius Cicero Bo 2. p7. 41/59, 5. p4. 2/3; ~ **Cithero/Scithero** F.Fkl 722. Cf. **Tullius.**
Mardochee Mordecai E.Mch 1373.
Marie (Seinte) 1. St. Mary the Virgin B.ML 641, 841, B.Pri 1880, C.Pard 308, E.Mch 2418; in oaths B.Sh 1592, C.Pard 685, E.Mch 1899, G.CY 1062, HF 573. **2.** St. Mary the Egyptian B.ML 500.
Marmorike Marmarica in north Africa Bo 4. m3. 9/12.
Marrok Morocco B.ML 465.
Marte Mars A.Kn 2021, TC 2. 435, 988, LGW 2244. **Martes** gen. A.Kn 2024, D.WB 619, F.Sq 50, TC 3. 437, HF 1446.
Massinisse Masinissa of Numidia PF 37.
Maudelayne Magdalene **1.** name of a ship A.Prol 410. **2.** the treatise De Maria Magdalena LGW 428.
Mecene/Messene Messenia, in Greece F.Fkl 1379.
Megera Megaera, one of the Furies TC 4.24.
Melan Milan B.Mk 3589.
Mercenrike the kingdom of Mercia B.NP 4302.
Messene see **Mecene.**
Met(h)amorphoseos Ovid's Metamorphoses B.ML 93.
Michias Micah I.Pars 201.
Myda Midas D.WB 951, TC 3.1389.
Middelburgh Middelburg, in Holland A.Prol 277.
Milesie Miletus F. Fkl 1409.
Minerva BD 1072, TC 2.1062, **Minerve** TC 2.232, LGW 932.
Myrra Myrrha TC 4.1139.

Moises Moses D.Sum 1885, F.Sq 250, I.Pars 195, ABC 89. gen. B.Pri 1658.
Monesteo Mnestheus TC 4.51.

Nabugodonosor Nebuchadnezzar B.Mk 3335, 3752, I.Pars 126, HF 515.
Narcisus Narcissus A.Kn 1941, F.Fkl 952, BD 735, RR 1468, etc.
Narice Ithaca Bo 4. m3. 2 (L Neritii (ducis), var Naricii: Ovid used dux Neritius for Ulysses).
Naso P. Ovidius Naso, Ovid LGW 725, 928, 2220.
Nembrot Nimrod FormA 59.
Neptune LGW 2421, **Neptunus** F.Fkl 1047, TC 2.443, 4.120.
Nero A.Kn 2032, B.Mk 3653, etc., B.NP 4560, Bo 2. m6. 2/3, **Neroun** B.Mk 3727.
New(e)gate Newgate prison A.Co 4402.
Nicerates gen. of Niceratus F.Fkl 1437.
Nichanor(e Nicanor **1.** a general of Antiochus IV of Syria B.Mk 3781. **2.** an officer of Alexander the Great F.Fkl 1432.
Ninive(e Nineveh B.ML 487, G.CY 974, BD 1063.
Noe Noah A.Mil 3534, etc., I.Pars 766. **Noe(e)s** gen. A.Mil 3518, 3616.
Northfolk Norfolk A.Prol 619.
Note, Seint(e St. Neot A.Mil 3771.
Nothus Notus, the south wind Bo 2. m6. 18/25, 3. m1. 6/8.
Nowelis comic distortion of Noes A.Mil 3818, 3834.

Octovian Octavian **1.** the Roman emperor later Augustus LGW 624; cf. **Cesar. 2.** the hero of the romance Octovian Imperator BD 368.
Odenake/Onedake Odenathus of Palmyra B.Mk 3462, etc.
Oëtes Aeëtes of Colchis LGW 1438, 1593.
Olofern(e Holofernes B.Mk 3746, 3757, **Olofernus** B.ML 940, B.Mel 2289, E.Mch 1368.
Ome(e)r(e Homer F.Fkl 1443, TC 1.146, 5.1792, HF 1466, 1477; cf. Bo 5. m2. 1.
Onedake see **Odenake.**
Orcades the Orkney islands TC 5.971.
Oreb Horeb D. Sum 1891.
Orewelle Orwell Haven, Suffolk A.Prol 277.
Origines Origen LGW 428.
Orion Arion HF 1205.
Orliens Orleans F.Fkl 1118, etc.
Osenay/-eye Osney near Oxford A.Mil 3274, 3400.
Oxenford Oxford A.Prol 285, A.Mil 3187, 3329, D.WB 527, E.Cl 1, Astr prol 8/10.

Padowe Padua E.Cl 27.
Palatye Palathia, in Anatolia A.Prol 65.
Palimerie Palmyra B.Mk 3437.
Palladion the Palladium, a sacred image of Pallas Athena TC 1.153, etc.
Pamphilles Pamphilus, author of De Amore B.Mel 2746, etc.; cf. F.Fkl 1110.
Panik a county near Bologna E. Cl 764, 939.
Papinian Aemilius Papinianus, a Roman jurist Bo 3. p5. 36/50.
Parcas Fates TC 5.3.
Parnaso/Per- Mount Parnassus F.Fkl 721, Anel 16, TC 3.1810, HF 521.
Parthonope(e Parthenopaeus, one of the Seven against Thebes Anel 58, TC 5.1503.

Pathmos Patmos B.Pri 1773.
Paul see **Poul.**
Paulin Paulinus Bo 1. p4. 68/93.
Pavie Pavia E. Mch 1246, RR 1654.
Pedmark see **Penmark.**
Pegasee Pegasean (horse), Pegasus F.Sq 207.
Pelleus Peleus of Thessaly LGW 1397, etc.
Pemond Piedmont E.Cl 44.
Pene Punic lands, Carthage Bo 3. m2. 6/8 (L *Poeni*).
Penmark/Pedmark Penmarch in Brittany F.Fkl 801.
Penneus *gen.* of Peneus A.Kn 2064.
Perotheus Pirithous A.Kn 1191, etc.
Perse/Perce Persia B.Mk 3442.
Peter (Seint(e) St. Peter A.Prol 697, B.Mel 2691, I.Pars 142, etc.; in oaths B.Sh 1404, D.WB 446, D.Fri 1332, G.CY 665, HF 1034. **Petres** *gen.* A.Mil 3486, D.Sum 1819.
Petrak Petrarch B.Mk 3515, E.Cl 31, 1147.
Petro Pedro **1.** of Spain, **2.** of Cyprus B.Mk 3565, 3581.
Pharao/Pharo(o Pharaoh B.NP 4323, I.Pars 443, HF 516. *gen.* BD 282.
Phasipha Pasiphaë D.WB 733.
Phebus Phoebus **1.** Apollo H.Mcp 105, TC 1.70, *gen.* LGW 986. **2.** the sun A.Kn 1493, B.ML 11, C.Phs 37, F.Sq 48, TC 2.54, LGW 773.
Pheton Phaëthon TC 5.664, HF 942.
Philomene Philomela LGW 2274, etc.
Philotetes Philoctetes LGW 1459.
Phitonissa Pythoness, the witch of Endor D.Fri 1510.
Phitoun the Python H.Mcp 109, 128.
Pictagoras/Pithagores Pythagoras BD 667, 1167, Bo 1. p4. 186/260.
Piers Alfonce/Alphonce Petrus Alphonsus, author of *Disciplina Clericalis* B.Mel 2243, 2408, etc.
Pirous Pyroeis, one of the horses in the chariot of the sun TC 3.1703.
Pirrus Pyrrhus, son of Achilles B.ML 288, B.NP 4547, HF 161.
Pyse/Pize Pisa B.Mk 3597, etc.
Plato A.Prol 741, G.CY 1448, etc., **Platon** HF 759.
Pleynt(e of Kynde *De Planctu Naturae* by Alanus de Insulis PF 316.
Polixene/-a Polyxena, daughter of Priam BD 1071, TC 1.455, 3.409, LGW 258.
Polymite(s Polynices, one of the Seven against Thebes TC 5.938, 1488, 1507.
Polym(n)ya the Muse Polyhymnia Anel 15.
Polynestor(e Polymnestor TC 4.52.
Pompe(e / Pompei / Pompeye / Pompeus Pompey B.ML 199, B.Mk 3874, 3883, HF 1502.
Poo the river Po E.Cl 48.
Popering Poperinghe near Ypres B.Th 1910.
Porcia Portia F.Fkl 1448.
Portingale Portugal B.NP 4649.
Poul (Seint) St. Paul D.WB 73, D.Fri 1647, I.Pars 162; **Paul** B.Mel 2179, B.NP 4631, C.Pard 521, **Paulus** C.Pard 523. **Poules** *gen.* D.Sum 1819; St. Paul's Cathedral A.Prol 509, *attrib.* A.Mil 3318, B.NP 3970.
Proigne Progne or Procne, sister of Philomela TC 2. 64, LGW 2248, etc.
Protheselaus Protesilaus F.Fkl 1446.
Pruce/Pruyse Prussia A.Prol 53, BD 1025.
Ptolome(e/Tholome(e Ptolemy D.WB 182,

324, Bo 2. p7. 23/33, LGW 580, Astr 1.17.6/9.

Quiryne Quirinus, Romulus TC 4.25.

Ravenne Ravenna Bo 1. p4. 90/125.
Razis Rhazes, an Arabian physician A.Prol 432.
Remedie of Love Ovid's *Remedium Amoris* B.Mel 2166.
Reynes Rennes in Brittany BD 255.
Richard, King 1. Richard I B.NP 4538. **2.** Richard II LSt 22 rubr.
Ripheo Riphaeus or Rhipeus TC 4.53.
Rochel(e, the La Rochelle C.Pard 571.
Rodogone Rhodogune, daughter of Darius F.Fkl 1456.
Rodopeya/-e the Rhodope mountains in Thrace LGW 2438, 2498.
Roger Ruggieri degli Ubaldini B.Mk 3606.
Romeward in *to* ~ towards Rome B.ML 968; see **toward.**
Ronyan/Ronyon Ronan C.Pard 310, 320.
Rosarie the *Rosarium Philosophorum,* a treatise on alchemy G.CY 1429.
Rouchestre Rochester, Kent B.Mk 3116.
Rouncivale the hospital of St. Mary Roncevall at Charing, Westminster, a cell of Roncevaux Priory in Navarre A.Prol 670.
Rowland Roland BD 1123.
Ruce Russia A.Prol 54, **Russye** F.Sq 10.
Rufus a Greek physician A.Prol 430.

Sagittar(i)e the zodiacal sign Sagittarius Astr 2. 6. 11/17, etc.
Sayne/Seyne Seine F.Fkl 1222, RR 118.
Salamon/Salomon Solomon A.Kn 1942, A.Mil 3529, A.Co 4330, B.Mel 2187, etc., D.WB 35, E.Cl 6.
Saluce(s Saluzzo in northern Italy E.Cl 44, 420, etc.
Sampsoun Samson A.Kn 2466, B.ML 201, B.Mk 3205, etc., C.Pard 554, D.WB 721.
Santippe (Boccaccio *Santippo*) Antipus or Xantipus TC 4.52.
Sapor Shapur, King of Persia B.Mk 3510.
Sarra Sarah E.Mch 1704.
Sarray Sarai, capital of the Mongol Batu Khan near the present Volgograd F.Sq 9, 46.
Satalye Attaleia in Pamphylia, near modern Antalya on the south coast of Turkey A.Prol 58.
Sathanas Satan A.Mil 3750, B.Pri 1748, B.Mk 3195, D.Fri 1526, D.Sum 1686, *gen.* B.ML 598; **Sathan** B.ML 365, etc.
Scariot Judas Iscariot B.NP 4417.
Scipioun Scipio Africanus Minor BD 286, PF 31, etc., HF 514, **Scipio** 916; **Cipioun** B.NP 4314, RR 10.
Scithero see **Marcus Tullius.**
Scithia Scythia A.Kn 867, **Cithe/Cithia** Anel 23, 37.
Scotlandward in *to* ~ towards Scotland B.ML 718; see **toward.**
Seint Denys St-Denis, a suburb of Paris B.Sh 1191, etc.
Seint Jame see **Jame.**
Seys see **Ceys.**
Semyram(e/Semyramis/-us Semiramis, queen of Assyria B.ML 359, PF 288, LGW 707.

Senec/Senek Seneca B.ML 25, B.Mel 2174, etc., D.WB 1168, D.Sum 2018, E.Mch 1376, Bo 3. p5. 34/47; cf. B.Mk 3693, I.Pars 144, 759.

Septe Ceuta, opposite Gibraltar B.ML 947.

Septem triones 'the Seven Plough-oxen', the stars of the Wain Bo 2. m6. 15/21.

Sesiphus/Cesiphus Sisyphus BD 589.

She(e)ne now Richmond, Surrey LGW 497.

Sibyle/Sibille 1. the Cumaean Sibyl HF 439. **2.** Cassandra TC 5.1450.

Sidingborne Sittingbourne, Kent D.WB 847.

Signifer the zodiac TC 5.1020.

Silla Scylla, who loved Minos PF 292.

Symacus Symmachus Bo 2. p4. 20/26.

Simo(u)n 1. St. Simon the apostle D.Sum 2094. **2.** Simon Magus I.Pars 783, HF 1274. **3.** Simon the Pharisee (Luke 7: 39 ff.) I.Pars 504.

Sino(u)n Sinon, betrayer of Troy B.NP 4418, F.Sq 209, HF 152, LGW 931.

Sisile Sicily Bo 3. p5. 17/24.

Sitheo Sichaeus LGW 1005.

Sitho extracted from Ovid's *Sithonis* 'Thracian' LGW 2508.

Soler Halle prob. King's Hall A.Rv 3990.

Soran(a)s *n.pl.* men like the Stoic Soranus Bo 1. p3. 41/56.

Southwerk Southwark A.Prol 20, 718, A.Mil 3140.

Stace Statius A.Kn 2294, Anel 21, TC 5. 1792, HF 1460.

Stilbo(u)n a name for Mercury substituted for *Chilon* of John of Salisbury's *Polycraticus* C.Pard 603.

Stimphalides Stymphalis F.Fkl 1388.

Stix Styx TC 4.1540.

Surrye Syria B.ML 134, etc.

Susanne/-a Susannah B.ML 639, I.Pars 797.

Sweto(u)n/Swetonius Suetonius B.Mk 3655, 3910.

Tantale Tantalus BD 709; cf. Bo 3. m12. 27/38, TC 3.593.

Tarquin Tarquinius F.Fkl 1407, LGW 1863, **Tarquiny** LGW 1837; cf. LGW 1682, 1698, etc.

Tars Tarsia in Chinese Turkestan A.Kn 2160.

Taur/Tawr the constellation Taurus D.WB 613, E.Mch 1887; **Taurus** a sign of the zodiac B.NP 4384, LGW 2223, Astr 1. 8. 2/3, etc.

Termagaunt a heathen idol B.Th 2000.

Tertulan Tertullian D.WB 676.

Tesbe(e *see* Tisbe(e.

Tessalye Thessaly LGW 1396, 1461, etc.; cf. B.Mk 3869.

Tewnes Tunis BD 310.

Thelophus Telephus F.Sq 238.

Theofraste Theophrastus D.WB 671, E.Mch 1294, etc.

Thesbe *see* Tisbe(e.

Thesiphone Tisiphone, one of the Furies TC 1.6, 4.24.

Thobie 1. Tobit B.Mel 2307. **2.** Tobias I.Pars 906.

Tholome(e *see* **Ptolome(e.**

Thomas, Seint 1. of India, the apostle D.Sum 1980, E.Mch 1230. **2.** of Kent, St. Thomas Becket A.Prol 826; in oaths A.Mil 3291, 3425, 3461, D.WB 666, HF 1131.

Tybre the river Tiber B.Mk 3666.

Ticius Tityus TC 1.786.

Tyle Thule Bo 3. m5. 5/7.

Timeo/Thymeo Plato's *Timaeus* Bo 3. p9. 142/192.

Timothee/Thymothee Timothy I.Pars 32.

Tyresie Tiresias Bo 5. p3. 94/133.

Tirie Tyre Bo 2. m5. 3. m4. 2/3.

Tyro *adj.* of Tyre B.ML 81.

Tisbe(e/Tesbe(e/Thesbe Thisbe, loved by Pyramus B.ML 63, E.Mch 2128, PF 289, LGW 261, 725, etc.

Titus 1. Livy LGW G. 280, LGW 1873, ~ **Livius** I.Pars 1, BD 1084, LGW 1683. **2.** error for **Dyte** HF 1467.

Trace Thrace A.Kn 1638, Anel 2, Bo 3. m12. 3/4, HF 391, LGW 432.

Tramissene Tremessen, Tlemcen in Algeria A.Prol 62.

Trigwille Triguilla Bo 1. p4. 43/59.

Trist(r)am Tristan PF 290, Rosem 20.

Trophee B.Mk 3307 unidentified.

Tubal Tubal-Cain, son of Lamech (should be Jubal) BD 1162.

Tullius 1. Cicero B.Mel 2355, etc., PF 31. *gen.* Scog 47. Cf. **Marcus Tullius. 2.** Tullus Hostilius, King of Rome D.WB 1166.

Ulixes Ulysses Bo 4. m3. 1, m7. 13/18, etc.

Urban Pope Urban I G.SN 177, 179, etc.

Vache, Sir Philip (de) la Truth 22 *var.*

Valerie 1. Valerius Maximus B.Mk 3910, **Valerius** D.WB 1165. **2.** prob. *Epistola Valerii ad Rufinum ne uxorem ducat,* ascribed to Walter Map D.WB 671, LGW G. 280.

Venyse Venice E.Cl 51, HF 1348.

Verone Verona Bo 1. p4. 154/214.

Vesevus/Visevus Vesuvius Bo 1. m4. 6/8.

Vesulus Monte Viso E.Cl 47, 58.

Vincent of Beauvais, author of *Speculum Historiale* LGW G. 307.

Vitulon Witelo, a Polish mathematician F.Sq 232.

Vulcano Vulcan HF 138, **Vulcanus** A.Kn 2222, 2389.

Wade a legendary Germanic hero, OE *Wada* E. Mch 1424, TC 3.614.

Walakye Wallachia BD 1024.

Ware, Hertfordshire A.Prol 692, A.Co 4336.

Windesore Windsor RR 1250.

Xantippa Xantippe D.WB 729.

Xristus for *Christus* ABC 161.

Zacharie/Zak- Zechariah I.Pars 434, ABC 177.

Zanzis Zeuxis C.Phs 16, TC 4. 414.

Zepherus/Zephirus the west wind A.Prol 5, BD 402, Bo 1. m5. 15/22, TC 5.10, LGW 171.